Using Word for Windows 2
Special Edition

D0932634

RON PERSON
KAREN ROSE

with
ROBERT VOSS, PH.D.
RALPH SOUCIE
SHAREL MCVEY
SHERRY ERSKINE

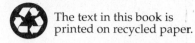
Publisher: Lloyd J. Short

Acquisitions Manager: Rick Ranucci

Product Development Manager: Thomas H. Bennett

Managing Editor: Paul Boger

Book Designers: Scott Cook and Michele Laseau

Production Team: Jeff Baker, Claudia Bell, Brad Chinn, Michelle Cleary, Mark Enochs, Brook Farling, Denny Hager, Audra Hershman, Betty Kish, Phil Kitchel, Laurie Lee, Anne Owen, Juli Pavey, Joe Ramon, Linda Seifert, Louise Shinault, John Sleeva, Kevin Spear, Bruce Steed, Suzanne Tully, Johnna VanHoose, Allan Wimmer, Phil Worthington, Christine Young

CREDITS

Product Director
Shelley O'Hara

Production Editor
Lori A. Lyons

Editors
Jo Anna Arnott
Susan M. Shaw
Colleen Totz

Technical Editors
Mark Hagerty
Roger Jennings

Composed in Cheltenham and MCP Digital by Que Corporation.

RON PERSON

Ron Person has written more than twelve books for Que, including *Using Excel 3 for Windows; Using Microsoft Windows 3,* 2nd Edition; *Windows 3 Quick Start;* and *Using 1-2-3 Release 3.* Ron is the principal consultant for Ron Person & Co. He has an M.S. in physics from The Ohio State University and an M.B.A. from Hardin-Simmons University.

KAREN ROSE

Karen Rose is a senior trainer for Ron Person & Co. She has written four books for Que, including *Using Microsoft Windows 3,* 2nd Edition; *Windows 3 Quick Start,* and *Using WordPerfect 5.0/5.1.* Karen teaches Word for Windows and desktop publishing for Ron Person & Co. and has taught for the University of California, Berkeley Extension, and Sonoma State University.

Ron Person & Co., based in San Francisco, has attained Microsoft's highest rating for Microsoft Excel and Word for Windows consultants—Microsoft Consulting Partner. The firm's consulting and development experience includes financial, marketing, and executive information systems based on Microsoft Excel and office automation systems based on Word for Windows. Ron Person & Co. delivers training and licenses training materials to corporations nationwide and is well known for its macro developer courses.

For more information about consulting, training, or training materials, contact Ron Person & Co. at:

Ron Person & Co.
P.O. Box 5647
Santa Rosa, CA 95402
(707) 539-1525

TRADEMARK ACKNOWLEDGMENTS

Que Corporation has made every effort to supply trademark information about company names, products, and services mentioned in this book. Trademarks indicated below were derived from various sources. Que Corporation cannot attest to the accuracy of this information.

AutoCAD is a trademark of Autodesk, Inc.

CorelDRAW is a trademark of Corel Systems Corporation.

dBASE III Plus and dBASE IV are trademarks of Ashton-Tate.

IBM and IBM PS/2 are registered trademarks of International Business Machines Corporation.

Lotus and 1-2-3 are registered trademarks of Lotus Development Corporation.

Micrografx Designer is a trademark of Micrografx Inc.

Microsoft, Microsoft Excel, and Windows are registered trademarks of Microsoft Corporation.

Polaris PackRat is a trademark of Polaris Software.

PageMaker is a registered trademark of Aldus Corporation.

PC Paintbrush IV Plus is a trademark of ZSoft Corporation.

PostScript is a registered trademark of Adobe Systems.

Q+E is a trademark of Pioneer Software.

Superbase 4 is a trademark of Precision Software.

WordPerfect is a registered trademark of WordPerfect Corporation.

WordStar is a registered trademark of WordStar International Incorporated.

ACKNOWLEDGMENTS

Using Word for Windows 2, Special Edition, was created through the work and contributions of many professionals. We want to thank the people who contributed to this effort.

Thanks to everyone at Microsoft. Their energy and vision have opened new frontiers in software—software that is more powerful, yet easier to use. The accessibility of Word for Windows to all levels of users shows the benefit of Microsoft's usability labs and testing.

> Laurel Lammers took a tough job and handled it with skill and knowledge. She kept us informed and up to date while working with numerous Word for Windows beta sites. She is a conscientious professional.

Thanks to the software consultants and trainers who helped us write *Using Word for Windows 2*, Special Edition.

> Robert Voss, Ph.D., deserves special thanks for his help in bringing this book together. In addition to writing on numerous topics, including headers, footers, tables of contents, and large document assembly, Robert helped in final edits and in applying a business perspective to the writing. Robert is a senior trainer in Microsoft Excel and Word for Windows for Ron Person & Co.

> Ralph Soucie, long-time contributing editor to *PC World*, and author of a popular book on Microsoft Excel, is also a Microsoft Excel consultant. Ralph works out of Lake Oswego, Oregon. Ralph wrote on the topics of editing techniques, form letters, mail merge, and customizing Word for Windows 2.0.

> Sharel McVey put her long experience as a corporate trainer to work on the tutorial, as well as editing tools, tables, and columns. Sharel lives in San Francisco and trains corporations throughout Northern California on Word for Windows and Microsoft Excel.

Sherry Erskine wrote in-depth chapters on programming in WordBASIC. Due to the book's size, her chapters were reduced to an introduction to macros. Sherry is a principal in Pivotal Computer Systems, Inc., a Windows consulting and programming firm in San Francisco that has extensive experience developing custom applications in WordBASIC.

Matt Fogarty is the talented artist who drew the pictures of the horse race and character study of an old man's face, using Microsoft Draw. Matt is a student at Santa Rosa High School in Santa Rosa, California.

Technical editing was done by two very capable Windows consultants; however, the responsibility for any errors that may have slipped through their knowledgeable gaze lies solely with us.

Roger Jennings is the principal of OakLeaf Systems, Inc., a database and publishing programming firm based in Oakland, CA. Roger is a leader in database publishing systems, WordPerfect to Word for Windows conversion, and VisualBASIC.

Mark Hagerty is a full-time corporate trainer based in Livermore, California. Mark is dedicated to training beginning through advanced levels of Windows, Microsoft Excel, and Word for Windows.

The editors ensure that our books are consistent and easy to read. That they succeed in their jobs is evident by the comments of our corporate clients on the quality and value of Que books.

Shelley O'Hara was the product director who managed the arduous process of getting *Using Word for Windows 2*, Special Edition, into print.

Lori Lyons worked with us on an almost daily basis to ensure that we didn't get too far behind schedule and to give us feedback on style and content. Lori was assisted with the editing by Jo Anna Arnott, Susan M. Shaw, and Colleen Totz.

With the rush of consulting, training, and book development going on in our office, we could not have kept our heads above the disks and printouts were it not for our assistant, Wilma Thompson.

TABLE OF CONTENTS

II Using Advanced Features

18 Automating with Field Codes 451

III Using Graphics and Charts

Introduction

Word for Windows is the most powerful word processor available. In competitive reviews, Word for Windows has received the highest rating from every major reviewer and magazine. Its features range from those of an easy-to-use word processor to those that make it the most powerful and customizable word processor.

Why You Should Use This Book

This book contains the combined input of six consultants and trainers who work with businesses that use Word for Windows. This is not just a rehash of the manual by writers who aren't familiar with Word for Windows. This team works with a spectrum of Word for Windows users—from training business people who have just started learning but need results quickly, to helping corporate developers who program in WordBASIC, the programming language built into Word for Windows. These writers are familiar with communicating the power and nuances of Word for Windows. They have seen the confusion caused by some areas in the manuals and have expanded and clarified these areas. They also have expanded on procedures and techniques that the manuals allude to, but do not cover.

Throughout the book, tips and notes highlight combinations of features or tricks that make you more productive. These tips and notes are set off from the text so that you can get at them quickly without having to wade through a swamp of black ink.

Word for Windows 2 is an extensive upgrade from the original Word for Windows. Areas of change display a Version 2 icon. If you used Word for Windows before, watch for these icons so that you can quickly learn about new features.

Using Word for Windows 2, Special Edition, includes extensive sections on how to get the most out of WordArt, Microsoft Draw, Microsoft Graph, and the Equation Editor—applications you can use to create publishing titles, draw or import art, create charts and graphs, or insert equations.

If you are new to Word for Windows, you'll be especially interested in Chapter 2's quick start tutorial. The quick start guides you from starting Windows through creating and formatting a simple business letter. With Chapter 2, you can quickly become familiar with Word for Windows and the basics of all Windows programs.

Why You Should Use Word for Windows

Many reasons exist for choosing Word for Windows as your word processor, including its wide array of features, its accessibility, its power, and its ability to exchange data and graphics with other Windows applications. For those of you standardizing on a word processor, the choice of Word for Windows is an easy one. For those of you already using one or more word processors, Word for Windows can increase productivity and decrease support costs. Because of its capability to coexist with other word processors, you can begin a gradual transition toward Word for Windows.

Word for Windows Has Accessible Power

Word for Windows is the most powerful word processor, but it has features that make it the easiest to use and easiest to get help.

Most people do not need or use advanced word processing features regularly. On most days, you want a convenient word processor with advanced features that don't get in the way when they aren't needed. Word for Windows' capability to customize the screen display and its command system makes the program straightforward and easy to use. When you do need an advanced feature, however, you want to be able to learn it quickly.

The toolbar and ribbon shown in figure I.1, for example, enables you to click on a button to do the most frequently used commands such as opening or saving files, inserting bulleted lists, making tables or columns, or formatting for bold with centered alignment. You can even customize the toolbar to fit your needs by adding or removing commands.

FIG. I.1.

The toolbar and ribbon give you instant access to the most frequently used commands.

Word for Windows Works in the Windows Environment

If you know any other Windows application, you already know how to use Word for Windows' menus and commands, choose from dialog boxes, use the Help window, and operate document windows. Another advantage of Windows is that you can easily transfer data between applications, embed graphics or text in a Word for Windows document, or link graphics or text between applications. Figure I.2 shows a Word for Windows document linked to Microsoft Excel charts and tables. You can easily switch between the two applications.

Word for Windows gives you access to the power of Object Linking and Embedding (OLE). With OLE you can embed text, graphics, and charts into a Word for Windows document and not have to worry about misplacing the file that the text, graphics, or charts came from. The data is embedded along with the result. Double-click on an embedded picture, like the ambulance in figure I.3, and the Microsoft Draw program appears making it easy for you to edit the picture. *Using Word for Windows 2*, Special Edition, covers in detail the applets that come with Word for Windows.

Word for Windows Shows You Results

Word for Windows enables you to zoom from a 25% to 200% view of your document—exactly as it will appear when printed. You can edit and format text or move framed objects while you are in any zoomed view. If you are using TrueType, you are guaranteed to see what will print. Figure I.4 shows a page zoomed out to show almost an entire page.

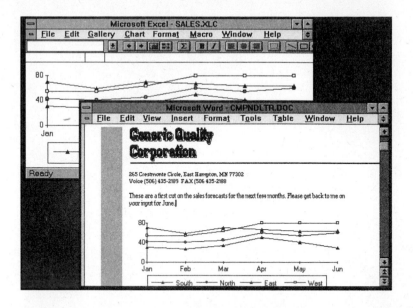

FIG. I.2.

Word for Windows enables you to link with data and charts in other applications.

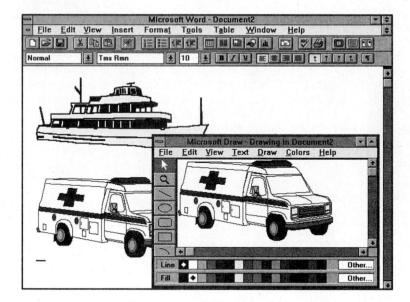

FIG. I.3.

One of Word for Windows add-in applications.

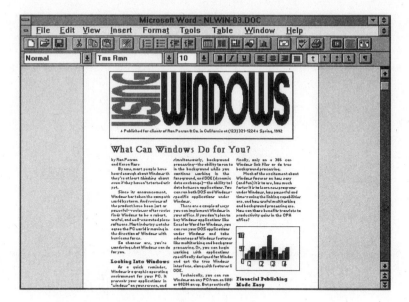

FIG. I.4.

You can view, edit, format, and move objects while pages are zoomed from 25% to 200%.

Word for Windows Reduces Support

Word for Windows contains extensive help files you can use to get an overview of a procedure. To get help, just press the F1 key. When the Help window appears, you can click on topics about which you want additional information. Press Alt+F4 to put the Help window away. In fact, anytime a dialog box or alert box appears and you want more information, just press F1. When you need more extensive help or tips and tricks, refer to this book.

Word for Windows Helps WordPerfect Users

Word for Windows not only does a good job of translating WordPerfect documents and graphics, it can help you learn Word for Windows. When you install Word for Windows, or at any later time, you can turn on the capability to use WordPerfect menus and navigation keys. While the WordPerfect help system is on, you can press a WordPerfect key such as Ctrl+F8 for fonts and the WordPerfect Help dialog box, shown in figure I.5, will appear with the appropriate WordPerfect menu. (The figure shows the highest level WordPerfect menu.) Use the same keystrokes you would use in WordPerfect. When you finish making menu choices, Word for Windows displays a *stick-em* note describing what to do, or actually makes the Word for Windows menu and dialog choices for you. As you watch it make the correct choices, you learn how to use Word for Windows.

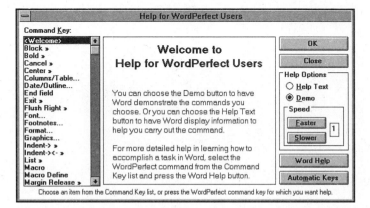

FIG. I.5.

With WordPerfect Help you can make an easy transition to Word for Windows.

If you are the professional typist that likes a clean, clear screen to work on, you can remove the status bar, scroll bars, ruler, ribbon, and toolbar so that the Word for Windows screen is clear except for the single menu bar.

Working with Word for Windows

Word for Windows has features that fit many working environments. Even beginning and intermediate-level operators can customize Word for Windows to fit specific job needs. This section includes several examples of the many types of documents you can produce with Word for Windows.

Word Processing in Daily Business

Word for Windows makes repetitive work very easy. As a professional typist doing daily business work, you can use some of the following Word for Windows features:

- Use print preview or page layout views to see results before you print.
- Use the mail-merge capabilities that guide you through mailings and labels.
- Automatically generate envelopes.
- Use templates to hold repetitive documents, glossaries, and short-cut keys.
- Choose the symbol you need from a table.
- Insert tables for numbers or lists by clicking on a toolbar button.
- Format numbered and bulleted lists by clicking on a toolbar button.
- Add toolbar buttons for the commands you use frequently.
- Portrait (vertical) and landscape (horizontal) pages in the same document.

Word Processing for Legal and Medical Documents

Legal and medical documents present unique word processing requirements that Word for Windows is built to handle:

- Glossaries to eliminate typing long words and repetitive phrases
- One of the best outliners available
- Tables of authorities and automatic cross-referencing
- Annotations, hidden text, and revision marks
- Numbered lines with adjustable spacing

Word Processing for Scientific and Technical Documents

When you write scientific or technical papers, you need to include references, charts, tables, graphs, equations, table references, footnotes, and endnotes. Word for Windows will help your technical documents with the following:

- An equation editor that builds equations when you click on equation pieces and symbols
- Drawing and graphing tools built into Word for Windows
- The capability to insert CGM and AutoCAD files
- Spreadsheet-like tables for data

Word Processing for Financial Documents

The reader's initial impression of a financial report comes when the cover page is turned. Word for Windows gives you on-screen tables, similar to spreadsheets, and links to Microsoft Excel and Lotus 1-2-3 for Windows worksheets and charts. You will find the following productive features:

- Commands and structure similar to Microsoft Excel
- Operate Microsoft Excel or Lotus 1-2-3 and Word for Windows simultaneously and switch between them
- Row-and-column numeric tables that can include math
- Borders, shading, and underlining to enhance columnar reporting
- Tables and charts linked to other Windows applications

Word Processing for Graphics Artists and Advertising

Until now, testing page layouts and advertising design required two applications: a word processor and a desktop publishing program. Word for Windows combines both. Although Word for Windows doesn't have all the "free form" capabilities of a publishing application like Aldus PageMaker, Word for Windows still gives you many features, such as the following:

- Wide range of graphic file import filters
- Text wrap-around graphics
- Movable text or graphics
- Borders and shading
- Parallel or snaking columns that include graphics
- Print preview or an editable page layout view that zooms 25% to 200%
- Compatibility with PostScript typesetting equipment
- Linking of body copy and graphic files into a single, larger master document

Word Processing for Specific Industries

Word for Windows is the only fully customizable word processor available for Windows. Therefore, industry associations, custom software houses, and application developers can tailor Word for Windows features to fit the needs of specific vertical industries or to integrate with their own custom applications. To aid developers, Word for Windows includes the following:

- WordBASIC, an extensive macro programming language with more than 400 commands
- A macro recorder and editing tools
- Customizable toolbars, menus, and shortcut keys
- Glossaries for industry-specific terms
- Customized templates to package documents with customized features
- Personal and foreign language dictionaries
- Integration and data exchange with other Windows applications

How This Book Is Organized

Word for Windows is a program with immense capability and a wealth of features. It can be straightforward and easy to learn if approached correctly. This book is organized to help you learn Word for Windows quickly and efficiently.

If you use Word for Windows Version 1.0 through 1.1a, then you should scan the table of contents for new features and look through the book for pages marked with the Version 2 icon that marks new features.

Using Word for Windows 2, Special Edition, is organized into four parts:

- Part I: Learning the Basics
- Part II: Using Advanced Features
- Part III: Using Graphics and Charts
- Part IV: Customizing Word for Windows

Part I helps you learn the fundamentals of Word for Windows that you will need for basic letters. If you are new to Windows and Word for Windows, you should start at Chapter 1 and learn the basics of operating a Windows application. After you read Chapter 1, work through the quick start tutorial in Chapter 2. It guides you through creating a simple business letter. If you are familiar with Windows, but are not familiar with Word for Windows, you should start on the quick start in Chapter 2. It will get you producing documents quickly. Chapters 3 through 8 describe simple editing and formatting techniques. Chapter 9 describes editing tools such as Word's spelling checker and thesaurus or how to search and replace words, or how to sort lists. Chapter 10 closes Part I by showing you how to print.

Part II teaches features that help you become more productive and work faster. You learn features related to specific tasks. Two of the most useful chapters in Part II are Chapters 11 and 12. Chapter 11 covers styles, which are useful to anyone who uses a format repetitively, for headings, titles, and so on. Chapter 12 describes tables, one of the handiest features in Word. For anyone who works with lists or budgets, the tables are a real time saver.

In Part III you learn how to use the drawing and graphics programs and the *applet* programs that come with Word for Windows. These programs add extensive graphic capability. Word for Windows' capability with graphics puts it almost at the level of desktop publishing software. For most business needs that don't require color control or precise alignment of images, Word for Windows fits the bill.

Turn to Part IV when you want to learn how to customize Word for Windows. You learn how to customize the toolbar, create templates for repetitive documents, and record macros that do automated procedures. Chapter 29 shows you how to use the Tools Options command to customize the appearance and operation of Word for Windows. If you use the same documents frequently, read Chapter 30 and learn how to create templates. When you want to add your own buttons to the toolbar or record your own automated procedures, turn to Chapter 31.

The appendixes contain infrequently used information about installing Word for Windows, converting files from other Word Processors, and managing your use of fonts with Windows and Word for Windows.

Conventions Used in This Book

Conventions used in this book have been established to help you learn to use the program quickly and easily. As much as possible, the conventions correspond with those used in the Word for Windows documentation.

Letters pressed to activate menus, choose commands in menus, and select options in dialog boxes are printed in boldface type: **F**ile **O**pen. Names of dialog boxes are written with initial capital letters, as the name appears on-screen. Messages that appear on-screen are printed in a special font: Document 1.

Two different types of key combinations are used with this program. For combinations joined with a comma (Alt,F), you press and release the first key and then press and release the second key. If a combination is joined with a plus sign (Alt+F), you press and hold the first key while you press the second key.

An icon is used throughout this book to mark features new to Version 2 of Word for Windows.

Learning the Basics

Learning Word for Windows Basics

The basics of using Word for Windows are the same as the basics for using any other Windows program. If you are familiar with another Windows application, such as Microsoft Excel, you may not need to read this "basics" chapter (or perhaps a quick scan is all you need). If you are a new Windows user, however, you will find this chapter important for two reasons: you will become comfortable navigating Word for Windows; and you will have a head start on the next Windows program you learn.

In this chapter, you learn how to control not only Word for Windows menus and dialog boxes but also the windows that contain Word for Windows and its documents. By the time you finish this chapter, you will be able to use the mouse and the keyboard to choose commands from menus, select options from dialog boxes, access the extensive help system, and manipulate windows on-screen. Beyond these basic tasks, you should be able to organize windows so that you can access and use multiple documents at once or "clear away your desktop" so that you can concentrate on a single job.

Starting Windows and Word for Windows

To start Word for Windows, follow these steps:

1. Start Windows by typing *WIN* at the DOS prompt and pressing Enter.

2. Activate the group window that contains Word for Windows. This window is the Microsoft Word for Windows 2.0 group or a group in which a Word for Windows program item has been created.

   Figure 1.1 shows the Microsoft Word for Windows 2.0 group window and the Word for Windows program item selected within. On your screen the group window may be open (as are the Main group window and the Word for Windows 2.0 group window in fig. 1.1) or closed (as are the four group icons at the bottom left of the Program Manager window in fig. 1.1).

   Mouse: Click on the open group window or double-click on the closed group icon that contains the Word for Windows program item icon.

   Keyboard: Press Ctrl+Tab until the desired open group window is active or until the title of the closed group icon is highlighted. Press Enter to restore the group icon into a window.

3. Start Word for Windows.

   Mouse: Double-click on the Word for Windows program item icon.

   Keyboard: Press the arrow keys until the title of the Word for Windows program item icon is highlighted, then press Enter.

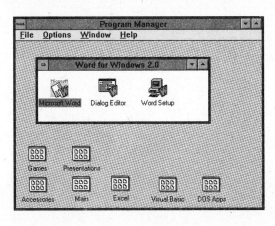

FIG. 1.1.

The open Microsoft Word for Windows group window.

If you are at the DOS prompt (usually C:>) and want to start Windows and Word for Windows together, do the following:

1. Type *WIN C:\WINWORD\WINWORD.EXE*.

2. Press Enter.

T I P

If you always want to start Windows and Word for Windows together, you can add a RUN or LOAD command line to your WIN.INI file. When you type a path name and an application file name after *load=*, Windows loads and minimizes the specified application to an icon. When you type a path name and an application file name after *run=*, Windows loads and runs the specified application. Use Notepad (or any text editor) to add a *run* or *load* line to the *[windows]* segment of your WIN.INI file. The file is located in the \WINDOWS subdirectory. A modified WIN.INI file for WINWORD.EXE in the C:\WINWORD directory may appear as follows:

```
[windows]
run=c:\winword\winword.exe
load=c:\excel\excel.exe
Beep=yes
Spooler=yes
```

After changing the WIN.INI file, save the file to the same directory from which you opened the file. Restart Windows to make your changes take effect.

Understanding the Word for Windows Screen

If you are new to Windows applications, you must learn some of the terms that describe parts of the screen. Study figure 1.2 and table 1.1 to learn the parts of application and document screens. These terms are used throughout this book and other books on Windows applications.

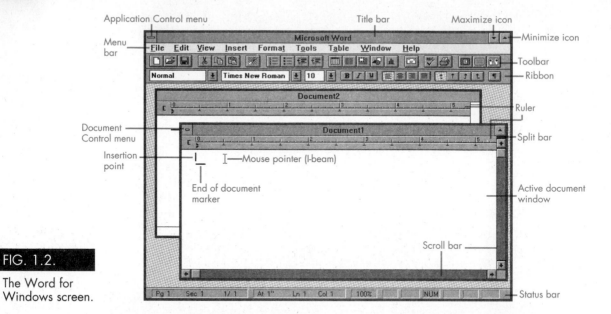

FIG. 1.2.

The Word for Windows screen.

Table 1.1. Components of the Word for Windows Screen

Term	Description
Application window	The window within which Word for Windows runs. If you are running Windows, you may run multiple Windows applications, each in its own window. An application window can fill the entire screen.
Document window	The window within which each document appears. Word for Windows can have multiple document windows. A document window can fill all or a portion of the interior of Word for Windows' application window.
Application Control menu	The menu used to manipulate the application window. To activate this menu, press Alt, space bar or click the control icon.
Document Control menu	The menu used to manipulate the active document window. To activate this menu, press Alt, hyphen (-) or click the control icon.
Title bar	The bar at the top of a window, containing the application or document title.
Active window	The window that accepts entries and commands. This window with a solid title bar is normally the window on top.

Term	Description
Inactive window	Any window you are not working in, which has a cross-hatched or gray title bar.
Mouse pointer	The on-screen pointer that shows the mouse location.
Insertion point	The point where text appears when you type.
End of document marker	The point beyond which no text is entered.
Menu bar	A horizontal list of menu names displayed beneath the application title bar.
Ribbon	A bar containing buttons and text boxes that indicate formatting style, font, font size, font style, paragraph alignment, and tabs at the insertion point's (cursor) location. The ribbon can be used with the mouse to format characters quickly.
Ruler	A bar containing a scale that indicates tabs, paragraph indents, and margins in the paragraph where the insertion point (cursor) is located. The ruler can be used with the mouse to format paragraphs quickly.
Toolbar	A customizable bar containing buttons that enable you to carry out many of the most commonly used commands without using the menus.
Minimize icon	The pictorial equivalent of the Minimize command to shrink a window to an icon.
Maximize icon	The pictorial equivalent of the Maximize command to enlarge a window to full-screen size.
Restore icon	The pictorial equivalent of the Restore command to restore a maximized or minimized window to its previous size and shape.
Scroll bar	A horizontal or vertical bar with arrows used to scroll the document under mouse pointer control.
Split bar	A bar you can drag down to split the active window into two parts, or drag back up to restore.
Status bar	The bar at the bottom of the screen that shows command prompts or indicators.

Using the Toolbar

The *toolbar* enables you to directly access several of the most commonly used commands with the mouse, bypassing the menus. For example, you can start a new document, save a document, cut, copy, and paste text, and create numbered or bulleted lists each with a click of the mouse. To turn on the toolbar, choose the View **T**oolbar command. With the mouse, click **V**iew; then click **T**oolbar. With a keyboard, press Alt,V,T. When the Toolbar is active, a check mark appears next to the command **T**oolbar in the **V**iew menu.

T   I   P   If you forget the function of a particular button on the toolbar, highlight the button and hold down the mouse button. A brief explanation of what that button does appears in the status bar. If you do not want to carry out the command, pull the pointer away from the button before you release the mouse button.

T   I   P   Word for Windows gives you the capability to customize the toolbar to match your needs. You can add up to four macros or commands to the toolbar and replace any existing button's command with any of the commands available in the macros or menus. See Chapter 29 for detailed information on customizing the toolbar.

Table 1.2 summarizes the functions of each of the buttons appearing in the toolbar.

Table 1.2. Toolbar Functions

Button	Function
	Opens a new file using the normal template (default settings). Equivalent to the **F**ile **N**ew command.
	Displays the File Open dialog box so that you can open an existing file. Equivalent to the **F**ile **O**pen command.
	Saves the current document or template. Equivalent to the **F**ile **S**ave command.

Button	Function
	Cuts and places the current selection in the Clipboard. Equivalent to the **E**dit Cu**t** command.
	Copies the current selection into the Clipboard. Equivalent to the **E**dit **C**opy command.
	Inserts the contents of the Clipboard at the insertion point. Equivalent to the **E**dit **P**aste command.
	Reverses the last action. Equivalent to the **E**dit **U**ndo command.
	Creates a numbered list. Equivalent to the **T**ools **B**ullets and Numbering command with Numbered **L**ist option selected.
	Creates a bulleted list. Equivalent to the **T**ools **B**ullets and Numbering command with **B**ullets option selected.
	Moves the left and first line indents of selected paragraph(s) one tab stop to the left.
	Moves the left and first line indents of selected paragraph(s) one tab stop to the right.
	Inserts a table. Dragging the mouse over the sample table determines the number of rows and columns in the table. Equivalent to the **T**able **I**nsert Table command.
	Changes the number of columns in the current section. Equivalent to the **F**ormat **C**olumns command.
	Inserts a frame (text or graphics) at the site of the insertion point (cursor) or around the current selection. Equivalent to the **I**nsert **F**rame command.
	Starts Microsoft Draw so that you can insert a drawing at the insertion point. Equivalent to the **I**nsert **O**bject Microsoft Drawing command.
	Starts Microsoft Graph so that you can insert a graph at the insertion point. Equivalent to the **I**nsert **O**bject Microsoft Graph command.
	Creates an envelope using the selected address as the addressee and prints the envelope with the document. Equivalent to the **T**ools Create **E**nvelope command.
	Checks the spelling in the active document. Equivalent to the **T**ools **S**pelling command.
	Prints the active document using the current defaults. Equivalent to the **F**ile **P**rint command.
	Displays an entire page in page layout view. Equivalent to the **V**iew **Z**oom **W**hole Page command.

continues

Table 1.2. *(continued)*	
Button	**Function**
⊞	Scales the view to 100% in normal view. Equivalent to the **View Z**oom command with **1**00% option selected.
⊞	Scales the view to display the entire width of the page. Equivalent to the **View Z**oom **P**age Width command.

Using the Ribbon and Ruler

The *ribbon* and *ruler* indicate character and paragraph formatting at the insertion point's (cursor's) location. The ribbon appears under the toolbar (if displayed), and a ruler appears at the top of each document window. You can use the mouse with the ribbon and ruler to make formatting changes to documents quickly. You can format characters and paragraphs and set margins and tabs without accessing the menus.

Table 1.3 summarizes the functions accessible from the ribbon. Detailed information on using the ribbon and ruler is available in each chapter that describes commands and features available from the ribbon and ruler.

Each of these ribbon buttons *toggles* a feature on or off. Selecting the button changes the selected text or graphic to the opposite of its current setting for that feature.

Table 1.3. The Ribbon	
Button or list box	**Function**
Style list box	Selects or displays the style for the paragraph in which the insertion point (cursor) is located.
Font list box	Selects or displays the font for the currently selected text or for text typed at the insertion point (cursor).
Point size list box	Selects or displays the point size for the selected text or for text typed at the insertion point.
B	Boldfaces the selected text or text typed at the insertion point.
I	Italicizes the selected text or text typed at the insertion point.
U	Underlines the selected text or text typed at the insertion point.

Button or list box	Function
	Aligns the selected paragraph(s) to the left.
	Centers the selected paragraph(s).
	Aligns the selected paragraph(s) to the right.
	Fully justifies the selected paragraph(s), aligning text to the left and right.
	Inserts a left-aligned tab stop at locations selected on the ruler with the mouse.
	Inserts a center-aligned tab stop at locations selected on the ruler with the mouse.
	Inserts a right-aligned tab stop at locations selected on the ruler with the mouse.
	Inserts a decimal-aligned tab stop at locations selected on the ruler with the mouse.
	Toggles the display of nonprinting characters (such as paragraph and tab markers) off and on.

Using the Mouse

The *mouse* is a hand-held device that, when moved, moves a pointer on-screen. The buttons on the mouse enable you to tell Word for Windows when the mouse is correctly positioned on a menu, text, or a command. When you press one of these mouse buttons, some action occurs depending on the location of the pointer.

The mouse is especially useful for selecting large blocks of text, copying and moving text, selecting commands, exploring menus, changing the sizes and locations of windows, selecting options in dialog boxes, and drawing or charting. You will find that using a combination of mouse movements, touch typing, and shortcut keys is the most productive way to work.

Moving the Mouse

The mouse, shown in figure 1.3, is a small device that fits comfortably under your palm. As you move the mouse across your desk, the *mouse pointer*—usually an arrow shape—moves in the same relative direction across the screen. You find that using the mouse to "point" to an item on-screen becomes a natural process.

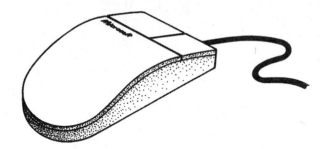

FIG. 1.3.

A Microsoft mouse.

When you hold the mouse, the cord should project forward, away from your arm, so that the buttons are under your fingers. Make sure that you keep the device oriented so that moving the mouse away from you moves the pointer up the screen. This method makes the mouse easier to use. A mouse may have two or three buttons; however, Word for Windows uses only two buttons. You will use the left mouse button most often.

T I P   If you are left-handed, use the Control Panel application found in the Main group of the Program Manager to reverse the actions of the left and right mouse buttons.

Do not operate the mouse on a dusty or dirty surface or over paper. Lint and dirt can build up inside the mouse and cause the pointer to skip.

Understanding the Mouse Pointer

The *mouse pointer* shows more than the pointer's position on-screen. Depending on its location, the pointer changes appearance to tell you what you can do in that location. Table 1.4 shows and explains the different shapes of the pointer.

Table 1.4. Mouse Pointer Shapes

Pointer Appearance	Screen Location	Function
	Menu	Select commands
	Scroll bars	Scroll through document
	Objects or selected text	Move, size, or select objects
	Left edge of text	Select lines or paragraphs
	Selected text with mouse button depressed	Mouse moves selected text
	Text	Type, select, or edit text
	Window corner	Resize two sides of window
	Window edge	Resize single side of window
	Corner or side handle of selected frame or object	Resize selected picture, frame, or object picture
	Window center object edge	Move window or object
	Top of table	Select column
	Left or right edge of any cell in a table	Widen or narrow column
	Split bar	Split window into two panes
	Anywhere	Get help specific to next item selected
	Help window	Select help items
	Anywhere	Wait while processing

Selecting with the Mouse

Three basic techniques are used for selecting items with the mouse:

- *Click* to select an item, such as a menu, command, cell, or graphic object. Clicking in some screen locations, such as over a word, produces a shortcut to a command. To click, move the mouse pointer inside the text or put the pointer on an object, menu name, command name, or dialog box object; then press and release the mouse button once.

- *Double-click* to select a dialog box option and choose OK simultaneously. Double-clicking in some screen locations produces a selection shortcut. To double-click, move the mouse pointer onto the item and rapidly click the left button twice.

- *Drag* to select multiple text characters or to move an object. To drag, move the mouse pointer onto the item, hold down the mouse button while you move the mouse pointer to the new location, and release the mouse button.

To choose a command with the mouse, click the menu name in the menu bar, and then click the command name in the pull-down menu.

T I P   You cannot access some menu items at all times. Until you make a selection in your document, for example, the **Edit Cut** and **Edit Copy** commands are not available. Unavailable commands are dimmed in the menu.

In text, to relocate the flashing vertical cursor, known as the insertion point, follow these steps:

1. Move the I-beam pointer to the spot where you want to insert or edit text.

2. Click once to relocate the insertion point.

To select text, follow these steps:

1. Move the I-beam pointer to the left of the text you want selected.

2. Hold down the mouse button.

3. Drag the I-beam pointer to the right or down across the text you want selected. (Selected text is highlighted.)

4. Release the mouse button.

Using the Keyboard

Word for Windows does not limit you to using only the mouse. With the keyboard, you can execute commands or make selections by using the following techniques:

- Typing the underlined letter in each command or dialog box
- Pressing arrow keys to choose menus and commands
- Pressing shortcut keys
- Pressing function keys

Word for Windows follows the conventions recommended by Microsoft for all Windows applications. When you learn how to select menus and choose items in Word for Windows, you know how to control other Windows applications that follow the recommended conventions.

Using Key Combinations

Throughout this book, you see pairs of keys combined with a plus sign (+), as in Alt+F. This notation means that you must hold down the Alt key as you press the letter key. Do not try to press the two keys simultaneously. After pressing the second key—F in this case—release both keys. (Just press the F key; do not hold down the Shift key for the capital F unless the Shift key also is indicated specifically.)

Keystrokes separated by commas are pressed in sequence. When the text says to "press Alt, space bar," for example, press and release Alt, and then press and release the space bar. Table 1.5 describes the keystrokes, combinations, and sequences of keystrokes you use for making selections from Windows and Word for Windows menus.

Table 1.5. Using the Keyboard To Select from Menus and Dialog Boxes

Key(s)	Action
Alt	Activates the menu bar
Letter (after Alt)	Opens the menu whose name contains the underlined letter, or chooses the command from the pull-down menu
Alt+letter (in dialog box)	Selects or deselects an option or check box in a dialog box. Letter indicates the underlined letter in the item's title.

continues

Table 1.5. *(continued)*

Key(s)	Action
Alt, space bar	Displays the Application Control menu
Alt, - (hyphen)	Displays the Document Control menu
Up/down arrow keys	Moves the selection up or down in the menu or moves among option (round) buttons in a dialog box
Left/right arrow keys	Selects the adjacent menu or moves among option buttons in a dialog box
Enter	Within the menu bar or a menu, chooses the highlighted menu or command; within a dialog box, chooses the button that has bold edges
Esc	Cancels a selection or dialog box
Tab	Activates the next check box, button, or group of options in a dialog box
Space bar (in dialog box)	Selects or deselects the active check box in a dialog box

Choosing Menu Commands with the Keyboard

In the menu bar, the name of each menu contains one underlined letter, which is used to activate that menu from the keyboard. Each command in a menu also contains a single underlined letter, which is used to activate that command.

To choose a command from a menu by the keystroke method, follow these steps:

1. Press the Alt key to activate the menu bar.

2. Press the underlined letter of the menu you want to open.

3. Press the underlined letter of the command in the pull-down menu.

After you activate the menu bar by pressing Alt, you also can move among different menus and commands by pressing the arrow keys. To choose a command with this method, select the menu you want by pressing Alt and the appropriate letter, press the down-arrow key to highlight the command you want to choose, and then press Enter.

Press Esc or click on the menu name to back out of a menu without making a choice. Press Esc or click the Cancel button to back out of a dialog box without making a choice.

T I P

If the Status bar appears at the bottom of the screen, you see a description of the selected menu or command as you move the selection on the menu bar or menu.

T I P

Using Shortcut Keys

You can speed your work in Word for Windows by using shortcut keys, which execute commands without taking you through the menus. Many shortcuts involve key combinations, such as Shift+Del rather than **E**dit **Cut**, or Alt+Backspace rather than **E**dit **U**ndo. Table 1.6 describes the keys that control most Windows applications, including Word for Windows application and document windows. Many other shortcut keys are available for commands and functions. A more complete list of shortcut keys is provided on the command chart at the back of this book and in the appropriate sections that describe the commands.

Table 1.6. Shortcut Keys for the Control Menu

Function	Document Window Shortcut	Word Window Shortcut
Close	Ctrl+F4	Alt+F4
Restore	Ctrl+F5	Alt+F5
Move	Ctrl+F7	Alt+F7
Size	Ctrl+F8	Alt+F8
Minimize	N/A	Alt+F9
Maximize	Ctrl+F10	Alt+F10

T I P In each chapter of this book, you find the shortcut keys that pertain to the subjects being discussed. Besides using the many built-in keyboard shortcuts that Word for Windows provides, you can create your own shortcut keys with macros. See Chapter 31 for more information on macros.

Using Dialog Boxes

When Word for Windows needs more information to complete a command, the application displays a dialog box in which you can enter additional information or request options. A command that displays a dialog box appears in a pull-down menu with an ellipsis (...). For example, figure 1.4 shows the File menu. Notice the **Print** command. Figure 1.5 shows the dialog box that appears after you choose the **File Print** command. For your convenience, the components of the dialog box are labeled. Table 1.7 summarizes these components.

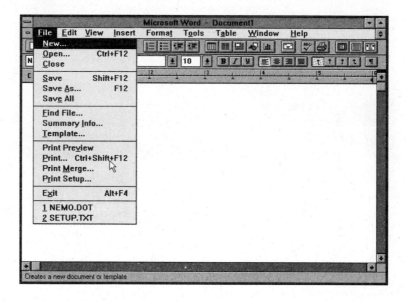

FIG. 1.4.

The File menu.

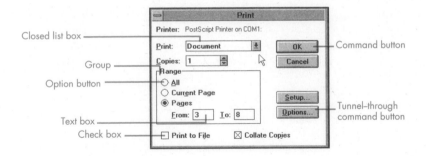

Closed list box

Command button

Group

Option button

Text box

Check box

Tunnel–through
command button

FIG. 1.5.

The Print dialog
box.

Table 1.7. Examining a Dialog Box

Component	Description
Text box	Box in which you type text or numbers.
Option button	Round button used to select a single option from multiple options in a group.
Group	An associated group of option buttons from which only one option button can be selected.
Check box	Used to select one or more options. The status of the check box toggles on or off.
List box	Displays a scrolling list of alternatives. Open list boxes remain open at all times (as in the File Open dialog box). Closed list boxes open when selected to display a scrolling list (see fig. 1.6).
Command button	Used to execute or cancel the command or extend the dialog box for more options.
Tunnel-through command button	Used to move to another dialog box related to the current dialog box.

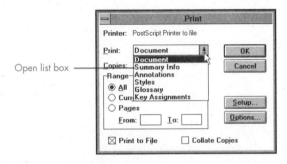

Open list box

FIG. 1.6.

The Print dialog
box with Print list
expanded.

Upon first appearance, a dialog box shows the current option selections and settings for the selected text, picture, or insertion point (cursor location). When selected, check boxes contain an X and option buttons appear with a darkened center. In figure 1.5, for example, the Print options are set as follows:

Option	Setting
Print	Document
Copies	1
Range	Pages
From	3
To	8
Print to File	Off
Collate Copies	On

A dashed line surrounds the active box, option, or group of options in a dialog box.

Use one of the following techniques to select or unselect options, text boxes, list boxes, and so on, in a dialog box:

- Click the item with the mouse pointer.

- Press Alt+*letter*, where *letter* is the underlined letter in the item name.

- Press the Tab key until the item is enclosed in a dashed line; then press the space bar. Press Shift+Tab to select an item in the reverse direction.

Working with Text Boxes

Text boxes accept text or numbers that you type. You can edit the text within a text box the same way you edit text in any Windows application. The typing cursor where your typing appears is a small flashing vertical bar, known in Word for Windows as the *insertion point*. The mouse pointer appears as an *I-beam* when moved within a text area.

Keep in mind that the I-beam is not the cursor. The insertion point and the I-beam are separate. The I-beam is used by the mouse to reposition the insertion point or to select text.

After you select the text box by clicking the box or pressing Alt+letter, use the mouse actions and keys shown in table 1.8 to move or edit text.

Table 1.8. Text-Editing Actions

Mouse Action	Result
Click I-beam in text	Moves the insertion point (flashing cursor) to the I-beam location
Shift+click in text	Selects all text between the current insertion point and the I-beam
Drag	Selects all text over which the I-beam moves while the mouse button is held down

Keyboard Action	Result
Left/right-arrow key	Moves the insertion point left/right one character
Shift+arrow key	Selects text as the insertion point moves left or right
Ctrl+left/right-arrow key	Moves the insertion point to the beginning of the preceding/next word
Shift+Ctrl+left/right-arrow key	Selects from the insertion point to the beginning of the preceding/next word
Home	Moves the insertion point to the beginning of the line
Shift+Home	Selects from the insertion point to the beginning of the line
End	Moves the insertion point to the end of the line
Shift+End	Selects from the insertion point to the end of the line

To insert text in a text box using the mouse, click the I-beam at the location where you want the text, and then type the text. If you use a keyboard, press the Alt+letter combination or the Tab key to activate the text box, and then press one of the cursor-movement keys shown in table 1.8 to position the insertion point. Then type.

To delete characters in a text box, follow these steps:

1. Position the insertion point.

   Mouse: Click the I-beam in text.

   Keyboard: Select the text box option and press an arrow key.

2. Press Del to delete a character to the right of the insertion point.

   or

   Press the Backspace key to delete a character to the left of the insertion point and to close up the space.

To replace text or to delete multiple characters in a text box, follow these steps:

1. Select the text box.

   Mouse: Click the text box.

   Keyboard: Press the Alt+*letter* combination or Tab until the text box is selected.

2. Select the text you want to replace.

   Mouse: Drag the I-beam over the text you want to replace. In some text boxes, you can double-click to select the entire contents.

   Keyboard: Press the arrow keys to move the pointer so that the pointer rests before the first character you want replaced. Press Shift+right-arrow key to select each character you want replaced.

3. Type the replacement text.

   or

   Press Del to delete the text.

Text you type replaces the selected text only when the **T**yping Replaces Selection option is selected from the **T**ools **O**ption General **C**ategory dialog box.

T   I   P   Pressing Tab activates each option or box in a dialog box and selects all text in an active text box. All the characters appear white on a black background. If you type then, you replace all the characters. If you press the Del key, you delete all the characters. If you accidentally delete characters and want to start over, press Esc to remove the dialog box and start over with the original text.

Working with List Boxes

With *list boxes*, you can choose from lists of alternatives, such as file names, fonts, or sizes. List boxes save you time and prevent typing errors.

Figure 1.7 shows the Open dialog box, which contains the File **N**ame list box. Use this list box to select a file to be retrieved. This type of list box always remains open so that you can see the list. Scroll through the list by clicking the up and down scroll bar arrows displayed on the right side of the list box or by pressing the up- or down-arrow key. You can move quickly to an alternative by clicking once in the box and then typing the first letter of the alternative you want. The list scrolls to names that begin with that letter. When you see the item you want to select, click the item or press an up- or down-arrow key until the item is highlighted.

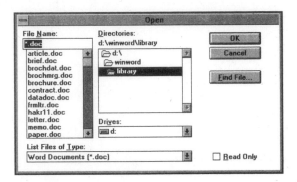

FIG. 1.7.

The Files list box in the Open File dialog box.

Not all list boxes remain open permanently. Figures 1.5 and 1.6 (shown earlier) show the Print dialog box and the **P**rint list box, which is used to select which parts of the document to print. Notice that in figure 1.5, the **P**rint list box is closed, but in figure 1.6, the box is open.

A closed list box does not immediately show its list but drops down the list when you select the box. To open a list box with the mouse, click the down arrow displayed to the right of the box. From the keyboard, press Alt+letter to select and open the box.

After the box opens, use the mouse to click the choice you want. From the keyboard, press the down-arrow key to select a choice in the list. Then press Tab to move to the next set of options, or press Enter to choose OK and execute the command.

T I P

With a mouse, you can double-click selections in some open list boxes or double-click some option buttons to make a selection and simultaneously choose OK. Experiment to see which boxes and buttons respond to this technique.

NOTE Make sure that the name you want to select in a list box is highlighted (appears white on black) and is not just surrounded by a dashed line. When you press the Tab key, dashes may surround a name, but the name is not selected until you press the space bar or an arrow key.

Working with Option Buttons and Check Boxes

You can choose from two types of options in dialog boxes: the round option buttons or the square check boxes. With the *round option buttons*, you can make only one choice from among a group of option buttons. Round option buttons are selected when they contain a solid circle.

To choose an option button, use one of these procedures:

Mouse: Click the option button or its name.

Keyboard: Press Alt+*letter*, where *letter* is the underlined letter in the name of the option you want. If one of the option buttons in the group is active, you can move the selection within the group by pressing the arrow keys or by typing the underlined letter. The active option has a dotted box around it.

The square *check boxes* enable you to turn on more than one option within a group of check boxes. Check boxes are selected when they contain an X. The result of turning on multiple check boxes is a combination of the options selected. You may choose, for example, character formatting to be **B**old and *I*talic.

To change a check box (toggle on or off), use one of these procedures:

Mouse: Click the check box.

Keyboard: Press Alt+*letter*, where *letter* is the underlined letter in the name of the option you want. If the option is selected (has a dotted box around it), you can toggle the option on or off by pressing the space bar.

To change the status of an option button or check box, select the option again.

Working with Command Buttons

Command buttons execute commands, cancel dialog boxes, or extend dialog boxes to display more options. A few command buttons "tunnel through" to a dialog box that you ordinarily access by directly choosing a command from a menu. If you select Find File in the Open File dialog box (refer to fig. 1.7), for example, the dialog box in figure 1.8 (or one similar to it) appears to help you find a file that you may have misplaced. You ordinarily access the Find File dialog box by choosing the Find File command from the **F**ile menu.

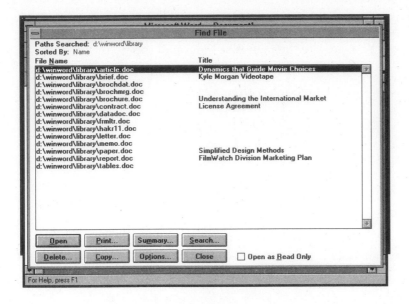

FIG. 1.8.

The Find File
dialog box.

Choose any command button with a click. If you use the keyboard, use
the following keypresses:

Press	To choose
Enter	The bold bordered button (usually OK)
Esc	Cancel
Alt+*letter*	Any other button, where *letter* is the underlined letter in the button name

Some buttons may appear gray when they are not available for selection.

Getting Help

Windows and Word for Windows have Help information to guide you
through new commands and procedures. Word for Windows' extensive
Help files explain topics that range from parts of the screen to commands, dialog boxes, and many specific procedures.

To get help in Word for Windows or other Windows programs, choose
a command from the **H**elp menu or press F1. The Help Index command
or F1 displays the window shown in figure 1.9. From this window you

can learn how to use Help or see the index of topics. Notice that Help has three different ways in which you can access or control help information. You can use the menus at the top of the Help window, use the buttons under the menus for quick browsing through Help information or for jumping forward or backward through related topics, or choose any underlined words to go directly to information on that topic.

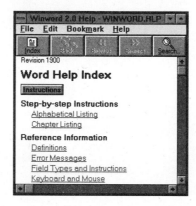

The following list describes the menu commands available in Help:

Command	Action
File Open	Opens a Help file to another program (usually located in the program directory).
File Print Topic	Prints the current Help topic to the current printer.
File Printer Setup	Sets up the printer.
File Exit	Exits the Help program.
Edit Copy	Copies the active Help window's text contents into the clipboard so that you can paste this information into other documents.
Edit Annotate	Displays a notepad in which you can type your own notes to attach to the current Help topic. Topics with custom notes show a paper clip icon at the top to remind you that these topics have annotations. (To learn more about annotations, refer to Chapter 15.)
Bookmark Define	Creates a bookmark name that attaches to the current Help topic. You can return quickly to this topic by selecting the name from the list in the Bookmark Define list or by choosing the name from under the Bookmark menu. Bookmarks in Help are like bookmarks in Word for Windows. (Refer to Chapter 4 to learn about bookmarks.)

Command	Action
Bookmark # *name*	Lists by numbered name the available bookmarks so that you can choose one and quickly go to the topic where that bookmark is located. (# *name* is not a visible command until bookmarks have been created.)
Help Using Help	Shows you information about how to use Help.
Help About	Shows the copyright and version of your Help file.

You can use the Bookmark and Edit Annotate commands to customize Help. By marking the location of interesting topics and annotating those topics with notes, you can customize Help to fit your work.

T I P

Command buttons located under the menu help you to move through the Help topics. Choose a button by clicking on the button or by pressing Alt+*letter*. The following command buttons help you move through information:

Button	Action
Index	Shows the Help Index.
Back	Returns to the preceding Help topic. With this button, you can retrace the topics you have viewed back to the initial Help Index.
Browse <<	Shows the preceding related topic. If no more related topics exist, the button dims.
Browse >>	Shows the next related topic. If no more related topics exist, the button dims.
Search	Displays a list of key words from which you can choose a topic. The Search dialog box enables you to search for topics within the Help file.

Jumping to Linked Topics

"Hot" words or phrases appear within the actual Help text. These words or phrases have a solid or dashed underline, meaning that the word or phrase is linked to additional information.

To jump to the topic related to a solid underlined word, click on the word, or press Tab until the word is selected and press Enter. To see the definition of a word with a dashed underline, hold down the mouse button on the word, or tab to the word and press the Enter key.

Any time that the Help window is active, you can return to the Help index by choosing the **I**ndex button. When the Index appears, you can display information about a linked topic by selecting an underlined topic.

Searching for a Topic

The Search dialog box enables you to find topics related to the subject with which you need help. To use Search, choose the Search button; the dialog box shown in figure 1.10 appears.

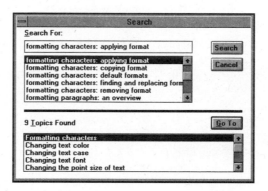

FIG. 1.10.

Searching for
help by topic.

Mouse: Scroll through the **S**earch For list and click on a topic. Then click on the Search button. The lower box, **T**opics Found, fills in with related topics. Scroll through these topics, click on the topic you want more information about, then click on the **G**o To button. The Help window for that topic appears.

Keyboard: Press Alt+S to choose the **S**earch For list. Type a topic in the text box. As you type, the list scrolls to topics that start with the letters you type. If you want to scroll through the list, press Tab until a topic in the list is enclosed with dashes, then press the up- or down-arrow keys. Press Enter, and the Go To list fills with related topics. Press the up- or down-arrow keys to select a topic, and then press Enter.

Displaying Help on Error Messages

You can get help for any dialog box or error message that appears in Word for Windows. Figure 1.11 shows the message box that appears when you try to expand a glossary entry that does not exist. When such a dialog box or error message appears, press F1 or press the Help button to get context-sensitive help. Figure 1.12 shows the Help screen that appears when you press F1 or the Help button after the error message in figure 1.11 appears.

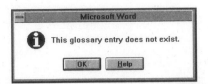

FIG. 1.11.

A message box warning of an error.

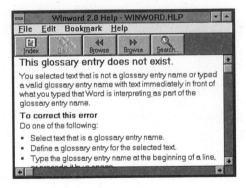

FIG. 1.12.

The Help screen for the error message box.

Displaying Context-Sensitive Help

To learn what a command does or how a portion of the screen works, press Shift+F1, then choose the command (using standard keyboard or mouse techniques) or choose a portion of the screen by clicking. Notice that the mouse pointer changes to a question mark that overlays the pointer. Pressing Shift+F1 enables you to ask a question about the item you choose.

Closing the Help Window

Because Help is an actual program, you must close its window when you are done. To remove the Help window, double-click on the Control menu icon to the left of the Help title bar, or press Alt, space bar, then C for **C**lose (Alt+F4) or choose the **F**ile E**x**it command.

Getting Help for WordPerfect Users

Word for Windows has built-in help features to aid WordPerfect users during the transition to Word for Windows. One of the help features enables you to use WordPerfect navigation keystrokes. The other enables you to use the WordPerfect keystrokes you have memorized while you learn how to operate Windows programs. You can get a help window describing what to do or see a demonstration on your document of how to do the equivalent Word for Windows technique. Figure 1.13 shows the WordPerfect Help dialog box.

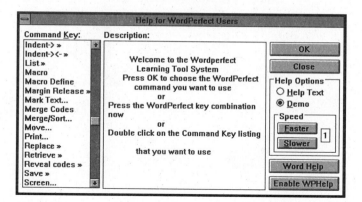

FIG. 1.13.

The WordPerfect Help dialog box.

You can display the WordPerfect Help dialog box in two ways. If you normally want to use Word for Windows menus, then choose the **H**elp **W**ordPerfect Help command to display the dialog box. If you want to use WordPerfect command keystrokes while learning Word for Windows, you can choose settings described later so that the WordPerfect Help dialog box appears as soon as you press a WordPerfect command keystroke.

To use WordPerfect Help, follow these steps:

1. Choose the **H**elp **W**ordPerfect Help command.

    or

Press a WordPerfect function key if you have that feature enabled. (Enabling WordPerfect keystrokes is described later in this section.)

The WordPerfect Help dialog box appears.

2. Select the **H**elp Text option if you want to see a scrolling list of information over your document.

or

Select **D**emo if you want Word for Windows to demonstrate on your document how to do the equivalent command. Select **F**aster or **S**lower speed options for the rate of the demonstration.

3. From the Command **K**ey list, choose the WordPerfect command in one of the following ways:

Press the appropriate WordPerfect command or function key.

Use the Tab and arrow keys or click on an item, then choose the OK button.

Double-click on an item.

As you make selections, the dialog box shows help information in the middle window.

If you select the **H**elp Text option, when you choose OK Word for Windows displays another Command **K**ey list from which you must select another option, or a moveable list of information over the top of your Word for Windows document, as shown in figure 1.14.

WordPerfect Help

Refer to the following information while performing the commands in Word.

To change the point size

1. If the ribbon is not displayed, choose Ribbon from the View menu.
2. Select the text you want to format, or position the insertion point where you want to begin typing in the new size.
3. Click the arrow next to the font size box on the ribbon.
4. Select the point size you want.

Close

FIG. 1.14.

The movable scrolling help list.

You can type in your document as you read the help information. Because this window is an actual program window, you must close the window by clicking the Close button or by activating it and pressing

Alt+F4 or double-clicking on the Application control icon at the window's top left.

If you select the **D**emo option, the dialog box disappears when you choose OK, and Word for Windows demonstrates how to do the equivalent command to your request using Word for Windows commands and features. This is an excellent way to see where features are located and to learn Word for Windows concepts.

Another way to use WordPerfect Help is to turn on a feature that enables you to use WordPerfect command or navigation keys while in Word for Windows. Select the Automatic Keys button in the Help for WordPerfect Users dialog box. Now anytime you're working on a Word for Windows document, you can press a WordPerfect command to display the WordPerfect Help box (if you chose the **H**elp text option) or a demonstration of how to execute the command in Word for Windows (if you selected the **D**emo option). You can disable this feature later by selecting the Disable Automatic button (which replaces the Automatic Keys button when selected).

Another way to use WordPerfect commands while you are working in Word for Windows is through the Options dialog box. Follow these steps:

1. Choose the **T**ools **O**ptions command.

2. Select the General **C**ategory.

   The dialog box shown in figure 1.15 is displayed.

3. If you want to use WordPerfect keystroke methods for moving in the document, select the WordPerfect Document Navigation Keys check box.

4. If you want to use WordPerfect keystrokes for Word for Windows equivalent demonstrations or help, select the **W**ordPerfect Help check box.

5. Choose OK or press Enter.

When WordPerfect Help is enabled, the WPH indicator appears in the status bar. When WordPerfect Document Navigation Keys is selected, the WPN indicator appears in the status bar. When both options are selected, WP appears in the status bar.

If you have **W**ordPerfect Help selected in the General Category of the Tools Options dialog box, then pressing a key such as Ctrl+F8 (the Fonts key in WordPerfect) displays the WordPerfect Help dialog box at the appropriate WordPerfect Font menu, as shown in figure 1.16.

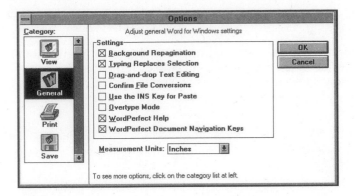

FIG. 1.15.

The Options dialog box with General Category selected.

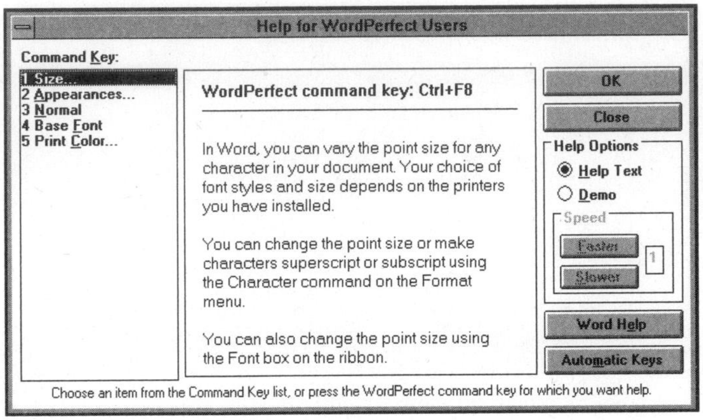

FIG. 1.16.

The appropriate level of WordPerfect menu displays when you press a WordPerfect function key.

Manipulating Windows

When you use Word for Windows, you can display and run more than one application or work with more than one Word for Windows document. Seeing that much information on your screen can be confusing unless you keep your windows organized on-screen.

You see two types of windows on-screen. An *application window* contains an application, such as Word for Windows, Microsoft Excel, Q+E, or Aldus PageMaker. Applications display data in *document windows*, which appear within the application window.

Selecting the Active Window

Your work is done in *active* document and application windows. The active window generally has a solid title bar. If windows overlap, the active window is usually on top. Notice the differences between the windows in figure 1.17.

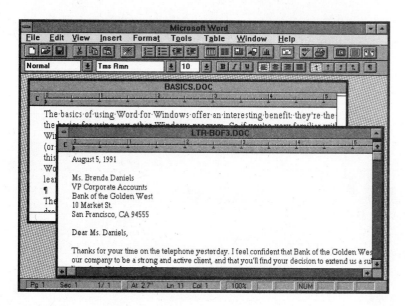

To change between document windows with the mouse, click anywhere on the window you want to activate. With the keyboard, open the **Win**dow menu, which lists and numbers the documents on-screen, and choose the appropriate window number. The document with the check mark by its name is the active document. Alternatively, you can switch between document windows by pressing Ctrl+F6.

You can run other applications at the same time as Word for Windows. You can switch among applications by pressing Alt+Esc or Alt+Tab, or you can press Ctrl+Esc to open the Task List and select the desired application from the list of open applications. If you can see another application window, click on the window to activate and bring it to the top.

Moving a Window

To move an application window or document window with the mouse, drag the window title bar until the shadowed outline of the window is where you want to relocate the window. Then release the mouse button.

From the keyboard, open the Application Control menu by pressing Alt, space bar, or open the Document Control menu by pressing Alt, - (hyphen). Press M to select **M**ove. When the four-headed arrow appears in the title bar, press the arrow keys to move the shadowed outline of the window. Press Enter to relocate the window, or press Esc to retain the original location.

Sizing a Window

When working with multiple applications or documents, you may want to see only part of an application window or a document window. You can do so by changing the window size. Follow these steps:

1. Activate the window.

   Mouse: Click on and move the window so that the edge or corner you want to change is visible.

   Keyboard: Press Alt,W to open the **W**indow menu. Press the number that appears to the left of the window you want active.

2. Select the window edge you want to move.

   Mouse: Move the mouse pointer over the edge or corner you want resized until the pointer changes to a two-headed arrow.

   Keyboard: Press Alt, - (hyphen) to open the Document Control menu, or press Alt, space bar to open the Application Control menu. Then press S to choose the **S**ize command. Press the arrow key that points to the edge you want sized. If you want to size a corner, first press the arrow key that points to one side of the corner, and then press the arrow key that points to the other side of the corner.

3. Resize the window.

   Mouse: Drag the two-headed arrow until the shadow of the window's edge is in its new location. Release the mouse button.

   Keyboard: Press the arrow key(s) in the direction you want the edge or corner moved. When the shadow of the edge is in its new location, press Enter.

Minimizing, Maximizing, and Restoring Windows

You soon find that your computer desktop can become as cluttered as your real desktop. To gain more space, you can put unused applications temporarily on hold by *minimizing* them so that they become small symbols (icons) at the bottom of the screen. (Document windows cannot be minimized to icons.) When you need a minimized application, you can *restore* its icon to an application window at the original location and size. You *maximize* a window to fill the entire available screen area. The icons for minimizing and maximizing are shown earlier in figure 1.2.

 NOTE When an application or document is in a window, the maximize icon appears as an up arrow at the top right corner of the window. The maximize icon changes when the window is maximized (as large as possible). The application maximize icon changes to the double-arrow restore icon so that you can return the application to a window.

To maximize an application window or a document window with the mouse, click the maximize icon for the active window, or double-click the window's title bar.

To maximize a window from the keyboard, press Alt, - (hyphen) to display the Document Control menu, or press Alt, space bar to display the Application Control menu. Press X to choose Maximize from either menu.

To shrink an application window to an icon that appears at the bottom of the screen, click the minimize icon. From the keyboard, press Alt, space bar to display the Application Control menu and then press N to choose Minimize. You cannot minimize a document window in Word for Windows.

Whether Word for Windows' application window has been maximized to fill the screen or minimized to appear as a small icon, you always can restore the window to its last size. If the application is a small icon at the bottom of the screen, and you want the application in a window, double-click the application's icon. If the application fills the screen, click the restore icon at the upper right corner of the maximized window. With a keyboard, select the Application Control menu by pressing Alt, space bar and then choose **R**estore.

Closing a Document Window

When you finish with an application or a document, you should close the document window to remove the window from the screen and to free memory. If you have made a change since the last time you saved the document, Word for Windows asks whether you want to save the changes.

To close the file contained in the active document window, follow these steps:

1. Close the document window.

    Mouse: Choose the **F**ile **C**lose command. This command closes the file even if the file is open in more than one document window.

    or

    Click the Document Control icon, then click **C**lose. As a shortcut, double-click the Document Control icon.

    Keyboard: Press Alt, F, then C to close the file. To close the active window, press Alt,-,C to choose **C**lose.

2. If a dialog box appears, confirm whether you want to save changes made since the last save.

    Mouse: Click the **Y**es command button to save the document, **N**o to close without saving, or Cancel to return to the document.

    Keyboard: Press Y to save the document, N to close without saving, or Esc to return to the document.

3. If you choose Yes and the document previously has not been named, enter a new file name in the Save dialog box that appears.

    Mouse: Type the new name and click the OK command button.

    Keyboard: Type the new name and press Enter.

To learn more about saving a document, see Chapter 3.

Quitting Word for Windows

To quit Word for Windows, follow these steps:

1. Choose the **F**ile **E**xit command.

    Mouse: Click **F**ile; then click **E**xit.

    Keyboard: Press Alt+F,X or press Alt+F4.

2. If a dialog box appears, confirm whether you want to save changes to documents made since the last save.

   Mouse: Click the **Yes** command button to save the document, **No** to close without saving, or Cancel to return to the document.

   Keyboard: Press Y to save the document, N to close without saving, or Esc to return to the document.

3. If you choose Yes, enter a new file name in the Save dialog box that appears.

   Mouse: Type the new name and click the OK command button.

   Keyboard: Type the new name and press Enter.

4. Repeat steps 2 and 3 for each document name that appears in an alert box. The dialog box asking whether you want to save appears for each on-screen document that has been changed.

T I P Double-click the Application Control menu icon to the left of the Microsoft Word title bar to exit Word quickly. From the keyboard, press Alt+F4. Word for Windows quits immediately if you haven't made any changes since the last time you saved your documents. If you have made changes, you are asked whether you want to save.

T I P Choose the **F**ile Sa**v**e All command if you want to save all open files, macros, and glossaries. A dialog box appears for each one, asking whether you want to save.

From Here . . .

After reading this chapter, you should do the quick start tutorial in Chapter 2. The quick start builds a sample business letter and quickly teaches you the basics of entering, editing, and formatting so that you immediately can become productive with Word for Windows.

Quick Start: Creating a Business Letter

This quick start chapter covers the fundamentals of Word for Windows so that you can become productive quickly. Figure 2.1 shows the business letter you will create. In this chapter, you learn the following:

- Display the ruler, ribbon, and toolbar
- Set page margins
- Type and edit text
- Set tab stops and tab alignments
- Save and retrieve documents

- Select and change character fonts and sizes
- Center selected text
- Draw borders around paragraphs
- Move text to a new location
- Preview the appearance of printed documents
- Print documents

Generic Quality Corporation
324 Vineyard Rd.
Santa Rosa, CA 95409

August 18, 1992

Mr. Jim Runell
Generic Quality Corporation
1298 California St.
San Francisco, CA 94467

Subject: Automated Reports

Dear Jim,

This letter is to thank you for your recommendation to move to Windows and Excel. The Xanix project was a big success!

We completed the Xanix project on time and with excellent results. The client was very pleased. Your recommendation to bring everyone up to speed on Word for Windows and Excel before starting the project was excellent. Everyone on the project felt they were more productive than they were with our older software. Word's ability to hot-link data with other applications, such as our engineering design package, the database in dBASE, and our spreadsheets in Excel, was astounding.

You might like to see the following list of some of our forecast and actual completion dates.

Project	Scheduled	Actual
Initial Report	April 20, 92	April 16, 92
Design	May 18, 92	May 15, 92
Completion	July 20, 92	July 10, 92

Your recommendation of Microsoft Word for Windows and Excel contributed to our quick completions and polished results. Thanks for helping us work even better.

Sincerely,

Ms. Jan Bosco
Senior Project Manager

FIG. 2.1.

The sample
business letter.

This quick start explains how to use the mouse and the keyboard. Later chapters explain in greater detail the different techniques for editing, selecting, and choosing commands in Word for Windows. Approximately halfway through this quick start, you learn how to save a file. If necessary, you can quit Word for Windows at that time and continue the quick start later.

Starting Word for Windows

Before you can start Word for Windows, you must be in Windows. If you are not familiar with Windows, consult your Windows documentation to get acquainted with a few basics.

To start Word for Windows, follow these steps:

1. Type *win* at the DOS prompt.

2. Start Word for Windows.

   Mouse: Double-click on the Word for Windows icon, which is located in the Word for Windows 2.0 group window (see fig. 2.2). If the Word for Windows group window is reduced to an icon, double-click on the icon to open the window.

   Keyboard: Press Ctrl+Tab until the Word for Windows 2 group window or icon is selected. If the Word for Windows 2 group is an icon, press Enter. Press the arrow key until the Word for Windows icon is selected and press Enter.

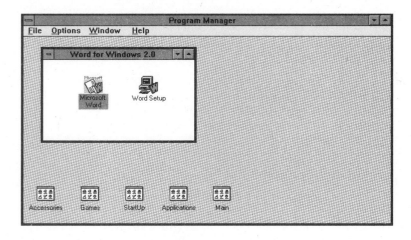

FIG. 2.2.

The Word for Windows icon in the Program Manager.

When Word for Windows starts, your screen looks similar to figure 2.3. Word for Windows can appear full-screen or in a window. If someone used the program before you, that user may have customized Word for Windows' appearance differently.

The next section instructs you how to display the ribbon, ruler, toolbar, and status bar. The ribbon, ruler, and toolbar buttons are accessed most easily with a mouse. These items enable you to quickly and easily access frequently used commands.

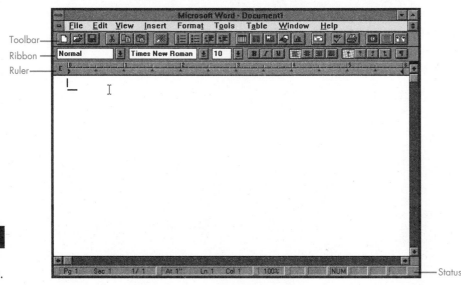

FIG. 2.3.

The Word for Windows screen.

Changing the Screen Appearance

The toolbar and ribbon appear under the menu bar. The *toolbar* gives you quick access to frequently used commands such as copying, inserting bullets, and printing. The *ribbon* gives you quick access to formatting commands such as font type and size, bold, or italic. The *ruler* displays at the top of each document window and shows tab settings, margins, and column or table margins. The *status bar* appears at the bottom of the Word for Windows window. The status bar displays messages relevant to commands you are using and information about the location of the insertion point (for example, the column, line, page, and section numbers). The status of certain keys—the Caps Lock and Num Lock keys, for example—is also displayed in the status bar.

To turn on the ribbon, ruler, toolbar, and status bar, follow these steps:

1. Choose the **View Ribbon** command.

   Mouse: Click **View**; then click **Ribbon**.

   Keyboard: Press Alt,V,B.

2. Choose the **View R**uler command.

    Mouse: Click **V**iew; then click **R**uler.

    Keyboard: Press Alt,V,R.

3. Choose the **View T**oolbar command.

    Mouse: Click **V**iew; then click **T**oolbar.

    Keyboard: Press Alt,V,T.

4. Choose the **T**ools **O**ptions command.

    Mouse: Click **T**ools; then click **O**ptions. Select View from the **Cat**egory list. Click on the Status **B**ar option and click OK.

    Keyboard: Press Alt,O,O. Use the arrow keys to select View from the **C**ategory list and then press Alt,B. Press Enter.

A check mark appears next to the Ri**b**bon, **R**uler, and **T**oolbar commands in the **V**iew menu when those items are displayed. Each time you choose one of these commands, you toggle the item's display on or off.

If you want Word for Windows to fill the entire screen so that you have more room to type and work, you can maximize the application window by doing the following:

> **Mouse:** Click on the up arrow at the far right side of Word for Windows' title bar. If you find a down arrow and a double arrow only, the Word for Windows window already is maximized.

> **Keyboard:** Press Alt+space bar. (Hold down the Alt key as you press the space bar.) Press X to choose the Ma**x**imize command. If the Ma**x**imize command is grayed, the Word for Windows window already is maximized.

For additional information on manipulating windows, see Chapter 1.

Changing Document Formatting

A letter's appearance strongly influences the reader's initial impression. You can increase your letter's acceptance and make the letter more readable by adjusting its appearance through formatting. Word for Windows uses the following four levels of formatting:

Page Set Up   Controls document format

Section Layout   Controls chapter—or section—type formatting within the document

Paragraph	Controls line and paragraph formatting
Character	Controls individual character appearance

To set the page margins, follow these steps:

1. Choose the Format Page Set Up command.

   Mouse: Click on Format, then click Page Set Up.

   Keyboard: Press Alt,T,U.

   The Page Setup dialog box appears, showing current document settings.

2. Select the Margins option.

   Mouse: Click on the Margins option button at the top of the dialog box.

   Keyboard: Press Alt+M.

   The Page Setup dialog box shows options and settings for margins (see fig. 2.4). In this dialog box, you set formatting that affects the entire document. Other options are paper Size and Orientation and Paper Source.

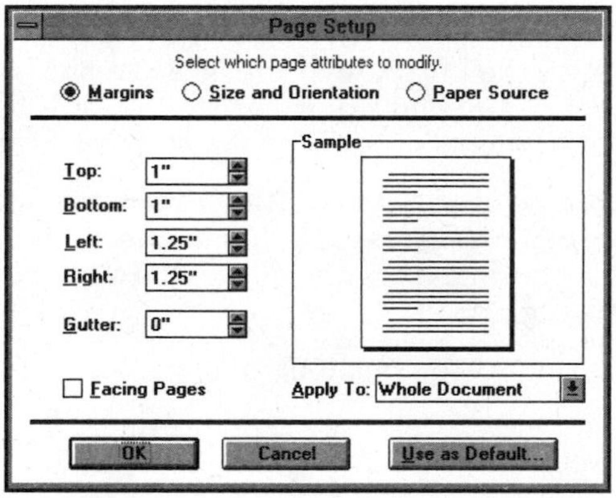

FIG. 2.4.

The Page Setup dialog box showing Margin settings.

3. Change the top margin from 1 inch to 1.5 inches.

   Mouse: Position the I-beam in the text box and double-click to select the Top text box. Type *1.5* to replace the selected 1 " in the box.

   Keyboard: Press Alt+T to select the Top text box. (Hold down the Alt key as you press T.) Type *1.5* to replace the selected 1 " in the box.

4. Choose OK or press Enter.

The entire document now uses 1.5-inch top-of-page margins.

> Read the options in dialog boxes to learn Word for Windows as you
> work. If you are unclear about the contents of the dialog box on the
> screen, press F1. Word for Windows on-line help appears with an
> explanation of the dialog box. To close a help dialog box, press
> Alt+4.
>
> **T I P**

Changing Character Formatting

Follow these steps to enter the company name in bold typeface:

1. Choose a bold character format.

   Mouse: Choose the **B** button in the ribbon. Notice that the button
   appears highlighted. Choose OK.

   Keyboard: Press Ctrl+B to turn on bold or Alt,T,C to choose the
   Forma**t** **C**haracter command. The Character dialog box appears
   (see fig. 2.5). Press Alt+B to select the **B**old option. When Bold is
   on, the Bold check box appears with an X. Press Enter.

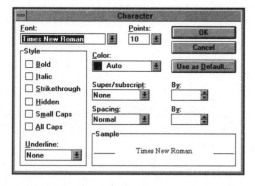

FIG. 2.5.

The Character
dialog box.

2. Type the company name: *Generic Quality Corporation*.

3. Choose normal character format and move to the next line.

   Mouse: Click on the **B** button in the ribbon again. Notice that the
   button no longer appears highlighted. Press Enter to move to the
   next line. Choose OK.

Keyboard: Press Ctrl+B to unselect the bold command, or press Alt,T,C to choose the Forma**t** **C**haracter command. Then press Alt+B to remove the X from the Bold check box. Press Enter.

T   I   P   The character fonts, sizes, and type styles available in Word for Windows may be different than those formatting commands used in the quick starts. Your work, therefore, may look slightly different than the figures. Your available fonts, sizes, and styles depend on whether you use TrueType, your printer's capabilities, the font cartridges or soft fonts installed in your printer, and which of these options you selected during printer installation or from the **F**ile **P**rinter Setup command.

Typing the Text

Using a word processor is different from using a typewriter. Do not press Enter (carriage return) at the end of each line. When you type in Word for Windows, type continuously until you reach the end of a paragraph. The words in a sentence wrap to the next line as they pass the right margin. (This function is called *word wrap*.) Do not press Enter at the end of a line unless you want that line to stand alone as a paragraph. Press Enter to mark the end of a paragraph or create a blank line. Word for Windows considers a paragraph to be any text that you end by pressing Enter.

Type the following text. Notice that the copy contains mistakes. Type the mistakes; you will correct them later when you learn how to edit text. If you make accidental errors, ignore them and continue, or use the Backspace key to erase them.

After pressing Enter at the end of the last line of the company address, press Enter two more times to add two blank lines.

Generic Quality Corporation
324 Vineyard Rd.
Santa Rosa, CA 95409

Mr. Jim Runell
Generic Quality Corporation
1298 California St.
San Francisco, CA 94467

Subject: Automated Reports

Dear Jim,

This letter is to thank you for your recommendation to move to for Windows and Excel. The Xanix projectt was a big success!

We completed the Xanix project on time and with excellent re- sults. The client was very pleased. Your recommendation to bring everyone up to speed on Word for Windows and Excel before starting the project was excellent. Everyone on the project felt they were more productive than they were with our older soft- ware. Word for Windows' ability to hot-link data with other appli- cations, such as our engineering design package, the database in dBASE, and our spreadsheets in Excel, was astounding. Thanks for helping us work even better.

You might like to see the following list of some of our forecast and actual completion dates.

Setting Tabs

One way to align text in columns is to use tabs. The following section of this letter is organized as tabular data.

Word for Windows begins with default left tab stops every 1/2 inch from the left margin. The default tab stops appear as small inverted Ts under the ruler's scale (refer to fig. 2.3). The following instructions describe how to enter customized tab stops to align the text as shown in figure 2.6.

When you set a tab stop on the ruler, all default tab stops to the left of the one you set are removed. To align the data as shown in the letter, a left-align tab is set at 1 inch, and right-align tabs are set at 3-1/2 inches and 5 inches. In the letter, the left-align tab will align the column titled *Project*, and the two right-align tabs will align the columns titled *Sched- uled* and *Actual*.

To set tab stops, use the Format **T**abs command or the tab buttons on the right side of the ribbon. The ribbon contains four tab buttons, rep- resented by upward pointing arrows.

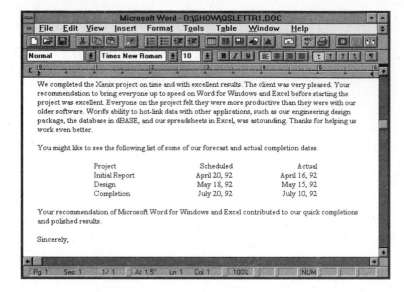

FIG. 2.6.

Using tabs to
align text.

Button	Function
↑	Aligns left edge of text (default)
↑	Centers text on tab stop
↑	Aligns right edge of text
↑.	Aligns decimal with tab stop

Tab stops apply to the paragraph containing the insertion point or the paragraphs selected. To apply new tab stops to data you already have typed, select the paragraphs containing the data, and then set the tab stops.

In Word for Windows, paragraph formatting, such as tab stops, is stored in the paragraph mark at the end of each paragraph. To carry paragraph formatting forward to the next paragraph, press Enter. This procedure is useful when you want formatting to continue as you work.

If you do not want the next paragraph to use this formatting, move the insertion point down to the next paragraph with the down arrow. Do not press Enter. If you are at the end of the document, press Enter and reformat the new paragraph as desired.

Press the arrow keys to move the insertion point to where you will type the tabbed table.

To set tabs with a mouse, follow these steps:

1. Click on the left-align tab button on the ribbon.

2. Position the mouse pointer directly underneath the 1-inch mark on the ruler and click the left mouse button.

   A small left tab arrow appears on the scale. You can drag the tab icon right or left to reposition it. To remove the icon, drag it off the ruler and release the button.

3. Repeat steps 1 and 2 for the second and third tabs. Be sure that you select the right-align tab button for these tabs. Set them at 3.5 and 5 inches.

To set tabs with the keyboard, follow these steps:

1. Choose the Format Tabs command by pressing Alt,T,T.

   The Tabs dialog box appears (see fig. 2.7).

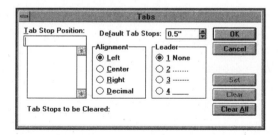

FIG. 2.7.

The Tabs dialog box.

2. Press Alt+T to select the Tab Stop Position text box. The insertion point flashes in the box.

3. Type *1* for the first tab location (1 inch from the left margin).

4. Press Alt+L to select Left alignment for the first tab stop.

5. Press Alt+S to choose the Set button to set the first tab stop.

   Notice that the tab stop now appears in the Tab Stop Position list box. When you select the position of a tab stop from this list, the Alignment and Leader options reflect their settings for that position.

6. Repeat steps 2 through 5 to enter the second and third tab stops. Set the second tab at 3.5 inches and the third tab at 5 inches. Use a right-align tab for these stops (press Alt+R). Remember to choose Set after entering the tab stop information for each tab.

Figure 2.8 shows the Tabs dialog box with the entries completed for these tab stops.

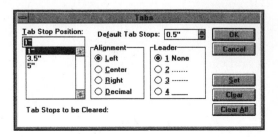

FIG. 2.8.

The completed
Tabs dialog box.

7. Press Enter.

Notice that the tab stops showing in the ruler change after you set the tab stops. If you move to a different paragraph, the tab stops change back to the tab stops for the paragraph that contains the insertion point. Make sure that you are on the line (paragraph) that contains the new tab stops.

Entering Tabular Data

Now that you have set the tab stops, you are ready to enter the tabular data by following these steps:

1. Press Tab and type the first column heading, *Project*.

2. Press Tab and type the second column heading, *Scheduled*.

3. Press Tab and type the third column heading, *Actual*.

4. Press Enter to start the next line. The tab formatting carries forward to the next paragraph. (Tabs are a form of paragraph formatting.)

5. Repeat steps 1 through 4 for the following three rows of text.

Initial Report	April 20, 91	April 16, 91
Design	May 18, 91	May 15, 91
Completion	July 20, 91	July 10, 91

6. Press Enter twice after the last line.

If you frequently create tables of numbers, text, or pictures, become familiar with the **Table** commands in Word for Windows. Tables built with the **Table** commands give you greater ease and flexibility in editing and formatting than tables built with tabs. Chapter 12 discusses table features.

T   I   P

Completing the Letter

Now type the last paragraph and closing. (This paragraph is different from the one shown in fig. 2.1. You will be correcting the paragraph later.)

> Your recommendation of Microsoft Word for Windows and Excel contributed to our quick completions and polished results.

> Sincerely,

> Ms. Jan Bosco

> Senior Project Manager

Editing Text

Now that you have completed your letter, you need to edit it. To edit, you have to reposition the cursor. In Windows applications the cursor is called the *insertion point*. To reposition the insertion point in your document, use the mouse or the keyboard.

New mouse users often confuse the I-beam pointer with the insertion point. The *I-beam* pointer shows where the mouse is positioned. The *insertion point* (cursor) is the flashing vertical bar in the text that doesn't move as you move the mouse. The insertion point shows where your typing or editing takes place. Remember to click the mouse button when you want to reposition the insertion point at the I-beam's location.

T   I   P

Many techniques are available for inserting and deleting text. To insert *Word* in the first sentence of your business letter so that the sentence reads ...*related to Word for Windows and Excel*, follow these steps:

1. Position the insertion point directly before the *f* in *for*.

   Mouse: Move the mouse so that the I-beam is directly before the *f* in *for*, then click. Move the I-beam away to see the repositioned insertion point.

   Keyboard: Press the arrow keys on the keyboard to move the insertion point directly before the *f* in *for*.

2. Type *Word* and press the space bar.

Deleting characters is one of the most common forms of editing. To delete the extra *t* in *project* in the second line, follow these steps:

1. Position the insertion point before or after the *t* you want to delete.

   Mouse: Move the mouse so that the I-beam is directly to either side of the *t*, then click. Move the I-beam away to see the repositioned insertion point.

   Keyboard: Press the arrow keys to move the insertion point directly to either side of the *t*.

2. Press the Backspace key to delete the character to the left of the insertion point; press Del to delete the character to the right of the insertion point.

T I P   Word for Windows has a command that enables you to undo your last action. If you inadvertently delete some crucial text or choose the wrong command, you can reverse the last action with the **Edit Undo** command. You must catch your error right away. The **Edit Undo** command reverses only your last typing, deletion, or command. With the mouse you can click on the Undo button in the Toolbar. (The Undo button looks like the eraser end of a pencil.)

Saving Your Document

You should save your work every 15 to 20 minutes. To save the active document into the current directory, follow these steps:

1. Choose the File Save command.

   Mouse: Click on the Save button in the toolbar. (It looks like a disk.)

   Keyboard: Press Alt,F,S.

   The first time you save a file, the Save As dialog box appears with the File **Name** text box selected (see fig. 2.9). After saving the file once, choosing the File **S**ave command or the Save button will save the file with the same name, without displaying the Save As dialog box.

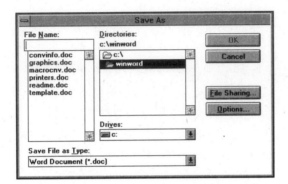

FIG. 2.9.

The File Save As dialog box.

2. Type the file name *QSLETTER* in the File **Name** text box.

3. Choose OK or press Enter.

   Depending on Word for Windows' settings, a document summary box may appear.

4. If you prefer, enter document summary information in the summary box, then choose OK or press Enter. Document summary information can help you find a document when you need to retrieve it according to specific information you recorded in the summary.

When you save a file, Word for Windows adds the extension DOC to the file name. You can type your own extension if you want.

By saving before you quit, you can come back to the quick start later and not lose the work you already have completed.

If you need to quit Word for Windows now, choose the File Exit command. If you saved the most current version of your document, the program quits immediately. If you changed the document since you last saved, a dialog box appears, asking whether you want to save the changes. When you want to return to the quick start, start Word for Windows and go to the next section, "Opening a Document."

To continue the quick start without quitting Word for Windows, close the current document by choosing the **File Close** command. (Click on **File**, then on **Close**, or press Alt,F,C.) Notice that when you close a document, its window and ruler disappear. Closing the document at this point is not necessary during normal operation, but it prepares you for the next part of the quick start.

Opening a Document

Use the **File Open** command when you want to open and work on a document saved to disk. To open the document you created in the first half of the quick start, follow these steps:

1. Choose the **File Open** command.

   Mouse: Click on the Open button in the toolbar. (The Open button is on the left and looks like an open folder.)

   Keyboard: Press Alt,F,O.

   The Open dialog box appears (see fig. 2.10). Notice that the current disk drive and directory appear under the File Name text box. The files currently are saved in this directory and are opened from this directory.

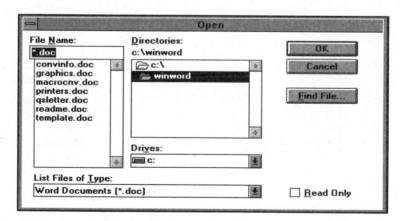

FIG. 2.10.

The Open dialog box.

2. Select the file named QSLETTER.DOC. File names are listed in alphabetical order.

   Mouse: Click on the up or down arrows on the scroll bars by the File Name box to scroll the list of files until the QSLETTER.DOC file name scrolls into view. Click on the name, then choose OK or press Enter.

Keyboard: Press Alt+N to select the File **N**ame box. Press the up- or down-arrow key until QSLETTER.DOC is selected. Or press Q to go to the first file starting with Q; then select QSLETTER.DOC. Press Enter.

The document stored in QSLETTER.DOC appears on-screen, with the insertion point positioned at the beginning of the first line.

You can press Shift+F5 to move the insertion point to its location when the document was last saved.

T I P

Enhancing Existing Characters

You can enhance characters as you type, as you did when typing the company name, or you can make enhancements to existing text. To enhance existing text, select the text you want to change, and then choose the command that makes the change.

To increase the size of the already boldface company name, follow these steps:

1. Select the company name, *Generic Quality Corporation*, as shown in figure 2.11. (Refer to the section title "Selecting Text" for instructions on selecting text.)

   Mouse: Click directly to the left of *Generic*, hold down the mouse button, and drag across the title until the company's name is selected. Release the mouse button.

   Keyboard: Move the insertion point to the left of *Generic*, then press Shift+right arrow or Shift+Ctrl+right arrow to select text to the right. (Shift+Ctrl+right arrow selects a word at a time to the right.)

2. Display a list of available font sizes.

   Mouse: Click on the down arrow by the Pts pull-down list on the ribbon. A list of sizes drops down (see fig. 2.12).

   Keyboard: Press Ctrl+P and then the down arrow to display the pull-down list on the ribbon, or press Alt,T,C to choose the Forma**t** **C**haracter command.

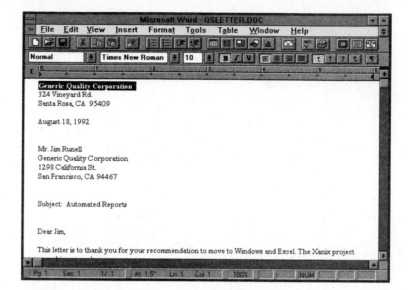

Selecting
Generic Quality
Corporation.

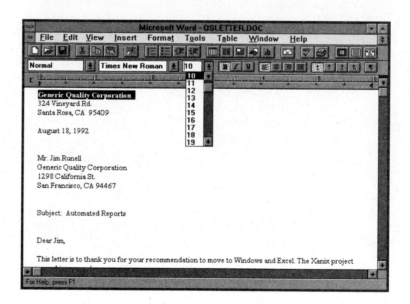

A list of font sizes
displays from the
ribbon.

3. Select a larger point size from the **P**oints box.

   Mouse: Click on the point size you want from the list that appears
   from the ribbon. The font size changes. Skip step 4.

   Keyboard: Use the down-arrow key to select a point size from the
   pull-down list on the ribbon, or press Alt+P to display the Pts list

in the Character dialog box (see fig. 2.13). Then press the up- or down-arrow key to select from the list, or type the size you want.

Your printer and its fonts may have point sizes different from those sizes shown in figure 2.12 and 2.13.

4. If you used a keyboard, press Enter.

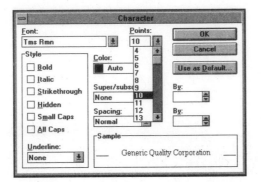

FIG. 2.13.

The Character dialog box also contains a list of available font sizes.

To ensure that your screen display and available fonts match your current printer's capabilities, select the LineBreaks and Fonts as Printed check box from the View Category of the Tools Option command.

T I P

Formatting Paragraphs

You can format paragraphs to align left, right, or center within margins. You can indent paragraphs and vertically space them from other paragraphs so that information stands out. You can even put borders around paragraphs and shade their backgrounds.

You do not have to select a complete paragraph to format it with a Format Paragraph command. If you select part of the paragraph or position the insertion point in the paragraph, the formatting works.

To format the paragraphs containing the company's letterhead so that the text is centered, follow these steps:

1. Select the three lines composing the letter's heading.

Mouse: Click to the left of the first character in the heading, hold down the left mouse button and drag down and right until the heading is selected.

Keyboard: Move the insertion point before the first character, then press Ctrl+right arrow to select a word at a time.

2. Center the heading.

Mouse: Click on the Center button (a miniature page of centered text) in the ribbon. No further action is needed.

Keyboard: Press Alt,T,P.

The Paragraph dialog box displays the current paragraph settings (see fig. 2.14).

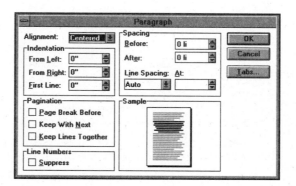

FIG. 2.14.

The Paragraph dialog box.

3. Select the Centered option in the Alignment pull-down list.

Keyboard: Press Alt+G to select the Alignment pull-down list. Press the up- or down-arrow key until Centered is selected.

4. Choose OK or press Enter.

Adding a Border

The Border Paragraphs dialog box enables you to apply formatting commands such as borders and shading to paragraphs. To put a border around the tabular data in the letter, follow these steps:

1. Select the four lines of tabbed material in the quick start letter.

2. Display the Border Paragraphs dialog box.

Mouse: Click on Format, then click on the Border command.

Keyboard: Press Alt,T,B.

3. Select Preset **B**ox to specify a box around the paragraphs (see fig. 2.15). Notice that the sample in the top left corner of the dialog box changes to reflect your selections.

   Mouse: Click on the **B**ox example in the Preset section of the dialog box.

   Keyboard: Press Alt+B to select the **B**ox example in the Preset section of the dialog box.

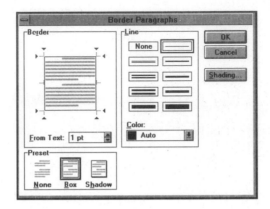

FIG. 2.15.

The Border
Paragraphs
dialog box.

4. Select a thick line style from the **L**ine style section of the dialog box. Watch the sample as you make your changes.

   Mouse: Click on the first thick line style in the line section.

   Keyboard: Press Alt+L. Press the up-, down-, right-, or left-arrow key until the first thick line style is selected.

5. Choose OK or press Enter.

The tabbed columns in your letter now should look similar to figure 2.16.

Moving Text

Moving text is one of the most powerful capabilities of any word processor. You can write thoughts as they come to you and later reorganize the document so that your sentences are coherent and form a logical conclusion.

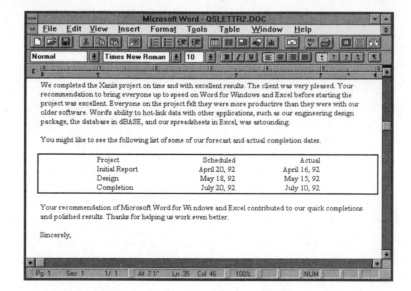

FIG. 2.16.

Putting borders around paragraphs or tabbed data makes it more presentable and easier to read.

To move the last sentence of the second paragraph of the business letter to the end of the last paragraph, follow these steps:

1. Scroll the window so that the second paragraph is in view.

   Mouse: Click on the up arrow at the top of the vertical scroll bar to the right side of the window.

   Keyboard: Press the up-arrow key or Pg Up key.

2. Select the last sentence of the paragraph, *Thanks for helping us work even better.* (Refer to earlier sections on how to select text.)

3. Cut the selected text.

   Mouse: Click on the Cut button on the toolbar. (The Cut button appears as a pair of scissors.)

   Keyboard: Press Alt,E,T.

   This step cuts the selected text from the screen and places the text in a special part of your computer's memory called the clipboard. The text stays in the clipboard so that you can paste it in another location. Choosing the **E**dit Cu**t** or **E**dit **C**opy command replaces the contents of the clipboard with the new cut or copied material.

4. Move the insertion point to the end of the last paragraph.

5. Paste the contents of the clipboard at the insertion point's location.

Mouse: Choose the Paste button on the toolbar. (The Paste button looks like a clipboard.)

Keyboard: Press Alt,E,P.

6. Insert spaces as necessary so that the pasted sentences do not run together.

The text is inserted at the insertion point's location. To preserve the original text and move a copy to a new location, use the **E**dit **C**opy and **E**dit **P**aste commands. Cutting, copying, and editing are discussed in detail in Chapter 4.

Previewing and Printing

You need to print only once because Word for Windows enables you to view your document on-screen as it will appear when printed on the selected printer. You also can drag the margins to a new location.

To preview your document, follow these steps:

1. Preview the document.

   Mouse: Choose the **F**ile Print Pre**v**iew command.

   Keyboard: Press Alt,F,V.

   Your document appears on-screen. Notice the buttons that appear above the preview page (see fig. 2.17). With these buttons, you can print, change margins, see facing double pages, return to page view, or cancel and return to the view you were using.

2. Choose Cancel or press Esc to return to the previous view of the document. You also can choose the **P**rint button if you like the results on-screen and want to print the document. The next procedure describes how to print from the menu.

With the **F**ile **P**rint command, you can go directly to the Print dialog box without previewing the document. To print a document without going through the preview, follow these steps:

1. Print the active document.

   Mouse: Click on the Print button on the toolbar. (The Print button looks like a printer.)

   Keyboard: Press Alt,F,P.

   The Print dialog box that appears shows you which printer is currently selected. You can change the number of copies you want printed and designate which pages to print. The **O**ptions button gives you choices about things such as printing in reverse page order or printing in draft mode.

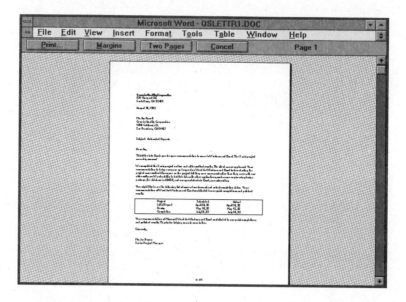

FIG. 2.17.

Previewing your document before printing.

2. Choose OK or press Enter.

If the printed document does not look like its screen preview appearance, you may have used a character font that your printer is unable to print. For more information on printer fonts, see Appendix C.

Exiting Word for Windows and Windows

To exit Word for Windows when you are finished working, follow these steps:

1. Exit the Word for Windows program.

    Mouse: Double click on the application control menu icon at the far left corner of the Word for Windows title bar.

    Keyboard: Press Alt,F,X.

    If you made changes to the document since you last saved, a dialog box appears and asks whether you want to save.

2. Choose Yes to save changes made to the document since the last change. Choose No to exit the program without saving the changes. Choose Cancel to void the exit command and return to the document.

If you were prompted to save changes, and you responded with Yes, Word for Windows saves the document with the same file name you used previously. To save the document under a different name or a name with a version number, choose the File Save As command before exiting and type a new name.

From Here . . .

Now that you have worked through this chapter, you have enough basic knowledge to start creating your own documents with Word for Windows. The many features in Word for Windows make it one of the most powerful word processors available. The chapters that follow discuss in detail these features and many shortcuts.

Creating and Saving Documents

Word processing basics begin with opening a new document, typing the text, and saving the document. Beyond those simple basics, a high-performance word processor such as Word for Windows gives you the tools to accomplish many advanced editing and formatting tasks. Before you tackle those advanced features, however, start with this "beginner's" chapter to learn how to create, save, close, and reopen a document. A slightly more advanced section in this chapter teaches you helpful techniques for finding files, even if you don't know the file names or where they are stored on your disk.

Creating a New Document

When you first start Word for Windows (see Chapter 1), you see a blank document, ready for typing (see fig. 3.1). This new document is named Document1 to indicate that the document is the first one you have created since starting the program.

If your new document isn't the first one you have seen since starting Word for Windows, however, the document is numbered accordingly: the second new document is called `Document2`, the third is `Document3`, and so on.

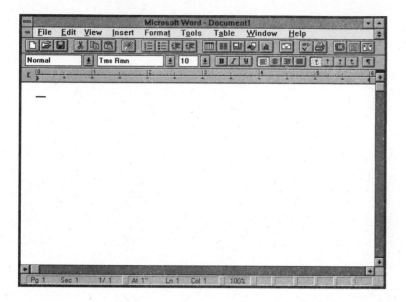

FIG. 3.1.

A blank document, ready for typing.

To start a new document, you must use a menu command, as in the following steps:

1. Choose the **File New** command or choose the File New button on the toolbar (the first button on the left). The New dialog box appears (see fig. 3.2).

FIG. 3.2.

The New dialog box.

2. Choose OK or press Enter.

Using Templates

In the New dialog box, the Template list box contains one or more se-lections. A *template* is a predefined set of formatting characteristics, such as type style, margin width, tab settings, and so forth. You must choose one of these templates as the basis for your new document.

The Normal template, built into Word for Windows, always appears in the New dialog box, but you also can create your own templates. For example, you may want to base your document on a special template you have created called Letters that includes formatting to match your company's letterhead. Unless you choose otherwise, however, Word for Windows bases new documents on the Normal template.

To learn more about creating and using templates, refer to Chapter 30.

Adding Summary Information

Summary information includes descriptive notes that can ease the task of organizing and finding files later, after you have created many files. You can attach summary information to your document at three differ-ent times: when you first create the file, while you work on the file, or when you save the file. Whichever method you choose, including sum-mary information is a wonderful time-saver. Later, this chapter dis-cusses one way summary information can be useful, by helping you locate misplaced files or files whose names you don't quite remember.

You can include any text—up to 255 characters—in any of the Sum-mary Info fields. No naming or character restrictions exist.

To add summary information when you create a new document, follow these steps:

1. In the New dialog box, select **S**ummary. The Summary Info dialog box appears (see fig. 3.3).

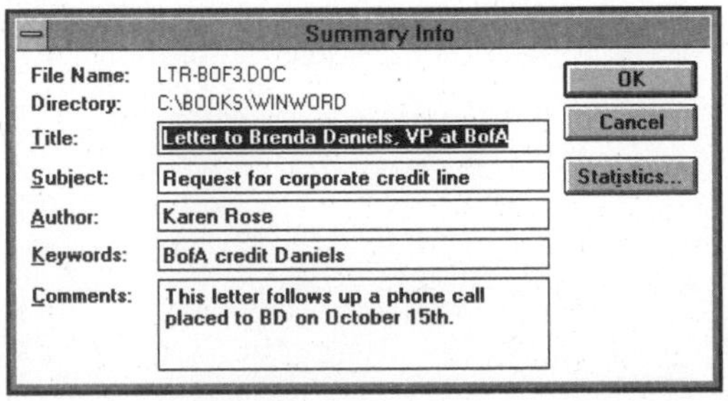

FIG. 3.3.

The Summary Info dialog box.

2. Fill in any of the fields with descriptive text. Include as much (up to 255 characters) or as little information as you like.

3. Choose OK or press Enter.

You can edit the summary information at any time by choosing the **File Summary Info** command to display the Summary Info dialog box. If you want to include summary information when you save a file, you can select an option to display the Summary Info dialog box whenever you choose the **File Save As** command. For details, refer to "Saving for the First Time" later in this chapter.

T   I   P   Filling in the Summary Info box may seem like a nuisance. But try the box before giving up. When you learn how to use the powerful **Find File** command, you see that summary information helps you find files much more easily than by using the cryptic eight-letter DOS file name. Besides, if you absolutely don't need the information in the Summary Info dialog box for an unimportant file, you can bypass the box quickly by selecting OK or pressing Enter.

Another useful feature of the Summary Info box is the Statistics option, which tells when you created the document, when the document most recently was saved, and how many pages, words, and characters the document contains. Follow these steps to see the statistics:

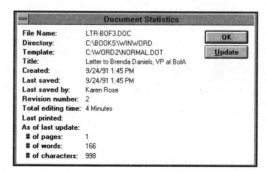

FIG. 3.4.

The Document Statistics dialog box.

1. In the Summary Info dialog box, select Statistics. The Document Statistics dialog box appears (see fig. 3.4).

2. If you have edited the document, select Update to bring the statistics up-to-date.

3. Take note of the statistics that interest you.

4. Choose OK or press Enter.

Typing Text

When you create a new document in Word for Windows, you see a blank typing screen (except for the helpful tools at the top, bottom, and right). A vertical bar, the *insertion point*, flashes at the top left. Below the insertion point is a horizontal line—the document end mark. When you begin typing, your characters appear on-screen to the left of the insertion point, which moves to the right as you type.

If you have never typed in a word processor before, you immediately become aware of one difference from typing on a typewriter: you don't have to press the Enter key at the end of every line. You continue typing past the end of the right margin, and Word for Windows wraps sentences around to fit within the margins.

Press the Enter key *only* to mark the end of a paragraph or to insert a blank line. Pressing Enter inserts a paragraph mark. (Normally you don't see paragraph marks; if you want to see them, see Chapter 4.)

Press Enter only when you want to end a paragraph for two important reasons. First, if you add or delete text from the paragraph, the word-wrap feature ensures that the paragraph stays intact. If instead you press Enter at the end of each line, then add or delete text, each line ends where you pressed Enter—whether that's at the beginning or middle of the line. Second, as you learn in Chapter 6, a paragraph is a special set of text with its own useful formatting commands, such as alignment, indents, line spacing, and tabs.

When you type text on-screen, you can use all characters on your keyboard. Besides the normal characters you see on your keyboard, however, Word for Windows offers many special characters you can type, including bullets, typesetting quotes, wide dashes, and many others. For details about entering these characters, see Chapter 5.

When you type in Word for Windows' *insert* mode, you add text to an existing document between the existing words. In some cases you may prefer to type in the *overtype* mode so that new text types over existing text.

If you want to switch from the insert to the overtype mode, press the Insert (or Ins) key on your keyboard. OVR appears in the status bar at the bottom of the screen. Press the Insert key a second time to return to insert mode. If your status bar isn't displayed, you don't see a screen message reminding you that you're in the overtype mode. (To display the status bar, choose the Tools Options command and select the view Category. In the Window group, select Status Bar so that an X appears in the check box.)

If you prefer to use the overtype mode all the time, you can customize Word for Windows to do so (see Chapter 29).

Saving a Document

By now you probably have heard the lecture advising you to save your document frequently. Saving your work stores the work as a file on disk. Until you save, your work exists only in your computer's memory. Thus, if the electricity goes off, even for a very short time, your computer's memory is lost—along with your work.

Saving frequently also reduces the time required for Word for Windows to store your work on disk. In effect, you save time by saving often.

Saving for the First Time

Because a new document has no name and no home, you must name and assign the document to a disk drive and directory. Word for Windows files use standard MS-DOS file names. Remember these simple rules when naming files:

- A DOS file name can have an extension (or last name) up to three characters long.

- A DOS file name can be from one to eight characters long (excluding the three-letter extension).

- You can use letters A through Z (upper- or lowercase), numbers 0 through 9, hyphens (-), underscores (_), and exclamation marks (!).

- You cannot use periods (.) or blank spaces. A period separates a file's first name and extension. Substitute legal characters for blanks.

- You cannot use characters such as asterisks (*), plus signs (+), equal signs (=), and some punctuation marks in file names. Legal characters include !, @, #, $, %, ^, &, (,), _, -, {, and }. Use the exclamation mark or another legal character as the first character in a name when you want the name to be first in the alphabetical listing of names.

- Word for Windows provides its own extension name, DOC. You can override this default when you name your file by including a period and an extension. Using Word for Windows' default extension is better, however, because the extension helps you to identify each file's type and eases the task of opening files. (By default, Word for Windows lists only files with its own DOC extension in the Open dialog box).

To save and name a file, follow these steps:

1. Choose the **F**ile Save **A**s command. The Save As dialog box appears (see fig. 3.5).

   Instead of performing step 1, you can choose the **F**ile Save **A**s command by pressing F12.

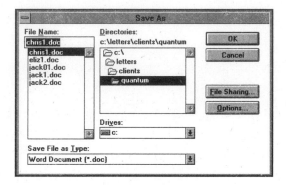

FIG. 3.5.

The Save As dialog box.

2. In the File **N**ame box, type a file name.

3. In the **D**rives list, select the drive where you want to save your file. Use this option to save your file to a floppy disk in drive A or B, for example, or to save the file to a different drive on your hard disk. (See "Changing Directories and Drives" later in this chapter to learn how.)

4. In the **D**irectories list box, select the directory where you want to save your file. (Selecting directories is discussed later in this chapter.)

5. Choose OK or press Enter.

Saving Files with a New Name

You can use the **F**ile Save **A**s command to save a named file with a new name, which creates a backup of your file. If you have a file called LETTERA.DOC, for example, you can save your file a second time, giving it the name LETTERB.DOC. You then have two versions of the same file, each with a different name. You can save the new version of your file in the same location as the original, or in any other directory or drive.

Revising your file slightly before saving it with a new name is more common. You then have the original file and the second, slightly revised file, each with a unique name.

To save a named file with a new name, choose the File Save **As** command, change the file name in the File **N**ame box, change the drive or directory if you want, and then choose OK or press Enter.

T I P   You can use the File Save **As** command to make sequential backups of important documents. The first time you save a file, name the file with a number, such as FILE01. Then each time you save the file again, rename the document with the next higher number: FILE02, FILE03, and so on. The file with the highest number is always the most recent version. And when you finish the project, you can delete the files with low numbers.

Be sure to name the files FILE01 and FILE02—including the zero—so that the files stay in order in dialog box lists. If you don't, FILE11 is listed before FILE3 because files are listed alphabetically and numerically. This rule is especially important in the Open dialog box, where you want to be sure you open the most recent version of your file.

Changing Directories and Drives

The first time you save a document, Word for Windows assumes that you want to save the document in the Word for Windows directory. Instead, you usually want to save the file in a work directory or subdirectory. You must tell Word for Windows where you want to save your file—whether that location is a different directory or subdirectory, a different drive on your hard disk, or a floppy disk in drive A or B. To switch directories or drives, use the appropriate list boxes in the Save As dialog box (shown earlier in fig. 3.5).

Your file is saved in the selected directory and drive, both of which are shown in the path statement listed above the **D**irectories list box. If you see the path C:\LETTERS\AUGUST, for example, you know your file is saved on drive C, in the directory LETTERS, and in the subdirectory AUGUST. A backslash separates drives and directories.

The **D**irectories list box includes all directories and subdirectories on the selected drive. An icon that resembles a file folder represents each directory. Open file folders indicate open directories; closed file folders indicate closed directories. If you want to save your file to a subdirectory contained within a directory, you first must open the directory.

To change disk drives or directories, follow these steps:

1. Choose the **File Save As** command. The Save As dialog box appears (refer to fig. 3.5).

2. Scroll the Drives list to display the drive where you want to save your file.

   Mouse: Click the down arrow at the right side of the Drives list.

   Keyboard: Press Tab to advance to the Drives list, then press the up- or down-arrow key.

3. Select the drive where you want to save your file if it is not already selected.

   Mouse: Click the drive letter. Word for Windows immediately changes to that drive.

   Keyboard: Press the up- or down-arrow keys to select the drive letter, and then press Enter. Word for Windows changes to that drive.

4. Scroll the **Directories** list to display the directory where you want to save your file.

   Mouse: Click on the down arrow at the bottom right of the **Directories** list box. (Click on the arrow and hold the mouse button to scroll continuously.)

   Keyboard: Press Tab to advance to the Directories list; press the down- or up-arrow keys to scroll the list.

5. If necessary, open a directory to display the subdirectory where you want to save your file.

   Mouse: Double-click on the directory you want to open.

   Keyboard: Press the up- or down-arrow keys, then press Enter to select and open the directory.

6. Select the directory or subdirectory where you want to save your file.

   Mouse: Click once on the directory or subdirectory.

   Keyboard: Press the up- or down-arrow keys to advance to the directory or subdirectory.

7. In the File **Name** box, type the file name. (Word for Windows supplies the extension DOC.)

8. Choose OK or press Enter to save the file.

T I P   If you are familiar with directory path names, you can save a file into another directory by typing the path name and file name in the File Name box of the Save As dialog box. To save a file named REPORTS into the CLIENTS directory on drive C, for example, type the following path name and then choose OK or press Enter:

C:\REPORTS\CLIENTS

Saving a Different File Type

When you save a file in Word for Windows, the document is saved in Word for Windows format. Word for Windows, however, enables you to save your file in many formats. You may need to save a file into another format, such as WordPerfect format. Other times you may need to save the file in Text (ASCII) format so that you can import the file into a different type of program.

To save your file in a non-Word for Windows format, follow these steps:

1. Choose the File Save As command. The Save As dialog box appears (refer to fig. 3.5).

2. In the File Name box, type the file name without an extension.

3. Scroll the Save File as Type list box to display the file format you want.

   Mouse: Click the down arrow at the right side of the Save File as Type list box.

   Keyboard: Press Tab to advance to the Save File as Type list, then press the down-arrow key.

4. Select the format in which you want to save your file.

   Mouse: Click the format.

   Keyboard: Press the up- or down-arrow keys to highlight the format.

5. Choose OK or press Enter to save your file.

Word for Windows assigns an appropriate extension to the file name. (The extensions for each file type are listed in the Save File as Type list box.) To learn more about saving a file to a different file format, refer to Appendix C.

Word for Windows displays in the Save File as Type list box only the types for which converters have been installed. If the word processor you need doesn't appear, reinstall Word for Windows using the custom installation option. You will be given the chance to install converter files without reinstalling all of Word for Windows.

Protecting Shared Files

If you share files or your PC with other users, you may want to prevent people from opening some files or from modifying others. To prevent users from opening a file, you can assign the file a password. The next time you open the file, you must type in the password. (Be careful: If you forget your password, *you* cannot open the file either.) To prevent users from modifying a file, you can lock the file for *annotations*, or notes appended to a file in a special annotation window. With annotations, users can add annotations but otherwise cannot modify your file. (Chapter 15 discusses annotations in more detail.)

To assign a password or lock a file for annotations, follow these steps:

1. Choose the File Save **As** command (or press F12).

2. Select **F**ile Sharing. The File Sharing dialog box appears (see fig. 3.6).

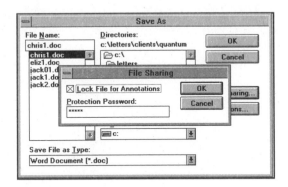

FIG. 3.6.

The File Sharing
dialog box.

3. To lock a file for annotations, select the **L**ock File for Annotations option.

   Mouse: Click the box to the left of **L**ock File for Annotations so that an X appears.

   Keyboard: Press Tab to advance to the **L**ock File for Annotations option, then press the space bar so that an X appears inside the box.

4. To assign your file a password, select the **P**assword Protection option and type in a password. As you type, you see only aster-isks—no written record of your password exists anywhere.

   Mouse: Type the password inside the **P**assword Protection text box.

   Keyboard: Press Tab to advance to the **P**assword Protection text box and type in the password.

5. Choose OK or press Enter. If you have entered a password, Word for Windows prompts you to re-enter the password to confirm.

6. Choose OK or press Enter at the Save As dialog box to save the file.

When someone tries to modify a file with annotations locked, they can-not. If that user uses your PC, however, then as far as Word for Win-dows knows, that user is you. Annotations, therefore, only protect you when you share your file with someone else on a disk or over a network.

When a file is password protected, however, no one can open that file without the password—including you. Don't forget your password.

To turn off the **L**ock File for Annotations feature, follow the same proce-dure, but select the box so that no X appears. (Option boxes toggle: an X means the feature is turned on; no X means the feature is turned off.)

To change or delete a password, follow the same procedure, but delete the existing password (which still appears only as a string of aster-isks) and type in the new password (or not, if you want to remove the password).

Using the Save As Options

Word for Windows offers many options when you save and name a file using the **F**ile Save **A**s command. Options include automatic file back-ups, fast saves, prompting for summary information each time you save, and automatic saving. You can turn on or off each of the following Save As Options:

Option	Description
Always Create **B**ackup Copy	Each time you save a file, Word for Windows creates a backup using the same file name, but adding the exten-sion BAK. The backup copy is not the current version of your file, but the preceding version.

Option	Description
Allow **F**ast Saves	With this option selected, Word for Windows saves faster because the program saves only the changes, not the entire document. Fast saves only occur with the **S**ave command, not the Save **A**s command. (Some other programs may not be capable of opening fast-save files.)
Prompt for Summary Info	Each time you save a file, you are prompted for summary information, including title and key words. For more information on summary information, see "Adding Summary Information" earlier in this chapter.
Auto **S**ave Every ____ **M**inutes	Word for Windows saves the file as frequently as you specify in the Minutes box. The first Auto Save is a complete save; subsequent Auto Saves are Fast Saves.

Auto Save files are saved with a name different from your file name, but always with the ASD extension. Auto Save files are saved in the directory specified in the AUTOSAVE line in the Microsoft Word for Windows 2.0 section of your WIN.INI file (by default, the WINDOWS\TEMP directory).

To use the Save As options, follow these steps:

1. Choose the **F**ile Save **A**s command (or press F12).

2. Choose the **O**ptions button in the Save As dialog box. The Options dialog box appears (see fig. 3.7).

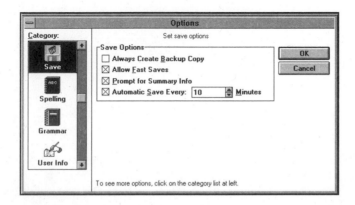

3. Select the option you want turned on, or unselect the option you want turned off.

   Mouse: Select the check box by clicking it.

   Keyboard: Press Tab to advance to the check box, then press the space bar.

4. To specify the number of minutes between automatic saves if you turn on the Auto **S**ave option, select the up or down arrow in the **M**inutes box.

   Mouse: Click the up arrow to increase the number of minutes.

   Keyboard: Press Tab to advance to the **M**inutes box, then type in the number of minutes you want between automatic saves.

5. Choose OK or press Enter.

You also can access the Options dialog box through the T**o**ols menu (refer to Chapter 30).

T I P   If you lose power during a work session in which Auto Save is turned on, use the **F**ind File command to locate and open the most recently created file with the extension ASD. That file is the automatically saved version of the file you were working on when the power went out. (See the section "Finding Files" later in this chapter.)

Saving Many Documents At Once

If you have several documents open at once, you can save them all simultaneously by showing the **F**ile Sav**e** All command.

Files you normally don't see, including glossary and macro files, also are saved when you use this command.

Saving without Renaming

Every time you save a document with a unique name, you create a new file on disk—a good way to keep backups of your document. Not all files are so important, however, that you need multiple backups. In that case, you can save the document to its existing file name, replacing the current version of the file.

CAUTION   Remember that when you save without renaming, you
erase and replace the existing file with the new file.

To save without renaming, choose the File Save command. To choose
the File Save command, press Shift+F12 or choose the File Save button
on the toolbar (the third button from the left, which looks like a floppy
disk).

Closing a Document

After you finish working on a document and save the file, you may want
to close the document, especially if you have several documents open.

To close a document, choose the File Close command. If the document
is in a window, you can close it by double-clicking on the dash icon at
the top left corner of the document window. When a document is maximized to full screen, the dash icon appears in the menu bar to the left
of File.

If you have made changes since you last saved, Word for Windows asks
whether you want to save your changes. Choose Yes to save them. (If
you haven't named the document, the Save As dialog box appears, and
you must name the file.) Choose No to discard changes. Choose Cancel
to cancel the close, or choose Help to access the Word for Windows
help window.

Opening an Existing Document

The great advantage to word processors is that you can use the same
files repeatedly.

Finding a file involves locating the file in a drive and directory and
knowing what type the file is. Word for Windows, by default, lists in the
Open dialog box only Word for Windows files that end in the extension
DOC. The program also can open other files: template files, which end
in the extension DOT; and files created by other programs, which have
various extensions. To open a file with an extension other than DOC,
you must specify the extension you want to list by choosing the file
type in the List Files of Type box or by typing the extension in the Open
File Name box and then pressing Enter.

You can use wild cards to help you locate the type of file you want—an
asterisk (*) means any character or characters, and a question mark (?)
means any single character. If you want to locate all files that end in the

extension EXT, type *.*EXT* in the Open File **N**ame box. If you want to list files with any name that ends in any extension, type *.* in the Open File **N**ame box.

To open an existing document, follow these steps:

1. Choose the **F**ile **O**pen command (or press Ctrl+F12, or choose the File Open button on the toolbar—the second button from the left, which looks like an open file folder). The Open dialog box appears (see fig. 3.8).

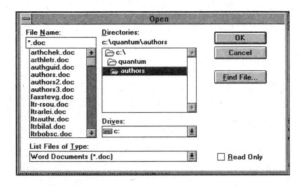

FIG. 3.8.

The Open
dialog box.

2. If necessary, select a different disk drive in the **D**rives list.

3. If necessary, select a different directory in the **D**irectories list.

4. If necessary, select a different file type in the List Files of **T**ype box.

5. Select the **R**ead Only option if you want to prevent changes to the original document.

   This option prevents the use of the **F**ile **S**ave command, which replaces the original version with the changed document. Documents opened with **R**ead Only must be saved with the **F**ile Save **A**s command and a new file name.

6. In the Open File **N**ame text box, type the name of the file you want to open, or select the file you want to open from the Open File Name list.

7. Choose the OK button or press Enter.

Through the Open dialog box, you can access the **F**ind File command, which uses summary information to help you locate files, which you then can open, print, delete, or copy. For details about the Find File command, see "Finding Files" later in this chapter.

You can open and use many files at once. To open additional files, repeat the process of opening a file. For details about working with multiple files, see "Working with Multiple Documents" later in this chapter.

T I P

Opening a Recently Used File

Word keeps track of the last four documents you used and enables you to reopen them quickly. To reopen one of the last four files you have closed, follow these steps:

1. Choose the **File** menu.

2. Select the file name from the bottom of the menu.

   Mouse: Click on the file you want to reopen.

   Keyboard: Type the number (1 through 4) of the file you want to reopen.

Opening Non-Word for Windows Files

Word for Windows can open files created by other programs such as the Windows Notepad (or any other application that creates a text file), WordPerfect, DOS Word, WordStar, Windows Works, and others. You use the normal **File Open** command, but then you must identify the file type so that Word for Windows can convert the file into its own format. (Word for Windows proposes the file type the program thinks the file should be, and the proposed type usually is correct.)

To open non-Word for Windows files, follow these steps:

1. Choose the **File Open** command.

2. Select the drive and directory containing the file you want to open.

3. In the File **Name** box, specify the extension of the file you want to open. (For example, to list all files ending in the extension WP5, type *.WP5*.)

4. From the list of files in the File **Name** box, select the file you want to open.

5. Choose OK or press Enter. The Convert File dialog box appears (see fig. 3.9).

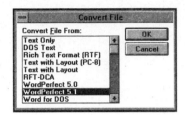

FIG. 3.9.

The Convert File dialog box.

6. Select the format of the file you're opening.

7. Choose OK or press Enter.

If a converter does not appear for the file type you need, return to the Program Manager and run the Word for Windows setup program. You will have the chance to install additional converters found on Word for Windows installation disks.

Starting Word for Windows While Opening a Document

From the File Manager, you can start Word for Windows and open a file at the same time. To do so, follow these steps:

1. In the File Manager, display the window containing the Word for Windows document you want to open.

2. Open the file. Word for Windows starts, with your file on-screen.

   Mouse: Double-click on the file name.

   Keyboard: Press the arrow keys to advance to the file, then press Enter (or choose the **F**ile **O**pen command).

Finding Files

PCs suffer from an annoying limitation—files can have only eight-character names (plus a three-character extension). Because of the eight-character limit, you can end up with some pretty cryptic file names. Luckily, Word for Windows offers a command that searches for files using other criteria besides the file name. The command is **F**ind File, located in the **F**ile menu.

The first time you choose the Find File command from the File menu, Word for Windows searches for all the Word for Windows files in the current directory. The program then lists the files in the Find File dialog box (see fig. 3.10). The next time you choose the Find File command, Word for Windows displays the preceding list in the Find File dialog box, and you must use the Search command to change the list. You can search for files by directory, name, type of file, date created or saved, or any of the information you have entered in the Summary Info dialog box.

FIG. 3.10.

The Find File dialog box.

You can find files based on any combination of criteria. You can find files in a particular directory that contain certain words in their summary information, for example, and that are created within a certain range of dates. The more you narrow your search, the faster the search is performed, and the quicker you see your list.

A list of files often contains more files than you actually want to use. To narrow the list, you must select the files you want from the list.

After you list and select the file or files you want using various search criteria, you can sort, open, delete, print, or copy them—one at a time or in groups—all from one convenient central Find File dialog box.

To find and select files, follow these steps:

1. Choose the File Find File command. The Find File dialog box appears.

2. Select the files you want to sort, open, delete, print, or copy.

   Mouse: Click on the single file you want, or hold Ctrl and click multiple file names. If you want to select several sequential files, hold Shift and click the first and last file you want. (Hold Ctrl and click a second time to unselect any file you select by mistake.)

   Keyboard: Press the up- or down-arrow keys to move to the single file you want to select.

   To select multiple noncontiguous files, press Shift+F8, then move to each file you want to select and press the space bar. Press Shift+F8 again to turn off the multiple selection mode. To select multiple contiguous files, press the up- or down-arrow key to select the first file, hold Shift, then press the up- or down-arrow key to extend the selection.

To close the Find File dialog box, choose the Cancel or Close button.

Opening Found Files

After you use the Find File command to find and select a file, you can open the file from the Find File dialog box. You also can open more than one file.

To find and open documents, do the following:

1. Choose the File Find File command. The Find File dialog box appears (refer to fig. 3.10).

2. Select the file or files you want to open.

3. If you want to prevent yourself from modifying the file or files you open, select the Open as Read Only option.

4. Choose the Open button.

When you choose the Open button, all files open, each in its own document window. See "Working with Multiple Documents" later in this chapter for details about switching between windows.

Printing Found Files

You can use the File Print command to print the open document. If you want to print several documents with the same printing parameters at once, however, use the File Find File command to first find and then print the files.

To print documents from the Find File dialog box, follow these steps:

1. Choose the File Find File command. The Find File dialog box appears.

2. Select the file or files you want to print.

3. Choose the Print button. The Print dialog box appears.

4. Select the printing options you want and choose OK or press Enter.

If you select multiple documents to print, they all print with the parameters you identify in the Print dialog box. For more details about printing, see Chapter 10.

Deleting Found Files

You can use the Find File command to do some file management tasks, such as deleting files you no longer need. The command is handy because you don't have to leave Word for Windows to perform file management.

To find and delete files, follow these steps:

1. Choose the File Find File command. The Find File dialog box appears (refer to fig. 3.10).

2. Select the file or files you want to delete.

3. Choose the Delete button. A dialog box asks you to confirm the deletion.

4. Choose the Yes button to delete the file or files or No if you don't want to delete them. (Select Help to find out more about deleting files.)

You cannot delete a file that is open now or a file from which you cut or copied text during the current work session.

Copying Found Files

You can use Find File to copy selected files from one location to another. Similarly, you can use a combination of techniques to move files, first by copying them to their new location, then by deleting them from their original location.

To find and copy files, follow these steps:

1. Choose the File Find File command. The Find File dialog box appears.

2. Select the file or files you want to copy.

3. Choose the Copy button. The Copy dialog box appears (see fig. 3.11).

FIG. 3.11.

The Copy
dialog box.

4. Select the directory to which you want to copy the file or files, or type in the path name.

5. Choose OK or press Enter.

Files are copied to a new location with their original name and extension.

T I P   Using Find File to copy files is a good way to make backups onto a floppy disk.

Sorting Files

Before you open, print, delete, or copy any of the files listed in the Find File dialog box, you may want to sort them into a different order besides the alphabetical order in which they are listed by default. You also may want to see different information about your files besides their titles, which appear by default.

To find, sort, and list files with different criteria, follow these steps:

1. Choose the File Find File command. The Find File dialog box appears (refer to fig. 3.10).

2. Choose the Options button. The Options dialog box appears (see
   fig. 3.12).

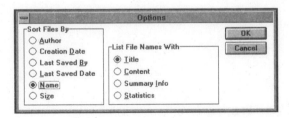

FIG. 3.12.

The Options
dialog box.

3. Select the Sort Files By option that you want.

Option	Files are listed
Author	Alphabetically by author
Creation Date	Chronologically by the file creation date (most recent date first)
Last Saved By	Alphabetically by name of person who saved the files
Last Saved Date	Chronologically by the date files are saved (most recent date first)
Name	Alphabetically by name (default choice)
Size	Numerical order by file size

4. Select the List File Names With option that you want.

Option	Displays files with
Title	Just their titles (default choice)
Content	A reduced view of their contents
Summary Info	Summary information
Statistics	The statistics contained within the summary information

5. Choose OK or press Enter.

   The Find File dialog box divides in two, with all the file names
   listed on the left side and the List File Names With option on the
   right for only the selected file. To display the List File Names With
   option for a different file, select a different file.

T I P Displaying files' contents is handy, but can slow down the operation of Find File. For faster operation, display files with just their titles.

Searching for Files

Often you want to list files in some other directory than the directory now listed, you want to list other types of files, or you may want to list files by some criteria other than where the files are located. You can tailor your list by searching for files that are in certain locations, contain certain types of information, or have certain attributes.

One of the most useful ways to search for files is to list them by the information contained in the Summary Info dialog box. (You can add Summary Information to a file when you create a new file, when you save a file with a new name, or while you edit a file. See "Adding Summary Information" earlier in this chapter.) Summary information includes title, subject, author, key words, and comments.

When you search for files by different criteria, Word for Windows lists the found files in the Find File dialog box. You can choose whether to add the new list of files to the existing list or to replace the existing list of files with the new list.

Searching for Specific Files or Different File Types

By default, Word for Windows searches for all the Word for Windows files in the specified path (or in the specified drive if no path has been specified). But you also can search for a specific file or different types of files. If the files are compatible with Word for Windows, you can open or print them; whether or not the files are compatible with Word for Windows, you can copy or delete the files you find.

To search for different file types, follow these steps:

1. Choose the **F**ile **F**ind File command. The Find File dialog box dialog box appears (refer to fig. 3.10), listing the files meeting the current search criteria.

2. Choose the **S**earch button. The Search dialog box appears (see fig. 3.13).

```
┌─────────────────────────────────────────────────────────────────┐
│ ─ □                            Search                              │
├───────────────────────────────────────────────────────────────────┤
│ File Name: [*.doc      ]  Type: [Word Document (*.doc)   ▼]  ┌──────────────┐ │
│ ┌─Location──────────────────────────────────────────────┐  │ Start Search │ │
│ │ Drives:  [📂 Path Only          ▼]    [ Edit Path... ] │  ├──────────────┤ │
│ │ Path:  [c:\quantum\authors;c:\quantum\jul         ]    │  │    Close     │ │
│ └────────────────────────────────────────────────────────┘  └──────────────┘ │
│ Title:    [guide                      ]   ┌─Date Created─┐                     │
│ Subject:  [                           ]   │ After:  [   ] │                     │
│ Keywords: [                           ]   │ Before: [   ] │                     │
│ Any Text: [                           ]   ┌─Date Saved───┐                     │
│ Author:   [              ] Saved By: [   ]│ After:  [   ] │                     │
│                                           │ Before: [   ] │                     │
│ Options:  [Create New List        ▼]   □ Match Case                            │
└───────────────────────────────────────────────────────────────────────────────┘
```

FIG. 3.13.

The Search dialog box with the Options list displayed.

3. In the File **N**ame box, type the name of the file you want to search for. You can use wild cards if you don't know the exact name: use an asterisk (*) to represent a group of unknown characters, or use a question mark (?) to represent one unknown character.

4. Select the down arrow in the **T**ype box to display a list of file types, and select the file type for which you want to search.

   or

   In the File **N**ame box, type the extension of the file type you want to search for. Use wild-card characters if you like. An asterisk (*) represents any string of characters, so you can search for all files ending with the extension TXT by typing *.*TXT*. A question mark (?) represents any one character, so you can search for *LETR?.DOC* to search for all files named LETR1.DOC, LETR2.DOC, LETRB.DOC, and so forth.

5. Choose one of the following from the Opt**i**ons list at the bottom of the Search dialog box:

Option	Description
Create New List	Replaces the existing list
Add Matches to List	Adds the new list to the existing list
Search Only in List	Searches for criteria only in the existing list. This option does not apply when you search a different drive or directory.

6. Choose the **S**tart Search button or press Enter.

Searching Different Drives or Directories

You can search for a list of files in a different drive or directory. To search an entire drive, you can select the drive to search from the **Drives** list in the Search dialog box. To search different directories or multiple drives or directories, however, you must edit the path.

The path identifies your file's location. If a file named JAN15.DOC is on your hard drive C, in a directory called LETTERS, and in a subdirectory called BANK, then the path is C:\LETTERS\BANK\JAN15.DOC. As always in Word for Windows, you can use icons in a dialog box to locate the file's path, or you can type the path in the **P**ath type box. If you type the path name, be sure to use a backslash (\) to separate the drive, directory, subdirectories, and file name. In the Search **P**ath box, you can include many different paths, separated with a semicolon (;).

The **Drives** list overrides the **P**ath name in the Search dialog box. If you specify **D**rive A and select the **P**ath C:\LETTERS\BANK, for example, then the resulting list shows only files in drive A. Select a drive only if you want to search an entire drive, but edit the path to search part of a drive.

You may want to search an entire drive when you're looking for a specific file but don't remember where the file is located. If you don't specify search criteria when you search a drive, your search may take a long time because Word for Windows lists all the files on the drive.

To search an entire drive, follow these steps:

1. Choose the **F**ile **F**ind File command and choose the **S**earch button. (The Search dialog box is shown in fig. 3.13.)

2. Select a drive from the **Drives** list.

3. Choose OK or press Enter.

If you search only part of a drive, you must specify which directories to search. You can edit the path or paths to search from the Edit Path dialog box (shown in fig. 3.14). Each path you add (by selecting the directory or subdirectory and then selecting the **A**dd button) is appended to the existing **P**ath in the Search dialog box. (Multiple paths are separated by a semicolon.) Word for Windows uses the path or paths specified in the **P**ath box in the Search dialog box to conduct the search. You also can delete paths from the search path.

To change the search path, follow these steps:

1. Choose the **F**ile **F**ind File command and choose the **S**earch button. (The Search dialog box is shown in fig. 3.13.)

2. Select Path Only from the **Drives** list.

3. Choose the **Edit Path** button. The Edit Path dialog box appears (see fig. 3.14).

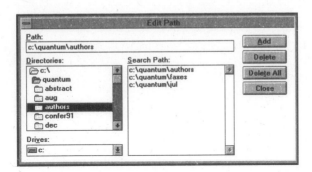

FIG. 3.14.

The Edit Path dialog box.

4. In the **Path** box, type a path.

   or

   In the **Directories** box, select a directory.

5. Select **A**dd to add the path to the **S**earch Path list box. The files listed are included in the path to be searched.

6. Choose the Close button to close the Edit Path dialog box.

To delete from the search path, follow these steps:

1. Choose the **File Find** File command and choose the **S**earch button. (The Search dialog box is shown in fig. 3.13.)

2. Select Path Only from the **D**rives list.

3. Choose the **E**dit Path button.

4. From the **S**earch Path list box, select the path you want to delete.

5. Choose the De**l**ete button.

6. Choose the Close button.

If you're familiar with paths, you can bypass the Edit Path dialog box and type the path to search in the **P**ath box in the Search dialog box.

To type a path, type the drive letter followed by a colon and backslash, then type the directories, subdirectories, and file name, separating each with a backslash. To search multiple paths, separate the paths with a semicolon.

T I P

T I P   Be sure to include the full path of *all* directories and subdirectories you want to search in the Edit Path dialog box. If you're looking for a file you think is located in the subdirectory BANK, which is located inside the directory LETTERS, which is on drive C:, for example, you won't list that file if you search for C: or even C:\LETTERS. You must include the full path, C:\LETTERS\BANK, to list a file contained within the subdirectory BANK.

Searching by Summary Information or Text in the File

One of the greatest advantages to including summary information in all your files is that you can search for files by the text contained in any of the summary information's fields. Because you can search through files by summary information and then open the files, Word for Windows gives you a way to override the DOS limitation of an eight-character file name. You also can search for files based on any of the text contained in the file.

To search by summary information or any text in the file, follow these steps:

1. Choose the **F**ile **F**ind File command.

2. Choose the **S**earch button. The Search dialog box appears.

3. Type the summary information to search for in the following text boxes:

Text box	Searches for
Title	Text in the summary information Title box
Subject	Text in the summary information Subject box
Keywords	Text in the summary information Keywords box
Any Text	Any text in the body of the document
Author	Text in the summary information Author box
Saved By	Text in the summary information Saved By box

4. Select Match **C**ase to match upper- and lowercase exactly.

5. Select **S**tart Search or press Enter.

A few rules exist for searching files by summary information or by text in the file. You can type up to 255 characters in any of the summary information fields in the Search dialog box (shown in fig. 3.13). You can use partial words or any combination of upper- and lowercase letters. If you type *ba* or *Ba* in the Title field, for example, you list files containing the words *bank* or *abandon* or any other word containing the letters *ba* in their titles. (Select the Match Case option to match upper- and lowercase exactly.) If you want to search for a phrase such as *bank loan*, then enclose the phrase in double quotation marks: *"bank loan"*. You can use wild cards in your search, and you can combine words, as shown in the following table:

To search for	Type in the Text box
Any single character	? (question mark); for example, type *ba??* to find *bank* or *band*
Any string of characters	* (asterisk); for example, type *ba** to find any word that begins with the letters *ba*
A phrase (such as *bank loan*)	" " (quotation marks enclosing phrase); for example, type *"bank loan"*
one word or another word	, (comma); for example, type *bank,loan* to find files containing *bank* or *loan*
one word and another word	& (ampersand) or space; for example, type *bank & loan* or *bank loan* to find files containing *bank* and *loan*
files not containing this word or letter	~ (tilde); for example, type *bank~loan* to find files containing *bank* but not *loan*

Editing Summary Information

You can use the **F**ind File command to edit summary information for a selected file, as in the following steps:

1. Choose the **F**ile **F**ind File command.

2. Search for and select the file for which you want to edit summary information.

3. Choose the Su**m**mary button. The Summary Info dialog box appears.

4. Edit the summary information.

5. Choose OK or press Enter.

Searching by Date Saved or Created

You can search for files based on the date you created or saved them. This feature is especially handy when used in combination with other search criteria. For example, you can search for files containing the title words *bank* and *letter* that were created between June 1 and June 30 of last year.

To search for files by date saved or created, follow these steps:

1. Choose the File Find File command and choose the Search button. The Search dialog box appears.

2. In the Date Created After box or the Date Saved After box, type the beginning date in the range of dates you want to search. Use the format mm/dd/yy (for example, 6/1/91).

3. In the Date Created Before box or the Date Saved Before box, type the ending date in the range of dates you want to search. Use the format mm/dd/yy (for example, 6/30/91).

4. Choose the Start Search button.

Working with Multiple Documents

In Word for Windows, you can work with several documents simultaneously. Each new document you create or each existing document you open resides in its own document window on your screen. (For details on the difference between the program window and document windows, and on moving and sizing windows, see Chapter 1.

One great benefit to working with multiple documents simultaneously is that you can easily copy or move text between them. This feature eases the task of creating two different versions of one basic document or borrowing from an existing document as you build a new one. For details about copying and moving text, see Chapter 4.

As you open successive documents, they appear in document windows that hide the previously opened documents. To work with these documents, you can switch between them in this full-screen mode, or you can arrange the windows so that you can see at least a portion of each of them. The only active, or selected, window at any time is the window on top, the one with the solid title bar.

To arrange multiple document windows, choose the **W**indow **A**rrange All command.

Word for Windows reduces the size of each window so that you can see them all on-screen. You can resize or move these windows using normal Windows techniques. To switch between the windows, click on the window you want to select, or press Ctrl+F6 to select the next window. To restore any window to its full-screen size, click the maximize arrow at the top right of the window, or choose the Control Maximize command (Ctrl+F10).

To switch between full-screen document windows, do the following:

1. Choose the **W**indow menu, which lists all currently open files.

2. Select the name of the file you want to switch to.

As an alternative to using the **W**indow menu to switch between open documents, you can press Ctrl+F6. This method is the quickest when you have only two files open.

To open a second copy of the current file, follow these steps:

1. Choose the **W**indow menu, which lists all currently open files.

2. Select **N**ew Window.

When you open multiple copies of the same file, the first ends with :1, the second with :2, and so forth. You can switch between these windows in the same way you switch between any document windows, but any edits you make to one are made to all, and when you save or close one document, they all save or close.

From Here . . .

In Chapter 4 you learn how to select and edit the documents you create. Chapters 5-8 show how to improve the appearance of your documents with character enhancements such as bold and italic, with paragraph formatting such as tabs and indents, and with section and document formatting such as columns and margins. Chapter 9 explains many advanced editing techniques that are surprisingly simple to use—and useful. And when your document looks right, go on to Chapter 10 to print your document.

Editing a Document

As you begin working with Word for Windows, start by gaining a solid understanding of the basics. For example, several different options exist for viewing your document: you can work very fast in draft mode, or you can slow down and zoom in to do detailed work by choosing the page layout view and enlarging it up to 200 percent. You can move around in your document in may ways, using the mouse and keyboard techniques. You should understand one of the most important principles in working with Word for Windows: "Select, then do." You can move and copy text and objects from one part of your document to another, from one document to another, or even from one application to another.

In this chapter you learn these basics (and more) and many handy shortcuts you will use now and as you become a more experienced Word for Windows user.

Controlling Your Document's Appearance On-Screen

In Word for Windows, you can display your document in the way that best fits what you need to do. As you work, you can use normal view to see the body text as it will print, use draft view for fast typing, use outline view for outline expansion or contraction, and use page layout view to see the entire page exactly as it will print, including columns, headers, footers, and page numbers. In all these views you can type, format, and edit. (A fifth view under a different menu, print preview, shows thumbnail pictures of how pages will print, but you cannot edit in this view. For more information on print preview, see Chapter 10.)

The following sections describe the various Word for Windows views. Keep in mind that you can add or remove screen elements, such as scroll bars and status bars, to these views. Screen elements are controlled by selections you make with the **Tools Options** command (see the section "Changing the Display with the Options Command" later in this chapter).

Editing in Normal View

Use *normal view* for most of your typing and editing. In this view, which is Word for Windows default view, you see character and paragraph formatting as they will print. Line and page breaks, tab stops, and alignments are accurate. The area outside the text body—the area containing headers, footers, footnotes, page numbers, margin spacing, and so on—does not show. You also cannot see the exact placement of such features as snaking columns, positioned paragraphs, or text wrapping around fixed paragraphs or objects. Figure 4.1 shows a document in normal view.

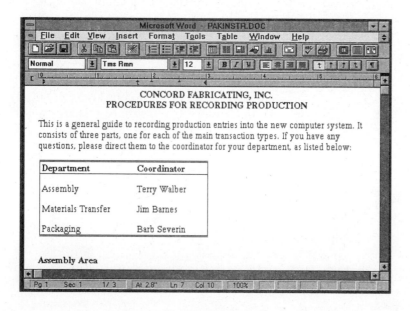

FIG. 4.1.

A document in normal view.

To type in normal view, make sure that in the **View** menu the **Normal** command is selected and that the **Draft** command is not selected. (Remember that a selected option appears with a bullet or a check mark to the left of the option.) To unselect a checkmarked view, select the corresponding command again.

Editing in Page Layout View

In *page layout view*, your document shows each page as it will appear when printed. You can scroll outside the body copy area of the page to see such items as headers, footers, footnotes, page numbers, and margin spacing. Snaking columns and text that wraps around fixed position objects appear as they will print. Although you can see exactly how the page will print, you still can type and make formatting changes.

To change to the page layout view, choose **View** **P**age **La**yout. Figure 4.2 shows a document in the page layout view. Notice how you can see the actual position in which the table will print and how the text will wrap around it.

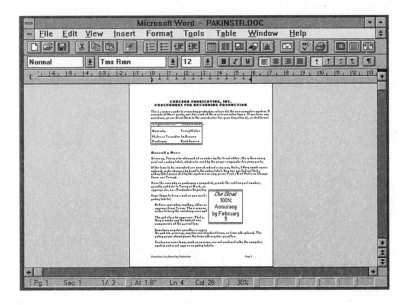

FIG. 4.2.

A document in page layout view.

Editing in Draft View

Work in the *draft view* when you need quicker response. Draft view enables you to type and scroll faster. In draft view, your document appears in "draft" characters, all the same size, rather than in the fonts you have selected. Enhanced characters in different fonts or styles appear underlined. Only the borders of pictures show. You can use draft view to type quickly and partially format your document. You then can switch to page layout view to see exactly how the document will appear and to add final enhancements and formatting.

To change to draft view, choose **View Draft**. (If you are in page layout view when you choose **View Draft**, Word for Windows switches to normal view.) Figure 4.3 shows a document in draft view.

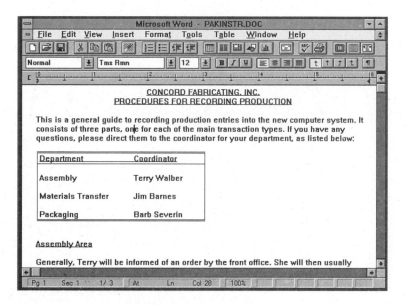

FIG. 4.3.

A document in draft view.

Zooming In or Out

To see more of your document, use the **View Zoom** command to change the scale, as in the following steps:

1. Choose the **View Zoom** command.

2. When the Zoom dialog box shown in figure 4.4 appears, select the desired magnification. The lower the magnification, the more of your document appears on-screen.

Naturally, you can zoom in for a closer look by selecting **2**00% magnification. This could be useful if you work with small font sizes. If none of the preset magnification options (200%, 100%, 75%, and 50%) meets your needs, you can enter your desired magnification in the **C**ustom box.

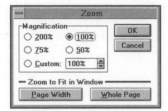

FIG. 4.4.

The Zoom dialog box.

Choosing the **W**hole Page button at the bottom of the Zoom dialog box shrinks the display so that one screen is equal to one printed page. Figure 4.5 shows a page zoomed to **W**hole Page in page layout view. You also can zoom to **W**hole Page in normal view.

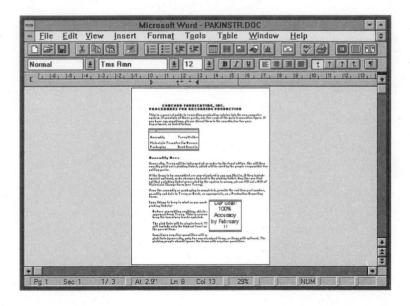

FIG. 4.5.

The display after choosing the Whole Page option in the Zoom dialog box (page layout view).

You also can zoom in and out by using one of the three Zoom buttons on the toolbar (these are the three buttons that appear at the right end of the toolbar—see fig. 4.6). The left button of the three buttons is the View Zoom Whole Page button, which zooms to a view of the whole page in page layout view (as shown in fig. 4.5). The center button is View Zoom 100, which shows a full-size page in normal view (Word for Windows' default view). The rightmost button is View Zoom Page Width, which zooms the page to show the full width of the text (in normal view) or the full width of the page (in page layout view).

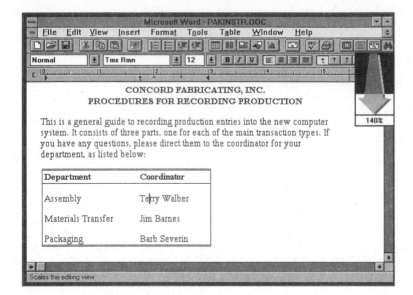

FIG. 4.6.

The three built-in
Zoom buttons
and the added
View Zoom
button.

T I P You can add commands to the toolbar, assigning them to the button of your choice. A handy command to add is View Zoom (see Chapters 29 and 31 to learn how to customize the toolbar). When you click on the View Zoom button, the button drops down like a menu, displaying a large arrow (see fig. 4.6). Drag downward on the arrow to select the zoom scale you want, watching the percentage displayed at the bottom of the arrow. When the scale you want is displayed, release the mouse button.

Editing in Outline View

In *outline view*, your document shows the levels of outline structure. The outline bar appears at the top of the screen to enable you to promote and demote outline topic levels (see fig. 4.7). Outlining is described in Chapter 14. To change to the outline view, choose **View Outline**.

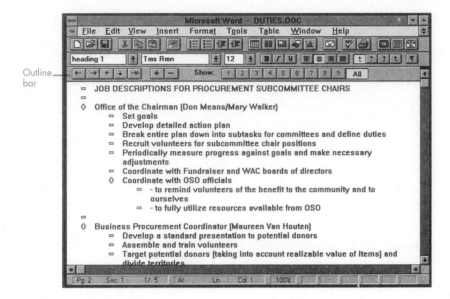

Outline bar

FIG. 4.7.

Outline view.

Displaying the Toolbar, Ruler, and Ribbon

The toolbar offers "one-button" access to Word for Windows' most commonly used commands. The ruler and ribbon are similarly useful, providing a quick and easy visual access to the most frequently used formatting commands operations.

Occasionally, however, you may need all the screen space you can get, or you may prefer to work with a screen that displays only the menu bar and text. You can remove the toolbar, ruler, and ribbon by choosing the appropriate command from the View menu. Table 4.1 describes each of these screen items and lists the corresponding menu commands.

Choosing the command removes the item from the screen (if it is not currently displayed) and removes the corresponding check mark from the View menu. When an item is not displayed, choosing the same command redisplays it on the screen.

Table 4.1. Optional Screen Formatting Tools

Item	Location	Command	Function
Toolbar	Below menu bar	**View Toolbar**	Accesses a wide range of commands
Ribbon	Below toolbar	**View Ribbon**	Formats text, sets alignment and tabs, and views hidden text
Ruler	Above document window	**View Ruler**	Views and changes indents, margins, tabs, and column widths

Modifying the Screen Display

With the **Tools Options** command, you can further modify the display to fit your preferences. You can, for example, request that tab and paragraph marks display as special characters, that margins display as dotted lines, or that horizontal and vertical scroll bars display.

To change your screen's appearance, follow these steps:

1. Choose the **Tools Options** command. The Options dialog box appears, as shown in figure 4.8.

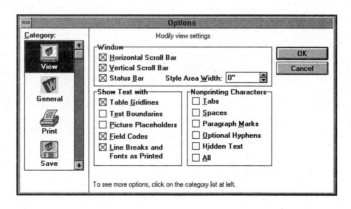

2. Select the appropriate options (see table 4.2).

3. Choose OK or press Enter.

Table 4.2. View Options in the Options Dialog Box

Option	Function
Window	
Horizontal Scroll Bar	Displays horizontal scroll bars
Vertical Scroll Bar	Displays vertical scroll bars
Status **B**ar	Displays status bar
Style Area **W**idth	Controls width for the area by the left margin where the style name is displayed.(If the width is too narrow, the name is cut off.)
Show Text With	
Table **G**ridlines	Displays the lines marking a table's grid
Text Boundaries	Displays margins and fixed-position boundaries as dotted lines
Picture Placeholders	Displays pictures or graphics on-screen
Field codes	Displays field code type and switches (if any in field braces)
Line Breaks and Fonts as Printed	Displays the document as it will print with your printer and its fonts (you can turn this option off only in normal view)
Nonprinting Characters	
Tabs	Displays tabs as right arrows
Spaces	Displays spaces as dots
Paragraph **M**arks	Displays paragraph marks as ¶
Optional Hyphens	Displays optional hyphens as ➡
Hi**d**den Text	Varies, depending on the particular type of hidden text
All	Displays all marks along with text boundaries

Figures 4.9 and 4.10 show two screens of the same document in page layout view. Each screen uses different options in the view mode Options screen.

T I P   You can format and enhance documents with features your printer cannot handle, which gives you the power to create documents that later can be printed on other printers or typesetting equipment. But with this power you must exercise caution. You may create a document that will not print on your printer as the document appears on-screen. If you use fonts unavailable in your printer, the printer will substitute fonts for those it doesn't have, and your pictures and graphs may not print.

To ensure that you are using only fonts, features, and graphics that your printer is capable of printing, choose the **Tools Options** command and select the **Line Breaks and Fonts as Printed** option.

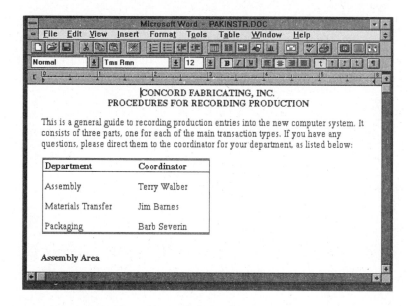

FIG. 4.9.

A document displayed with scroll bars, no status bar, and no control characters visible.

T I P   To quickly show all special formatting marks, click the ¶ button at the right end of the ribbon or press Shift+Ctrl+* (Show All). To remove the marks, click the ¶ button again or press Shift+Ctrl+* again.

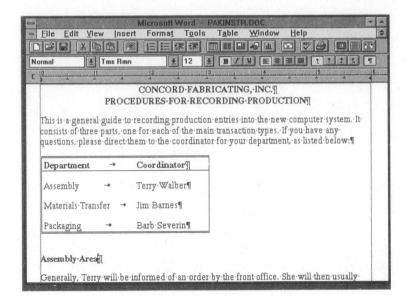

FIG. 4.10.

A document
displayed with
no scroll bars, no
status bar, and
all control
characters
visible.

Moving in the Document

If you're familiar with word processing, you will learn to move efficiently through a Word for Windows document in no time at all. But
don't stop trying to learn more, because Word for Windows provides a
number of unique methods to cut your visual search time to the abso-
lute minimum.

Moving and Scrolling with the Mouse

To relocate the insertion point by using the mouse, scroll the view so
that you can see the location you want, and then click the I-beam
pointer at the character location where you want the insertion point.

Using your mouse pointer in the horizontal and vertical scroll bars
enables you to scroll the document easily so that a new area displays.
Figure 4.11 shows the parts of the scroll bars, which include the scroll
box and page icons. The scroll box shows the screen's location relative
to the entire document's length and width. Page layout view displays
page icons, which you can click to turn a page.

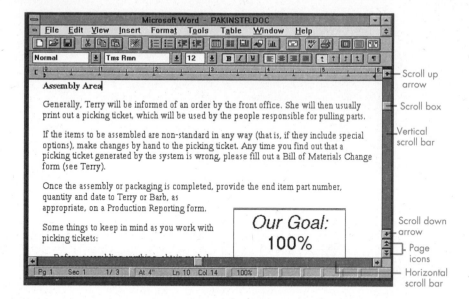

FIG. 4.11.

Parts of the scroll bar.

T I P If you use a mouse, display the horizontal and vertical scroll bars so that you can scroll with the mouse. If you use the keyboard, turn off the horizontal and vertical scroll bars to have more room on the typing screen.

Table 4.3 lists the scrolling methods you can use with the mouse and the scroll bars.

Don't forget to click the I-beam at the new typing location after the text you want to edit scrolls into sight. If you scroll to a new location and leave the insertion point at the old location, your typing or editing appears at the old location.

Moving and Scrolling with the Keyboard

The arrow keys ($\uparrow$, $\downarrow$, $\leftarrow$, and $\rightarrow$) and cursor-movement keys (PgUp, PgDn, Home, and End) move the insertion point as you would expect. Combine these keys with the Ctrl key, however, and they become powerful editing allies. Table 4.4 shows cursor movements you can make with the keyboard.

Table 4.3. Using the Mouse and the Scroll Bars

To move	Click
One line	Up or down scroll arrow
One screen up or down	Gray area above or below the scroll box in the vertical scroll bar
One page	Page icons (in page layout view)
Large vertical moves	Drag vertical scroll box to a new location
Horizontally in small increments	Right or left scroll arrow
Horizontally in relative increments	Drag horizontal scroll box to a new location in the horizontal scroll bar
Into left margin	Left scroll arrow while holding Shift (normal view); left scroll arrow (page layout view)

Table 4.4. Moving and Scrolling with the Keyboard

To move	Press
One character left	Left-arrow key
One character right	Right-arrow key
One line up	Up-arrow key
One line down	Down-arrow key
One word to the left	Ctrl+left arrow
One word to the right	Ctrl+right arrow
To end of a line	End
To beginning of a line	Home
One paragraph up	Ctrl+up arrow
One paragraph down	Ctrl+down arrow
Up one window	PgUp key
Down one window	PgDn key
To bottom of window	Ctrl+PgDn
To top of window	Ctrl+PgUp
To end of document	Ctrl+End
To start of document	Ctrl+Home

Going to a Specific Page

When you need to move to a specific page number, use the **E**dit **G**o To command. The **E**dit **G**o To command works with page numbers only when the document has been paginated either automatically or with the **T**ools Rep**a**ginate Now command.

With the mouse, follow these steps to move to a specific page:

1. Choose the **E**dit **G**o To command. The dialog box shown in figure 4.12 appears. (Your dialog box may appear with names in the Go To list. The use of Bookmark names to mark locations is described later in this chapter in the section "Using Bookmarks.")

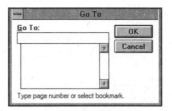

FIG. 4.12.

The Go To box.

2. Type a page number in the **G**o To text box.

3. Choose OK.

From the keyboard, move to a specific location by following these steps:

1. Press the F5 (Go To) key.

2. At the Go To prompt in the status bar, type the page number.

3. Press Enter.

As an alternative, you can press the F5 key twice to display the Go To dialog box. Use the box according to the instructions for the mouse.

Going to a Bookmark

Bookmarks are locations in a document or sections of a document to which you assign a name. If you are familiar with Microsoft Excel or Lotus 1-2-3, bookmarks are similar to range names. You can go to a bookmark using the Go To procedures by following these steps:

1. Choose the **E**dit **G**o To command or press the F5 key twice. The dialog box shown in figure 4.13 appears. The bookmarks in the document appear in the Go To list.

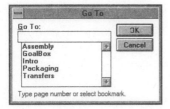

FIG. 4.13.

The Go To box
with bookmarks
listed.

2. Select one of the bookmarks.

3. Choose OK.

As an alternative, you can go to a bookmark by pressing F5, typing the bookmark name at the Go To prompt that appears in the status bar at the bottom of the screen, then pressing Enter.

"Using Bookmarks" later in this chapter describes how to create bookmarks.

In many scrolling lists, like the list of names in the Go To list, double-clicking on an item in the lists selects the item and chooses the OK button. In the Go To list, for example, double-clicking on one of the names takes you immediately to the name without having to click OK.

T I P

Moving the Insertion Point a Relative Distance

You can move a relative distance from the insertion point's current location. The move can be in increments of pages, lines, sections, footnotes, or annotations. You can even move to a location that is a certain percentage of the way through the total document.

To move a relative distance, follow these steps:

1. Choose the **Edit G**o To command or press F5 twice to display the Go To dialog box.

   or

   Press F5 to display the Go To prompt in the status bar.

2. Type one of the move codes listed in table 4.5 in the Go To text box.

3. Choose OK or press Enter.

Sections, footnotes, and annotations are numbered from the beginning of the document. For example, f9 is the ninth footnote in the document, but f+9 is the ninth footnote forward from the current one.

Table 4.5. Codes to Go To a Relative Location

To move insertion point	Type
To page n	pn or n
Forward n pages	p+n
Backward n pages	p-n
To next line	l
To line n	ln
Forward n lines	l+n
Backward n lines	l-n
To next section	s
To section n	sn
Forward n sections	s+n
Backward n sections	s-n
To next footnote	f
To footnote n	fn
Forward n footnotes	f+n
Backward n footnotes	f-n
To annotation n	an
Forward n annotations	a+n
Backward n annotations	a-n
n percent through document	%n or n%

NOTE n is the number of units (pages, lines, sections, footnotes, or annotations) you want to move forward or backward from the current location. Typing *p+3* in the Go To box, for example, moves the insertion point three pages forward. If you type nothing, the insertion moves to the next page.

Moving to Previous Insertion Points

Return the insertion point to the last three locations where an action occurred by pressing Shift+F5. Each of the first three presses moves the insertion point to the immediately preceding place of action. Pressing a fourth time returns the insertion point to the starting location.

Pressing Shift+F5 after opening a document returns the insertion point to its location when you last saved the document.

Selecting Text

Word for Windows uses the principle common to all good Windows software: Select, then do. Whether you want to delete a word, format a phrase, or move a sentence, you must select what you want to change before choosing the command. As with other commands and features, you can use the mouse or the keyboard to select text. Many shortcuts and tips also are available for selecting text quickly.

Selecting Text with the Mouse

Selecting text with the mouse is easy and convenient. You can select any amount of text from a single character to the entire document. You also can combine mouse and keyboard selection techniques. Use whichever method or combination is effective for you.

To select a small amount of text with the mouse, follow these steps:

1. Click and hold the insertion point at the beginning of the text.

2. Drag the insertion point in any direction across the text you want selected.

If the insertion point touches the edge of the window as you are dragging, the window scrolls in that direction if more text exists.

To select from the current insertion point to a distant location, follow these steps:

1. Click the I-beam at the beginning of the text to relocate the insertion point.

2. Hold down the Shift key or press the F8 (Extend Selection) key.

   While you are in extend-selection mode, EXT appears on the status bar at the bottom of the screen.

3. Scroll the screen so that the end of text you want selected shows.

4. Click the I-beam at the end of the text.

5. Release the Shift key if you held it down in step 2, or press Esc if you pressed the F8 key in step 2.

As an alternative, position the insertion point where you want to start the selection, scroll until the end of the text is visible, and then hold the Shift key while you click the I-beam where you want to end the selection.

To unselect text, click the mouse button anywhere in the document.

You can select specific units of text, such as words, sentences, lines, paragraphs, or the whole document, by using one of the techniques listed in table 4.6. Notice that clicking or dragging in the selection bar, as indicated in figure 4.14, is a shortcut for selecting text. The selection bar is the blank vertical space on the left side of the Word for Windows document. Text never extends into this area.

If you frequently select the same block of text or need to select text under macro control, use a bookmark. Bookmarks are described later in this chapter.

Table 4.6. Selecting Blocks of Text with the Mouse

Text to select	Mouse action
Word	Double-click the word
Sentence	Press Ctrl and click in sentence
Line	Click in selection bar (blank margin to left of text)
Multiple lines	Click in selection bar and drag up or down
Paragraph	Double-click in selection bar
Document	Press Ctrl and click in selection bar

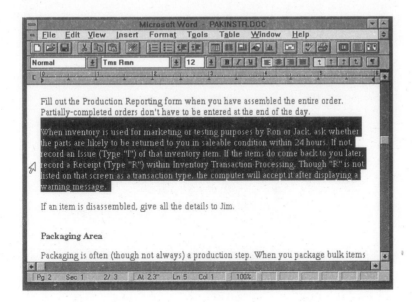

FIG. 4.14.

The selection bar with a paragraph selected.

> **T I P**
>
> The usual technique for selecting text selects the full width of the page—all the text from margin to margin. If you want to select a vertical area of text (such as all the numbers in a numbered list), however, drag across the text while holding the *right* mouse button instead of the left.

Selecting Text with the Keyboard

If you are a touch typist, you don't need to move your fingers from the keyboard to select text. Word for Windows enables you to select varying amounts of text quickly and conveniently.

The method most convenient for selecting text is to hold down the Shift key as you move the insertion point. Some of these key combinations are listed in table 4.7. You can select text by using Shift in combination with any move key.

To select large amounts of text or an amount relative to your current location, combine the F8 (Extend Selection) key with the F5 (Go To) key and a move code. Follow these steps:

1. Move the insertion point to the beginning of the text to be selected.

2. Press F8 (Extend Selection).

3. Press F5 (Go To).

4. Type a move code representing the relative location of the end of your selection, as described earlier in the section "Moving the Insertion Point a Relative Distance."

5. Press Enter.

6. Press Esc to end the selection.

Table 4.7. Selecting Text with the Shift Key

To select	Press
A word	Shift+Ctrl+left- or right-arrow key
To beginning of line	Shift+Home
To end of line	Shift+End
One line at a time	Shift+up- or down-arrow key
To beginning of document	Shift+Ctrl+Home
To end of document	Shift+Ctrl+End

To select the next 20 lines in your document, for example, you press F8 (Extend Selection) and F5 (Go To), type *l+20*, and then press Enter. Press Esc to exit extend-selection mode.

T I P Press Ctrl+5 to select the entire document. This shortcut works only with the 5 key on the numeric keypad. Num Lock can be on or off.

T I P To select an entire table, place the insertion point inside the table and press Alt+5 on the numeric keypad. Num Lock must be off.

Another way of selecting text with the keyboard is to use the F8 (Extend Selection) key to select text the insertion point moves over. To select from the insertion point to a distant location using the F8 (Extend Selection) key, follow these steps:

1. Move the insertion point to the beginning of the text you want to select.

2. Press F8 (Extend Selection).

3. Press one of the keys listed in table 4.8.

4. Press the Esc key to exit extend-selection mode.

Table 4.8. Selecting Text in the Extend-Selection Mode

To select to	Press
Next or preceding character	Arrow key
A character	That character
End of line	End
Beginning of line	Home
Top of next screen	PgUp
Bottom of next screen	PgDn
Beginning of document	Ctrl+Home
End of document	Ctrl+End

When out of extend-selection mode, you can press any arrow key to unselect the selected text.

You also can use extend-selection mode to select specific units of text, such as a word, sentence, or paragraph, by following these steps:

1. Move the cursor into the text.

2. Press F8 (Extend Selection), as indicated in this chart:

To select current	Press F8
Word	2 times
Sentence	3 times
Paragraph	4 times
Section	5 times
Document	6 times

If the insertion point is in a field code when you press the F8 key, the field code and then the next larger block of text are selected. (Field codes are hidden codes used to automate Word for Windows processes. Reading Chapters 15, 16, and 18 will help you understand field codes.)

To select a unit of text smaller than the current selection, press Shift+F8 as many times as needed to decrease the selection.

Remember, press the Esc key, and then move the insertion point to get out of extend-selection mode.

Creating Bookmarks

A *bookmark* in Word for Windows is a specific named item. The item can be a portion of the document, including text, graphics, or both; or it can simply be a specific location. Spreadsheet users will readily recognize the concept—bookmarks are similar to named ranges in a worksheet.

Use bookmarks to move quickly to a given point in a document, or to mark text or graphics for efficient moving, copying, or cross-referencing. Bookmarks also are vital when you create a macro that performs an operation on a specific portion of a document.

To create a bookmark, follow these steps:

1. Position the insertion point at the location you want to name, or select the text or graphic you want named.

2. Choose the **Insert Bookmark** command. The Bookmark dialog box displays so that you can name a new bookmark or redefine an existing one (see fig. 4.15).

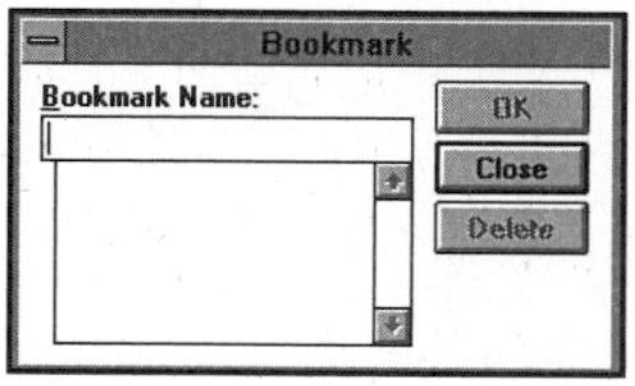

FIG. 4.15.

The Bookmark dialog box.

3. Type a new name for the bookmark in the **Bookmark** Name text box or select from the list an existing name that you want to redefine.

4. Choose OK or press Enter.

Bookmark names can be up to 20 characters long. A name must begin with a letter but can include numbers, letters, and underlines. Do not use spaces, punctuation marks, or other characters.

Rather than choose the **Insert Bookmark** command to create a Bookmark, you can position the insertion point or select an area, press Ctrl+Shift+F5, and type the bookmark name. (No dialog box appears, but a prompt appears in the status bar.)

T I P

One way in which bookmarks can save you time is in selecting text or graphics that you frequently copy, move, or reformat. By naming the text or graphic with a bookmark, you can select the text or graphic no matter where you are in the document. Bookmarks are important when constructing macros in which a portion of text must always be found, then acted on.

T I P

If you want to quickly go to and select items or a location named by a bookmark, choose the **Edit Go** To command or press the F5 key twice, select the name, and choose OK. This is described in more detail in the earlier section on moving within a document.

When you want to delete a bookmark, follow these steps:

1. Choose the **Insert Bookmark** command.
2. Select the name you want to delete.
3. Choose the **Delete** button.
4. Choose the **Close** button.

Deleting Text

Effective writing doesn't come easily, and good writers spend a great deal of time deleting text. Deleting is a simple operation in Word for Windows, but you should be aware of some nuances.

To delete text, first select it, using any selection technique or shortcut, and then press the Del or Backspace key. You can use one of the following key combinations to delete specific units of text:

To delete	Press
Character to right of insertion point	Del
Character to left of insertion point	Backspace
The next word	Ctrl+Del
The preceding word	Ctrl+Backspace

T I P To make editing quick and easy, use the F8 or Shift key combinations to select text; then press Del or Backspace. To delete a sentence, for example, press F8 three times and then press Del. Press Esc to turn off extend mode.

Replacing Text

One helpful feature in Word for Windows—a feature not available in many word processors—enables you to replace selected text with your typing. Before you can replace selected text with text you type or paste from the clipboard, you may need to select a custom setting by doing the following:

1. Choose the **T**ools **O**ptions command. This brings up the Options dialog box in figure 4.16.

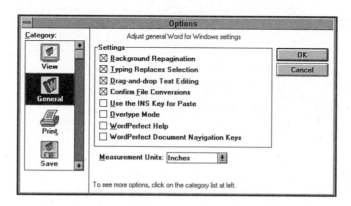

FIG. 4.16.

The Tools Option dialog box with the General Category selected.

2. Select the General option from the **C**ategory group.

3. Select the **T**yping Replaces Selection option.

4. Choose OK or press Enter.

Anything you type or paste replaces whatever is selected.

If you accidentally type over selected text, you can undo your mistake by immediately choosing the Edit Undo command or pressing Ctrl+Z or Alt+Backspace.

T I P

CAUTION If you're in overtype mode, typing replaces the selection and text following the selection. You cannot undo overtyping, so be very careful if you're working in this mode. (You can toggle overtype mode on or off by pressing the Ins key or by selecting Overtype Mode in the General Settings section of the Options dialog box.)

Undoing Edits

The Undo command reverses the most recent action (assuming that action can be reversed). You can undo most editing actions, such as deletions. Other actions that you can undo are Insert commands (except Insert Page Numbers), Format commands (Style), and Tools commands (except Options).

You must choose the Undo command immediately after you make the mistake. If you continue working, you cannot undo your error. To undo the last action, such as a deletion, choose the Edit Undo command, or press the Undo keys, Ctrl+Z or Alt+Backspace.

Moving, Copying, and Linking Text or Graphics

With Word for Windows' move and copy commands, you can reorganize your thoughts to make your writing flow smoothly and logically.

Word for Windows also has the powerful capability to link text or graphics within a document or to other documents. This feature enables you to link text or graphics in one location to another location in the same document. When you change the original, the linked copy changes simultaneously.

Word for Windows incorporates *OLE*, Object Linking and Embedding. This enables you to link documents and data such as an Excel chart into a Word for Windows document. When you want to update the Excel chart, you can double-click on the chart to bring up Excel so that the chart can be edited. The OLE features of Word for Windows are described in detail in Chapter 21.

Understanding the Clipboard

A section of text or a graphic being moved or copied is kept in a temporary area of memory known as the *clipboard*. The clipboard holds an item while it is being moved to a new location in the same or a different document. In fact, you can even move or copy text from Word for Windows to other Windows or DOS applications.

If you cut or copy something and want to see it in the clipboard, follow these steps:

1. Select the Application Control menu by pressing Alt, space bar, or by clicking the Application Control icon at the left of the Microsoft Word title bar.

2. Choose the R**u**n command.

3. Select the **C**lipboard option.

4. Choose OK or press Enter.

The clipboard displays in its own window, as shown in figure 4.17. The window's heading shows the type of contents in the clipboard. The clipboard may be empty if you have not cut or copied something to it. Some commands clear the clipboard after executing. Close the clipboard by pressing Alt, space bar, and then C.

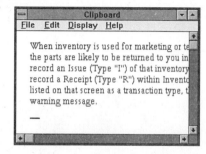

FIG. 4.17.

The Clipboard
window.

Moving Text or Graphics

You probably are familiar with the concept of moving text or graphics. A portion of text or a graphic is "cut" from the original location and then "pasted" into a new location. The existing text at the new location moves to accommodate the new arrival.

To move text or graphics, follow these steps:

1. Select the text or graphic you want to move.

2. Choose the **E**dit Cu**t** command. The selection is stored in the clipboard.

3. Reposition the insertion point where you want the item to reappear.

4. Choose the **E**dit **P**aste command. The selection is pasted into its new location.

If you need to accumulate and move multiple pieces of text to the same location, you will want to use the spike. The *spike* enables you to cut several pieces of text, move all of them to a new location, and paste them in the order they were cut. Chapter 9 describes how to use Word for Windows' glossary feature to spike your selections.

Copying Text or Graphics

Copying text uses a process similar to moving text. The difference is that copying retains the original text and inserts a duplicate in the new location. You can even copy information from one document and paste the information into another document.

To copy text or graphics to a new location, follow these steps:

1. Select the text or graphic you want copied.

2. Choose the **E**dit **C**opy command. The selection is stored in the clipboard.

3. If you want to paste into another document, open that document now. If it is already open, make it active by choosing it from the Window menu or by clicking any portion of that document if you can see it.

4. Reposition the insertion point where you want the copy to appear.

5. Choose the **E**dit **P**aste command.

You can make repeated pastes of the same item until you cut or copy a new item to the clipboard.

Shortcut keys for moving and copying text or graphics can save you time. Table 4.9 lists available shortcuts for moving and copying text or graphics quickly.

Table 4.9. Using Shortcut Keys To Move and Copy	
Key	Function
Ctrl+X or Shift+Del	Cuts the selected text or graphic to the clipboard. This shortcut works the same as the Edit Cut command.
Ctrl+C or Ctrl+Ins	Copies the selected text or graphic to the clipboard. This shortcut works the same as the Edit Copy command. You can paste the copied material multiple times.
Ctrl+V or Shift+Ins	Pastes the clipboard's contents at the cursor's location. This shortcut works the same as Edit Paste.
Shift+F2	Copies the selected text or graphic one time without using the clipboard. To use this shortcut, select what you want to copy and then press Shift+F2. The prompt Copy to where? appears at the bottom of the screen. Move the insertion point to the new location, and press Enter.

Using the Mouse To Move and Copy Items

With Word for Windows, you can move, copy, and link items within a document by using only the mouse. This feature enables you to quickly move paragraphs or sentences, copy phrases, or drag pictures to new locations.

T I P Word for Windows now enables you to *frame* graphic objects or any amount of text, and then pick up the frame and place it somewhere else in the document. You can, for example, drag pictures to the center of a page and the text will wrap around them, or you can drag a paragraph to the side, enclose it in borders and use it as a "pull quote." To learn how to use these desktop publishing features in Word for Windows, refer to Chapters 24 and 28.

To move text or a graphic to a new location using the mouse, follow these steps:

1. Select the text or graphic you want to move. (If you are dragging a picture to a new location, change to page layout view before dragging.)

2. Move the mouse pointer over the selected text or graphic. The mouse pointer changes from an I-beam into a pointer over selected text or into a four-headed move pointer over graphics.

3. Hold down the left mouse button and drag to where you want the text or graphic located.

   The text pointer becomes an arrow pointer combined with a small gray box. The text insertion point appears as a grayed vertical bar. The graphic will appear as a grayed outline as it is dragged to a new location.

4. Release the left mouse button to insert the selected text or graphic.

To move text or graphics quickly, select the text or graphic you want to move. Then scroll to the screen area where you want to move the text or graphic. Hold down the Ctrl key as you click the right mouse button at the target location.   **T I P**

Linking Text

A special technique exists for forging a link between the source and the destination when you copy text or an object between or within documents. By linking the object as you copy it, you can automatically update the destination each time you make a change to the source. For example, a CPA might maintain a library of boilerplate paragraphs to borrow from when writing individual letters to clients advising them about tax matters. If tax laws change, the CPA can change the source (boilerplate) document, and by simply selecting a command or pressing a key, update the destination document to reflect the changes.

To copy and link text or an object, follow these steps:

1. Select and copy the text or object in the source document.

2. Position the insertion point where you want to link the text or object in the destination document.

3. Choose the **E**dit Paste **S**pecial command. The Paste Special dialog box appears (see fig. 4.18).

4. Choose the Paste Link check box.

Word for Windows inserts a field code that displays in the destination document the contents of the linked selection from the source document.

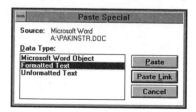

FIG. 4.18.

The Paste Special dialog box.

The advantage of linking text is the ease of transferring changes between the original and the linked text. Linked text actually is created by inserting a hidden field code that links the original text to the location you indicate. An example of such a field code linking within the same document is as follows:

```
{REF INTERN_LINK4 \* mergeformat}
```

Chapter 21 describes in detail links created to other documents or applications. To learn more about field codes, refer to Chapter 18.

You can edit and format linked text just as you would normal text. When the linked text is updated, however, it changes to reflect the current status of the original text.

To update linked text to match any changes made to the original text, select across the entire linked text, making sure to exceed at least one end of the linked text. Press the F9 key to update all field codes within the selection. You will see the linked text update to match the changes in the original.

You can unlink linked text from its original by selecting all of the linked text and pressing Shift+Ctrl+F9. This changes the link into normal text.

To update the linked text or object (to reflect the changes made in the original), select the object to update and choose the Edit Links command. In the Links dialog box, choose Update Now. To cancel the link, choose Cancel Link.

T I P

When you update a link, Word for Windows looks for the source document in the same location where it was when you created the link. If it's not there, the link cannot be updated unless you tell Word for Windows where to find the source document. To do that, change the source document's path in the field code that is entered when you link text or an object (to see and edit the path, choose the **View** Field **C**odes command).

Working with Multiple Windows

You can have up to nine documents open at one time in Word for Windows. Each document occupies its own window. You can arrange these windows within Word for Windows just as you place pieces of paper on a desk. With the **W**indow **A**rrange All command, you can arrange all open windows so that each has a portion of the screen. You can even open more than one window onto the same document when you need to work on widely separated parts of the same document. And as mentioned previously, you can even cut or copy from one document and paste into another.

Viewing Different Parts of the Same Document

If you are working with a long document, you may want to see more than one part of it at the same time. This can be useful when you need to compare or edit widely separated parts of the same document.

You can expand your view in two ways. The first method is to open a new window by choosing the **W**indow **N**ew Window command. This technique creates a second window containing the same document. With two windows holding the same document, each window has a title bar showing the file name, a colon, and then the number of the window—for example, PAKINSTR.DOC:1 and PAKINSTR.DOC:2. Figure 4.19 shows two windows displaying the same document. Notice their titles.

To close a new window, choose the document control menu and select **C**lose or press Ctrl+F4.

You also can split a window so that you can see two different areas of a document in the same window. This approach is helpful when you type lists. You can split the document's window so that the upper part shows column headings and the lower part shows the list you are typing. As you scroll the list, the headings stay in place.

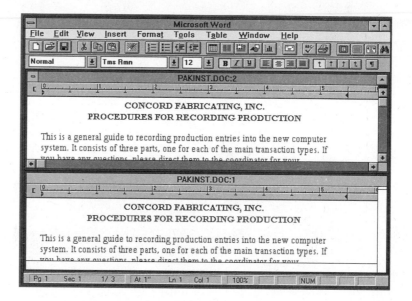

Two windows showing the same document.

To split a window with the keyboard, press Alt,- (hyphen) to choose the Document Control menu, select Split, press the up- or down-arrow key to position the horizontal gray line where you want the split, and press Enter. To remove the split, choose the Split command again and move the line all the way up or down, and then press Enter.

To split the window with the mouse, look for the black bar above the up arrow in the vertical scroll bar. Drag this black bar down and release the mouse button to position the split. To remove the split, drag the black bar all the way up or down, and then release the button.

T I P   Double-click the split bar to split the screen in half. Double-click the split bar when the window is split, and you remove the split. (You must double-click the bar in the vertical scroll bar, not the line separating the window panes.)

Cutting and Pasting between Documents

When you have several documents on-screen, you can move from one document window to the next in the stack by pressing Ctrl+F6. Press Ctrl+Shift+F6 to move to the preceding document window. Displaying two or more documents on-screen at one time can be useful. If you have two similar contracts to prepare, for example, you can use **E**dit **C**opy to copy paragraphs from one contract, press Ctrl+F6 to switch to the other contract, and then paste the paragraphs in the second contract by choosing **E**dit **P**aste.

If you have many documents open, you may want to directly activate the document you want. To do this, choose the **W**indow menu. At the bottom of the menu is a list of all open documents. Select the document you want active.

Working with Pages

Before you print your document, be sure that it's paginated correctly. You don't want a page to break right below a title, for example, and you may not want certain paragraphs separated onto two pages. You can let Word for Windows manage page breaks for you, or you can control them yourself.

Repaginating a Document

By default, Word for Windows repaginates whenever you make a change in your document. Word for Windows calculates how much text fits into a page and inserts a "soft" page break, which appears as a dotted line in normal view, or as the end of a page in page layout view. This feature is called *background repagination*. You can have Word for Windows repaginate for you, or you can repaginate manually with a command. To change background repagination, follow these steps:

1. Choose the **T**ools **O**ptions command.

2. Select the **G**eneral Category.

3. Select the **B**ackground Repagination option to repaginate as you work and keep the page numbers in the status bar current.

4. Choose OK or press Enter.

Word for Windows operates faster with background repagination turned off. To update page breaks if you have background repagination turned off, choose the **T**ools Rep**a**ginate Now command.

Word for Windows repaginates automatically whenever you print, when you choose the **View P**age Layout or **F**ile Print Preview commands, or when you compile or update an index or table of contents.

Inserting Manual Page Breaks

As you work on a document, Word for Windows breaks pages every time you fill a page with text or graphics. These are automatic or *soft page breaks*. If background repagination is on, Word for Windows recalculates the amount of text on the page and adjusts soft page breaks as you work.

You can insert page breaks manually whenever you want to force a page break at a particular spot—at the beginning of a new section, for example. Page breaks you insert are called *hard page breaks*, and they appear as a heavy dotted line. When you insert a hard page break, Word for Windows adjusts the soft page breaks that follow. Word for Windows cannot move hard page breaks; you must adjust them yourself.

To insert a hard page break, press Ctrl+Enter or choose the **Insert Break** command, select the **P**age Break option, and choose OK. Delete a hard page break by moving the cursor to the dashed line created by the page break and pressing the Del or Backspace key.

If you find a page break difficult to delete, check the Forma**t P**aragraph command for the paragraphs after the page break. If any of the options in the Pagination group are selected (**P**age Break Before, Keep With **N**ext, or **K**eep Lines Together), they may be causing a page break before the paragraph. Try unselecting these options.

From Here . . .

This chapter contains many editing shortcuts and options. Don't expect to learn them all at once. Learn what you need now and check back occasionally to find more ways of streamlining your work.

You can look forward to learning other useful editing tools in Chapter 9, which covers search and replace, and glossaries. In Chapter 15, you learn to revise your summary document information and to use headers and footers. In Chapter 12 you learn how to work with tables—a powerful time-saving feature.

Formatting Characters

Characters—individual letters, numbers, punctuation marks, and symbols—are the smallest unit of text you can format. You can apply formatting styles such as bold, italic, or a different font to as little as one character or to as much as a whole document. Many character formatting options can be combined; for example, you can make a word bold and italicized. You also can use as many different types of character formatting in a document as you want. Your document's title, for example, can be a different font or a larger size, subheadings can be boldfaced, and paragraphs of text can be plain text with italic for occasional emphasis.

Character formatting options include fonts, sizes, boldface, italic, strikethrough, hidden text, colors, superscript and subscript, upper- and lowercase, small caps, underlines, and character spacing.

Word for Windows also has many special characters to include in your document. You can create a list using bullets or decorative dingbats, for example, or you can include a copyright or trademark symbol in your document. This chapter covers all the character formatting options.

Viewing Formatted Characters

The way characters appear on-screen depends on several factors. One factor is the selected document view. In normal view, which is the default view, you see accurate character formatting (boldface appears **bold**, for example). But in draft view, which is faster for typing, you see only plain text that displays no formatting. Select the view you want from the **V**iew menu.

Another factor controlling how text appears on-screen is the printer selected. If your printer doesn't support a font or size you use to format your text, Word for Windows may substitute the closest possible font and size. (This feature can be turned on or off.)

A final factor controlling screen appearance is screen fonts (which control screen appearance) and printer fonts (which the printer uses). If you have printer fonts for which no corresponding screen fonts are available, fonts on-screen may look blocky (because they're scaled up or down from the nearest font or size) even though they print just fine. For more details on printer and screen fonts, see Appendix C.

If you format text with fonts your printer cannot print, you may end up with a screen that doesn't match printed output. To be sure your document looks the same on-screen as printed, select the **T**ools menu and choose the **O**ptions command. In the Options dialog box, select the View category, and select the **L**inebreaks and Fonts as Printed option. Appendix C describes how to improve the correspondence between what you see on-screen and the printed result.

T I P   The fonts list in the ribbon includes a printer icon to the left of each font that is available for printing on your printer. For best results, always use one of these fonts.

Using Different Character Formatting Techniques

Word for Windows offers no shortage of techniques for applying character formatting. If you have a mouse, you can format using buttons and lists on the ribbon. If you prefer the keyboard, you can access format commands from the menu. Many helpful mouse and keyboard shortcuts also exist.

No matter what technique you use, you can format characters as you type or after you finish typing. To format characters as you type, choose the formatting command, type the text, and then choose the formatting command a second time to turn off the command. To format characters after you finish typing, select the text to format, then choose the formatting command.

Either way, you must remember that most character formatting commands *toggle* on and off—you turn them on the same way that you turn them off. If you select and boldface a word, then want to remove the boldface, select the word a second time and choose the bold command again. Toggling applies no matter which technique (mouse, keyboard, or shortcut) you use to apply or remove the formatting.

Using Menu Commands To Format Characters

Using a menu command is probably the most basic technique for formatting characters. Using the menu has two primary advantages: the Character dialog box displays all the character formatting commands at once, and you can apply several types of character formatting simultaneously with the Character dialog box.

To format characters using a menu command, follow these steps:

1. Select the text to format, or position the insertion point where you want formatting to begin.

2. Choose the Forma**t C**haracter command. The Character dialog box appears (see fig. 5.1).

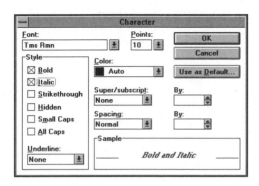

FIG. 5.1.

The Character dialog box, showing options selected.

3. Select the formatting option or options you want.

4. Choose OK or press Enter.

The Character dialog box contains the following options. (Those options marked with asterisks are detailed later in this chapter.)

Group	Option	Description
Font*	Varies depending on printer	A typeface style. Common fonts include Times Roman, Helvetica, and Courier.
Style	**B**old	Heavy text: **Bold.** Often used for document titles or subheadings.
	Italic	Oblique, or slanted, text: *Italic*. Often used for book or magazine names, or for emphasis.
	Strikethru	Text crossed with a line: ~~Strikethru~~. Often used when making revisions.
	Hidden*	Text that doesn't appear or print unless you want the text to. Often used for private notes; also used by Word for Windows for index and table of contents entries.
	Small Caps	Short uppercase letters: SMALL CAPS. Used for emphasis or for graphic effect.
	All Caps	All uppercase letters: ALL CAPS. Used for emphasis or for graphic effect. Harder to read than format combining upper- and lowercase.
Underline*	None	Normal text. Used to remove underlining.
	Single	<u>Single underline</u>. The space between words is underlined.
	Words only	<u>Single</u> <u>underline</u>. The space between words is not underlined.

Group	Option	Description
	Double	<u>Double underline</u>. The space between words is underlined.
Points*	8, 10, 12, etc.	Character size. An inch consists of 72 points (a typesetting measurement).
Color*	Auto, Black, Blue, Red, Yellow, etc.	Changes the color of text on-screen if you have a color monitor. Prints in color if you have a color printer.
Super/subscrip**t***	None	Normal text. Used to remove super/subscript.
	Superscript	Text raised above the baseline.
	Subscript	Text lowered below the baseline.
B**y**:	3 pt (default), or enter your own amount	Number of points by which superscript text is raised or subscript text is lowered.
Spacin**g***	None	Normal text. Used to remove spacing.
	Expanded	Space between characters expanded.
	Condensed	Space between characters condensed.
B**y**:	3 pt (default), or enter your own amount	Number of points by which text is expanded or condensed. Measured in increments of 1/4-point.
Use as **D**efault	n/a	Applies selected formatting to Normal template and current document.
Sample	n/a	Shows a sample of text formatted with selected options.

The Character dialog box shows formatting for the currently selected characters. If selected text is bold, for example, the **B**old box has an X in it. If the selection includes various formatting options, check boxes appear gray and text boxes display no text.

Because any formatting options you select apply to all the selected text, you can use the Character dialog box to turn on or off formatting for large areas of text, even if the text includes a variety of formatting. Suppose that your whole document has bold text scattered throughout and that you want to remove all of the boldface at once. Select all of the text, then choose Format Character (the Bold check box is gray). Select the **B**old option once to toggle boldface on for all the selected text (an X appears in the Bold box); then select the **B**old option a second time to toggle boldface off for all the selected text (the Bold box is now empty).

Using Keyboard Shortcuts

You can use the keyboard in two ways to format characters. The first is to press Alt,t,C to display the Character dialog box, which you can use to select character formatting options. The second is to use a control-key shortcut.

To format characters using control-key shortcuts, follow these steps:

1. Select the text to format, or position the insertion point where you want formatting to begin.

2. Press the appropriate control-key combination:

Format	Shortcut
Bold	Ctrl+B
Italic	Ctrl+I
Single underline	Ctrl+U
Word underline	Ctrl+W
Double underline	Ctrl+D
SMALL CAPS	Ctrl+K
ALL CAPS	Ctrl+A
Hidden text	Ctrl+H
Superscript (3 pts.)	Shift+Ctrl+= (equal sign)
Subscript (3 pts.)	Ctrl+= (equal sign)
Remove formatting	Ctrl+space bar

Using the Ribbon

The *ribbon* is a handy tool for quick character formatting (see fig. 5.2). You can change the style, font, or size of text and format characters with bold, italic, or single underline. Paragraph formatting commands also are included on the ribbon. For more details about paragraph formatting, refer to Chapter 6.

Paragraph mark display button

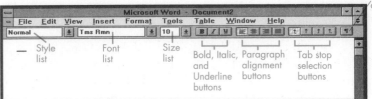

FIG. 5.2.

The ribbon is useful for quickly formatting characters.

The ribbon includes a styles list, a font list, a point size list, a bold button, an italic button, and an underline button. General instructions for formatting with the ribbon are included here; more detailed instructions for using styles, bold, italic, and underline are described later in this section. Techniques for using the ribbon to format fonts and sizes are described in the sections "Changing Fonts" and "Changing Font Size" later in this chapter.

To format characters using the ribbon, follow these steps:

1. Display the ribbon by choosing the **View Ri**bbon command. (Do this step only if the ribbon is not displayed now. If you choose **View Ri**bbon when the ribbon already is displayed, you turn the feature off.)

2. Select the text to format, or position the insertion point where you want formatting to begin.

3. Select a style from the style list.

   or

   Select a font from the font list.

   or

   Select a select a size from the point size list.

   or

   Choose the Bold, Italic, or Underline button.

No matter how you apply formatting to text—whether you use a menu command, a shortcut, or the ribbon—the ribbon displays the formatting for selected text.

Notice that the ribbon also includes paragraph formatting options. For details about using these options, see Chapter 6.

Selecting Styles with the Ribbon

A *style* is a set of "memorized" formatting commands. Although styles apply to entire paragraphs, they often contain character formatting. Word for Windows uses the Normal style to apply default formatting, but you can change the style easily by following these steps:

1. Position the insertion point inside the paragraph you want to format with a style.

2. **Mouse:** Select a style from the Styles list box.

   Keyboard: Press Ctrl+S to select the Styles list box, press the down-arrow key to select the style you want, and press Enter. Or press Ctrl+S, type the name of the style you want, and press Enter.

You can apply a style even if the ribbon isn't displayed by pressing Ctrl+S and typing the style name. (You must type the name accurately.)

For details about creating and using styles, see Chapter 11.

Selecting Bold, Italic, or Underline with the Ribbon

The three-dimensional buttons on the ribbon appear depressed when selected and raised when not selected. If selected text is boldfaced, for example, the Bold button appears to be depressed. If your selection includes more than one formatting choice, then the buttons are dimmed. Raised, depressed, or dimmed, selecting a button applies (or removes) formatting to all selected text.

To apply bold, italic, or underline with the ribbon, follow these steps:

1. Select the text to format, or position the insertion point where you want the formatting to begin.

2. Choose the Bold, Italic, or Underline button for the formatting you want to use.

Remember that these buttons toggle on and off. If you select a bold-faced word and choose the Bold button, the bold formatting is removed from the selected word. If you select a bold word and a normal word and choose the Bold button, however, both words are formatted as bold.

Changing Fonts

A *font* is a style, or appearance, of text. Three basic types of fonts exist: *serif*, with strokes at the ends of letters; *sans serif*, with no strokes; and *specialty*, such as symbols and script fonts.

Common fonts include Times Roman, a serif font; Helvetica, a sans serif font; and Zapf Chancery, a script font. These and other fonts are shown in figure 5.3.

Times Roman

Helvetica

Palatino

Bookman

Zapf Chancery

Script

Symbol: σ ψ μ β o λ

FIG. 5.3.

A selection of different fonts.

The fonts you have available to use depend on the printer (or printers) you have installed and selected. The HP LaserJet II, for example, includes Courier and Line printer. A PostScript printer usually includes Times Roman, Palatino, Bookman, New Century Schoolbook (serif fonts), Helvetica, Avant Garde (sans serif fonts), Zapf Chancery (a script font), and Zapf Dingbats (a symbol font). The selected printer determines which fonts you see listed in the Fonts list box. (Built-in Windows fonts such as the symbol fonts, Symbol and Fences, also are listed. For more information about fonts available in Windows, see Appendix C.)

If your printer doesn't have enough fonts to suit you, you can add more. You can buy software fonts (which tend to print slowly) and download them to a printer or buy font cartridges to insert into an HP LaserJet printer. The popular Z1A cartridge for the HP LaserJet II, for example, includes Times and Helvetica in several sizes and styles.

Because Word for Windows and other Windows programs use printer and screen fonts, you can select screen fonts in your document that your printer cannot print. If you do, what you see on-screen isn't necessarily what you get when you print. To make sure that your screen displays what you actually get when you print, select the T**o**ols menu and choose the **O**ptions command. In the Options dialog box, select the View category and the **L**inebreaks and Fonts as Printed option.

T I P You can use the Edit Replace command to search for and replace fonts (without changing the text). For details, see Chapter 9.

You can change fonts in two ways: using a menu command or using the ribbon.

Changing Fonts with Menu Commands

To change the font using a menu command, follow these steps:

1. Select the text in the font you want to change, or position the insertion point where you want the new font to begin.

2. Choose the Format Character command.

3. Select the Font list.

4. **Mouse:** Select the font you want.

   Keyboard: Press the up- or down-arrow key to select the name of the font you want (or type in the font name).

5. Choose OK or press Enter.

Changing Fonts with the Ribbon

The ribbon's Font list shows all the fonts available for your printer. To apply a font using the ribbon, follow these steps:

1. Select the text in the font you want to change, or position the insertion point where you want the new font to begin.

2. **Mouse:** Select a font from the Font list box.

   Keyboard: Press Ctrl+F to select the Font list box, press the down-arrow key to select the font you want, and press Enter. Alternatively, press Ctrl+F, type the name of the font you want, and press Enter.

T I P Even if the ruler isn't displayed, you can change the font by pressing Ctrl+F, which displays a status box at the bottom of the screen, asking Which font name? Accurately type in the font name and press Enter.

Changing Font Size

Font sizes are measured in *points*, the traditional typesetting measuring unit. An inch consists of 72 points; thus, an inch-high letter is 72 points, and a half-inch-high letter is 36 points. Text in a book may be 10 or 11 points.

Like fonts, your printer determines what font sizes you can use. An HP LaserJet II printer equipped with the popular Z1A cartridge includes Times and Helvetica fonts in pre-set sizes ranging from 8 to 14 points. PostScript printers and HP LaserJet III printers include scalable fonts, which can be printed from as small as a barely readable 4 points to as tall as a page. (For more information about fonts and font sizes, see Appendix C.)

Screen fonts (created without TrueType), which are included in Windows rather than in the printer, don't come in all sizes, even if your printer has scalable fonts. If you change text to an odd size such as 17 points, the text looks blocky on-screen because Word for Windows substitutes a scaled-up version of the next closest font size for the missing screen font (see fig. 5.4). The blocky appearance occurs even if you select the **Linebreaks and Fonts as Printed** option.

You can change font sizes in three ways: with the menu command, the ribbon, or shortcuts.

Changing Sizes with Menu Commands

To change the font size using the menu command, follow these steps:

1. Select the text to resize, or position the insertion point where you want the new font size to begin.

2. Choose the Forma**t C**haracter command.

3. Select the **P**oints list.

4. **Mouse:** Select the point size you want.

   Keyboard: Press the up- or down-arrow key to select the point size you want, or type in the point size.

5. Choose OK or press Enter.

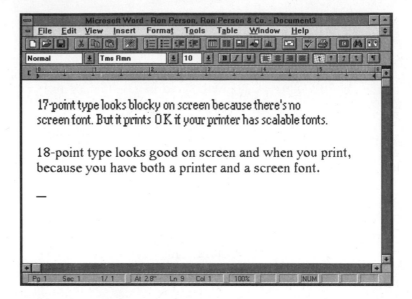

FIG. 5.4.

Fonts in an in-between size look blocky.

Changing Sizes with the Ribbon

The ribbon provides a quick way to change font size without using a menu command. The ribbon first must be displayed before using it. To display the ribbon, choose the **V**iew Ri**b**bon command.

To change font size using the ribbon, follow these steps:

1. Select the text to resize, or position the insertion point where you want the new size to begin.

2. **Mouse:** Select a size from the Point Size list box.

   Keyboard: Press Ctrl+P to select the Point Size list box, press the down-arrow key to select the point size you want, and press Enter. Alternatively, you can press Ctrl+P, type the point size you want, and press Enter.

T I P   Even if the ruler isn't displayed, you can change point size by pressing Ctrl+P, which displays a status box at the bottom of the screen, asking Which font size? Then type the font size and press Enter.

Changing Sizes with Shortcuts

Another shortcut is available for increasing or decreasing point size to the next size listed in the Points list on the ribbon or in the Character dialog box. If sizes 9, 10, and 12 are listed, for example, you can increase 10-point text to 12 points, and you can decrease 10-point text to 9 points.

To use keyboard shortcuts to change point size, do the following:

1. Select the text to resize, or position the insertion point where you want the new size to begin.

2. Press Ctrl+F2 to increase the point size.

   or

   Press Ctrl+Shift+F2 to decrease the point size.

> You can replace a font size in your document just as you can replace text. If all of your headlines in a report are 14 points and you want to change them to 12 points, for example, you can use the Edit Replace command to make the global change quickly (see Chapter 9).

T I P

Applying Special Character Formatting Options

Many formatting options are simple and straightforward. A font is a specific character set design. Size is measured in points. Boldfaced text is heavier than normal text. Other options, however, aren't quite so obvious. To use them, you often can specify some criteria that further controls the option. For example, you can specify how high you want superscript text to appear in relation to the text baseline.

Some of the character formatting options described in this section toggle on and off. Others must be turned off: to remove subscripting, you must select the subscripted text, choose the Character dialog box, and select Super/Subscript None.

Hiding Text

At times, you may want to include hidden text in your document—text that disappears until you choose a command to display it. When displayed, hidden text appears with a dotted underline (see fig. 5.5). Hiding text doesn't affect the text formatting.

You can format any text, such as notes to yourself, as hidden text. Word for Windows also uses hidden text to format table of contents entries, index entries (as shown in the fig. 5.5), and annotations.

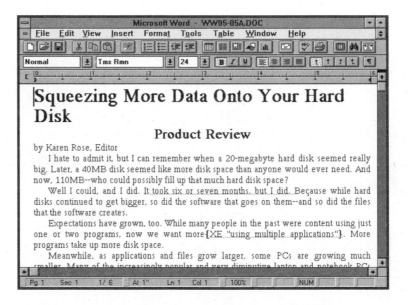

FIG. 5.5.

Hidden text appears with a dotted underline.

To hide text, follow these steps:

1. Select the text to hide, or position the insertion point where you want hidden text to begin.

2. Choose the Format Character command.

3. Select the **H**idden option.

   To apply the Hidden option to selected text without using steps 1 through 3, press Ctrl+H.

To display hidden text, follow these steps:

1. Choose the Tools Options command.

2. Select the View Category. The Options dialog box appears (see fig. 5.6).

3. Select the Hidden Text option.

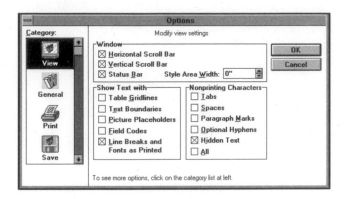

FIG. 5.6.

The Options
dialog box.

If you want to print hidden text (whether or not the text is displayed), you can use the **O**ptions command or select a printing option. To print hidden text all the time, choose the **T**ools **O**ptions command and, in the Print **C**ategory, select the **H**idden Text option. To include hidden text only when you print the current document, choose the **F**ile **P**rint command, choose **O**ptions, and select **H**idden Text.

> You can format any character as hidden text, even a page break or paragraph mark; but doing so affects the page numbering in a table of contents. For an accurate page count, remove the hidden formatting by using the **E**dit **F**ind command to locate the hidden character and remove the hidden formatting. For details about finding and replacing formatting, refer to Chapter 9.

T I P

Changing Character Colors

If you have a color monitor, you can make good use of the 16 different colors available for text in Word for Windows. On an office task list, for example, you can format each person's duties in a different color so that they easily can see who must do which job. You also can format different levels of priority as different colors: for example, red items must be done right away; blue can wait. If you have a color printer, you can print text in color.

To color text, follow these steps:

1. Select the text to color, or position the insertion point where you want the new color to begin.

2. Choose the Forma**t C**haracter command.

3. From the Color list, select the color you want.

4. Choose OK or press Enter.

Auto color, also listed in the Color list, is the color you selected for Window Text in the Colors section of the Control Panel. Auto color is usually black.

Using Superscript and Subscript

Superscript and subscript are useful for scientific typing and for references such as trademark or copyright symbols. In calculating where superscript and subscript appear in relation to normal text, Word for Windows begins with the text baseline. By default, Word for Windows raises superscript 3 points above the baseline and lowers subscript 3 points below the baseline. You can change that distance, however, in the Character dialog box.

To create superscripts and subscripts, follow these steps:

1. Select the text to raise or lower, or position the insertion point where you want raised or lowered text to begin.

2. Choose the Format Character command.

3. In the Super/Subscript list box, select Superscript to raise text, or select Subscript to lower text.

4. In the By box, accept 3 points as the default distance to raise or lower text, click the up or down arrows to change the distance, or type in a new amount.

5. Choose OK or press Enter.

T I P   To superscript text by 3 points, select the text and press Shift+Ctrl+= (equal sign). To subscript text by 3 points, select the text and press Ctrl+= (equal sign).

To remove superscript or subscript, select the raised or lowered text, choose the Format Character command, and select None from the Super/Subscript box.

Using Three Types of Underlines

Word for Windows offers three types of underlines: single, which underlines words and the space between words; words only, which underlines words but not the space between words; and double, which double-underlines words and the space between words.

To underline text, follow these steps:

1. Select the text to underline, or position the insertion point where you want underlining to begin.

2. Choose the Format Character command.

3. In the Underline list box, select Single, Words Only, or Double.

4. Choose OK or press Enter.

> To underline text quickly, select the text and press Ctrl+U for single underline, Ctrl+W for word underline, or Ctrl+D for double underline.
>
> **T I P**

To remove underlining, select the underlined text, choose the Format Character command, and select None from the Underline list box. For single underlines, select the underlined text and choose the Underline button in the ribbon to toggle the underlining off. You can toggle off all underlines by selecting the underlined text and pressing the Ctrl+U, Ctrl+W, or Ctrl+D shortcut keys.

Changing Spacing between Characters

The normal spacing between letters in a word is just right for most typing. Occasionally, however, you must fit more text on a line. Condensing the line can make the text fit. Sometimes, such as in large headlines, you also must condense the space between two individual letters to improve the headline's appearance. This is known as *kerning*. In other instances, you may want to increase the space between letters, to fill out a line, or to create a special effect. Expanding makes text wider. For examples of condensed and expanded text, see figure 5.7.

By default, Word for Windows expands the spacing between characters by 3 points and condenses the space between characters by 1.75 points. You can change the distance in increments of .25 of a point. For kerning, this level of precision is needed.

This text is condensed by 1 point.

This text is expanded by 3 points.

FIG. 5.7.

Condensed and
expanded text.

Letter pairs that might need kerning: AV   Ty   Pd
After kerning: AV   Ty   Pd

In the Character dialog box, watch the Spacing sample box to see how your text looks after condensing or expanding.

To condense or expand the space between characters, follow these steps:

1. Select the text to condense or expand, or position the insertion point where you want condensed or expanded text to begin.

2. Choose the Format Character command.

3. In the Spacing box, select Expanded or Condensed.

4. In the By box, accept the default, click the up or down arrows to increase or decrease the amount, or type in a new amount.

To return expanded or condensed text to normal, select the text, choose the Format Character command, and in the Spacing box select None.

Switching between Upper- and Lowercase

You can use a Word for Windows shortcut to change letters from uppercase to lowercase, or vice-versa. The result depends on the case of selected text.

To change the letter case, follow these steps:

1. Select the text to change or position the insertion point in or to the left of the word whose case you want to change.

2. Press Shift+F3 to change the case with these results:

Capitalization	Result
All lowercase	All uppercase
First character lowercase	All uppercase
All uppercase	First character of each word to uppercase, all other characters to lowercase
First character uppercase	All lowercase

You can see by the chart that two steps are required to change text from all uppercase to all lowercase. The first time you select the text and press Shift+F3, the text changes to first-character uppercase. Leave the text selected and press Shift+F3 a second time to change the text to all lowercase.

To use a menu command to change case, refer to the section "Using Menu Commands To Format Characters" earlier in this chapter.

 NOTE The terms *uppercase* and *lowercase* come from the days when type was set by hand from individual letters molded from lead. The capital letters were stored in the upper case above where the typesetters assembled their text, and noncapital letters were stored in the lower case.

Changing the Default Character Formatting

Word for Windows uses the Normal style (contained in the Normal template) to control the default character and paragraph formatting choices for all documents. The Normal style's default type font, Times Roman, has a default size of 10 points. If you always work with some other character formatting settings, you can apply those settings to the Normal style. Your new defaults take effect for the current document and for all future documents (but not for existing documents).

To change default character formatting, follow these steps:

1. Choose the Format Character command.

2. Select the new defaults you want to use.

3. Choose the Use as Default button.

Because you have requested a change to the Normal template, when you exit Word for Windows you see a message box asking whether you want to save changes to Word for Windows. Choose Yes. For more information about styles, see Chapter 11.

Repeating and Copying Character Formatting

If you do much repetitive character formatting, you can save some time by repeating or copying formatting between characters.

To repeat character formatting, immediately after formatting characters, select the new text to format and press F4, or choose the Edit **Re**peat formatting command. To use this technique, you must perform the repeat immediately after performing the edit that you want to repeat.

Remember that the **R**epeat command repeats only the *one* most recent edit. If you use the Character dialog box to apply several formatting choices at once, the **R**epeat command repeats all those choices because they are made as a single edit. But if you use the **R**epeat command after making several formatting choices from the keyboard or with the ribbon, only the one most recent choice is repeated.

To copy character formatting, select the text you want to format, point to the formatting you want to copy, hold Ctrl+Shift, and click the left mouse button.

You also can copy paragraph formatting. Instead of pointing to the character whose formatting you want to copy, move the mouse pointer to the left margin, where the pointer turns into an arrow pointing to the paragraph whose formatting you want to copy. Then hold Ctrl+Shift and click the left mouse button.

Inserting Special Characters and Symbols

You can include many special characters in your document. Symbol fonts such as Symbol and Zapf Dingbats, for example, contain *dingbats* (decorative characters such as bullets, stars, and flowers) and scientific symbols. Foreign language characters such as umlauts (ü) and tildes (ñ) are available, as are ANSI characters such as bullets and *em dashes* (wide hyphens used in punctuation). You also can use invisible characters such as discretionary hyphens (which appear only when needed) and nonbreaking spaces that prevent two words from separating at the end of a line.

Two techniques give you access to special characters. One is the Symbol dialog box, which shows a keyboard of special characters to choose from. The other is a series of special keystrokes.

Using the Symbol Dialog Box

The symbol dialog box gives you access to symbol fonts and ANSI characters (see fig. 5.8). A symbol font, Symbol, is included with Word. Others may be built into your printer; for example, most PostScript printers include Zapf Dingbats. ANSI characters are the regular character set that you see on your keyboard, plus another hundred or so characters including a copyright symbol, a registered trademark symbol, and many foreign language symbols.

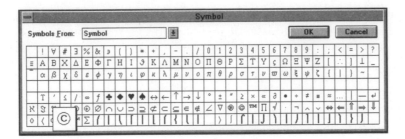

FIG. 5.8.

The Symbol dialog box.

To insert symbols from the Symbol dialog box, follow these steps:

1. Position the insertion point where you want the symbol to appear.

2. Choose the **Insert Symbol** command. The Symbol dialog box appears.

3. From the Symbols From list box, select the font for which you want to see symbols. (Select Normal Text to see ANSI characters.)

4. Click on a symbol to select, or press the cursor-movement keys to move the selection to the symbol you want.

   To enlarge a symbol, click and hold the left mouse button, or press the cursor-movement keys to move the selection, enlarging each symbol in turn.

5. Choose OK or press Enter.

   To select a symbol from the symbols box and exit the box simultaneously, double-click on the symbol.

Be sure to scan through all the interesting and useful symbols available in the Symbol and the Normal Text fonts.

T I P

Inserted symbols are actually field codes embedded in your document. This prevents you from accidentally selecting your symbol and changing it to a different font, which could change it back to a letter (for example, if you format text as Zapf Dingbats to include square bullets in your document, and then change the bullets to Times Roman, the bullets turn into *n*s). To delete an inserted symbol, you first must select it, and then press the Del key. You cannot position the insertion point to the right of the symbol and press Backspace.

Inserting Special Characters from the Keyboard

You can insert special characters from the keyboard in two ways, without accessing the Symbol dialog box. But you must know the ANSI character number or the corresponding character for the symbols you want.

To insert ANSI characters from the keyboard, do the following:

1. Position the insertion point where you want the symbol to appear.

2. Press Num Lock on the numeric keypad (so that numbers appear when you type).

3. Hold the Alt key and type 0 (zero) on the numeric keypad, followed by the ANSI code for the symbol you want. To type the fraction 1/4, for example, press Alt+0188 on the numeric keypad.

To see a complete list of these characters, refer to your Windows book or manual.

If you have a symbol font such as Zapf Dingbats or want to use a special character from the Symbol font, you can type and format the corresponding character with the Zapf Dingbat or Symbol font. To type a solid square (■), for example, you can type and format the letter *n* as Zapf Dingbats.

Inserting Hyphens and Nonbreaking Spaces

Other special characters you may need in your document are more subtle than symbols and dingbats. They include optional hyphens, which remain invisible until they are needed to hyphenate a word at the end of a line; nonbreaking hyphens, which prevent a hyphenated word (like a name) from splitting at the end of a line; and nonbreaking spaces, which prevent two words from separating at the end of a line. To insert these characters, type the following control-key combinations:

Character	Shortcut
Regular hyphen	- (hyphen key)
Optional hyphen	Ctrl+-
Nonbreaking hyphen	Shift+Ctrl+-
Nonbreaking space	Shift+Ctrl+space bar

Word for Windows can hyphenate text (see Chapter 9), but sometimes adding your own optional hyphens is easier, especially in words like a long proper name that Word for Windows doesn't hyphenate automatically. The optional hyphen doesn't appear unless needed to hyphenate the word.

From Here . . .

This chapter outlines many different techniques for formatting characters. You can use a menu, the mouse, or keyboard commands. Often you can choose from several different methods for accomplishing the same formatting result.

One method mentioned only briefly in this chapter is to use styles for formatting. With styles, you can format your document quickly; even more importantly, you can make global formatting changes just by redefining a style. Although styles apply to paragraphs, they often contain character formatting and are useful for applying character formatting to paragraphs of text (such as body copy and headlines). To learn more about styles, see Chapter 11.

Text sometimes can function as a graphic. For example, you can create a box, type text inside, add borders, and move the box around on the page so that the rest of the text on the page wraps around the box. For details, see Chapter 24. For ideas about using text in a graphical way, see Chapter 28.

Formatting Paragraphs

In literature, a paragraph is a series of sentences linked together to convey a single thought or idea, or to describe a single image. In Word for Windows, the definition of a paragraph is less lyrical: a *paragraph* is any amount of text—or no text at all—that ends when you press the Enter key. A paragraph may be the title of a story, an item in a list, a blank line between other paragraphs, or a series of sentences linked together to convey a single thought or idea.

In Word for Windows, a paragraph is also a formatting unit. Just as you format individual characters with character formatting options such as bold and italic, you can format paragraphs with paragraph, tab, and border formatting options, such as the following:

- *Alignment*. Lining up the text of a paragraph to the left, center, right, or both margins.

- *Indents*. Indenting the left edge, right edge, or first line of a paragraph in from or out from its margin.

- *Tabs*. Creating columns of text that line up perfectly and can be adjusted easily.

- *Spacing*. Adding spaces between lines and paragraphs.

- *Pagination*. Keeping paragraphs positioned properly on a page.

■ *Lines, borders, and shading.* Adding graphic interest to paragraphs with lines next to paragraphs, borders surrounding paragraphs, and shading to fill a border.

Paragraph formatting affects the entire paragraph and is stored in the paragraph marker that ends every paragraph. If you delete one of these paragraph markers, the text preceding the marker becomes part of the following paragraph. If the paragraph marker you delete contains formatting selections, that formatting also is lost. The new paragraph formed of two merged paragraphs takes on the formatting applied to the second of the two paragraphs.

Displaying Paragraph Markers

When paragraph markers are hidden, you don't see them at the end of a paragraph. You can display paragraph markers, however; they look like reverse P's (see fig. 6.1). If you expect to do much text editing, you should display the paragraph markers to avoid accidentally deleting one of them and thereby losing your paragraph formatting.

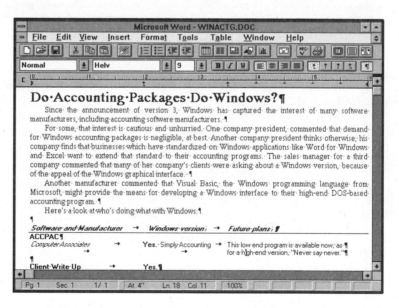

FIG. 6.1.

Paragraph markers look like reverse P's.

To display paragraph markers, do one of the following:

■ Click the Show Paragraph Markers button on the ribbon.

■ Press Ctrl+Shift+8.

■ Choose the Tools Options command, select the View Category, and under Nonprinting Characters select Paragraph Marks.

Using Paragraph Formatting Techniques

Every new document you create based on the default Normal template is controlled by the Normal style. The Normal style formats paragraphs as left-aligned and single-spaced, with left-aligned tab stops every half inch. If you usually choose different paragraph formatting selections, change the Normal style to reflect your preferences. For details about changing styles, see Chapter 11.

You can format a paragraph at two times: before you begin typing or after you finish typing. To format after typing, you must select the paragraph or paragraphs you want to format. If you format only one paragraph, instead of selecting the entire paragraph you can position the insertion point anywhere inside the paragraph before making your formatting selections. Paragraph formatting commands apply to the entire paragraph.

Word for Windows offers several alternative techniques for formatting paragraphs. You can use the Format Paragraph command to select many formatting options at once and to get the widest possible range of paragraph formatting options. You can use the ribbon and toolbar to access paragraph formatting commands individually. You can use the ribbon and ruler to set tabs and indents quickly. With keyboard shortcuts, you can format as you type.

Formatting Paragraphs with Menu Commands

The Paragraph dialog box offers the greatest number of options for formatting paragraphs and shows a sample of how the formatting you select affects your paragraph (see fig. 6.2). Because the dialog box provides quick access to the Tabs dialog box, you also can do quite a bit of formatting at once using the Format Paragraph command.

Specific instructions on using the Paragraph dialog box appear throughout this chapter.

FIG. 6.2.

The Paragraph
dialog box.

Formatting Paragraphs with the Toolbar

The Word for Windows toolbar provides a quick way to select certain paragraph formatting options, if you have a mouse (see fig. 6.3). Default paragraph formatting buttons on the toolbar include Numbered List, Bulleted List, Unindent, and Indent. To use the toolbar, select the paragraph to format and click the button. When selected, the buttons appear depressed.

FIG. 6.3.

The toolbar.

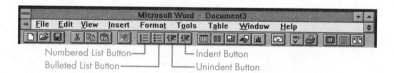

The toolbar is optional but useful to display if you do much formatting. If you want more typing space on-screen, however, remove the toolbar. To display the toolbar, choose the View Toolbar command; to remove, choose the View Toolbar command a second time. When the toolbar appears, a check mark appears to the left of the Toolbar command on the View menu.

You can add any command to the toolbar, filling in blank spaces in the toolbar or replacing existing tools. For more details, see Chapter 29.

In this chapter, the sections "Setting Indents" and "Creating Bulleted or Numbered Lists" give specific instructions on using the toolbar.

Formatting Paragraphs with the Ribbon

The ribbon includes buttons for controlling a paragraph's alignment, selecting tab styles, and displaying paragraph markers (see fig. 6.4). To use the ribbon for alignment, select the paragraph or paragraphs to align and choose the appropriate alignment button: Left, Centered, Right, or Justified (both margins aligned). To select tab styles (Left, Centered, Right, or Decimal) or to display paragraph markers, click on the appropriate buttons. Selected buttons appear depressed. You need a mouse to use the ribbon.

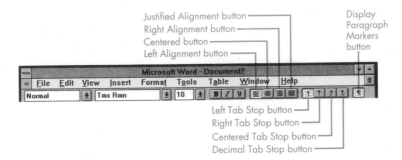

FIG. 6.4.

The ribbon.

Like the toolbar, the ribbon is an optional screen object. To display the ribbon, choose the View **R**ibbon command; to remove, choose the View **R**ibbon command a second time. When the ribbon is displayed, a check mark appears to the left of the **R**ibbon command on the **V**iew menu. If you're doing much formatting, try to display the ribbon. If you want more typing space on-screen, however, remove the ribbon.

The sections "Setting Paragraph Alignment" and "Setting Tabs" in this chapter discuss using ribbon buttons.

Formatting Paragraphs with the Ruler

The ruler is useful for quickly setting paragraph indentations and tabs with a click of the mouse (see fig. 6.5). Often you use the ruler with the ribbon to set tabs. By default, tabs are left-aligned, but if you want a different tab style, you must select that style from the ribbon before positioning the tab on the ruler.

FIG. 6.5.

The ruler.

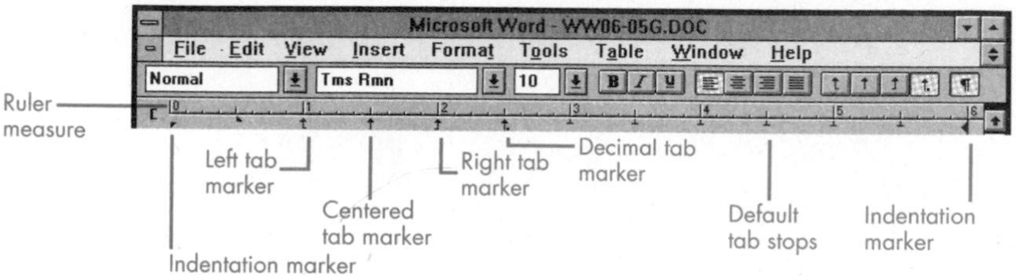

Like the toolbar and ribbon, the ruler is also optional. To display the ruler, choose the **View R**uler command; to remove, choose the **View R**uler command a second time. The ruler command has a check mark to its left when displayed. Displaying the ruler can speed up formatting if you have a mouse; removing the ruler gives you more room on-screen.

Duplicating Paragraph Formatting

The easiest way to duplicate paragraph formatting is to carry the formatting forward as you type. As you arrive at the end of the current paragraph and press Enter, the current paragraph ends and a new one begins—using the same formatting as the preceding paragraph. If, however, you use the mouse or cursor-movement keys to move out of the current paragraph, you move into a different paragraph, which may have different formatting.

Another way to duplicate formatting is to use the **Edit R**epeat command or press F4. Remember that this command duplicates only your one most recent action. The command works best when you format with the Paragraph, Tabs, or Borders dialog box, making multiple formatting choices at once.

If you have a mouse, use this handy shortcut for duplicating paragraph formatting:

1. Select the paragraph or paragraphs you want to format, or position the insertion point inside the paragraph you want to format.

2. Move the mouse to the left margin of the paragraph that has the formatting you want to copy. The mouse must turn into an arrow pointing to the paragraph whose formatting you want to copy.

3. Hold Ctrl+Shift and click the left mouse button.

Probably the most powerful way to duplicate paragraph formatting is to use styles. A *style* is a set of formatting commands that you can apply all at once and can change globally later. Styles are easy to create—especially when you use the "styles by example" technique—and easy to use. Styles are explained in detail in Chapter 11.

Setting Paragraph Alignment

Paragraph alignment refers to how the left and right edges of a paragraph line up (see fig. 6.6). Left-aligned paragraphs line up on the left edge but are ragged on the right (the Word for Windows default). Right-aligned paragraphs line up on the right edge but are ragged on the left. Centered paragraphs are ragged on both edges, centered between the margins. Justified paragraphs are aligned on both edges.

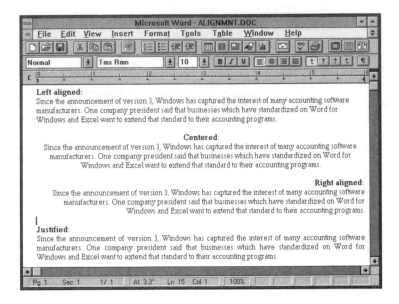

FIG. 6.6.

Examples of Paragraph alignment.

Paragraphs are aligned to the margins if no indentations are set for paragraphs. If paragraphs are indented, they align to the indentation.

You can set paragraph alignment while typing or while editing your document. If you set alignment as you type, the alignment carries forward when you press Enter (like all paragraph formatting selections). If you set alignment later, your setting applies only to the selected paragraph or paragraphs.

Using the Paragraph Command To Set Alignment

You can use the Format Paragraph command to set alignment with a mouse or your keyboard. To set alignment using the Paragraph dialog box, follow these steps:

The tab stop appears as an arrow in the same style as the tab style you selected from the ribbon. If you don't get the tab arrow in just the right place on the ruler, position the pointer on the arrow, hold the left mouse button to select the arrow, and drag the tab arrow to the correct position. Figures 6.8 and 6.9 show the ruler with tab stops added.

T I P To use the ruler to change a tab stop's alignment or to add a leader, double-click the tab stop to display the Tabs dialog box. The tab stop on which you double-clicked is selected. Make whatever changes you want and choose OK or press Enter.

Removing a Tab Stop

To use the mouse to remove a tab arrow from the ruler, point at the tab arrow, drag the arrow down off the ruler, and release the mouse button.

Setting Tabs with the Keyboard

If you don't have a mouse, you still can set tab stops on the ruler from the keyboard. By default, the left-aligned tab stop is selected on the ribbon, so using this technique inserts a left-aligned tab on the ruler. If you select a different type of tab stop (either on the ribbon or in the Tabs dialog box), however, that tab stop is inserted on the ruler.

To set tabs with the keyboard, follow these steps:

1. Select the paragraph (or paragraphs) for which you want to set tabs, or position the insertion point where you want the new tab settings to begin.

2. Press Ctrl+Shift+F10 to activate (or display) the ruler. A square "ruler cursor" appears at the left end of the ruler (see fig. 6.11).

3. Press the right-arrow key to move the ruler cursor where you want the left-aligned tab. Alternatively, you can press the left- or right-arrow keys to move the ruler cursor over a tab stop you want to delete.

4. Press the Ins (Insert) key to insert the tab stop, or press the Del (Delete) key to delete a tab stop.

5. Press Enter to return to the document.

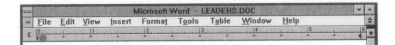

FIG. 6.11.

The ruler cursor
sets tabs and
indents.

Setting Indents

A document's margins are determined by selections made in the Page
Setup dialog box. Margins apply to the entire document or to sections
within the document. But individual paragraphs or groups of paragraphs can be indented from those margins, and therefore appear to
have their own margin settings.

Although only two side margins (left and right) are available, you can
indent a paragraph in many ways (see fig. 6.12). You can indent from
the left, right, or both margins. You can indent just the first line of a
paragraph, a technique that often substitutes for pressing Tab at the
beginning of each new paragraph. You can create a hanging indent,
which "hangs" the first line of a paragraph to the left of the rest of the
paragraph; hanging indents often are used for bulleted or numbered
lists. You also can create nested indents—indentations within
indentations.

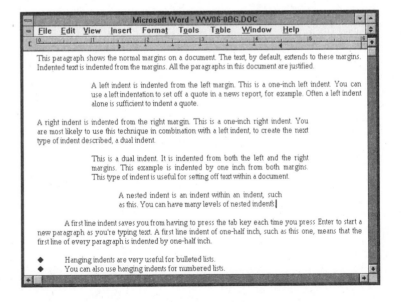

FIG. 6.12.

Different indent
types.

Several techniques exist for creating indents. You can use the Paragraph dialog box, typing in the amount of indent for the selected paragraph or paragraphs. You can use the ruler, dragging indent icons left and right. You can use a button on the toolbar to indent or unindent paragraphs quickly or to create lists with a hanging indent. You also can use keyboard shortcuts.

Whichever technique you use, indenting belongs to the paragraph and is carried forward when you press Enter at the end of a paragraph. Alternatively, you can return to a paragraph later and format the text with an indent.

Note that numbered and bulleted lists are a special type of indented list. They are described later in this chapter under "Creating Numbered or Bulleted Lists."

Using the Paragraph Command To Set Indents

You can use the Paragraph dialog box to set any type of indent, measured precisely. The Indentation list in the Paragraph dialog box lists three options: From **L**eft, From **R**ight, and **F**irst Line (see fig. 6.13).

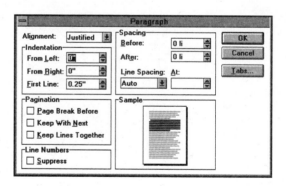

FIG. 6.13.

The Indentation group.

The indentation options give the following results:

Option	Result
From Left	Indents selected paragraph or paragraphs from left margin. If the number is positive, the paragraph is indented inside the left margin; if the number is negative, the paragraph is indented outside the left margin.

From **Right**	Indents selected paragraph or paragraphs from right margin. If the number is positive, the paragraph is indented inside the right margin; if the number is negative, the paragraph is indented outside the right margin.
First Line	Indents first line or lines of selected paragraph or paragraphs from left indent (or margin, if no indent is made). If the number is positive, the first line is indented inside the left indent. If the number is negative, the first line is indented outside the left indent (like in a hanging indent).

To set indentations using the Paragraph dialog box, follow these steps:

1. Select the paragraph (or paragraphs) to indent, or position the insertion point where you want the new indentation to begin.

2. Choose the Forma**t P**aragraph command.

3. Select the From **L**eft, From **R**ight, or **F**irst Line Indentation option.

4. To increase or decrease the indentation value, click the up or down arrows. The numbers in the indentation option boxes are incremented in decimal tenths.

   or

   If you want a measurement other than in tenths, type a new value in decimal numbers. For example, if you want a quarter-inch first-line indent, type the decimal value *.25*. (For a negative indent, precede the number with a minus sign.)

5. Choose OK or press Enter.

You can create indents in measurements other than decimal inches. To create a 6-point indent, for example, type *6 pt* in either indentation box. (An inch consists of 72 points.) To create an indent of 2 centimeters, type *2 cm*; to create an indent of 1 pica, type *1 pi* (six picas per inch; 12 points per pica).   **T I P**

Creating a Hanging Indent

A hanging indent is really a combination of indents. Creating a hanging indent involves indenting the left edge of the whole paragraph, then creating a negative indent for the first line of the paragraph. To create a hanging indent in which the first line of the paragraph starts at the left margin, and the rest of the paragraph is indented to one-quarter inch from the left margin, type these indentation settings in the Paragraph dialog box:

From **L**eft:	0.25"
From **R**ight:	0"
First Line:	−0.25"

To use a hanging indent, type a number or bullet at the left margin, press the Tab key to advance to the left indent, then begin typing the text of the paragraph. When text reaches the end of the line, the paragraph wraps around to the left indent, not the left margin. This technique is useful for numbered and bulleted lists. (You can create hanging indents for numbered and bulleted lists automatically with the toolbar or the Bullets and Numbering dialog box. See "Creating Numbered and Bulleted Lists" later in this chapter.)

Symbol fonts such as Symbol and Zapf Dingbats are full of interesting dingbats you can use as bullets in a list. For details about using these characters, see Chapter 5.

Using the Ruler or Toolbar To Set Indents

With the ruler, you can easily create indents of any kind. With the toolbar, you can indent a selected paragraph to the next available tab stop.

The ruler contains black triangular markers, called *indentation markers*, at the left and right margins. You can drag them left and right on the ruler to set indents. The black triangle at the left edge of the ruler splits into a top and a bottom part. The top half of the triangle represents the first-line indent, whereas the bottom half represents the left indent (see fig. 6.14). The triangle at the right margin represents the paragraph's right indent.

T I P   Usually, when you drag the bottom half of the left indentation triangle, the top half moves also, creating a left indentation. But if you want to move the bottom half independently, hold the Shift key as you drag the left indentation marker. This technique is ideal for creating hanging indents.

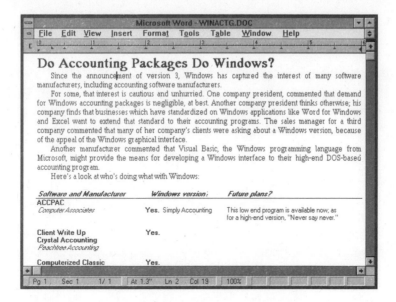

FIG. 6.14.

The left indenta-
tion triangle is
split, showing a
first-line indent of
one-quarter inch.

To set indents with the ruler, you must display the ruler. Choose the
View Ruler command to display the ruler.

To set indentations with the ruler, follow these steps:

1. Select the paragraph (or paragraphs) to indent, or position the
   insertion point where you want the new indentation to begin.

2. To set a left indent, drag the bottom half of the indentation triangle to the ruler position where you want the indentation. (Notice the top half of the triangle moves with the bottom half.)

   or

   To set a right indent, drag the right indentation triangle to the
   position where you want the indentation.

   or

   To set a first-line indent, drag the top half of the left indentation
   triangle to the position where you want the first-line indentation.

   or

   To set a hanging indent with the first line at the left margin, hold
   the Shift key and drag the bottom half of the left indentation triangle to a new position on the ruler.

The toolbar includes two buttons for indenting a selected paragraph to
the next tab stop: the Indent and Unindent buttons (refer to fig. 6.3 to
see the location of these two buttons on the toolbar). These buttons

are used to create left indents only, not first-line or hanging indents. To use this technique, be sure the toolbar is displayed, using the **View Toolbar** command.

To indent or unindent paragraphs using the toolbar, follow these steps:

1. Select the paragraph (or paragraphs) to indent, or position the insertion point where you want the new indentation to begin.

2. To indent the paragraph, click the Indent button.

   or

   To unindent the paragraph, click the Unindent button.

You can click the Indent button as many times as you want to continue moving the left indentation to the right. Therefore, the Indent button is an easy way to create nested paragraphs, which are like indents within indents (refer to fig. 6.12).

Using Keyboard Shortcuts To Set Indents

If you're a touch typist, you will appreciate being able to create indents using keyboard shortcuts. Just as when you use the toolbar to create indents, keyboard shortcuts rely on existing tab settings to determine the position of indents. If you have not changed Word for Windows' default tab stops so that they still are set every half inch, for example, using the shortcut keys to create a hanging indent leaves the first line of the paragraph at the margin but moves the left edge for the remaining lines of the paragraph to one-half inch.

To set indents using keyboard shortcuts, follow these steps:

1. Select the paragraph (or paragraphs) to indent, or position the insertion point where you want the new indentation to begin.

2. Use one of these keyboard shortcuts to indent your text:

Shortcut	Indentation type
Ctrl+N	Moves the left indent to the next tab stop
Ctrl+M	Moves the left indent to the preceding tab stop
Ctrl+T	Hanging indent

Another way to use the keyboard to set indents is to operate the ruler from the keyboard. Follow these steps:

1. Select the paragraph (or paragraphs) to indent, or position the insertion point where you want the new indentation to begin.

2. Press Ctrl+Shift+F10 to activate (or display) the ruler. A square ruler cursor appears at the left margin.

3. Press the right- or left-arrow keys to move the ruler cursor to the position where you want left, first-line, or right indents.

4. Press one of the following keys to set the indent:

Key	Indentation type
F	First Line Indent
L	Left Indent
R	Right Indent

5. Press Enter to return to your document.

Just as you use shortcuts to format a paragraph, you can use a shortcut to remove formatting. Press Ctrl+Q to reset a paragraph to normal formatting (as defined by the Normal style).

T I P

Adjusting Line and Paragraph Spacing

Like all word processing and typesetting programs, Word for Windows spaces lines of text far enough apart so that lines don't crash into each other. If something large is on the line, such as a graphic or an over-sized character or word, Word for Windows leaves extra space.

But you're not limited to using Word for Windows' automatic spacing. You can add extra space between lines and paragraphs.

Spacing is an excellent candidate for using *styles*, which are sets of remembered formatting commands that you easily create and apply. If your document's style includes subheadings preceded by extra space, for example, then create a style for your subheadings that includes extra space and apply the style to each subheading. For details about using styles, see Chapter 11.

T I P

Adjusting Paragraph Spacing

You can adjust paragraph spacing by adding extra lines before or after the selected paragraphs. After you press Enter, Word for Windows skips the specified amount of space before starting the next paragraph. This tool is useful when your document's style requires extra spacing between paragraphs, before new sections, or around graphics. Adding extra spacing before or after paragraphs is like pressing the Enter key a second time each time you finish typing a paragraph (see fig. 6.15).

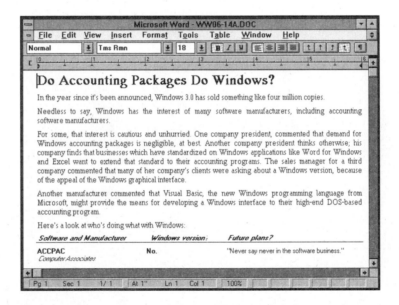

FIG. 6.15.

Extra spacing after paragraphs.

When printing, if you format a paragraph to include extra space before, and the paragraph appears at the top of a new page, Word for Windows ignores the extra space so that the top margins of your document always remain even.

The Sample section of the Paragraph dialog box shows the effect of your selected spacing.

To adjust paragraph spacing, do the following:

1. Select the paragraph (or paragraphs) to add spacing before or after, or position the insertion point where you want the new spacing to begin.

2. Choose the Format Paragraph command.

3. To add line spacing before the selected paragraph or paragraphs, type a number in the Spacing Before box or click the up or down

arrows to increase or decrease the spacing amount in increments of half a line (see fig. 6.16).

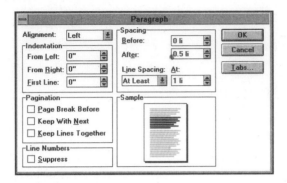

FIG. 6.16.

The paragraph spacing options in the Paragraph dialog box.

4. To add line spacing after the selected paragraph or paragraphs, type a number in the Spacing After box, or click the up or down arrows to increase or decrease the spacing amount in increments of half a line.

5. Choose OK or press Enter.

T I P

Like indents, you can use measurements other than decimal inches to specify spacing. To add 6-point spacing, for example, type *6 pt* in the **B**efore or Aft**e**r box. To add spacing of 2 centimeters, type *2 cm*, and to add spacing of 1 pica, type *1 pi*.

Adjusting Line Spacing

Typesetters call the spacing between lines in a document *leading* (pronounced "ledding"). Typesetters have great control over precisely how much space appears between lines. They know that long lines need more spacing so that the eye doesn't lose its place in moving from the right margin back to the left. They know that font styles with small letters require less spacing between lines than fonts with big letters.

Word for Windows gives you a typesetter's control over spacing between lines in your document. The feature begins with automatic spacing and enables you to increase spacing, reduce spacing, permit extra spacing for a large character or superscript on the line, or control the spacing exactly.

Spacing is measured by lines. Normal text has Auto spacing of one line, but if you request spacing of .5, you get half-line spacing. Lines formatted this way are condensed. If you request spacing of 1.5, then the paragraph has an extra half-line between lines (see fig. 6.17).

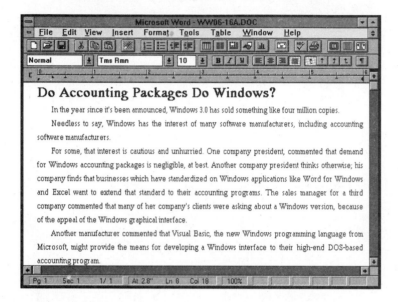

FIG. 6.17.

Extra spacing between lines.

To adjust spacing between lines, follow these steps:

1. Select the paragraph (or paragraphs) to space, or position the insertion point where you want the new spacing to begin.

2. Choose the Format Paragraph command.

3. Select an option in the Line Spacing box.

Option	Spacing
Auto	Automatic line spacing (lines are spaced far enough apart to accommodate the largest character in each line)
Single	Single-line spacing (12-point line spacing)
1.5 Line	Line-and-a-half spacing (extra half line between lines)
Double	Double spacing (extra full line between lines)
At Least	At least the amount of spacing you specify in the At box. (Word for Windows adds extra spacing, if necessary, for tall characters, big graphics, or super/subscript.)

Exactly	The exact amount of spacing you specify in the **At** box. (Word for Windows does not add extra spacing for anything. Some text may disappear if enough space isn't available.)

4. If you want to specify your own line spacing, type the spacing amount in the **At** box (with decimal numbers, such as 1.25 for an extra quarter-line of space between lines), or click the up or down arrows to increase or decrease the amount.

   You can select a spacing amount in the **At** box without first selecting from the Line Spacing list. Word for Windows assumes that you want at least this spacing and provides extra spacing if needed for large characters, superscript, and so forth.

5. Choose OK or press Enter.

If you want to return to automatic line spacing, select the paragraph or paragraphs, choose Forma**t P**aragraph, and select Auto Line Spacing.

A "line" in Word for Windows' **At** box—which you use to set line spacing—is defined as a 12-point line. So if you set line spacing for 12-point text at `Exactly 2 lines`, you get double spacing. For 48-point text, however, a setting of `Exactly 2 lines` crashes the lines together because the letters are much larger than the 12-point spacing. To space lines of large text, use points rather than lines. For example, try setting 48-point type with a line spacing of `Exactly 48 pt`. Experiment to get the look you want.

T I P

Controlling Pagination

The Paragraph dialog box offers many techniques for controlling a paragraph's appearance. Sometimes, however, you also want to control where the paragraph appears.

The Pagination options enable you to specify that a certain paragraph always appear at the top of a new page, that it always stays on the same page with the following paragraph, or that the paragraph itself keeps together without breaking across two pages.

To control paragraph position on the page, follow these steps:

1. Select the paragraph to position.

2. Choose the Format **P**aragraph command.

3. Select a Pagination option.

Option	Effect
Page Break Before	Inserts a page break before the selected paragraph so that the paragraph always appears at the top of a page
Keep with **N**ext	Keeps the selected paragraph with the following paragraph so that both appear on the same page
Keep Lines Together	Keeps the lines of the selected paragraph together so that the paragraph doesn't break at the end of a page

4. Choose OK or press Enter.

Using Bookmarks for Cross-References

Bookmarks can be used in combination with fields to create cross-references to page numbers and text. If you mark some text in a document with a bookmark, for example, you can refer to that bookmark in another part of your document and have Word for Windows insert either the text itself or the page number on which that text begins.

Fields are codes you can place in your document to automate certain procedures, such as the insertion of the dates, and the creation of indexes and table of contents entries. See Chapter 18 to learn more about the power of field codes.

To create a cross-reference to the page number of marked text, follow these steps:

1. Insert a bookmark at the location, picture, object, or segment of the document that you want to refer to by page number.

2. Position the insertion point where you want the cross-reference to be inserted.

3. Press Ctrl+F9 to insert field characters, {}.

4. Type *pageref* inside the field characters, followed by a space and the name of the bookmark you want to refer to. For example, type the following:

    {pageref CompanyNames}

5. To update the field you just created, move the insertion point between the field characters and press F9.

When the field is updated, the page number on which the marked text begins will replace the field code. If you continue to see the field code after updating the field, turn off the View Field Codes command.

To create a cross-reference to marked text, follow these steps:

1. Insert a bookmark for the location or segment of the document that you want to reference.

2. Position the insertion point where you want the cross-reference to be inserted.

3. Press Ctrl+F9 to insert field characters, {}.

4. Type *ref* inside the field characters, followed by a space and the name of the bookmark you want to refer to.

5. To update the field, move the insertion point between the field characters and press F9.

When the field is updated, the marked text will replace the field code. If you continue to see the field code after updating the field, turn off the View Field Codes command.

If you want to replace either field code with its result, page reference or text, select the field, and then press Shift+Ctrl+F9 (the Unlink Field key).

Suppressing Line Numbers

An option in the Paragraph dialog box offers the chance to suppress line numbers that are applied as part of section formatting. (This option does not suppress line numbers applied in creating a numbered list, described later in this chapter).

To suppress line numbers, follow these steps:

1. Select the lines for which you want to suppress line numbering.

2. Choose the Format Paragraph command.

3. Select the Line Numbers Suppress option.

4. Choose OK or press Enter.

To learn how to create line numbers in a section, see Chapter 7.

Creating Bulleted or Numbered Lists

A bulleted or numbered list is a special type of list formatted with a hanging indent. Bulleted lists have a bullet at the left margin; numbered lists have a number and are numbered sequentially (see fig. 6.18).

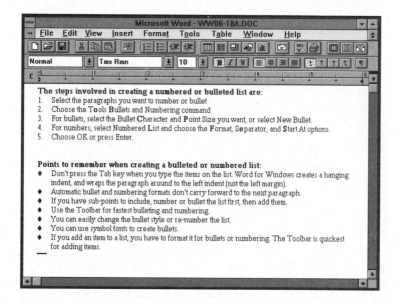

FIG. 6.18.

Bulleted and numbered lists.

Before you create a bulleted or numbered list, you first must type the list without bullets, numbers, or tabs. When you select and format the list as a bulleted or numbered list, Word for Windows sets a one-quarter-inch hanging indent and adds the bullets or numbers. You cannot add another bulleted item to a bulleted list by pressing Enter at the end of the last line. Instead, you must type the new line as usual and format the line as a bulleted list. To add to a numbered list, you must reselect and reformat the entire list as a numbered list so that the numbers remain sequential.

By default, Word for Windows offers two bullet shapes, round and diamond, in a range of sizes. If you want to use a heart or some other symbol as your bullet, however, Word for Windows gives you the option of selecting a character from the Symbol dialog box. (To learn more about the Symbol dialog box, see Chapter 5.)

You can create a bulleted or numbered list in two ways: with a menu command and with a toolbar shortcut. As usual, with the menu command you have many more options.

Creating Bulleted Lists with Menu Commands

To create a bulleted list with menu commands, follow these steps:

1. Type the list at the left margin.

2. Select the list you want to format with bullets.

3. Choose the Tools Bullets and Numbering command. The Bullets and Numbering dialog box appears (see fig. 6.19).

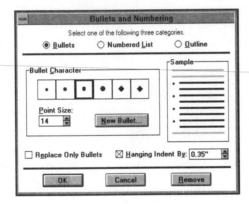

FIG. 6.19.

The Bullets and Numbering dialog box, with Bullets selected.

4. Select the Bullet Character you want from the bullets shown. (The choices include four round bullets in different sizes and two diamond-shaped bullets.)

5. Select the Point Size you want (if the size shown is not what you want).

6. Select New Bullet if you want to use a bullet other than those shown.

   You advance to the Symbol dialog box. Select the symbol font you want from the Symbols From list, then select the symbol you want to use for your bullets.

7. If you want to change the hanging indent distance, select **By** and type in a new distance, or click the up or down arrows to increase or decrease the hanging indent amount in decimal increments of tenths of an inch.

8. Choose OK or press Enter.

If you prefer a bulleted list with no hanging indent, select the **H**anging Indent option in the Bullets and Numbering dialog box so that no X appears inside the box. Word for Windows sets no indent, and bullets are separated from the text by one space.

If you want to replace an existing bulleted list with new bullets, reselect the list, choose the T**o**ols **B**ullets and Numbering command, and select a different bullet. If you want to replace bullets with numbers, select the list and refer ahead in this section for instructions on creating a numbered list. Word for Windows asks you to confirm that you want to replace bullets with numbers.

To add bulleted items to a bulleted list, you must type the new items on your list and format them as bulleted text.

T I P Sometimes items on a list contain subsets of information that you don't want bulleted. First, type the primary items on your list, leaving out the subsets of information. Format the list for bullets. Then return to your list and add the subsets of information. Because Word for Windows does not add bullets automatically when you press Enter, the subsets are not bulleted. Later if you want to change the bullets on your list, you can select the entire list, choose T**o**ols **B**ullets and Numbering, select the new bullet style, select the **R**eplace Only Bullets option, and choose OK or press Enter.

Creating Bulleted Lists with the Toolbar

With the toolbar, you can easily set up a bulleted list by clicking the Bulleted List button (refer to fig. 6.3). The Bulleted List button uses the options selected most recently in the Bullets and Numbering dialog box.

To create a bulleted list with the toolbar, follow these steps:

1. Display the toolbar (if not already displayed) by choosing **V**iew **T**oolbar.

2. Type the list at the left margin, without pressing the Tab key.

3. Select the list you want to format with bullets.

4. Choose the Bulleted List button from the toolbar.

Creating Numbered Lists with Menu Commands

Numbered lists are much the same as bulleted lists; however, they are numbered sequentially rather than bulleted. You have several numbering styles to choose from.

To number a list, follow these steps:

1. Type and select your list. Don't use the Tab key to indent the items on your list.

2. Choose the Tools Bullets and Numbering command. The Bullets and Numbering dialog box appears.

3. Select the Numbered List option. The Bullets and Numbering dialog box changes to show numbers instead of bullets (see fig. 6.20).

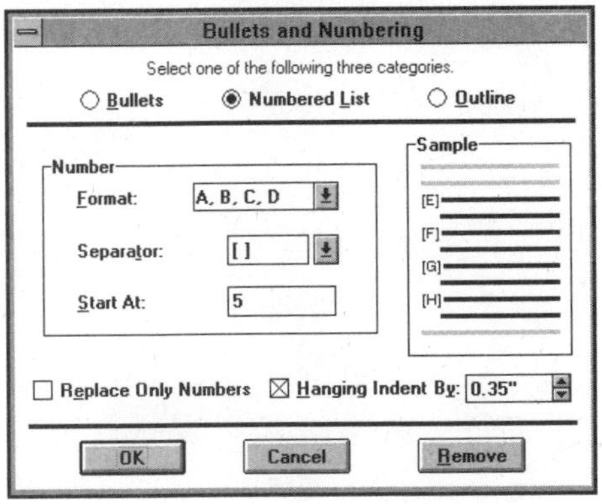

FIG. 6.20.

The Bullets and Numbering dialog box, with Numbered List selected.

4. Select the numbering style you want from the Format list. Your choices include Arabic numbers, Roman numerals, and letters.

5. Select the character you want to appear after the number in the Separator list, or type in the separator you want. Choices included in the list box are None (to remove separator character), period (.), parenthesis ()), colon (:), bracket ([]), parentheses surrounding the number ((1)), brackets surrounding the number, ([2]), and hyphens surrounding the number (-3-).

6. Select the starting number for your list from the **S**tart At list. (If you're doing a series of lists, the starting number may be something other than 1.)

7. If you want to change the hanging indent distance, select B**y** and type in a new distance, or click the up or down arrows to increase or decrease the hanging indent amount in decimal increments of tenths of an inch.

8. Choose OK or press Enter.

To renumber a list to which you add items, reselect the list and repeat the process of numbering your list just as though you are numbering for the first time. A shortcut later in this section shows how to use the toolbar to number a list.

If you prefer a numbered list with no hanging indent, select the **H**anging Indent option in the Bullets and Numbering dialog box so that no X appears inside the box. Word for Windows sets no indent, and numbers are separated from the text by one space.

If you want to replace an existing numbered list with new numbers, reselect the list, choose the **T**ools **B**ullets and Numbering command, and select a different number style. If you want to replace numbers with bullets, select the list and refer back in this section for instructions on creating a bulleted list. Word for Windows asks you to confirm whether you want to replace numbers with bullets.

T I P   Sometimes items on a list contain subsets of information that you don't want numbered. First, type the primary items on your list, leaving out the subsets of information. Number the list, then go back and add the subsets of information. Because Word for Windows does not number inserted items when you press Enter, the subsets are not numbered. Later if you want to change only the numbers on your list, you can select the entire list, choose **T**ools **B**ullets and Numbering, select the new numbering style, select the **R**eplace Only Numbers option, and Choose OK or press Enter.

Creating Numbered Lists with the Toolbar

An even quicker way to number a list is to use the Numbered List button on the toolbar. Like with bullets, using the toolbar is the easiest way to add items to the end of a numbered list because you can add the item, select the list, and click the Numbered List button to number sequentially.

To number a list using the toolbar, follow these steps:

1. Display the toolbar (if not already displayed) by choosing **View Toolbar**.

2. Type the list at the left margin.

3. Select the list you want to number.

4. Choose the Numbered List button from the toolbar.

By default, Word for Windows uses Arabic numbers and a quarter-inch hanging indent to format lists with the Numbered List button on the toolbar. If you recently selected different options in the Bullets and Numbering dialog box, however, Word uses those selections instead.

Removing Bullets or Numbering

If you want to remove bullets or numbering from a list, you must use a menu command. Follow these steps:

1. Select the list from which you want to remove bullets or numbering.

2. Choose the Tools Bullets and Numbering command.

3. Choose the **R**emove button.

The Bullets and Numbering dialog box also contains a third option, called **O**utline. To learn how to number an outline, see Chapter 14.

Hierarchical Numbering of Paragraphs

When you use the outline option for numbering paragraphs, Word for Windows looks for different heading styles or indent levels to determine how to number each paragraph. Paragraphs formatted with the heading 1 style, for example, are numbered with the first outline level (I., II., III.), paragraphs with the heading 2 styles with the second level (A., B., C.), and so forth. Word for Windows provides four outline numbering formats for these different levels:

■ Legal (1, 1.1, 1.1.1, and so on)

■ Outline (I., A., 1., a), (1) and so on)

- Sequence (1., 2., 3., and so on)
- Outline All (I., I.A, I.A.1, and so on)

In addition, Word for Windows has a Learn By Example option in which it learns from a number or letter you insert before the first paragraph of a given level and numbers the remaining paragraphs in the same format.

For outline numbering to work correctly, the paragraphs must be in an outline, or have outline heading styles, or use indents that match their level in the hierarchy. You can apply heading styles by promoting or demoting the paragraphs in the outline view (see Chapter 14), by applying the appropriate heading styles (see Chapter 11), or by indenting paragraphs (see Chapter 6). If you don't apply heading styles or indents, the paragraphs will be numbered in sequence format.

Word for Windows provides two ways to number paragraphs—automatically or manually. If you number paragraphs automatically, Word for Windows numbers them by inserting a field code at the beginning of each paragraph. Field codes are hidden text that automates processes in Word for Windows. (Field codes are described in Chapter 18.) This method has one big advantage: when you delete or rearrange paragraphs the paragraphs are renumbered automatically.

If you number paragraphs manually, Word for Windows inserts a number instead of a field code at the beginning of each paragraph. To renumber the paragraphs, you must select them and repeat the paragraph numbering procedure. This method also has an advantage: it enables you to include several individually numbered lists in a document. Figure 16.21 shows a document that includes two manually numbered lists; if automatic numbering had been used instead, the second list would have been numbered from 6 to 8.

To number paragraphs with outline numbering, follow these steps:

1. Select the paragraphs to number.

2. Choose the Tools Bullets and Numbering command.

3. Select the Outline option to display the dialog box shown in figure 16.22.

4. Select the format you want to use from the Format list box.

5. Select Auto Update if you want paragraphs to update automatically when changes are made.

   Numbered lists normally offset the text from the number with a hanging indent. You can control the amount of indent or turn off the indent.

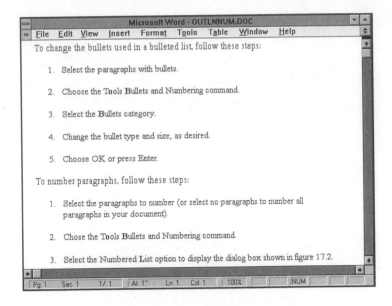

FIG. 6.21.

A document with manually numbered lists.

FIG. 6.22.

The Bullets and Numbering dialog box with the Outline option selected.

6. Select the **H**anging Indent check box if you want the text indented. Type or adjust the amount of indent in the B**y** text box.

7. Review the Sample view shown on the right side of the dialog box. If you do not like the numbering format or the indent, you can make changes at this point.

8. Choose OK or press Enter.

Creating Custom Numbering

Word for Windows can learn a new numbering format if you want to use something other than legal, outline, or sequence. First, number a paragraph in each level with the format you want—for example, change *1.* to *a.*). Next, select the paragraphs you want to number and choose the **T**ools **B**ullets and Numbering command. Select the **O**utline option, select Learn by Example from the **F**ormat list box, and choose OK.

An alternative to this approach is to enter the desired formatting directly into the **F**ormat text box in the Bullets and Numbering dialog box. For example, type *I. A. 1. a.* to modify the separators in the outline format. Enter a space between each level.

Updating Numbered Paragraphs

Paragraphs numbered with the **A**uto Update check box renumber automatically when you reorder or delete paragraphs. If you do not select **A**uto Update, however, the numbers are entered as though you typed them and will not update automatically. You can quickly update these numbers, however, with the following procedure:

1. Select the paragraphs you want to update.

2. Choose the **T**ools **B**ullets and Numbering command.

3. Select the **O**utline option.

4. If you want to renumber only those paragraphs that already have numbers, select the **R**eplace Only Numbers option.

   Unnumbered paragraphs occurring among numbered paragraphs will not be numbered if you select this option.

5. Choose OK or press Enter.

Being able to renumber only the numbered paragraphs, as described in step 3, has a real advantage. Suppose that your document contains several lists, each of which has been numbered manually, so each begins again. Between each pair of lists is a paragraph or more of unnumbered text (much like in this book). You rearrange some or all of the lists and want to renumber them, but you don't want to number the text between the lists. Select all the rearranged lists, and be sure to select **R**eplace Only Numbers in the Bullets and Numbering dialog box when you renumber the paragraphs. Word for Windows skips any unnumbered paragraphs. Using this technique, you don't have to select and renumber each list individually.

Removing Paragraph Numbers

You can remove outline numbering by selecting the paragraphs from which you want to remove the numbering and choosing the **R**emove button in the Bullets and Numbering dialog box (with the Outline option selected).

Applying Paragraph Borders

For a finishing touch, you can add paragraph borders and shading to your document. A *border* may be a box surrounding a paragraph (or paragraphs) on all sides or a line that sets a paragraph off on one or more sides. A border may include shading, which fills a paragraph with a pattern. Boxes and lines can be solid black, shading can be gray, or, if you have a color monitor, they can be more colorful than a rainbow.

Borders are particularly useful in setting special paragraphs apart from the rest of your text for emphasis or wonderful graphic effects (see fig. 6.23). If you use Word for Windows for desktop publishing, you find boxes, lines, and shading to be helpful tools. For examples of text enhancement, see Chapter 28.

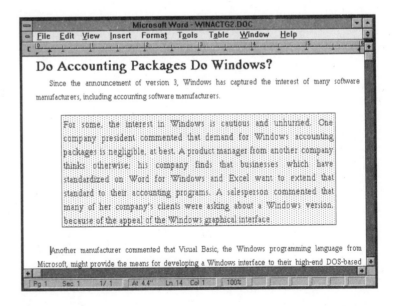

FIG. 6.23.

Borders, lines, and shading can set paragraphs apart.

Creating colored lines, boxes, and shading is easy if you have a color monitor. If you have a color printer, you also can print colored lines, boxes, and shading.

T I P   Service bureaus in many cities offer color printing for a per-page fee. If you want to print your document with colored lines, boxes, and shading, use your own printer to proof the pages, then bring a floppy disk containing your file to the service bureau to have the final pages printed in color.

Borders, like all forms of paragraph formatting, belong to the paragraphs to which they're applied. They are carried forward when you press Enter at the end of a paragraph. Thus, if a group of paragraphs are formatted with a box around them and you press Enter at the end of the last paragraph, your new paragraph falls within the box. To create a new paragraph outside the border, move the insertion point outside the border before you press Enter. If you're at the end of the document and have nowhere to go outside of the border, then create a new paragraph and remove the border.

If you delete the paragraph marker (which stores all the paragraph formatting), then the current paragraph merges with the following one, assuming its formatting. If you accidentally remove borders in this way, immediately choose the **Edit Undo** command to undo your mistake.

Adding Boxes and Lines

A box fully surrounds a paragraph or selected group of paragraphs. Two types of preset boxes are available: box and shadow. A line appears on one or more sides of a paragraph or selected paragraphs, or may appear between selected paragraphs. You have 10 line styles to choose from and can use any line style to create a line, a box, and or a shadowed box.

In the Border Paragraphs dialog box, which you use to create boxes, lines, and shadows, you have several choices to make (see fig. 6.24). An outline of these choices follows:

Option	Effect
Border	A line on one or more sides of the selected paragraph(s). Dotted lines at the corners and sides of the sample indicate where the lines appear; when selected, arrows point to these dotted lines. The sample displays each border as added.
From Text	The distance between the line or box and the text, measured in points. Because 72 points make up an inch, select 9 points for an eighth-inch distance or 18 points for a quarter-inch distance.

Preset **N**one	No box. Use this option to remove an existing box. (This option is used often with the **S**hading option to create a shaded box with no border.)
Preset **B**ox	A box with identical lines on all four sides.
Preset **Sh**adow	A box with a drop shadow on the bottom right corner.
Line None	No line. Use this option to remove individual lines.
Line (other options)	A line or box with the selected line pattern. Options on the left side of the box include double lines in widths of 1 point (with 1 point between lines), 2 points (with 2 points between lines), 3 points (with 3 points between lines), and a single line in 6-point width. Options on the right side include single lines in widths of 1, 2, 3, 4, and 8 points.
Color	A line or box in the selected color. Sixteen colors and gray shades are available. If you select paragraphs of various colors, the Auto option leaves all the colors as they are.
Shading	Shading in the selected paragraph. Use this option with or without a box or border. (The next section discusses shading.)

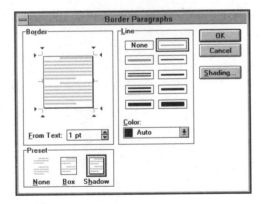

FIG. 6.24.

The Border Paragraphs dialog box.

To create a line or box, follow these steps:

1. Select the paragraph or paragraphs for which you want to create a box or line.

   If you create a box for more than one paragraph, the box encloses the paragraphs as a group, with no borders between them.

2. Choose the Forma**t B**order command. The Border Paragraphs dialog box appears.

3. To create a box, select the Preset **B**ox or Preset **Sh**adow option.

   To create a line, use one of the following techniques:

   Mouse: To create a line, in the Bo**r**der group click the side of the paragraph where you want the line. To select multiple sides, hold the Shift key while you click each side. If multiple paragraphs are selected, you can create a line between them by clicking the horizontal line between paragraphs in the Bo**r**der box.

   Keyboard: Press any cursor-movement key to scroll through various line combinations.

4. Select the line style you want from the Line box.

   Selecting the line style before you create borders ensures that borders take on the appearance of the selected line style. (If None is selected as the line style, borders have no line.)

5. To set the spacing between a box or line and the text, select a distance in the **F**rom Text box.

6. To apply color to all your boxes and lines, select a color from the **C**olor list.

7. Choose OK or press Enter.

The width of a paragraph border (box or line) is determined by the paragraph indent. (If no indent exists, width is determined by the page margins.) If you want a paragraph's border (or line) to be narrower than the margins, indent the paragraph.

If you select and box several paragraphs that have different indents, each paragraph appears in its own separate box (instead of all appearing together in one box). To make paragraphs with different indents appear within a single box, you must create a table and put each paragraph in a row by itself, then format a box around the table (see Chapter 12).

T I P   When paragraphs extend exactly to the margins of your page (as they always do if you do not indent the paragraphs), then borders extend slightly outside the margins. If you want borders to fall within or exactly on the margins, you must indent the paragraph. To make borders fall on the margins, indent the paragraph by the width of the border: for example, if the border is the double 1-point line, which adds up to a total of 3 points in width, then indent the paragraph by 3 points. Type *3 pt* in the left and right indentation boxes in the Paragraph dialog box.

> Remember the definition of a paragraph: any amount of text—even no text—that ends when you press the Enter key. If you format groups of paragraphs to have lines between them, those lines apply to blank spaces between paragraphs if you create those blank spaces by pressing the Enter key an extra time. To avoid extra lines between paragraphs, use the Spacing After command to add blank space between paragraphs. (See "Adjusting Line and Paragraph Spacing" earlier in this chapter.)
>
> **T I P**

You can remove borders all at once or line by line. Changing the line style of existing borders is essentially the same process.

To remove or change a box or line, follow these steps:

1. Select the paragraph or paragraphs for which you want to remove or change boxes or lines.

2. Choose the Forma**t B**order command.

3. To remove all borders, select the Preset **N**one option.

   or

   To remove selected lines, select the line you want to remove and select the **L**ine None option.

4. To change all borders, select a different line style or **C**olor from the Line group.

   or

   To change selected lines, select the line you want to change and select a different option from the **L**ine group.

5. To change the Preset border style, select **B**ox or **Sh**adow.

6. Choose OK or press Enter.

Shading Paragraphs

Paragraphs can be shaded as well as bordered. Shading comes in various percentages of black or the selected color, and in patterns (see fig. 6.25). Percentages of black appear as grays of various intensities. For each shade or pattern, you can select a foreground or background color. Shades create a blended effect: a foreground of yellow and a background of blue creates the effect of green. But in patterns, the effect is more dramatic: in a Light Grid pattern, for example, the yellow foreground forms a light grid pattern over a blue background.

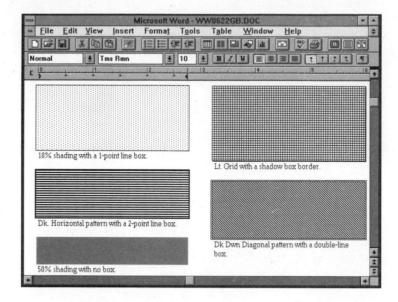

FIG. 6.25.

Shading comes
in many styles.

T I P   Before concocting patterns that you hope to use behind text, be sure
to test whether the text is readable with that pattern behind it.

You can use shading with borders so that a paragraph is surrounded
by a line and filled with shading, or you can use shading alone so that
no border goes around the shaded paragraph. Watch the Sample box in
the Shading dialog box to see the effect of the patterns and colors you
select.

To shade paragraphs, follow these steps:

1. Select the paragraph or paragraphs you want to shade.

2. Choose the Format **B**order command.

3. If you want borders around your selected paragraph, select bor-
    der options.

4. Choose the **S**hading button. The Shading dialog box appears (see
    fig. 6.26).

5. Select an option from the **P**attern list. Options include Clear (uses
    the background color), Solid (uses the foreground color), percent-
    ages, and striped and checkered patterns such as Dk Horizontal
    (for dark horizontal stripes) and Lt Grid (for a grid made of light
    cross-hatching).

Percentage patterns consist of foreground and background colors. The result appears in the Sample box. For best results in creating colors, however, look first for the color you want in the **Fore**ground list.

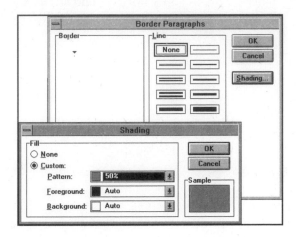

FIG. 6.26.

The Shading dialog box.

6. To color a percentage pattern or a pattern foreground, select a color from the **F**oreground list.

7. To color a percentage pattern or a pattern background, select a color from the **B**ackground list.

8. Choose OK or press Enter.

To remove shading, follow these steps:

1. Select the paragraph or paragraphs from which you want to remove shading.

2. Choose the Forma**t B**order command.

3. Choose the **S**hading button.

4. Select **N**one from the Fill group.

5. Choose OK or press Enter.

From Here . . .

In this chapter you learned how to format paragraphs. You also learned how to align the lines within a paragraph, set tabs and indents, adjust spacing between lines and paragraphs, control pagination, create lists, and add borders and shading.

To learn how to position paragraphs exactly where you want them on a page, see Chapter 24. To learn how to format paragraphs quickly with styles and reformat them globally, see Chapter 11. To learn how to use paragraphs as graphic elements in a newsletter or other publication, see Chapter 28. To learn how to apply borders and shading to objects other than paragraphs, see Chapters 12, 23, 25, 26, and 27.

Formatting Sections

If you've been reading through this book sequentially—no doubt eagerly anticipating each upcoming chapter as the mysteries of Word for Windows unfold before your eyes—by now you're aware of two levels of formatting: character, in which you control the appearance of as little text as a single character; and paragraph, in which you control the appearance of paragraphs, defined as any string of text that ends when you press the Enter key.

A third level of formatting, section formatting, encompasses an even broader selection of text. *Sections* are divisions within your document that separate the document into parts, each of which can be formatted with separate margins, paper size or orientation, columns, page numbers, headers and footers, line numbering, and footnote locations.

To divide your document into sections, you can use a command that inserts a section break (which looks like a double dotted line across the width of a page). Alternatively, you can select a section or document formatting command and specify that the section break be applied from the current position of the insertion point forward in your document. Word for Windows inserts the section break for you.

Sections are especially important in creating two types of documents: those with chapters and those that fall into the desktop publishing category. Sections are useful for chapters because you can force a section to start on a right-facing page (as most chapters do) and can change headers, footers, page numbers, line numbering, and so on for each chapter. Sections also are indispensable for desktop publishing, where you often need to vary the number of columns on a single page.

A fourth level of formatting, document formatting, controls the appearance of your entire document. Section and document formatting are closely related: unless you divide your document into sections, the document has, by default, only one section, and thus section formatting applies to the whole document. Many document-level formatting commands also can be applied to sections. You learn about document-level formatting in the next chapter in this book.

Inserting and Removing Section Breaks

Section breaks divide your document into sections. The breaks appear as double dotted lines when your document is in normal view but do not appear in page layout view or when you print your document (see fig. 7.1). A section break marks the point in your document where new section-level or document-level formatting begins. This new formatting can begin in your document immediately, on the next page, or on the next even-numbered or odd-numbered page. You determine where the new section formatting begins when you insert the section break, or later, when you format the section layout.

To insert a section break, follow these steps:

1. Position the insertion point where you want the section break.

2. Choose the **Insert Break** command. The Break dialog box appears (see fig. 7.2).

3. Select from the following Section Break options:

Option	Section start
Next Page	Top of the next page in document
Continuous	Insertion point (causing no apparent break in the document)

Option	Section start
Even Page	Next even-numbered page in document (generally a left-facing page)
Odd Page	Next odd-numbered page in document (generally a right-facing page)

FIG. 7.1.

A section break appears as a double dotted line when your document is in normal view.

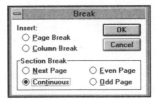

FIG. 7.2.

The Break dialog box.

4. Choose OK or press Enter.

Use the Continuous section break when you create a newsletter that has different-width columns on the same page (such as a full-width title followed by a three-column story). Use the Odd Page section break for chapters when you want them to start always on a right-facing page (assuming page numbering in your document starts with page 1 on a right-facing page).

Word for Windows inserts section breaks for you on two occasions: when you format a document for columns and specify that the columns take effect from "This Point Forward" or "Selected Sections" rather than for the entire document; and when you change the page setup and specify that your changes take effect from "This Point Forward" or "Selected Sections" in your document. For more information on columns and page setup, see "Using Sections with Columns and Desktop Publishing" and "Using Sections with Page Setup" later in this chapter.

In the same way that paragraph markers store paragraph formatting, section break markers store section formatting. Although you can easily remove a section break, remember that when you do, you also remove all section formatting for the section preceding the section break marker that you remove. The preceding section then merges with the following section, taking on its formatting characteristics. If you accidentally delete a section break marker, immediately choose the **E**dit **U**ndo command to retrieve the marker.

To remove a section break, follow these steps:

1. Position the insertion point on the section break.

2. Press the Del (Delete) key.

As alternatives, you can position the insertion point just after the section break marker and press the Backspace key; you can select the section break and press Backspace or Delete; or you can choose the section break marker and choose the **E**dit **C**ut command.

Formatting the Section Layout

Several formatting commands apply specifically to sections. They include defining where the section starts, establishing the section's vertical alignment, suppressing footnotes, and numbering lines.

To format a section (without line numbers), follow these steps:

1. Position the insertion point inside the section you want to format.

2. Choose the Forma**t S**ection Layout command. The Section Layout dialog box appears (see fig. 7.3).

The Section Layout dialog box.

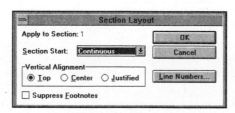

3. From the Section Start list, select an option if you want to change the section's current starting point:

Option	Section starting point
Continuous	No break in text
New Column	Beginning of next column
New Page	Beginning of next page
Even Page	Beginning of next even-numbered page
Odd page	Beginning of next odd-numbered page

4. Select an option from the Vertical Alignment group.

Option	Alignment
Top	Text in section aligns to top margin
Center	Section text is centered between top and bottom margins
Justified	Text in section spaces out to stretch from top to bottom margin

Usually, you want to align a section to the top margin. As an alternative, however, you can align to the center of the page or align justified, which adds space between lines and paragraphs to make the section fill out a page from top to bottom. Aligning a section as justified is a good way to even up the edges of columns at the bottom of a page.

5. If you want to suppress footnotes in the section, select the Suppress Footnotes check box. (This box is gray unless you have created footnotes that are to print at the end of the section.) Footnotes are discussed at the end of the next section.

6. Choose OK or press Enter.

NOTE You don't see the effect of centered or justified alignment in the normal or page layout views; you must choose the File Print Preview command to see how your page looks when printed.

Numbering Lines

A final section formatting alternative is line numbering, which causes lines in the section to be numbered. Line numbers are useful in preparing manuscripts or legal documents, for reference, or if you simply need to know how many lines of text are on a page, in a poem, or in a document. You can choose the starting number for line numbering, the distance between numbers and text, the interval at which line numbers appear, and whether line numbering restarts with every new page or section or continues throughout your section. (You can suppress line numbering for a specific paragraph or paragraphs; see Chapter 6.)

To number lines in a section, follow these steps:

1. Position the insertion point inside the section in which you want line numbers.

2. Choose the Format Section Layout command.

3. Choose the Line Numbers button. The Line Numbers dialog box appears (see fig. 7.4).

FIG. 7.4.

The Line
Numbers dialog
box.

4. Select the Add Line Numbering option. Change the following default line numbering settings if you want.

Option	Setting	Then Type
Start At #	Starting line number	Type a new starting number in the box, or click the up or down arrows to increase or decrease the starting line number. (By default, line numbering begins with number 1.)

Option	Setting	Then Type
From Text	Distance between line numbers and text	Type a distance in the box, or click the up or down arrows to increase or decrease the distance by tenths of an inch. (The Auto option places line numbers one-quarter inch to the left of single-column text, or one-eighth inch to the left of multiple-column text.)
Count By	Interval between printed line numbers (all lines are numbered, but only those numbers specified here print)	Type an interval in the box, or click the up or down arrows to increase or decrease the interval.

5. To establish when line numbers restart at the first number, select an option from the Restart At group:

Option	Restart Point
Every New Page	Beginning of each new page
Every New Section	Beginning of each new section
Continue	None; number lines continuously throughout document

6. Choose OK or press Enter.

You cannot see line numbering in the normal or page layout views. To see line numbers, choose the File Print Preview command or print your document.

Copying Section Formatting

The section break that appears as a double dotted line in the normal view stores section formatting. (In the page layout view, you don't see the line, but you do see the effects of your section formatting.) You can duplicate section formatting quickly by selecting, copying, and then pasting the section break elsewhere. When you paste the section break, the preceding text takes on the formatting of the copied section break.

Another way to duplicate section formatting is to copy and store a section break as a glossary. That way the break becomes available in all new documents and can be applied quickly and easily. To learn how to create and apply glossaries, see Chapter 9.

A final way to duplicate section formatting is to include the formatting in a template—even the Normal template. Remember that by default, a new document includes only one section. That section carries certain default formatting characteristics: one column, .5 inch space between columns (if columns are selected), no footnote suppression, and no line numbers. If you always format sections differently, modify the Normal template or create a new template that includes your own custom section formatting selections. To learn about templates, see Chapter 30.

Understanding the Usefulness of Sections

Sections give you a way to apply document-level formatting commands, such as commands to create columns and establish margins, to the entire document. This chapter gives you an overview of how you can use sections. Other details on specific topics such as columns, page setup, headers and footers, footnotes, and desktop publishing appear throughout the book.

T I P   If you are formatting your document with many sections, select the section formatting that applies to most of them before you insert section breaks. That minimizes the amount of extra formatting you have to do for each individual section.

Using Sections with Columns and Desktop Publishing

One of the most common uses for sections is to separate a document into different parts that have different numbers of columns. A newsletter is an excellent example. Usually a newsletter begins with a large title, or *masthead*, that spans the width of the page and includes a subhead with a date. Following the masthead may be the title of the first story, also as wide as the page. The masthead and title are formatted as a separate section with no column breaks. Below the masthead and title (following a Continuous section break) the text of the first story begins, formatted with multiple columns.

On subsequent pages of the newsletter, similar scenarios may occur. A wide title is in a section by itself, followed by multicolumn text, followed by yet another section with a wide title, followed by another section with multicolumn text. The first section on this hypothetical page is formatted with a New Page section break, ensuring that the title starts at the top of the new page. The remaining section breaks on the page are Continuous, ensuring that the text stays on the same page. For an example of section formatting used in a newsletter, see figure 7.5.

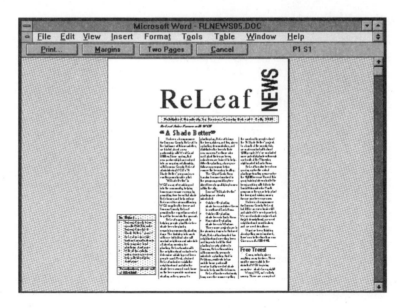

FIG. 7.5.

Section breaks are helpful with desktop publishing.

T   I   P   Inserting a Continuous section break balances the columns of text preceding the break. If the last page of a newsletter doesn't fill up the page, you can insert a Continuous section break at the end of the text to balance the columns.

Because columns so frequently work with section breaks, the Columns dialog box gives you the option to apply columns to the current section, from "This Point Forward" in the document, or to the whole document. If you know where you want a different number of columns to start, position the insertion point there and choose the Format Columns command. Choose the number of columns you want, and from the Apply To list, select This Point Forward. Word for Windows inserts a continuous section break just before the insertion point. By using this technique, you don't have to use the Insert Break command to insert your section break (but be sure to position the insertion point exactly where you want the break to appear).

To learn more about using sections with columns, see Chapter 13. To learn more about desktop publishing, see Chapter 28.

Using Sections with Page Setup

Page setup includes three types of settings that in past word processing programs usually applied to the entire document. These settings include margins, paper size and orientation, and paper source. You can apply each setting to the current section, to "This Point Forward," or to the whole document. As with columns, if you apply the page setup settings to "This Point Forward" in your document, Word for Windows inserts a continuous section break just before the insertion point.

Varying the page setup throughout a document is used frequently in desktop publishing and in creating reports. One example of how to vary setup is in the "ReLeaf News" newsletter shown in fig. 7.5. The newsletter's masthead has a wider left margin setting than the following text; that way, the masthead is inset from the left to line up with the second column of text. (In this example, you can achieve the same effect by indenting the paragraph containing the masthead.)

Another example of how you can vary margins is when you add borders that you want to line up with the edges of the surrounding text, rather than projecting into the margins. Isolate the bordered text into a separate section, then increase its margins by the amount that the border is offset from the text. To learn more about page setup options, see Chapter 8.

Using Sections with Headers, Footers, and Page Numbers

In a single-section document, headers and footers are the same on every page, although page numbers may change. In a multiple-section document, however, you can have different headers and footers in each section.

In a multiple-section document, any header or footer you insert repeats in all following sections, but not in preceding sections. If you type a footer in section 2, the same footer appears in sections 3, 4, and so on, but not in section 1. You can modify the header or footer in any section to make it unique.

If your header or footer changes only in part from section to section, create the basic header or footer before you divide your document into sections. Then modify the header or footer for each section.

Varying headers and footers throughout a document is useful when you create a document with chapters. The first chapter may have a footer reading "Chapter One: Choosing the Right Tree for Your Location"; whereas Chapter 2 may have a footer reading "Chapter Two: Recent Innovations in Tree-Planting Techniques."

Page numbers also can restart with each new section—another feature often useful for creating chapters.

For more about creating headers, footers, and page numbers, see Chapter 15. For more about page numbers, see Chapter 18.

Using Sections with Footnotes

When you create footnotes, Word for Windows gives you the option of printing them at the bottom of each page, just below the text, at the end of each section, or at the end of the document. You make this choice when you create the footnote. If you print footnotes at the end of each section but want to suppress them for a single section, position the insertion point inside the section for which you want to suppress footnotes, choose the Format Section Layout command, and select the Suppress Footnotes option. The footnotes appear at the end of the following section.

If you want footnotes to appear at the end of the document, select that option when you create each footnote. (These footnotes often are called *endnotes*.) For more about footnotes, see Chapter 15.

From Here . . .

In this chapter, you learned how sections can be useful for dividing a document into parts consisting of different margins, paper size or orientation, columns, page numbers, headers and footers, line numbering, and footnote locations.

For more about working with sections and columns, see Chapter 13. For more about using desktop publishing techniques to create newsletters, fliers, and other publications, see Chapter 28. For more about creating separate headers and footers for each section in your document, or about using footnotes in sections, see Chapter 15. For more details about using sections to separate chapters in long documents, see Chapter 20.

Formatting Page Setup

Of the four levels of formatting—character, paragraph, section, and page setup—page setup is the broadest. Page setup often encompasses formatting choices that affect the entire document. In a change from tradition, however, Word for Windows enables you to apply page setup formatting selections to portions of the document known as sections (Chapter 7 covers sections).

Page setup formatting options include margin settings, paper size, paper orientation, and paper source. You can use the Format Page Setup command to apply these options to some—or all—of your text. By default, page setup options apply to the entire document. Alternatively, you can apply these options to a designated section of text, or from the position of the insertion point forward in your document. Being able to specify where page setup options apply gives you great flexibility in designing your document.

For example, you can include an envelope and a letter in a single document by specifying different margins, paper size, paper orientation, and paper source for the first page of the document—the envelope—than you specify for the remaining pages—the letter. (The Create Envelope button on the toolbar does this automatically.) You also can set up the pages of a multiple-page letter to have different margins—wider margins to accommodate letterhead on the first page, and standard margins for printing the following pages on plain paper.

All new documents are based on a template, and unless you choose a different template, Word for Windows bases new documents on the Normal template, which contains default page setup choices. Because these default choices may not be exactly what you want, Word for Windows gives you the chance to change them by applying your own page setup options to the Normal template. Thus, you can use your own page setup choices as defaults. You can change the default margins, for example, if you always print on paper that requires different margin settings than those supplied by the Normal template. You can change the defaults for all page setup options—margin, page size and orientation, and paper source.

Setting Margins

Margins are the borders on all four sides of a document page, within which the text of your document is confined. Margins aren't necessarily blank, however; they may contain headers, footers, page numbers, footnotes, or even text and graphics.

Word for Windows' default margins are 1 inch top and bottom and 1.25 inches left and right. You can change the margins for the entire document (if the document contains only a single section) or for parts of the document (if you divide the document into sections). If you use different margin settings regularly, you can send your settings to the Normal template so that they become the new defaults.

Different document views in Word for Windows show different perspectives on your margins. In the normal view, you don't see the margins, but you see the space between them, where your text appears. In the page layout view, you see the page as it will print, margins and all. Select that view if you want to see headers, footers, page numbers, footnotes, and anything else that appears within the margins. To select the page layout view, choose the View Page Layout command.

You can change the margins in your document in three ways. First, you can choose the Format Page Setup command and make selections from the Page Setup dialog box. A second technique is to use the ruler, which contains margin markers. Third, you can change margins with the Print Preview screen, which shows how your new margins look (and also gives a readout of their measurements).

Setting Margins with the Page Setup Command

Using the Page Setup command to set margins gives you the greatest number of options. You can set the margins to precise measurements, establish facing pages and gutters for binding (later in this chapter), set varying margins for different sections of your document, and apply your margin settings to the Normal template so that they become the new default settings.

If you want to apply margin settings to your entire document, the insertion point can be located anywhere in the document when you set your margins. If you want to apply margins to only one part of your document, however, you must do one of two things: to apply margins to a selected portion of your text, select that text before you set the margins; or to apply margins from a specific point forward in your document, position the insertion point where you want the new margins to start. If you apply margins to selected text, Word for Windows inserts section breaks before and after the selected text. If you apply margins from the insertion point forward, Word for Windows inserts a section break at the insertion point. (Chapter 7 discusses using sections.)

As you select your margin settings, notice that the Sample box in the Page Setup dialog box shows you how your page or pages look.

To set margins using the Page Setup command, follow these steps:

1. Position the insertion point inside the section for which you want to set margins. (The margins will apply to the entire document unless the document has multiple sections.)

   or

   Select the text for which you want to set margins.

   or

   Position the insertion point where you want new margins to begin in your document.

2. Choose the Format Page Setup command. The Page Setup dialog box appears (see fig. 8.1).

3. Select the Margins option, if necessary. (The option may be selected already.)

FIG. 8.1.

The Page Setup
dialog box.

4. Select your margin settings. For each setting, type in the amount
   of the margin, or click the up or down arrow (or press the up- or
   down-arrow key) to increase or decrease the margin setting by
   tenths of an inch.

Option	Margin setting
Top	Top of page
Bottom	Bottom of page
Left	Left side of page
Right	Right side of page
Gutter	Extra space on pages for binding (see the following section)

5. From the Apply To list, select the section to which you want to
   apply margins (choices on the list vary depending on the amount
   of text currently selected).

Option	Applies margins to	When
This Section	Current section (no section break inserted)	Insertion point is located within a section
Selected Sections	Multiple sections (no section breaks inserted)	At least part of more than one section is selected

Option	Applies margins to	When
This Point Forward	Insertion point forward to end of document (new-page section break inserted at insertion point)	Insertion point is where you want new margin to start
Selected Text	Selected text (new-page section breaks inserted at beginning and end of selected text)	Text is selected
Whole Document	Entire document (no section break inserted)	Insertion point is anywhere

6. Choose OK or press Enter.

Margins usually are measured in decimal inches, unless you change your default measurement system through the Tools Options command (see Chapter 29). Nonetheless, you can create margins in a different measurement system by typing in amounts such as *36 pt* for 36 points (half an inch—72 points make up an inch), *3 cm* for 3 centimeters, or *9 pi* for 9 picas (one and one-half inches—6 picas make up an inch). If you use the inch measurement system, the next time you open the Page Layout dialog box you see that your measurements have been converted back to inches.

T I P

If your document contains different margin settings, it must be divided into different sections. You can create sections with different margins in several ways. You can insert section breaks manually and then format the text between the breaks (or after a break) with different margin settings (see Chapter 7 to learn about inserting section breaks). Alternatively, you can use the Format Page Setup command to apply margins to only the selected text, or from the insertion point forward in your document. If you do include sections with different margins in your document, remember that if you delete the section break, you delete the section and thus lose its margins. If you accidentally delete a section break, choose Edit Undo, or if you don't catch your mistake quickly enough, create and format the section again.

Creating Facing Pages and Gutters

Facing pages in a document are the left and right pages of a double-sided document, like in a book or magazine. You can set up your document for facing pages when you set margins. Facing pages are ideal when you plan to print your document on both sides of the paper and want wider margins on the inside than on the outside edges.

The first change you notice in the Page Setup dialog box when you select the **F**acing Pages option is that you no longer have left and right margins; instead, you have inside and outside margins. On the left page, the inside margin is on the right side; on the right page, the inside margin is on the left side. The second change you notice is that the sample box displays two pages side by side.

With facing pages, you can have different headers and footers on each page and can position page numbers on opposite sides of the facing pages. In a newsletter footer, for example, you may want to position page numbers below the outside margins and the date below the inside margins.

Whether you're working with normal pages that have left and right margins or facing pages that have inside and outside margins, you can add a gutter to your pages to leave extra space for binding. A gutter on normal pages adds space at the left edge of the page; a gutter on facing pages adds space at the inside edges of each page. For example, to leave an extra half-inch for binding, include a gutter of .5. A gutter doesn't change your document's margins, but it does reduce the printing area.

Like margins, facing pages and gutters apply to sections. You can insert section breaks before selecting facing pages or gutters, or you can create sections as part of the process. (For details, see the earlier instructions on setting margins.)

To set facing pages and a gutter, follow these steps:

1. Position the insertion point inside the section for which you want facing pages or a gutter. (The change applies to the entire document unless the document has multiple sections.)

2. Choose the Forma**t** Page Set**u**p command.

3. Select the **M**argins option (if not selected already).

4. Select the **G**utter option and type in the amount by which you want to increase the left margin (if you select facing pages) or the inside margin (if you do not select facing pages). Alternatively, click the up or down arrows (or press the up- or down-arrow key)

to increase or decrease the gutter amount by tenths of an inch. Notice that the Sample box shows a shaded area where the gutter appears (see fig. 8.2).

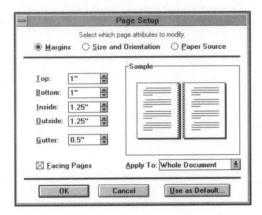

5. Select the Facing Pages option. Notice that the Left and Right margin options change to Inside and Outside, and that the Sample box shows side-by-side pages.

6. Choose OK or press Enter.

Changing the Default Margin Settings

If you always use different margin settings from Word for Windows' default margins, use the Page Setup dialog box to change the Normal template. Then each new document you create based on the Normal template has your new default margins.

To change the default margin settings, follow these steps:

1. Choose the Format Page Setup command.

2. Select Top, Bottom, Left, and Right margin settings. Set a Gutter and select Facing Pages if you want.

3. Choose the Use as Default button. A dialog box asks you to confirm that all new documents based on the Normal template are affected by the change. Choose OK or press Enter.

If you change defaults, when you quit the program, Word for Windows asks whether you want to save global glossary and command changes. Choose Yes to save your changes to the Normal template or No to discard your changes.

Setting Margins with the Ruler

A quick way to set margins for your document or for a section in your document is to use the ruler with a mouse.

To use the ruler to set margins, the ruler must be displayed. (Choose the **View** **R**uler command if the ruler is not displayed now.) Next you must switch to the ruler's margin view. By default, the ruler displays the indent view, which enables you to change the indent for the current paragraph or paragraphs. But at the left edge of the ruler, left of the zero point, you see a bracket-like symbol—the Margin Scale symbol. If you click the symbol, the indent markers on the ruler change to left and right margin markers (see fig. 8.3). You can drag the margin markers on the ruler to change the margins for the currently selected section or sections.

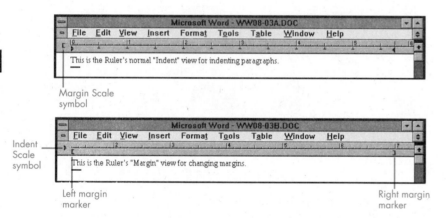

FIG. 8.3.

When you click on the Margin Scale symbol on the ruler, the indent symbols change to Margin Scale symbols.

Notice that when you click the Margin Scale symbol to change the indent markers on the ruler to margin markers, the Margin Scale symbol changes to an Indent Scale symbol. To return indent markers to the ruler, select the Indent Scale symbol.

Using the ruler doesn't insert any section breaks into your document; it sets the margins for the entire document or for the section containing the insertion point. If you want to use the ruler to create various margins for multiple sections in your document, insert section breaks before you begin.

To change margins with the ruler, follow these steps:

1. If the ruler is not displayed, choose the **View** **R**uler command.

2. Position the insertion point inside the section where you want to change margins.

3. Click the Margin Scale symbol at the left end of the ruler to change the indent markers on the ruler to margin markers (margin markers look like brackets; refer to fig. 8.3).

4. To change the left margin, drag the left margin marker to a new position on the ruler. To change the right margin, drag the right margin marker to a new position.

If you want to change the margins for just one or a few paragraphs, use indents instead (see Chapter 6 for details). Use the ruler to change margins only when you want to change margins for the entire document or for a large section.

T I P

Setting Margins in the Print Preview Screen

If you're a visually oriented person, the easiest way to set margins is to use the Print Preview screen and a mouse. You drag dotted lines representing the margins on a reduced picture of your page. You can see the effect that changing the margins has on your document.

Just like when you set margins by using the ruler, margin settings you apply in the Print Preview screen apply to the currently selected section or sections, or to the entire document, if it has no sections.

If your document has facing pages, be sure to display two pages (by choosing the Two Pages button in the Print Preview status bar) so that you can see the effect of any change you make to the inside margins. If you change the inside margin on one page, all pages in the section reflect that change.

To set margins in the Print Preview screen, follow these steps:

1. Choose the File Print Preview command. The Print Preview view appears (see fig. 8.4).

2. Choose the Margins button to display the margin borders. (If two pages are displayed, margin borders appear on the left page; click the right page to display the margin borders there.)

   Margin borders appear as dotted lines at the top, bottom, left, and right edges of the page. Small black selection squares appear at the ends of each of these dotted lines.

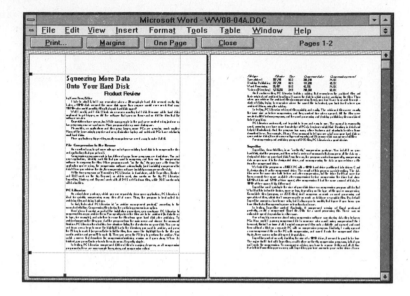

FIG. 8.4.

The Print
Preview view.

3. Change any margin.

   Mouse: Move the arrow pointer over the selection square at the end of the margin you want to change. The arrow turns into a crosshair. Click and hold the left mouse button, and drag the margin to a new location.

   Keyboard: After pressing M to choose the **Margins** button, press the Tab key enough times to select the margin you want to change. Press the arrow keys to move the margin.

   Notice that as you drag the margin border, its current position appears numerically at the right end of the Print Preview status bar at the top of the screen.

4. Display the effect of your change.

   Mouse: Click anywhere outside the page to see the effect of your change.

   or

   Choose the **Margins** button a second time to display the effect of your change and to hide the margin borders.

   Keyboard: Press the M key again (to choose the **Margins** button) to see the effect of your change.

5. Choose the **Close** button (by clicking on it or pressing C) to return to your document.

Setting Paper Size and Orientation

You can change the paper size or orientation for your entire document or for part of your document. You may select a different paper size to create something smaller than usual, like an invitation. You may select landscape (horizontal) orientation instead of the usual portrait (vertical) orientation for something like a brochure or envelope.

Word for Windows offers several predefined paper sizes, including letter, legal, note, A4 and B4 (European standard paper sizes), small letter, and small A4. But if none of those sizes suits your needs, you can select a custom size instead and enter your own measurements.

Paper size and orientation settings apply to the current section, just like margin settings. If you haven't divided your document into sections, your settings apply to the whole document, unless you choose to apply them to the currently selected text or from the insertion point forward in your document. If you apply settings to selected text, Word for Windows inserts a new-page section break before and after the selection. (The new-page section break isolates the section on a separate sheet of paper. When you're changing paper size and orientation, this format is probably what you want.) If you apply settings to the insertion point forward, Word for Windows inserts a new-page section break at the insertion point's current position.

To set paper size and orientation, follow these steps:

1. Position the insertion point inside the section for which you want to set paper size and orientation. (The change applies to the entire document unless the document has multiple sections.)

    or

    Select the text for which you want to change paper size and orientation.

    or

    Position the insertion point where you want new paper size and orientation to begin in your document.

2. Choose the Format Page Setup command. The Page Setup dialog box appears.

3. Select the Size and Orientation option. The Page Setup dialog box changes to display size and orientation options (see fig. 8.5).

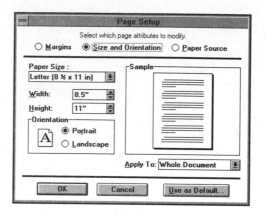

The Page Setup dialog box, showing Size and Orientation options.

4. From the Paper Size list, select a predefined paper size.

   or

   In the **Width** box and **Height** box, type the width and height of your custom paper size. As an alternative, you can click the up or down arrows (or press the up- or down-arrow keys) to increase or decrease the paper size by tenths of an inch.

5. For a vertical, upright page, select the Portrait option.

   or

   For a horizontal, sideways page, select the Landscape option.

6. From the **Apply To** list, select the section to which you want to apply paper size and orientation settings (different options appear on this list, depending on how much text is selected in the document).

Option	Applies settings to	When
This Section	Current section (no section break inserted)	Insertion point is located within a section
Selected Sections	Multiple sections (no section breaks inserted)	At least part of more than one section selected
This Point Forward	Insertion point forward to end of document (new-page section break inserted at insertion point)	Insertion point is where you want new size or orientation to start

Option	Applies settings to	When
Selected Text	Selected text (new-page section breaks inserted at beginning and end of selected text)	Text is selected
Whole Document	Entire document (no section break inserted)	Insertion point is anywhere

7. Choose OK or press Enter.

If you want to apply the paper size and orientation settings to the Normal template so that they become the default settings, select your settings and choose the Use as Default button.

Note that if you create custom size paper, the paper measurements you type are usually in inches, unless you change the default measurement system using the Tools Options command (see Chapter 29). You can override the default inches by typing your measurement using text that describes a different measurement system. For example, to set a paper width of 36 picas, type *36 pi*; to set a paper height of 24 centimeters, type *24 cm*.

Selecting the Paper Source

You not only can alter margins, paper size, and paper orientation for your document or for a section of your document, but you also can specify where your printer finds the paper.

Many printers have different options for storing paper. For example, most laser printers have a default paper tray and a manual feed. You can specify that one section of your document be printed from the manual feed, while the rest of the document be printed from paper in the default paper tray. Some printers have two paper trays; you can specify that one section, such as the first page of a letter, be printed on letterhead in the first tray, while the remaining pages be printed on plain paper from the second tray (see fig. 8.6).

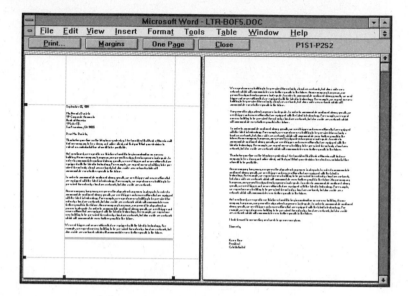

FIG. 8.6.

You can select
different paper
sources for
different pages.

As with all page setup options, you can insert section breaks before
you select paper source, or Word for Windows can insert section
breaks for you.

To select a paper source for your document, follow these steps:

1. Position the insertion point inside the section for which you want
   to set paper source. (The change applies to the entire document
   unless the document has multiple sections.)

   or

   Select the section for which you want to set paper source.

   or

   Position the insertion point where you want new-paper source to
   begin in your document.

2. Choose the Format Page Setup command.

3. Select the Paper Source option. The Page Setup dialog box
   changes to show paper source options (see fig. 8.7).

4. From the First Page list, select the paper source for the first page
   of your document.

5. From the Other Pages list, select the paper source for the remaining pages of your document.

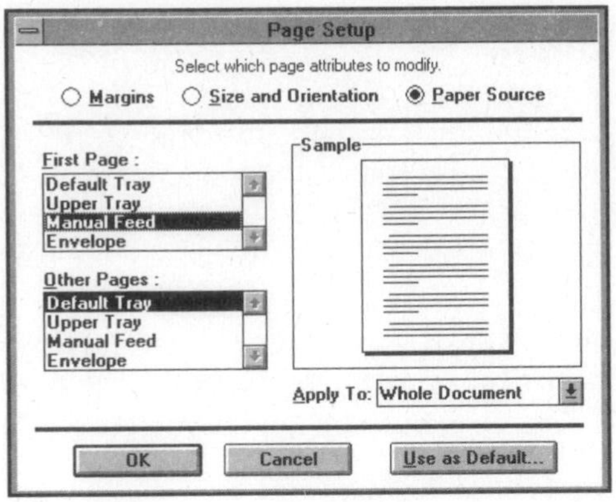

FIG. 8.7.

The Page Setup
dialog box,
showing paper
source options.

6. From the **A**pply To list, select the section to which you want to apply paper source settings (the list will display different options, depending on how much text is selected in the document).

Option	Applies settings to	When
This Section	Current section (no section break inserted)	Insertion point is located within a section
Selected Sections	Multiple sections (no section breaks inserted)	At least part of more than one section is selected
This Point Forward	Insertion point forward to end of document (new-page section break inserted at insertion point)	Insertion point is where you want new paper source to start
Selected Text	Selected text (new-page section breaks inserted at beginning and end of selected text)	Text is selected
Whole Document	Entire document (no section break inserted)	Insertion point is anywhere

7. Choose OK or press Enter.

When you print a document with various paper sizes, orientations, or sources, your printer may pause at the end of each page and wait for you to indicate that it should continue. In some cases, you may need only to access the Print Manager and "Resume" the print (see Chapter 10). In other cases, you may need to press a button on the printer. Newer laser printers work well with varying paper sizes and orientations, but if you experience difficulties, check your printer manual.

If you want to apply your paper source selections to the Normal template so that they become the default settings, choose the **Use** as Default button rather than pressing Enter.

T I P   Be sure you have installed the correct printer driver for your printer in Windows so that Word for Windows knows which paper trays your printer has available. Refer to your Windows book or manual for details.

From Here . . .

In this chapter you learned how to change the margins, paper size, paper orientation, and paper source for your document. You learned that you can vary all of these settings within a single document—a powerful new feature of Word for Windows. When you're working with your page setup, be aware of the different possible views of your document. In normal view, you don't see what's in the margins; while in page layout view, you see the document as it actually will print. (To learn more about views, see Chapter 1.) The print preview view really shows how your document looks on paper; to learn more about other options the Print Preview screen offers, see Chapter 10.

You can select margin settings that apply to the whole document or to sections within the document, but if you want to change the margins in just a paragraph or two, then indents may be a better choice. See Chapter 6 to learn how to set paragraph indents. See Chapter 7 to learn how to create and work with sections.

Columns are affected by margin settings. To learn more about columns, see Chapter 13.

Using Editing and Proofing Tools

By now you're probably familiar with most of the basics of Word for Windows—how to create, edit, format, and save your document. You also can use many tools to ease text entry, to ensure accuracy, and to make your document not only look good, but also read well.

Glossaries can save you time when you are entering repetitive text. By defining selected text as a glossary and assigning it an abbreviation, you can type the abbreviation and press the F3 key to enter the entire text.

With Word for Windows, you can find and replace text, formatting, special characters, and styles.

Before you print your document, check its spelling. Your eyes are trained to correct obvious spelling errors when you read them, but you still can miss a mistake when you proof a document. Use the spelling checker to catch mistakes you missed and to correct spelling when you make an error. You also can use Word for Windows' grammar checker to check sentence construction and style.

If you collaborate on a document, you can share files rather than printed copies, using the revision marking feature to show you where your co-author suggests changes.

You can use the sorting command when you create lists. You can sort lists of names, for example, when you're using the mail-merge feature to send letters to a long list of people. You can sort by any field in your list (last name, city, or zip code).

Using Glossaries

Glossaries are like word processing shorthand. They save you time by storing selected text and graphics (and their formatting) that are used repeatedly. If you have a long company name which you frequently must type in documents, for example, you can abbreviate it as a glossary and insert it quickly into your document. Glossaries also ensure that repetitive material is typed correctly and consistently. If you create templates for standardized documents, you should consider including in the templates glossaries of frequently used words, phrases, template formats, or pictures. (To learn more about templates, see Chapter 30.)

Glossaries do not have to be limited to text. They can contain pictures and graphics of digitized signatures, graphic letterheads, logos, or symbols. If you frequently use a table with special formatting, you can make it a glossary entry.

Creating a Glossary Entry

To add text or graphics to a glossary (or to change an existing glossary), follow these steps:

1. Select from your document the text, graphic, table, or combination of items that you want to add to the glossary.

2. Choose the **E**dit Gl**o**ssary command. The Glossary dialog box appears.

3. In the Glossary **N**ame box, type an abbreviated name for the text (see fig. 9.1). Use an abbreviation you can remember easily. To change an existing glossary entry, select the name of the entry from the list and edit it.

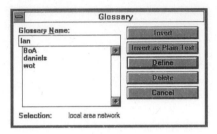

FIG. 9.1.

The Glossary
dialog box.

4. Choose the **D**efine button.

Glossary entries belong to your current document and to a template. If the document in which you define a glossary is based on a template other than the Normal template, a dialog box appears after you choose the **D**efine button asking whether you want to store your glossary entry as **G**lobal or **T**emplate. If you choose **G**lobal, your glossary entry is stored in the Normal template; if you choose **T**emplate, it is stored in the current document's template. When you exit Word for Windows after a session in which you created glossary entries, a dialog box appears asking if you want to save global glossary and command changes. Choose **Y**es to keep your glossary entries and **N**o to discard them.

Inserting Glossary Entries

To insert a glossary entry into your text, follow these steps:

1. Position the insertion point where you want the glossary entry to appear.

2. Type the abbreviation you gave the glossary entry.

3. Press F3, the Glossary key.

When you press F3, Word for Windows replaces the glossary abbreviation with the glossary text. (The glossary abbreviation you type in your document must be at the beginning of a line or preceded by a space.)

If you cannot remember the glossary abbreviation, follow these steps:

1. Position the insertion point where you want the glossary entry to appear.

2. Choose the Edit Glossary command.

3. In the Glossary Name box, type the glossary name, or select it from the list.

4. Choose the Insert button, or choose the Insert as Plain Text button to insert the glossary entry without its formatting (it takes on the formatting in your document).

Deleting a Glossary Entry

A glossary can store up to 150 entries. To delete a glossary entry, follow these steps:

1. Choose the Edit Glossary command.

2. In the Glossary Name box, type the name to delete, or select the name from the list.

3. Choose the Delete button.

Using the Spike

The *spike* is a special type of glossary entry that enables you to remove selected items from different places in your document, collect them, and insert them into your document as a group. The term *spike* comes from the old office spikes that impaled bills and invoices until they could all be dealt with at once. Contents stored in the spike glossary entry are inserted just as you would insert a regular glossary entry. You also can empty the contents of the spike and make it available to store another collection of text and graphics.

To add text or graphics to the spike, follow these steps:

1. Select the text or graphics you want to add to the spike.

2. Press Ctrl+F3, the Spike key. Word for Windows cuts the selected text or graphic and adds it to the spike glossary entry.

3. Select additional items in the order you want them added to the spike and repeat step 2.

After you create a spike entry, you will see it listed as Spike in the Glossary dialog box list when you choose the Edit Glossary command.

Note that spiked selections are cut from your document—not copied.

To insert the spike's contents into your document, follow these steps:

1. Position the insertion point where you want the spike's contents to appear.

2. Press Shift+Ctrl+F3, the Unspike key, to paste in the spike and remove its contents from memory.

   or

   Type *spike*, and then press F3 (Glossary) to paste in the spike and retain its contents so that you can paste them again.

Printing Glossary Entries

If you do not use certain glossary entries regularly, you soon will forget what the abbreviation in the glossary list does. To see a more complete view of each glossary entry, including its format, print a list of glossary entries. To print a list of glossary entries, open a document based on the template containing the glossary. Choose the **File P**rint command and select Glossary in the **P**rint list; then choose OK or press Enter.

Using Find and Replace

Being able to find and replace text, formatting, styles, and special characters is an important time-saver (and a good way to make sure you catch every occurrence of whatever you need to find or replace). The **E**dit **F**ind command finds and selects the text, formatting, style, or special character you specify, making it easy to locate a certain phrase or a particular type of formatting in your document. The **E**dit **R**eplace command enables you to find and replace text, formatting, and characters. You can replace items selectively or globally (changing your entire document all at once).

Finding Text

With Word for Windows' Find feature, you can quickly find a specific word or phrase or a special formatting character in a document that is many pages long. The text can be as brief as a single letter or as long as a sentence up to 256 characters. You also can search for special characters, such as tabs, page breaks, line numbers, footnotes, or revision marks within your document, or you may want to search for a particular format or style.

To find text (up to 256 characters), empty space, or special characters, follow these steps:

1. Choose the **Edit Find** command. The Find dialog box appears (see fig. 9.2).

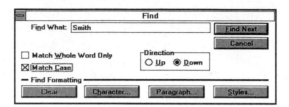

2. In the Find What text box, type the text or special characters you want to search for (refer to table 9.2 in the section "Finding and Replacing Special Characters" for a list of special characters).

   The text scrolls to the right if you enter more text than will fit in the box. You can enter up to 256 characters.

3. Select one or more of the options in the Find dialog box.

Option	Effect
Match **W**hole Word Only	Finds whole words only. Do not select this option if you want to find all occurrences of the text.
Match **C**ase	Matches the text exactly as you have typed it—including capital letters. Do not select this option if you want to find all occurrences of the text, whether letters are upper- or lowercase.
Direction **U**p	Searches between the insertion point and the beginning of the document.
Direction **D**own	Searches between the insertion point and the end of the document. This is the default direction.

The Find Formatting options at the bottom of the dialog box include **C**haracter, **P**aragraph, and **S**tyles. The dialog box expands to display the various types of formatting for each formatting option. (Refer to the section "Finding and Replacing Formatting and Styles" in this chapter for more information on these options.)

Choose the Clear command to remove any formatting codes displayed beneath the text box from a previous find operation (unless you want these codes to affect the current search).

4. Choose the Find Next command or press Enter to begin the search.

When Word for Windows finds the first occurrence of the text, it scrolls to and selects the text. The dialog box remains open so that you immediately can continue to search for other occurrences of the text by choosing Find Next or pressing Enter again. If you want to edit the found text, choose Cancel or press Esc and edit the selected text. You then can repeat the search by pressing Shift+F4 or choosing the Edit Find command again, and choosing Find Next.

If Word for Windows cannot find the text, the program displays a dialog box that says, The search text is not found. Choose OK and try again.

If you're unsure of spelling, try using question marks, or *wild cards*, in place of letters you're not sure about. If you want to find *Smith*, for example, but aren't sure whether it's spelled with an *i* or a *y*, search for *Sm?th*. Or search for part of a word, like *Smi* and make sure that the Match Whole Word Only check box in the Find dialog box is turned off.

If the insertion point isn't at the beginning of your document when you start the search and Word for Windows reaches the end of the document without finding the text, you see a dialog box asking whether you want to continue the search from the beginning of the document. Choose Yes to continue or No to cancel the search.

If you want to search for or replace text in only a portion of your document, select that portion of the document, and then follow the general instructions for finding and replacing.

Replacing Text

Besides searching for text, formatting, or special characters, you also can replace them automatically. If you finish your document and realize that *Mr. Smith* really should have been *Ms. Smythe*, you can use a simple menu command to search for every occurrence of the incorrect spelling and replace it with the correct spelling. If your typist underlined every title in a long list of books and you decide you want book titles to be italicized, for example, you can search for every occurrence of underlining and replace it with italic.

Replacing text works much the same way as finding text. The only major difference is an additional Replace With text box that enables you to enter the text to replace the text you find. The Replace dialog box enables you to confirm each replacement, or you can replace all occurrences of the text with a single command.

To replace text, follow these steps:

1. Choose the Edit Replace command. The Replace dialog box appears (see fig. 9.3).

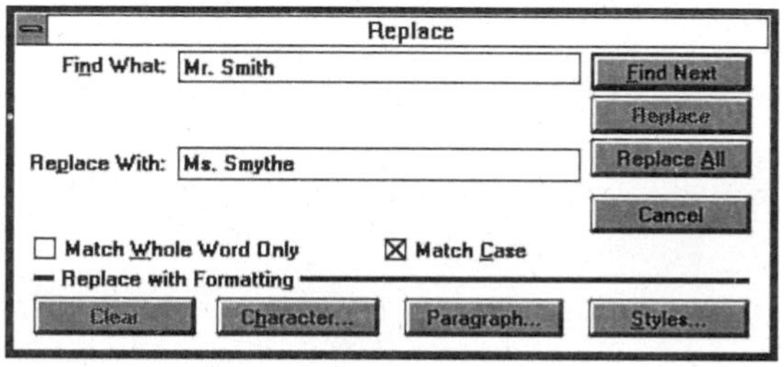

FIG. 9.3.

The Replace dialog box.

2. In the Find What text box, type the text you want to replace.

3. In the Replace With box, type the new text.

4. If you want, you can select either or both of the Match Whole Word Only or Match Case options.

5. Choose the Find Next or Replace All button.

   If you want to confirm each change, choose Find Next. When an occurrence of the text is found, choose the Replace button to change the text or choose the Find Next button again (or press Enter) to continue the search without changing the selected occurrence. (If the dialog box is covering up the selected text, you can move the dialog box by dragging its title bar or pressing Alt, space bar, m, and then pressing any arrow key.)

   If you want to change all occurrences of the specified text without confirmation, choose the Replace All button.

6. Choose Close to return to the document.

If the insertion point isn't at the beginning of your document when you start the search and Word for Windows reaches the end of the document, you see a dialog box asking whether you want to continue the search from the beginning of the document. Choose Yes to continue, and No to cancel the search.

If Word for Windows cannot find the text at all, you see a message dialog box that says, The search text is not found.

If you want to search for or replace text in only a portion of your document, select that portion of the document, and then follow the general instructions for finding and replacing. To cancel a search-and-replace operation, press Esc.

> Choosing the Replace All button saves time but can be risky. You may want to start by confirming the first few replacements. When you are sure that you want to change all remaining occurrences of the text, choose Replace All. If you select Replace All and then realize you made a mistake, immediately choose Edit Undo.

T I P

Unless you specify otherwise, Word for Windows applies the original formatting to the new replacement text. If you replace the boldface word *Roger* with the plain name *Ms. Smith*, for example, the replacement is a boldface **Ms. Smith**. To override this feature, specify formatting as part of your replacement (see this chapter's section on finding and replacing formatting).

You can undo a replacement by choosing **Edit Undo Replace**. If you have confirmed each replacement, the **Edit Undo Replace** command undoes only the last replacement. If you selected the Replace **All** button and made all the replacements at once, the **Edit Undo Replace** command undoes all the replacements.

> You can paste text copied to the clipboard with the **Edit Copy** command into the text boxes in the **Edit Find** and **Edit Replace** dialog boxes. This feature enables you to insert large amounts of text or text using noncontiguous formats. To use the contents of the clipboard, position the insertion point in the Find What or Replace With text box and press Ctrl+V.

T I P

Finding and Replacing Fonts, Formatting, and Styles

Finding and replacing fonts and formatting is similar to finding and replacing text. Suppose that you have a document with many underlined titles, and you want to italicize them instead. Or suppose that an article is sprinkled with boldface phrases, and you want to remove the boldface formatting. You can choose to change just the text, just the formatting, or both the text and the formatting.

You also can replace paragraph formats and styles. A centered paragraph, for example, can be replaced with right-alignment formatting, or a style such as Heading 1 can be replaced with another style such as Heading 2.

Finding and Replacing Formats

To find or replace fonts and formatting, follow these steps:

1. Choose the **E**dit **F**ind or the **E**dit **R**eplace command. The Find or the Replace dialog box appears.

2. Select the Fi**n**d What box and type the formatted text you want to find or leave the box blank to find a font or formatting only.

3. To find a font or character formatting, select the C**h**aracter button. The Find Character dialog box appears (see fig. 9.4). It looks the same as the Character dialog box used for formatting characters. Select the font or formatting options you want to find and choose OK or press Enter.

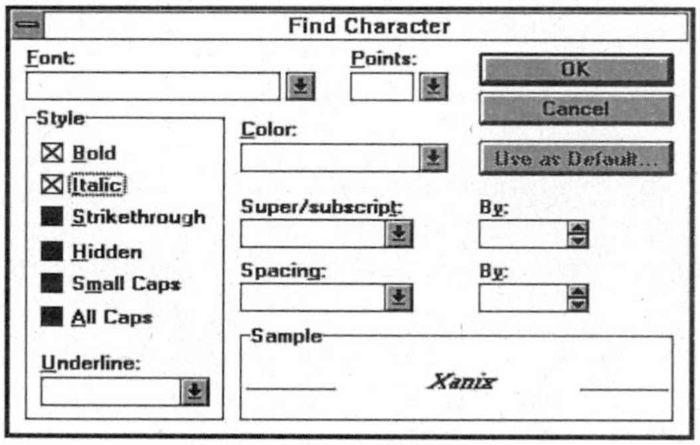

FIG. 9.4.

The Find Character dialog box.

To find paragraph formatting, choose the Para**g**raph button. The Find Paragraph dialog box appears. It looks the same as the Paragraph dialog box used for formatting paragraphs. Select the paragraph formatting options you want to find and choose OK or press Enter.

The font and formatting options you select are listed under the Fi**n**d What box.

4. To replace a font or formatting, select the Replace With box, and type the replacement text or leave the box blank to replace the contents of the Find What box with only a font or formatting.

5. To replace the contents of the Find What box with a font or character formatting, choose the Character button. The Replace Character dialog box appears. Select the replacement font or formatting options. Choose OK or press Enter.

   To replace the contents of the Find What box with paragraph formatting, select the Paragraph button. The Replace Paragraph dialog box appears (see fig. 9.5). Select the replacement paragraph formatting options and choose OK or press Enter.

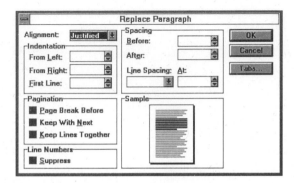

FIG. 9.5.

The Replace
Paragraph
dialog box.

The font and formatting options you select are listed under the Replace With box.

6. To find the next occurrence of the specified text, font, or formatting, choose Find Next.

   If you're replacing a font or formatting, choose Find Next to find the next occurrence and then choose Replace, or choose Replace All to find and replace all occurrences.

7. When the find or replace operation is complete, choose Cancel (or press Esc) to close the Find dialog box, or choose Close (or press Esc) to close the Replace dialog box.

Initially, check boxes are grayed and text boxes are blank, indicating that these fields are not involved in the search or replace operation. Clicking once on a check box option selects that option. Clicking a second time clears the option. In this case, the option is still involved in the search or replace operation, but you have specifically unselected that option, removing that format. Clicking a third time grays the option again so that the option is no longer involved in the search or replace operation.

If you want to remove boldface from all occurrences of a certain word, for example, type the word into the Find What box, choose the Character button, and click the Bold option to select it. Choose OK to return to the Replace dialog box and type the same word into the Replace With box. Choose the Character button and click the Bold check box twice to unselect this option. If you leave this box grayed, the formatting will not be removed.

The font and formatting selections you make for the Find What and the Replace With boxes remain in effect until you change them. In other words, they will be there the next time you open the Find or Replace dialog box. To remove all formatting options, select either Find What or Replace With and choose Clear.

> **CAUTION** You may want to always confirm the first occurrence of your search and replace operations before preceding with a global replace.

> **T I P** You can use the shortcut keys for formatting characters and paragraphs in the Edit Find and Edit Replace dialog boxes. To specify bold formatting, for example, press Ctrl+B. To specify a font, press Ctrl+F repeatedly, until the font you want is selected. See the reference card for a list of the shortcut keys.

The find and replace feature in Word for Windows is flexible, enabling you to replace text only regardless of formatting, both text and formatting, or just the formatting. You also can replace text with nothing (that is, delete specified text) or remove formatting. Table 9.1 outlines replacement options available when using the Find and Replace commands.

Replacing Styles

A style is a combination of several formatting commands. You may have a style called Title, for example, that includes the formatting commands for Times Roman font, 24-point size, centered, underlined, and bold. A style enables you to apply all these formats with a single command. (For more information on styles, see Chapter 11.) You can use Word for Windows' replace command to replace a format with a style or replace one style with another. When you replace formatting or a style with a style, all paragraphs formatted by the replacement style take on that style's formatting.

Table 9.1. Find and Replace Options

If you replace	With	You get
Text, format, or both	Text	New text, old format
Text	Format	Old text and format plus new format
Format or text and format	Format	Old text, new format
Text	Text and format	New text, old format, plus new format
Format or text and format	Text and format	New text, new format
Text	Nothing	Remove text
Format or text and format	Nothing	Remove text and format

The procedure to replace a format with a style or a style with a style works the same as the procedure described for replacing one format with another format. When you choose the **S**tyles button in the Replace dialog box, the Find Style or Replace Style dialog box displays all the defined styles (see fig. 9.6). When the style is selected in the **F**ind What Style or Replace with Style list, the formatting commands that make up the selected style appear below the list.

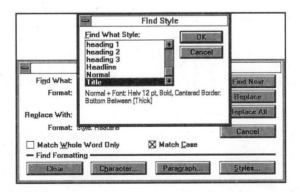

FIG. 9.6.

The Find Style dialog box.

T I P Make sure that the formatting or style name indicated under the Find What and Replace With boxes is correct. Each time you use the Find or Replace command, Word for Windows remembers the last words and formatting you searched for or replaced. Choose the Clear button in the dialog box to clear formatting selections.

Finding and Replacing Special Characters

Searching for and replacing text in your document is handy and easy. Sometimes, however, you want to search for and replace other things. By getting acquainted with a few special codes, you can learn how to find and replace many special characters, including a wild-card character (?), a tab mark, a paragraph mark, section marks, or a blank space. If you open a text (or ASCII) file with carriage returns at the end of every line, you can replace each of those paragraph marks with a space. Or, if you have a list that contains spaces instead of tabs, you can replace multiple spaces with tabs. Always be careful to confirm your changes at least once so that you don't inadvertently make an incorrect replacement.

Table 9.2 lists the codes that represent the special characters you can find and replace. To use these codes to find special characters, choose the Edit Find or Edit Replace command as usual, and type the appropriate code in either the Find What or the Replace With box. (Type the caret (^) character by holding down the Shift key and pressing 6.) Choose the Clear button if you do not want the formats to influence the action of the find or replace command.

If you want to find or replace special characters, you should display nonprinting characters, such as paragraph marks and tab marks. To display nonprinting characters, choose the Show/Hide button on the ribbon (the button on the far right) or choose the Tools Options command and select the All check box in the dialog box.

After you enter your text, and you're pretty sure that the words are right, you should do at least one last thing before you print your document: check the spelling. You can easily overlook spelling mistakes when you proofread your document, and you may find a word or two you spelled wrong.

Table 9.2. Codes for Special Characters

Code	Special Character
?	Any single character (Find only)
^?	Question mark
^w	White space (any space—one space, multiple spaces, tab spaces—bordered by characters) Find only.
^t	Tab
^p	Paragraph mark
^n	New line character
^d	Section mark or hard page break
^s	Nonbreaking space
^-	Optional hyphen
^~	Nonbreaking hyphen
^^	Caret
^1	Any graphic
^2	Footnote(1)
^3	Footnote separator
^5	Annotations
^19	Any field
^c	Clipboard contents (Replace only)
^0nnn	An ANSI character (where nnn is the ANSI number)
^m	Adds Search text to replacement text (Replace only). If you search for *Bill*, and replace with ^m *Smith*, all *Bills* are replaced with *Bill Smith*.

Checking Your Spelling

Word for Windows' spelling checker quickly pinpoints words in your document that don't match words in its dictionary, in the user dictionary, or in your own custom dictionary. When you aren't sure about a word, you can ask Word for Windows to suggest alternative spellings.

The program searches its dictionary for a match and offers you a list of other spellings. It can even suggest one as the most likely choice.

Word for Windows' spelling checker also looks for double words (the the), oddly capitalized words (mY), words that should be capitalized (california), and words that should be all capitals (ZIP). You also can set additional options in the Spelling dialog box.

Spell checking begins at the insertion point and works forward through your document. You can check spelling in a smaller area of text by first selecting that area (it can be as little as a single word) and then checking the spelling as usual.

T I P   A good spelling checker gives you the confidence of knowing that your work is accurate. But be careful. No spelling checker can tell you when you have misused words, perhaps typing *for* when you meant *four*, or *thought* when you meant *though*. A spelling checker is an important tool, but it cannot replace good, old-fashioned proof-reading.

Checking Your Document's Spelling

To check spelling in your document, follow these steps:

1. Select the word or section of your document you want to spell check. If nothing is selected, Word for Windows checks the entire document from the insertion point forward.

2. Choose the Tools Spelling command, or choose the Spelling button on the toolbar. (The Spelling button looks like an ABC with a checkmark.)

   Word for Windows scrolls through your document, matching each word against the main dictionary. The program selects words it does not recognize, and the Spelling dialog box appears. The un-recognized word is highlighted in the text and displayed in the Not In Dictionary box (see fig. 9.7). You can move the spelling dialog box if it is hiding the selected word.

3. Correct the misspelled word in the Change To text box, or select the correct word from the Suggestions list

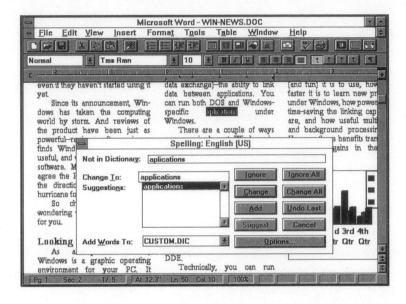

FIG. 9.7.

The Spelling
dialog box.

If the Always **S**uggest option is turned on and Word for Windows
can suggest an alternative spelling, that suggestion is displayed
in the Change **T**o box. Other possible words will appear in the
Suggestions list. If the Always Suggest option is turned off, the
selected word appears in the Change To text box. (For more information on using Always Suggest, see the section "Setting Spelling
Options" later in this chapter.)

If the Always **S**uggest option is turned off, the Suggestions list will
be empty. Choose the **S**uggest button to display a list of possible
words; then select the correct word from the list.

4. When the correct spelling appears in the Change **T**o box, choose
   the **C**hange button and the selected word changes to the spelling
   displayed in the Change **T**o box. Choose Change All to change all
   occurrences of the misspelled word in your document.

   or

   Choose **I**gnore to leave the word as is. Choose I**g**nore All to ignore
   all future occurrences of the word in your document.

   or

   If Word for Windows finds a word it thinks is misspelled and you
   want to add that word to the dictionary, choose the **A**dd button.
   The word is added to the selected dictionary displayed in the Add
   Words To box.

5. Word for Windows continues searching. Choose Cancel to discontinue the spell checking. You also can undo up to five of the previous corrections by choosing the **Undo Last** command.

6. A message dialog box displays when the spell checker reaches the end of the document or the end of the selection. If you are spell checking a word or a selected section, a dialog box asks whether you want to check the remainder of the document. Choose **Yes** or **No**.

If you started spell checking after the document beginning, when the end of the document is reached, you are asked whether you want to continue checking from the beginning of the document.

T I P   If you want to halt the spelling check to edit your document without closing the spelling check dialog box, drag the Spelling dialog box out of the way of where you want to edit, and then click in the document or press Ctrl+Tab to activate the document window. After editing your document, choose the **Start** button in the Spelling dialog box to proceed with spell checking at the point where you left off.

You can use wild-card characters such as * or ? when you are looking for the spelling of a word. In the Change **To** text box of the Spelling dialog box, type the word using either an * as a wild card for multiple unknown characters or the ? as a wild card for a single unknown character. If you are not sure whether the correct spelling is *exercise* or *exercize*, for example, type *exerci?e* in the Change **To** text box and choose the **Suggest** button. Word for Windows displays the correct spelling of the word.

Another way to access Word for Windows' spelling check feature is to press F7, the shortcut key. When you use this method, Word for Windows bypasses the Check Spelling dialog box and begins checking the spelling in the selected area or checks the selected word. If nothing is selected, Word for Windows checks the word following the insertion point.

You can undo all spelling changes made during a spell check. Choose the **Edit** Undo Spelling command immediately after you complete the spell checking.

Finding Double Words

When Word for Windows' spelling checker finds double words, the Not In Dictionary box changes to the Repeated Word box, and the repeated word is displayed. To delete the repeated word, leave the Change To box blank and choose the Delete button. Be sure to delete spaces that may be left.

Adding Words to a Dictionary

You can add words to a custom dictionary as part of the spell-checking process. When Word for Windows selects an unrecognized word, choose the dictionary to which you want to add the word from the Add Words To list and choose the Add button. Be careful—don't accidentally add misspelled words to the dictionary!

Setting Spelling Options

One of the buttons that appears in the Spelling dialog box is the Options button. Choosing the Options button enables you to use a non-English dictionary or to check spelling against a custom dictionary you create. (See the next section for information on creating a custom dictionary.)

Spell checking options can be set at any time. To set options while spell checking, choose the Options button. To set options before you spell check, follow these steps:

1. Choose the Tools Options command and select the Spelling Category. The Options dialog box for adjusting spelling options appears (see fig. 9.8).

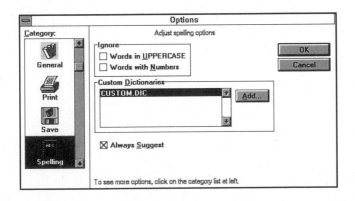

FIG. 9.8.

The Options dialog box with the Spelling Category selected.

2. Under Ignore, select the class of words you want Word for Windows to skip during every spell check, as follows:

Option	Function
Words in UPPERCASE	Ignores words in all uppercase letters
Words with Numbers	Ignores words that include numbers

3. Select from the Custom Dictionaries list the dictionaries you want open. Up to four custom dictionaries can be open. You may have many custom dictionaries available, but Word for Windows checks spelling against only open custom dictionaries.

4. Select the Always Suggest option if you want Word for Windows to always suggest corrections. Unselect this option if you don't always want suggestions (and if you want the spell checker to work faster).

5. Choose OK or press Enter.

Creating a Custom Dictionary

Each time you run the spell checker, it checks each word in your document against the words in the dictionary. Word for Windows' standard dictionary contains thousands of commonly used words, but certain words you use frequently may not be included—words common in your profession, for example, or your company's name, or the names of products your company sells. You can create custom dictionaries and specify that Word for Windows consult them each time you check your spelling. To learn how to open these dictionaries so that they're used when you check spelling, refer to the preceding section, "Setting Spelling Options." To learn how to add words to your custom dictionary, refer back to "Adding Words to a Dictionary."

To create a custom dictionary, follow these steps:

1. Choose the Tools Options command and select the Spelling Category.

2. Choose the Add button in the Custom Dictionaries section. A dialog box prompts you for the name of the dictionary file.

3. Type a name for the new dictionary ending with the extension DIC. Your dictionary is stored in the Word for Windows directory.

4. Choose OK or press Enter.

5. Choose OK or press Enter to close the Options dialog box.

> You can remove a word from a custom dictionary by opening the custom dictionary file (by default, Word for Windows saves it in your WINWORD directory). The file lists all dictionary entries alphabetically. Delete the words you no longer want, and save the file in "Text Only" format (don't change the file's name or location).
>
> **T I P**

Checking Your Grammar

When you are creating a document, you may be uncertain whether your sentence structure is grammatically correct. You may use the phrase *between you and I*, for example, when the grammatically correct phrase is *between you and me*. Word for Windows' grammar checker is used to spot grammatical errors and suggest how to correct the errors. The Grammar dialog box provides several choices for making changes.

If nothing is selected, Word for Windows checks the entire document beginning at the insertion point. If text is selected, only the selection is checked. A selection must contain at least one sentence.

By default, Word for Windows checks spelling and grammar. If you want to check only grammar, turn off the Spelling Errors option in the Grammar Category of the Options dialog box. (To learn how, see the upcoming section on "Selecting Grammar Rules.")

To check a document's grammar, follow these steps:

1. Choose the T**o**ols **G**rammar command.

   The Grammar dialog box appears when Word for Windows finds a sentence with a possible grammatical error or questionable style (see fig. 9.9). The grammatically questionable words appear in bold.

2. Select an option in the Grammar dialog box.

If possible, the S**u**ggestions box offers ideas on how you can correct the questionable sentence. You can update the sentence with a suggested correction by selecting the correction in the Suggestions box and choosing the **C**hange button. If the Change button is dimmed, the Grammar checker is unable to suggest a change. You can make a change directly in the document.

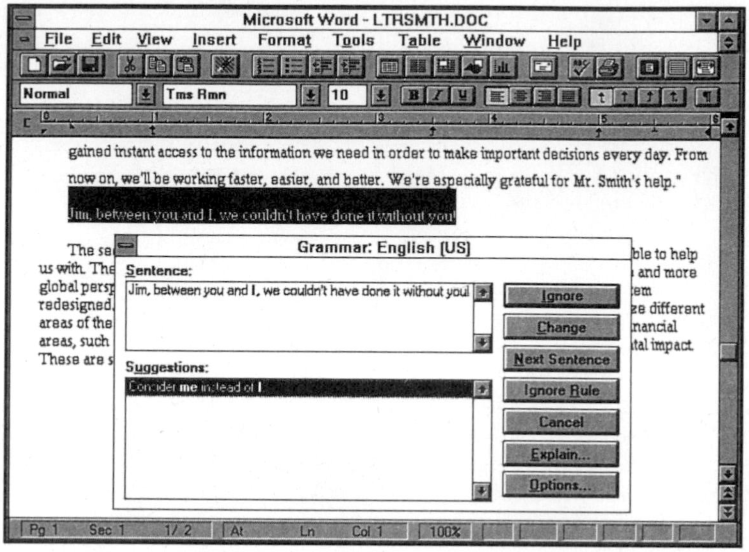

FIG. 9.9.

The Grammar
dialog box.

To temporarily leave the Grammar command to make a change in the document, choose the document window by clicking it or by pressing Ctrl+Tab. Edit the sentence in the document and choose the **S**tart button that appears in the Grammar dialog box to restart checking from the insertion point after you have edited your document.

Ignore the questioned word or phrase by choosing the **I**gnore button. To skip other similar occurrences breaking the same grammatical or style rule, choose the Ignore **R**ule button.

Leave the sentence unchanged and move to the next sentence by choosing the **N**ext Sentence button.

Request more information about the error by choosing the **E**xplain button. A dialog box appears describing the relevant grammatical or stylistic rule. After you read the information, press Esc to clear the dialog box and return to the Grammar dialog box.

Select different rules of grammar and style by choosing the **O**ptions button. A dialog box appears enabling you to select an option button for the rule group you want to observe for the remainder of the check. Choose the **Cu**stomize Settings button to select which rules you want to observe and which rules you want to disregard. Choose OK or press Enter twice to continue with the grammar check using the custom settings.

When the grammar checker reaches the end of the document, you see a message asking whether you want to continue checking from the beginning. Choose **Y**es to continue. Choose **N**o to end the grammar check. If the entire document or the selected section has been checked, you see a message indicating that the grammar check is completed. Choose OK or press Enter to return to your document.

If the Show **R**eadability Statistics After Proofing option is turned on, a dialog box displays the information about the document. (Readability is covered later in the section "Testing the Readability of a Document.") Choose OK or press Enter to return to your document.

Selecting Grammar Rules

You can choose the rules of style and grammar to be used during grammar checks. Depending on your audience, your style, and the material, you may want to follow some rules and disregard others. When you choose the **T**ools **O**ptions command and select the Grammar **C**ategory, you can choose from among three predefined rule groups (see fig. 9.10). The three groups are **S**trictly (All Rules), For **B**usiness Writing, and For **C**asual Writing. The **S**trictly rule group applies all grammar and style rules. The **B**usiness group applies fewer rules. The **C**asual group applies the least number of rules. You can customize rule groups by selecting or clearing grammar and style options.

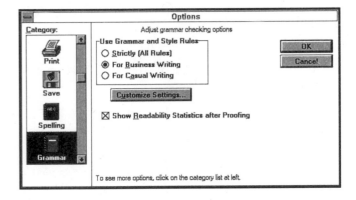

FIG. 9.10.

Options dialog box with the Grammar Category selected.

To customize a rule group, follow these steps:

1. Choose the **T**ools **O**ption command and select the Grammar **C**ategory. If you already started grammar checking, choose the **O**ptions button in the Grammar dialog box.

2. Select the rule group you want to change under the Use Grammar And Style Rules option group.

3. Choose the **C**ustomize Settings button. The Customize Grammar Settings dialog box appears (see fig. 9.11).

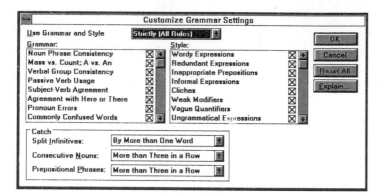

4. Select the rule check boxes for rules you want Word for Windows to observe. Clear check boxes for rules you want ignored.

5. Select from the pull-down lists in the Catch group how you want to control Split **I**nfinitives, Consecutive **N**ouns, and Prepositional **P**hrases.

6. Choose OK or press Enter.

Testing the Readability of a Document

Readability statistics measure how easy your writing is to read. Writing that is easier to read communicates more clearly. The Wall Street Journal, for example, writes at the eighth grade level, and Hemingway wrote at the sixth grade level. Writing need not be boring when it's readable. Hemingway used intriguing subject matter, active writing, colorful descriptions, and variable sentence lengths to make his writing interesting.

The Readability Statistics appear at the end of grammar checking when the option is on. If it is off, you can display Readability Statistics after you use the Grammar command by following these steps:

1. Choose the **T**ools **O**ptions command.

2. Select the Grammar **C**ategory.

3. Select the Show **R**eadability Statistics After Proofing check box.

4. Choose OK or press Enter.

Word for Windows' readability statistics are based on the Flesch-Kincaid index. This index assigns a reading ease score and grade level based on the average number of words per sentence and the average number of syllables per 100 words.

Using the Thesaurus

When you're not sure of the meaning of a word or when you think you're using a certain word too often, take advantage of Word for Windows' thesaurus. It defines selected words and offers alternative words (synonyms). For example, Word for Windows' synonyms for the word *information* include *intelligence*, *data*, and *facts*.

The thesaurus looks up one word at a time. If a word is selected or the insertion point is in a word, the thesaurus looks up that word; if the insertion point is outside a word, the thesaurus looks up the word before the insertion point.

To display a list of synonyms and definitions for a word in your document, follow these steps:

1. Select the word for which you want to locate a synonym.

2. Choose the **T**ools **T**hesaurus command or press Shift+F7. The Thesaurus dialog box appears (see fig. 9.12).

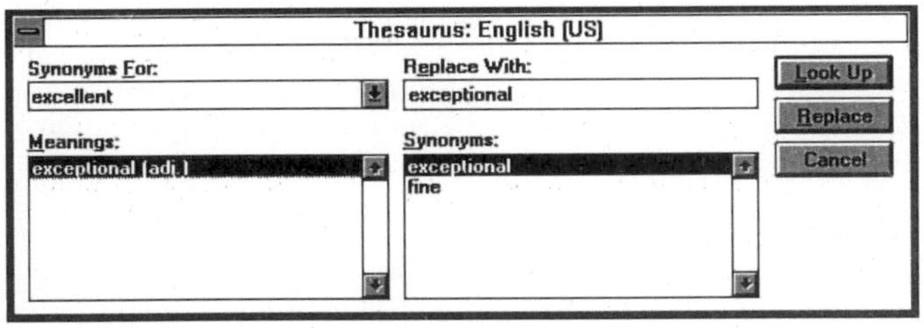

FIG. 9.12.

The Thesaurus dialog box.

The selected word is displayed in the Synonyms **F**or text box. The first meaning is displayed in the **R**eplace With text box and its definition appears in the **M**eanings box. The **S**ynonyms box lists synonyms.

3. You have several options at this point:

■ Select one of the synonyms from the **S**ynonyms list. (It moves into the **R**eplace With box.)

■ Select a different meaning from the **M**eanings list to display a new list of synonyms in the **S**ynonyms box, then select a word from this list.

■ If the words Related Words or Antonyms display in the Meanings list, select either to display the Related Words or Antonyms list box from which you can select.

■ Look up other words by selecting the word from the **M**eanings or **S**ynonyms list and choosing **L**ook Up. You also can type a word in the **R**eplace With text box and choose the **L**ook up button.

4. Choose the **R**eplace button to replace the selected word in the document with the word in the **R**eplace With box, or choose the Cancel button.

Proofing in Other Languages

If you're reading this book in English, most of your typing is probably in English. But your document may contain some text in Spanish, French, or some other language. You can select that text, assign to it a language other than English, and all the Word for Windows proofing tools—spell checker, hyphenation, thesaurus, and grammar checker—will use the other language dictionary you specify to proof that text.

Before the language command is available, you must purchase and install the appropriate language-proofing tools for the language you will be using. If you want to check the spelling of French text, for example, you must install a French dictionary. Contact Microsoft Corporation or other vendors for information on the many language-proofing tools available.

To proof text in another language, follow these steps:

1. Select the text written in another language.

2. Choose the Forma**t** **L**anguage command to display the Format Language dialog box.

3. Select the language from the **M**ark Selected Text As list. To change the language for all the text you proof, choose the **U**se As Default button.

   You can select "no proofing" if you want the proofing tools to skip the selected text. This feature is useful for technical material containing terms not listed in any of the standard spelling dictionaries.

4. Choose OK or press Enter.

Using the Revision Marks Feature

Revising a document is often a job shared by two people or even by a group of people. A contract or proposal may be written by one person, for example, but then reviewed by others. Revision marks show the originator where the document has been changed.

Adding revision marks is simple. Before making revisions, the editor chooses the Tools Revision Marks command and selects the Mark Revisions option. Revisions to the document then are marked according to the type of mark selected. For example, new text may be underlined and deleted text lined through (see fig. 9.13).

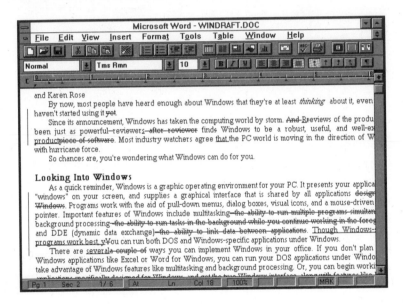

FIG. 9.13.

An example of text marked with revisions.

When the writer opens the edited file, the editorial revisions are obvious. Revisions can be accepted, discarded, or evaluated.

Another way to check revisions is to compare two versions of the same file. All the editor's changes are marked according to the current selections in the Mark Revisions dialog box.

Marking Revisions

Revision bars appear in the margin adjacent to any lines containing altered text. Revision marks indicate the actual text that has changed— new text is emphasized and deleted text has a line through it. You can turn on revision bars and revision marks, or you can turn on one or the other.

To mark revisions in your document, follow these steps:

1. Choose the Tools Revision Marks command. The Revision Marks dialog box appears (see fig. 9.14).

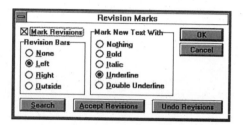

2. Select Mark Revisions.

3. Select an option from the Revision Bars list as listed in table 9.3.

4. Select an option from the Mark New Text With list as shown in table 9.3.

5. Choose OK.

Table 9.3. Revision Marks Dialog Box Options

Revision Bars Option	Effect
None	No revision bars in the margin
Left	Revision bars in the left margin
Right	Revision bars in the right margin
Outside	Revision bars in the outside margins of the printed pages and in the left margins on-screen

Mark New Text With Option	Effect
Nothing	No revision marks for new text.
Bold	Boldfaces new text
Italic	Italicizes new text
Underline	Underlines new text
Double Underline	Double-underlines new text

Deleted text always has a line through it.

To turn off revision marking, select the **T**ools Revision Mar**k**s command and unselect the **M**ark Revisions check box.

As you insert text into a document with Revision **M**arks turned on, new text is marked according to the Mark New Text With option you select (for example, new text may be underlined). Deleted text has a line through it. If you delete new text—text marked with an underline, for example—the deleted new text simply disappears. Only existing text—not new text—appears with a line through it.

Accepting All Revisions

Word for Windows makes accepting revisions easy. To accept all revisions, choose the **T**ools Revision Mar**k**s command and select **A**ccept Revisions. When prompted to accept the revisions, answer Yes, and then choose OK. All the deleted text disappears, the new text is incorporated, and the revision marks are removed.

You cannot undo this command. As a safety measure, save your file with a new name before you accept all revisions. You then have a copy of the revised edition for later reference or comparison.

Discarding All Revisions

To discard all revisions, choose the **T**ools Revision Mar**k**s command and select Undo Re**v**isions. When prompted to undo all revisions, answer Yes, and then choose OK.

Be careful. Save your file before undoing revisions. You cannot use **E**dit **U**ndo to undo this command.

Accepting or Rejecting Individual Revisions

In most cases, you will find that some of the revisions made to your document are acceptable and some are not. You can search through your revised document revision-by-revision, choosing whether to accept or reject each change.

To accept or reject individual revisions, follow these steps:

1. Choose the Tools Revision Marks command.

2. Select Search.

3. When the first revision is highlighted, choose Accept Revisions to accept it or Undo Revisions to reject it.

4. Select Search to locate the next revision.

Another way to locate revisions is to choose the Edit Find command, select the Find What text box and press Ctrl+N to search for new text. Choose OK. You can press the repeat search keys, Shift+F4, to repeat the search quickly.

Hyphenating Words

Hyphenation joins words used in combination or splits long words so that they can break to the next line. Splitting long words with hyphens reduces the ragged appearance of your right margin or the amount of white space between words in justified text. Word for Windows has three types of hyphens: optional, regular, and nonbreaking.

Inserting Regular and Nonbreaking Hyphens

Use regular hyphens when you want to control where a hyphen is inserted or to join two words used in combination. A regular hyphen breaks the word, when necessary, so that it can wrap at the end of a line. Use a nonbreaking (or *hard*) hyphen to join words or acronyms that you do not want broken at the end of a line. (Optional hyphens are discussed in the next section.) Table 9.4 summarizes the three types of hyphens available in Word for Windows.

Table 9.4. Types of Hyphens

Hyphen	Keystroke	Appearance	Function
Regular	Hyphen	-	For words that are always hyphenated and can be split at line breaks.
Optional	Ctrl+Hyphen	¬	To split words at the end of a line. Not displayed unless the word appears at the end of the line.
Nonbreaking	Ctrl+Shift+Hyphen	—	For words that are always hyphenated and you do not want to split at the end of the line.

Inserting Optional Hyphens throughout a Document

The Tools Hyphenation command automatically inserts optional hyphens throughout your document. It identifies the first word in each line and, if the word can be hyphenated, Word for Windows inserts an optional hyphen. The first part of the word then is moved to the end of the preceding line of text. Optional hyphens are printed in your document only if they are needed to break a word at the end of a line.

You normally don't see optional hyphens unless they are used to break a word. To see all optional hyphens, choose the Tools Options command, select the View Category, and select either the All or Optional Hyphens check boxes in the Nonprinting Characters group. Optional hyphens appear as a dash with a crook.

Hyphenation should be used after you finish writing, editing, and proofreading your document. To hyphenate a document, follow these steps:

1. Select the text you want hyphenated, or move the insertion point to the top of the document. The Hyphenation command hyphenates text from the insertion point to the end of the document if no text is selected.

2. Choose the **T**ools **H**yphenation command. The Hyphenation dialog box appears (see fig. 9.15).

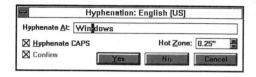

FIG. 9.15.

The Hyphenation dialog box.

3. Select from among the options in the dialog box:

Option	Function
Confirm	Confirms each hyphenation.
Hyphenate CAPS	Hyphenates words in all caps.
Hot **Z**one	The space at the right margin within which a word can be hyphenated. To increase the number of hyphenated words and decrease right-margin raggedness, lower the number in the Hot **Z**one box. Increase the number for less hyphenation with a more ragged right margin.

4. Choose OK or press Enter.

5. If you select the **C**onfirm option, Word for Windows stops at each word to be hyphenated, displaying the word in the Hyphenate **At** text box. A vertical gray line in the word indicates the margin. For each word you can do the following:

   ■ Choose the **Y**es button to hyphenate the word at the suggested location.

   ■ To choose a different hyphenation point, move the insertion point in the word displayed in the Hyphenate **At** box to a new location and choose the **Y**es button. The word is hyphenated at the insertion point.

   ■ Choose the **N**o button if you do not want the word to be hyphenated.

   If you did not start at the beginning of the document, a dialog box appears asking if you want to continue from the beginning of the document.

6. Choose **Y**es to continue the hyphenation process or Cancel to stop. When a dialog box appears telling you hyphenation is complete, choose OK.

Sorting Text

Word for Windows' Sorting command is a quick and easy method for arranging selected data in alphabetical or numerical order. Data can be sorted in ascending (smallest to largest) or descending order (largest to smallest). The Sorting command can be used to sort the records in a print merge file. If you are doing a bulk mailing, for example, you can sort the records by ZIP code before carrying out the print merge operation.

To sort selected text, follow these steps:

1. Select the text to be sorted.

2. Choose the **T**ools Sor**t**ing command. The Sorting dialog box appears (see fig. 9.16).

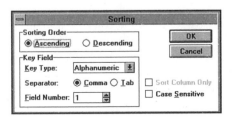

FIG. 9.16.

The Sorting dialog box.

3. Select **A**scending or **D**escending to specify the sorting order.

4. Select from the **K**ey Type list the type of characters being sorted. The default selection is Alphanumeric. The other alternatives are Numeric or Date.

5. Select Separator type **C**omma if the selected data is separated by commas or select **T**ab if data is separated by tabs.

6. Select the Case **S**ensitive check box to list capitalized words before lowercase words.

7. Enter the Field Number you want to sort on in the Field Number box. Each segment of text separated by a comma or a tab is considered a field. The first field is 1.

8. Choose OK or press Enter.

Refer to Chapter 12 to learn about sorting rows and columns in tables.

Comparing Two Versions of a Document

Another way to check revisions is to compare the current document to an earlier version. When you compare two documents, Word for Windows applies revision marks to your current document wherever it differs from the earlier version. To compare two versions of a document, open the document in which you want to see revisions. Choose the Tools Compare Versions command, and in the File Name box select a file to which you want to compare the current file. Choose OK or press Enter. Word for Windows compares the two documents, and based on options selected in the Revision Marks dialog box, marks any revisions that appear in the current document.

From Here . . .

This chapter has taught you the basics of editing and proofing a document using Word for Windows' built-in features. You learned how to find and replace text, special characters, formatting, and styles in your document. You also learned how to check spelling, add supplemental dictionaries to the spelling checker, use the grammar checker, and use the thesaurus to find alternative words. You were introduced to glossary entries, pagination, and inserting manual page breaks. Additionally, you learned how to mark, accept, and reject revisions to a document and you learned how to compare versions of a document.

To learn about how you can apply hyphenation to a layout with columns, see Chapter 13. To find out more about how you can use the tools described in this chapter with desktop publishing projects, see Chapter 28. To learn how to use other tools Word for Windows included in the Tools menu, refer to Chapter 6 for Bullets and Numbering; Chapter 19 for Creating Envelopes; Chapter 31 for macros, and Chapter 29 for customization options.

Previewing and Printing a Document

I n the early days of word processing, printing was pretty simple but time consuming. You chose a print command, sent the job to your dot-matrix printer, and got the printed pages. Previewing pages—that is, seeing on-screen what your document will look like when printed—was impossible.

Fortunately, word processing has matured. Although printing with Word for Windows can be as simple as opening a document, choosing a print command, and starting the printing operation, Word for Windows gives you many additional options. You can preview your document and change its margin in the preview. You can print all or part of an open document. You can print a draft or a final version. You can print normal copy and graphics or print hidden text and field codes. You also can print multiple documents without opening them.

Selecting a Printer

Microsoft Windows is the common denominator that makes printing with Word for Windows easy. Any printer you install to use with Windows can be used with Word for Windows.

Word for Windows prints on whichever installed printer currently is selected. You can find out which printer is selected by choosing the File Print command and looking at the top of the Print dialog box, as shown in figure 10.1.

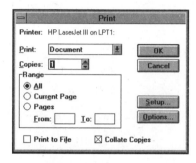

FIG. 10.1.

The Print dialog box.

To select a printer, use the File Print Setup command. If you use only one printer, select that printer the first time you print a document with Word for Windows. After you print, your printer stays selected. If you switch between printers, you must select a printer each time you change printers.

When you select a printer, Word for Windows shows you a list of printers to select from in the Print Setup dialog box (see fig. 10.2). This list includes all printers installed for use with Windows. If the printer you want to use is not on the list, you must install it in Windows. To install a printer, see the following section, "Installing a Printer in Windows."

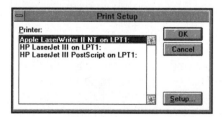

FIG. 10.2.

Choosing a printer from the list of installed printers.

To select a printer, follow these steps:

1. Choose the File Print Setup command.

2. Select a printer from the list in the Print Setup dialog box.

3. Choose OK or press Enter.

The next time you choose the **F**ile **P**rint command, you see your selected printer listed at the top of the Print dialog box.

Setting Up Your Printer

Windows manages most details of setting up a printer. Three tasks,
however, are left up to you: selecting the printer you want to use in
Word for Windows, installing the printers you want to use in Windows,
and changing the printer setup for special printing needs.

Installing a Printer in Windows

Selecting a printer in Word for Windows is simple—if the printer is
listed in the Print Set**u**p dialog box. If your printer is not listed, Windows does not have that printer installed. You can install a printer in
Windows from within Word for Windows.

To install a printer in Windows, follow these steps:

1. Choose the Control menu (Alt+space bar); then choose **Ru**n.

2. Select the Control **P**anel option; then choose OK.

3. Choose the Printers icon from the Control Panel dialog box by
   double-clicking on the icon or by pressing the arrow keys until
   selected, and then pressing Enter (see fig. 10.3 for the Windows
   3.0 Control Panel). This action brings up the Printers dialog box.
   The control panel is the same one you access from the Main
   Group in the Program Manager.

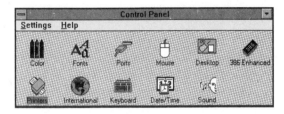

FIG. 10.3.

The Control
Panel.

4. Choose the **A**dd Printer button. The Printers dialog box expands
   to reveal a list of available printer drivers at the bottom, as shown
   in figure 10.4 (for Windows 3.0).

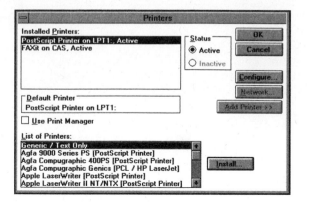

FIG. 10.4.

Available printers
listed in the
Printers dialog
box.

5. Select the printer you want to install from the **List of Printers** list, and then choose the **Install** button.

   If your printer is not listed and you receive a printer driver—a DRV file—from the printer manufacturer, select Unlisted Printer at the end of the list. If your printer is not listed and you do not have a driver, you may be able to use the driver of a compatible printer model or you can select the Generic/Text Only driver found at the top of the list. This driver does not support special fonts or graphics.

   A dialog box prompts you to insert one of the original Windows installation disks or the disk issued by the printer manufacturer. (Drive A is shown as the default, but you can enter another drive letter.)

6. Insert the disk, and then choose OK.

   If Windows does not find the driver on the disk, the dialog box reappears. Insert a different disk from the one requested and choose OK again. The printer driver may be on one of the other Windows installation disks.

7. Choose the **C**onnect button.

8. Select the port you want for that printer; then choose OK.

   If another printer is connected to the port you want to use, change its connection to NONE. Alternatively, you can change the printer to inactive status by selecting that printer and choosing the **I**nactive option in the Status box.

9. Choose the **S**etup button. The setup dialog box appears (the setup dialog box varies from one printer to another).

10. Select the settings you use most frequently, such as printing in portrait (vertically) or landscape (sideways), the resolution, paper source, printer memory, and font cartridges. Choose OK or press Enter.

    A single printer driver program often is used for a whole family of printers. In that event, you must select your specific printer model from a list box. If your printer model is not listed, select a compatible printer driver.

11. Choose OK again to complete the setup operation.

12. Choose **S**ettings E**x**it to close the Control Panel.

Using Special Print Setups

For the most part, after you install a printer in Windows, Word for Windows completes the rest of the process of setting up the printer. Because Word for Windows makes certain assumptions, you do not have to choose those options. For a laser printer, Word for Windows assumes that you are printing in portrait orientation on standard-size paper. You may want to print in landscape (horizontal) orientation, however, or on legal-size paper; you may want a different graphic resolution; or you may want to scale your print to be smaller or larger than normal. You can make these changes by using the **F**ile **P**rint Setup command in Word for Windows.

If you use a laser printer, you may need to specify which font cartridge to use and how much memory is in the printer. These settings affect the capabilities of your printer, so do not neglect to set them. You can change many aspects of your printer setup, depending on what type of printer you have.

The setup dialog boxes may appear differently, depending on which printer you have selected; the concepts and selections still are appropriate, whichever version you use.

T I P

To change the printer setup, follow these steps:

1. Choose the **F**ile **P**rint Setup command. The Print Setup dialog box appears (see fig. 10.5).

2. Select the printer to set up.

3. Choose the **S**etup button.

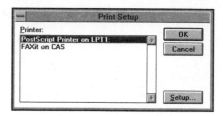

FIG. 10.5.

The Print Setup
dialog box.

4. Make the appropriate choices from the Setup dialog box, and then
    choose OK or press Enter. When you choose **S**etup, the choices
    you see listed in the window depend on the printer you are using.
    Figure 10.6 shows the Setup dialog box for a PostScript printer;
    figure 10.7 shows the Setup dialog box for a Hewlett-Packard
    LaserJet Series III printer.

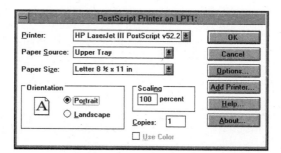

FIG. 10.6.

The Setup dialog
box for a
PostScript printer.

FIG. 10.7.

The Setup dialog
box for a
Hewlett-Packard
LaserJet Series III.

T I P

Many laser printers access additional fonts through cartridges inserted into the printer. You can select two cartridges simultaneously from the Cartridges list box (when you set up an HP LaserJet capable of using two cartridges). If you use a mouse, select each cartridge with a click. If you use the keyboard, Press Tab to move to the Cartridges list and press the up- or down-arrow key until the focus is on the cartridge you want. Press the space bar to select that cartridge. Press the up- or down-arrow key to move the focus to the second cartridge and again press the space bar, which selects or deselects cartridges from the list. Remember to turn your printer off and back on after replacing cartridges.

T I P

You can change certain print options—such as document size and paper source—in the Print Setup dialog box and the Page Setup dialog box. The File Print Setup command with the Setup button displays the Print Setup dialog box to set your global default preferences. The Format Page Setup command displays the Page Setup dialog box. The Size and Orientation and Paper Source settings in this box affect only the current document; these settings override the defaults for this specific document.

Matching Format and Fonts to the Printer Capabilities

A significant advantage to using Windows applications is that you can see on-screen how your document prints. If you use incorrect settings, however, you can format a document or use fonts on-screen that your printer cannot produce. The result is a printout that has little resemblance to the on-screen document.

To ensure that your document's on-screen fonts and formatting match your printer's capabilities, follow these steps:

1. Choose the View Normal command.

2. Choose the Tools Options command.

The Options dialog box appears, showing different Categories of Options in the list at the left (see fig. 10.8).

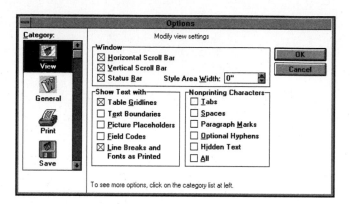

FIG. 10.8.

The View Category in the Options dialog box.

3. Choose the **View** icon from the Category list.

4. Select the **Line** Breaks and Fonts as Printed check box to ensure that what you see is what prints.

5. Choose OK or press Enter.

6. Return to the view you want to work in.

T I P   To learn more about how Word for Windows works with fonts, about TrueType, and about font management, read Appendix C.

Previewing Pages before Printing

Word for Windows offers you two alternatives for viewing your document before you print. These alternatives are the page layout view or Print Preview.

The advantages of using the page layout view to preview your printing follow:

■ You can scale your view using the **View Zoom** command.

- You can edit and format in the document.

- You can frame and then drag text or graphics to new locations and see the body copy wrap around.

- You see formatting, graphics, charts, tables, and columns exactly as they will print.

The advantages to using the Print Preview mode follow:

- You can display facing pages so that you can preview the appearance of binding space, headers, and footers on facing pages.

- You can drag boundaries and page breaks to new locations.

The major disadvantages of the Print Preview mode are that you cannot scale the miniature page (which cannot be read) or edit or format in the page.

Using Page Layout View

To view the document as it will print, use the page layout view, as follows:

1. Open the document you want to preview.

2. Choose the **View P**age Layout command (if the command is not selected already.)

3. Choose the **View Z**oom command.

    The Zoom dialog box shown in figure 10.9 enables you to specify the size of the document you want to preview.

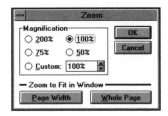

FIG. 10.9.

Specify the percentage of the document's magnification with the Zoom dialog box.

4. Choose the **P**age Width button to zoom the page so that its boundaries touch the sides of the windows. This view displays everything in its place and is a large enough view to make editing easy, but you cannot see the whole page at once.

    or

Choose the **W**hole Page button to zoom the page so that the entire page shows. With this view, you can easily see the proportions and layout of the page, but editing is difficult because you cannot read the text.

5. Choose OK or press Enter.

After you finish previewing, return to the View **Z**oom command or the zoom tool in the toolbar and restore the view to a size that is comfortable to work in.

Using Print Preview Mode

The other method of seeing how your document prints is to use the Print Preview mode. To see the entire document in Print Preview mode, follow these steps:

1. Open the document you want to preview.

2. Choose the **F**ile Print Preview command. You see a screen like the one in figure 10.10.

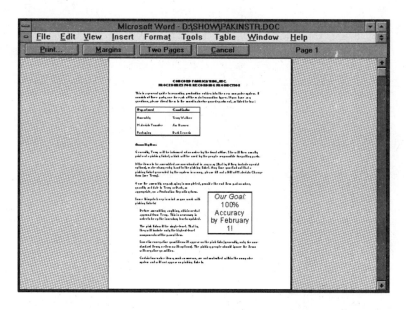

FIG. 10.10.

The Print Preview screen.

If your document is more than a page long, you can view more pages by clicking the arrow or gray area in the scroll bar or pressing the PgUp or PgDn keys to view another page.

In the Print Preview screen, you cannot edit the text. You can, however, change margins and reposition headers and footers. You also can save or print your document.

Using the Preview Icon Bar

Across the top of the Preview screen is a button bar. The buttons on the bar can be used for the actions listed in table 10.1.

Table 10.1. Preview Screen Buttons

Button	Effect
Print	Displays the Print dialog box, from which you can print your document, with the usual printing options.
Margins	Displays dotted lines showing margins, page breaks, and header and footer margins. You can move any formatting margins by dragging them with the mouse pointer or by pressing Tab to select them and then pressing the arrow keys to move them. After moving the margins, click outside the document to update the screen or choose the Margins button again to hide the margins and update the screen.
One Page/ Two Pages	Toggles between displaying one or two pages at once. This option is useful for seeing how even and odd headers and footers appear or how even and odd pages balance their text and margins.
Cancel or Close	Returns to your document. (Cancel appears before you make changes to your document; Close appears after.)

The button bar also provides information. To the right of the Cancel/ Close button is an indicator telling you what page(s) and section(s) of your document you now are viewing. When you move a margin, the indicator displays the coordinates of your margin.

Printing from Print Preview

You can print all or part of your document from the Print Preview screen. Choosing the Print command gives you the normal Print dialog box.

To print from Print Preview, follow these steps:

1. Choose the **P**rint button on the Print Preview icon bar. If you are using the keyboard, press P.

2. Make the usual printing selections in the dialog box.

3. Choose OK or press Enter.

Formatting Margins in Preview

While in Print Preview mode, you can display and move margins and page breaks. When you display your document's margins, you see dotted lines surrounding all headers, footers, margins, and page breaks. You can move any margin to a different place on the same page by using the mouse or the keyboard.

To display, select, and move margins, follow these steps:

1. Choose the **M**argins button from the Print Preview icon bar. Click the button or press M.

2. Press Tab repeatedly to select different margins or click the margin you want to select.

3. Press the arrow keys to move selected margins, or drag the margin you want to move. If you use the keyboard, press Enter when the margin reaches the desired position.

4. Choose the **M**argins button again to update the screen, or click on the background somewhere outside the page.

If you don't have a mouse, you can change margins only on the left page in two-page view. Pressing PgDn, however, moves the former right-hand page over to the left side, where you can work with the page. Mouse users can select either page at any time with a click.

Viewing One or Two Pages

You can view on-screen up to two pages at once. Select One P**a**ge to view a single page; select Two P**a**ges to view two pages. To choose the button, click it or press A. Figure 10.11 shows a view with two pages of a newsletter. All other selections in the icon bar work as usual.

Making Menu Edits in Preview

You can use certain menu commands while you are in the print preview mode. Table 10.2 lists these commands.

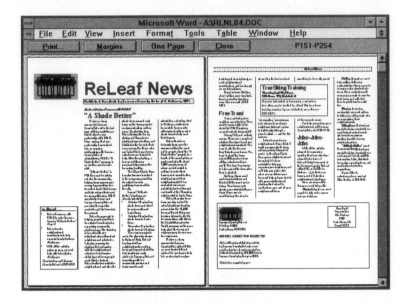

FIG. 10.11.

Print Preview
enables you to
see left and right
pages.

Table 10.2. Menu Commands Available in Print Preview Mode

Menu	Commands
File	**C**lose, **S**ave, Save **A**s, Sav**e** All, Print Preview (to return to document), **P**rint, E**x**it
View	**N**ormal, **O**utline, **P**age Layout, **D**raft (all return you to document)
Forma**t**	**P**age Set**u**p
T**o**ols	Rep**a**ginate Now, **R**ecord Macro
Help	All commands

Making Keyboard Edits in Preview

Table 10.3 lists the keys and key combinations of print preview mode.

Making Mouse Edits in Preview

When Margins are turned on, you can reposition margins on the page.
To update the page to reflect your new page layout, select **M**argins
from the icon bar, or click outside the page. If you need to edit text and

move graphics, you may want to choose the View **P**age Layout command and work in layout view (described in "Using Page Layout View," earlier in this chapter).

Table 10.3. Print Preview Keys

Key	Function
Alt+letter key	Activates any available menu command
Tab	Selects margins and objects when **Margins** is turned on—repeatedly pressing Tab rotates through margins and objects, selecting one after another
Enter	Updates changed margins
Shift+Tab	Moves backward through margins
Arrow keys	Moves selected margin
PgUp, PgDn	Turns to different page
P	Selects Print button from button bar
M	Selects Margins button from button bar
A	Selects One Page or Two Pages button from button bar
C or Esc	Cancels or closes Print Preview screen

Canceling or Closing the Print Preview Screen

To return to your editable document, select **C**ancel or **C**lose from the icon bar. (The button reads **C**ancel if you have not made any changes to your document, **C**lose if you have.)

Printing the Current Document

The simplest way to print is to open a document and choose the **F**ile **P**rint command. By default, Word for Windows prints one copy of all pages of the currently open document on the currently selected printer without printing hidden text.

To print one copy of a document, follow these steps:

1. Open the document you want to print.

2. Choose the **F**ile **P**rint command, click the Printer button in the toolbar, or press Ctrl+Shift+F12.

3. Choose OK or press Enter.

To cancel printing while the Print dialog box is displayed, press Esc or click the Cancel button. (The status bar at the bottom of the screen displays a message telling you when you can cancel the print job.) If the Print dialog box is no longer displayed and you are using the Windows Print Manager, the complete print job may already have been sent to the Print Manager. In this case, you must press Ctrl+Esc to display the Task List, activate the Print Manager, and stop your print job. If you are not using the Print Manager and the Print dialog box is no longer displayed, the print job already may have been sent to the printer.

Printing Multiple Copies

With Word for Windows' Print dialog box, you can print more than one copy of your document. In fact, you can print 32,767 copies of your document (but you may want to plan a trip to Hawaii while all those copies print). By default, Word for Windows collates the copies—a handy feature for long documents. Figure 10.12 shows the settings for printing three copies of pages 1 through 3 of your document.

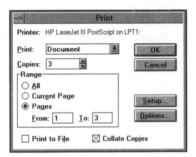

FIG. 10.12.

Printing multiple pages or a range of pages.

To print multiple copies of your document, follow these steps:

1. Open the document you want to print.

2. Choose the **File Print** command or press Ctrl+Shift+F12.

3. Select the **C**opies box in the Print dialog box and enter the number of copies you want to print.

4. Choose OK or press Enter.

If print time is important, you can turn off the Collate Copies option at the bottom of the dialog box. This step enables Word for Windows to run multiple documents through the printer faster. You pay for this later, however, when you have to recollate all the copies by hand.

Printing Part of a Document

Word for Windows provides two ways to print part of a document. You can select the portion of your document you want to print and then issue the print command. You also can print a specific range of pages.

Printing a selected area is handy when you want to print a section of a larger document but don't know on which page or pages the section is located.

To print a selected area of text, follow these steps:

1. Select the text to print.

2. Choose the **File P**rint command or press Ctrl+Shift+F12.

3. Select the Range Se**l**ection option.

4. Choose OK or press Enter.

If you know exactly which pages you want to print, you can print a range of pages. Suppose that you make changes to the first three pages of a long document. In that case, you may want to print from pages 1 through 3.

To print a specific range of pages, follow these steps:

1. Choose the **File P**rint command or press Ctrl+Shift+F12.

2. Select the Pages **F**rom option and type the starting page number.

3. Select the Pages **T**o option and type the ending page number.

4. Choose OK or press Enter.

Printing Different Types of Document Information

Word for Windows documents contain associated information such as summary information, glossaries, styles, and hidden text. You can choose to print this information with the document or separately. The first method describes how to print ancillary information separately. The second method describes how to print information with the document.

Instead of printing the text, you may want to print non-displaying text associated with your document (such as annotations), or you may want to print associated files (such as glossaries). Word for Windows gives you the options of printing the following types of information:

- Document
- Summary information
- Annotations
- Styles
- Glossaries
- Key assignments

As shown in figure 10.13, these printing choices are included in a pull-down list in the Print dialog box. If you select Annotations in the **Print** list box, for example, Word for Windows prints a list of the annotations associated with your document. (You can use this option to see a list of the annotations a reviewer has made to your document.)

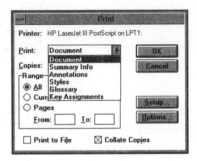

FIG. 10.13.

Selecting printing options from the Print list.

To print any special type of information, follow these steps:

1. Choose the **File Print** command or press Ctrl+Shift+F12.

2. Select the option in the **Print** pull-down list (see table 10.4).

3. Choose OK or press Enter.

Alternatively, you may want to print ancillary document information at the same time that your document prints. Word for Windows enables you to include the following hidden attributes as part of your printed document:

- Summary information
- Field codes
- Annotations
- Hidden text

Alternatively, you can print separate lists of some types of hidden information. See "Printing Different Types of Document Information" earlier in this chapter.

Table 10.4. Print List Box Options

Option	Effect
Document	Prints the document
Summary Info	Prints a summary of information about the document, including author, subject, print date, and number of pages, words, and characters
Annotations	Prints a list of annotations reviewers have attached to your document, with page number headings indicating where each annotation occurs
Styles	Prints the current document's style sheet (opens a template to print its style sheet)
Glossary	Prints a list of glossary entry names and contents, in alphabetical order
Key Assignments	Prints a keyboard reference sheet

To print any of these special types of information, follow these steps:

1. Choose the **F**ile **P**rint command.
2. Choose the **O**ptions button.
3. Select one or more of the options given in table 10.5.
4. Choose OK or press Enter to close the Options dialog box.
5. Choose OK or press Enter to print the selected items.

Table 10.5. Special Printing Options

Option	Effect
Summary Info	Prints summary of information about document—including author, subject, print date, and number of pages, words, and characters—on separate pages at end of document
Field Codes	Prints field codes rather than their results
Annotations	Prints list of annotations at end of document
Hidden Text	Prints any hidden text, such as table of contents entries, where text appears in document

Controlling Printing Options

Word for Windows offers you many printing options. You can print the pages in reverse order or save time by printing a draft copy. You can print text that usually is hidden, separately or as part of your document. You can update fields as you print, or you can print from paper in a specified bin if your printer has more than one paper source.

To access these printing options, you must choose the **O**ptions button in the Print dialog box. Follow these steps:

1. Choose the **File P**rint command or press Ctrl+Shift+F12.

2. Choose the **O**ptions button. The Options dialog box appears (see fig. 10.14).

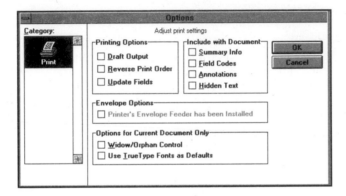

FIG. 10.14.

The Print Options.

The following sections describe the available options.

Printing Pages in Reverse Order

Some printers, such as Hewlett-Packard LaserJets, have a collator that produces printed pages stacked in the correct order. Other printers, such as the Apple LaserWriter and LaserWriter Plus, stack pages with the last page on top. If your printer stacks with the last page on top, you may want to select the **R**everse Print Order option to stack your pages in the correct order.

To print in reverse order, choose the **File P**rint command, select **O**ptions, and then select **R**everse Print Order. Choose OK or press Enter. You can print all or part of the document in reverse order.

Printing a Draft

Sometimes you need a quick, plain printed copy of your document. Perhaps someone else must edit the copy, or you want to take the copy home from work to review. For a quick, unadorned print, choose a draft copy. A draft prints quickly, without formatting. Enhanced characters are underlined rather than in boldface or italic, and graphics print as empty boxes. (The exact result of a draft print depends on your printer; for example, not all printers can print underlining.)

To print a draft copy of your document, choose the File Print command, select Options, and then select the Draft Output check box. Choose OK or press Enter.

Updating Fields

Word for Windows files can include field codes that instruct Word for Windows to insert special information into the document. A date field, for example, inserts the current date when the document is printed. But some fields may not be updated during the printing process. To update those fields when you print, you must choose a special command. In most cases you want this option turned on.

To update fields when you print, choose the File Print command, select Options, and then select Update Fields. Choose OK or press Enter.

To learn more about fields and how they are updated, refer to Chapter 18.

Printing from a Different Paper Source

If your printer has multiple bins or can accommodate manually fed paper or envelopes, you can specify the paper source with the Format Page Setup command. (This option is explained in Chapter 8.)

T I P On many single-bin laser printers, such as the HP LaserJet Series II, you can slide your letterhead into the manual tray as far as the letterhead goes and leave your bond paper in the paper bin. When you choose OK from the Print dialog box, the letterhead is pulled in first and the bond pulled in for following sheets. On printers like the HP LaserJet Series II, therefore, you do not need to go through a series of steps. Just print.

Printing Multiple Unopened Documents

Occasionally, you may want to print an unopened document or several documents simultaneously. The Find File command in the File menu enables you to open and print several documents at once or search for documents whose names have characteristics you specify.

To print one (or more) unopened documents, follow these steps:

1. Choose the Find File command from the File menu.

2. Select the file or files to print.

3. Choose the Print button.

4. Select any print options.

5. Choose OK or press Enter.

Select a file to print by clicking with the mouse. To select a single file with the keyboard, press the up- or down-arrow key until the file is selected.

To select multiple contiguous files with the mouse, click the first file, hold down the Shift key, and click the last file. To select noncontiguous files, hold down the Ctrl key while you click the files. To select multiple contiguous files with the keyboard, use the arrow keys to move to the first file, hold down the Shift key, and use the arrow keys to move to the last file. To select noncontiguous files with the keyboard, use the arrow keys to select the first file, press Shift+F8, use the arrow keys to select the next file, and press the space bar. Use the arrow keys and space bar to select as many files as you want.

To learn more about the Find File command, see Chapter 3.

Using Other Print Options

To prevent Word from leaving a single line at the beginning or end of a printed page, turn on widow and orphan control. Choose the Tools Options command, and then choose the Printer Category and select the Widow and Orphan check box. Choose OK or press Enter.

Certain options in the expanded File Print dialog box are covered in other parts of this book. The Envelope options are discussed in Chapter 19. The option to Use TrueType Fonts as Defaults is explained in Appendix C.

When you have two documents you want to combine into one, use Word for Windows's File Print Merge command. The two most useful applications for this command are form letters and mailing labels, which are created when you merge a file containing name and address records with a file containing a letter or a label format. To learn about Print Merge, see Chapter 19.

Printing to a File

Someday you may need to print a document to a file and not to a printer. One way this can be useful is to print a document setup for a PostScript printer to a file. The resulting encapsulated PostScript (EPS) file can be taken to a printer to be printed on a Linotronic typesetting machine for very high-quality documents.

Another use for printing to a file is to create a file that can be taken to a computer that has a printer but no copy of Word for Windows. If the file has been created for that printer, you can use the DOS COPY command to copy the Word for Windows file to the LPT1 printer port. The file prints even though Word for Windows is not running.

To print to a file, follow these steps:

1. Choose the File Print command.

2. Select the Print to File option; then choose OK or press Enter.

3. Type the full path name of the file to contain the document; then choose OK or press Enter.

You see the disk light come on as the information sent to the printer is stored in a file with the name you entered in step 3.

When you want to resume printing to your printer, turn off the Print to File option in the Print dialog box.

T   I   P   You can easily create a text file in Word for Windows. Just choose the File Save **As** command; then select the Save File as **T**ype pulldown list and select one of the text file format files that Word for Windows creates. In most cases you should choose the Text Only (*.TXT) format.

From Here . . .

In this chapter, you learned how to manage printing and about the four steps to printing: connecting and installing the printer, setting up the printer, selecting the printer, and printing. You learned that you can preview your pages before you print, saving yourself time and paper.

An important part of printing and formatting is understanding how your printer works with fonts. You may want to make sure that the fonts and formatting on-screen match those your printer can use. See Appendix C for more information on fonts and TrueType.

File Print Preview is a powerful command for viewing your page before you begin printing. Other commands in the **V**iew menu (**P**age Layout and **Z**oom)—not to mention the zoom buttons in the toolbar—can be just as useful, however.

Merging is a special type of printing that is extremely useful when you want to create form letters or labels. You can learn more about merging in Chapter 19.

P A R T

II

OUTLINE

Using Advanced Features

Formatting with Styles

What gives your document style? For the most part, style is the appearance of your document: the arrangement of text on pages, the shape of the paragraphs, the characteristics of the letters, the use of lines and borders to give your document emphasis. All these elements of style are formatting choices you make while working with Word for Windows.

Style involves more than just appearance, however. Style is also readability and consistency. When your document's style is appropriate to its content and is consistent from one section to the next, the reader's job of gleaning information from your text becomes much easier.

Word for Windows offers you tools designed to make the task of developing and maintaining your document's style much easier. Appropriately, these tools are called *styles*. In Word for Windows, a style is a set of formatting instructions you save to use again and again. Styles include character and paragraph formatting, tab settings, paragraph positioning, borders and shading, and language used for spell checking.

Using styles instead of directly formatting each paragraph or page individually offers several savings. First, you save time. You can format one paragraph the way you like it and copy that formatting to other paragraphs. Second, you preserve consistency. By using styles to format your document, you can be sure that each paragraph looks the same as others of its type. Third, you reduce the effort required when you want to change your document's appearance. By changing a style, you also change all the paragraphs associated with that style. See figure 11.1 for an example of how styles can give your document a consistent appearance.

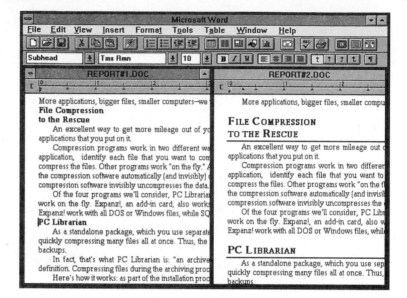

FIG. 11.1.

Using styles for a consistent appearance within and between documents.

Defining Styles

The process of using styles involves two steps. First you create the style, specifying formatting choices like paragraph indentations, line spacing, font, and font size. Then you apply that style—along with all your formatting choices—to other paragraphs in your document. You can create styles in two ways: by example (using the ribbon or a keyboard shortcut), or by menu command. Creating a style by example is so easy that even a beginner can do it. Using a menu command gives you more options, and isn't difficult when you understand the concept of styles.

Similarly, you can apply styles in two ways: by choosing a style from the ribbon (or with a keyboard shortcut); or by using the menu command. You mostly will use just the ribbon.

When you apply a style to text, remember that styles are paragraph-level formatting commands—even though they can contain character formatting. Any style you apply to text formats the entire paragraph (or the group of selected paragraphs). If a style includes character formatting, it too is applied to the entire paragraph.

You're always using at least one style when you work with Word for Windows. The Normal style, built into Word for Windows, gives your document its default formatting choices. If you have the ribbon displayed when you start a new document, you can see that the Normal style already is selected (see fig. 11.2). The Normal style's formatting selections are basic: it includes a font and font size (12-point MS Serif, 10-point Times Roman, or different, depending on your printer), left alignment, and single-line spacing. You learn how you can change the Normal style if you prefer different default formatting choices in the section "Redefining Standard Styles" later in this chapter.

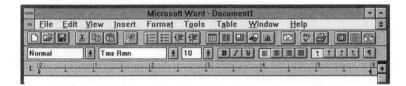

FIG. 11.2.

The Normal style is displayed in the ribbon when you start a new document.

Styles are saved with the document or template in which you create them. You can share styles with other documents, however. (Refer to the section "Sharing Styles among Documents" later in this chapter.)

Creating and Applying Styles by Example

The simplest way to get started using styles is to define a style by example, using the ribbon or a keyboard shortcut. You format a paragraph the way you want it, and then create a style based on the formatting contained in that paragraph.

As you format your first paragraph (the one you will use as an example to create a style), remember that although styles are paragraph-level formatting commands, they also can contain character formatting. If your example paragraph contains left and right indents and a border, those formatting choices will be part of your style. If your entire paragraph is formatted as bold, then bold formatting also will be part of your style. If your paragraph includes only one word formatted in bold, however, then bold will not be part of your style.

Character-level formatting is included in your style only if the majority of characters in your example paragraph (more than half) include that formatting.

T I P The processes of creating, applying, and redefining styles by example are all similar. If you get an unexpected result, choose **Edit Undo** immediately, and then review the steps carefully to see what you may have done wrong. If you think you're creating a new style, but you use the name of an existing style, for example, then you will be applying the existing style to your paragraph instead of creating a new style.

Creating a Style By Example

You can create a style by example by using the ribbon or by using a keyboard shortcut with or without the ribbon displayed. Either way is easy.

You should remember that a new style name must be unique. If you try to create a new style with an existing name, you apply the existing style to your paragraph instead of creating a new style. If that happens, choose **Edit Undo** and try again. Be aware that Word for Windows includes quite a few built-in styles (like Normal and Heading 1 through Heading 9); don't create new styles using their names. For a list of built-in styles, refer to the section "Using Word for Windows' Standard Styles" later in this chapter.

As you're naming your style, remember these rules:

- A style name can contain up to 24 characters.
- The name can contain spaces and most punctuation marks (you will see a message if a character is illegal).
- Characters in the name can appear as upper- or lowercase.

Choose a style name that makes sense to you so that you will remember it later, and so that you can use it consistently in other documents. If you frequently create lists in your documents and you always format them the same way, for example, create a style called List in all the documents where you want to create identically formatted lists.

Creating a Style with the Ribbon

To create a style by example using the ribbon, follow these steps:

1. Display the ribbon (if it isn't already displayed) by choosing the **View Rib**bon command.

2. Format your example paragraph.

   You can include character or paragraph formatting, borders and shading, frames and positioning, tabs, and a language for spell checking. (Your style will include character formatting only if you apply it to more than half of your example paragraph.)

3. With the insertion point still inside your example paragraph, select the entire name of the existing style in the ribbon's Style box (see fig. 11.3).

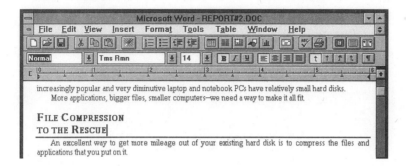

FIG. 11.3.

Select the current style name in the ribbon's Style box.

4. Type the name of the style you want to create (see fig. 11.4).

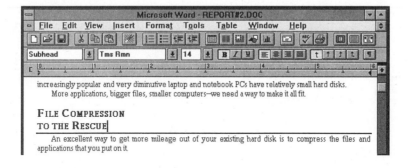

FIG. 11.4.

Type the new style name to create a style by example.

5. Press Enter to create the style.

After you create your style, look in the ribbon's Style box—you see your new style displayed, indicating that its formatting choices control the appearance of your example paragraph.

Creating a Style with the Keyboard

With or without the ribbon displayed, you can create a style by example using the keyboard. If the ribbon is not displayed, watch the status bar at the bottom of your screen (a status bar will appear if it wasn't displayed before you started).

To create a style by example using the keyboard, follow these steps:

1. Format your example paragraph.

2. Press Ctrl+S.

   If the ribbon is displayed, Word for Windows selects the current style in the Style box. If the ribbon is not displayed, Word for Windows displays a message in the status bar at the bottom of your screen asking Which style?.

3. Type the name of the style you want to create (see fig. 11.5).

4. Press Enter to create the style.

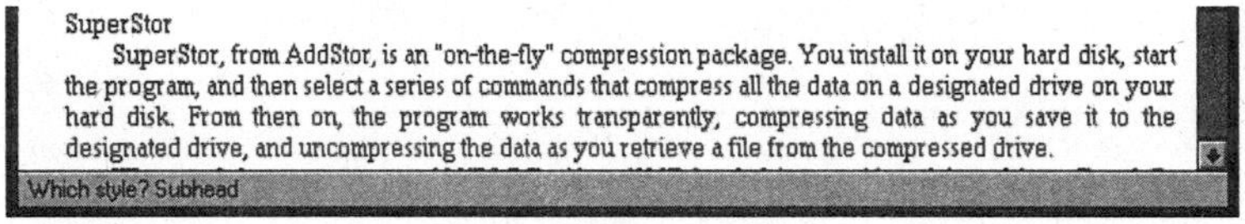

FIG. 11.5.

If the ribbon is not displayed, the new style name displays at the Which Style? prompt in the status bar.

SuperStor

SuperStor, from AddStor, is an "on-the-fly" compression package. You install it on your hard disk, start the program, and then select a series of commands that compress all the data on a designated drive on your hard disk. From then on, the program works transparently, compressing data as you save it to the designated drive, and uncompressing the data as you retrieve a file from the compressed drive.

Which style? Subhead

Look at the Style box in the ribbon to see that your new style is now selected for your example paragraph. (If the ribbon isn't displayed, you won't be able to tell by looking at your screen which style is applied to your paragraph—unless you display the style area. Refer ahead in this chapter to the section on "Viewing and Applying Styles Using the Style Area" to learn how to use the style area.)

Applying a Style with the Ribbon or Keyboard

The power of styles becomes apparent when you use them to apply consistent formatting to paragraph after paragraph in your document. Using the ribbon or keyboard, applying styles is as easy as creating them.

To apply a style using the ribbon, follow these steps:

1. Display the ribbon (if it is not displayed currently) by choosing the **View Ri**bbon command.

2. Position the insertion point inside the paragraph, or select text in the paragraphs you want to format with a style.

3. Click the down arrow at the right side of the Style box in the ribbon to display a list of available styles.

4. Select the style you want to apply to the paragraph or selected paragraphs (scroll the list if necessary).

If you use the keyboard shortcut to apply a style, you don't need the ribbon displayed.

To apply a style using the keyboard, follow these steps:

1. Select the paragraph or paragraphs you want to format with a style.

2. Press Ctrl+S.

   If the ribbon is displayed, the current style is selected in the Style box. If the ribbon is not displayed, the status bar displays the message Which style?.

3. If the ribbon is displayed, press the down-arrow key to select the style you want to apply.

   or

   If the ribbon is not displayed, accurately type the name of the style you want to apply to the selected paragraph or paragraphs.

4. Press Enter.

In the second part of step 3, the word *accurately* is critical: if you type the name of a style that doesn't exist, you will create a style based on the example of the selected paragraph or paragraphs rather than applying a style. This is another argument in favor of simple, memorable style names.

Redefining a Style by Example

By redefining a style, you can change the appearance of your entire document—all at once. Suppose that you're editing an article that contains many subheadings formatted with the style Subhead. Currently the Subhead style is bold and a larger point size than the text of the article, but now you want all your subheadings to be larger, in small caps, and underlined. By changing the text in one of your subheadings, and then redefining the style Subhead using the changed subheading as an example, you instantly can change all the subheadings based on the style Subheading.

To redefine a style by example, follow these steps:

1. If you want to use the ribbon, and it currently isn't displayed, display it by choosing the **V**iew Ri**b**bon command.

2. Reformat the paragraph you will use as an example for the redefined style. Select the paragraph (or some portion of the paragraph).

3. In the ribbon, select the current style name, or just position the insertion point to its right.

   or

   Press Ctrl+S and accurately type the name of the style you want to redefine.

4. Press Enter.

   You see a message asking if you want to redefine the current style based on the selection (see fig. 11.6).

5. Select **Yes** to redefine the style.

FIG. 11.6.

You can easily redefine a style by example.

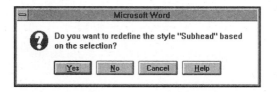

Using Word for Windows' Standard Styles

Word for Windows includes a great number of standard, or built-in styles. You already are familiar with the Normal style, which Word for Windows uses to apply default formatting to all new documents based on the default Normal template. Other standard styles include those that provide formatting for outline headings, headers, footers, page numbers, line numbers, index entries, table of contents entries, annotations, and footnotes.

You can apply the standard styles in the same way you apply your own styles. In a new document, for example, you see the styles Normal, Heading 1, Heading 2, and Heading 3 listed in the ribbon's Style list box, and you can apply these styles to selected paragraphs just by selecting the paragraph and then selecting the standard style from the list. You are more likely to apply the standard styles automatically—by creating headers, footers, index entries, and so on—all of which are formatted automatically, using standard styles. After you use these styles in your document, their names appear in the ribbon's Style list box.

Many standard styles do more than just format text. When you use the automatic heading styles (Heading 1 through Heading 9), for example, you later can collect these headings into a table of contents. Or, if you insert table of contents entries (formatted with the styles Toc 1 through Toc 8), you later can collect these entries as a table of contents. Similarly, if you insert index or footnote entries into your document, Word for Windows collects them where you have specified they are to appear in your document.

Table 11.1 lists Word for Windows' standard styles.

Table 11.1. Word for Windows' Standard Styles

Standard style or style family	Default formatting	How applied
Normal (used by default to format all new text)	10- or 12-point serif font (varies with printer), left-aligned, single line spacing	Applied to all text automatically in a document that is based on the Normal template.
Normal Indent (indents paragraphs)	Normal + 1/2-inch left indent	Manually
Heading 1 through Heading 9 (formats outline headings)	Formatting ranges from large and bold (Heading 1) to indented and italic (Headings 7-9)	Outline view
Annotation Reference (creates hidden annotation references)	Normal + 8 point font	Insert Annotation command
Annotation Text (formats annotation text)	Normal	Typing annotation text in the annotation pane
Footer (formats footers)	Normal + 3-inch centered tab, 6-inch right tab	View Header/ Footer command
Footnote Reference (formats footnote references)	Normal + 8-point font, 3-point superscript	Insert Footnote command
Footnote Text (formats footnote text)	Normal	Typing footnote text
Header (formats headers)	Normal + 3-inch centered tab, 6-inch right tab	View Header/ Footer command

continues

Table 11.1. (continued)

Standard style or style family	Default formatting	How applied
Index 1 through Index 7 (formats index entries)	Normal + increasing indents	Insert Index command
Index Heading (formats optional heading separators in index)	Normal command	Insert Index
Line Number (formats line numbers)	Normal	Format Section Layout
Toc 1 through Toc 8 (formats table of contents entries)	Normal + indent and dot-leader tab at 5 3/4 inches, right tab at 6 inches (indents increase)	Insert Table of Contents command

In table 11.1, notice that the formatting for many standard styles is based on the Normal style. In other words, many styles include all the formatting contained in the Normal style plus additional formatting choices. The index styles, for example, are the Normal style plus indentations. The header and footer styles are Normal style plus tab settings.

If you change the Normal style, any other style based on the Normal style also changes. If you change the Normal style to double spacing, for example, headers, footers, index entries, and all other styles based on Normal also will include double spacing.

To learn how to base your own styles on another style—or how to avoid doing this—refer to the section "Basing a Style on Another Style" later in this chapter.

Redefining Standard Styles

Standard styles come with predefined formatting, but you can easily redefine them. Suppose that you want to use the standard header styles (Heading 1 through Heading 9) to format your document because you can use the outline mode to apply these styles, and because you want to collect the headings later as a table of contents. Unfortunately, you don't like the default formatting choices Word for Windows has made for the heading styles. Redefine the styles, using either the styles by example techniques described previously in this chapter, or by using the Format Styles command, described in the next section.

(To learn more about using the outline view to apply heading styles, refer to Chapter 14. To learn more about creating a table of contents from heading styles, refer to Chapter 16.)

You can redefine a standard style, but you cannot delete a standard style.

T I P

Creating and Applying Styles with a Menu Command

If you want to create styles before you use them, rather than creating them by example, you need the Format Style command. Using this command, you name a style, define its formatting characteristics, and select options such as whether to base the style on another style, whether to follow it with another style, and whether to add the style to the current template.

Creating styles by using the menu command is a good way to take advantage of one of the greatest benefits of styles—the consistency between documents that styles can ensure. Suppose that you regularly produce documentation for new products your company manufactures, or suppose you're in charge of editing the company's biweekly employee newsletter. In both cases, you want a consistent appearance from publication to publication. Before Word for Windows, you probably wrote out a style guide and tucked it in your desk drawer so that you could reference it each time you started a new publication. But with Word for Windows styles, you can create your style guide on your computer instead.

To create your style guide, create a template (refer to Chapter 30), and in the template, create all the styles you need for your document. Each time you begin a new document, begin with your customized template, rather than with the default Normal template. The styles will be there for you in your new document. If you need to change a style later, you can change it in the template and then merge it into the document you're currently working on (see "Sharing Styles among Documents" later in this chapter). If you design a new style, you can add it back to the template from within the document.

When you create a style by using the menu command, you have the option to apply the style to the currently selected paragraph, or simply to add it to the style sheet or list of styles you created for your document (or for your template).

T I P

The group of styles associated with a template or document is called a *style sheet*. If you want to print a document's style sheet (along with a description of each style), choose the **File Print** command, select Styles in the Print box, and then choose OK or press Enter.

In the Style dialog box, all new styles you create are based on the style of the currently selected paragraph. In the section "Basing One Style on Another Style," you learn how you can base your new style on any other style.

Creating a New Style

To create a style by using the menu command, follow these steps:

1. Choose the Format Styles command. The Style dialog box appears (see fig. 11.7).

   Notice that the Description box displays the formatting characteristics of the currently selected paragraph.

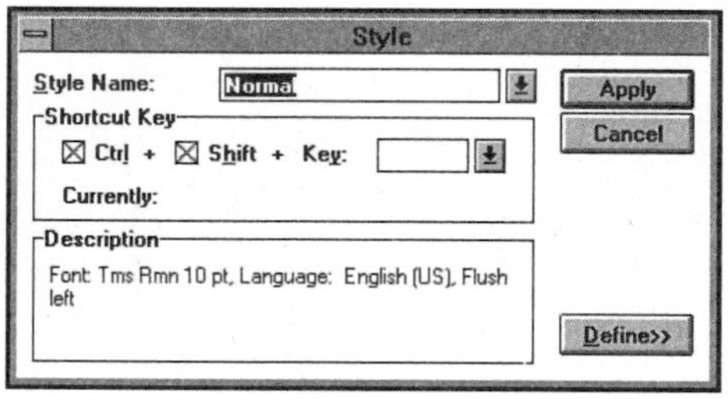

FIG. 11.7.

The Style dialog box.

2. In the **S**tyle Name box, type the name of your new style.

   Now only the style name of the currently selected paragraph appears in the Description box.

3. Choose the **D**efine button. The Style dialog box expands to show options (see fig. 11.8).

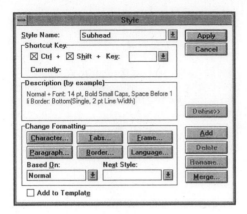

FIG 11.8.

The expanded
Style dialog box
with options.

4. Choose any button in the Change Formatting group to display the dialog box that enables you to select formatting options for your style. If you want to include bold formatting as part of your style, for example, choose the **C**haracter button to display the Character dialog box, then select the **B**old option.

Button	Formatting options
Character	Font, style (bold, italic, underline), size, color, super/subscript, and character spacing
Tabs	Tab stop position, alignment, and leaders, or clear tabs
Frame	Text wrapping, frame size or position, or remove frame
Paragraph	Paragraph alignment and indentation, pagination, line numbers, line spacing
Border	Border location, style, color, and paragraph shading
Language	The language the spell checker, thesaurus, and grammar checker should use for the current paragraph

5. Choose the **A**dd button.

   To create additional styles, you can repeat steps 2 through 5 before closing the dialog box.

   (Note that the **A**dd button reads Change when you change an existing style.)

6. To apply your new style to the currently selected paragraph, choose the Apply button.

   or

To exit the Style dialog box without applying the style to any paragraph, choose the **C**lose button or press Esc.

 When you type the name of your new style in step 2, be sure that it is a unique name. If you type the name of an existing style and then make formatting choices, you will redefine the existing style. Any text formatted with the existing style then will take on this redefined formatting.

As part of the process of creating a style, you can assign shortcut keys to make the style easy to apply. See the later section "Using Style Shortcut Keys."

Creating a Style by Example

You can use the menu command to create a style by example. You might do this, for example, if you want to use a formatted paragraph as the basis for a style, but you also want to add additional formatting choices to the style.

To define a style by example using the menu command, follow these steps:

1. Format the paragraph you want to use as an example for your style, and leave the insertion point inside the paragraph.

2. Choose the Forma**t** St**y**le command.

3. In the **S**tyle Name box, type the name of your new style.

   Notice that the Description box changes to show the selected paragraph's formatting.

4. Choose the **D**efine button and make additional formatting choices.

5. Choose the **A**dd button.

6. Choose the **C**lose button.

Renaming or Deleting a Style

At some point, you may decide you no longer need a style. You can delete it, and all text associated with the deleted style will revert to the Normal style. You also can rename a style, which does not affect the associated text, but changes the style name throughout your document.

To delete or rename a style, follow these steps:

1. Choose the Format Style command.

2. In the Style Name list box, select the style you want to delete or rename.

   If you have selected a paragraph containing the style you want to delete, the style already will be selected in the Style Name list box.

3. Choose the Define button.

4. To delete a style, choose the Delete button. You see a message asking whether you want to delete the style. Choose Yes.

   To rename a style, choose the Rename button. You then see the Rename Style dialog box. In the New Style Name box, type the style's new name, and then choose OK or press Enter.

5. Choose the Close button.

Applying Styles with the Format Styles Command

The easiest way to apply a style is to select it from the Style box on the ribbon, or to use the Ctrl+S shortcut and type the style's name (or if the ribbon is displayed, press the up- or down-arrow key to select the style from the Style box). When you use the ribbon, any style you created for your document or your template is listed in the ribbon's Style box.

You sometimes may want to use the menu command to apply a style, especially if you want to apply one of Word for Windows' standard styles not listed in the Style box on the ribbon.

To apply a style using the menu command, follow these steps:

1. Select the paragraph or paragraphs to which you want to apply the style.

2. Choose the Format Style command.

3. From the Style Name list, select the style you want to apply.

   Press Ctrl+Y if you want to list all the standard styles.

4. Choose the Apply button.

Redefining Styles with the Format Styles Command

You can redefine any style—including standard styles. When you redefine a style, something important happens: all the text formatted with that style updates to reflect the changes you have made. Suppose that you finish a 35-page report with many subheadings formatted with a style called Subhead which includes 18-point, bold, Helvetica, centered text. Now your company's publications committee decides subheadings should be smaller and underlined. Just redefine the style Subhead to reflect the new formatting, and all the subheadings in your text will change (refer to fig. 11.1).

To redefine a style using the menu command, follow these steps:

1. Choose the Format Style command.

2. From the Style Name list, select the style you want to redefine.

3. Choose the Define button.

4. Select any formatting options you want to add to your style, and unselect any options you want to remove.

5. Choose the Change button.

    Repeat steps 2 through 5 if you want to redefine additional styles.

6. Choose the Close button.

Creating Style Shortcut Keys

Another way to apply a style is with a shortcut key, which you can assign as part of the process of creating or redefining a style. The shortcut keys usually include pressing the Ctrl key plus the Shift key plus a letter that you designate. You could assign the shortcut Ctrl+Shift+S, for example, to a style called Sub. You can use other key combinations if you want, but they may conflict with shortcut keys preassigned to Word for Windows' built-in macros. (Word for Windows uses the built-in macro Ctrl+S, for example, to enable you to create or apply a style quickly, so you wouldn't want to assign Ctrl+S to your style Sub.) To learn more about built-in macros, refer to Chapter 31.

To create shortcut keys for styles, follow these steps:

1. Choose the Format Style command.

2. From the Style Name list, select the style for which you want to create shortcut keys.

3. From the Shortcut Key group, select the Ctrl option to include the Ctrl (Control) key in your shortcut, and select the Shift option to include the Shift key. When selected, an X appears in the option box.

   To unselect the Ctrl key option or the Shift key option, select them so that no X appears in the option box.

4. From the Key list, select or type a character or key to include in your shortcut. You can use the letters A through Z, the numbers 0 through 9, any function key, or the Ins or Del key.

   The Currently message line at the bottom of the Shortcut Key group displays any shortcut currently assigned to the selected style. If no shortcut is assigned, the Currently message line displays [unassigned]. In addition, the message warns you if the shortcut key combination you have selected is already in use by another style or macro.

5. Choose the Define button.

6. Choose the Change button.

7. Choose the Close button.

To remove a shortcut key (if you discover later that your shortcut overrides a favorite macro, for example) simply delete the letter, number, function key, or Ins or Del key in the Key box.

To apply a style with a shortcut key you have assigned:

1. Select the paragraph (or paragraphs) to which you want to apply the style.

2. Hold down the Ctrl or Shift keys while you type the shortcut letter, number, function key, Ins, or Del key. (If your shortcut is Ctrl+Shift+C, for example, hold Ctrl and Shift while you press C.)

Basing a Style on Another Style

Unless you specify otherwise, a new style is based on the style of the currently selected paragraph. Often, that's the Normal style. You have the option, however, to base any style on any other style. When you do, any changes you make to the base style carry through to all styles based on that style. If you change Normal, those changes are reflected in any style based on the Normal style.

This often can be to your advantage. Suppose that you work in a legal office and you regularly type certain court documents that must always be double-spaced, in a certain font and size, and have specific margins.

To help automate this task, you can create a template with the correct margins, and then modify the template's Normal style to include the correct font and size and double-spacing. You then can create additional styles based on that redefined Normal style, and they too will use the specified font and size and be double-spaced.

Keep in mind that Word for Windows' automatic styles are based on the Normal style, and if you alter the Normal style, your alterations will apply to all the automatic styles as well.

If you don't want to alter your Normal style, you can create a base style in your document and use it as the basis for additional styles.

To base one style on another style, follow these steps:

1. Choose the Format Style command.

2. Type the name of your new style in the Style Name box, or select an existing style from the Style Name list.

   When you type a new style name, you see the style name for the currently selected paragraph listed in the Description box. Your new style automatically is based on that existing style, unless you specify a different style.

3. Choose the Define button.

4. From the Based On list, select the style on which you want to base your style (see fig. 11.9). The name of this style is now listed in the Description box.

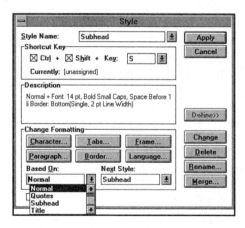

FIG. 11.9.

The Based On list.

5. Choose any of the Change Formatting buttons to add additional formatting options to your style.

6. Choose the **A**dd button if you are creating a new style, or choose the Ch**a**nge button if you're changing an existing style.

7. Choose the **C**lose button.

or

Choose the **A**pply button if you want to apply your new style to the currently selected paragraph. After choosing **A**pply, you can make additional selections in the Style dialog box before you choose **C**lose.

Following One Style with the Next Style

One of the most useful style options is the ability to follow one style with another. Suppose that you're editing a complex document with many subheadings, all formatted with styles. Text formatted with the Normal style follows each subheading. You would save time and effort if you didn't have to apply the Normal style each time you finished typing a subheading—which is exactly what happens when you follow one style with another. If the style Subhead is followed by the Normal style, for example, when you finish typing a subhead and press Enter, the Normal style is applied automatically to the next paragraph. You can see this process in action by watching the Style box in the ribbon.

By default, Word for Windows follows each style with that same style so that when you press Enter, the style carries forward. In many cases, that's what you want. When you finish typing a paragraph formatted with the Normal style, you want the next paragraph also to be formatted with the Normal style. All of Word for Windows' automatic styles are followed by the next style Normal.

To follow one style with another style, follow these steps:

1. Choose the Forma**t** St**y**le command.

2. Type a new style name in the **S**tyle Name box (if you're creating a new style), or select an existing style from the list.

3. Choose the **D**efine button.

4. In the Ne**x**t Style list, select the style that you want to follow the current style (see fig. 11.10).

    If you select no style, your style will be followed by itself.

5. Choose the **A**dd button if you're creating a new style, or choose the Ch**a**nge button if you're redefining an existing style.

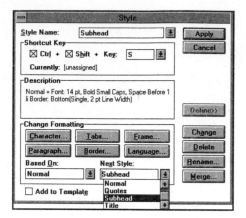

FIG. 11.10.

The Next Style
list.

The **Add** and **Change** buttons toggle; the button reads **Add** if
you're creating a new style, but it reads **Change** if you're redefining an existing style.

6. Choose the **Close** button.

Creating a Nonparagraph Line Break

When you type a paragraph formatted by a style that is followed by a
next style and you press Enter, the next paragraph is formatted with
the next style. Sometimes, however, you may not be ready to change to
the next style. If you have a two-line subheading, for example, you may
want to be able to press Enter after the first line and still be in the subheading style rather than switching to the next style.

Word for Windows provides a trick: to end a line without inserting a
paragraph marker, press Shift+Enter.

Pressing Shift+Enter breaks a line without breaking the paragraph.
When you finish typing your two-line subheading, press Enter in the
usual way to end the paragraph, and begin the following paragraph
with the next style.

If you press the Paragraph button at the far right end of the ribbon to
display paragraph markers, you see that the line end markers at the
ends of lines where you pressed Shift+Enter look like left-facing arrows
rather than paragraph markers (see fig. 11.11).

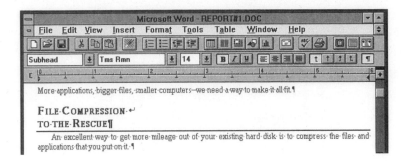

FIG. 11.11.

Line end markers display as left-facing arrows rather than paragraph markers when you press the Paragraph button.

Sharing Styles among Documents

Every document you create includes styles—even if it's only the Normal style and Word for Windows' other automatic styles. This collection of styles is called a *style sheet*. Each document's style sheet is provided by its template—whether that's the Normal template or a custom template you create.

In its simplest sense, using a template is the basic way you can share styles among documents. You create a template that contains certain styles you need, and then base your documents on that template. You may, for example, have a template called Letters that contains styles for formatting letters to be printed on your company's letterhead. If you regularly produce several different types of documents, you may create a template for each of them. (For details about creating templates, refer to Chapter 30.)

At some point, however, you may want to use the styles from one document or template in a different document or template. You can do that by merging style sheets.

A likely scenario for sharing styles is the big, multidocument publication that undergoes design revisions as the project progresses. In the beginning of the project you create a template containing styles for formatting each document. Because all documents are based on the same template, they contain identical formatting, which preserves consistency. Later, the publications committee issues major design changes. One way to change your documents is to open each one and revise its styles. But an easier way to make the changes is to revise the styles in the template instead, and then merge the template's revised styles into each document. The template's revised styles replace the document's identically named styles, and any text associated with those styles changes to reflect the revisions.

You can merge style sheets to or from any document or template. (You cannot merge individual styles—only the document or template's entire style sheet.) Identically named styles from a style sheet replace the styles in the sheet you're merging to; new styles from a style sheet are added to the style sheet you're merging to.

To merge style sheets, follow these steps:

1. If you're merging style sheets *from the current* document or template *to another* document or template, *open both* the current and the other document or template. (One exception is that if you're merging style sheets to the current document's own template, you do not have to open the template.)

   or

   If you're merging style sheets *to the current* document or template *from another* document or template, *open only the current* document or template.

2. Choose the Forma**t S**tyle command.

3. Choose the **D**efine button.

4. Choose the **M**erge button. The Merge Styles dialog box appears (see fig. 11.12).

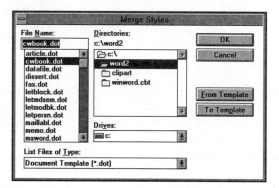

FIG. 11.12.

The Merge Styles dialog box.

5. In the **D**irectories list, select the directory containing the document or template from which or to which you want to merge a style sheet (or just type the path name in the **D**irectories box).

6. In the File **N**ame box, select the document or template from or to which you want to merge a style sheet (or just type the name in the File **N**ame box).

   To list files of a particular type (document or template), select Word Document (*.doc) or Document Template (*.dot) from the List Files of **T**ype box.

7. To merge a style sheet from the selected file, choose the **From Template** button.

   or

   To merge a style sheet to the selected file, choose the To Template button.

   Word for Windows responds by warning you that current styles will be replaced with new styles of the same name, and asking if you want to continue. Choose **Yes**.

8. Choose the Cancel button to close the Merge Styles dialog box.

Although the Merge Styles dialog box contains buttons reading **From Template** and To Template, you can merge style sheets from and to both templates and documents.

T I P

Merging styles using the Format Style command merges entire style sheets between documents. A sneaky way to merge a *single* style into a document is to copy into your document a paragraph formatted with a different style from another document. Be careful, though. Copying styles into your document this way does not override existing styles (as merging style sheets does). If, for example, you copy in a paragraph formatted with a style called List, and your existing document also contains a style called List, the new paragraph will take on the formatting of the existing List style. Other commands for inserting text into a document, such as Glossary and Paste Link, also can bring in new styles. You can copy in up to 50 paragraphs that contain unique style names—if you copy in more than 50, then Word for Windows merges in the document's entire style sheet.

Using the Style Area

If you're working with styles extensively, you can display the style area on your screen to list each paragraph's style name in the left margin (see fig. 11.13).

Using the style area, you can see at a glance which style is applied to each paragraph. If you have a mouse, you also can use the style area to apply and redefine styles quickly; you double-click on the style name to display the Styles dialog box. From there you can apply, create, or redefine a style.

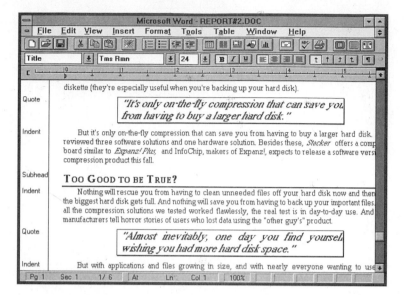

FIG. 11.13.

The style area
lists each
paragraph's style
name.

The width of the style area varies. When you first display the style area, you set its width. After it's displayed, however, you can vary its width by using a mouse to drag the line separating the style area from the text to the left or right. You can close the style area entirely by dragging the arrow all the way to the left edge of the screen, or by resetting the style area width to zero.

To display the style area, follow these steps:

1. Choose the Tools Options command.

2. From the Category list, select View (it may be selected already). The Options dialog box lists all the view settings you can modify (see fig. 11.14).

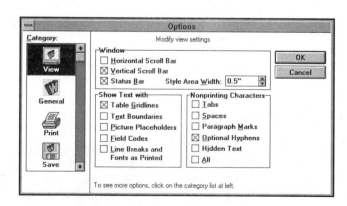

FIG. 11.14.

The Options
dialog box with
the View
Category
selected.

3. In the Style Area **W**idth box, type the style area width you want in decimal inches.

or

Click the up or down arrows at the right end of the Style Area **W**idth box to increase or decrease the style area width by tenths of an inch.

4. Choose OK or press Enter.

By clicking on the style name in the style area, you quickly can select an entire paragraph.

T I P

If you frequently display the style area, you can record a simple macro that turns on the style area. For quick access to your macro, you can assign it to a shortcut key. (If you get a little braver, you can edit your macro so that it toggles the style area on and off. To learn about recording and editing macros, turn to Chapter 31.)

T I P

Overriding Styles with Manual Formatting

Although you can do most of your formatting with styles, at times you will need to override the formatting in a style you have already applied. You may want to do something simple, like making one word in a paragraph bold, or maybe something more substantial, like italicizing a whole paragraph. You can modify the formatting in a paragraph without changing the style.

Be aware, however, of what effect your formatting will have on the paragraph if you later reapply the style. Reapplying the style may cancel some of the manual formatting changes you have made. Manual formatting works with styles as follows:

■ If the reapplied style contains formatting choices in the same category as those you have applied manually, the style's choices override the manual formatting. If you have manually applied double line spacing, but the style specifies single line spacing, for example, then the double line spacing is cancelled when you apply the style.

■ If the reapplied style contains formatting choices unrelated to the formatting you have applied manually, the style won't affect manual formatting. If you add a border to a paragraph and then reapply a style that doesn't specify borders, for example, the border will remain.

■ Some character formatting choices toggle on and off—you select bold to turn it on in the same way you select bold to turn it off. If you apply a style containing bold to a paragraph with one or two words that are bold, for example, then all of the paragraph will be bold except the one or two words that you formatted as bold manually (the style toggles them off). On the other hand, if you make a whole paragraph bold, then reapply a style that contains bold, Word for Windows leaves the paragraph bold rather than toggling off the bold.

■ If you want to remove all your manual character formatting from a paragraph formatted with a style, press Ctrl+space bar.

From Here . . .

In this chapter you learned how to format your documents with styles. Using styles can save you time and can help ensure a consistent appearance within and between documents. Templates work well with styles—you can create a special template containing styles you need for a particular type of document, and base all your documents on that template. To learn about creating and using templates, refer to Chapter 30.

In this chapter, you also learned how to apply styles, but many times Word for Windows applies styles itself—when you create an outline, for example, or insert index or table of contents entries, or add headers and footers to your document. To learn how to use an outline, refer to Chapter 14. To learn about headers and footers, refer to Chapter 15. To learn about indexes and tables of contents, refer to Chapter 16.

Macros are a great way to automate some of the things you do repeatedly, like displaying the style area. To learn how to create and edit macros, refer to Chapter 31.

12

Creating and Editing Tables

Tables give you an excellent way of working with columns or tabular data. If you have worked with a spreadsheet application, such as Microsoft Excel or Lotus 1-2-3, you will find working with tables similar to working with a spreadsheet. A *table* is simply a grid of columns and rows. The intersection of a column and a row is a rectangular box referred to as a *cell*. Each cell is independent and can be sized or formatted.

Tables can have text, numbers, pictures, or formulas in a cell. A table enables you to present text in columns and align paragraphs or graphics. If you enter text in a cell, the text wraps to the next line according to the width of the cell. If you adjust the width of the cell or column, the text adjusts to the new width.

A table also can be formatted with borders to add a professional touch to your document. In this chapter you learn how to create, edit, and format a table.

This entire chapter covers features new with Version 2 of Word for Windows.

Figure 12.1 shows an example of a table containing text and numbers in seven columns and five rows.

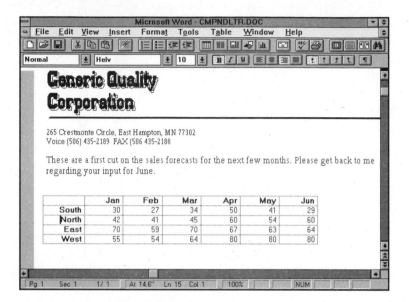

FIG. 12.1.

This simple table makes it easy to present a sales forecast.

You can use tables to show lists of data, personal rosters, financial information, scripts, and procedural steps. Tables can even include pasted illustrations that explain steps in a list.

T I P   If you need to position your table anywhere on the page and have text wrap around it, frame your table and drag it to the location you want. To learn how to frame and move tables, text, charts, or pictures, refer to Chapter 24.

Creating a Table

You can create tables with a menu command or with a button from the toolbar. Using the Table button on the toolbar is the easiest way to insert a table. Using the Table Insert command enables you to size the column widths at the time you insert the table. Tables created with the toolbar must have their column widths adjusted later.

Before you create a table, you must have a rough idea of the number of columns needed. You can insert and delete columns and rows, however, after the table is created.

Using the Table Button

The easiest way to create a table is with the Table button located in the toolbar. The Table button looks like a miniature spreadsheet (grid) with a black top border. Using the Table button is almost like drawing the table into your worksheet.

To create a table with the Table button, follow these steps:

1. Move the insertion point to where you want the table in the document.

2. Click the Table button and drag down and to the right.

   As you drag the mouse pointer, the Button expands to create a grid of rows and columns like a miniature table. As long as you continue to hold down the mouse button, you can move the pointer within the grid to select the size of the table you want inserted. Figure 12.2 shows the Table button expanded and a table size selected.

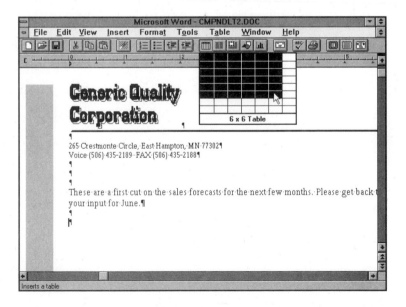

FIG. 12.2.

The Table button enables you to draw the size of table you want inserted.

3. Release the mouse button when the selected grid is the size of the table you want.

If you decide you do not want to insert a table, but you have already begun the selection process with the Table button, continue to hold down the mouse button and drag the pointer to the left until it is outside the grid, and then release the button. You also can drag up until the pointer is over the button and then release.

T I P   Tables, like text, can be stored as a glossary entry. If you use the same type of table repeatedly, you can save considerable time by storing the table as a glossary. To store a table as a glossary, select the entire table and choose the Edit Glossary command. Type a name for the table glossary and choose OK. To later insert the table glossary, type the table glossary name and press F3.

Using the Table Insert Command

To insert a table in a document, follow these steps:

1. Position the insertion point where you want the top left corner of the table.

2. Choose the Table Insert Table command. The Insert Table dialog box shown in figure 12.3 appears.

FIG. 12.3.

The Insert Table
dialog box.

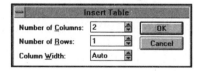

3. Type the number of columns you want in the Number of Columns text box.

4. If you know the number of rows you will need, type the number of rows in the Number of Rows text box.

   If you are unsure, don't worry. You can easily add rows to the end of a table or in the middle of the table.

5. If you know how wide you want all columns, adjust the Column Width box.

Column widths can be easily changed if you are unsure of the column width or later want to adjust the table.

6. Choose OK or press Enter.

The table appears in your worksheet. It may be invisible, or it may show because table gridlines have been turned on. The insertion point appears in the first cell.

Hiding Gridlines and End Marks

Table gridlines can show you the outline of your cells and table, which makes working in tables easier. Figure 12.4 shows a table in which the gridlines and end marks are turned off. Figure 12.5 shows the same table with the gridlines and end marks turned on. You can see how they help you see the table. Gridlines do not print.

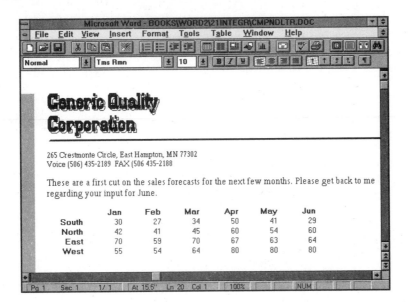

FIG. 12.4.

In this table, gridlines and end marks are turned off.

If you want gridlines on or off, choose the Table Gridlines command. This command toggles gridlines on or off. A check mark appears to the left of the command if gridlines are turned on. To turn end marks on or off quickly, press Shift+Ctrl or click on the paragraph mark in the ribbon.

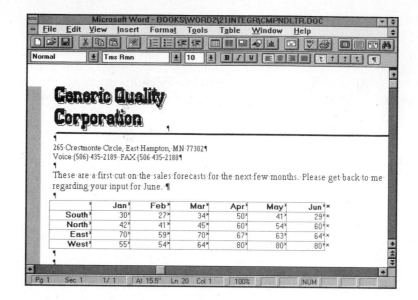

FIG. 12.5.

This table is easier to see and edit because gridlines are turned on.

As an alternate method for hiding or displaying gridlines and end marks, follow these steps:

1. Choose the Tools Options command.

2. Select the View Category. The Options dialog box for view settings is shown in figure 12.6.

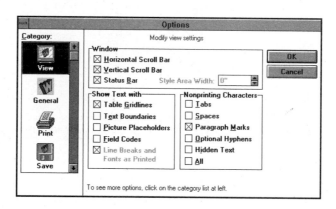

FIG. 12.6.

The View Categories options enable you to turn on gridlines.

3. Select or clear the Table Gridlines check box under the Show Text With group.

4. Select or clear Paragraph Marks under Nonprinting characters.

5. Choose OK or press Enter.

If you need to switch back and forth between showing and hiding the gridlines, you may want to add a custom button to the toolbar. Use the methods described in Chapter 29 to add the TableGridlines macro to a button you designate on the toolbar. With that button, you can toggle the gridlines on or off with a click.

T I P

Typing and Moving in a Table

When you create a new table, the insertion point flashes in the first cell—the cell at the upper left corner of the table. To insert text or numbers in the cell, just start typing.

As you enter text into a cell, you may type more characters than fit in one line. Characters simply wrap to the next line in the cell. In a Word for Windows table, the entire row of cells expands downward to accommodate the text. The same thing happens if you press Enter in a cell. The insertion point moves to the next line down, and the row becomes taller. Each cell acts like a miniature word processing page.

If you type more text in a row than will fit on a single page, the text that exceeds the page is not printed. To avoid this problem, limit the text within the cell to less than the page length or consider entering text in multiple rows. Page breaks can be inserted between rows. If a cell will not fit on the page, a page break is inserted above the row containing the cell. A page break cannot be inserted within a cell.

T I P

To move forward through the cells in the table, press the Tab key. Press Shift+Tab to move backward through the cells. To move with the mouse, click in the cell at the point where you want the insertion point to appear.

If you reach the last cell in the table (the lower right cell) and press Tab, you create a new row of cells at the end of the table and move the insertion point into the first cell of that row. To leave the table, you must press an arrow key or use the mouse to move the insertion point outside the table.

T I P   Don't be concerned with the number of rows in a table. Additional rows are added to the end of the table by pressing the Tab key when the insertion point is in the last cell of the table.

Arrow keys also help you move around in a table. Table 12.1 summarizes these keyboard movements and includes several other handy shortcuts to help you move around in a table.

Table 12.1. Shortcut Keys Used To Move in a Table

Key combination	Function
Tab	Moves insertion point right one cell; inserts a new row when pressed in the bottom right cell.
Shift+Tab	Moves insertion point left one cell.
Arrow key	Moves insertion point character by character through a cell and into the next cell when the insertion point reaches the end of the current cell.
Alt+Home	Moves insertion point to the first cell in the row.
Alt+End	Moves insertion point to the last cell in the row.
Alt+PgUp	Moves insertion point to the top cell in the column.
Alt+PgDn	Moves insertion point to the bottom cell in the column.

Editing a Table

To format your table, you will need to select cells, rows, or columns. Tables often need to have additional rows or columns inserted or to have rows sorted.

Selecting and Editing Cells

After you enter text, numbers, or graphics in your table, you probably need to format or edit the table. You have two ways to select the contents of a table: by character, for which you use Word for Windows' usual character-selection techniques; and by cell, for which Word for Windows offers special techniques.

When the entire cell or cells is selected, the entire cell appears darkened (see fig. 12.7). Word for Windows has techniques that enable you to easily select an entire row, an entire column, or the entire table.

	Jan	Feb	Mar	Apr	May	Jun
South	30	27	34	50	41	29
North	42	41	45	60	54	60
East	70	59	70	67	63	64
West	55	54	64	80	80	80

FIG. 12.7.

A selected cell.

Selecting by Menu

You can select rows, columns, or the entire table by using commands from the menu. Follow these steps:

1. Move the insertion point into the cell containing the row or column you want selected. Any cell will do if you need to select the table.

2. Choose either Table Select Row, Table Select Column, or Table Select Table.

Selecting by Mouse

You also can use a mouse to select the contents of a cell. Just drag across characters or double-click words in the usual way. As with the keyboard, you can extend the selection beyond the cell: as soon as the selection reaches the border of a cell, you begin selecting entire cells rather than characters. In addition, each cell contains special selection areas, which you can use with the mouse. If you move the I-beam mouse pointer to the left or upper edge of a cell, the I-beam turns into an arrow pointer. When you click or double-click the arrow, you select cells, rows, or columns. When you drag the arrow, you select groups of cells. Table 12.2 summarizes the mouse selection techniques.

Table 12.2. Using the Mouse To Select Groups of Cells

Item to select	Mouse action
Characters	Drag across characters.
Cell	Click the cell selection area at the left inside edge of the cell.
Group of cells	Select first cell or characters; then drag to the last cell.
Horizontal row	Click the selection area to the left of the table; drag down for multiple rows.
Vertical column	Click the top line of the column; drag to either side for multiple columns. (Pointer appears as a solid black down arrow when positioned correctly.)
Vertical column	Click the right mouse button anywhere in the column; drag to either side for multiple columns.
Table	Click in selection area to left of top row and drag down to select all rows or Shift-click to the left of the last row.

Selecting with the Keyboard

Word for Windows provides several other keyboard techniques for selecting cells and groups of cells. These methods are listed in table 12.3.

Table 12.3. Using Shortcut Keys To Select Cells

Key combination	Selects
Tab	Next cell
Shift+Tab	Previous cell
Shift+arrow key	Character by character in the current cell, and then the entire adjacent cell
F8+up or down arrow	Current cell and cell above or below (press Esc to end the selection)

Key combination	Selects
F8+left or right arrow	Text in current cell (character-by-character), and then all of adjacent cell (press Esc to end the selection)
Alt+5 (on numeric keypad)	Table

When you select with an arrow key, you first select each character in the cell. As soon as you go beyond the border of the cell, however, you begin selecting entire cells. If you change arrow directions, you select groups of adjacent cells. If you use Shift+right arrow or F8+right arrow to select three adjacent cells in a row and then you press the down-arrow key once, for example, you extend the selection to include the entire contents of the three cells below the original three.

Editing and Deleting Cell Contents

To edit selected text, use Word for Windows' usual text-editing techniques. These character and word selection techniques are discussed in Chapter 4.

You also can delete selected cells. When you select and delete the contents of one or several cells by using the Edit Cut command, the Del key, or the Backspace key, the cells are left empty, but the cells themselves remain. To delete the cell grid and its contents, refer to the section "Adding or Deleting Cells" later in this chapter.

> To delete a table, select the table and at least one line of text outside the table. Then choose Edit Cut, or press Del or Backspace.
>
> **T I P**

Formatting Cell Contents

You can format the contents of a cell or an entire table, using the ruler and ribbon or the same Format Character and Format Paragraph commands you use in the body copy. You can select the contents of a row and make it boldface, for example, or you can select and center all the text in a column of cells. Use Word for Windows' usual selection techniques (such as pressing Shift+arrow or double-clicking to select a word), or use the table-selection techniques from this chapter. Character and paragraph formatting choices apply to your selection—individual cells, groups of cells, or the entire table.

Moving, Copying, and Linking Cells and Tables

Unless you do everything perfectly the first time, you will need to reorganize data in your tables. Word for Windows gives you all the flexibility of moving and copying in a table that you have with text. With Word for Windows, you also can link cells in a table or link two tables in a document. After you change one table, you only need to update the document to change the other table automatically.

Using the Mouse to Drag and Drop Cells

The mouse shortcuts that work with text in body copy also work on cell contents, cells, or an entire table.

To move or copy the characters in a cell or one or more cells and their cellular structure, follow these steps:

1. Select the characters or entire cell(s) you want moved.

2. Move the mouse pointer over selected characters until it changes from an I-beam to an arrow pointed up and to the left, as shown in figure 12.8. (The pointer still may be an arrow if you have not moved it out of the selected area.)

FIG. 12.8.

Use the pointer to drag cells, rows, or columns.

	Jan	Feb	Mar	Apr	May	Jun
South	30	27	34	50	41	29
North	42	41	45	60	54	60
East	70	59	70	67	63	64
West	55	54	64	80	80	80

3. To move, hold down the left mouse button. To copy, hold down Ctrl and then the left mouse button. Notice the message in the status bar.

4. Position the grayed insertion point where you want the moved or copied characters or cells to appear. Position the pointer over the top left cell of the place where you want a range of cells to appear.

   The insertion point will appear gray and display a gray box at its bottom end.

5. Release the mouse button.

Using Commands

The **Edit Cut**, **Copy**, and **Paste** commands work much the same way in a table as they do with text outside a table. These commands enable you to move or copy cells within a table or copy a table to another location. You can cut and copy a single cell, multiple cells, or an entire table.

If you select only the text, number, or picture within a cell, then you will copy or cut what you have selected, just as you would in a document's body copy. But if you select the entire cell or multiple cells, you will copy the cell boundaries as well.

If you select an entire cell, the **Copy** command copies the entire cell to the clipboard. The **Cut** command moves the entire contents of the cell to the clipboard. The cell's boundaries remain in the table. When you paste cells from the clipboard, the cell containing the insertion point receives the first cell on the clipboard. The original cells in the table will be replaced by the contents of the cells on the clipboard, as shown in figures 12.9 and 12.10.

	Jan	Feb	Mar	Apr
South	30	27	34	50
North	42	41	45	60
East	70	59	70	67
West	55	54	64	80

FIG. 12.9.

These selected cells are being copied.

	Jan	Feb	Mar	Apr	Apr
South	30	27	34	50	50
North	42	41	45	60	60
East	70	59	70	67	67
West	55	54	64	80	80

FIG. 12.10.

The same cells pasted into a blank area.

When you paste cells, the **Paste** command becomes **Paste Cells**, and the cells are pasted as cells in a table. If you copy an entire row or column, the command becomes **Paste Row** or **Paste Column**, respectively. When you paste cells into an area not formatted as a table, they arrive as a table. When you paste a group of cells into an existing table, the table expands, if necessary, to accommodate the new cells.

You also can paste text from outside a table into a single cell in a table. Just copy or cut the text, move the insertion point inside a cell, and choose the **Edit Paste** command.

To move or copy cells, follow these steps:

1. Select the cells you want to move or copy.

2. Choose the **Edit Cut** command if you want to move the cells. Choose the **Edit Copy** command if you want to copy the cells.

3. Select an area in the table that matches the shape and size of the area you selected in step 1.

Word will warn you if the shape and size of the copied cells do not match the shape and size of the cells being pasted into.

4. Choose the Edit Paste Cells command.

Using the Outliner

The Word for Windows outline view provides another option for reorganizing rows, columns, and cells. Switching to outline view enables you to move an entire row of selected cells by dragging the selection to the location where you want the data to appear. To move a row of cells, follow these steps.

1. Choose the View Outline command.

A small box, called a *body text symbol*, appears to the left of each row (see fig. 12.11).

2. Select the row by clicking the body text symbol.

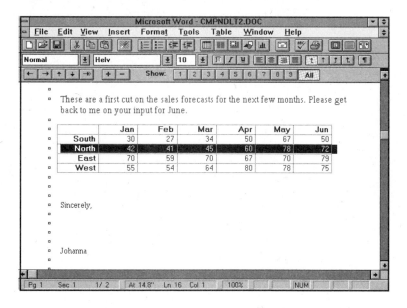

FIG. 12.11.

Drag the body text symbol for a row to a new location.

3. Select the up or down arrows in the outline bar or drag the body text symbol up or down to move the selected row to the desired location.

A real shortcut for moving table rows up or down is to select the entire row, and then press Shift+Alt+up or down arrow. You do not have to be in outline mode for this to work, nor does the document need an outline.

T I P

Adding or Deleting Cells, Rows, and Columns

Word for Windows enables you to change the structure of a table by adding and deleting cells, rows, and columns. You can add or delete one or many cells, rows, or columns with a single command. The Table menu changes its Insert command, depending on what you have selected.

If a cell is selected, the Table menu displays Insert Cells and Delete Cells commands. If a column is selected, the Table menu displays the Insert Column and Delete Column commands. If a row is selected, the menu displays Insert Row and Delete Row.

Adding or Deleting Cells

To add cells to or delete cells from an existing table, follow these steps:

1. Select the cells you want to add or delete.

2. Choose the Table Insert Cells command or Table Delete Cells command.

   The Insert Cells or Delete Cells dialog boxes appear, depending on which command you choose (see figs. 12.12 and 12.13).

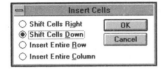

FIG. 12.12.

This dialog box appears if you are inserting cells.

340 USING ADVANCED FEATURES

FIG. 12.13.

This dialog box
appears if you
are deleting
cells.

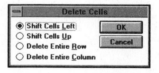

3. Choose the appropriate option button that corresponds to shift-
ing the existing cells to the position you want. You also have the
option of inserting or deleting an entire column or row.

Choosing the **I**nsert Cells command inserts blank cells at the location of the selected cells and shifts the selected cells either down
or right.

Choosing the **D**elete Cells command deletes the selected cells and
shifts adjacent cells either up or left to fill the vacancy.

4. Choose OK or press Enter.

T I P If you want to delete cell contents without deleting the actual cell,
select the cell contents you want to delete and press the Del key or
the Backspace key.

Adding or Deleting Columns and Rows

Columns and rows can be inserted and deleted from a table using the
same commands you used to insert or delete cells. Columns and rows
can be added to the end of the table or they can be inserted within the
table.

If the insertion point is positioned at the last position in the last cell,
press Tab to insert a new row at the end of the table. If you need to
insert or delete rows through the middle of an existing table, follow
these steps:

1. Select the row(s) where you want to insert or delete.

2. Choose the T**a**ble **I**nsert Row or T**a**ble **D**elete Row command.

When you insert a row, the selected row is shifted down and a
blank row is inserted (see fig. 12.14). When you delete a row, the
selected row is deleted and lower rows move up.

	Jan	Feb	Mar	Apr	May	Jun
South	30	27	34	50	67	50
North	42	41	45	60	78	72
East	70	59	70	67	70	79
West	55	54	64	80	78	75

FIG. 12.14.

After inserting
at the selected
rows.

> If the Table Insert or Delete command for rows or columns does not appear on the menu, you have selected only cells. You must select the rows or columns you want to work with so that Word for Windows will know which Insert or Delete command to add to the menu.

T I P

To insert or delete one or more columns within a table, follow these steps:

1. Select one or more columns where you want columns inserted or deleted.

   When you insert columns, the selected columns shift right to make room for the inserted blank columns. When deleting, selected columns are removed and columns to the right shift left to fill the gap.

2. Choose the Table Insert Column or Table Delete Column command.

If a column is inserted, the table looks like it does in figure 12.15. If a column is deleted, the table looks like it does in figure 12.16.

	Jan	Feb	Mar	Apr		May	Jun
South	30	27	34	50		67	50
North	42	41	45	60		78	72
East	70	59	70	67		70	79
West	55	54	64	80		78	75

FIG. 12.15.

Inserting a
column shifts
existing
columns right.

	Jan	Feb	Mar	Apr	Jun
South	30	27	34	50	50
North	42	41	45	60	72
East	70	59	70	67	79
West	55	54	64	80	75

FIG. 12.16.

Deleting a
column shifts
existing
columns left to
fill the gap.

Inserting a column as the last column requires a different procedure. To insert a column to the right of a table, follow these steps:

1. Position the insertion point at the end of a table row outside the table. This places it in front of an end-of-row mark.

If gridlines and end marks and are not displayed on your screen, refer to the earlier section in this chapter, "Hiding Gridlines and End Marks."

2. Choose the Table Select Column command.

3. Choose the Table Insert Column command.

To insert additional columns to the right of the table, choose the Edit Repeat command.

T I P If you want to quickly insert multiple columns at the right edge of the table, select from the existing table as many columns as you want to insert. (Dragging across with the right mouse button is a quick way to do this.) Choose the Edit Copy command. Move the insertion point to the end of the first row of the table and choose the Edit Paste command. Reselect these new columns and press the Del key to clear them.

Sorting Tables

Tables often are created to arrange data in columns and rows. To sort a table, follow these steps:

1. Select the whole table if you want to sort the whole table based on the first column. Alternatively, select only the rows you want to sort. If you want to sort the table on a column other than the first column, select that column.

2. Choose the Tools Sorting command.

3. Select from the Ascending or Descending options and the Key Type.

4. If you selected more than one column, you can type the number of the column you want to base the sort on in the Field Number box.

5. If you want to sort only the selected column and not the entire table, select the Sort Column Only check box. This option is grayed (unavailable) if more than one column is selected.

6. Choose OK or press Enter.

The Edit Undo command reverses the Sorting command if used immediately after sorting. You may want to save your document before sorting so that you can return to it if it is sorted incorrectly.

Merging Multiple Cells

Sometimes you will want text or a figure to span the width of multiple cells. A heading is an example of text you may want to stretch across several columns. Word for Windows enables you to merge multiple cells in a row into a single cell. Merging cells converts their contents to paragraphs within a single cell.

To merge multiple cells in a row into a single cell, follow these steps:

1. Select the cells you want to merge (see fig. 12.17). Only cells in a single row can be merged.

		Sales Forecast			
	Jan	Feb	Mar	Apr	Jun
South	30	27	34	50	50
North	42	41	45	60	72
East	70	59	70	67	79
West	55	54	64	80	75

FIG. 12.17.

Select cells you want to merge.

2. Choose the **Ta**ble **M**erge Cells command.

   The selected cells condense into a single cell (see fig. 12.18). You may need to reformat the contents so that the cell aligns correctly.

		Sales Forecast			
	Jan	Feb	Mar	Apr	Jun
South	30	27	34	50	50
North	42	41	45	60	72
East	70	59	70	67	79
West	55	54	64	80	75

FIG. 12.18.

Merge cells to put text such as titles into a single, wider cell.

Cells that have been merged can be returned to their original condition. To split merged cells, follow these steps:

1. Select the cell that was merged previously.

2. Choose the **Ta**ble **Sp**lit Cells command.

If the selected cell has not been merged, the **Sp**lit Cells command will not be available.

Changing Column Width

When a table is first created, the columns are sized equally to fill the area between the right and left margins. You can set column or cell widths in three ways: drag the right cell border of the column in the table, drag the T column marker on the ruler, or choose the Table Column Width command.

When you change a column's width, the columns to the right shift. This means that if you increase a column's width, the width of the table increases. If you decrease a column's width, the width of the table decreases.

Dragging Cell Borders

To change the width of a column using the mouse, position the pointer on the right border of the column. The pointer changes to a vertical double bar when it is positioned properly. (The pointer changes even if the gridlines are turned off.) Drag this column marker to the desired column width and release the mouse button.

If you want to keep the size of the table the same and just change the cell width, hold down the Shift key as you drag. If you want to keep the size of the table the same and change all cells to the right an equal amount, hold down the Ctrl key as you drag.

If the entire column is selected or if cells are not selected, the entire column adjusts to the new width. If cells within the column are selected, only the selected cells adjust to the new width.

Figure 12.19 shows the shape of the pointer when it is correctly positioned to drag a cell wider.

	Jan	Feb	Mar	Apr	Jun
South	30	27	34	50	50
North	42	41	45	60	72
East	70	59	70	67	79
West	55	54	64	80	75

Using the Ruler To Change Column Width

When the insertion point is positioned in a table, you can make T column width markers appear on the ruler. If the ruler is not turned on, choose the View Ruler command. If the T column markers do not show on the ruler, click at the far left end of the ruler until they appear. Drag the column width marker of the column you want to adjust to the desired width and release the mouse button. If the entire column is selected or nothing in the column is selected, the entire column adjusts to the new width. If cells within the column are selected, only the selected cells adjust to the new width.

If you want to change the width of a column without affecting the size of the table, hold down the Shift key as you drag a column width marker; the overall width of the table will remain the same. The column to the right of the adjusted column will change its width to accommodate the column width you are adjusting.

If you have multiple columns to the right of the adjusted column, and you want all columns to the right to split the difference and adjust equally, hold down the Ctrl key as you drag the column width marker.

Using the Column Width Command

The Table Column Width command is useful if you want to change the width of multiple columns with a single command or if you want to define the width of columns by specific amounts. The Table Column Width command also enables you to change the distance between columns.

To change column width using the Column Width command, follow these steps:

1. Select the columns or cells whose width you want to change.

2. Choose the Table Column Width command.

   The Column Width dialog box appears (see fig. 12.20).

	Jan	Feb	Mar	Apr	Jun
South	30	27	34	50	50
North	42	41	45	60	72
East	70	59	70	67	79
West	55	54	64	80	75

FIG. 12.20.

The Column Width dialog box.

3. Select or type a number in the Width of Columns text box.

4. Select or type a number in the Space between Cols text box.

   The space you set in this box is divided between the left and right margins within the cell—just as though the cell were a small page and you are entering the combined value for the left and right margins.

5. If you want to adjust other columns, choose the **Previous** Column or **N**ext Column buttons to keep the dialog box open and move to the next column. The **W**idth of Columns label will change to tell you which row you are formatting.

6. Choose OK or press Enter.

Changing Column Spacing

The Column **W**idth dialog box enables you to control the amount of space between columns. When a table is first created, the number of columns you choose for the table are of equal size and span the distance between margins. Included in the column width is a default column spacing setting of .15 inches. To change the spacing between columns, follow these steps:

1. Select the columns you want to adjust. Select a row if you want to adjust all columns in the table.

2. Choose the **T**able Columns **W**idth command.

3. Select or type a number in the **S**pace Between Cols text box.

4. Choose OK or press Enter.

The column spacing will affect the cell's usable column width. If a column width is 2 inches and the column spacing is set to 0.50 inch, for example, the column width available for text and graphics is 1.5 inches.

Using Indents and Tabs in a Cell

Cells contain indents the same as a normal text paragraph. You can format these indents using the same techniques you would use to format a paragraph. Use the ruler or the Format **P**aragraph command. To change the indent or first line indent within a cell, follow these steps:

1. Select the cell.

2. Choose the Format **P**aragraph command.

   or

   Click in the ruler at the far right corner until you can see the double triangles that indicate the indent and first-line indent.

3. Set indents in the dialog box, and then choose OK, or drag the indent and first-line indent markers to a new location.

Pressing the Tab key moves you from one cell to the next in a table. Pressing Shift+Tab moves you to the previous cell. You also can set tabs within a cell. Select the cell or cells in which you want tabs, and set the tab stops in the usual way—using the ruler or the Format **Par**agraph or Format **T**abs commands. To move the insertion point to the tab stop within the cell, however, press Ctrl+Tab rather than just Tab.

Changing Row Height and Position

All rows are equal in height when a table first is created. The text and amount of paragraph spacing you add changes the height of the row. The **T**able Row **H**eight command enables you to set how far a row is indented from the left margin, the height of the row, and the alignment of the row between margins.

Setting Row Height

To set row height, follow these steps:

1. Select the rows whose height you want to adjust.

2. Choose the **T**able Row **H**eight command.

   The Row Height dialog box appears (see fig. 12.21).

	Jan	Feb	Mar	Apr	Jun
South	30	27	34	50	50
North	42	41	45	60	72
East	70	59	70	67	79
West	55	54	64	80	75

   FIG. 12.21.

   The Row Height dialog box.

3. Select a **H**eight of Row option.

Option	Result
Auto	Row height automatically adjusts to the size of the text or graphic up to the height of the page. Maximum height is the height of the page.
At Least	Sets minimum row height. Automatically adjusts row if text or graphic exceeds minimum.
Exactly	Sets a fixed row height. Text or graphics that exceed the fixed height are cut off on-screen and at printing.

4. If you choose At Least or Exactly in step 3, enter the number of lines you want specified in the **A**t box.

5. Choose the **P**revious Row or **N**ext Row button if you want to format other rows. The **H**eight of Row label will change to tell you which row you are formatting.

6. Choose OK or press Enter.

Changing Row Spacing

A little extra vertical spacing between rows can make your table easier to read. The amount of space between rows can be adjusted using the paragraph spacing icon on the ruler or by choosing the Format **P**aragraph command. To add space between rows, follow these steps:

1. Select the rows to which you want to add spacing.

2. Choose the Forma**t P**aragraph command.

3. Type or select a spacing in the Spacing **B**efore or the Spacing After boxes. You can use lines (li) or point (pt) measurements by typing the number and space and then the abbreviation.

4. Choose OK or press Enter.

Indenting Rows or Aligning Rows

With Word for Windows, you can control the position of a table by changing the alignment of rows. You also can indent selected rows to align with other text in your document. Row alignment and indentation does not affect the alignment of text within the cells.

To align rows between page margins, select the rows you want to align. Choose the **T**able Row Height command and select a Left, **C**enter, or **R**ight alignment. Choose OK or press Enter.

The Row Height dialog box also enables you to indent selected rows. When you indent a row, the entire row shifts right by the amount you specify, just as though you were indenting a paragraph. To indent a row, select the row, choose the **T**able Row **H**eight command, and enter the number of inches of indent you want in the **I**ndent from Left box.

You also can indent rows by selecting them and dragging the indent marker on the ruler. If you are unfamiliar with the indent marker, refer to Chapter 4.

Formatting a Table

Borders and shading can make a table more attractive and more read-able. Word for Windows enables you to add borders around the table or around selected cells. You also can draw gridlines within the table. To enhance the appearance or make important data stand out, you can use colored borders or shaded or colored backgrounds. In addition, 26 different shades and patterns are available for black-and-white laser printers—an important feature when you have to make a good impres-sion with your document.

> **T I P**
>
> If you spend a lot of time formatting tables with borders, shading, text alignment, and other formatting commands, you can create a style that combines the table formatting commands into a single style name. This style then can be applied to other tables with a single command. Applying a style not only saves you time but ensures consistency if a table must adhere to a specific format. Styles are discussed in Chapter 11.

To add borders or shading to all or selected parts of your table, follow these steps:

1. Select the entire table or the cells you want to shade or border.

2. Choose the Format Borders command.

   If you select the entire table, the Border Table dialog box appears, as shown in figure 12.22. If you select cells or part of the table, the Border Cells dialog box appears, which includes the same options as the Border Table dialog box.

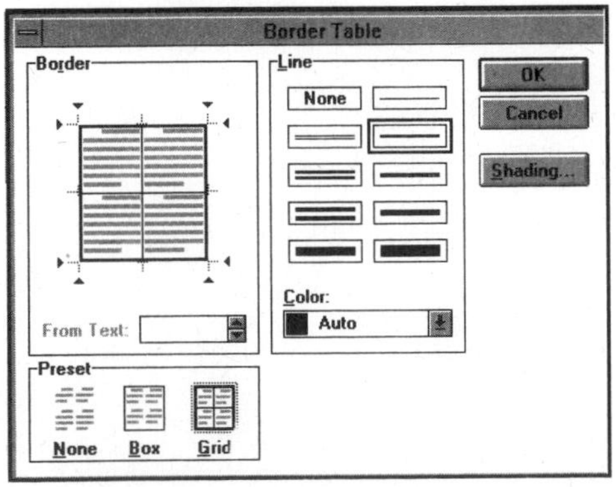

FIG. 12.22.

The Border Table dialog box.

3. Select and apply the border type. (The steps for this are described in the next section.)

4. Choose the **S**hading button and select the shading and colors you want. (The steps for this procedure are described in section "Selecting Shading and Colors.")

5. Choose OK or press Enter.

Figure 12.23 shows a table formatted with multiple border styles.

FIG. 12.23.

A table formatted with border styles.

	Jan	Feb	Mar	Apr	Jun
South	30	27	34	50	50
North	42	41	45	60	72
East	70	59	70	67	79
West	55	54	64	80	75

Selecting Border Formats

Using the mouse or keyboard, you can apply different line types and line weights to any border or line in the table. Two factors control which lines are formatted: the cells you select from the table, and the lines you select in the Border portion of the Border Cells dialog box. The number of cells you select defines how many cells are affected; the Border selection in the dialog box defines which edges or interior lines within the selection are affected.

You can apply borders using the defaults of no borders, borders around edges, or borders around edges with interior gridlines. You also have the choice of custom borders that can be applied to any line.

With the Border Cells dialog box open, follow these steps to apply default border settings:

1. Select the **L**ine weight.

   Mouse: Click the line type you want.

   Keyboard: Press Alt+L, and then use the arrow keys to move to your preferred line type.

2. Select a line color from the **C**olor list.

3. Select one of the Preset border patterns, **N**one, **B**ox, or **G**rid.

4. Watch the appearance of the sample shown in the Border box. If you do not like its appearance, return to step 1 or use the custom techniques that follow.

5. Choose OK or press Enter.

If you want to specify custom combinations of border types, weights, and colors, you can select from the Border box which lines will be affected by your Line and Color selections. Follow these steps:

1. Select the line type and weight from the **Line** options as described.

2. Select the line color from the **Color** list.

3. Select the line or edge you want affected from the sample in the Border box. Figure 12.24 shows the arrow head handles that point to the lines which can be affected by Line and Color.

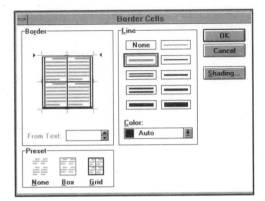

FIG. 12.24.

You can select any combination of individual edges or the interior gridlines to change.

Mouse: Click the line or outside border you want changed. To change multiple lines or edges at one time, hold down the Shift key and click the lines. After lines are selected, click a line type from the **Line** options.

Keyboard: Press Alt+R to move the focus to the Border box. Press the up- or down-arrow keys to cycle through combinations of selected lines. Stop on the combination you want and press the space bar to change them to the current Line and Color selections. You can alternate among the Line, Color, and Border options until you get the right combination.

4. Watch the sample in the Border box to see the result of your choices. If you do not like the sample appearance, return to step 1.

5. Choose OK or press Enter.

Selecting Shading and Colors

A table or selected cells can be enhanced with shading. Shading draws attention to a particular section of a table or it can be used to create reserved areas on office forms.

With the Border Cells dialog box on-screen, follow these steps to shade the selected cells:

1. Choose the **S**hading button. The Shading dialog box appears.

2. Select **N**one to remove shading or **C**ustom to apply shading.

3. If you select **C**ustom, select the pattern or percentage of shading from the **P**attern list. Figure 12.25 shows the 20% shading. Many shades are available.

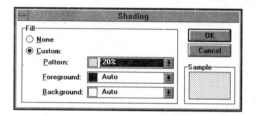

4. Select a foreground color from the **F**oreground list. Select Auto or Black if you are printing to a black and white printer.

5. Select a background color from the **B**ackground list. Select Auto or White if you are printing to a black-and-white printer.

6. Check the pattern you have created in the Sample box. If it is what you want, choose OK; otherwise return to step 3 and make other selections.

The background of selected cells are shaded when shading is applied. You can control the type of shading you want by setting the shading percentage. If you want lighter shading, choose a lower shading percentage. A higher percentage applies darker shading.

Your printer's resolution controls shading patterns. The higher the resolution—dots per inch (dpi)—the finer the shading. The resolution at which your printer prints graphics and shading is an option within the Printer Setup dialog box available under **F**ile **P**rint Setup. Experiment with the Pattern, Foreground, and Background options in the Shading dialog box to find the shading pattern that looks best.

Converting a Table to Text

You can convert the cell contents of a table to comma-separated or tab-separated text, or you can convert the contents of each cell into one or more paragraphs. To convert a table to text, follow these steps:

1. Select the rows of the table you want to convert to text or choose the entire table.

2. Choose the Table Convert Table To Text command.

   The Convert Table To Text dialog box appears.

3. Select a Convert To option from the dialog box. Each cell's contents can be separated by Paragraph Marks, Tabs, or Commas.

4. Choose OK or press Enter.

Converting Existing Text to a Table

When you copy data from another application or convert a file from a word processor that did not have tables, your data may be in tabbed columns. Converting it to Word tables will make it much easier to work with.

To convert text to a table, follow these steps:

1. Select the lines of text or paragraphs you want to convert to a table.

2. Choose the Table Convert Text to Table command.

   If Word for Windows is not sure how to convert the text, a dialog box like the one in figure 12.26 appears, listing the Convert Text to Table options.

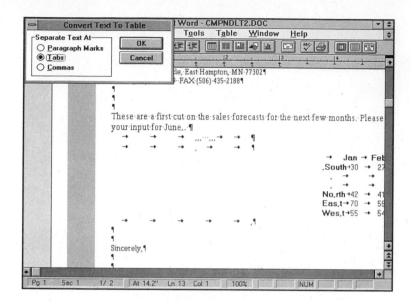

FIG. 12.26.

This dialog box appears if Word cannot determine how to convert text to a table.

Choose one of the following options from the dialog box:

Option	Result
Tabs	A tab character separates information in a cell. Word for Windows converts each paragraph and each line ending in a hard line break (created by pressing Shift+Enter) into a row. The number of columns is determined by the greatest number of Tab characters in the paragraphs or lines.
Paragraph Marks	A paragraph separates information to be in a cell. Each paragraph becomes its own row.
Commas	A comma separates information in a cell. Word for Windows converts each paragraph and each line ending in a hard line break (created by pressing Shift+Enter) into a row. The number of columns is determined by the greatest number of commas in the paragraphs or lines.

3. Choose OK or press Enter.

Inserting Text between Rows

You may have an occasion when you need to insert a paragraph or heading between rows in a table. If you start a table at the very top of a document and later decide you need to insert some text before the table, Word for Windows enables you to split the table and insert text between rows. To insert text above the table or between rows, follow these steps:

1. Position the insertion point in the row below where you want to insert the text. Position the insertion point in the first row of the table if you want to enter text above the table.

2. Choose the Table Split Table command or press Ctrl+Shift+Enter.

   A paragraph mark formatted with the Normal style is inserted above the row.

From Here . . .

Tables are one of the most useful features in Word for Windows. They are considerably better than using tabs for creating columns of lists, rosters, or tables of data. Word for Windows provides many other productivity enhancers that are simple to use. If you frequently use the same formats, see Chapter 11. You can easily create a style using an existing text, borders, or shading format. If you frequently enter the same titles, text, tables, or even pictures, you should examine how to use glossaries. Glossaries are discussed in Chapter 9. When you need to include tabular data from a worksheet, see Chapter 21 to learn how to import or link the data from the worksheet file into your Word for Windows documents.

Creating and Editing Columns

Sometimes what you have to say isn't best said in line after line of margin-to-margin text. Often you can help keep your reader interested and make your prose look a little more inviting by dividing the text into columns. Research has shown that text of newspaper column width is much faster to read. Columns not only make information more attractive, but also more readable.

In Word for Windows, you can create two types of columns: the *snaking columns* of text you see in newspapers, magazines, and newsletters; and the *parallel columns* of text and numbers you see in lists and tables. Chapter 12 discusses tables, which consist of columns and rows of text, numbers, or dates. Tables work well for parallel columns or for data that you want to keep aligned. This chapter discusses snaking columns, in which the text wraps continuously from the bottom of one column to the top of the next column. Figure 13.1 shows an example of a desktop published newsletter with newspaper columns. (To learn more about the desktop publishing capabilities of Word for Windows, refer to Chapter 28.)

♦ Published for clients of Ron Person & Co. in California at (123) 321-1224 ♦ Spring, 1992

What Can Windows Do for You?

by Ron Person
and Karen Rose

By now, most people have heard enough about Windows that they're at least *thinking* about it, even if they haven't started using it yet.

Since its announcement, Windows has taken the computing world by storm. And reviews of the product have been just as powerful--reviewer after reviewer finds Windows to be a robust, useful, and well-executed piece of software. Most industry watchers agree the PC world is moving in the direction of Windows with hurricane force.

So chances are, you're wondering what Windows can do for you.

Looking Into Windows

As a quick reminder, Windows is a graphic operating environment for your PC. It presents your applications in "windows" on your screen, and supplies a graphical interface that is shared by all applications designed for Windows. Programs work with the aid of pull-down menus, dialog boxes, visual icons, and a mouse-driven screen pointer. Important features of Windows include multitasking--the ability to run multiple programs

simultaneously, background processing--the ability to run tasks in the background while you continue working in the foreground, and DDE (dynamic data exchange)--the ability to link data between applications. You can run both DOS and Windows-specific applications under Windows.

There are a couple of ways you can implement Windows in your office. If you don't plan to buy Windows applications like Excel or Word for Windows, you can run your DOS applications under Windows and take advantage of Windows features like multitasking and background processing. Or, you can begin working with applications specifically designed for Windows, and get the true Windows interface, along with features like DDE.

Technically, you can run Windows on any PC from an 8088 or 80286 on up. But practically speaking, you ought to have at least a 386SX, and a 386 (or 486) is best. One reason you need a more powerful PC to run Windows is speed--the graphic interface will run slowly on an 8088 or a 286. Another reason is memory--on a 386 you can access up to 16MB of memory, while you're limited to 640K on a 286 or an 8088. And

finally, only on a 386 can Windows link files or do true background processing.

Much of the excitement about Windows focuses on how easy (and fun) it is to use, how much faster it is to learn new programs under Windows, how powerful and time-saving the linking capabilities are, and how useful multitasking and background processing are. How can those benefits translate to productivity gains in the CPA office?

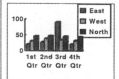

Financial Publishing Made Easy

One of the great advantages to working with Windows is that it's easy to copy information between files--even if the files are in different programs. For example, you can copy a Lotus worksheet or an Excel chart into a financial report you're putting together in WordPerfect or Word for

Using Windows—Ron Person & Co.—Spring, 1992—Page 1

FIG. 13.1.

A newsletter formatted with columns.

Creating Columns

To create columns, you divide the text into multiple columns of equal width, with equal spacing between the columns. The width of the columns depends on the number of columns you choose, your margins, and the amount of space you set between columns. If you have 1-inch left and right margins on a standard 8 1/2-inch paper width, for example, and you divide your text into three columns with 1/4 inch between them, you get three 2-inch-wide columns.

When you create columns, they apply to part of or the whole document, depending on how you create columns and whether you include section breaks in your document:

■ By default, columns apply to the whole document if your document includes no section breaks.

■ Columns apply to the current section if you divide your document into sections. (Columns apply to multiple sections if multiple sections are selected.)

■ You can position the insertion point where you want columns to start in your document, and apply columns from that point forward. Word for Windows inserts a section break at the insertion point.

■ You can select the text you want in columns and apply columns to just that selection. Word for Windows inserts a section break before and after the selected text.

The number of columns you can create depends on several factors, including the document margins, page orientation, column width, spacing between columns, size of the font, and the default tab settings. The smaller the text and the more space available for text on the page, the more columns you can have.

Word for Windows gives you two methods of creating columns: the Format Columns command and the Columns button on the toolbar.

Defining Sections

A new document based on the default Normal template is a single section with a one-column format. Sections are divisions within a document that can be formatted independently of one another. Sections are used to separate parts of a document so that they can have different numbering systems, different numbers of columns, different headers and footers, or different footnotes. Sections are described in detail in Chapter 7.

Additional sections are created by inserting section breaks. If the entire document uses the same number of columns, you may not need to insert section breaks. If different sections of the document have different numbers of columns, you need to insert section breaks that divide the document into sections and then format each of these sections with a different number of columns.

You can specify how Word for Windows handles section breaks (see Chapter 7). You can specify that sections run continuously so that you can have a different number of columns on the same page, or you can specify that each section start on a new page or on the next even-numbered or odd-numbered page.

In normal view, a section break appears as a double dotted line. Although columns appear in the correct width in normal view, they do not appear side by side. A section break does not appear at all in page layout view, but if that section is formatted for multiple columns, the columns are displayed.

T   I   P   All column formatting is stored in the section break mark at the end of a section, just as paragraph formatting is stored in the paragraph mark. If you delete a section break mark at the end of the section, that section takes on the column formatting and section formatting of the section below it.

Creating Columns with the Columns Button

You can use the Columns button to format columns. Columns apply to the entire document if you haven't formatted your document to include sections, or to the currently selected section (or sections) if you divided your document into sections. The Columns button enables you to create as many columns as are possible for the selected text or section.

To create columns with the Columns button, follow these steps:

1. If the toolbar is not displayed, choose the View Toolbar command.

2. Position the insertion point in the section you want to format into multiple columns. If the document has only one section, the entire document is formatted.

3. Move the pointer over the Columns button on the toolbar.

4. Click and drag the mouse down and right within the column pull-down box to select the number of columns you want. Figure 13.2 shows the Columns button with three columns selected.

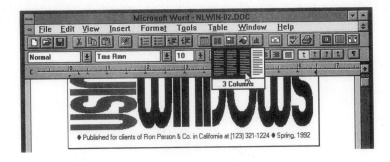

FIG. 13.2.

The Columns
button on the
toolbar.

The section is formatted with the number of columns you selected. If
you did not insert section breaks in the document, the entire document
is formatted with the number of columns you selected.

Creating Columns with the Columns Command

Although you can easily format your document with columns by using
the toolbar's Columns button, you get more options when you choose
the Format Columns command instead.

When you create columns with the Format Columns command, you can
specify whether columns apply to the whole document, the current
section(s), the insertion point forward, or the selected text (if text is
selected). If you choose columns for the entire document, all sections
are formatted with columns. If you already divided your document into
sections, Word for Windows assumes that you want to apply columns
to the currently selected section(s). If no text is selected, you have the
option to apply columns from the insertion point forward in your document, and Word for Windows inserts a section break at the insertion
point. If you select text before choosing the command, Word for Windows inserts a section break before and after the selected text and
applies the column format only to the selected text.

Using the Format Columns command, you also can specify how much
space you want between your columns and whether you want a vertical
line to appear between columns (the line appears only in the print preview view of your document and when you print; it does not appear in
normal or page layout views).

To create multiple columns with the Format Columns command, follow
these steps:

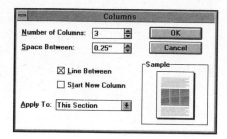

FIG. 13.3.

The Columns
dialog box.

1. Select the text you want to format into multiple columns, or position the insertion point inside the section you want to format or at the point where you want a new number of columns to begin.

2. Choose the Format Columns command.

   The Columns dialog box appears (see fig. 13.3).

3. Type or select the number of columns you want from the Number of Columns box.

4. Type or select the space you want between columns in the Space Between box.

5. Select the Line Between option if you want a line between the columns.

6. Select from the Apply To pull-down list the amount of text you want to format. The options shown in the Apply To list change depending on whether text is selected or whether your document contains multiple sections.

Option	Function
Selected Sections	Appears only when multiple sections are selected. Formats the sections you selected with columns.
Selected Text	Appears only when text is selected. Formats the text you selected with columns. Puts a section break before and after the selection.
This Point Forward	Appears only when no text is selected. Formats with columns from the insertion point forward. Puts a section break at the location of the insertion point.
This Section	Appears only when the insertion point is inside one of multiple sections. Formats with columns the section containing the insertion point.
Whole Document	Formats entire document with columns.

7. Choose OK or press Enter.

T I P

A column must be at least as wide as the default tab stop. The default tab stop is normally 0.5 inch, but you can change your document's default tabs by modifying the normal style. For more information, see Chapter 11.

Viewing Columns

Word for Windows has several ways to view a document. Views include normal, draft, page layout, and print preview. Depending on which view you are in, columns appear differently on your screen.

Normal view is faster for text entry but does not display columns side by side as they will appear when printed. The text appears in the same width as the column, but in one continuous column (see fig. 13.4). Normal view displays section breaks as a double dotted line and column breaks as a single dotted line. Normal view with Draft turned on is the fastest mode for data entry, but you do not see an accurate display of formatted text.

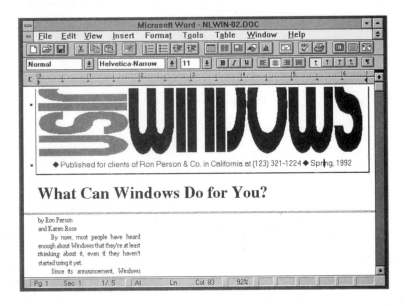

FIG. 13.4.

Normal view shows a single column and section breaks.

Page layout view displays columns side by side (see fig. 13.5). You can edit, insert column breaks, and adjust column widths with the ruler. Vertical lines between columns do not appear in this view.

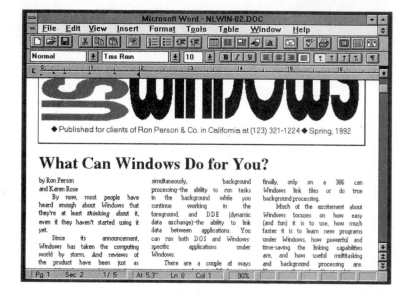

FIG. 13.5.

Page layout view shows side-by-side columns.

Print preview gives an overview of the page as it will appear when printed (see fig. 13.6). This view can display vertical lines between columns and enables you to adjust margins and page breaks.

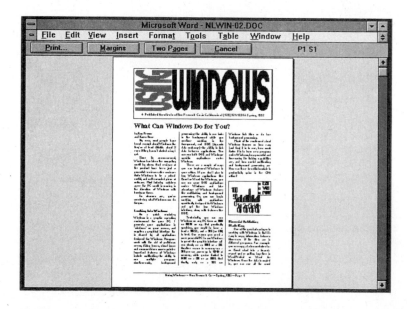

FIG. 13.6.

Print preview view of a page.

When you are editing a document, you may need to view a particular section up close. At other times you may need an overview of the entire page. The toolbar includes three buttons that enable you to magnify or reduce the size of the display (see fig. 13.7). The Zoom Whole Page button shows you a miniature view of the whole page in page layout view. The Zoom 100% button shows you a full-size page in normal view. The Zoom Page Width button shows you the full width of the page in whichever view you're currently working.

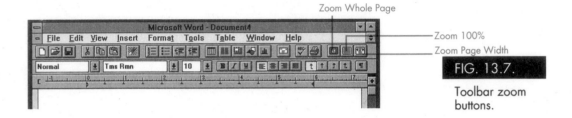

Zoom Whole Page

Zoom 100%

Zoom Page Width

FIG. 13.7.

Toolbar zoom buttons.

If you are viewing your document in normal or page layout view, you can zoom in on a section of your document or zoom out to display the entire page on the screen. You can select magnification of 25 to 200 percent with the View Zoom command. For more information on zooming the view, see Chapter 4.

Formatting Columns

The width of columns depends on the number of columns you choose, your document margins, and the amount of space you set between columns. When you divide a 8.5-inch-wide page that has 1-inch left and right margins into three columns with .25 inches of space between them, for example, you get three 2-inch-wide columns. If you increase the page margins or the spacing between columns, then the width of the columns decreases. Word for Windows columns are always of equal width and equal spacing. If you change the width or spacing of one column, all other columns in the section adjust to the same width and spacing.

If you want columns of uneven widths, you must convert the column text to a table. Refer to Chapter 12 to learn how to make parallel columns of uneven widths.

Columns are the length of the current section, or of the current page if there are no sections. The final column on the final page of your document may be shorter, however, than the preceding columns. By inserting a continuous section break at the end of columns that end unevenly on the last page of your document, you can balance the columns.

Adjusting Column Width and Spacing with the Ruler

You can easily adjust the width of columns by using the margin markers on the ruler. When you're working in columns, notice that the ruler changes to reflect column width, rather than page width. In the ruler's default indent view, you see indent markers, which you can use to change the indents for any selected paragraph. If you change to the ruler's margin view, however, you can see margin markers for each column (see fig. 13.8). In normal or page layout view, you can drag these markers left and right to change the width of the columns in the selected section. In page layout view you see the columns side by side, and therefore can change the column width and the space between the columns. All columns in the section adjust to be the same width.

FIG. 13.8.

Margin markers on ruler in columns.

To use the mouse and the margin marker on the ruler to adjust column width, follow these steps:

1. If the ruler is not displayed, choose the **View R**uler command.

2. Choose the **View P**age Layout command if you want to display columns side by side.

3. Position the insertion point in the section with the formatted columns. If both margin markers ([ ]) are not displayed on the ruler above each column, click on the margin icon ([) at the left end of the ruler to display them.

4. Drag the left and right column margin markers ([and]) for *one* column to adjust the column width and the spacing between *all* columns.

All other columns and the spacing between columns adjust to reflect the change.

Adjusting Spacing between Columns

Column width also can be adjusted by changing the spacing between columns. To adjust spacing between columns, follow these steps:

1. Position the insertion point in a column in the formatted section.

2. Choose the Format Columns command.

3. Enter the spacing you want between columns in the Space Between box. The default setting is 0.5 inch. Spacing can be set in inches ("), centimeters (cm), points (pt), or picas (pi).

4. Watch the sample box to see an approximate image of the effect from the spacing change. If you do not like the change, return to step 3 and set a new spacing.

5. Choose OK or press Enter.

If you enter a spacing that extends the formatted columns beyond the width of your document page, a message dialog box appears warning you that margins, spacing, or paragraph indents are too wide. Choose OK to clear the dialog box and enter a smaller measurement. Choose OK again.

Balancing Column Lengths

On pages where the text in columns continues on to the next page, Word for Windows automatically balances (lines up) the last line of text at the bottom of each column. But when columnar text runs out on a page, you may be left with two full-length columns and a third column that's only partially filled. You can balance column lengths so that the bottom of all the columns are within one line of each other. Figure 13.9 shows balanced and unbalanced columns.

To balance the length of multiple columns, follow these steps:

1. Position the insertion point at the end of the text in the last column of the section you want to balance.

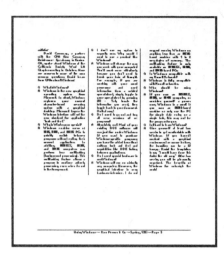

FIG. 13.9.

Unbalanced columns leave a ragged end; balanced columns are even.

2. Choose the **Insert B**reak command.

3. Select the Continuous Section Break option.

4. Choose OK or press Enter.

Typing and Editing Text in Columns

Typing and editing text in columns follows all the same rules—and takes advantage of the same shortcuts for typing, selecting, and editing any other text. (Refer to Chapter 4 for details.) Two tips will help you as you move around in and select columnar text:

■ To move from one column to the top of the next column using the keyboard, press Alt+down-arrow key. To move to the top of the previous column, press Alt+up-arrow key.

■ The selection bar that normally appears at the left margin of a page now appears at the left margin of each column in page layout view. When you move the mouse pointer into this area, it turns into an arrow you can use to select lines and paragraphs within a column.

As you type and edit columns, you sometimes may want to specify where a column will start or stop. A column break forces text to start at the top of the next column; a page break forces a column to start at the beginning of the next page.

Inserting Column Breaks

When Word for Windows creates columns, it automatically breaks the columns to fit on the page. But sometimes the column may break inappropriately. On a three-column page, for example, column two may end with a heading that should be at the top of column three. By inserting a column break directly before the heading, you shift the heading to the top of the next column, keeping the heading and its following text together.

To insert a column break, press Ctrl+Shift+Enter or follow these steps:

1. Position the insertion point where you want the new column to start.

2. Choose the **Insert Break** command.

   The Break dialog box appears (see fig. 13.10).

3. Select the **Column Break** option.

4. Choose OK or press Enter.

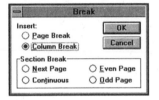

FIG. 13.10.

The Insert Break dialog box.

Another way you can force text to start at the top of the next column is to insert a continuous section break and then select the Start New Column option in the Columns dialog box.

> If you format a new section to start on a new column, and the section has a different number of columns from the preceding section, the new section starts on a new page.
>
> **T I P**

Inserting a Page Break

If you want a column to start on a new page, you can insert a page break. To insert a page break, press Ctrl+Enter or follow these steps:

1. Position the insertion point where you want the break.

2. Choose the **Insert** **B**reak command. The default selection is **P**age Break.

3. Choose OK or press Enter.

   The section continues on a new page.

From Here . . .

Columns are used extensively in desktop publishing to create newsletters, fliers, brochures, and much more. Tables are often called into play as well. To learn more about how to use Word for Windows as a desktop publishing program, refer to Chapter 28.

Working with Outlines

Many writers feel comfortable organizing their thoughts and even their schedules with outlines. If you're among that group of organized people, you are going to enjoy working with Word for Windows' outlining feature. In Word for Windows, an outline is a special view of your document that consists of formatted headings and body text. Nine possible outline heading levels are available: Heading 1, Heading 2, Heading 3, and so on through Heading 9. Each heading level can have one level of body text. Assigning each heading level a different formatting style enables you and the reader to quickly discern the organization of your document.

Having an outline for your document is useful in many ways. For one thing, an outline can help you organize your thoughts as you compose a new document. At a glance, you quickly can see an overview of your document that shows only the headings. Later, an outline can help you reorganize and edit your document. By "collapsing" parts of your document so that only the headings show, you can easily move an entire section—heading, subheadings, and any associated body text. But

Word for Windows has some other, not-so-obvious uses for outlines: you can easily number the parts of a document, change heading level formatting (each heading level has its own specific style), and use headings to generate tables of contents and other lists.

Viewing an Outline

To view an outline, choose the **View O**utline command. Figure 14.1 shows the first page of a document in the normal editing view, and figure 14.2 shows the same document in outline view with headings displayed. Figure 14.3 shows the document in an expanded outline view, with text and subheadings displayed.

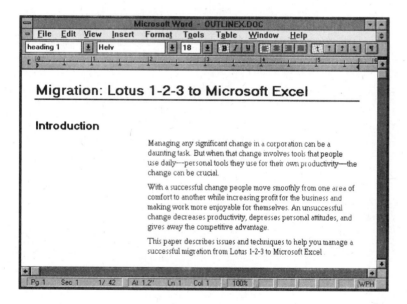

FIG. 14.1.

A document in normal view.

You can see that the outline view looks different from the normal editing view in several ways. First, the *outline bar* has replaced the ruler. Second, the formatted headings and body text paragraphs are indented to different levels. Third, + or – icons display to the left of each heading and paragraph.

When you are in the outline view, you have the option of viewing headings at different levels or of viewing the entire document, including all body text. You also have a choice of displaying headings at selected levels or displaying headings and text. Seeing a large document as only headings gives you an opportunity to get a global perspective. You also can see where topics have been missed or where they are misplaced.

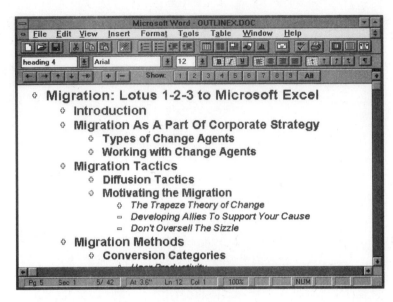

FIG. 14.2.

Outline view can show an over-view of contents by headings only.

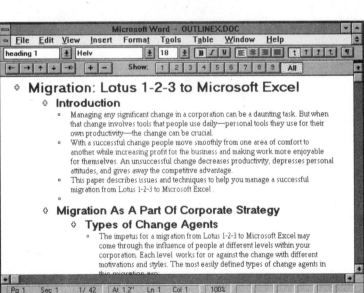

FIG. 14.3.

Outline view also can show detailed contents by expanding the outline.

The outline bar includes tools you can use to assign heading levels to text, to promote or demote headings, and to hide or display headings. Table 14.1 summarizes the functions of the individual buttons in the outline bar.

Table 14.1. The Functions of the Outline Bar

Buttons and Icons	Function
←	Promotes the heading (and its body text) by one level; promotes body text to the heading level of the preceding heading
→	Demotes the heading by one level; demotes body text to the heading level below the preceding heading
↑	Moves the selected paragraph(s) before the first visible paragraph that precedes selected paragraph(s)
↓	Moves the selected paragraph(s) after the first visible paragraph that follows selected paragraph(s)
→»	Demotes a heading to body text
+	Expands the first heading level below the currently selected heading; repeated clicks expand through additional heading levels until body is expanded
−	Collapses body text into heading, then lowest level headings into higher level headings
Buttons 1 through 9	Display all headings and text through the lowest level number you click
All	Displays all text if some is collapsed; displays only headings if all text is expanded

In the sections that follow, you learn how to use these buttons to create and reorganize your outline.

In figure 14.2, note that two different types of screen icons display to the left of the headings and paragraphs in the outline. A + (plus sign) means that subordinate headings (those at a lower level than the heading being examined) or paragraphs of body text are associated with the heading. A − (minus sign) indicates that no headings or paragraphs are beneath the heading.

Creating an Outline

Creating an outline does two things: organizes your work by heading, subheading, and body text; and applies formatting to each heading level. Styles define the formatting applied to each heading level. The first level of heading is formatted by the style Heading 1, the second level is formatted by Heading 2, and so on, through Heading 9. Body text is formatted by the Normal style. The Heading and Normal styles are predefined by Word for Windows; however, you can redefine any of those styles using the Format Style command (see Chapter 11).

Word for Windows provides two ways to create an outline. The first method is to select the outline view and assign heading levels to your text by using the tools on the outline bar (while creating or after creating the document). This chapter describes this method. The second method is to work in the normal (or draft or page layout) view of your document and assign appropriate styles such as Heading 1 or Heading 2 to headings. To learn how to apply styles to text, see Chapter 11.

To create an outline in a new or existing document, follow these steps:

1. Choose the **View Outline** command.

2. Type a heading or select the text you want to convert to a heading. Select the heading by moving the insertion point anywhere within the heading's text, or by clicking to the left of the heading (but not on the plus or minus icon).

   If you're creating an outline from scratch (in a new file), the level 1 heading is applied as you begin typing.

3. Assign the appropriate heading level by clicking in the outline bar or by pressing a shortcut key, as follows:

Result	Mouse action	Shortcut key
Promote heading one level	Click on left arrow	Press Shift+Alt+ left-arrow key
Demote heading one level	Click on right arrow	Press Shift+Alt+ right-arrow key
Convert heading to body text	Click on double arrow	Press Shift+Alt+5 (with Num Lock off)
Convert body text to heading	Click on right or left arrow	Press Shift+Alt+left- or right-arrow key

4. Press Enter to end the heading (or body text) and start a new heading (or body text) at the same level.

While you work in your document in normal or page layout view, you may come to text that should be a heading in the outline. You can stay in the normal or page layout view and create this heading. One way is to format the paragraph with a heading style. Another method is to move the insertion point into the heading text and press Shift+Alt+left-arrow key. The paragraph containing the insertion point is formatted to the same heading level as the preceding outline heading in the document. Use Shift+Alt+left-arrow key or Shift+Alt+right-arrow key to adjust the heading to the level you want.

Formatting Your Outline

When you create an outline, you're actually applying styles to the headings in your document. The styles determine your document's formatting. Unless Heading 1 has been redefined in your document, for example, the style applies the Helvetica font in 12-point size, boldfaced and underlined, with a 1-line space before the heading.

If you want the headings in your document to be formatted differently from the predefined heading styles, you must redefine the heading styles. If you want the first-level headings in your outline to be formatted differently, for example, you must redefine the Heading 1 style. You can redefine styles by formatting an example or by choosing the Format Style command, choosing the **D**efine button, and then redefining a style. (To learn more about defining styles, see Chapter 11.) When you redefine a style for a heading, the format change cascades through all headings at that level.

Promoting and Demoting Headings

Promoting a heading means raising its level in the outline. You may promote a Heading 3 to a Heading 2, for example, to make the indent smaller. *Demoting* does just the opposite. When you promote and demote headings, Word for Windows assigns the appropriate heading style for that level.

Using the Mouse To Promote/Demote Headings

You can use the mouse to promote or demote headings in two ways. One method uses the buttons in the outline bar. In the other method, you drag the heading's + or − icon left or right until the heading is at the level you want.

If you want to use the mouse and promote or demote only the selected heading(s) or text, follow these steps:

1. Choose the **View O**utline command (if you haven't already).

2. Select the paragraphs to promote or demote.

3. Click the left-arrow button in the outline bar to promote the heading.

   or

   Click the right-arrow button to demote the heading.

   or

   Click the double-arrow button to convert the heading to body text.

Headings are treated independently; associated subheadings are not promoted and demoted along with the headings. Body text, however, always remains associated with its heading. This method is useful for changing only the selected heading level while leaving subordinate text or levels alone.

To promote or demote a heading and have all subordinate headings and text change at once, follow these steps:

1. Choose the **View O**utline command.

2. Move the mouse pointer over the + or − icon that appears to the left of the heading you want to promote or demote (the pointer becomes a four-headed arrow). Click and hold the mouse button.

3. Drag the icon to the left to promote the heading and its subordinate subheadings and body text, or drag the icon to the right to demote. (Drag all the way right to demote a heading to body text.)

When you drag a heading to a new level, the mouse pointer becomes a two-headed arrow and a gray vertical line appears as you drag across each of the heading levels.

Using Keyboard Shortcuts To Promote/Demote Headings

You also can use keyboard shortcuts to promote and demote individual headings (and body text). You needn't be in the outline view to use this method; any view works.

To use shortcut keys to promote or demote a heading or portion of body text, follow these steps:

1. Select the heading(s) or body text to promote or demote.

2. Press Shift+Alt+left-arrow key to promote one level.

   or

   Press Shift+Alt+right-arrow key to demote one level.

   or

   Press Shift+Alt+5 (on the numeric keypad with Num Lock off) to demote to body text.

   Only selected headings and text are affected; associated subheadings are not promoted and demoted along with selected headings.

No matter which method you use, when you return to the normal editing view and display the ruler, you see that the appropriate heading styles have been applied to your outline headings.

Collapsing and Expanding an Outline

A *collapsed* outline shows only the headings down to a specific level. When an outline is *expanded* to a specific level, you see all headings down to that level as well as body text. You can collapse an outline all the way down so that only first-level headings show, or you can expand the outline all the way so that all the headings and body text show.

Collapsing and expanding your outline can help you to write and edit. By collapsing your outline, you can see an overview of your entire document and can move around quickly in the outline. To move to a particular section, just collapse to the level of the heading to which you want to move, select the heading, and then expand the outline. Also, you can use shortcuts to move entire headings and all their subordinate headings and text to new locations in the outline.

To collapse or expand the entire outline, use the numeric buttons on the right side of the outline bar. Click the lowest level you want to display in your outline. If you want to show levels 1, 2, and 3 but no lower levels, for example, click the 3 button. To display all heading levels but no body text, click the 9 button. To display all levels, including body text, click All. Clicking a number in the outline bar collapses or expands your entire outline uniformly. Figure 14.4 shows the outline in figure 14.2 with only two levels of headings displayed.

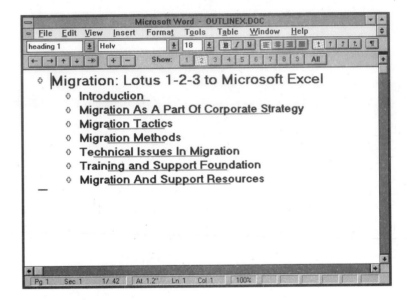

FIG. 14.4.

Collapsing an outline shows only higher levels of headings.

Using the Mouse To Collapse/Expand Headings

You also can use the mouse and the + and – icons in the outline bar to selectively collapse or expand headings, as in the following procedures:

- Collapse headings and body text into the selected heading by clicking the – icon in the outline bar.

- Expand heading's contents of selected headings by clicking on the + icon in the outline bar.

- Expand or contract a heading's contents by double-clicking on the + icon to the left of the heading in the outline view.

Using Keyboard Shortcuts To Collapse/Expand Headings

If you don't have a mouse or if you work faster on the keyboard, you can collapse and expand your outline by using shortcut keys. One shortcut enables you to save space by displaying only the first line of each paragraph designated as body text. Table 14.2 lists the shortcut keys available. Before using a shortcut key, you must select the heading or text you want to collapse or expand.

Table 14.2. Using Shortcut Keys To Collapse and Expand

Shortcut Key	Function
Alt+Shift+- (hyphen)	Collapses the selected heading's lowest level and collapses all body text below the heading. Repeated presses collapse additional levels.
Alt+Shift++ (plus sign)	Expands the selected heading's next lower level. Repeated presses expand additional levels and, after all headings are expanded, body text.
Alt+Shift+F	Shows only first line of each paragraph of body text (entire outline). Pressing the key combination again displays all text.

Reorganizing an Outline

You can select outline headings in any of the normal ways, using Word for Windows' selection techniques. The outline view, however, offers a shortcut for selecting that can be a real time saver. When you select an outline heading by clicking its icon in the outline view, you select the heading and its subordinate headings and body text.

Even if you don't use an outline to organize your thoughts before you begin writing, you can use an outline later to reorganize your document quickly. After you click a heading's + or – icon, you can move all the subordinate headings and text as a unit. (If you select only the words in an expanded heading, you move only the heading.)

You can move selected headings (along with associated subheadings and body text) by using the mouse or the keyboard. To move a selected heading upward (toward the first page) or downward (toward the last page), you can use any one of these methods:

- Press Alt+Shift+up- or down-arrow key.
- Drag the heading's icon up or down.
- Click the up or down arrow in the outline bar.

By selecting multiple headings and paragraphs, you can move them as a unit.

Numbering an Outline

If you need numbered outlines for legal documents, bids, or proposals, you can have Word for Windows add the numbers for you.

To number your outline (from any view), use the T**o**ols **B**ullets and Numbering command. You will have a choice as to whether you want to use an outline numbering method. You also can choose to create numbering that automatically updates itself as headings are reorganized. Figure 14.5 shows some of the numbering options available. Figure 14.6 shows an outline numbered using the legal numbering style. For detailed information on numbering, see Chapter 16.

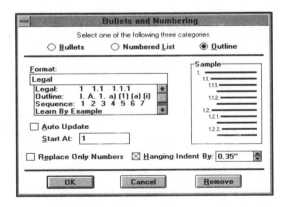

FIG. 14.5.

Use the Outline option to renumber outlines.

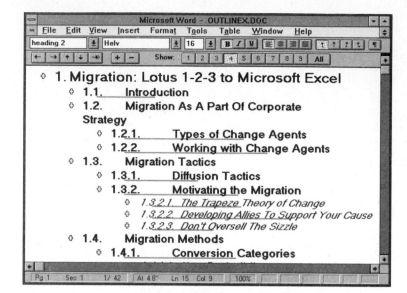

FIG. 14.6.

Automatic numbering makes legal and proposal documents easy to construct.

Using Outline Headings for a Table of Contents

If you need a table of contents, Word for Windows can build one from the outline. Word for Windows constructs tables of contents by accumulating outline headings and their page numbers.

To create a table of contents from outlining, use the Insert Table of Contents command. Chapter 16 goes into detail about how to use the Table of Contents dialog box shown in figure 14.7 to create a table of contents like the one shown in figure 14.8.

FIG. 14.7.

From this dialog box you can create a table of contents.

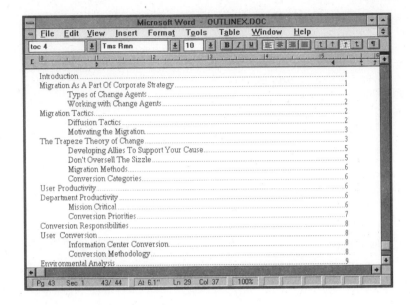

FIG. 14.8.

The finished table
of contents uses
outline headings
and document
page numbers.

> If you want to create a table of figures or references quickly, assign
> an unused outline heading level, such as Heading 9, to figure descrip-
> tions or references. When you choose the Insert Table of Contents
> command, specify that you want a table of contents using only
> Heading 9.
>
> T I P

Printing an Outline

You can print your document as seen in View Outline. To print the outline, choose the View Outline mode, display the levels of headings and
body text you want to print, and then choose the File Print command.

From Here . . .

The outlining capability of Word for Windows is one of the best available in a word processor. If you left school with a hatred of outlines,
you may want to check out what's available under View Outline before
you set your beliefs in concrete.

Outlining works well with Word for Windows' styles and table of contents features. You can learn how to reformat headings quickly throughout your document by examining styles in Chapter 11. If you need a list or table of contents of information associated with your outline, review the commands in Chapter 16.

Inserting Headers, Footers, and Document References

This chapter covers features in Word that enhance the appearance of your documents and make them easier to use. You learn how to add page numbers to your documents. You also learn to add headers and footers, which contain text and graphics that repeat on every page of your document; for example, you can include the chapter titles and page numbers in the header of a book manuscript. Footnotes are an essential part of many types of documents. Inserting, editing, and formatting footnotes is easy in Word. If several people are working on a document, they can use Word's annotation feature to add initialed comments to a document, and the comments will not be incorporated into the text.

Creating Headers and Footers

Headers and footers contain information repeated at the top or bottom of the pages of a document. The simplest header or footer may contain only a chapter title and page number. More elaborate headers or footers can contain a company logo (or other graphics), the author's name, the time and date when the file was saved or printed, and any other information that may be needed.

Headers and footers can be formatted like any other part of the document, but they usually are positioned within a page's top and bottom margins, although Word for Windows enables you to position them anywhere on the page. Word for Windows also gives you the option of having a different header or footer on the first page of a document or section of a document. You also can have different headers and footers on even and odd pages. This is a useful feature for chapter headers in books and manuscripts. Each section of a document—a chapter, for example—can have its own headers and footers.

Use the View Header/Footer command to add headers and footers to your document. When you add or edit a header or footer in the normal view, you work in a separate pane that appears at the top or bottom of the screen. In page layout view, headers and footers appear at the top or bottom of the page just as they would when they print. They can be edited and formatted in that location as with any other text.

Adding Headers and Footers

To add a header or footer to a document, follow these steps:

1. Choose View Normal if you are not already in normal view.

2. Choose View Header/Footer to display the Header/Footer dialog box shown in figure 15.1.

3. If you want a different header or footer on the first page or on the odd and even pages, check the appropriate boxes in the Header/Footer dialog box.

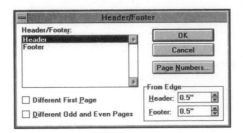

FIG. 15.1.

The Header/
Footer dialog
box.

4. Select either Header or Footer from the Header/Footer list and choose OK.

5. If you are in normal view and you select either or both of the Different First **P**age or the **Di**fferent Odd and Even Pages options, the Header/Footer list changes to give you the option to edit your choice of the First Header, First Footer, Even Header, Even Footer, Odd Header, or Odd Footer. Select the header or footer that you want to add or edit and choose OK.

6. Type the text for the header or footer. In normal view, type into the pane that appears as shown in figure 15.2. The field code for the page number was inserted by selecting the page number button (see the following section).

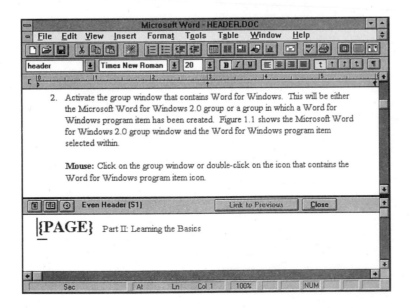

FIG. 15.2.

The Header/
Footer pane.

7. When you finish entering the text, choose the **C**lose button, or press Alt+Shift+C or Shift+F10, C.

When you are in normal view, you cannot see headers or footers without opening the Header/Footer pane. To view the placement of headers and footers as they will appear on the printed page, choose View **P**age Layout. Figure 15.3 shows the header from figure 15.2 as it will appear on the printed page.

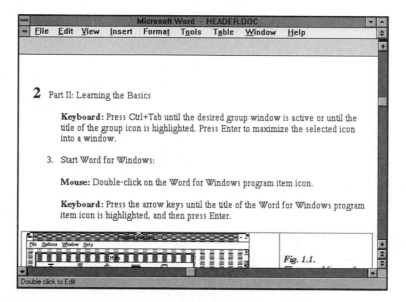

FIG. 15.3.

The header as it will appear on the printed page.

You also can add or edit a header or footer while in page layout view. When you first add a header of footer in page layout view, choosing the View **H**eader/Footer command places the insertion point into an empty header or footer at the top or bottom of the page. After you add the header or footer, you can edit it by scrolling directly to the top or bottom of the page and working on the text as you would any other text.

T I P   If you want the header or footer on the first page of a document or section to be blank, select the Different First **P**age option in the Header/Footer dialog box, and leave the First Header or First Footer blank.

Inserting Page Numbers, Dates, and Times

The Header/Footer pane in normal view contains buttons to easily insert field codes for the page number, date, and time (the date and time are updated at printing). You also can use three default tab stops for aligning text on the left, center, and right of the page. To insert a code in normal view, click the appropriate icon or press one of the following combinations:

To Insert	Press
Page numbers	Shift+Alt+P or Shift+F10, P
Current date	Shift+Alt+D or Shift+F10, D
Current time	Shift+Alt+T or Shift+F10, T

Headers and footers have default tabs set at the center and aligned to the right. To put page numbers, dates, or times in the center of the page or at the right side, press the Tab key and then choose a button to insert a field.

If you are in page layout view, use the **Insert Field** command to insert a code for the Date, Page, or Time. You can insert many other field codes into headers or footers besides those for the page number, date, and time that are inserted with the icons in the Header/Footer pane. You can, for example, insert fields to print the author's name (*{author}*), the file name of the document (*{filename}*), and the number of pages in the document (*{numpages}*). See Chapter 18 for additional information on using fields and field codes.

Editing Headers and Footers

Whether you work in the Header/Footer pane by choosing the **View Header/Footer** command while in normal view or work directly in the header or footer in page layout view, you edit and format headers and footers as you do any other text. You can use the menu commands such as Forma**t C**haracter, the ribbon, ruler, and toolbar, or the shortcut keys to apply character and paragraph formatting.

The default template, NORMAL.DOT, includes styles for headers and footers. Amazingly enough, the styles are named *header* and *footer*. You can modify the formatting of your headers and footers by redefining these styles using the Forma**t** Style command instead of directly formatting the Header/Footer text. See Chapter 11 for more information on styles.

To delete a header or footer, open the Header/Footer pane (in normal view) or scroll to the top or bottom of the document (in page layout view) and delete the text. Choose **C**lose (or press Alt+Shift+C or Shift+F10, C) if you are in the Header/Footer pane.

Each section in a document with multiple sections can have unique headers and footers. This is helpful if you format each chapter in a book as a separate section. When you create a new section, Word for Windows creates headers and footers for that section which are the same as for the previous section, if there are any. If you want different headers or footers for that section, place the insertion point in that section and edit the header or footer.

After you create a header or footer for a section, if you decide you want the header or footer to be identical to the one in the previous section, choose the **L**ink to Previous button in the Header/Footer pane and choose Yes when the message box appears. (The Link button is only active when the section's header or footer is different from that of the previous section's. If you are using a keyboard, press Shift+Alt+L for the **L**ink button.) See Chapter 7 for more information on working with sections.

Positioning Headers and Footers

Word for Windows enables you to position headers and footers in a number of different ways. You can change the vertical positioning of headers and footers—the distance from the top or bottom edge of the page—by using the **V**iew **H**eader/Footer or **F**ile Print Preview commands. The horizontal positioning can be adjusted using the paragraph formatting options on the ribbon and ruler (that is, the alignment buttons on the ribbon and the indent markers on the ruler) or by using the Forma**t** **P**aragraph command.

Vertical Position

To change the vertical positioning of headers and footers using the **V**iew **H**eader/Footer command, follow these steps:

1. Choose **V**iew **H**eader/Footer.

2. Select the header or footer you want to position from the Header/Foote**r** list box.

3. Increase or decrease the **H**eader or **F**ooter setting in the From Edge text box by clicking on the up or down arrows or select the text box and type in the desired measurement.

4. Choose OK or press Enter.

T I P

You can place a header or footer anywhere on the pages designated for the header or footer. While in the page layout view, select the header or footer and then choose **Insert Frame.** You then can drag the header or footer to the position where you want it to appear on every page.

To drag an image of the header or footer to a new vertical position *within the margins of the print preview*, follow these steps:

1. Choose the **File Print Preview** command.

2. Choose the **Margins** button from the Print Preview icon bar.

   When you choose the **Margins** button, you see dotted lines indicating all headers, footers, margins, and page breaks. Figure 15.4 shows the Print Preview screen with the boundaries displayed and the header selected.

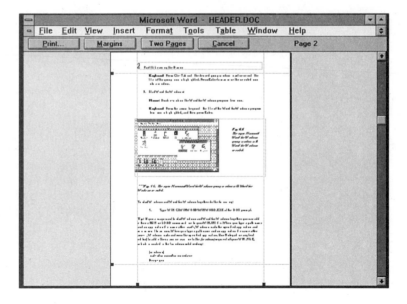

FIG. 15.4.

The Print Preview screen enables you to drag the header or footer to a new vertical location.

3. Move the mouse pointer over the header or footer you want to reposition. The pointer changes to a crosshair.

   or

   Press Tab repeatedly until the header or footer that you want to move is selected (that is, the crosshair appears over it).

4. Drag the header or footer up or down to its new position outside the page margins and within the header or footer side margins.

or

Use the arrow keys to reposition the header or footer and press Enter.

5. Click anywhere off the page to update the screen display.

As you drag the header or footer, the vertical position is displayed on the right side of the icon bar, helping you to position the header or footer exactly. The new vertical position is reflected in the From Edge setting in the Header/Footer dialog box.

T I P To increase the space between the header or footer and the document text, you can change the setting for the top or bottom margin or press Enter to add blank lines before or after the header or footer text. As you add blank lines, Word for Windows adjusts the text margins, although these adjustments are not reflected in the margins settings displayed in the Format Page Setup dialog box or in Print Preview.

Horizontal Position

You can change the horizontal positioning of a header or footer, in either the normal header or footer pane or at the top or bottom of the page in the page view mode. Either way, you can change horizontal positioning with the alignment buttons on the ribbon or with the Format Paragraph command. Use the indent markers on the ruler or choose the Format Paragraph command to change the indentation of the text in the header or footer.

If you have used the default tab stops (left-, center-, and right-aligned), you can reposition these tabs, using the ruler or the Format Tabs command. To extend header or footer text beyond the margins, use negative indent settings.

Inserting Page Numbers

You can use two approaches for adding page numbering to a document in Word for Windows. The first approach uses the Insert Page Numbers command. This is the method to use if you want only page numbers to appear in the header or footer and do not want a page number to appear on the first page of the document. If you want additional text to appear in the header or footer, or you want a page number to appear on the first page of the document, use the View Header/Footer command, described earlier. With either method, the page number is inserted in the header or footer.

Word for Windows provides many options for customizing the numbering of pages:

- Page numbers can be positioned both vertically and horizontally.

- Several number formats are available from which to select (for example, a, b, c, or i, ii, iii).

- The starting page number can be altered. You can, for example, restart page numbering in a new chapter.

- Page numbering in different parts of a document can be treated differently by dividing the document into sections and applying different numbering schemes to each section.

Using the Insert Page Numbers Command

Use the Insert Page Numbers command if you want page numbers to appear only in the header or footer and you do not want a page number on the first page of the document or section.

To add page numbering using the Insert Page Numbers command, follow these steps:

1. Choose the Insert Page Numbers command to display the Page Numbers dialog box, shown in figure 15.5.

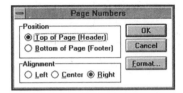

FIG. 15.5.

The Page Numbers dialog box.

2. Select the **T**op of Page or **B**ottom of Page position option.

3. Select one of the three alignment options (**L**eft, **C**enter, **R**ight).

4. Choose OK or press Enter.

Word for Windows provides several formats for page numbers. You can use lowercase roman numerals (i.e., i, ii, iii), for example, for an introduction. You also can change the starting page number.

To change the number format or the starting page number, follow these steps from within the Page Numbers dialog box:

1. Choose the **F**ormat button in the Page Numbers dialog box to display the Page Number Format dialog box shown in figure 15.6.

2. Select a new format from the Number **F**ormat list box.

3. Enter a new starting number in the **S**tart At text box or use the mouse to scroll to a new number with the up and down arrows.

FIG. 15.6.

The Page
Number Format
dialog box.

Using the View Header/Footer Command

If you want to insert additional text besides the page number into the header or footer—for example, *Page 1*—use the View **H**eader/Footer command. You also must use this method if you want a page number to appear on the first page of the document or section. The View **H**eader/Footer command also enables you to customize the positioning of the page numbers. In a document that will be bound, for example, you can position the page numbers differently on the odd and even pages so that they always appear next to the outside margin.

To insert page numbers using the **H**eader/Footer command, follow these steps:

1. Choose the View **N**ormal command if your document is not in normal view already.

2. Choose the View **H**eader/Footer command.

3. If you want a different header or footer for the first page or for odd and even pages, check the appropriate box.

4. Select from the Header/Footer list box the header or footer in which you want to insert page numbering.

    You can change the format of the page numbers or the starting page number by choosing the Page Numbers command button from within the Header/Footer dialog box. Select the desired number format or change the starting page number and choose OK.

5. Choose OK or press Enter to display the Header/Footer pane used in the normal view, as shown in figure 15.2.

6. Use the Tab key, alignment commands, or spaces to position the insertion point where you want the page number to appear. You can set new tab stops on the ruler as you would in the document.

7. Select the Page Number button from the top of the header/footer pane to insert a page number.

    You can add any other text you want to the header or footer, as described in the "Creating Headers and Footers" section earlier in this chapter.

8. When you finish creating the header or footer, choose the Close button, or press Alt+Shift+C.

> **T I P**
>
> When you insert a page number using the page button in the Header/Footer pane, Word for Windows actually inserts a field code for the page number ({page}). To see the code rather than the number, choose the View Field Codes command.

> **T I P**
>
> A number of field codes can be used in headers and footers. You can create a header that displays the total number of pages as well as the current page—for example, Page 1 of 12. To create this header, type the word *Page* followed by a space, and then click on the page icon in the Header/Footer pane. Next, type a space, the word *of,* and then another space. Finally, press Ctrl+F9 to insert a pair of field characters and type *numpages* inside the brackets. Use the right-arrow key to move outside the field code. See Chapter 18 for additional information on using field codes.

Inserting Dates and Times

With Word for Windows, you can easily insert the date and time by using the Insert Date and Time command. When you use this command, Word for Windows inserts a field code that returns the current date or time. You can update the date or time by using the F9 (Update Field) key, or you can have the field updated automatically when you print the document. This is useful if you want to create a document (for example, a business letter) that will be printed at a later date, and you want the date at the time of printing to appear in the document.

To insert the date or time into a document, follow these steps:

1. Position the insertion point where you want the date or time to be inserted.

2. Choose the Insert Date and Time command to display the Date and Time dialog box shown in figure 15.7.

3. Select the desired format from the Available Formats list box.

4. Choose OK or press Enter.

```
┌─ Date and Time ──────────────┐
│ Available Formats:           │
│ 9/16/91              ┌──────┐│
│ 16 September, 1991   │  OK  ││
│ September 16, 1991   └──────┘│
│ 16-Sep-91            ┌──────┐│
│ September, 91        │Cancel││
│ Sep-91               └──────┘│
│ 9/16/91 8:49 AM              │
│ 8:49 AM                      │
│ 8:49                         │
└──────────────────────────────┘
```

FIG. 15.7.

The Date and Time dialog box.

If you need a date or time format that is different from those that appear in the Date and Time dialog box, you can create your own. To customize the format, display the field codes by choosing the View Field Codes command. A date and time field inserted by the command will appear similar to the following:

$\{$TIME \@ "*d MMMM, yyyy*"$\}$

The term within quotes defines the format the TIME field code will display. The *d* represents a single day number, *dd* represents a number with a leading zero, *ddd* represents the three letter text abbreviation such as *Tue*, and *dddd* represents the full word *Tuesday*. You can create your own date-time formats by using different combinations of formatting letters and separators. Chapter 18 goes into more detail on formatting field code results.

T I P

To update date and time fields automatically when the document is printed, choose the **File Print** command and choose the **Options** command button. Check the **Update Fields** box and choose OK or press Enter. You can print the document at this time by choosing OK, or you can return to the document by choosing the Close button. The Update Fields option remains in effect from session to session until you unselect it.

To prevent a date or time field from being updated, you can unlink the field. Select the field and press Ctrl+Shift+F9 (the Unlink Field key). The field changes to text.

Creating Annotations

If you share documents with other people in a work group or you routinely send your documents to other people for review, you will find annotations useful. An *annotation* is an initialed note or comment attached to your document in a separate Annotations pane. As the author, you can choose whether to incorporate the annotation into your document. Annotations become part of your document only when you copy them from the Annotations pane.

Inserting Annotations

You (or your reviewers) enter annotations in a special Annotations pane on-screen. A hidden field appears in your document where the annotation is attached. To see these fields, you must display hidden text; to read the annotations, you must open the Annotations pane. An annotation can be of any length, and it can be formatted in any way.

To insert an annotation, follow these steps:

1. Position the insertion point where you want the annotation.

2. Choose **Insert Annotation.**

   An annotation mark appears in your document, and the Annotations pane opens at the bottom of your screen.

3. Type the annotation text in the Annotations pane.

The annotation mark in your document shows your initials and the number of the annotation. In figure 15.8, for example, the annotation mark in the document is [RP1]; it represents the first annotation created by RP. The Annotations pane includes the annotation mark and the annotation text.

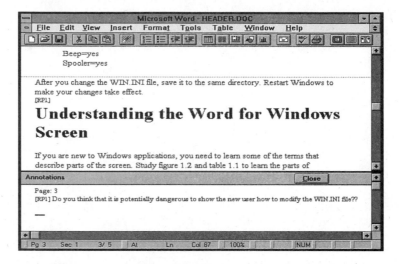

FIG. 15.8.

The Annotations
pane showing the
reviewer's initials
and the text of
the annotation.

The initials assigned to annotations come from the Tools Options User Info Category dialog box. You can change your initials, and therefore change the annotation initials, but you cannot change the initials in annotations that have already been entered. The Tools Options User Info Categories commands are global; they apply to all documents you create on your PC. When someone else edits your document on another PC, the other user's initials are assigned to that user's annotations.

To move between the Annotations and document panes, press F6 or move the insertion point with the mouse. The Annotations pane scrolls with the document so that you can see the text of any annotation when the annotation mark is visible in your document.

Creating an annotation opens the Annotations pane. After you create one or more annotations, you can display the pane by choosing View Annotations or by holding down the Ctrl key and using the mouse to drag the split bar down. (Remember that the split bar is the small black bar above the up arrow in the right scroll bar.) To close the Annotations pane, choose View Annotations again or drag the split bar back up (or drag it down off the bottom of the screen).

A shortcut for quickly opening the Annotations pane from the document is to double-click an annotation mark. To close the pane, double-click the annotation mark in the Annotations pane.

T I P

The annotation mark is hidden text, so unless you choose Tools Options View Category and turn on Hidden Text, you will not be able to see the marks in your text after you close the Annotations pane. (Even if Hidden Text is turned off, Word for Windows displays the marks while the pane is open.)

Finding Annotations

The easiest way to find an annotation in your text is to use the Go To menu command or the Go To shortcut key, F5. Word for Windows gives you precise control over where to look for an annotation.

To find an annotation, choose the Edit Go To command or press F5 (Go To). Next, type *A* and then press Enter to jump to the next annotation mark. Or be more specific in describing the annotation you're looking for: type *a4* to go to the fourth annotation mark; type *a+3* to go to the third annotation mark from the insertion point; type *a–5* to go to the fifth annotation mark behind the insertion point.

You also can find a specific annotation mark on a specific page or section. For example, choose Edit Go To or press F5, and type *a3p2* to find the third annotation on the second page; type *a5s3* to find the fifth annotation in the third section; or type *a1s2p3* to find the first annotation in the second section, page 3. Any combination works. Press F5 twice as a shortcut for displaying the Go To dialog box (see fig. 15.9).

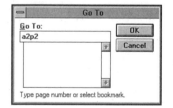

FIG. 15.9.

Using the Go To dialog box to locate an annotation quickly.

Incorporating and Deleting Annotations

One of the main purposes for annotations is so that other people can suggest changes to your document. You may want to add their revisions to your text, or you may want to delete their suggestions. Doing either is easy.

To incorporate an annotation into your document, follow these steps:

1. Display the annotation in the Annotations pane.

2. Select the text you want to move into your document using normal selection techniques.

3. Use **Edit C**opy or press Ctrl+C to copy the text.

4. Move the insertion point to the place in your document where you want the text inserted.

5. Use **Edit P**aste press or Ctrl+V to paste the text.

To remove an annotation, locate the annotation mark in your document, select it, and press Del. The annotation text is deleted along with the mark. You cannot delete an annotation by deleting the text in the Annotations pane.

Locking Your Document

If you give your document to someone else to review, you may want to prevent the other user from changing your document. That's the purpose of locked annotations: enabling reviewers to suggest without changing.

To lock your document, follow these steps:

1. Choose the **File Save As** command.

2. Choose the **File Sharing** button.

3. Select **L**ock File for Annotations.

4. Choose OK or press Enter twice.

When a document is locked, anyone opening it can add annotations but cannot edit the document's text. Only the document's author (or someone using the author's computer) can unlock a document.

Printing Annotations

Annotations never print as part of your document. Annotations are separate from your document unless you copy them in. But you can print a list of annotations, including each annotation's page number, author's initials, number, and the text of the annotation. You can print the list separately or at the end of your document.

To print a separate list of annotations, follow these steps:

1. Choose the **F**ile **P**rint command.

2. Select Annotations from the **P**rint list box in the Print dialog box, shown in figure 15.10.

3. Specify the number of copies or a range to print.

4. Choose OK or press Enter.

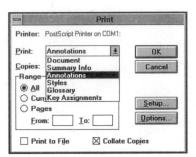

FIG. 15.10.

Printing annotations as a separate list.

To print annotations at the end of your document, follow these steps:

1. Choose the **F**ile Print command.

2. Select **O**ptions in the Print dialog box.

3. Select **A**nnotations from the Include With Document group in the Options dialog box (see fig. 15.11).

4. Choose OK or press Enter.

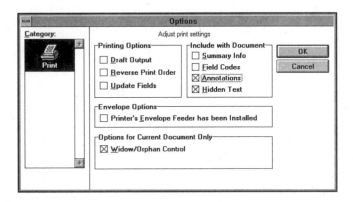

FIG. 15.11.

Printing annotations as part of your document.

T I P
If you work with editorials or contracts that must be reviewed and revised, you may find *revision* marking helpful. It marks changes to an original document. You then can go through and accept or reject revisions. Accepted revisions are incorporated in the document; rejected revisions are cleared.

Revisions are different from annotations in that annotations are usually comments that are not designed to be shown in the document—in most cases they are not included. Revisions, however, usually are designed to be included. You want to easily accept or reject a revision and be able to print a copy of text with or without revisions. To learn more about marking and accepting revisions, see Chapter 9.

Creating Footnotes

Footnotes have long been a staple of academic treatises—supplying additional information about a topic in the text or providing a reference. Footnotes save you from having to clutter the text of your document with every single bit of information you have. Instead, you can include parenthetical or reference information as a footnote listing. Because each footnote is referenced in the text, finding this extra information when you need it is easy.

T I P
If you have selected a typeface other than the default for the template in use, make sure that you change the style for footnote references and footnotes before inserting them. If you don't, they will not match the typeface you have selected.

Basically, a *footnote* consists of two parts: a footnote reference in the text (usually a superscripted number after the text) and the footnote entry at the bottom of the page or at the end of the section or document, set apart from the text by a footnote separator. The process of creating footnotes involves two basic steps. First, you insert the footnote reference and type the footnote entry (customizing the footnote separator if you prefer). Second, you specify where the footnotes should appear in your document.

Inserting Footnote References

When you insert a footnote, Word for Windows places the footnote at the bottom of the same page on which the reference mark appears (unless you choose to have the footnotes placed at the end of the section or document), adjusting the document text as necessary.

To insert a footnote reference and create a footnote entry, follow these steps:

1. Position the insertion point after the text to footnote or select a portion of text.

   Word for Windows inserts the reference mark at the insertion point, unless you have selected text, in which case it positions the mark before the selection.

2. Choose the Insert Footnote command.

   The Footnote dialog box appears (see fig. 15.12).

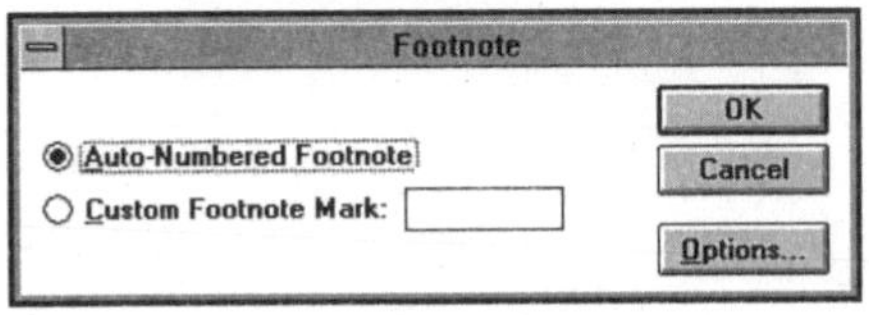

FIG. 15.12.

The Footnote dialog box.

3. Accept the default Auto-Numbered Footnote to have Word for Windows number your footnotes.

   With this option selected, footnotes are renumbered when footnotes are added, deleted, moved, or copied.

   or

   Select Custom Footnote Mark to type a reference mark of your own. Your custom reference mark doesn't interfere with any automatically numbered footnote references already in your document. You can use up to 10 characters, such as asterisks or daggers.

   To change an existing reference mark, select the mark, choose Insert Footnote, and type a new mark in the Custom Footnote Mark text box.

4. Choose OK or press Enter.

5. Type the text of your footnote.

    If you're in the draft or normal view of your document, you type in a special Footnotes pane, which appears when you choose OK in step 4. At this point your screen is divided into two parts: the text of your document on top, showing the footnote reference, and the Footnotes pane below, showing the footnote entry (see fig. 15.13).

    If you're in the page layout view of your document, you don't see the Footnotes pane. Instead, you type the footnote directly on the page (see fig. 15.14).

    The footnote text can be formatted and edited just like any other text. You can use the ribbon, ruler, toolbar, and menu commands for formatting footnotes. The default point size is 10 point for the footnote text and 8 point for the reference superscript.

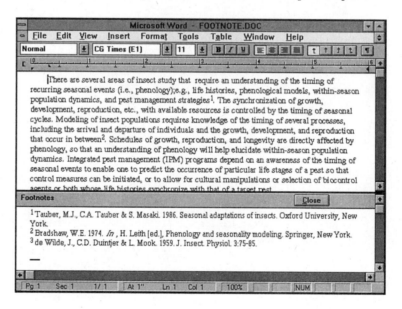

FIG. 15.13.

The Footnotes pane at the bottom of the screen.

6. If you are in normal view, leave the Footnotes pane visible and press F6 to move back to the document window or close the Footnotes pane by choosing the Close button in the icon bar or choosing **View** **F**ootnote (which is turned on when you insert a footnote).

    or

    If you are in page layout view, you can use Shift+F5 (the Go Back key) to return to where you inserted the reference.

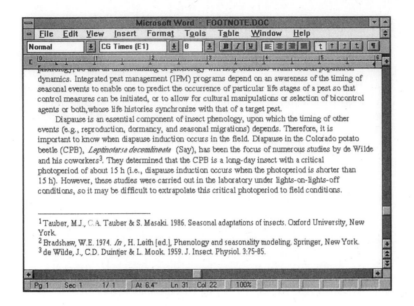

FIG. 15.14.

Footnotes as
they appear in
page layout
view.

If you choose to leave the Footnotes pane open, it will scroll along with
the document to display the footnotes that correspond to the footnote
references displayed in the text.

> **T I P**
>
> You can easily change the formatting of all your footnotes by redefin-
> ing the Footnote Reference and Footnote Text styles. Choose **Format
> Style** and select either Footnote Text or Footnote Reference from the
> **Style** Name list. Choose the **D**efine command button, and then
> choose the appropriate command button from the Change Format-
> ting group. Make the desired formatting changes in the dialog box
> that is displayed and choose OK. Choose Change and then Yes.
> Finally, choose the **C**lose button. See Chapter 11 for more informa-
> tion on working with styles.

Word for Windows offers some handy shortcuts for opening and
closing the Footnotes pane. If you have a mouse, you can open the
Footnotes pane by double-clicking any footnote reference in your document, and you can close the pane by double-clicking any footnote entry
in the pane. You also can open the Footnotes pane by holding down the
Shift key while you drag the split bar down. (The split bar is the black
bar above the up arrow in the right scroll bar.) Close the pane by dragging the split bar back up or by double-clicking the split bar.

Finding Footnotes

If you are in page layout view, you can use Shift+F5 to return to where you inserted the reference. You can return to the footnote associated with a reference by double-clicking the reference mark. The combination of using the Go Back key while in the footnote and double-clicking the reference mark in the text allows you to quickly move back and forth between the document and the footnote while in page layout view. You can edit footnotes in page layout view just like any other text; simply scroll to the footnote and make the desired changes.

You can use the F5 (Go To) key to locate footnotes. Press F5 and type one of the following notations:

Type	Result
f	go to next footnote
f-	go to previous footnote
fn	go to footnote number n
f+n	move forward n footnotes
f-n	move backward n footnotes

Deleting, Copying, and Moving a Footnote

To delete a footnote, you must select the reference mark for the footnote and press Del. Deleting the footnote text leaves the reference mark in the text.

 Be careful about deleting text that contains footnotes. If you select and delete text that contains a footnote marker, you also delete the footnote.

To copy a footnote, select the reference mark for the footnote, choose **E**dit **C**opy (or press Ctrl+C), position the insertion point where you want to copy the footnote reference, and choose **E**dit **P**aste (or press Ctrl+V). To move a footnote, use the **E**dit **Cu**t command (or press Ctrl+X) instead of the **E**dit **C**opy command. Word for Windows copies or moves the footnote text to the appropriate place and numbers the footnotes.

Customizing Footnotes

You can override the default footnote settings to suit your particular needs in several ways. You can customize the separator—the line that separates footnotes from the document text and from each other if they continue across more than one page. You also can add a continuation notice specifying that a footnote continues on the next page.

By default, footnotes appear on the bottom of the page in which their reference marks appear. If you want, you can specify that footnotes are printed at the end of a section or the end of the document. If the text on a page does not extend to the bottom, you can specify that the footnotes be printed just below the last line of text.

Finally, you can change the numbering scheme for footnotes. You can change the starting number for footnotes or choose to have footnote numbering restart on each page or at the beginning of each section, rather than having the footnotes numbered sequentially from the beginning of the document.

Customizing the Footnote Separator

To customize the footnote separator, follow these steps:

1. Choose the **I**nsert Foot**n**ote command.

2. Choose the **O**ptions button to display the Footnote Options dialog box shown in figure 15.15.

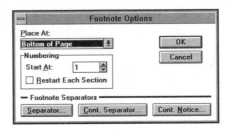

FIG. 15.15.

The Footnote Options dialog box.

3. Choose the **S**eparator or **C**ont. Separator button to open the Footnote Separator pane, which appears at the bottom of the document window.

   The **S**eparator option represents the separator between your document and footnotes on any page that includes footnotes. Word for Windows proposes a two-inch line. You can keep the line, delete it, or add text before or after the line that extends out from the left margin. You can change the characters that are used as the separator or use graphics characters if you want.

The Cont. Separator option represents the separator between the document text and the remainder of a footnote that continues across more than one page. Word for Windows proposes a margin-to-margin line. You can edit this line the same way as the separator line.

4. Choose the Close button, or press Alt+Shift+C.

To add a continuation notice, follow these steps:

1. Choose Insert Footnote.

2. Choose the Options button.

3. Choose the Cont. Notice button from Footnotes separators group.

    The continuation notice pane opens up where you can type a continuation notice for footnotes that continue past a page, such as *continued next page*.

4. Choose the Close button, or press Alt+Shift+C.

To reset the default settings for the footnote separators or continuation notice, open the appropriate pane and choose the Reset button, and then choose OK or press Alt+Shift+C.

Placing Footnotes

You can specify where the footnotes you create are to appear in your document. Traditionally, they appear at the bottom of the page. Word for Windows places them at the bottom margin, below the footnote separator. You can move all footnotes to the end of a section or document, however, if you prefer. Footnotes at the end of a document usually are called *endnotes*.

To change the position of footnotes, follow these steps:

1. Choose the Insert Footnote command.

2. Choose the Options button. The Footnote Options dialog box appears (refer to fig. 15.15).

3. Select one of the following options from the Place At list box:

Option	Function
Bottom of Page	Places the footnotes at the bottom margin of the page on which the footnote references appear (the default setting).
Beneath Text	Prints the footnotes after the last line of text. This style is handy when the text is much shorter than a page.
End of Section	Prints the footnotes at the end of the section.
End of Document	Prints footnotes at the end of the document.

Figure 15.14 shows a document with the footnotes placed at the bottom of the page, just below the document text. Figure 15.16 shows the same document with the footnotes collected at the end of the document.

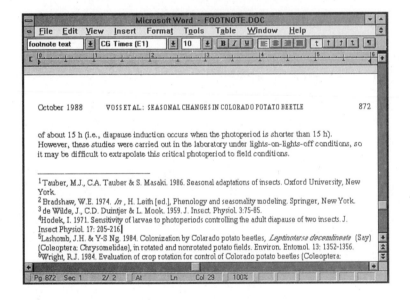

FIG. 15.16.

A document in page layout view showing footnotes collected at the end of the document.

If you specify footnotes to appear at the end of each section, you can choose to print the footnotes at the end of the current section (the choice Word for Windows proposes), or you can save them for a later section. Choose the Format Section Layout command. Select Suppress Footnotes (so that an X appears in the box) to save footnotes for the next section, or unselect Suppress Footnotes (so that the box is empty) to include the footnotes with the current section.

Customizing Numbering

You can change how you number your footnotes. To customize the numbering of footnotes, follow these steps:

1. Choose Insert Footnote.

2. Choose the Options button. The Footnote Options dialog box appears.

3. To change the starting number, type a new number in the Start At text box, or scroll the up and down arrows to select a new number.

4. To have footnote numbering restarted at each section, select the Restart Each Section option.

   Depending on which of the Place At options is selected, Word for Windows restarts the numbering of footnotes on each page, in each section, or at the beginning of each document.

5. Choose OK or press Enter.

From Here . . .

Many other topics in this book can be helpful when you're working with document reference aids. Other topics that are helpful for professional and academic documents include outlines, tables of lists or contents, and indexes. These are covered in Chapter 16.

Many academic treatises also include equations and tables of data. Word for Windows' equation editor is simple to use but very powerful (see Chapter 17). Tables containing text, numbers, math operations, or pictures and graphs are described in Chapter 12.

Creating Indexes and Tables of Contents

I n this chapter, you learn how to build references for a document so that it is easy for people to use. Imagine trying to locate a specific topic in a long reference book with no table of contents, or trying to get information from a long technical document without a good index, or trying to remember where you saw a useful chart or table in a book with no list of figures. Word for Windows is equipped with powerful tools for creating these reference aids.

Creating Indexes

An index, such as the one found at the end of this book, lists topics covered in a book or document and provides the page numbers where you can find the topics. Without an index, your readers will have difficulty locating information in a long document or one that is filled with references.

In Word for Windows, creating an index involves two steps. First, you must identify in the document each entry you want indexed. Second, you must collect these entries into an index.

Word for Windows has the ability to create simple indexes, such as the following:

> Printing, 5, 12, 25
> Publishing, 37, 54, 68

Word for Windows also can create indexes that use subentries so that specific topics are easier to locate:

> Printing
>   Envelopes, 37, 39
>   Merge, 43-45

If you need more in-depth or complex indexing, Word for Windows is capable of creating indexes that include different characters as separators, unique formatting, and multiple levels of subentries, as in the following example:

> Printing
>   Envelopes: 37, 39-42
>   Mail Merge
>   Data document: 54-62
>   Main document: 50-55, 67, 72
>   Conversion, *see also* WordPerfect conversion

Creating Index Entries

Identifying an entry, such as a word, to be included in your index can be as simple as selecting the word and choosing a command. As an alternative, you can position the insertion point where you want the entry referenced, choose a command, and type the word to index. This second method gives you the flexibility to decide how the topic will appear in the index.

T I P   When creating index entries, you should select the entire word or phrase to be indexed. Remember that you can select entire words by double-clicking the word or by moving to the beginning of the word and pressing Shift+Ctrl+right arrow.

To create an index entry in your document, follow these steps:

1. Select the word or words to index or position the insertion point where you want the entry.

2. Choose the **Insert Index Entry** command.

   The Index Entry dialog box includes the selected word or words (see fig. 16.1). If no word or words are selected, type the index entry.

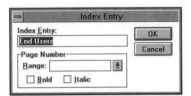

FIG. 16.1.

The Index Entry dialog box.

3. In the Index **E**ntry text box, make no change if the index entry looks the way you want it; or type the index entry as you want it to appear in the index.

4. Select among the Page Number options.

   Select **R**ange and type or select the name of a bookmark from the list if you want the index entry to refer to the range of pages spanned by the bookmark.

   Select **B**old to print the index page numbers in boldface text.

   Select **I**talic to print the index page numbers in italic text.

5. Choose OK.

Repeat these steps for every index entry in your document.

Including a Range of Pages

As you create an index, you probably will want to reference a range of pages for an index entry—for example:

> Desktop Publishing, 51-75

To do this, you first must select the range of pages and assign a bookmark to the selection (see Chapter 4 for more information on using bookmarks). Then, when you insert the index entry, you use the bookmark name in the Page Number **R**ange text box to indicate the range of pages for the entry.

The reason you want to use a range name to mark the span of pages rather than an actual number of pages is that editing, insertions, and deletions may move the topic so that it spans different page numbers than those typed. By using a bookmark, Word for Windows calculates the new location of the bookmark so that the index will be up to date.

To reference a range of pages, first create the bookmark by following these steps:

1. Select the pages you want to reference in the index entry.

2. Choose Insert Bookmark.

3. Type a name of up to 20 characters in the Bookmark Name text box.

4. Choose OK or press Enter.

Now create the index entry and use the bookmark to describe the page range involved in the reference:

1. Position the insertion point where you want to insert the index entry.

2. Choose the Insert Index Entry command.

3. In the Index Entry text box, make no change if the index entry looks the way you want it, or type an index entry.

4. Type the bookmark name in the Page Number Range text box.

5. Select other options as necessary.

6. Choose OK or press Enter.

Customizing Index Entries

When you choose the Insert Index Entry command, enter descriptive text, and choose OK, you actually are entering a hidden field code into the document at a point directly after the insertion point or the selected text. These field codes are a powerful feature that can help you automate Word for Windows and customize the results of some commands, like the Insert Index Entry command.

To see the hidden text of the field codes inserted by the Insert Index Entry command, choose the Tools Option command, then select the View Category. Select Hidden Text from the Non-Printing Characters group and choose OK. Unselect this check box when you want to hide the {XE} characters.

> **T I P**
>
> If you use the View Category command often, you may want to refer to the chapters on macros (Chapter 31) or customizing Word for Windows (Chapter 29) to learn how to add this command to a shortcut key, the tool bar, or to a menu command so that it is more accessible.

Some example field codes for index entries are as follows:

Field Code	Result in Index
{XE "Printing"}	Printing, 56
{XE "Printing:Envelopes" \r "PagesEnv"}	Printing Envelopes, 72-80
{XE "Printing:Envelopes" \b \i}	Printing Envelopes, *56*

You can modify and edit these codes to give them more capabilities or formatting than is built into the Insert Index Entry command. The section "Formatting an Index" later in this chapter covers formatting in detail.

Assembling a Simple Index

After you create an entry for each index entry or subentry you want collected into an index, you can compile the index. Follow these steps to create your index:

1. Position the insertion point where you want the index.

    Turn off the display of hidden text and field codes so that the document will be repaginated properly before the index is created.

2. Choose the Insert Index command.

    The Index dialog box shown in figure 16.2 appears.

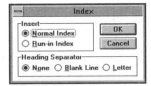

FIG. 16.2.

The Index dialog box collects your entries into an index.

3. Choose from two types of indexes: normal or run-in. Select **N**ormal Index to indent subentries under major entries in the index as in the following example:

> Printing
>   Envelopes, 56

Select **R**un-in Index to include subentries on the same line as their major entries, with words wrapping to the next line if necessary, as in the following example:

> Printing: Envelopes, 56

4. Select among three Heading Separator options.

Select N**o**ne if you want no break between letter categories in the index (when you get to the end of the As, the Bs begin).

Select **B**lank Line to include a line between the letter categories in the index (when you get to the end of the As, one blank line is inserted before the Bs begin).

Select **L**etter to include a single letter at the beginning of each letter category in the index (an A before the As, a B before the Bs, and so on). The letter heading will be formatted by the automatic style named index heading, which you can change if you want.

5. Choose OK.

Figure 16.3 shows a sample index.

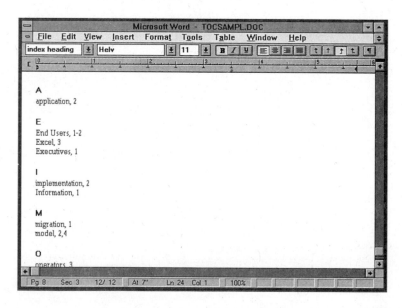

A sample index.

When you choose the Insert Index command, you are actually inserting a hidden field code, {INDEX}. Field codes are described in detail in Chapter 18.

Formatting an Index

You can change the appearance of an index by using styles. Word for Windows supplies automatic styles for index entries: Index heading, Index 1, and so on through Index 7. Index heading is the style Word for Windows uses to format the letters at the beginning of each section of your index. In figure 16.3, the index heading style has been changed to add one blank line before the paragraph so that a space falls between sections in the index. To redefine a style, choose the Format Style command and then the Define button. For more information on using styles, see Chapter 11.

You also can format the index directly, using the Format commands, the ribbon, and the ruler. If you update your index, however, you will lose all direct formatting changes. For this reason, you should redefine the styles for your index to make formatting changes.

> You can access several formatting options for indexes by using switches in the INDEX field. For example, you can specify which characters are used to separate index headings using the \h switch, or you can change the characters used to separate the index text from the page numbers (the default is a comma plus a space) with the \e switch. To add these switches, choose View Field Codes to display the field codes, position the insertion point inside the INDEX field, and type in the desired switches. See Chapter 18 for more information on the switches you can use with the INDEX field.

T I P

Updating an Index

If you later add index entries to your document and want to update your index, simply reissue the Insert Index command. Word for Windows asks whether you want to replace the existing index. Respond OK to update the selected index.

T   I   P   Another way to update an index is to move the insertion point within the {INDEX} field code (or the text that results from the code) and then press F9 (the Update Field key). Word for Windows replaces the index without prompting you first, as it does when you use the Insert Index command.

Deleting an Index

To delete an index, select the index and press Del. You can select the entire index quickly by clicking the mouse button in the margin to the left of the last entry in the index. To select and delete an entire index quickly using the keyboard, place the insertion point to the left of the first entry, press F8, press the down-arrow key once, and press Del. Another alternative is to select View Field Codes to display the {INDEX} code, select the code, and press Del.

Fixing an Index as Text

An index is actually created with a hidden field code, {INDEX}. As long as the field code is there, you can quickly update the index by selecting the code and pressing F9.

In some cases, you may want to change the field code to its text result so that the index cannot be changed or updated. You may want to fix the field code so that you can reformat the index and formatting is not lost if someone selects the document and presses F9 to update other fields, or so that you can save the document to another word processing format while preserving the index.

To fix the index field code so that it changes to text, select the index or field code so that the entire index is selected. This is most easily done by dragging across one end of the index, which causes the entire index to be selected. Then press Shift+Ctrl+F9, the Unlink Field key combination.

Creating Multiple-Level Index Entries

If you have ever looked up a topic in an index and found the topic listed with a dozen or so page numbers, you know the value of a multiple-level index. When you expect to have several occurrences of a topic, you can help your reader by using categories and subcategories to divide the topic into more specific references. In Word for Windows, these entries are called *multiple-level index entries*, and they're easy to create.

The following is an example of the difference between a regular and a multiple-level index:

Regular index	Multiple-level index

Computers, 1, 6, 17, 25, 33-37, 54	Computers hard disk drives, 6
	    modems, 17
	    software, 1, 25
	    processor types, 33-37, 54

To create a multiple-level index entry, follow these steps:

1. Position the insertion point where you want the index entry.

2. Choose the **Insert Index Entry** command.

3. In the Index Entry text box, type the name of the main category, type a colon, then type the name of the subcategory.

4. Select among other options as needed and choose OK.

Follow this procedure for each index entry. To create a multiple-level index entry, for example, you type the following line in the Index Entry box in step 3:

    Computers:hard disk drives

You also can create sub-subentries, as in the following example:

    Computers:hard disk drives:maintenance
    Computers:hard disk drives:performance
    Computers:processors

These entries could appear in an index as follows:

    Computers
        Hard disk drives
            Maintenance, 54
            Performance, 65
        Processors, 102

Creating Cross-Reference Index Entries

The **Insert Index Entry** command is a shortcut for entering a field code for each item you want indexed. To create a more complex index, like a cross-reference index, you must use field codes to create the index entries. A cross-reference index gives the reader information such as "Modem, see Computers."

Before you begin creating cross-reference index entries, make sure that the Hidden Text option in the View category of the Tools Options command is turned on. You will create a manually entered Index Entry field that appears as follows:

```
{XE "Graphics" \t \i "see also Desktop Publishing"}
```

To create this field code for cross-referenced indexes, follow these steps:

1. Position the insertion point where you want the index entry.

2. Press Ctrl+F9, the Insert Field key combination.

3. Inside the field characters, { }, type *XE* and press the space bar once.

4. Type the index entry (enclose it in double quotation marks if it includes more than one word), and press the space bar once.

5. Press \ at the end of the index entry.

   You can add the *i* switch to the *t* switch to italicize the cross-reference.

6. Type the cross-reference text (enclose it in double quotation marks if it includes more than one word).

Another way to select Index entry from the Insert Field Type list is to use the Insert Field command and type the index information shown earlier, minus the braces and field name, in the Field Code box:

```
"Graphics" \t \i "see also Desktop Publishing"
```

Do not include the braces or the field name, XE. Note that you must select Index Entry, not Index, from the Insert Field Type box.

Creating Tables of Contents, Tables of Figures, and Tables of Authorities

A table lists selected items included in your document, along with their page numbers. Building a table of contents at the beginning of a document is probably the most common use of this feature. You also can create tables of figures, photos, tables, or other items. Figure 16.4 shows one of the types of tables of content you can create.

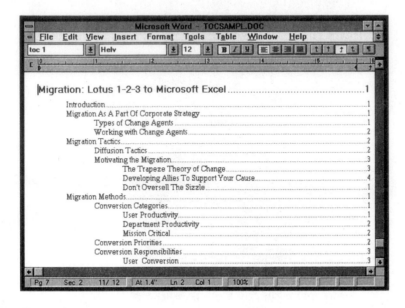

FIG. 16.4.

Word for Windows can create tables of content in many forms and for different items.

You have two ways to create a table of contents: by using heading styles or by using special table of contents entry fields. The easiest way to create a table of contents is to collect headings styles. (Styles are discussed in Chapter 11.)

Creating a Table of Contents Using Headings

If you know you want a table of contents, you may want to format your document headings using the built-in heading styles—heading 1, heading 2, and so on. When you want to compile a table of contents, Word for Windows recognizes these heading styles and uses the text with those styles to create the table of contents. Word for Windows provides nine heading levels, heading 1 through heading 9, and you can choose which heading levels to use when creating a table of contents.

The heading styles used to create tables of contents or lists are the same heading styles used automatically when you create an outline. If you prefer to work with Word for Windows' outliner, you may want to outline your document before or while you write, and then use the outline headings to create your table of contents. Chapter 14 describes how to create and use outlines.

Before you can create a table of contents, you should apply heading styles to each of your headings, figure descriptions, or list items you want in the table of contents. You can apply heading styles in many ways. For all of these methods, you first move the insertion point into the text and then use one of the following methods, which are listed from the easiest to most complex:

- Select the desired heading style from the style list box in the ribbon.

- Press Shift+left or right arrow to change a paragraph into a heading style and move it to a higher or lower style.

- Choose the Format Style command and select the desired heading style from the Style Name list and choose OK.

- Press Ctrl+S, type the name of the heading style into the status bar (heading 1, for example), and press Enter.

You can apply heading styles as you type in the headings, using either the mouse or keyboard methods.

To create a table of contents from headings formatted with heading styles, follow these steps:

1. Position the insertion point where you want the table of contents to appear in your document.

2. Choose the Insert Table of Contents command.

   The Table of Contents dialog box shown in figure 16.5 appears.

FIG. 16.5.

Use the Insert Table of Contents command to create a table of contents using heading styles or outline levels.

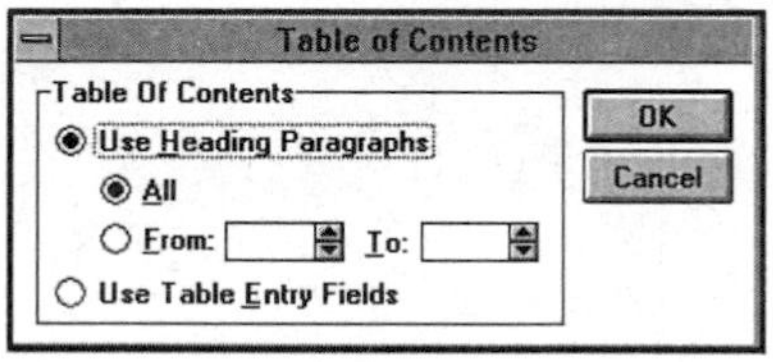

3. Select Use Heading Paragraphs.

4. Select All to collect all headings into a table of contents.

   or

   Select From and To and type in the lowest and highest heading levels you want to use in your table of contents.

5. Choose OK or press Enter.

Figure 16.4, shown earlier, shows a table of contents built from heading styles.

Creating a Table of Contents from Any Text

Some documents don't lend themselves to heading styles, or you may want to include references to items that don't have headings. In those cases, you can insert a table of contents field code, along with a descriptive entry, at the beginning of each appropriate section in your document (or wherever you want the listing to be referenced in the table of contents). Word for Windows then can collect these fields and descriptions into a table of contents. You must use table of contents fields if you want to include more than one list in a document (for example, a table of contents and a table of figures) that can be updated automatically.

A *field* is a hidden code enclosed in special characters that look like braces ({ and }). They are used to automate features of Word for Windows. Field codes were used earlier in this chapter for indexes. For more information on fields, see Chapter 18.

Marking Table of Contents Entries

To insert table of contents fields into your document, follow these steps:

1. Position the insertion point where you want the table of contents entry.

2. Choose the **Insert Field** command.

3. Select the Field Code text box, delete the equal sign (=), and type *tc*.

   or

   Press T to select TC from the Insert Field Type list box. Pressing the letter T advances you to the first field type beginning with a T; in this case, it is TC (see fig. 16.6).

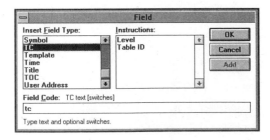

FIG. 16.6.

Creating a table of contents from field codes.

4. Position the insertion point in the Field Code box, leaving one space after the tc entry.

5. Type an opening quotation mark ("), type the text of the table of contents entry, and type a closing quotation mark.

   To create the first entry in the table of contents shown in figure 16.4, for example, type the following in the Field Code box:

   tc "Migration: Lotus 1-2-3 to Microsoft Excel"

6. Choose OK.

Repeat these steps for each table of contents entry you want. The field codes you insert will not appear in your document unless you have turned on the Hidden Text option in the View Category of the Tools Options command.

T I P You can bypass using the Insert Field command by using the Insert Field key combination, Ctrl+F9. Position the insertion point where you want the table of contents entry, press Ctrl+F9 (a pair of field characters will appear), and type *tc "text"*, where *text* is the text you want to appear in the table of contents.

Creating the Table of Contents

To collect {tc} field codes into a table of contents, follow these steps:

1. Turn off the display of hidden text and field codes to ensure that the document repaginates correctly when you insert the table of contents.

2. Position the insertion point where you want the table of contents to appear in your document.

3. Choose the Insert Table of Contents command.

4. Select Use Table Entry Fields.

5. Choose OK or press Enter.

Creating Tables of Figures, Tables of Authorities, and Other Tables

You can create tables of other things besides contents—figures, photos, tables, or any other items. The easiest way to assemble any table is to use heading styles. For example, you can assign all your figures to heading style 6. You then can collect a table of figures that includes only level 6 headings.

 CAUTION A document can contain only one table of contents at a time. Before you create a table of contents for heading style 6, therefore, make sure that you unlink or fix any previous table of contents by selecting it and pressing Shift+Ctrl+F9.

Another way to collect special tables is to use field codes instead of the styles associated with headings. These field codes will do three things:

- They mark the spot in the text you want to reference by page number.
- They include the text you want to appear in the table.
- They include an identifier that defines into which table they should be accumulated.

You can type these field codes directly into a document or use a command to insert them. The field codes you insert look similar to the following:

```
{tc "Automated publishing" \f p}
```

In the command, *tc* is the field code, *"Automated publishing"* is the text that appears in the table, and the \f switch indicates that the table will be built from fields. The *p* is an identifier that associates this entry with other entries with the same identifier. This entry will be accumulated in a table with other field codes that have the *p* identifier.

The letters you use are up to you. The code for tables, for example, could be simply *t*. Some examples of how you may group items in different tables are as follows:

Item	Field code identifier
Authorities	a
Charts	c

continues

Item	Field code identifier
Figures	f
Lists	l
Pictures	p
Tables	t

Marking Other List Entries

To insert field codes that mark what will be included in tables, follow these steps:

1. Position the insertion point on the page where you want the table to reference.

2. Choose the **Insert Field** command.

3. Select Field **C**ode, delete the =, and type *tc*.

   or

   Press T to select TC from the Insert Field Type list box.

   Make sure that you do not select TOC. TOC is the field code that accumulates the TC codes into a table.

4. Position the insertion point in the Field Code text box, leaving one space after *tc*.

5. Type a quotation mark, type the text of the table entry, and type another quotation mark to close the quotation.

6. Press the space bar once, type \f, (the *f* indicates that the table is being built from fields).

7. Press the space bar to insert a space, then type a single-character list identifier, such as *g*, for graphs. Use the same single-letter character for all items to be accumulated in the same table.

8. Choose OK or press Enter.

Repeat these steps for each entry that should appear in your table of contents. Figure 16.7 shows a sample entry in the Insert Field dialog box. Your TC field code should look similar to the following:

```
{TC "Graph Showing Learning Retention" \f g}
```

Another, and often quicker, way to enter the field code is to position the insertion point, press Ctrl+F to insert the field code braces, {}, and then type the code and text inside the braces.

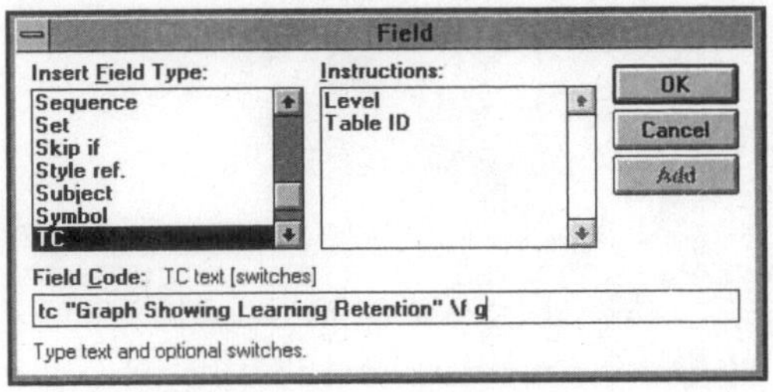

FIG. 16.7.

Entering a field code to mark the location of a graphic using the *g* identifier.

Creating the Table

To create a table that accumulates all the items belonging to a single identifier, such as *f* for figures or *g* for graphs, follow these steps:

1. Turn off the display of hidden text and field codes so that the document repaginates using only the text that will print.

2. Position the insertion point where you want the table to appear.

3. Choose the **Insert Fiel**d command.

4. Select Field **C**ode, delete the =, and type *toc.*

   or

   Select TOC from the Insert **F**ield Type list box.

5. Position the insertion point to the right of *toc* in the Field **C**ode text box.

6. Leaving one space after *toc*, type \f, (the *f* indicates that the table of contents is being built from fields).

7. Press the space bar to insert a space, and then type the list identifier—for example, *g* for graphs.

8. Choose OK or press Enter.

If you display the resulting field code with **V**iew **F**ield Codes, it should appear similar to the following:

```
{toc \f g}
```

By using different list identifiers, you can include multiple tables for different entries in a document (for example, contents, tables, figures, and so on).

Updating Tables of Contents and Other Items

If you are using heading styles to create your table of contents and you add new headings, you can update the table of contents by simply repeating the process of creating the table. Word for Windows asks whether you want to replace the existing table. Because you can easily update the table in this way, don't hesitate to create a table of contents early in the process of developing your document—the table can help you quickly find a section in a long document.

If you create a table of items using field codes and identifiers, you can update that list by selecting the field code and pressing F9 (Update Fields). Select the field by clicking in the middle of the field code or dragging across one end of the table of contents, which causes the entire table to be selected.

Tables of contents that have been unlinked so that they no longer can be updated must be re-created if you want an updated version.

Before updating the table of contents, hide hidden text using the **T**ools **O**ptions command (Category View) and hide field codes using the **V**iew **F**ield Codes command. This ensures that the pagination will be based on only those pages that will actually print.

T I P   Create a table of contents early in your work, then you can use it to navigate through your document. If you put the table of contents at the end of the document, you can press Ctrl+End to go to the end, check the table of contents to identify the page number you want, and then use the Edit Go To command (or press F5) to go quickly to the page.

To delete a table of contents, just select it and press Del, or turn on **V**iew Field **C**odes and delete the TOC field.

Limiting Tables of Contents and Other Tables

If you need to create a table of contents or list for part of a document, you need to modify the field codes with switches. To modify the field codes, choose the **View Field Codes** command so that you can see the TOC field codes, and then type the switches inside the field code braces as shown in the following table. After modifying the field code, return to the document, select the TOC field code, and press F9 to update the table. For more information on modifying field codes, refer to Chapter 18.

Switch	Argument	Use
\b	bookmarkname	`{toc \o \b NewIdeas}` The table of contents that is built is only for the area named NewIdeas. The \o indicates that the table of contents is built from heading styles.
\o	1-4	`{toc \o 1-4}` The table of contents is built from a limited selection of heading styles, Heading 1 through Heading 4.

For more information on page numbering or limiting the scope of a table of contents, refer to Chapter 20.

Formatting Tables of Contents and Other Tables

If you format a table directly, using the format commands or the ribbon and ruler, that formatting will be lost if you update the table. You can use two methods to format table of contents and other items so that formatting is not lost when tables are updated. With the first method, each level within a table of contents has a style—toc1, toc2, and so on. By redefining each of these styles, you can change the format for each level within a table of contents. The second method uses switches that are inserted within the TOC field to add or preserve formatting.

Formatting with Styles

Levels within a table of contents each have a specific style—TOC1, TOC2, and so on. By redefining these styles you can change the format of the table of contents, and that new format will still be used when you update the table of contents.

This method of changing styles is useful when you want to format one level of the table of contents differently from other levels. You may, for example, want the first level of the table, TOC1, to be in bold 12 point Times Roman without tab leaders (dots or dashes before the page number), but have all other levels use the Normal font with tab leaders.

Word for Windows' original TOC styles are based on the Normal style, with added indents, so your table of contents will look similar to the rest of your document. To redefine the TOC styles, choose the Format Styles command, then choose the Define button when the Styles dialog box appears. The dialog box expands to give you options for redefining styles. From the Style Name list, select the style you want to redefine, such as toc1 for the first level of table of contents entries.

Choose the Change Formatting button for the format you want to change. Make formatting changes to the style, and then choose OK. When the original Style dialog box reappears, choose the Change button. When prompted whether you want to change the standard (default TOC) style, choose the Yes button. You will be returned to the Style box where you can redefine styles for other toc. Choose Apply or press Enter from the Styles dialog box to return to the document. To see your changes, select the table of contents and press the F9 key to update the table of contents.

Formatting with Field Code Switches

The second method of formatting a table of contents so that formatting is preserved when you update the table employs switches you include with the TOC field code. You can use many switches to format the entire table of contents. These switches are discussed in more detail in Chapter 18.

To make changes, first display the field codes by choosing the View Field Codes command. Add your switch(es) inside the field code braces to tell Word for Windows how you want the table formatted after it updates. For example, if the TOC field code appears as

        {toc \f g * charformat}

the entire table of graphs uses the formatting applied to the first letter of toc. In this case, the bold and italic on *t* apply to the entire table. The * *charformat* switch applies the formatting of the first character in the field code to the entire result.

Some useful switches are as follows:

Switch	Argument	Use
*	charformat	`{toc \o \* charformat}` Apply formatting of first character in field code to entire result of field. For example, change the fonts of the entire table of contents.
*	mergeformat	`{toc \o \* mergeformat}` Retain formatting in field results that you applied manually. Formatting of updated results applies on a word-for-word basis. For example, change the tab leader throughout the table of contents.
*	upper	`{toc \f t \* upper}` Change all characters in the table of contents to uppercase.
*	lower	`{toc \f g \* lower}` Change all characters in the table of contents to lowercase.
*	firstcap	`{toc \o \* firstcap}` Change all words in the table of contents to use a capital for the first letter.
*	roman or * ROMAN	`{toc \o \* roman}` Change numbers in the table of contents to Roman numbers. *roman* produces iv; *ROMAN* produces IV.

After making changes in the toc field, you must select the field and press F9 (Update) to see the results of the changes.

From Here . . .

The topics in this chapter—tables of contents, other types of tables, and indexes—go beyond the normal business letter, but are an integral part of many professional documents. Documents that require these features usually also require headers, footers, footnotes or endnotes, and the other features used in professional typing. To learn more about these features, refer to Chapter 9 and Chapter 15.

This chapter gave you a brief glimpse of the flexibility available in Word for Windows when you modify the field codes that some commands insert in the document. To learn more about field codes and the way they can improve your work, read Chapter 18.

Entering Math and Equations

Have you ever wanted to perform a simple calculation while you were working in a document and use the results in your text? Or perhaps you would like to perform calculations on the numbers in a Word for Windows table that you created and have the results automatically updated if the figures in the table change, much as you would in a spreadsheet.

If you are a scientist or engineer, you may have longed for an easy way to enter equations into a document so that you are not faced with having to hand-draw equations into an otherwise polished-looking document. Word for Windows simplifies all these tasks with its built-in features. This chapter discusses these features.

Performing Calculations

You can use three methods to calculate numbers in Word for Windows. With the first method, you can perform basic math calculations by typing in the numbers and operators (+, -, *, or /, for example) for the calculation, selecting the expression, and choosing the Tools Calculate command. The results of the calculation are placed in the clipboard and can be inserted wherever you want. With the first method, you also can assign bookmark names to each of the numbers you want to use in the calculation. You then use those bookmark names and the math operators to write an expression for calculating the desired result.

The second method calculates the results within a field. *Fields* are codes you place in your document to automate certain procedures. (See Chapter 18 for more about field codes.) The second method is used if you are working in a table, similar to working in a spreadsheet. With this method, you can perform the calculations within the table, again, using fields.

Using the Tools Calculate Command

The simplest way to calculate a result is to write an expression using numbers and math operators, select the expression, and choose the Tools Calculate command. The results for the calculation are placed in the clipboard and can be inserted wherever you like. When you use the method, the results are not updated if any of the numbers in the expression are changed, and the numbers and operators must appear together within the text.

To perform simple mathematical calculations, follow these steps:

1. Enter the numbers and mathematical operators for the calculation anywhere in the text—for example, *5+6.*

    The mathematical operators you can use are as follows:

Operator	Operation
+	Addition
-	Subtraction
*	Multiplication
/	Division
%	Percentage
^	Power or root

2. Select the expression.

3. Choose the Tools Calculate command.

    Notice that the calculation result appears in the status bar at the bottom of the screen.

4. Position the insertion point where you want the result to appear and choose Edit Paste or press Ctrl+V.

When you are doing simple addition, the numbers you use in the calculation can appear in a row, a column (use the right mouse button to select a column of numbers), or within text. When the numbers appear within text, Word for Windows ignores the text and adds all the numbers within the selection. If one of the numbers has a dollar sign preceding it, Word for Windows includes a dollar sign in the result.

Some examples of simple calculations are as follows:

■ The quarterly profits for 1990 were $215,000, $325,090, $287,650, and $456,790, for a total profit of $1,284,530.00.

The total profit was calculated by selecting the four quarterly profit figures and choosing the Tools Calculate command. The result was pasted into the text.

■ (256,000/556,789) * 100 = 45.98

The expression on the left side of the equation was selected and calculated. The result, 45.98, was pasted into the right side of the equation.

■ 45
67
87
98
—
297

In this calculation, the numbers above the line were selected by dragging across them with the right mouse button, and the Tools Calculate command was chosen. The result was pasted below the line. When no operators are used, Word for Windows automatically adds the selected numbers.

Performing Calculations Using Bookmarks

To perform calculations on numbers scattered throughout a document and to allow the results of a calculation to be updated if any of the numbers change, you need to use bookmark names and fields to do the calculations. To use this method, follow these steps:

1. Using the Insert Bookmark command, assign a bookmark to each number you will use in the calculation. Use bookmark names that make sense, such as Profit, Expense, and Budget. (See Chapter 4 for more information on creating bookmarks.)

2. Position the insertion point where you want the result to appear and choose the **Insert Field** command.

3. Type the expression for calculating the desired result in the Field **C**ode text box, using bookmark names and mathematical operators.

    For a list of the mathematical operators you can use with bookmarks, look under the entry for the {=expression} field in Chapter 18.

4. Following the expression, add any formatting instructions. To add instructions, select a format from the **I**nstructions list box and choose the **A**dd button.

    For more information on formatting numeric results, see the topics on general switches in Chapter 18.

5. Choose OK or press Enter.

The results of the field (that is, the calculation) are displayed unless the **View Field C**odes command is selected, in which case the code itself is displayed. To update the field, select the field and press Ctrl+F9.

An example of using named fields is provided in the following example paragraph.

> Our budget for this quarter is $8,465 for travel and $2,500 for entertainment. This gives us $10,965.

In this example, the bookmark *Travel* was applied to $8,465 and the bookmark *Entertainment* was applied to $2,500. The field used to calculate the result is,

```
{=Travel+Entertainment \# "$#,##0"}
```

The advantage of using an expression field for this calculation is that, should the numbers change, you can quickly update the results. The numeric picture \# "$#,##0" was used to format the result without decimal places. Number formatting is described in Chapter 18.

T I P   When you assign a bookmark to a number, include the space on either side of the number as part of the bookmark. You then can change the number's first or last digit without destroying the bookmark, preventing an Undefined Bookmark error or a math error. If your bookmark includes only the number and you delete the first or last digit, the digits you type in as replacements will not be included in the new bookmark and the mathematical result will be wrong.

Performing Calculations in a Table

To carry out a calculation within a table, you use table references and special *reduction functions* to create a field expression for calculating the desired result. Reduction functions are mathematical functions that perform operations such as Sum or Average. To use this method, follow these steps:

1. Position the insertion point in the cell in the table where you want the result to appear.

2. Choose the **I**nsert Fiel**d** command or press Ctrl+F9 to insert field characters, {}.

3. Type the expression for calculating the desired result in the Field **C**ode text box or between the field characters, using cell references and reduction functions.

   To sum a column of numbers, for example, the expression might look like this:

   ```
   {=sum([r2c4:r10c4])}
   ```

   Sum is the reduction function for adding a range of numbers and *[r2c4:r10c4]* specifies the range of cells to be added; that is, the cells from row 2 to row 10 in column 4. Notice the use of square brackets to enclose the row and column range.

   For a list of operators and reduction functions you can use with table references, look under the entry for the {=expression} field in Chapter 18.

4. Following the expression, you can add formatting instructions. To add instructions, select a format from the Instructions list and choose the **A**dd button.

5. If you typed the reduction functions into the Insert Field dialog box, choose OK or press Enter.

The results of the field (the calculation) are displayed unless the **V**iew Field **C**odes command is selected, in which case the code itself is displayed. To update the field, locate the insertion point inside the field and press F9.

Creating Equations

Word for Windows comes with an Equation Editor that enables you to easily create publication-quality equations within a document. An equation created with the Equation Editor is inserted into your document as an object, just as you can insert pictures, graphs, and spreadsheet tables. To edit the equation, you must reopen the Equation Editor; you cannot edit the equation from within Word for Windows. You can, however, position and resize an equation from within a Word for Windows document, as with any object.

NOTE   If you did not choose to install the Equation Editor when you set up Word for Windows, it will not appear in the list of object types. You must run the setup program again to install the Equation Editor. You do not have to reinstall the entire program; you can tell the setup program to install only the Equation Editor.

You use the **Insert O**bject command to open the Equation Editor and create an equation. The equation you create will be inserted in the document wherever the insertion point was located when you chose the **Insert O**bject command. To insert an equation into a document, follow these steps:

1. Position the insertion point where you want to insert the equation you will create.

2. Choose the **Insert O**bject command.

3. Select Equation from the **O**bject Type list box and choose OK.

   When you choose OK, the Equation Editor opens, as shown in figure 17.1.

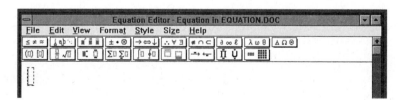

FIG. 17.1.

The Equation Editor window.

4. Create the equation in the Equation Editor (see the following sections for detailed instructions on creating an equation).

5. Choose **F**ile **E**xit to close the Equation Editor and return to the document. You are asked if you want to save the equation in the document.

   or

   Choose **U**pdate (or press F3) to insert the equation into the document without closing the Equation Editor window.

If you choose to update your equation without closing the Equation Editor, you can return to your document as you would switch to any other program—press Ctrl+Esc to use the Task List or press Alt+Tab until the document window is active.

When you first open the Equation Editor, you are presented with a screen containing a single *slot* (see fig. 17.1). Slots demarcate the different components of an equation. If you are entering a fraction, for example, a slot will be available for the numerator and a slot for the denominator. You move from slot to slot by clicking a slot or by pressing the arrow and tab keys, filling in the slots with text and symbols to create your equation.

The Equation Editor has several tools for simplifying the task of creating an equation. Just below the menu bar are several buttons that access the *template* and *symbol popups*. To access these popups, you point to the button and press and hold the mouse button. The template popups contain collections of ready-made templates that enable you to easily create the different components in an equation. For example, the second template from the left in the second row of buttons contains a collection of templates for entering fractions and roots (see fig. 17.2). The dotted areas within a template represent the slots into which you enter symbols and numbers. Several template popups contain a variety of templates for creating fractions, roots, summations, matrices, integrals, and many other mathematical expressions.

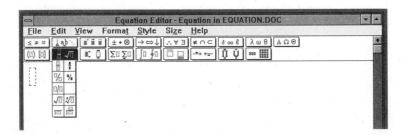

The Equation Editor with a template popup opened.

The Equation Editor also has several popups for entering symbols, including math operators, Greek symbols, arrows, and so on. The best way to become familiar with both the template and symbol popups is to experiment with them, running through them one-by-one and inserting either the template or symbol to see what it looks like.

Constructing an equation consists largely of using the template and symbol popups, and using the keyboard to assemble the equation piece by piece. Text and symbols are entered into slots, which are either part of a template, or on their own (for example, the slot that appears on-screen when the Equation Editor is first opened). Text or symbols are entered into whichever slot contains the insertion point. You use the arrow and Tab keys to move the insertion point from slot to slot.

The templates take care of most of the positioning and spacing aspects of equation building, although other commands are available to fine-tune spacing and alignment of the components of an equation. Commands also are available for controlling the font and font size of the various elements in an equation.

Figure 17.3 shows a partially completed equation in the Equation Editor. Notice the slots near the end of the equation into which characters have yet to be inserted.

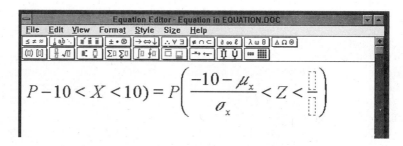

Typing in the Equation Editor

Typing in the Equation Editor is much like typing in a Word for Windows document, although with some important differences. Whenever you type in the Equation Editor, text is entered into the slot containing the insertion point. You can use the Backspace and Del keys to delete characters as you would in a Word for Windows document.

Unless you choose the Text style from the Style menu, the space bar will have no effect. The Equation Editor takes care of the spacing in an equation. When you type an equal sign, for example, the Equation Editor adds spacing before and after the equal sign. If you press the Enter key, a new line is started.

If you want to type regular text, choose the Text style from the Style menu or press Ctrl+Shift+E. You then can enter text as you normally would, using the space bar to insert spaces. Choose the Math style from the Style menu or press Ctrl+Shift+= to return to the Math style—the style you normally work with when creating an equation.

Selecting Items in an Equation

You may need to select an item within an equation—to change the point size or reposition the item, for example. To select characters within a slot, use the mouse to drag across characters, or with the keyboard, press the Shift+arrow key combination as you normally would. To select an entire equation, choose **E**dit Select **A**ll or press Ctrl+A.

To select embedded items (items not contained in a slot), such as character embellishments (such as carets, tildes, prime signs, and so on) or integral signs, hold down the Ctrl key and the mouse pointer changes to a vertical arrow. Point to the embedded item with the arrow and click to select the item.

Entering Nested Equation Templates

Complex equations involve templates nested within templates. The result is an equation involving many templates that are each nested within the slot of a larger template. To enter a template within an existing equation, follow these steps:

1. Place the insertion point where you want to insert the template.

2. Use the mouse to choose the desired template from one of the template popups. The template will be inserted immediately to the right of the insertion point.

   or

   Use one of the shortcut keys listed in table 17.1 to insert the template.

3. Type text or enter symbols into each slot in the template. The insertion point must be positioned in the slot before you begin entering text or symbols.

   To position the insertion point with the mouse, point to the desired slot and click.

   or

   Use the arrow and Tab keys to position the insertion point.

Table 17.1 lists the shortcut keys for inserting templates.

To use these shortcuts, press Ctrl+T and then the shortcut key. The items marked with an asterisk can be inserted by pressing the Ctrl key and then the shortcut key—you do not have to press T first.

Table 17.1. Shortcut Keys for Inserting Templates

Template	Description	Shortcut key
(⋮⋮)	Parentheses*	(or)
[⋮⋮]	Brackets*	[or]
{⋮⋮}	Braces*	{ or }
|⋮⋮|	Absolute Value	|
▯	Fraction*	F
▯/▯	Slash Fraction*	/
▦⌐	Superscript (high)*	H
▦∟	Subscript (low)*	L
▦⌐	Joint sub/superscript*	J
√⎺⎺	Root*	R
∜⎺⎺	Nth Root	N
Σ▯	Summation	S
∏▯	Product	P
∫▯	Integral*	I
⊞	Matrix (3×3)	M
▯	Underscript (limit)	U

Entering Symbols

Many fields of mathematics, science, and medicine use symbols to represent concepts or physical structures. The Equation Editor can insert symbols into slots with the following procedure:

1. Position the insertion point where you want to insert the symbol.

2. Use the mouse to select the desired symbol from one of the symbol templates.

   or

   Use one of the shortcut keys listed in table 17.2 to insert the symbol.

Table 17.2 lists the shortcut keys for inserting symbols. To use these shortcuts, press Ctrl+S and then the shortcut key.

Table 17.2. Shortcut Keys for Inserting Symbols

Symbol	Description	Shortcut key
∞	Infinity	|
→	Arrow	A
∂	Derivative (partial)	D
≤	Less than or equal to	<
≥	Greater than or equal to	>
×	Times	T
∈	Element of	E
∉	Not an element of	Shift+E
⊂	Contained in	C
⊄	Not contained in	Shift+C

Adding Embellishments

The Equation Editor has several embellishments you can add to characters or symbols, such as prime signs, arrows, tildes, and dots. To add an embellishment, follow these steps:

1. Position the insertion point to the right of the character you want to embellish.

2. Choose the embellishment icon from the Embellishment popup (third icon from the left in the first row of icons).

   or

   Use one of the shortcut keys listed in table 17.3 to add an embellishment.

Table 17.3. Shortcut Keys for Inserting Embellishments

Icon	Description	Shortcut key
	Over-bar	Ctrl+Shift+-
	Tilde	Ctrl+~ (Ctrl+" on some keyboards)
	Arrow (vector)	Ctrl+Alt+-
	Single prime	Ctrl+Alt+'
	Double prime	Ctrl+" (Ctrl+~ on some keyboards)
	Single dot	Ctrl+Alt+.

Controlling Spacing

Several spacing parameters can be modified by using the Format Spacing command (for example, line spacing, and row and column spacing in matrices). To modify the spacing setting used by the Equation Editor, follow these steps:

1. Choose the Format Spacing command.

   A dialog box displaying a scrolling list of dimensions appears.

2. Select the text box next to the dimension you want to modify. Use the scroll bar to move through the list of dimensions.

   The dimension you select will be displayed in the diagram at the right of the dialog box.

3. Type in a new measurement.

   The default unit of measure is points. You can specify other units by typing in the appropriate abbreviation from the following list:

Unit of measure	Abbreviation
Inches	in
Centimeters	cm

Unit of measure	Abbreviation
Millimeters	mm
Points	pt
Picas	pi

4. Choose the Apply or Enter button.

   Choosing Apply applies the modified dimension to the current equation and leaves the dialog box open, enabling you to continue modifications. Choosing Enter applies any modifications and closes the dialog box.

In practice, you probably should specify the spacing dimensions as a percentage of the point size specified for Full size type, which is set in the Size Define dialog box. The advantage to this approach is that if you change the type size, you don't have to redefine your spacing dimensions; spacing will always be proportional to the type size.

Unless you are using the Text style, the Equation Editor takes care of the spacing between elements in an equation. You can insert spaces manually if you desire, using the mouse or the keyboard. Four spacing symbols can be used for manually inserting spaces. These symbols are located in the second symbol popup from the left in the top row, or can be accessed with shortcut keys. The spacing symbols and shortcut keys are listed in table 17.4.

Table 17.4. Shortcut Keys for Inserting Spaces

Icon	Function	Shortcut key
	Zero space	Shift+space bar
	One point space	Ctrl+Alt+space bar
	Thin space	Ctrl+space bar
	Thick space (two thin spaces)	Ctrl+Shift+space bar

You can insert as many spaces together as you want. To delete a space, use the Del or Backspace keys, as you would with text.

Positioning and Aligning Equations

If you are not satisfied with the automatic positioning of the elements in an equation, you can fine-tune the positioning of any selected item using the Nudge commands. You first must select the item (see the section on selecting) and then use one of the following commands to move the item, one pixel at a time:

Keystroke	Function
Ctrl+left-arrow key	Moves item left one pixel
Ctrl+right-arrow key	Moves item right one pixel
Ctrl+down-arrow key	Moves item down one pixel
Ctrl+up-arrow key	Moves item up one pixel

The Equation Editor enables you to horizontally align the lines in an equation, or lines of equations, using either the Format commands or the alignment symbol. Lines can be aligned to the left, center, or right, or they can be aligned around equal signs, decimal points, or alignment symbols. You align a group of equations by simply choosing one of the Align commands from the Format menu. To align lines within an equation, position the insertion point within the lines and then choose one of the alignment commands.

To insert an alignment symbol, position the insertion point and choose the alignment symbol (top row, leftmost symbol) from the Spaces popup (top row of buttons, second button from the left). The alignment symbols are used as a reference point around which lines of equations or lines within an equation are aligned. They override the Format commands.

Selecting Fonts

When you normally work in the Equation Editor, you will use the Math style found in the Style menu. When you use the Math style, the Equation Editor automatically recognizes standard functions and applies the Function style (typeface and character formatting, for example) to such functions. The Variable style is applied otherwise. If the Equation Editor fails to recognize a function, you can select the function and apply the Function style manually. Other styles also are available, such as Text, Greek, and Matrix-Vector. Styles are simply a combination of font and character formatting assigned to selected characters or to characters about to be typed. You can modify the font and character formatting (that is, make the font bold or italic) of these styles using the Style Define dialog box.

To define the font and character attributes for a style, follow these steps:

1. Choose the **Style D**efine command.

2. Select the style you want to define.

3. Select the desired font from the list of available fonts.

4. Select the Bold or Italic boxes, if desired.

5. Choose OK or press Enter.

> Use the **T**ext style to type regular text. Selecting this style applies the Text style to the text you type and also enables the space bar so that you can enter spaces as normal. With the other styles, spacing is handled automatically by the Equation Editor.
>
> **T I P**

> Use the **O**ther style when you want to select a font and character format that is not one of the standard styles. Selecting this style opens a dialog box in which you can select a font and character format for selected characters or for the characters you are about to enter.
>
> **T I P**

Selecting Font Sizes

Just as the Equation Editor provides several predefined font styles, it also provides several predefined font sizes. The Full size is the choice you normally work with when you are building equations. You also have selections for subscripts, sub-subscripts, symbols, and sub-symbols. You can use the **O**ther size option for those cases in which you want to specify a size not defined by one of the standard sizes just listed.

To apply a font size to an equation, follow these steps:

1. Select the characters whose point size you want to modify.

If you do not select any characters, the size you choose will apply to characters you type subsequently.

2. Choose the Size menu.

3. Choose the desired size from the Size menu. If none of the defined sizes match your needs, choose Size Other and specify a size in the Other Size dialog box.

You can modify the default settings for each of the sizes listed in the Size menu by using the Size Define command, as in the following steps:

1. Choose the Size Define command.

2. Select the box to the right of the size you want to define.

   When you select a box, the element you are defining is highlighted in the diagram on the right side of the dialog box.

3. Type in a new size.

4. Choose OK or press Enter.

To apply a size, select the size from the Size menu, then type the characters you want the size applied to, or select the characters after they have been typed and then choose a size.

Working with Matrices

The Matrix template popup includes several vectors and matrices of predefined size. You also can select one of the template symbols in the bottom row of the popup to open up a Matrix dialog box, in which you can specify the dimensions of the matrix or vector and control several other matrix characteristics.

To insert a matrix template, click on the matrix template popup (the last popup in the second row) and drag the pointer to the desired popup. Release the mouse button. Selecting a template from the last row of icons will open up the Matrix dialog box (see fig. 17.4). In the Matrix dialog box, you can specify the dimensions of the matrix and make several other selections. You can specify how the elements in rows and columns are aligned and whether or not the column widths and row heights are equal (rather than based on widest or highest entry). By clicking in the space between the rows and columns in the dialog box, you can select one of three types of partition lines: solid, dashed, or dotted lines. As you click in the space, you cycle through the three types of lines and then back to no line. The spacing between rows and columns is controlled in the Format Spacing dialog box.

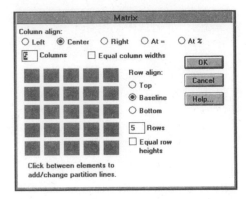

FIG. 17.4.

The Matrix
dialog box.

To format an existing matrix, select the entire matrix and choose the Format **M**atrix command. Make the desired selections from the dialog box. Choose OK or press Enter.

Viewing Equations

You can choose from three different views of the equation in the Equation Editor window. To change the view, open the **V**iew menu. To display the equation at the actual size it will appear in the document and on the printed page, select 100%. Select 200% and 400% commands to display the equation at twice and four times the actual size, respectively. These commands are useful when you want to fine-tune the spacing in an equation or get a close-up look at small items in an equation.

Editing an Equation

You must return to the Equation Editor to edit an equation. To open the Equation Editor, follow these steps:

1. Double-click on the equation you want to edit, or select the equation and choose **E**dit Equation Object.

2. Make the desired editing changes.

3. Choose **F**ile **U**pdate to update the equation without closing the Equation Editor.

   or

   Choose **F**ile E**x**it to close the Equation Editor and return to the document. You are asked if you want to save the equation in the document.

If you create the equation by using the {eq} field, you must edit the field code to change the equation. The Equation Editor cannot be used to edit equations made with field codes.

Printing Equations

It is not within the scope of this chapter to discuss the details of printing equations created in the Equation Editor. In short, to print equations you need to have a PostScript printer, an HP LaserJet printer that allows downloading of fonts, or a dot-matrix or HP DeskJet printer in conjunction with a font-scaling utility, such as TrueType or Adobe Type Manager. Appendix C describes the use of fonts in more detail. The Help facility in the Equation Editor contains extensive information on using printers and fonts with the Equation Editor. To access these help screens, follow these steps:

1. Choose the **Help** command in the Equation Editor.

2. Choose **I**ndex.

3. Select one of the topics under the Printers & Fonts category.

You can obtain a printout of the help screen by choosing **F**ile **P**rint Topic.

From Here . . .

In this chapter you learned three methods for performing calculations in a Word for Windows document. You also learned how to use the Equation Editor to produce publication-quality equations that can be embedded in your documents.

Several other chapters in this book cover Word for Windows features that can enhance your document. In Chapters 23 and 24, you learn how to insert and work with graphical objects in your documents. Chapter 21 explains how to share information with other applications—for example, how to link a table in a Word for Windows document with data in a Microsoft Excel worksheet.

Automating with Field Codes

Fields are a necessary, but often invisible, part of features such as a table of contents, an index, or a table of authorities. Fields also perform such simple tasks as inserting the date or displaying a data-entry box. The value you gain from using fields comes from the repetitive work they can automate for you.

Fields are hidden codes you type into a document or insert with commands from the Insert menu. You normally see the results of fields, such as dates, page numbers, text linked to other documents, or mail-merge data. By choosing the View Field Codes command, you can see and edit the fields that produce those results.

T I P

If you have used worksheet functions in Microsoft Excel or Lotus 1-2-3, you are familiar with the concept of fields. Fields are similar to functions. Worksheet functions are mathematically and financially oriented; Word for Windows fields are oriented toward words, document processing, and mail-merge functions.

In Word for Windows, most fields update to produce a new result only when you print, print merge, or select and then update the field. You can update fields individually or throughout the entire document.

Many of the other features described in this book use fields, although you may not have been aware of them. In Chapter 15, for example, the dates and page numbers in headers and footers are created with fields; in Chapter 16, the indexes and tables of contents are created with fields. Fields are used in Chapters 19, 20, and 21 to create mail-merge letters, assemble large documents, and integrate the output from different Windows applications.

With fields you can do the following:

- Build tables of contents, tables of authorities, and indexes
- Build mailing lists, labels, and form letters
- Prompt operators for information used repeatedly in a document
- Insert dates, times, or document summary information
- Link Word for Windows documents or data in other Windows applications with the current Word for Windows document
- Automatically update cross-referenced page numbers
- Calculate math results
- Enable operators to jump between related words or contents
- Start macros

This chapter gives you an introduction to fields, covering how to view, insert, update, edit, and format the fields. At the end of the chapter is an alphabetical reference list of field codes, a section on using general switches to format fields, and a table of shortcut keys that are helpful when you're working with fields.

Understanding the Basics of Fields

In this section you learn about the types of fields, their components, how to print fields, and how they appear in your documents.

Examining the Types of Fields

Fields can change your documents in a number of ways. Three types of Word for Windows fields are available: result fields, action fields, and marker fields.

Result fields produce a result in your document by inserting information. This information may be from the computer or document, such as the {author} and {date} fields. Other fields, such as {fillin}, display a dialog box that requests information from the operator and then inserts the information into the document.

Action fields do something to the document but don't insert visible text. The action is performed either when you update the field, as in the {ask} field, or when you click the field, as in the {gotobutton} and {macrobutton} fields. The {ask} field, for example, displays a dialog box and prompts you to enter information. But instead of displaying the information, Word for Windows stores it in a bookmark you designate.

Marker fields produce neither results nor actions. A marker field simply marks a location in the document so that you can find the location when you build such things as indexes and tables of contents. The index entry {xe} and table of contents entry {tc} fields are marker fields.

Understanding the Parts of Fields

Fields contain three parts: field characters, field type, and field instructions. A field may look like the following:

```
{date \@ "MMM d, yy"}
```

where the { and } are field characters, *date* is the field type, and \@ *"MMM d, yy"* is the field instruction.

Field characters define the beginning and end of a field. Although they look like braces, { and }, you cannot type the field characters. You create them by pressing Ctrl+F9 (Insert Field) or by choosing a menu command that creates a field.

The second part of a field, the *field type*, defines the type of action the field performs. The field type follows the first field character, {, and must be a field type (see "A Reference List of Field Codes"), an equal sign (=), or a bookmark name.

The third part of a field, the *field instructions*, defines the type of action performed. You can customize the action of some fields by giving different instructions.

Arguments are numbers, text, or graphics used to control a field's action or results. If an argument contains more than one word, the argument usually must be enclosed in quotation marks (" "). (Exceptions are described in each field's description.) For example, you can use the {ask} field to prompt the operator for text to be assigned to the bookmark First_Name as follows:

```
{ask First_Name "Enter the first name."}
```

T I P   If a field result, such as a fillin dialog box, shows only the first word of the text you typed, you have probably forgotten to enclose the rest of the argument in quotation marks. Word for Windows uses the first word of the argument, but doesn't see the rest unless it is in quotation marks.

Bookmarks in fields are the same as bookmarks you assign to text. They name a location or selection of text. Fields use bookmarks to take action on the text or object in the document having that bookmark name. Fields also can store information in a bookmark or use the page number or sequence value of a bookmark's location.

Identifiers distinguish between different parts of the same document. For example, you may use the letter F as an identifier of figures and the letter P as an identifier of pictures.

Text includes words or graphics used by the field. If you are entering a text argument with more than one word, you need to enclose all the text argument in quotation marks.

Switches toggle field results on or off. Type switches with a backslash (\) followed by the switch letter. Switches can be specific to a field or can be general and used by different fields. A field can contain as many as 10 field-specific switches and 10 general switches. Field-specific switches are described in "A Reference List of Field Codes" and general switches are described in the section "Using General Switches" later in this chapter.

Viewing Field Codes

Fields appear two different ways: as a field code and as the field result. Field results display as though they were typed. You normally don't see the field codes when you work in your document, but if they return text, you see their results after the fields have been updated. If the fields have not been updated, you see the fields' previous results.

Some fields produce no visible result. Instead, they produce an action that affects other field codes. The fields that do not produce results include {ask}, {data}, {nextif}, {next}, {rd}, {set}, {skipif}, {tc}, and {xe}. (See "A Reference List of Field Codes" later in this chapter for more information.)

To see the field codes so that you can review, delete, or edit them, choose the View Field Codes command. A check mark appears next to the Field Codes command in the View menu when field codes are displayed. Your document probably will change its word wrap when you reveal or hide field codes. This is due to the differences in length between the field codes and their results.

> A fast way to switch between displaying field codes or their results is to select the area containing the field or move the insertion point inside the field, and then press Shift+F9. This key combination toggles between displaying results and field codes in the selected range.

T I P

Figures 18.1 and 18.2 show two views of the same document. Figure 18.1 shows the field codes in the document. Figure 18.2 shows a document after the fields it contains have been updated. As you can see, the field codes create an automated document that can be used repeatedly.

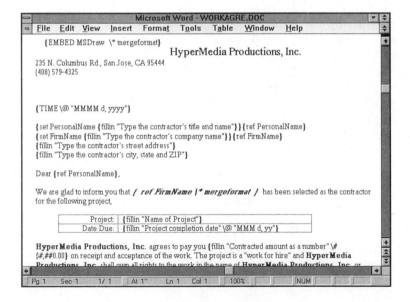

FIG. 18.1.

This view shows the field codes themselves.

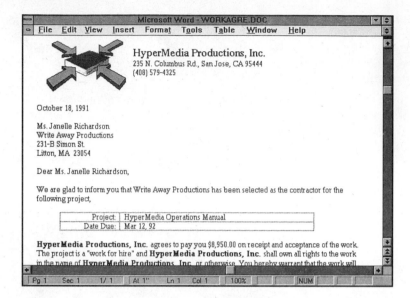

FIG. 18.2.

This view shows
the results of
field codes.

A few field codes do not display when you choose View Field Codes or select the area containing the field and press Shift+F9. The {xe} (index entry), {tc} (table of contents entry), and {rd} (referenced document) field codes are formatted automatically as hidden text. To see these codes when you display field codes, you must choose the Tools Options Category View and select the Hidden Text check box.

Most fields do not update automatically to show you the most current result. You must update fields manually or with a macro. When you load a document that contains fields, each field shows its previous result. This feature enables you to load a document, such as a contract or form letter, and update only the items you want changed.

Printing Fields

You probably should keep a printed copy of your documents and macros. These will help you if you ever lose the file or if someone else takes over your operation. To print a copy of the document so that you can see the field codes, follow these steps:

1. Choose the File Print command.

2. Choose the Options button from the Print dialog box.

3. Select the Field Codes check box under the Include with Document group.

4. Choose OK or press Enter to return to the Print dialog box, and then print your document.

Remember to unselect the **Field** Codes check box when you want to return to printing just the document.

Inserting Fields in Your Document

You can enter fields in a number of ways. Several commands enter field codes at the insertion point's position. Some of the commands that insert field codes include the following:

> **E**dit Paste **S**pecial Paste Link
> **I**nsert Foot**n**ote
> **I**nsert File
> **I**nsert Page N**u**mbers
> **I**nsert **A**nnotations
> **I**nsert **P**icture
> **I**nsert **O**bject
> **I**nsert Fiel**d**
> **I**nsert Index **E**ntry
> **I**nsert **I**ndex
> **I**nsert Date and **T**ime
> **I**nsert Table of **C**ontents
> **I**nsert **S**ymbol

You also can insert field codes into a document by using the **Insert Field** command, and then choosing the appropriate field codes from the Insert Field dialog box. Or you can type field codes directly into a document by pressing Ctrl+F9 (Insert Field) and typing between the field characters.

Using the Insert Field Command

To insert field codes with the **Insert Field** command, follow these steps:

1. Position the insertion point in the document at the location where you want the field result.

2. Choose the **Insert Field** command.

   Figure 18.3 shows the Field dialog box, from which you can select field types and instructions.

3. Select a field type from the Insert **F**ield Type list.

FIG. 18.3.

The Insert Field
dialog box
enables you to
see all the fields
and many of
their formatting
switches.

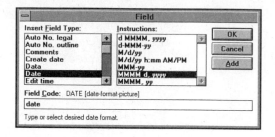

4. Select instructions to format or redefine the field type from the
   Instructions list. The Instructions list shows you the proper syntax for entering instructions and switches for the selected field
   type. Choose the **A**dd button to add the selected instructions to
   the field.

5. Edit the Field **C**ode text box to include additional instructions,
   such as switches or text, that modify the field.

6. Choose OK or press Enter.

When you choose OK or press Enter, some fields immediately update.
When you insert the {fillin} field, for example, Word for Windows displays the fillin dialog box that prompts you for an entry.

Inserting Field Codes Manually

Manually entered field codes are useful when you're creating form letters or building fields composed of multiple parts and many switches.
After you are familiar with the field code syntax, manual entry enables
you to enter the field codes quickly. To enter a field code manually,
follow these steps:

1. Position the insertion point in the document at the location where
   you want the field action or result.

2. Press Ctrl+F9.

   Even if fields are not displayed currently, Word for Windows
   shows the field characters you have just inserted. The insertion
   point appears between two field characters, {}.

3. Enter the field type followed by a space; then type the field instructions. Be sure to type two backslashes instead of a single
   backslash to separate directories in a path name.

4. Update the field code by pressing F9. An incorrect syntax in the
   field code causes a beep. Select the field and press Shift+F9 to see
   the results.

Another method of manually entering fields is to position the insertion point where you want the field, type the field type and instructions, select them, and then press Ctrl+F9. Word for Windows encloses the selection in field characters, { and }. This method works well when you need to nest fields inside other fields (see "Creating Complex Fields by Nesting" later in this chapter).

 NOTE Remember that although the field characters appear to be braces, they are not. Fields do not work if you type brace characters. You can create a matching set of field characters only by pressing Ctrl+F9.

Updating and Editing Fields

Different fields update at different times. Fields such as {date} update when the document opens. Fields such as {next} take affect only during print merge. Fields like {fillin} update when the field is selected and the F9 (Update) key is pressed.

You can change field codes after they are inserted by displaying them on-screen and then editing them. This method is how you add more complex formats and switches to give you more control over the results of fields.

Moving between Fields

You can find fields in two ways: use a shortcut key to find the next field, or use the **E**dit **F**ind command to find a specific field type.

To move to and select the next field after the insertion point, press F11 (Next Field). If you do not have an F11 key, press Alt+F1. To move to and select the preceding field before the insertion point, press Shift+F11 (Previous Field) or Alt+Shift+F1.

The F11 and Shift+F11 shortcuts do not find the {xe} (index entry), {tc} (table of contents entry), or {rd} (referenced document) fields. You can find these fields by first displaying hidden text with the **T**ools **O**ptions **C**ategory View command and selecting the Hidden Text check box. After the codes are visible, you can use the **E**dit **F**ind command.

T I P

To find a specific field code, follow these steps:

1. Choose the **View Field Codes** command to display field codes. With some field codes, you may have to display hidden text.

2. Choose the **Edit Find** command.

3. In the Find What text box, type the field type you want to find, such as *fillin*. Do not type the field characters.

4. Choose the Find Next button.

5. Choose Cancel or press Esc to edit the field.

6. Press Shift+F4 to find the next field of the same type.

   The insertion point moves to the next field of the type you requested.

Updating Fields

Updating a field produces a new result or action from the field—perhaps a change in text, numbers, or graphics. Some fields may not produce a visible change, but instead affect the results in other fields.

Some fields, such as {date}, update automatically when the document is loaded. Other fields, such as {ddeauto}, update when data in a linked application changes. Fields such as {fillin} update when you select them and press F9. Other fields update during printing, print merge, or repagination.

To update a field manually, select the field and press F9 (Update Field). You can select the field by selecting the text around it, using one of the selection methods described in previous chapters, or by pressing F11 (Next Field) or Shift+F11 (Previous Field) to move to and select the field. If field codes are visible, you can select a specific field by dragging across one of the field characters. You also can select a visible field code by moving the insertion point inside the field and pressing F8 (Extend Selection) until the field is selected.

If Word for Windows beeps when you attempt to update a field, that field is locked; there is a syntax error in the field code; or it is a field code that does not update—the fields that generate equations on-screen, for example.

If you want to update only part of a document, select only the portions of the document you want to update and press F9. To update fields in a table, select the portion of the table you want to update using any table selection method, and then press F9.

To update an entire document, select the entire document either by pressing Ctrl and clicking in the selection bar (the blank area to the left of the document), by choosing the **E**dit Select **A**ll command, or by pressing Ctrl+5 (on the numeric keypad). Press F9.

The following list shows fields unaffected by F9 (Update Field). Fields with an asterisk update automatically. Updating is not appropriate for the other fields.

Field	Use
*{autonum}	Automatic numbers with Arabic (1, 2, 3...) format
*{autonumlgl}	Automatic numbers with legal (1.1.1...) format
*{autonumout}	Automatic numbers with outline format
{eq}	Math formulas
{gotobutton}	On-screen buttons that jump to a location when double-clicked
{macrobutton}	On-screen buttons that run a macro when double-clicked
{print}	Send information to the printer

Undoing or Stopping Updates

You can undo field updates if you select the **E**dit **U**ndo Update Fields command (or press Alt+backspace or Ctrl+Z) immediately after updating one or more fields. This capability gives you a chance to make changes throughout a document, see how they affect the document, and then remove the changes if necessary.

If you are updating a document and want to stop the updates, press Esc, as indicated in the status bar at the bottom of the screen. This method is handy if you have selected the entire document and realize that you do not want to update all fields.

The status bar displays the percentage of updates completed. **T I P**

Locking Fields To Prevent Updates

When you want to prevent a field from changing, you can lock it. Locking fields is useful if you want to archive a file that will not change, to prevent accidental changes, or to prevent updating a link to a file that no longer exists. Word for Windows will not update a locked field. If you attempt to update a locked field, you hear a beep and see a warning in the status bar that an attempt was made to update a locked field.

To prevent a particular field from being updated while those around it are updated, lock the field. Select the field and then press Ctrl+F11 (Lock Field). To unlock the field, press Shift+Ctrl+F11 (Unlock Field). (If you do not have an F11 key, use Alt+Ctrl+F1 and Alt+Shift+Ctrl+F1, respectively.)

Locking a field is different from unlinking a field with Shift+Ctrl+F9. Unlinked fields replace the field code with the results. You are unable to return to a usable field code.

Editing Fields

You can manually edit field codes or their results. This is useful for correcting the results of a field or for changing the information or switches inside a field code after it has been created. By editing simple fields, you can change them into larger, nested fields containing multiple parts, which you then can use to accomplish complex tasks.

To edit a field code, follow these steps:

1. Choose the **View Field** Codes command or select the text enclosing the field and press Shift+F9 to display the field.

2. Move the insertion point inside the field.

3. Edit the field as you edit text. Make sure that you preserve the correct syntax of the parts within the field.

To see the results of your editing, select the field and press F9 (Update Field).

You can change the results of a field by editing the results on-screen as if you were editing normal text. You can even print this edited result. If the field updates, however, your edits disappear and the new results take their place. The solution is to lock edited field results before updating a document, printing, or doing a print merge (see "Locking Fields To Prevent Updates" earlier in this chapter).

> **T I P**
>
> Some fields, such as {include}, {dde}, and {ddeauto}, use DOS path names (directory names). When you type path names in fields, you must use double backslashes (\\) wherever the path name normally has a single backslash (\). Keep this fact in mind if you have to change the directory path name used in a field. Always use a backslash before any quotation mark (") within a quoted string. For example, the field
>
> ```
> {fillin "Who wrote \"Brahm's Lullaby\""}
> ```
>
> places quotation marks around the phrase "Brahm's Lullaby" when it appears in the prompt of a fillin dialog box.

Creating Complex Fields by Nesting

When you nest fields, you put one or more fields inside another field. This technique enables you to use the result of one field to change the actions of another. You can nest the {fillin} field inside the {set} field, for example, so that the typed entry in the {fillin} field can be stored by the {set} field in a bookmark. The text in the bookmark then can be redisplayed at other locations with the {ref} field:

```
{set Name {fillin "Type the name"}}
```

This method is used in the letter in figures 18.1 and 18.2.

To nest a field inside another field, follow these steps:

1. Display the field codes, if they are not already displayed, by choosing **View Field** Codes.

2. Insert the first field into the document by following the Insert Field procedure or by pressing Ctrl+F9 and typing the field type and its instructions.

3. Position the insertion point inside the existing field at the point where you want the nested field.

4. Insert the nested field by following the Insert Field procedure for this code, or by pressing Ctrl+F9 and typing the field type and its instructions between the field code characters, { }.

5. Insert additional fields or type additional field instructions.

6. Select the field and press F9 (Update Field) to check the results.

Deleting and Unlinking Fields

Delete a field by selecting it and pressing the Del key. A quick way to select and delete fields is to press F11 (Next Field) until the appropriate field is selected, and then press Del.

You may want to unlink fields and convert them to their fixed results. This freezes the result at its current value, removes the field code, and ensures that the result will not change if updated.

To unlink a field, select the field code and press Ctrl+Shift+F9 (Unlink Field).

Using Shortcut Keys

Table 18.1 lists shortcut keys that can make your work with fields much quicker and easier.

Table 18.1. Field Shortcut Keys

Key Combination	Function
Ctrl+Shift+F7	Transfer changes in the result back to the source Word document. Beeps if there is no link. See Chapter 21 for more information.
F9	Update fields in the selection
Shift+F9	Toggle the view between field codes and their results
Ctrl+F9	Insert field characters, { }
Ctrl+Shift+F9	Permanently replace a field with its last result
Alt+Shift+F9	Equivalent to double-clicking on a selected {gotobutton} and {macrobutton} fields
F11	Go to next field
Shift+F11	Go to previous field
Ctrl+F11	Lock field to prevent updates; field remains
Ctrl+Shift+F11	Unlock field to allow updates
Alt+Shift+D	Insert {date} field
Alt+Shift+P	Insert {page} field
Alt+Shift+T	Insert {time} field

A Reference List of Field Codes

Exploring all the power and possibilities available with field codes is beyond the scope of this book. But the following list of field codes shows the many fields available and some examples of their use. For additional examples on the use of fields, see Chapters 15, 16, 17, 19, 20, and 21.

This list shows some of the more frequently used field codes and their functions:

Function	Field Code
Date, Time, Summary Info	date, time, author, createdate
Index	xe, index
Linking, embedding, and importing	embed, import, include, link, dde, ddeauto
Mathematical calculations	eq
Mail merge	data, mergerec, mergefield, next, nextif, ref
Numbering	autonum, autonumlgl, autonumout
Page numbering	page, numpages
Prompting	ask, fillin
Reference figures, objects,	pageref, ref, seq, xe or locations
Symbol	symbol
Table of Contents	tc, toc

In the following list of field codes, the syntax of each field code shows whether the code contains field instructions, such as bookmarks, prompts, or switches. Remember that a *bookmark* is a name assigned to a selection or insertion point location. A bookmark also can be a name used to store information for future use by a field code. A *prompt* is a text message that appears on-screen when the field code updates. The prompt must be enclosed in quotation marks (" "). A *switch* alters the behavior or format of a field code in some manner. A field may use multiple switches. Included in some field code descriptions is an explanation of the specific switches used in that field code. A later section, "Using General Switches," explains how to use general switches to change a result's format.

In the following sections, the syntax shows the order in which information must be entered between field characters. Italicized words are information used by the field type. Optional information is enclosed in square brackets.

Getting Additional Help on Field Codes

The following sections in this chapter contain descriptions and examples of the more frequently used field codes and how they can be formatted. Field codes that are used less often have a brief description so that you can determine if it is a field code that you need to learn more about. To see a more extensive description and examples of a field code, do the following:

1. Choose the **Insert Field** command.

2. Select the field type you want information about from the Insert **F**ield Type list.

3. Press F1, the Help key.

4. Press Alt+F4 to close the Help application.

The Help window appears as shown in figure 18.4. The window contains the syntax, descriptions, and examples of how the field code can be used. For information on how to preserve the manual formatting you have applied to a field code or for information on how to use formatting switches within field codes, refer to the later sections in this chapter.

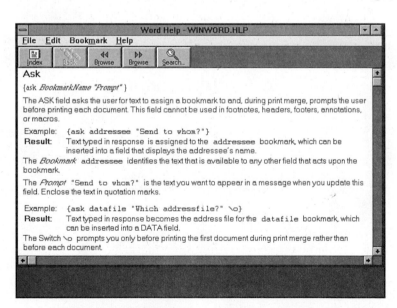

FIG. 18.4.

You can get descriptions and examples about a field directly from the Field dialog box.

{ask}

Syntax: {ask *bookmark prompt*}

Displays a dialog box asking the user to enter text. Word for Windows assigns that text to the bookmark, which then can be used throughout the document to repeat the typed text. For example, the following field code displays a dialog box asking the operator to enter the first name. Word for Windows stores the typed information in the bookmark named Firstname so that it can be used by other fields in the document:

```
{ask Firstname "Enter the first name"}
```

If you type *Mary* in response to the dialog box, you can repeat *Mary* throughout the document by using the field code {ref Firstname}.

Switch	Result
\o	Requests a response to the dialog box only at the beginning of the first document during a print merge.
\d	Defines default text for the dialog box. If no default exists, the last entry is repeated. Use \d" " if you want nothing as the default.

Updates during printing merge. You cannot use {ask} fields in footnotes, headers, footers, annotations, or macros.

If you want a dialog box for data entry, which you can update by pressing the F9 key, see the {fillin} field code.

{author}

Syntax: {author *[new_name]*}

Inserts or replaces the author's name as it appears in the document's Summary Info box.

The new name can be up to 255 characters long.

Updates when you press F9, or when you choose **F**ile Print **M**erge.

{autonum}

Syntax: {autonum}

Results in an Arabic number (1, 2, 3,...) when inserted at the beginning of a paragraph or outline level. Numbers display in the document in sequence and update as other {autonum} paragraphs are inserted or deleted.

{autonumlgl}

Syntax: {autonumlgl}

Displays a number using legal numbering (1.2.1) format when inserted at the beginning of a paragraph or outline heading. See {autonum}.

{autonumout}

Syntax: {autonumout}

Displays a number using outline number (I, A, 1, a,...) format when inserted at the beginning of a paragraph or outline heading. See {autonum}.

{bookmark}

Syntax: {*bookmark*}

Bookmarks are names that refer to text or graphics. Different field codes use bookmarks in different ways. Some fields return or display contents of the bookmark. Some fields return or display the page number where the bookmark's contents are located. You load data into a bookmark by using the **Insert Bookmark** command or by displaying an input box for operator entry using {ask} or {fillin} field control.

Bookmarks may be up to 25 characters in length and cannot include spaces. If you need to separate words, use an underline instead of a space.

If the bookmark *FirmName* contains the text *Generic Quality Corporation*, for example, the text appears in the document at every location of the field {ref FirmName}.

Updates when you press F9, when you choose File Print **Merge**, or when you choose **File P**rint the first time (when in a header or footer). See also {ref bookmark}.

{comments}

Syntax: {comments *["new_comments"]*}

Inserts or replaces comments from the document's Summary Info box appearing in the document.

Updates when you press F9, when you choose File Print **Merge**, or when you choose **File P**rint the first time (when in a header or footer).

{createdate}

Syntax: {createdate}

Inserts the date the document was created as shown in the Summary Info box. Formats according to the system's default format.

Updates when you press F9, when you choose File Print **M**erge, or when you choose **F**ile **P**rint the first time (when in a header or footer).

{data}

Syntax: {data *data_file [header_file]*}

Placed at the beginning of a merge document (form letter), the {data} field defines the file containing data to be merged by a print merge (mail merge). The field does not display after the data file has been attached.

{date}

Syntax: {date ["date_format_picture"]}

Results in the current date or time when the field was updated.

Updates when you select this field and press F9 or choose **F**ile **P**rint. Format with the date-time picture-switches listed in the section "Formatting Date-Time Results" later in this chapter.

{dde} and {ddeauto}

Syntax: {dde *app_name file_name [place_reference]*}

Syntax: {ddeauto *app_name file_name [place_reference]*}

The {dde} and {ddeauto} fields are inserted by the **E**dit Paste **S**pecial command with the Paste **L**ink button chosen.

Applications that have Dynamic Data Exchange (DDE) capability, but do not have Object Linking and Embedding (OLE) capability, can link data or graphics to Word for Windows using DDE fields.

```
{DDEAUTO Project1 Form1 Text1 \* mergeformat \t}
```

This link is to a Microsoft Visual BASIC where the BASIC program's name is *Project1*, the file name within the program is *Form1*, and the linked data within the file is a text entry box named *Text1*. The place reference name can be different for different types of source applications. In some applications it may be a row and column reference; in others it may be the name of a variable or data object. For more information, see Chapter 21.

Update {dde} fields by selecting the field and pressing F9. {ddeauto} fields update automatically when the linked data changes in the source application.

{edittime}

Syntax: {edittime}

Results in the number of minutes the document has been edited since its creation, as shown in the Summary Info box.

Updates when you press F9 or when you when you choose **File Print Merge**.

{embed}

Syntax: {embed object}

Results in embedding an object into a Word for Windows document. For example,

```
{embed ExcelChart \s  \* mergeformat}
```

embeds a Microsoft Excel chart into the document. For more information, see Chapter 21.

{eq}

Syntax: {eq formula_switches formula_text}

Displays an equation involving math symbols that cannot be typed directly from the keyboard, such as the square root symbol. This field code is for compatibility with previous versions of Word for Windows. If you have 2M of memory and available disk storage, you can create formulas more easily by using the Equation Editor. If you did not install the Equation Editor when you installed Word for Windows, you can run the Word Setup program from the Word for Windows group window in the Program Manager to install the Equation Editor.

{=expression}

Syntax: {= formula}

Displays the result of a mathematical calculation such as

    { = Sales - Cost}

Expressions can use bookmarks to define the locations of numbers or can use row and column locations (with R1C1 format) in document tables. See Chapter 4 to learn how to create bookmarks. Calculations on bookmarks can use common arithmetic operators, such as + (plus) and * (multiply). Calculations on row and column contents in a table use reduction functions such as Average, Count, Sum, and Product. Calculations are described in Chapter 17.

Updates when you press F9 or choose **File Print Merge**. If the expression is in the header or footer, it is updated once when you choose **File Print**.

Following are examples of expression fields:

Field Code	Result
{= Sales - Cost}	Subtracts the value in *Cost* from the value in *Sales*.
{= if (Sales > 450,Sales*.1,Sales*.05)}	Tests whether the value in *Sales* is greater than 450; if it is, the result is the Sales value multiplied by .1; if not, the result is the sales value multiplied by .05.
{= if (Sales > 450,Sales*.1,Sales*.05)*2}	Multiplies the result of the if statement by two.

If you need to create a large mathematical expression, build it in pieces within the field characters. As you complete each integral unit (one that can calculate by itself), select the entire field and press F9 to see whether the result is correct. Select the completed expression and press Ctrl+F9 to enclose that expression in another set of field characters. This method enables you to find errors in construction as you go rather than trying to find problems in a large completed expression.

T I P

T I P   Values in a document within a bookmark can lose their bookmark if you accidentally delete the characters (usually spaces) that enclose the number. If you are in doubt as to whether a bookmark still exists, press F5 twice and select the bookmark. See whether the correct value is selected in the document.

Use the following math operators with bookmarks only:

Operation	Operator
Plus	+
Minus	-
Multiply	*
Divide	/
Exponentiate	^
Less than	<
Less than or equal to	<=
Greater than	>
Greater than or equal to	>=
Parenthetical	()
Absolute value	Abs
Integer	Int
Sign	Sign
Test for error	Define
Modulus (remainder)	Mod
Round	Round
And	And
Or	Or
Not	Not

When you refer to a cell in a table, use the R1C1, row-column, format. If the expression is in the same table as the cells, only the R1C1 reference in brackets [] is needed. If the expression is outside a table, the table must be named and the cell reference must include that name, such as

    Budget[R2C7]
    Commission[R2C6]

Tables must use reduction functions for math operations. The following table lists reduction functions.

The following reduction functions and operators should be used for any math calculations within a table. Chapter 17 covers math in tables. Reduction functions can result to 1 for TRUE or 0 for FALSE.

Function	Name/ Example	Type/ Result
Abs	Absolute value	Operator
	`{= Abs -4}`	Results in 4
And	Logical and	Operator
	`{= And (Sales>500,Cost<300}`	Returns 1 if both arguments are true; 0 if either argument is false (maximum of two arguments).
Average	Averages arguments	Reduction function
	`{= Average (Budget[R1C1:R1C2])}`	Averages the content of cells in row 1, column 1 and row 1, column 2 from the table named Budget.
Count	Counts arguments	Reduction function
	`{= Count (Budget[C1])}`	Counts the number of numeric items in the cells of column 1 in the table Budget. Empty cells and text count as zero.
Defined	Checks for errors	Operator
	`{Defined (Sales)}`	Results in 1 if Sales bookmark exists and expression evaluates without error, otherwise results in 0.
Int	Results in integer	Operator
	`{= Int (Sales)}`	Deletes decimal fraction of an argument. To round numbers, use the Round operator.

Function	Name/ Example	Type/ Result
Max	Returns largest argument `{= Max (Budget[R1C1:R2C2])}`	Reduction function Returns the maximum value in the table named Budget within the range R1C1 to R2C2.
Min	Returns smallest argument `{= Min (Budget[R1C1:R2C2])}`	Reduction function Returns the maximum value in the table named Budget within the range R1C1 to R2C2.
Mod	Returns remainder `{= Mod (500,23.6)}`	Operator Returns the modulos. In the example, this is the remainder of 500 divided by 23.6.
Not	Reverses logical value `{= Not (Test)}`	Operator Returns 1 if the Test is 0 or if condition in Test is false; returns 0 if the Test is not zero or if condition in Test is true.
Or	Logical or `{=Or (Sales$mt500,Cost$lt300)}`	Operator Returns 1 if either condition is true, returns 0 if either condition is false.
Product	Multiplies all arguments `{= Product (Budget[R1C1:R2C1],2)}`	Reduction function Returns the product of values in the range R1C1 to R2C1 of the table Budget and the number 2.
Round	Rounds value to specified digits `{= Round (SalesTotal,2)}`	Operator Returns the value of SalesTotal rounded to two decimal places.

Function	Name/ Example	Type/ Result
Sign	Tests for sign of arguments `{= Sign (Profit)}`	Operator Returns 1 if Profit is positive, 0 if Profit is zero, -1 if Profit is negative.
Sum	Totals arguments `{= Sum(Budget[R1C1:R2C1])}`	Reduction function Returns the sum of values in the range R1C1 to R2C1 of the table Budget.

{filename}

Syntax: {filename}

Results in the file name as shown in the Summary Info box.

Updates when you press F9, when you choose File Print **M**erge, or if in the header or footer, when you choose File **P**rint.

{fillin}

Syntax: {fillin [*"prompt"*] *switch default_text*}

Produces a dialog box, like the one shown in figure 18.5, that displays a generic box used for data entry. Operators can type a response in the dialog box. The result appears at the field location or can be used by other fields in which {fillin} is nested. Enclose the prompt and default text in quotation marks. {fillin} is demonstrated in Chapter 19.

Updates when you press F9 or when you choose File **P**rint Merge. Updates once in header or footer when you choose File **P**rint.

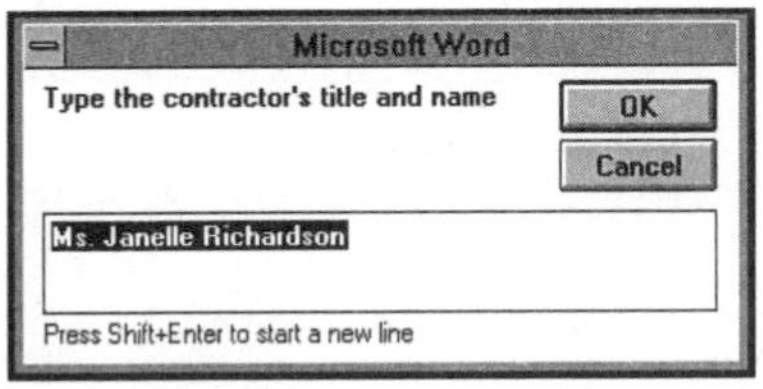

FIG. 18.5.

Use the fillin box to prompt for data entry.

Switch	Result
\d	Default text follows the switch. The default text appears in the text edit of the dialog box and is used if no entry is made. Enclose the default text in quotation marks. Use \d "" if you do not want any text to appear in the dialog box.

{ftnref}

Syntax: {ftnref *bookmark*}

This field inserts a footnote reference. The bookmark must be on the footnote reference number. Update by pressing the F9 key.

{glossary}

Syntax: {glossary *glossary_name*}

Displays the glossary contents for the term *glossary_name*. If the glossary includes the term *eir*, for example, the field

```
{glossary eir}
```

results in *environmental impact report* in the text.

Updates when you select the field and press F9; or if in the header or footer, when you choose **File Print**.

{gotobutton}

Syntax: {gotobutton *destination button_text*}

Produces a button in the document at the field's location. Double-clicking this button (or selecting the field and pressing Alt+Sift+F9) moves the insertion point to the *destination*. Use any destination you would when using F5 (Go To).

Create a button to surround the *button_text* by putting the field into a single-celled table or into a paragraph, and then formatting it to have a border. The *button_text* appears within the button. Do not enclose *button_text* in quotation marks.

{if}

Syntax: {if *expr1 oper expr2 if_true_text if_false_text*}

Use this field when you want Word for Windows to change a field action or result depending on some value or text in the document. The {if} field uses the operator, *oper*, to compare the value of *expr1* to *exper2*.

expr1 and *expr2* can be bookmarks of selected text, bookmarks assigned to store text, or R1C1 cell addresses from a table. *oper* is a mathematical operator separated from the *expr1* and *expr2* arguments by spaces. Allowed operators include the following:

=	equal
>	greater than
>=	greater than or equal to
<	less than
<=	less than or equal to
<>	not equal to

if_true_text is a result that produces text when the *expr1 oper expr2* statement is true. *if_false_text* is the result when the statement is false. If they are text, enclose them in quotation marks. Consider this example:

```
{if daysdue >= 30 "As a reminder, your account is more
than thirty days overdue." "Thank you for your busi-
ness."}
```

If the *daysdue* bookmark contains 12 when the field is updated, the field results in *Thank you for your business*. If the *daysdue* bookmark contains 45 when the field is updated, the field results in *As a reminder your account is more than thirty days overdue*.

Updates when you press F9 or when you choose File Print Merge. If in a header or footer, updates when you choose File Print. See also the {nextif} and {skipif} fields.

{import}

Syntax: {import *filename*}

Displays a bit-map image from an imported graphics file. The file prints using the graphic file to which the field is linked. The field is inserted when you select the Insert Picture command. Refer to Chapters 21 and 23 for more information on linking and updating links to picture files. The appropriate graphic files must be installed.

Updates when you select the field and press F9.

{include}

Syntax: {include *filename [place_reference] [\c converter]*}

Inserts the contents of the *filename* or a portion of the file indicated by *place_reference*. *place_reference* is the bookmark or range name that specifies a portion of the document to be included. Use *\c converter* to specify a converter file if the included file must be translated before being imported. The {include} is inserted with the Insert File command.

Switch	Result
\c	Specifies the converter file to be used for files Word for Windows does not convert automatically. The appropriate converter file must have been installed in Word.

{index}

Syntax: {index *[switches]*}

Accumulates all the text and page numbers from the {xe} (index entry) fields or from outline headings, and builds an index. Insert this field by choosing the Insert Index command. See also {xe}. You use switches to specify the range of the indexes or the separator characters:

Switch	Result
\b	Specifies the amount of text indexed
\e	Specifies the separator character
\g	Specifies the page range separator
\h	Specifies heading letter formats used to separate alphabetical groups
\l	Specifies the page number separator
\p	Specifies the alphabetical range of the index
\r	Puts sublevel indexes on the same level

{info}

Syntax: {[info] *type ["new_value"]*}

Results in information from the Summary Info dialog box according to the *type* you use. Available types include the following:

author	numpages
comments	numwords
createdate	printdate
edittime	revnum
filename	savedate
keywords	subject
lastsavedby	template
numchars	title

Updates when you press F9 or when you choose File Print **M**erge. If in the header or footer, when you choose File **P**rint.

{keywords}

Syntax: {keywords *["new_key_words"]*}

Inserts or replaces the key words from the Summary Info box.

Updates when you press F9, or when you choose **F**ile Print **M**erge. If in the header or footer, when you choose File **P**rint.

{lastsavedby}

Syntax: {lastsavedby}

Inserts the name of the last person to save the document, as shown in the Summary Info box.

Updates when you press F9, or when you choose **F**ile Print **M**erge. If in the header or footer, when you choose **F**ile **P**rint.

{link}

Syntax: {link *class_name file_name [place_reference][format]*}

Links the contents of a file into the Word for Windows document. The link is created using the **E**dit Paste **S**pecial command with the Paste Link button. This field updates when you press F9.

If the linked file cannot be updated, the results remain unchanged. See Chapter 21 to learn about creating links.

Switch	Result
\a	Updates link when source data changes.
\t	Inserts linked data as text.

Switch	Result
\r	Inserts linked data as RTF file (with converted formatting).
\p	Inserts linked data as a picture.
\b	Inserts a Windows bit map.

{macrobutton}

Syntax: {macrobutton *macroname instruction_text*}

Displays the *instruction_text* on-screen. The macro specified by *macroname* runs when you double-click the on-screen *instruction_text* or select it and press Alt+Shift+F9. Create a button to surround the text by putting the field into a single-celled table or into a paragraph and then formatting it to have a border. The *instruction_text* must fit on one line. Do not enclose *instruction_text* in quotation marks.

{mergefield}

Syntax: {mergefield merge_name}

Inserts data for the corresponding field name from the data file during a print merge. Created by attaching the data file and then choosing the Insert Merge **F**ield button from the print merge bar. See Chapter 19.

{mergerec}

Syntax: {mergerec}

Inserts the number of the current print merge record.

{next}

Syntax: {next}

No result appears, but the field instructs Word for Windows to use the next record in the data file. For example, {next} is used in mailing label templates to increment the mailing list from one record (label) to the next. {next} is inserted in labels created from the MAILLABL template.

The {next} field is demonstrated in Chapter 19.

Updates when you choose **F**ile Print **M**erge.

{nextif}

Syntax: {nextif *expr1 oper expr2*}

No result appears. {nextif} acts like a combination of the {if} and {next} fields. You can use {nextif} to specify a condition that data file records must satisfy before they are used for mail merge or form letters. See Chapter 19 for conditional mail merging information.

Updates during File Print Merge.

{numchars}

Syntax: {numchars}

Inserts the number of characters in the document as shown in the Summary Info box.

Updates when you press F9, or when you choose File Print Merge. If in a header or footer, updates when you choose File Print.

{numpages}

Syntax: {numpages}

Inserts the number of pages contained in the document when it was last printed or updated. The number comes from the Summary Info box. See also {page}.

Updates when you press F9, or when you choose File Print Merge. If in a header or footer, updates when you choose File Print.

{numwords}

Syntax: {numwords}

Inserts the number of words in the document as shown in the Summary Info box.

Updates when you press F9, or when you choose File Print Merge. If in a header or footer, updates when you choose File Print.

{page}

Syntax: {page *[page_format_picture]*}

Inserts the page number for the page where the field code is located. Use numeric picture or format switches to format the number (see "Using General Switches" later in this chapter).

Updates when you press F9, or when you choose **File Print**.

{pageref}

Syntax: {pageref *bookmark*}

Results in the page number on which *bookmark* is located. This field produces a cross-reference page number that updates itself.

Updates when you select it and press F9, or when you choose **File Print**.

{print}

Syntax: {print *"printer_instructions"*}

Sends the *printer_instructions* text string directly to the printer without translation. This field is used to send printer control codes to a printer or to send PostScript programs to a PostScript printer.

{printdate}

Syntax: {printdate *switch*}

Inserts the date on which the document was last printed, as shown in the Summary Info box. The default date format comes from the Control Panel. For other date formats, use a date-time picture, as described in the section "Formatting Date-Time Results" later in this chapter.

{quote}

Syntax: {quote *"literal_text"*}

Inserts the *literal_text* in the document. Update by selecting the field code and pressing F9 or by printing with print merge.

{rd}

Syntax: {rd *filename*}

No result appears. {rd} helps you create a table of contents or index for large documents that cross multiple files. See Chapter 20 for more information.

{ref}

Syntax: {[ref] *bookmark*}

Results in the contents of the *bookmark*, which specifies a selection of text. The formatting of the bookmark displays as in the original. You can use a bookmark within field characters, such as {datedue}, and produce the same result as {ref datedue}. You must use the {ref bookmark} form, however, to avoid using bookmark names that conflict with field types. If a bookmark's name conflicts with that of a field type—{ask}, for example—use {ref ask} whenever you want to refer to the bookmark.

Updates when you press F9, or when you choose **File Print Merge**. If in the header or footer, updates when you choose **File Print**.

{revnum}

Syntax: {revnum}

Inserts the number of times the document has been revised, as shown in the Summary Info box. This number changes when the document is saved.

Updates when you select the field and press F9, or when you choose **File Print Merge**. If in the header or footer, updates when you choose **File Print**.

{savedate}

Syntax: {savedate}

Inserts the date the document was last saved, as shown in the Summary Info box. To change formats, use a date-time-picture, as described in "Formatting Date-Time Results" later in this chapter.

Updates when you select the field and press F9, or when you choose **File Print Merge**. If in the header or footer, updates when you choose **File Print**.

{seq}

Syntax: {seq *seq_id [bookmark]*}

Inserts a number to create a numbered sequence of items. Use this field for numbering figures, illustrations, tables, and so on. *seq_id* specifies the name of the sequence, such as *Figure. bookmark* specifies a cross-reference to the sequence number of a bookmarked item. If you insert the following field wherever you need a figure number,

{ref chap}.{seq figure_num}

the field will produce an automatically numbered sequence of chapter number, period, and figure number—5.12. The bookmark *chap* must be defined at the beginning of the document and contain the number of the chapter. The *figure_num* is used to track only a specific sequence of items.

Updates the entire sequence when you select the entire document and press F9. Unlink (fix as values) the figure numbers by selecting them and pressing Shift+Ctrl+F9.

Switch	Result
\n	Inserts the next sequence number. If no switch is used, Word for Windows defaults to \n.
\c	Inserts the sequence number of the nearest preceding item in a numbered sequence.
\r	Resets the sequence number as specified. For example, the following field restarts the sequence numbering to 1 when it reaches 10:

{seq figurenum \r 10}

{set}

Syntax: {set *bookmark "data"*}

No result appears. Use this field to store text (data) in a bookmark. You then can use the bookmark in multiple locations to repeat that text. See {ref}

{set} is not allowed in annotations, footnotes, headers, or footers.

Updates when you select the field and press F9, or when you choose **F**ile Print **M**erge.

{skipif}

Syntax: {skipif *expr1 oper expr2*}

No result displays. This command is used in print merge to skip merges to meet specified conditions.

Updates when you choose **F**ile Print **M**erge.

{styleref}

Syntax: {styleref *"style_id" [switch]*}

Displays the text of the nearest paragraph containing the specified style, *style_id*. This field is useful for accumulating headings and topics that contain a specific style; for example, to create dictionary-like heading.

{subject}

Syntax: {subject *["new_subject"]*}

Inserts or replaces the subject found in the Summary Info box.

Updates when you select the field and press F9, or when you choose **File Print Merge.**

{symbol}

Syntax: {symbol *character*}

Inserts a symbol character. Inserted with the **Insert Symbol** command.

Switch	Result
\f	Font set used, {symbol \f "courier new bold" 169}.
\s	Font size used, {symbol \f Helv \s 12 169}.

{tc}

Syntax: {tc *"text" [switch] [table_id]*}

No result shows. {tc} marks the page and associates a text entry for later use when building a table of contents. See Chapter 16 for additional information. See also the discussion of the {toc} field in this chapter.

text is the text that should appear in the table of contents.

table_id is a single letter used to identify a distinct table. This letter should follow the \f switch, with one space between the switch and the *table_id* letter.

Switch	Result
\f	Defines this {tc} as belonging to the table indicated by the *table_id*. This switch enables you to accumulate tables of contents for different topics.
\l	Specifies the level number for the table entry. The default is 1.

{template}

Syntax: {template}

Inserts the name of the document's template as shown in the Summary Info dialog box.

Updates when you select the field and press F9, or when you choose **File Print Merge**. If in the header or footer, updates when you choose **File Print**.

{time}

Syntax: {time *[time_format_picture]*}

Results in the time or date when the field was updated. Reformat by using a *time_format_picture*, as described in the later section "Formatting Date-Time Results."

Updates when you select the field and press F9 or when you choose **File Print**.

{title}

Syntax: {title *["new_title"]*}

Inserts or replaces the document title as shown in the Summary Info box.

Updates when you select the field and press F9, or when you choose **File Print Merge**. If in the header or footer, updates when you choose **File Print**.

{toc}

Syntax: {toc *[switch] [bookmark] [tableid]*}

Shows a table of contents built by accumulating the text and page numbers of {tc} fields throughout the document. Constructing a table of contents based on {tc} fields is described in Chapters 16 and 20.

Switch	Result
\b	Builds a table of contents for the area of the document defined by the bookmark, as in {toc \b firstpart}
\f	Builds a table of contents from {tc} fields with specific *tableid*s. The following field builds a table of contents from only those fields with the *tableid* graphs: {toc \f graphs}
\o	Builds a table of contents from the outline headings. The following field builds a table of contents from the outline using heading levels 1, 2, and 3: {toc \o 1-3}
\s	Specifies that the following word names a sequence. See Chapter 20 for more information.
\d	Specifies the character to be used as a page number separator.

{xe}

Syntax: {xe *"index_text" [switch]*}

No result appears. Specifies the text and associated page number used to generate an index. You generate the index by choosing the Insert Index command. See Chapter 16 for examples.

Switch	Result
\r	Specifies a range of pages to be indexed.
\t	Specifies the use of text in place of page numbers.
\b	Toggles the page numbers for boldface.
\i	Toggles the page numbers for italic.

Formatting Field Results with Switches

Switches enable you to format the results of a field. To use a switch, include it in the field code after the field type. If you enter a field by choosing the **Insert Field** command, you frequently can select a switch from the **Instructions** list box in the **Insert Field** dialog box.

You can format field results in three ways:

■ * *mergeformat*. Format the field results with multiple formats by inserting this switch in the field, and then choosing Format **Char**acter or Forma**t** **P**aragraph commands.

■ * *charformat*. Format the field results with a single character format by inserting this switch in the field and then formatting the first character of the field type.

■ *General switches*. These switches enable you to format such things as date, time, and numeric formats. Enter a general switch within the field code, after the field type.

The * merge format and * charformat switches are described in the sections that immediately follow.

The general switches are listed in table 18.2. The sections that follow describe the switch types, numeric pictures, and date-time pictures used in the switches and explain how to use them in your fields.

Table 18.2. General Switches for Formatting Fields

Switch	Syntax	Effect
*	{field-type * switchtype}	Formats text result with case conversion, number conversion, or character formatting.
\#	{field-type \# numericpicture}	Formats numeric result to match a "picture" showing the pattern of numeric format.
\@	{field-type \@ date-timepicture}	Formats date or time result to match a "picture" showing the pattern of date-time format.
\!	{field-type \!}	Locks a field's results.

The following fields' results cannot be formatted with general switches:

{autonum}	{rd}
{import}	{eq}
{autonumlgl}	{tc}
{macrobutton}	{gotobutton}
{autonumout}	{xe}

> Always use a single space to separate the field instructions, like formatting switches, from the field type, such as *fillin*.
>
> **T I P**

Formatting Numbers, Dates, and Text Case

In the following sections, the {fillin} field is used to illustrate how each * switch works. The {fillin} field displays a dialog box in which you can type sample text or numbers. This enables you to type an entry and see the switch affect what you type.

To duplicate the examples, press Ctrl+F9, type *fillin*, type a space, then type the switch type and switch. To update the field and see the results, select the field and press F9. Remember that you can quickly switch between viewing the field codes and their results by pressing Shift+F9.

Preserving Manual Formats

The * charformat and * mergeformat switches are two of the most valuable switches. They enable you to retain formats you have applied to a field result. Without the use of these switches, your manual formatting of a field's result is removed when the field updates.

Switch Type	Effect
* charformat	Formats the field result the same as the format of the first character of the field type, the character after {. This format takes precedence over other formatting. For example, formatting the *f* in the {fillin} field as boldface produces a boldface field result.

Switch Type	Effect
* mergeformat	Preserves your manual formatting of a field's result.Character and paragraph formatting you apply to a field result are preserved after the field updates. The updated field results are reformatted on a word-by-word basis using the original formatting as a template. If the updated results have more words than the originally formatted result, the extra words use the format of the first character after the opening field character, {. If the previous field result was not formatted, mergeformat acts like charformat.

In the following example,

```
{fillin "Type a sample result" \* charformat}
```

format the first letter in fillin with the character format you want to apply to the entire result. Formatting remains even after updating the field.

In this example,

```
{fillin "Type a sample result" \* mergeformat}
```

format the results of the field with character or paragraph formatting. After the field updates, the * mergeformat field reapplies the formats you applied previously. Your formats are reapplied according to word-by-word locations. If the updated field contains words in a different order, the formatting may not coincide with the updated position of words.

T I P

When you first format a field that uses the * mergeformat switch, make sure that the field result has the maximum number of words you expect as a result for this field. Because mergeformat reapplies formatting on a word-by-word basis, this ensures that all subsequent field results with fewer words will be formatted as you expect.

Converting Upper- and Lowercase Text

The following switches change the capitalization of the field's results.

Switch	Result
* upper	Converts characters in the field results to all uppercase.
* lower	Converts characters in the field results to all lowercase.

Switch	Result
* firstcap	Converts the first letter of the first word in the field result to a capital, converts other letters to lowercase.
* caps	Converts the first letter of each word in the field result to a capital, converts other letters to lowercase.

Example: {fillin "Type a sample result" * upper}

Formatting Numeric Types

The following switches change how a numeric result displays:

Switch	Result
* Arabic	Uses Arabic cardinal numbers such as 1, 2, 3, and so on. If the field-type is {page}, the switch overrides the page-number formatting set by the Edit Header/Footer dialog box.
* ordinal	Converts a numeric field result to an ordinal Arabic number. When used with the {page} field, it produces page numbers such as 18th.
* roman	Converts a numeric field result to Roman numerals, such as XV for 18. Type the switch as * *Roman* for uppercase Roman numerals, or * *roman* for lowercase Roman numerals.
*alphabetic	Converts a numeric field result into its alphabetical equivalent. For example, the number 5 results in the letter e. Type the switch as * *Alphabetic* for uppercase letters, or * *alphabetic* for lowercase letters.

Example: {fillin "Type a number" * ordinal}

Formatting Numbers as Text

The following switches convert numeric results into a text equivalent. This process is useful for calculated numeric results that appear in documents—a check or invoice amount. Use the capitalization switches described earlier to change the capitalization of a number as text.

Switch	Result
* cardtext	Converts a numeric field result into text with the first letter in uppercase. For example, the number 35 results in Thirty Five.

Switch	Result
* ordtext	Converts a numeric field result to ordinal text. For example, the number 35 results in `Thirty Fifth`.
* hex	Converts a numeric field result into a hexadecimal number.
* dollartext	Converts a numeric field result into a text amount and fractional dollar. For example, 53.67 becomes `Fifty three and 67/100`.

Example: `{fillin "Type a number" \* cardtext \* upper}`

Formatting with Custom Numeric Formats

You can format numeric field results so that they appear in the numeric format you want. You can, for example, define your own custom formats that round results to the desired precision, display only significant numbers, include text, or have different formats for positive, negative, and zero results.

To format numeric results, you create a numeric picture. The switch for a numeric picture is \#. A numeric picture is a pattern that follows the switch and is composed of symbols that define placeholders, commas, and signs.

To format numeric fields with character formatting, such as boldface and italic, format the numeric picture. For example, formatting the negative portion of a numeric picture in italic produces italic formatting of negative results.

The examples use a fillin data-entry box that enables you to type into a data-entry box any number or text. To duplicate one of the examples, press Ctrl+F9 and then type *fillin* followed by a space. Type the \# switch and the numeric picture after the {fillin} field type. The result should look similar to the following:

```
{fillin \# $#,##0.00}
```

To update the field so that a dialog box asks for your entry, select the field and press F9. To toggle the display between showing field results and field codes, press Shift+F9.

You can use the following characters to generate numeric pictures:

```
0 # x . , - +
```

T I P

Use the general format (*) switches described in this chapter to change a number such as 35 into Thirty Five or Thirty Fifth. You can even change numbers such as 35.60 into Thirty Five and 60/100.

You also can specify formatting variations for positive, negative, and zero results and can include text, sequence names, and other symbols and characters in a numeric picture. The following sections describe how to use these characters in numeric pictures.

T I P

If you are familiar with how to create custom numeric and date formats in Microsoft Excel, you know how to create custom formats in Word for Windows.

Positive, Negative, and Zero Formatting Variations

You can specify three different numeric pictures that Word for Windows can use, depending on the sign of the field's result. The three numeric pictures must be separated by semicolons (;). If the field result is positive, Word for Windows uses the numeric picture to the left of the first semicolon. If the result is negative, Word for Windows uses the numeric picture between the two semicolons. And if the result is 0, Word for Windows uses the numeric picture to the right of the second semicolon. The numeric picture does not have to be in quotation marks if it contains only numeric formatting. If the numeric picture contains text or space characters, the entire numeric picture must be enclosed in quotation marks. For example, the numeric pictures in this field

```
{fillin \# #,##0.00;(#,##0.00);0}
```

produce 4,350.78 when the field result is 4350.776; 4,350.78 when the result is -4350.776; and 0 when the result is 0.

T I P

The right parenthesis,), accompanying a negative number can cause positive and negative numbers to misalign. If this problem occurs, align the numbers by using a decimal tab or insert a space in the positive format to the right of the last zero.

The 0 Placeholder

Put a 0 in a numeric picture wherever you want a 0 to display when a number is missing. The field {fillin \# 0.00}, for example, produces the following results:

Number	Result
.646	0.65
250.4	250.40

Most currency formats use two 0s to the right of the decimal.

The # Placeholder

The # character is a digit placeholder used when you do not want leading or trailing 0s in results. The field {fillin \# #.00}, for example, produces the following results:

Number	Result
0.6	.60
250.4	250.40

The x Placeholder

The x character is a digit placeholder that truncates, or cuts off, numbers that extend beyond the x position. For example,

```
{fillin \# #.#x}
```

produces .24 when the numeric result is .236.

The Decimal Point

Use the decimal point along with other numeric picture characters to specify the decimal location in a string of digits. Change the character used as the decimal separator by selecting a country from the International program in the Windows Control Panel.

The Thousands Separator

Use the thousands separator (usually a comma) along with the # or 0 numeric picture characters to specify the location of the thousands separator in a result. Change the character used as the thousands separator by selecting a country from the International program in the Windows Control Panel.

The Minus Sign (–)

Used in a numeric picture, this character displays a minus sign (–) if the result is negative and a blank space if the number is positive or 0.

The Plus Sign (+)

Used in a numeric picture, this character displays a plus sign (+) if the result is positive, a minus sign (–) if the result is negative, and a space if the result is 0.

Text

Use text formatting within a numeric picture to include measurements or messages along with the numeric result. Enclose text and the numeric picture in quotation marks (" "). The text displays in the field result in the same location as it appears in the numeric picture. For example, the numeric picture

```
{fillin \# "Amount owed is $#,##0.00"}
```

produces "Amount owed is $4,500.89" when the field result is 4500.89.

If the text string contains a character that Word for Windows might interpret as an operator or as field information, enclose that character in apostrophes (' '). In the following example, the dashes on either side of the zero, - 0 -, normally do not display for the 0 result. But by enclosing the entire numeric picture in double-quotation marks and the numeric picture for - 0 - in apostrophes, you can tell Word for Windows to display - 0 - for zero results:

```
{fillin \# "0.0;(0.0);'- 0 -'"}
```

If you use text in a numeric picture that includes positive, negative, and zero format variations, enclose the entire pattern in quotation marks, as in

```
{fillin \# "0.0;(0.0);Enter a non-zero number"}
```

If the text itself contains quotation marks, precede the text's quotation marks with a backslash (\), as follows:

```
{fillin "Who wrote \"Brahm's Lullaby\"?"}
```

Other Characters

You can use symbols and characters in the numeric picture, and they appear in the result. This feature is useful when you need to format a numeric result to include dollar signs, percent symbols, and international currency. A simple example is the use of the dollar sign, as in

```
{fillin \# $#,##0;($#,##0)}
```

or the percent sign, as in

```
{fillin \# #0%}
```

To enter ANSI characters such as the cent, pound, Yen, and section symbols, turn on the numeric keypad (press Num Lock until the Num Lock light is on) and hold down the Alt key as you type the appropriate four-number ANSI code. The character appears when you release the Alt key. Do not leave a space between the character entered and the numeric picture.

Formatting Date-Time Results

You can format date and time field results so that they appear in standard or custom formats. To format date-time results, you create a date-time picture. The switch for a date-time picture is \@. A date-time picture is a pattern composed of characters that define date and time formats such as month, day, and hour. Word for Windows uses the pattern as a sample format. For example, the field and pattern

```
{date \@ "MMMM d, yyyy"}
```

displays the computer's current date in the format December 24, 1992.

To format date-time pictures with character formatting such as boldface and italic, format the first letter of each portion of the date-time picture. In the preceding example, you can format the first capital M in boldface and italic to make the entire month boldface and italic but leave the day and year as they were.

You can use the following characters to generate date-time pictures:

M d D y Y h H m am pm AM PM

You also can include text, sequence names, and other characters and symbols in a date-time picture. The following paragraphs describe how to use these characters in date-time pictures.

The Month Placeholder

Uppercase M is the month placeholder (lowercase *m* designates minutes). The four formats are as follows:

M	1 through 12
MM	01 through 12
MMM	Jan through Dec
MMMM	January through December

The Day Placeholder

Upper- or lowercase *d* is the day placeholder. The four formats are as follows:

d or D	1 through 31
dd or DD	01 through 31
ddd or DDD	Mon through Sun
dddd or DDDD	Monday through Sunday

The Year Placeholder

Upper- or lowercase *y* is the year placeholder. The two formats are as follows:

yy or YY	00 through 99
yyyy or YYYY	1900-2040

The Hour Placeholder

Upper- or lowercase *h* is the hour placeholder. Lowercase designates the U.S. 12-hour clock. Uppercase designates the international 24-hour clock. The four formats are as follows:

h	1 through 12
hh	01 through 12
H	1 through 24
HH	01 through 24

The Minute Placeholder

Lowercase *m* is the minute placeholder (uppercase M designates months.) The two formats are as follows:

m	0 through 59
mm	00 through 59

Morning and Afternoon Indicators

Upper- or lowercase AM and PM are used with *h* or *hh* 12-hour clock formats to designate morning or afternoon. You can select characters other than AM/am and PM/pm by using the Control Panel to change settings in the International icon. The four formats are as follows:

\@ h AM/PM	8AM and 6PM
\@ h am/pm	8am and 6pm
\@ h A/P	8A and 6P
\@ h a/p	8a and 6p

Text Characters

Use text formatting in date-time pictures to include measurements or messages with the results. Enclose text and the date-time picture in quotation marks (" "). If the text includes characters that Word for Windows could interpret as field information characters, such as a minus (–) or zero (0), enclose those characters in apostrophes (' '). The text displays in the field result in the same location it appears in the date-time picture. For example, the field and date-time picture

```
{date \@ "Job complete at HH:mm"}
```

displays a result such as Job complete at 12:45.

Other Characters

You can use the colon (:), hyphen (-), and comma (,) in the date-time picture. These characters display in the result in the same position in which they are used in the date-time picture. For example, the date-time picture \@ "HH:mm" displays 23:15, and the date-time picture \@ "MMM d, yy" displays Jun 15, 92.

From Here . . .

This chapter described the field codes Word for Windows places in documents when you use some of Word for Windows' advanced features. Understanding field codes and editing them to fit your purpose gives you more control over Word for Windows' power.

For information about how field codes work when inserted from the menu, you may want to review Chapter 15 to learn more about using dates, times, and page numbering. Review Chapter 16 to learn about field codes used for bullets, numbered lists, indexes and tables of contents, or tables of items. Chapter 17 describes the use of field codes to do math.

Chapter 19 shows how mail merge and form letters use field codes. When you want to link multiple documents but produce a single table of contents and index, you should check the field code examples in Chapter 20. One of the truly powerful features of Windows becomes apparent when you read Chapter 21 and learn how field codes are the underlying fabric for linked data or embedded objects.

Mastering Mail Merge, Form Letters, and Envelopes

Successful businesses stay in touch with their clients and customers. Staying in touch with a lot of people is difficult, however, unless you learn how to create personalized form letters and envelopes with Word for Windows.

To make single letters easier to produce, Word for Windows has automated the process of printing an envelope. The envelope printing feature uses the address from a document to print an envelope, with or without a return address. The envelope can be printed separately or attached to the document with which it is associated. This feature is covered in the first section of this chapter.

Form letters broadcast information, yet add a personal touch to your work. You may produce only a few form letters each day, but they still can automate repetitive parts of your business and give you time to improve the creative end of your work. You also can generate invoices, appointment reminders, and so on. This chapter is challenging, but working through it will pay great dividends.

You can create two types of form letters: those that are filled in manually and those that are filled in from computer-generated lists. In this chapter, you learn to create an automated form letter that prompts you for information the document needs to create an invoice. You also learn how to fill in the "blanks" in a form letter by merging a mailing list with the main document. Finally, you learn Word for Windows' advanced techniques for document automation—including a form letter that combines manual fill in with merging of information.

 This entire chapter covers features new with Version 2 of Word for Windows.

Printing an Envelope

Word for Windows offers an easy and quick solution to a frequent word processing problem: printing envelopes. Word for Windows can print envelopes by themselves, attached to a document, or as part of a mass mailing.

To test the envelope feature, create a short letter like the one shown in figure 19.1.

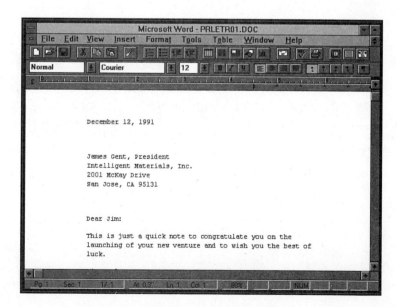

FIG. 19.1.

A form letter.

To create an envelope, load your manual sheet feeder or envelope feeder with envelope(s) and follow these steps:

1. Select the address in the letter. If the address is a contiguous block of three to five short lines near the beginning of the letter, you do not have to select it. Word for Windows automatically finds the address.

2. Choose the **To**ols Create **E**nvelope command or click the Envelope button on the toolbar (it resembles an envelope) to display the Create Envelope dialog box (see fig. 19.2).

Create Envelope

Addressed **T**o:

James Gent, President
Intelligent Materials, Inc.
2001 McKay Drive
San Jose, CA 95131

Print Envelope
Add to Document
Cancel

Return Address:

Dave O.Connor
Marlin & O'Connor
13200 Telegraph Road
Southfield, MI 48076

Envelope **S**ize:
Size 10 (4 1/8 x 9 ½ in)

☐ **O**mit Return Address

When prompted by the printer, place an envelope in your printer's manual feeder.

FIG. 19.2.

The Create Envelope dialog box.

3. If necessary, edit the Addressed **T**o information. To insert linefeeds (line breaks without a carriage return), press Shift+Enter.

4. If necessary, edit the **R**eturn Address information. If you do not want to print the return address (you may be working with pre-printed envelopes, for example), select the **O**mit Return Address check box.

5. If necessary, select an envelope size from the Envelope **S**ize list.

6. Choose the **P**rint Envelope button to immediately print an envelope.

   or

   Choose the **A**dd to Document button to add the envelope as a landscape-oriented section before the first page of your document.

You can change the default **R**eturn Address information. Choose the **T**ools **O**ptions command, then select the User Info **C**ategory. In the **M**ailing Address text box, add or edit a return address. This will be the default return address until you change it.

T I P

3. Type a customer address in the box. Press Shift+Enter to start a new line in the box (see fig. 19.8). Choose OK or press Enter to complete the box and insert your entry in the document.

The dialog box in figure 19.7 after entering the customer's name.

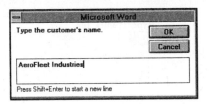

The entry you typed appears in the document in the same location as the field code. Text following the inserted entry is pushed down or right, just as if you had manually typed text in the location. Remember to choose View Field Codes to switch between displaying fields and their results.

T I P To update {fillin} fields throughout an entire document, select the entire document, then press F9 (Update).

Displaying Field Results

If you use field codes in form letters, you can request an input from the operator one time, but have that information appear in multiple locations. To reuse an entry from one fillin box in other locations in a form letter, you must use three field codes:

- {set bookmark data} assigns data to a bookmark, which stores information so that it can be reused later. In the next example, the data argument for {set} is a {fillin} field so that the operator's entry is stored in the bookmark name Custname. If the data is explicit text that does not change, such as *Montana*, you must enclose it in quotation marks. Do not include a space in the bookmark name.

- {fillin [prompt]} displays an input box in which the operator can enter data. The [] indicate that the prompt is optional.

- {ref bookmark} displays the contents of a bookmark at the field location. You enter this field to repeat a bookmark's contents in other locations within the document.

Figure 19.9 shows a field code that requests the customer's name and stores it in the Custname bookmark. The {fillin} field requests the name. The {set} field sets Custname equal to the {fillin} entry. The {ref} field displays the entry stored in Custname. You can use {ref} throughout the letter following the {set} field, even though the data was entered only once.

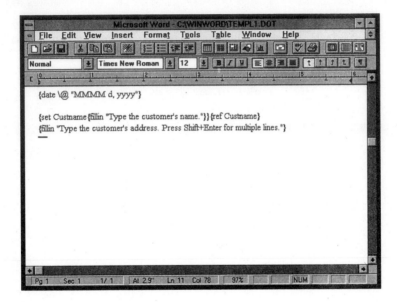

FIG. 19.9.

These field codes store a name in Custname so that it can be reused throughout the letter.

To enter the field for the customer's name, refer to figure 19.9. To build this *nested field* from the inside out, follow these steps:

1. Position the insertion point before where you need to use the entry.

   The {set} field occupies no space in the document, so you probably should put all the {set} fields at the beginning of a template.

2. Press Ctrl+F9, the Insert Field key.

3. Between the field characters, type *fillin*, a space, then a quoted prompt to the operator, such as *"Type the customer's name."*

4. Select the field you just typed. To select field characters and field contents, select a field character at either end.

5. Press Ctrl+F9 to enclose the selection in field characters.

This step nests your first field entirely inside another set of field characters. The insertion point moves directly after the first field character.

6. Directly after the first field character, type *set*, a space, then the appropriate bookmark, such as *Custname*.

   Leave a space after the bookmark, but do not leave spaces in the name.

This new nested field requests a name and stores it in the bookmark, but the entry does not appear on-screen. To see the field's result, follow these steps:

1. Move the insertion point to any location after the last field character of the nested field.

2. Press Ctrl+F9, the Insert Field key.

3. In the field characters, type *ref*, a space, then the appropriate bookmark, such as *Custname*.

To update both of these new fields and see the customer's name requested and displayed, follow these steps:

1. Select the entire line or lines containing both fields.

2. Press F9 (Update Fields).

   A dialog box appears and requests the customer's name (refer to fig. 19.7).

3. Type the entry as requested.

4. Choose OK or press Enter.

The {set} field stores in the bookmark the name you entered in the {fillin} field. The {ref bookmark} field displays the contents of a bookmark in the letter. You can enter a {ref bookmark} field in multiple locations in the document wherever you need the name repeated (see fig. 19.10). The new contents of {ref bookmark} do not appear, however, until each {ref bookmark} field is updated.

After you enter all of the field codes, choose **File Save As** and choose OK or press Enter to save the template.

These fields display data entered in the address block; they also request and display the type, model, and cost of the items the customer ordered. The switch * charformat used in the {ref bookmark * charformat} field formats the result of the updated field to match the format you apply to the letter *r* in *ref*. Chapter 18 provides more information on switches that format and control field results.

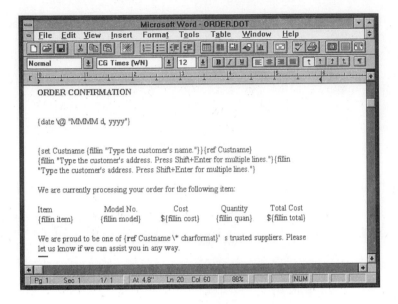

FIG. 19.10.

Inserted field codes that request data, display and repeat data, and format the results.

Saving and Naming the Template

This document must be saved as a template because you opened it as one. To save your template, choose the **F**ile Save **A**s command. Type an eight-letter name to describe your form in the File **N**ame text box. Notice that you cannot change many of the text or list boxes. Choose OK or press Enter. Word for Windows saves the template and adds the extension DOT. When you save a new template, give it a name that reflects the type of document it creates.

Updating Fields in a Form

To test the fields you entered, follow these steps:

1. Choose **F**ile **N**ew and select a template containing {fillin} fields. Choose OK or press Enter.

2. Move the insertion point to the top of the document, then press F11 to select the next field. (Press Shift+F11 to select the preceding field, or select the entire document to update all fields.)

3. Press F9 to update the selected field or, if the entire document is selected, each field in turn from the beginning to the end of the document.

4. Type the data requested and choose OK. (To preserve the previous entry, select Cancel; nothing is produced if no previous entry existed.)

If an error appears at a field's location, use the View Field **C**odes command to display the field codes. Check for correct spelling and spacing. Use one space between field types, instructions, and switches.

Creating a Macro To Update Fields Automatically

Because this type of fillin form is designed for repetitive use, you can have Word automatically prompt the user for the information as soon as the document is opened. You can do this with an automatic macro that updates all fields in the document when the document opens. With the fillin template as the active document, follow these steps:

1. Choose the **T**ools **R**ecord Macro command.

2. Type *AutoNew* in the Record Macro **N**ame box.

3. Enter a shortcut key if desired.

4. Enter a description, such as *Automatically updates all fields*, in the **D**escription box.

5. Choose OK or press Enter.

   The Macro dialog box appears.

6. Select the Store Macro in **T**emplate option so that the macro is available only to this template or to documents that originate from this template. (The option of where a macro is saved is described in Chapter 31.)

7. Choose OK or press Enter.

The indicator REC appears at the lower right corner of the screen, indicating that the recorder is on. Follow these steps to record a process that updates all fields in the document:

1. Press Ctrl+5 (numeric keypad) to select the entire document.

2. Press F9. A prompt generated by the first {fillin} field appears.

3. Choose the Cancel button for each {fillin} prompt.

4. Press Ctrl+Home to return the insertion point to the top of the document.

5. Choose the **T**ools Stop **R**ecorder command.

Choose File Save **A**ll to save the macro and close the template. To test the macro, follow these steps:

1. Choose the **File New** command.

2. Select the template from the Use Template list.

3. Choose OK or press Enter.

When you open the document, the AutoNew macro runs the update macro. Enter a response to each dialog box or choose Cancel. If the macro does not run correctly, record it again. If you rerecord using the same name (AutoNew), Word for Windows asks whether you want to replace the previous recording. Choose **Y**es.

Merging Mailing Lists and Documents

One of the most powerful and time-saving features available in any word processor is mail merge. Mail merge enables you to create multiple letters or envelopes by merging together a list of names and addresses with letters, envelopes, or address labels. Mail merge also can be used for tasks such as filling in administrative forms, creating invoices from accounting files, and so on. Anytime you keep a list or get a list from other programs and you need to put information into a Word for Windows document, you should be thinking about mail merge.

The time you save using mail merge can be tremendous. Instead of hand typing or modifying tens or hundreds of documents, Word can make all the documents for you. All you need to do is keep your list (names, addresses, and so on) up to date, and create a form letter in which the data will be inserted. In fact, you can even make each document pause during mail merge so that you can enter personalized information.

Understanding Form Letters and Data Files

You need two documents to create form letters or mailing labels. One document, called the *data file*, contains a precisely laid out set of data, such as names and addresses. The other document, the *main document*, acts as a form that receives the data. Most forms that receive data are form letters or multicolumn tables for mailing labels.

The first row of the data file must be one row of names. Below the row of names are rows of data. Each row of data is a *record*, and each piece of data in the row, such as a last name, is a *field*. The row of names in the first row of the documents is the *header record*. Each name in the first row is a *field name*. Each field can be referenced by the name for that field in the heading.

Only one row of field names can be at the top of the data file. Field names cannot contain blanks because Word for Windows uses the names as bookmarks. Do not start a field name with a number. (Although a number can be in the field name.) If you need to use a two-part field name, use an underscore rather than a space. Each field name must be unique.

The data in the data file merges with a main document. The main document is like a normal document except that it contains merge field codes that refer to the data file. You insert merge fields in the appropriate places in the form. After you create the data and main documents, you can merge data in the data file into the main document.

Understanding the Mail Merge Process

The process of creating a mailing list and mail-merge documents usually begins by creating a data file. After you create a data file, you insert in the main document MERGEFIELD field codes that specify where merged data will appear. In a normal form letter, for example, the data file is a mailing list of names and addresses and the main document is a form letter that needs names and addresses inserted.

Word for Windows helps you create and merge the data file and main document. To begin with, make your main document active, even if it is blank. You then choose the File Print Merge command. The dialog box shown later in figure 19.1 will display showing you a diagram of the different documents involved in a mail merge. Using the procedures in the following sections, you will attach a data file to the active document. When a main document has a data file attached, a mail-merge bar appears at the top of the document.

At that point you can begin or continue creating your main document. Your main document will consist of normal body copy and field codes for things such as the time or date. Because the main document is now attached to a data file, you can use the Insert Merge **F**ield button to insert MERGEFIELD codes wherever you want merged data. You can insert a MERGEFIELD code, <<Lastname>>, for example, where you want data from the LastName field to appear.

After your main document is complete, you can merge the data file into the main document. The result can appear as a new document on-screen, or you can print the results directly to the current printer. To merge you will choose either the **F**ile Print Merge command or click on one of the two mail-merge icons in the mail-merge bar.

Creating a Data File

You can create a data file in two ways. If you plan to keep the data in a Word for Windows document, you can create the data file in a Word for Windows document. Figure 19.11 shows a figure of a data file built in a Word for Windows document. If you create this document based on the DATAFILE.DOT template, you will have a built-in set of macros to help you manage your data file. If you are using another program such as Microsoft Excel or dBASE to manage and store your data, you can leave the data file in the native format (Microsoft Excel, dBASE, or others) and let Word for Windows convert the file as it merges.

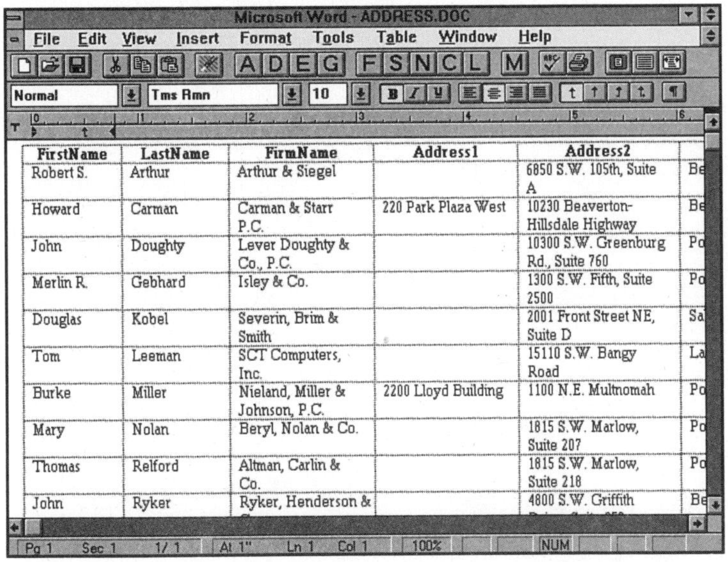

FirstName	LastName	FirmName	Address1	Address2	
Robert S.	Arthur	Arthur & Siegel		6850 S.W. 105th, Suite A	Be
Howard	Carman	Carman & Starr P.C.	220 Park Plaza West	10230 Beaverton-Hillsdale Highway	Be
John	Doughty	Lever Doughty & Co., P.C.		10300 S.W. Greenburg Rd., Suite 760	Po
Merlin R.	Gebhard	Isley & Co.		1300 S.W. Fifth, Suite 2500	Po
Douglas	Kobel	Severin, Brim & Smith		2001 Front Street NE, Suite D	Sa
Tom	Leeman	SCT Computers, Inc.		15110 S.W. Bangy Road	La
Burke	Miller	Nieland, Miller & Johnson, P.C.	2200 Lloyd Building	1100 N.E. Multnomah	Po
Mary	Nolan	Beryl, Nolan & Co.		1815 S.W. Marlow, Suite 207	Po
Thomas	Relford	Altman, Carlin & Co.		1815 S.W. Marlow, Suite 218	Po
John	Ryker	Ryker, Henderson &		4800 S.W. Griffith	Be

FIG. 19.11.

A data file containing a mailing list.

Creating a Data File Using Print Merge Commands

Word for Windows data files can be stored in documents. The data fields can be separated in columns within a table with 31 or fewer fields, or the data fields can be separated by commas. To create a data file, follow these steps:

1. Open a new document or a document that will be used as the main document.

2. Choose the File Print **M**erge command. The Print Merge Setup dialog box appears (see fig. 19.12).

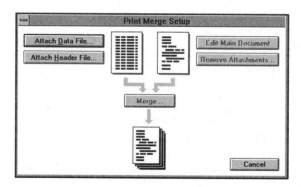

FIG. 19.12.

The Print Merge Setup dialog box.

3. Choose the Attach **D**ata File button. The dialog box in figure 19.13 appears.

4. Choose the **C**reate Data File button to be prompted through the creation of a data file. The Create Data File dialog box appears (see fig. 19.14).

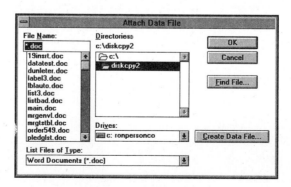

FIG. 19.13.

The Attach Data File dialog box.

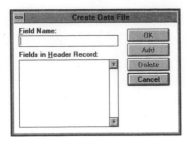

FIG. 19.14.

The Create Data
File dialog box.

5. Type a field name in the Field Name box, then choose the Add
button to add that field to the Fields in Header Record list. Continue to add or delete names that will be in the header record, the
first row of the data file.

Word for Windows uses 31 or less field names in the header
record. Names are used as bookmarks, so they should be assigned
with the same rules as bookmarks—no spaces, use underscore
characters instead; the first character must be a letter; and use no
more than 32 characters.

6. Choose OK when all the field names are entered, as shown in
figure 19.15.

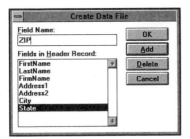

FIG. 19.15.

Enter the field
names used in
the header
record.

7. When prompted, enter a file name that Word will use to name the
file when it is saved.

The data file that Word for Windows creates is a table using the field
names you have entered for the first row (see fig. 19.16). The second
row is blank cells in which you can begin entering data.

Notice that the main document you have created, like the example
shown in figure 19.11, has special buttons in the toolbar. It also has two
additional commands in the Tools menu—the Record Management
Tools and Database Management Tools commands. These buttons and
commands will help you maintain your data file. The extra commands
and buttons are available because the document you created is based
on and attached to the DATAFILE.DOT template.

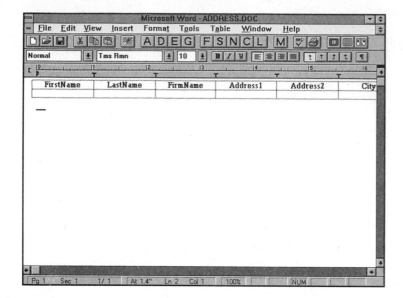

FIG. 19.16.

A data file that
Word for
Windows helps
you create.

Creating a Data File on Your Own

You may need to create a data file without the help provided by the print merge system described in the preceding section. You may need to do this if your system no longer has a copy of the DATAFILE.DOT template or if your mailing list requires more than 31 fields. (Tables, like that created by the earlier system, cannot have more than 31 columns.)

To create a data file manually, follow these steps:

1. Choose the **File New** command and open a new document based on the DATAFILE template if it is available, or the Normal template if DATAFILE is not available.

2. Position the insertion point at the top left corner of the document. The field names you will enter later must be in the first row.

3. If the number of fields in the data file is 31 or less, use the Table button or the **Table Insert Table** command to insert a table that is two rows deep and has as many columns as there are field names.

   or

   If the number of fields in the data file is greater than 31, use tabs or commas to separate fields. If you want to separate fields with tabs, set tab stops for the document.

4. In the first row, enter a field name for each field of data.

   If you are using a table, enter each field name in its own cell. If you are using tabs, press the Tab key between each field name. If you are using commas, separate each field name with a comma.

5. Save the document.

This data file now can have data added to it. When you open the main document that uses this data file, remember to attach the data file you have just created.

If you have data files created by importing files from earlier versions of Word for Windows or by copying data and pasting from another application such as Microsoft Excel or Lotus 1-2-3, you may want to paste the data into a new document opened from the DATAFILE template. This will give you access to the data management commands and toolbar buttons.

T I P

Entering Data in Your Data File

Data files contain data that are usually in table format. However, data may also be separated by commas or by tabs. No matter which format your data file uses, the data must be entered in the same sequence as the field names.

If your data file is a table, then enter data in each cell using the typing, moving, and selecting methods described in Chapter 12. Do not type blank spaces into an empty cell; these will appear in the merged document as a blank space and may throw off alignment or spacing. You can enter multiple lines within a cell by pressing the Enter key or inserting a line break (Shift+Enter). Fields that contain multiple lines of data will also merge as multiple lines of data. When you reach the end of a table, press Tab to add a new line. You can use any of the Table commands to alter or manage the table.

If your data file uses commas or tabs to separate data, then the data also must be entered with a comma or a tab between each field of data. A record of information is defined as being from the beginning of the first line until a paragraph mark (Enter key). Therefore, even if a record of data wraps to the next line, do not press Enter until you have typed all the data for that record.

Ensure that all records have the same number of tabs or commas as there are field names. This is an easy mistake to make when using tabs or commas. You can check whether they match after you attach a data file to the main document by clicking on the check mark in the print merge bar.

 If the text in a comma- or tab-separated data field contains a comma, tab, quotation marks, line break, or paragraph mark, then enclose that text within quotes (" ").

Managing Data in the Data File

Using the print merge system to create a data file or attaching a data file to the DATAFILE.DOT template gives you access to data management macros that make data entry and management easier. The new commands this template adds are as follows:

Tools menu	Toolbar button	Purpose
Record Management Tools		
Add New Record	A	Prompts you for new data and then the data is added
Delete Record	D	Deletes the selected record
Edit Record	E	Changes selected records
Goto Record	G	Goto a record of a specific number
Database Management Tools		
Add New Field	F	Inserts a new record
Sort Records	S	Sorts up to three records
Cleanup Database	C	Checks imported database records for correct format
Link to External Database	L	Links the data file to a file's original Windows application so that changes in the original application transfer immediately to the data file

NOTE Data files do not work with data brought into the data file with a DDE, DDEAUTO, EMBED, INCLUDE, or LINK field code. If you need to link data to an external file with an INCLUDE field, create the INCLUDE field with the **Insert File** command, then select the data and press Shift+Ctrl+F9 to unlink the data and freeze it. If you want to create an interactive data file linked to another Windows application, use the **Link to External Database** option from the **Database Management Tools** command that is added to the Tools menu. This command is available for data files based on or attached to the DATAFILE template.

Creating a Main Document

Creating a main document requires two steps. First you must attach the data file to the main document that will become your form letter, envelope, or label. Attaching the data file to the main document does three things: it shows Word the file name and path where the data will be located, it attaches a mail-merge bar with merge tools to the top of the main document, and it enables Word for Windows to read the field names used in the data file.

After the data file is attached to the main document, you can create a letter, document, envelope, or label by using normal typing and formatting features. Figure 19.17 shows a document containing body copy that will become a main document. Now that the data file is attached, you can use the Insert Merge Field button on the print merge bar to insert MERGEFIELD codes into the main document. These MERGEFIELD codes tell Word where to insert specific data from the data file.

To attach the data file to the main document and then insert MERGEFIELD codes, follow these steps:

1. With the main document active, choose the **F**ile Print **M**erge command. The Print Merge Setup box appears (refer to fig. 19.12).

2. Select the Attach **D**ata File button in the upper left of the dialog box. The Attach Data File dialog box appears (refer to fig. 19.13).

3. Select the desired data file. If you cannot find the file, choose the **F**ind File button and use the Find File dialog box to search the disk for the file. Select the file and choose **O**pen.

    Notice that a merge bar containing buttons and the names of data and form documents appears at the top of the document.

4. Move the insertion point to where you want the first merged data to appear.

5. Choose the Insert Merge **F**ield button from the toolbar that appears under the ribbon. The Insert Merge Field dialog box lists the fields you created when you created the data file (see fig. 19.18).

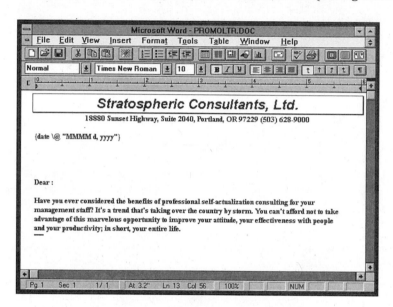

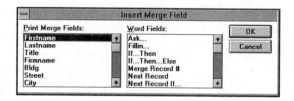

6. Select the field name from the **P**rint Merge Fields list.

7. Choose OK or press Enter.

Follow the same steps to insert all of the merge fields necessary for the form letter. With **V**iew Field **C**odes on, the form letter looks similar to figure 19.19 when you are finished. With **V**iew Field **C**odes off, the form appears as shown in figure 19.20. The {MERGEFIELD Firstname} field appears as <<Firstname>> when field codes are not displayed.

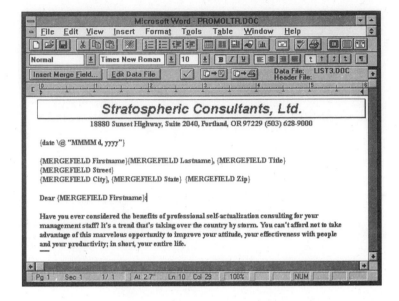

FIG. 19.19.

A form letter with
View Field Codes
on.

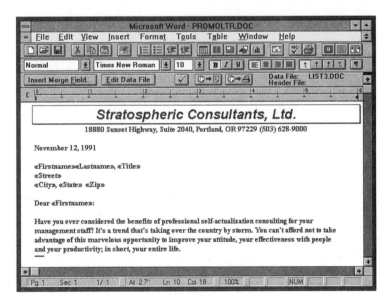

FIG. 19.20.

A form letter with
View Field Codes
off.

You can save your form letter as a document, or create and save it as a template.

To remove an attached data file, activate the main document, choose the **F**ile Print **M**erge command, and then choose the **R**emove Attachments button. Answer Yes when asked for verification.

Checking for Errors

Word for Windows has an error-checking button that appears as a check mark on the print merge bar (see fig. 19.21). When you click this button, Word for Windows reads your data file and checks for errors such as field names that do not meet the rules for bookmarks. Word for Windows also checks to ensure that the number of field names and number of fields in each record (row) are the same. You also are warned if the data file cannot be found. If Word for Windows finds errors, it displays the dialog box shown in figure 19.22. Choose the **Help** button shown in the dialog box for information specific to the problem.

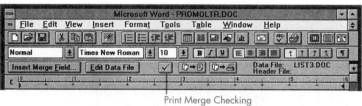

FIG. 19.21.

The print merge checking button.

Print Merge Checking
button

FIG. 19.22.

This error box appears when field names or merge fields are incorrect.

Microsoft Word

The following main document merge fields do not match any field names found in the header record of the data file or header file.

If you do not correct this problem, errors will occur during a Print Merge.

Title

Use Fields in Data File
Switch/Locate Data File...
Cancel
Help

To immediately fix the data file, choose the **S**witch/Locate Data File button. Word for Windows opens or activates the data document if it is a Word for Windows document. If the document is already open, Word for Windows activates it. Word for Windows then selects the field name that is incorrect. Fix the field name and save the data document. Choose the merge check button again to ensure that no other errors exist.

The guidelines in the following list can prevent errors that commonly cause problems:

- Field names must not have spaces. Use an underscore instead of a space.

- Field names must not start with a number, but can have a number in them.

- Field names must be in one row at the top of the data file.

- Field names must be unique—no duplicates.

- Each field (column) of data must have a field name.

- Number of fields in each record must match number of field names.

- If commas, tabs, or cells are missing from the data document, the number of fields in a record of data may not match the number of fields in the heading.

If the data document appears correct, change to the form, display the field codes, and check that the names in the MERGEFIELD codes match the data field names.

Changing the Data File

You may have one form letter you use with different mailing lists. When this happens, you will want to attach your main document to other data files. To attach the form letter to a different data file, choose the **F**ile Print **M**erge command and select the Attach **D**ata File option as you did when you set up the form letter for merging. Then select the data file to which you want to attach the form letter. If the field headers in the new data file do not match the field codes in the form letter, you have to make corrections.

Quickly Merging to Printer or Document

When you are satisfied with your main document, you can merge it with the data by choosing one of two merge buttons shown in figure 19.23. One button merges the data and main document and keeps the result in a new document; the other merges the data and main document and prints. These merge buttons enable you to merge quickly, but do not supply control of the number of records merged or other features. The next section describes how to merge documents with control of these features.

If you merge a large number of records, merge to the printer so that you do not exceed memory limits. To make manual edits to the merged result before printing, choose the merge button that merges to a new document. You may want to merge a few records to a new document before printing. This enables you to see if the merge is working correctly.

FIG. 19.23.

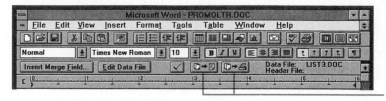

Merge buttons
enable you to
merge to screen
or to the printer.

Merge
buttons

Merging to a document results in one document with each letter separated from the next by a section break (a double-dashed line). This
document contains no field codes; you can treat it as you would any
typed document.

Controlling the Merge

Often you will not want to merge an entire data file into a letter. You
may want to do twenty letters at a time, or limit the merged data to
specific ZIP codes or job titles. Or you may want to merge one or two
letters as a text before running a large merge job.

To merge data and document while controlling which data merges,
follow these steps:

1. Prepare your data file and save it. Activate your main document.
   Ensure that the merge bar indicates that the main file is attached
   to the data file.

2. Choose the **File** Print **Merge** command. When the Print Merge
   Setup dialog box shown earlier in figure 19.16 appears, choose the
   Merge button.

   The Print Merge dialog box that appears enables you to control
   the merge process (see fig. 19.24).

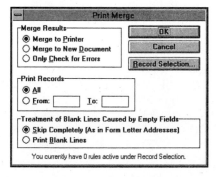

FIG. 19.24.

3. From the Merge Results group, select an option:

Merge to **P**rinter	Produces a printed result
Merge to New **D**ocument	Produces a new document
Only **C**heck for Errors	Checks the headings, but does not merge

4. From the Print Records group select the number of records:

All	Merges all records
From/**T**o	Limits the range of data according to the record (row) numbers in the data file

5. From the Treatment of Blank Lines Caused by Empty Fields group, select how blank fields are handled:

Skip Completely	Select this option if you do not want blank lines in addresses in letters.
Print **B**lank Lines	Select this option if you want blank lines to appear. Blank lines may be important for spacing in the completed merge result.

6. Choose OK or press Enter. You can further limit the records by making a set of rules. To do so, choose the **R**ecord Selection button and read the instructions in the next section.

Selecting Specific Records with Rules

Word for Windows enables you to select which records you want to merge. You can build *rules* that limit which data is merged. The rules form English statements specifying the data you want to merge. You can use this feature if you are doing a targeted mailing to a particular area (selected by ZIP code). For example, the statement *Lastname is equal to Smith* will merge only those records in which the name *Smith* appears in the lastname field.

To select specific records for merging, follow these steps:

1. Follow steps 1 through 5 in the preceding section.

2. Choose the **R**ecord Selection button.

   Use the Record Selection dialog box to build sentences that are rules for which data merges (see fig. 19.25).

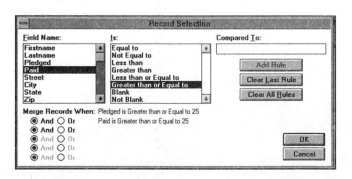

FIG. 19.25.

The Record
Selection dialog
box.

3. Select from the Field Name list the first field you want to limit.

4. Select from the Is list the type of comparison you want to make.

5. Type into the Compared To text box the numeric value or text you want compared to the field.

6. Choose the Add Rule button. Notice the English statement that appears to the right of Merge Records When group title.

7. To add another rule, repeat steps 3-6.

   When you add rules, they appear to the right of an And or Or option button. You must decide whether the rule should be related to the previous rule with an And or an Or. In other words, do both conditions have to be met or either condition for a record to be merged?

   When you finish creating rules, choose OK to complete the merge.

If you make a mistake, choose the Clear Last Rule button to clear your last entry. Choose the Clear All Rules button to start over.

When you build rules, a complete English statement is built that specifies how data from the data file is selected for merging. In figure 19.26, for example, the rule selects everyone who pledged $25 or more and paid $25 or more.

FIG. 19.26.

A completed
Merge Selection
dialog box.

Some tips for building rules are as follows:

■ Text is compared in the same way as numbers. For example, B is less than C.

■ Select ranges using *And*. A numeric range, for example, may be as follows:

ZIP is Greater than 95400

And

ZIP is Less than 95600

A text range may be as follows:

State is Greater than or equal to CA

And

State is Less than or equal to NY

■ Select individual names or numbers with Or. A numeric selection, for example, may be as follows:

ZIP is Equal to 95409

Or

ZIP is Equal to 95412

A text selection may be as follows:

Title is Equal to President

Or

Title is Equal to Manager

T I P

To personally select which records merge, create an extra field (column) with a field name such as Selection in your data document. In that column enter a *1* in the row of each record you want to merge. Use the Record Selection dialog box to specify that you want only records with a 1 in the Selection field to merge.

Using Letterhead

The first page of a form letter is usually on letterhead paper and needs a different top margin than the following pages. To create your normal documents and form letters to compensate for the difference in top margins, use a different header for the first page.

Choose the View Header/Footer command, then select the Different First Page check box. Select First Header from the Header/Footer list. Choose OK or press Enter. In the header editing pane that appears (or at the top of the page in page view), press Enter enough times to move the first line of body copy below the letterhead. This header is for the first page; the following pages begin body copy underneath the top margin set by the document format.

If your printer has double bins, like the HP LaserJet Series IID and IIID, you can pull letterhead paper from the letterhead bin. If your printer has only one bin, you can stack alternating letterhead and bond in the tray, or feed letterhead into the manual feed tray. If you push the letter-head far enough into the manual feed at the appropriate time, the LaserJet pulls from the manual feed before pulling from the bin. (The HP LaserJet accepts paper from the manual feed before pulling from the bin if the printer has the default menu settings.)

Merging Envelopes

With Word for Windows' automated envelope maker, you can create mail-merge envelopes or a document that merges mail-merge envelopes and documents at the same time.

To create mail-merge envelopes, create a data file and main document like the mail-merge form letter described in the earlier section, "Creating a Form Letter." Attach the data file to the main document. Be sure that the top of the main document contains a three-to-five-line address composed of MERGEFIELD codes. If you are not mailing a main document, create a blank letter with the MERGEFIELD codes in an address block. Your document will look similar to figures 19.19 and 19.20 shown earlier. The automatic envelope maker uses this document as a basis for its MERGEFIELD address information.

To make a mass mailing envelope based on your main document, follow these steps:

1. Activate your main document. Ensure that it has a three- to five-line address of MERGEFIELD codes and is attached to the data file.

2. Choose the Tools Create Envelope command or click on the Envelope button in the toolbar.

    The Create Envelope dialog box picks up the MERGEFIELD codes from the main document (see fig. 19.27).

3. Choose the Add to Document button to insert the envelope information and layout as a new section at the top of the main document.

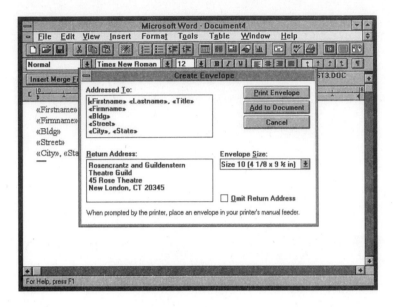

FIG. 19.27.

The Create
Envelope dialog
box.

4. To produce only mass mailing envelopes, delete the letter portion of the document. To alternate printing between envelopes and letters, keep them combined.

5. Save the document. Use the **F**ile Print **M**erge command to print.

The envelope is now a new section formatted as an envelope at the top of the main document. You can keep the letter and envelope together and merge them simultaneously, or delete the letter and merge only into the envelope. If you print the combined envelope and letter, you must feed the envelope manually (when the laser printer requests) or use an envelope bin.

Creating Mailing Labels

If you are sending many documents, mailing labels can save a great deal of time. With Word for Windows, you can easily update your mailing lists and print labels on demand.

Designing a form that prints multiple labels on a page is similar to creating the form letter described in the earlier section, "Creating a Form Letter." When designing a form, however, the label document is only one page. A table of cells with fixed row heights is used so that each label is in its own cell, and each cell after the first cell begins with a {next} field.

Figure 19.28 shows a three-column table of MERGEFIELD codes created for three-up labels. Each cell contains one label, although a label can have multiple lines. Figure 19.29 shows the resulting sheet of labels. Notice that some addresses do not include the building address. Word for Windows' merge feature can skip blank lines so that addresses do not contain blank lines.

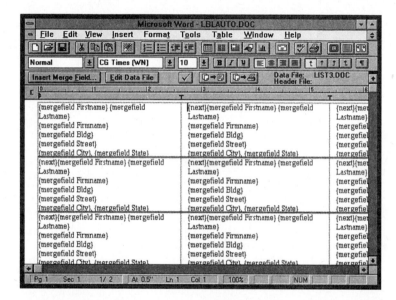

FIG. 19.28.

A multicolumn label document showing MERGEFIELD codes as they appear with View Field Codes off.

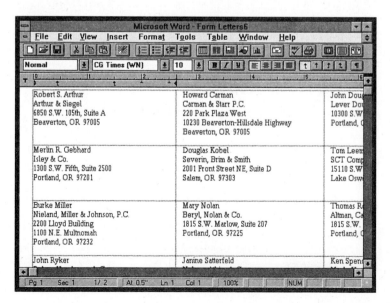

FIG. 19.29.

Sheet of labels after a merging with data.

Using the MAILLABL.DOT Template

The easiest way to create mailing labels is to use the template that comes with Word for Windows. To build a mailing label document using this template, follow these steps:

1. Choose the File New command and open MAILLABL.DOT.

2. The Mailing Labels dialog box appears. Choose the button for the type of printer you use, Laser or Dot Matrix.

    The Printer Label Sizes dialog box appears (see fig. 19.30).

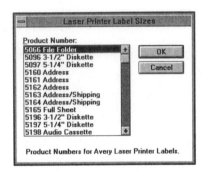

3. Select your type of label from the Product Number list. The labels shown are Avery product numbers. If you are not using Avery labels, use the Avery product number for the same size label or manually create the label document as described in the next section, "Creating Mailing Labels Manually."

    Word for Windows creates a table formatted for the type of labels you select.

4. Choose OK or press Enter.

5. To complete this mail-merge document, choose Multiple Labels from the dialog box that appears. Use the alternate button, Single Label, to enter labels manually into each cell in the table.

6. If you choose to create mail-merge labels, a prompt will appear. If the merge data is contained in two files, a header and data file, choose the Yes button. If the data file is one document, choose No.

    Dialog boxes for the Attach Data File (shown earlier in fig. 19.13) and, if appropriate, the Attach Header File appear.

7. Select the file(s) to be attached and choose OK.

The Layout Mailing Labels dialog box appears (see fig. 19.31). From this dialog box you can select or type items to be inserted into a cell. The Sample Mailing Label area of the dialog box shows the characters and MERGEFIELD codes used in the label.

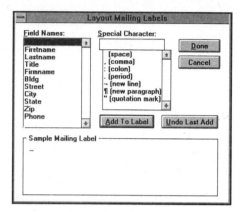

The Layout
Mailing Labels
dialog box.

8. Build a label in the Sample Mailing Label area by selecting from the **F**ield Names list or the **S**pecial Character list the items you want in your label. The label you build in the sample area is copied to all of the cells in the table. Characters not in the **S**pecial Character list can be typed in the **S**pecial Character text box. Choose the **A**dd to Label button to add the selected item in the **S**pecial Character list to the label. Choose the **U**ndo Last Add button to remove the last item.

   Use the ¶ (New Paragraph) option from the **S**pecial Character list to end lines in the label if you want Word for Windows to skip blank lines. Do not use the ➡ (New Line) option.

9. After you build a label similar to the one shown in figure 19.32, choose the **D**one button.

After you choose the **D**one button, Word for Windows copies the information from the Sample Mailing Label area into each cell in the document's table. All cells except the first cell begin their field codes with a {next} field followed by the MERGEFIELD codes in the Sample Mailing Label area. Figure 19.33 shows a mailing label document ready to be merged. You cannot see the {next} field or the MERGEFIELD code names because the **View Field C**odes command is off. (Turning off View Field **C**odes enables you to view the mailing label document more easily.)

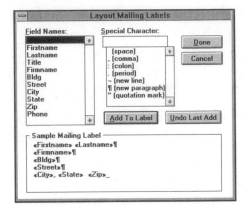

FIG. 19.32.

A sample label ready to be copied to all cells in the table.

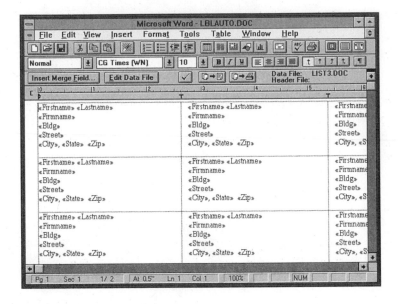

FIG. 19.33.

A finished label document built with the MAILLABL.DOT template.

Creating Mailing Labels Manually

You can create a mailing label document manually if your system does not have the MAILLABL.DOT template. You need to be familiar with creating and formatting tables and with the techniques for mail merging form letters described earlier in this chapter.

To create a mailing label document, measure one of your label sheets so that you know which margin settings, column positions, and row heights to use. Open a new document and set the document margins to match the label sheet's print area. Insert a table with one row and as many columns as the sheet needs. Choose the Table Row Height command. Select Exactly from the Height of Row list. In the At box set the height at the appropriate inches (") or lines (li) needed for each label and then choose OK. (If you use lines, the height varies with the font you use.) Press the Tab key to move to the last cell in the row. Continue pressing Tab to add enough rows to fill the page. To test the table's layout, format all cells with borders and print it over a page of labels. If necessary, adjust the table. Then remove the borders and save the page.

With this main document active, use the File Print Merge command to attach a data file. Then choose the Merge button. Use the techniques described in the section "Creating a Form Letter" to insert the MERGEFIELD codes into the top left cell in the table. The result appears similar to the top left cell in figure 19.35.

Copy the contents of the first cell and paste them into the second cell in the top row. Switch the View Field Codes to display field codes. Move before the first {MERGEFIELD} in the second cell, press Ctrl+F9 to insert field characters, and type *next* so that you have a {next} field. (Each cell after the first cell must begin with a {next} field code. The {next} field tells Word for Windows to get the next record in the data file. If you do not use a {next} field, all the MERGEFIELD on one page use the same record.)

Copy the contents of the second cell, including its {next} field, into the other cells in the table. Then save the document so that you can merge it using normal print merge procedures.

T I P   Do not use labels with adhesive backing designed for copiers in laser printers. Laser printers operate at high temperatures, which can melt and separate labels, creating a mess in your printer. Suppliers such as Avery have a complete line of labels of different sizes and shapes made especially for laser printers.

Getting the Most Out of Form Letters

Having worked through all of the basics of merging documents, you're now ready for a few of Word for Windows' most powerful features. One of these features eliminates blank lines in mail-merge addresses and labels, a feature that gives a more professional appearance. You also see how to use a main document with different data files, without having to re-create field names or MERGEFIELD codes. The secret is to use a header file that shows the field names. Another important topic is how to make merge documents pause and ask you for a customized entry. Finally, this section describes some of the databases you can use to manage large or complex Word for Windows mailing lists.

Suppressing Blank Lines in Addresses

Most business mailings include fields for information such as title, suite number, mail station, and so on. If some information is missing, however, blank lines can show up in your addresses or labels, producing an unfinished, unprofessional appearance. To ensure that blanks are skipped, choose the **F**ile Print **M**erge command, connect the data file, and choose the **M**erge button. In the Print Merge dialog box, select the **S**kip Completely (As in Form Letter Addresses) option from the Treatment of Blank Lines Caused by Empty Fields group (refer to fig. 19.24). Blank lines involving a MERGEFIELD are skipped if they end with a paragraph mark (¶). Lines ending with a line feed, Shift+Enter, are not skipped.

Maintaining Multiple Data Files with the Same Main Document

If you use a database program to maintain your mailing lists, you will appreciate this section. Your database program may generate data files that do not have a *header record*, the top row that contains field names. Instead of opening what may be a huge data file and adding a top row of field names, you can attach a header file. This also enables you to use many data files without having to change the MERGEFIELD in a main document. A *header file* contains a top row of field names, which are used with the data file. The header file can contain a single row of names or be an existing data file with the correct field names. The header file must have the same number of field names as there are fields in the data file.

To create a separate header file, follow these steps:

1. Be sure that the form letter is the active document.

2. Choose the **F**ile Print **M**erge command.

3. Choose the Attach **H**eader File button.

4. Choose the **C**reate Header File button. The Create Header File dialog box appears (see fig. 19.34).

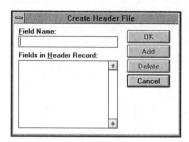

5. In the **F**ield Name box, type a field name, then choose the **A**dd button. Repeat this step for each field name you want in the header file. Enter the names in the left to right order in which data appears in the data file.

6. Choose OK or press Enter.

7. When the Save As dialog box returns, enter a name for the header file in the File **N**ame box, then choose OK or press Enter.

The header file you created is attached immediately to the active main document. You still must attach a data file to the main document. The data file itself should not contain a header record because Word for Windows will merge the row of names as it would a data record.

To print with separate header and data files, be sure that you attach the header and data files in the Print Merge Setup dialog box before you choose the **M**erge button.

Combining Merge Fields with Fillin Fields

Word for Windows can automate and personalize your written communication at the same time, but for truly personal form letters, put {fillin} fields in form letters so that you can type custom phrases into each mail-merge letter.

Figure 19.35 shows a main document with a {fillin} field in the second paragraph of the body text. During the merging operation, this field prompts the user to enter a personalized message to the recipient. The \d switch, and the text that follows, tells Word for Windows to display Go Blue against the Wildcats in the Silicon Bowl! as a default response.

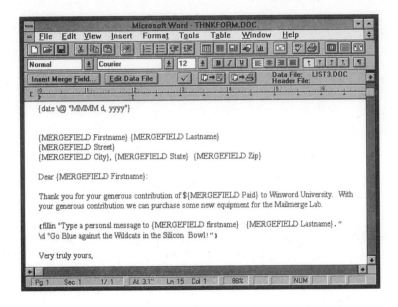

FIG. 19.35.

Use the {fillin} field when you want to type information in merged letters.

To create this {fillin} field, insert or type the following field code where you want the results to appear:

```
{fillin \d "Go Blue against the Wildcats in the Silicon
    Bowl!"}
```

Remember to use the Insert Field command or to press Ctrl+F9 to create the field characters, {}.

To personalize the letter, you need to know to whom you are sending it. To show in the fillin box the name of the person being addressed, type a prompt in quotes, then in the quotes, use the Insert Merge Field button to insert a MERGEFIELD of the person's name. The field should look like the following:

```
{fillin "Type a personal message to {mergefield
    Firstname} {mergefield Lastname}" \d "Go Blue against
    the Wildcats in the Silicon Bowl!"}
```

Notice that the MERGEFIELD code is inside the quotes that enclose the prompt. For more information on using prompts and defaults in {fillin} fields, see Chapter 18.

Managing Mailing Lists in Other Applications

Word for Windows can manage small mailing lists, but for large lists you may want to use a database application. Using a database application gives you more power to search, sort, and filter out information. The information stored in other applications, such as Microsoft Excel, Lotus 1-2-3, or dBASE, can be brought into Word for Windows using the file conversion filters that come with Word for Windows. These filters can be installed or reinstalled by running Word for Windows' setup program. You also can transfer smaller amounts of information to Word for Windows by copying it from one application and pasting it into a Word for Windows document. After you become proficient in Word for Windows' WordBASIC programming language, you can even transfer data to Word for Windows as it changes in the database program. For more information on integrating Word for Windows with other Windows applications, see Chapter 21.

Some Windows applications (such as Microsoft Excel, Q+E from Pioneer Software, Superbase 4 from Precision Software, Lotus 1-2-3 for Windows, and PackRat from Polaris Software) do more than maintain your data. They can manage large amounts of data and save it to a file for use as a mail-merge data file or link it directly into a Word for Windows document.

Contact these companies for more information:

Microsoft Excel	Microsoft One Microsoft Way Redmond, WA 98052-6399 (206) 882-8088
1-2-3 for Windows	Lotus Development 55 Cambridge Parkway Cambridge, MA 02142 (617) 577-8500
Q+E	Pioneer Software 5540 Centerview Drive, Suite 324 Raleigh, NC 27606 (919) 859-2220
Superbase 4	Precision Inc. 8404 Sterling Street A Irving, TX 75063 (214) 929-4888
PackRat	Polaris Software 1820 Escondido Boulevard, Suite 102 Escondido, CA 92025 (619) 743-7800

From Here . . .

You can do much more with print merge than explained here. Using computational fields, you can calculate amounts in a table to create invoices, reports on account status, or other documents containing computed numbers. By combining fields and recorded macros, you can create powerful systems that automate many challenging word processing tasks.

If you have questions about entering and editing fields, refer to Chapter 18. For more information on recording, typing, or editing macros, see Chapter 31.

Assembling Large Documents

You can work with any size document in Word for Windows, but several considerations dictate the most efficient approach to working with large documents. Large documents, and documents with many graphics, fields, bookmarks, and formatting, consume more memory and disk space. They can be slow to load, save, and work in, depending on how much memory you have and the speed of your computer.

Breaking up large documents into smaller components (like chapters) and working with these components individually until you need to print the final product is generally more efficient. You then can compose a large final document, the *master*, from the smaller *source* documents.

Although you can print small source documents as individual files, learning how to assemble small source documents into a master document has its advantage—you can get proper page numbers on pages and in tables of content and indexes.

You can use three approaches to assemble a master document from source documents. With the first technique, you use the Insert File command to insert a document into the master document. The inserted source documents become part of the master document, as if they were created there. This is useful for creating contracts or proposals by inserting paragraphs saved on disk. The inserted material is not linked back to the source. Two disadvantages to this method exist. If a source document changes, you must manually change the master. Also, the master document can become as large and as slow as if you had typed a large document.

With the second technique for creating a master document, you can link source documents on disk into a master document on-screen. You can update the master when a source document changes by updating the link. Again, this technique produces a large document in memory. You can handle paragraph numbering, footnotes, indexes, and tables of contents as you would in a normal document.

With the third technique, you leave individual files on disk and treat them separately. Because the files are never in memory at one time, Word for Windows operates more quickly. You can use a field code to create indexes and tables of contents that span the information contained in these separate files.

T   I   P   Documents of 20 or fewer pages give the best performance in Word for Windows. If your documents are significantly larger than 20 pages, you can segment the documents into multiple files and rejoin them using the techniques described in this chapter.

To ensure consistency when you or a team are writing large documents, read Chapter 30 on building templates and Chapter 11 on creating styles for consistent formatting.

Inserting Unlinked Files

With the first method, which doesn't link documents, you can assemble a large document from other files or portions of files. You can treat this new document as you would any other document. To insert one file inside of another, follow these steps:

1. Position the insertion point in the current document (called the destination document) where you want to insert the file.

2. Choose the Insert File command. The File dialog box appears (see fig. 20.1).

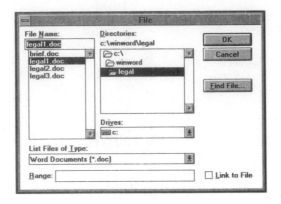

FIG. 20.1.

The File dialog
box.

3. Select the source file from the File Name list box.

   If the file you want to insert is located in another directory, select the correct directory from the **Directories** list box.

4. *Do not* select the Link to File check box.

5. If you are inserting a portion of the source file, type the bookmark name for that portion in the **R**ange text box.

The inserted file or portion of a file becomes an integral part of the document. You can insert a non-Word for Windows document, but the necessary word processing and graphic converters must be installed.

For detailed information on bookmarks, see Chapter 4.

Linking Files into a Master Document

With the second method for building a master document, you link files on disk into an active document. These linked files, or source files, create a *master* document. The master document consists of your basic document and INCLUDE fields that bring in other documents. Word for Windows sequentially numbers pages, paragraphs, footnotes, and so on, as in any Word for Windows document.

You can insert an INCLUDE field with the **Insert File** command or type it in as described in Chapter 18. You can print the large document with page numbering and create a table of contents and an index that use the page numbers.

Using the Insert File Command

Using the **Insert File** command is one of the easiest ways to assemble documents. To link a document, follow the same steps as those described in the preceding section for inserting a file but check the **Link to File** check box if you want the inserted file linked to the source.

You can link a range of a worksheet or a bookmarked area of a Word for Windows document by typing the range name of the worksheet or bookmark name in the **R**ange text edit box. You must assign the range name or bookmark in the source file and save the file before you can link to it. See Chapter 4 for detailed information on bookmarks.

The completed File dialog box looks similar to figure 20.2. This dialog box links a named portion of a larger file.

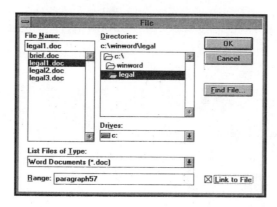

FIG. 20.2.

The completed dialog box links a named portion of a larger file.

For more information on exchanging data with other Windows applications, see Chapter 21.

If the source document is renamed, is moved to a different directory, or includes new or edited information, use the **Edit Links** command as described in Chapter 21 to edit the link or update the data.

When you select the **Link to File** check box, the file or portion of a file is inserted with an INCLUDE field. If the source document changes, you can update the master document by selecting the field code or the text around it and pressing F9, the Update Field key. Chapter 18 describes how to change views to see, edit, or update field codes.

Typing an INCLUDE Field

You can create a master document by typing INCLUDE fields. If you are familiar with the documents, this procedure may be faster than using the Insert File command with the Link to File option.

Insert an {INCLUDE} field where you want a linked file by pressing Ctrl+F9, the Insert Field key, and then typing *INCLUDE* inside the field characters, {}. Follow the INCLUDE field type with a space and the name of the first file that makes up the document—for example, {INCLUDE CHAPT1.DOC}.

If the source file you are including in the master document is located in a different subdirectory than the master document, the source file name must include the path for the file—for example, C:\\WINWORD\\BOOK\\CHAPT1.DOC. Note that you must use double backslashes when specifying a path in a field.

If the View Field Codes command is selected, the INCLUDE fields continue to be displayed in your document. To display the linked text, turn off the View Field Codes command.

Figure 20.3 shows how a master document might appear with the field codes displayed. These INCLUDE fields specify the file name, its path, and the bookmark (range) of the file to be inserted.

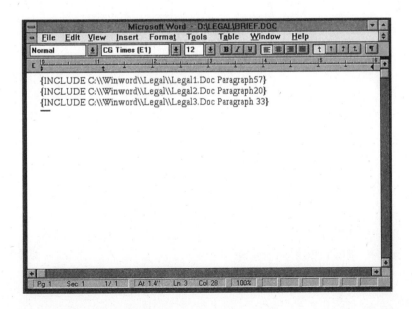

FIG. 20.3.

A master document with the field codes displayed.

T I P   If you move or rename a source file, use the Edit Links command described in Chapter 21 to update the link.

Updating a Source Document

You can update a source document from the master document if the source document is a Word for Windows file. Edit the text of a source document from within the master document. To update a source document, select the linked portion of the master document, and then press Ctrl+Shift+F7. Changes from the master document are copied back to the source documents. Select the entire document if you want all Word for Windows source documents updated.

Printing the Master Document

Before you print the master document, be sure that the INCLUDE fields are updated to reflect any changes made in the source documents. To update the fields, you can select all or parts of the master document and press F9, or you can update when printing.

To update when you print, choose the File Print command. Then choose the Options button and select the Update Fields option in the Options dialog box. Fields are updated when you print the master document; any changes in the source documents are reflected in the final document. Choose OK or press Enter twice to print the document.

Creating Chapter Numbers

In documents assembled with the INCLUDE field, you can use the SEQ field to print chapter numbers with the page numbers.

First you must put an SEQ field at the beginning of each chapter, as in the following steps:

1. Open the first source document you want to include in the master document.

2. Position the insertion point at the end of the document.

3. Choose the Insert Break command.

4. Choose the Next Page option.

5. Choose OK or press Enter.

   A section break is inserted at the end of the document so that when the master document is assembled, each chapter starts in a new section on a new page.

6. Move the insertion point to the beginning of the document.

7. Press Ctrl+F9 to insert a pair of field characters, {}.

8. Type *SEQ identifier \h* in the brackets.

   Identifier is a name you assign to the sequence (here, a chapter). The *h* code hides the result of the field so that it is not displayed in the document. The identifier may be a name such as *WordBook*. Use this identifier for all chapters in the same master document or book.

9. Repeat this process at the beginning of each subsequent chapter.

Now use this SEQ field to create a chapter/page number combination in each source document. For the first source document included in your master document, follow these steps:

1. Choose the **View H**eader/Footer command while in normal view.

2. Select header or footer from the list box, and choose OK or press Enter.

3. Position the insertion point where you want the chapter and page numbers to appear in the header or footer.

4. Press Ctrl+F9 and type *SEQ indentifier*.

5. Use the arrow key to move the insertion point outside the field bracket and type a dash or the character you want to separate the chapter number from the page number.

6. Click on the page button to insert a page field code.

   The entry in the header or footer will look similar to the following:

   ```
   {seq WordBook}-{page}
   ```

7. Choose the Close button.

8. Save the file.

You must set the starting page number for the second and subsequent files in the series of files included in the master document. When you use the INCLUDE field to assemble a large document, you usually do not have to set the starting page numbers because Word for Windows automatically assembles the final document into one file and numbers the pages sequentially. When the page numbering includes the chapter number, however, the page numbers have to restart at one for each chapter.

To set the page numbering in each subsequent chapter, follow these steps:

1. Choose the **View Header/Footer** command.
2. Choose the Page **N**umbers option.
3. Type or select 1 in the **S**tart At text box.
4. Choose OK or press Enter.
5. Choose the Close button.

In the individual files, the SEQ field that outputs the chapter number always results in the number one. When you assemble the master document and update the INCLUDE fields, however, the SEQ fields are updated, resulting in a sequence of chapter numbers.

Creating Indexes and Tables of Contents

When you use INCLUDE statements to assemble a large document from several source documents, you can create an index or table of contents by using the **I**nsert Index and **I**nsert Table of **C**ontents commands. These commands are described in Chapter 16.

Working with Individual Files

With the third technique for assembling large documents, you print the smaller documents separately as if they were for unrelated work. This technique is preferred for large documents that would overload memory if they were inserted or linked into one large master document.

When you use this technique, you must set the starting numbers for pages, paragraphs, footnotes, and so on for each of the individual files to maintain sequential numbering across the larger document.

Setting Starting Numbers

To set the starting numbers for the individual files, you start with the first file in the series. You repaginate the file, and then note the number of the last page and of any other sequentially numbered items, such as paragraphs, lines, footnotes, and items numbered using the SEQ fields (tables or figures, for example). Next, you open the second file in the series and use the appropriate commands to set the starting numbers for each sequentially numbered item in that document. This procedure is followed for each of the individual files. To save time, carry out this procedure after all editing changes have been made, to minimize the possibility of having to repeat the process of setting starting numbers.

To set the starting page numbers, follow these steps:

1. Choose the **T**ools Rep**a**ginate Now command.

2. Choose the **I**nsert Page N**u**mbers command.

3. Choose the **F**ormat option.

4. Type or select the appropriate page number in the **S**tart At text box (one higher than the number of the last page in the preceding file).

5. Choose OK or press Enter twice.

To set the starting footnote numbers, follow these steps:

1. Choose **I**nsert Foot**n**ote.

2. Choose the **O**ptions button.

3. Type or select the appropriate number in the Start **A**t text box (one higher than the number of the last footnote in the preceding file).

4. Choose OK or press Enter twice.

To set the starting line numbers, follow these steps:

1. Choose the Forma**t S**ection Layout command.

2. Choose the **L**ine Numbers option.

3. Type or select the appropriate line number in the Start **A**t # text box (one higher than the number of the last line in the preceding file).

4. Choose the **C**ontinue option in the Restart Field.

5. Choose OK or press Enter twice.

To set the starting number for paragraphs, follow these steps:

1. Select the group of paragraphs you want to renumber.

2. Choose the **T**ools **B**ullets and Numbering command.

3. Type the appropriate number in the **S**tart At text box (one higher than the number of the last numbered paragraph in the preceding file).

4. Choose OK or press Enter.

To set the starting numbers of items numbered using the SEQ field, follow these steps:

1. Choose the **V**iew Field **C**odes command to display field codes, if it is not already selected.

2. Find the first SEQ field and type in \r followed by the appropriate number (one higher than the last number in that sequence of items).

3. Repeat step 2 for each sequence in the document.

Creating Chapter Numbers

When you print the individual documents separately (not linking them with INCLUDE fields), you must insert the chapter number. To do so, you add the chapter number to the header or footer, next to the page number code. The entry in the header or footer for Chapter 2, for example, might look like this:

```
2-{page}
```

If the order of the chapters changes, you must edit the chapter numbers that appear in the header or footer to maintain the proper sequencing.

Printing Individual Files

After you set the starting numbers for each of the files, you can print them individually. To print several documents with one command, use the **F**ile **F**ind File command. When you choose this command, Word for Windows finds all the files in the path specified in the Search dialog box. You can edit this path if necessary (see Chapter 3). After you have a list of the correct files, follow these steps to print the desired files:

1. Hold down the Ctrl key and click on each of the files you want to print.

    or

    Press Shift+F8 and use the arrow keys to move to the file you want to print. Press the space bar to select the file. Repeat this step for each file you want to print.

2. Choose the **P**rint button.

3. Choose OK or press Enter to print the files.

Creating a Table of Contents

When you print the smaller documents separately, you must insert RD fields to create indexes and tables of contents. The RD fields are inserted into a document separate from the individual documents. Insert one RD field for each of the separate files that make up the larger document. You then use the Insert Index and Insert Table of Contents commands to create the index and table of contents from the document containing the RD fields. This document then contains only the index and table of contents, not the text of the documents. You can print the table of contents and index separately and combine it with the larger document.

To create a separate index or table of contents, follow these steps:

1. Open a new file to contain the RD fields.

2. Press Ctrl+F9, the Insert Field key.

3. Type *rd* followed by a space and the name and path of the first file that makes up the document. If the files are all in the current directory, you do not need to include the path (*rd chapt1.doc*, for example). Use the full path name if the files are located in different directories. Use a double backslash where a single backslash normally is used in a path name.

4. Use the arrow keys to move outside the field and press Enter to start a new paragraph.

5. Repeat steps 2 through 4 for each of the files that makes up the document.

6. Position the insertion point where you want to locate the table of contents and use the Insert Table of Contents command to create a table of contents.

7. Press Ctrl+Enter, the page break key, to separate the table of contents and index.

8. Position the insertion point where you want to locate the index and use the Insert Index command to create an index.

9. Use the Insert Page Numbers command to set the appropriate page numbers for the table of contents and index.

To set separate starting page numbers for the table of contents and the index, you must insert a section break between them. Choose the Insert Break command and select the Next Page option; choose OK or press Enter.

Figure 20.4 illustrates the field code view of a document set up to print the table of contents and index for a book.

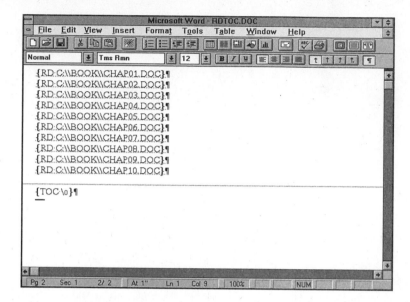

FIG. 20.4.

RD field codes
that will create a
table of contents.

Sometimes you may need to use RD fields to create a table of contents
or an index with documents you assemble by using INCLUDE fields.
You need to use RD fields, for example, if you run into memory limitations when you try to create a table of contents or index in a document
with INCLUDE fields that result in a lot of text and figures. In this case,
create a second master document in which you insert RD fields, and
create your table of contents and index in this document.

From Here . . .

Word for Windows can handle professional word processing. With
Word for Windows, you can produce large documents, manuals, books,
and assemble small documents into larger documents. Word for Windows also has many other professional features to aid authors, documentation writers, and legal staff.

Word for Windows has several tools that improve the consistency of
your work and decrease your workload. You can format styles, glossaries, and templates. For detailed coverage of styles, see Chapter 11.
Glossaries are covered in Chapter 9. For information on working
with templates, see Chapter 30. To learn how to edit links and use
information from other Windows applications in your documents see
Chapter 21.

Exchanging and Linking Data between Applications

One of the unique advantages of Windows applications is their capability to exchange and link information easily with other Windows applications. With Word for Windows, you also can import or link to files from many DOS applications, such as Lotus 1-2-3 worksheets and graphs, AutoCAD drawings, or dBASE database files. Figure 21.1 shows a letter with links to a Microsoft Excel worksheet and chart.

If you are used to working with a single application, the value of exchanging and linking data may not be immediately apparent to you. After you begin to link and exchange data, however, you will see how much your communication and use of the computer improves. You can use Word for Windows with other applications, for example, to do the following:

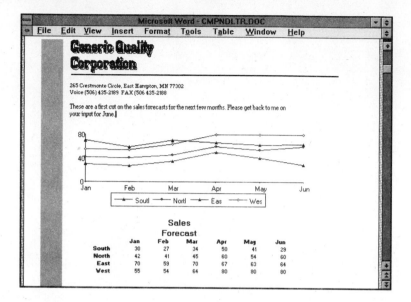

FIG. 21.1.

A document linked to a Microsoft Excel worksheet and chart.

■ Create mail-merge data documents from a mailing list file kept in dBASE, Microsoft Excel, or Lotus 1-2-3.

■ Create sales projections, financial analyses, inventory reports, and investment analyses with worksheets and charts in Microsoft Excel, and link or embed them into Word for Windows documents.

■ Keep client reminder letters and call backs by linking PackRat, a personal information manager, to Word for Windows through WordBASIC macros that come packaged with WordBASIC.

■ Produce proposals and contracts that include AutoCAD drawings.

■ Produce advertising or marketing materials that include artwork created in different Windows or DOS drawing and design applications.

Understanding Linking Terms and Concepts

This chapter includes references to *source* and *destination documents*. The source is the file on disk or document in an open application that supplies data. The destination is the document that receives the data.

You can look at the various methods of exchanging data in a number of different ways: you can evaluate whether the source of the data is a file or is in an active application; you can evaluate whether you are exchanging text or graphic data; or you can evaluate which of the different procedures can be used.

Word for Windows provides the ollowing three primary methods for exchanging data, depending on t ie location of the source data:

- *Embedded data.* The source data is encapsulated and inserted within the Word for Windows document. The advantage of this method is that the data, such as a drawing or a Microsoft Excel chart, is kept with the Word for Windows document. You control updating manually. Use embedded data to keep the source document with the destination document. Use this method when you do not need to share the source data with multiple destination documents.

- *Inserting or importing from a file.* The source data is located in and remains in a file on disk. Updating is controlled manually or can be automated through a macro. You do not need the source application because Word for Windows converts the file or graphic while inserting it. Changes to the source document may affect multiple destination documents.

- *Linking Data.* The source data is located in a source document in an open Windows application. Changes to source data are transmitted to the destination document automatically when source data changes or when the operator requests an update. Use this method when you want changes in a single source document to affect many destination documents.

The following commands are used for exchanging data:

- *File Open and conversion.* Use this command if the data is in a disk file, and you will transfer large amounts of non-graphic data infrequently. Use this method to load large dBASE files, text files, or entire worksheets as a new Word for Windows document. (See Appendix C for file conversion information.)

- *Insert File.* Use this command if the data is in a disk file and you need only portions of the file, or you want to insert the file within an existing Word for Windows document. Data can be brought in unlinked or linked to the disk file (source). Updates from the source on disk can be controlled automatically or manually.

- *Insert Picture.* Use this command for a graphic in a disk file. You can bring in graphics unlinked or linked to the disk file (source). Updates from the source on disk can be controlled automatically or manually. (Do not use this command with Microsoft Excel charts.)

- *Edit Paste*. Use this command to copy text or graphics from a running application and paste them into the document. Text transfers as if typed.

- *Edit Paste Special without linking*. If you use this command, text pastes as text. Graphics paste as embedded objects linked to the source application or to a Microsoft *applet* (a small application) such as Microsoft Drawing.

- *Edit Paste Special with linking*. Text or graphics are linked to the source application. Changes in the source document transfer to the pasted text or graphic. Double-clicking the item opens or activates the source application.

T I P   Before Word for Windows exchanges data with files or applications that use a data format other than Word for Windows or text, you must install the appropriate file converter. Before you can open dBASE files or insert portions of Microsoft Excel worksheets, for example, you must install the dBASE and Microsoft Excel converter files. If you did not install the converter files when you installed Word for Windows, you can rerun Word for Windows' installation program or run the Word for Windows Setup program item icon and install them without completely reinstalling Word for Windows. You will need your original installation disks.

Exchanging Data through Files

One of the easiest ways to bring large amounts of textual or numeric data into Word for Windows from another Windows or DOS application is to use the **File Open** command. This command is useful for opening dBASE files containing mailing list data or opening and formatting text files downloaded from a mainframe. Programs such as Aldus Page-Maker, the leading desktop publishing application, read Word for Windows files and import the style sheets, thereby saving you formatting time.

Chapter 3 describes how to change the List Files of **Type** pull-down list to the All Files (*.*) option. This option lists all files so that you can see and open non-Word for Windows files. If you installed the appropriate file converter, Word for Windows will open and convert the file simultaneously.

Inserting from Files on Disk

If you need to include in your Word for Windows document a graphic or portions of a file or worksheet, you should become familiar with the methods for inserting files and importing graphics. The advantages to linking with files on disk instead of pasting in data or graphics are as follows:

- The data resides in a disk file.

- All or part of a word processing, worksheet, or database file can be brought in.

- Only a source file on disk is required. The source application need not be open or even on the system. This means that you can use this method on computers that do not have enough memory to run two applications at once.

- The operator controls when the file or graphic data updates. This enables you to "freeze" the data in the destination document until you want an update. By not updating continuously, more computer power is left for your application.

- Files and graphics from DOS applications can be linked into Word for Windows documents.

Inserting from files on disk has the following disadvantages:

- Renaming or moving a source file can disturb the link. You then must edit the link so that the Word for Windows document can find it.

- Editing an inserted picture can break its link and change the graphic into an embedded object.

Refer to Chapter 20 to learn about creating large documents through inserting files. Refer to Appendix B for information on the file converters necessary to translate non-Word for Windows files.

Inserting Text or Worksheet Files from Disk

To insert within a document a file or a portion of a file that is on disk and for which you have an installed converter, follow these steps:

1. Position the insertion point in the destination document at the place where you want the source data to appear.

2. Choose the **Insert File** command. The File dialog box opens (see fig. 21.2).

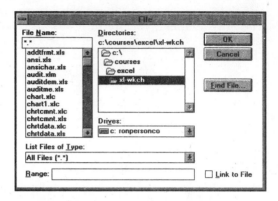

FIG. 21.2.

The File dialog box.

3. Change to the directory containing the source file. In the File **Name** box, type or select the name of the file you want to insert. If you do not see the file, change the List File of **Type** to `All Files (*.*)`.

4. To insert a portion of the file, type the name (for Microsoft Excel files), the bookmark (for Word for Windows files), or range name (for 1-2-3 files) in the **R**ange text box.

5. To link rather than insert the source document into the target document, select the **L**ink to File check box.

6. Choose OK or press Enter.

   The Convert File dialog box appears so that you can confirm the type of file conversion (see fig. 21.3).

7. Select the file type and choose OK. (You must have the appropriate converter installed to convert other word processing, worksheet, or database files.)

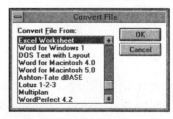

FIG. 21.3.

The Convert File dialog box.

If you are inserting a worksheet file and did not enter a range name, a dialog box appears from which you can select to insert the Entire Worksheet or select from the list of named ranges in the worksheet. When you later update the inserted worksheet, by selecting it and pressing F9, you again will have an opportunity to select the range to be updated.

Inserting a file without linking enters data as though it were typed. Worksheets are entered as Word for Windows tables.

If you insert a file with the Link to File check box selected, however, the program inserts an INCLUDE field code into the document. The following INCLUDE field, for example, links the Result range of the FORECAST.XLS worksheet found in the C:\FINANCIAL directory. The \c *MSBiff* switch tells Word for Windows which file converter to use (BIFF is the file format for Microsoft Excel, Lotus 1-2-3 is the format for Lotus files, and so on).

```
{INCLUDE C:\\FINANCIAL\\FORECAST.XLS Result \c MSBiff}
```

> Before you can use Insert File to insert data into a document, the source document must have been saved to disk.

T I P

For additional information on including and linking text or worksheet files as part of a large document, refer to Chapter 20.

Importing and Linking Graphics Files

Graphic files can be imported or linked into Word for Windows documents with the Insert Picture command. (This is described in detail in Chapter 23.) Inserting a picture without selecting the Link to File check box inserts a picture in the document that is not linked to the file. Inserting a picture with the Link to File check box selected, however, inserts an IMPORT field code in the document. The picture displays in the document at bit-map resolution but prints with the full resolution possible from the file on disk. If the picture in the file changes, you can update the link in the destination document by selecting the IMPORT field code or the picture and pressing the F9 key.

Be careful. If you double-click on a picture produced by an IMPORT field code, the Microsoft Draw program will start and load the picture. If you then update the picture from Microsoft Draw, the IMPORT field code changes to an EMBED field code. The picture will lose its link to the file on disk, and may also print at a lower quality. If you double-click on an Encapsulated PostScript (EPS) picture so that Microsoft

Draw starts, a warning dialog box appears with the warning `This pic-ture contains Encapsulated PostScript data, which cannot be retained`. If you want to preserve the EPS quality of the picture, do not update the picture from Microsoft Draw. To prevent accidentally changing an IMPORT field code to an EMBED field code, lock the picture. A section at the end of this chapter describes how to lock inserted pictures or files.

T I P   If you attempt to update an IMPORT field that refers to an incorrect directory or a file that cannot be found, the picture will be replaced with the error message, `Error! Cannot open file`. To repair this problem, use the **E**dit **L**inks command to re-create the link to the correct directory or file name. The use of **E**dit **L**inks is described later in this chapter. If the file is not available, immediately choose the **E**dit **U**ndo command to change the error message back to a picture. Select the picture (or its field code) and press Shift+Ctrl+F9 to convert the picture into a pasted drawing. This drawing is no longer linked to the original file, but it can be edited with Microsoft Draw or printed as part of the document.

Transferring Data with Copy and Paste

The simplest way to transfer small amounts of data or graphics from one application to another is to copy and paste in the same way that you move text or graphics in a document. To copy from one Windows application to a Word for Windows application, follow these steps:

1. Select the text, cells, or graphic in the source document.

2. Choose the **E**dit **C**opy command.

3. Press Alt+Tab until the title for Word for Windows appears on-screen. Release the Alt key to activate Word for Windows.

4. Position the insertion point where you want the data to appear in the document.

5. Choose the **E**dit **P**aste command.

Text is pasted into the document as formatted text; Microsoft Excel worksheet cells or ranges paste in as a table; graphics paste in as a bit-mapped picture. None of them are linked to their source document, however. If you double-click the picture, it will load into Microsoft Draw and become a Microsoft Draw embedded object.

Linking Data with Paste Special

Another way to link data between Windows applications is to use the Edit Paste Special command to create a communication channel between two open Windows applications. Data can be sent through this channel when information in the source changes or when you manually request an update.

The Edit Paste Special command is useful primarily when you want to link two Windows applications and use features in a source application to update data or graphics in your Word for Windows document. You might use the command if you have a financial worksheet and charts in Microsoft Excel, for example, and the results and charts are part of an integrated Word for Windows report. You need to be able to work in Microsoft Excel and use its functions and its links to mainframe data. When the worksheets and charts change, however, the changes should pass immediately to the integrated report in Word for Windows, where you can print them.

The advantages to using links created by Paste Special are as follows:

- You can link updates to a single source document to many destination documents.

- The data resides in the source application's document. You can use the source application and all its features to update the source document.

- The data or graphic is not embedded in the Word for Windows document—only the result is shown—so the document is much smaller than a document with embedded data.

- You can bring in all or part of a word processing, worksheet, or database file.

- Updates can be done automatically whenever the source data changes or manually when you request them.

Some disadvantages to using links created by Paste Special are as follows:

- Renaming or moving a source file can disturb the link. You must edit the link so that the Word for Windows document can find the source file.

- The source application and file must be on disk and available to Word for Windows if you want to edit the data or graphic.

- Not all Windows applications can link data.

- Automatic updates can slow down computer response time.

Creating a Link with Paste Special

Creating a link between Word for Windows and a Windows application is as easy as copying and pasting. When you give the paste command, you can make a link that updates automatically or a link that requires a manual update.

To create a link, follow these steps:

1. Open both Windows applications and their documents. Activate the source document.

2. Save the source document under the name that it will keep during all future transactions.

3. Select the text, range of cells, graphic, or database records you want to link.

4. Choose the **E**dit **C**opy command.

5. Activate the Word for Windows document and position the insertion point where you want the link to appear.

6. Choose the **E**dit Paste **S**pecial command.

   The Paste Special dialog box appears (see fig. 21.4). Notice that it displays the source of the link and lists the different ways that the linked data can appear or be linked.

FIG. 21.4.

The Paste Special dialog box.

7. From the **D**ata Type list, select the form in which you want your linked data.

Selecting some data types, such as a Microsoft Excel Object, disables the Paste Link button; when the program pastes in the data as an object, it stores all the source data (or graphic) in the Word for Windows document and doesn't keep a link to the original worksheet or graphic. Double-clicking the object starts or activates the application, in this case Microsoft Excel, and loads the embedded data or graphic.

8. Choose the Paste **L**ink or **P**aste button.

Choosing the Paste **L**ink button creates a link that updates automatically. To create a link that updates only when you manually request an update, see the section "Controlling Manual Versus Automatic Updates" later in this chapter.

When you create a link by pasting, the data from the source can appear in the Word for Windows document in different forms such as tabbed text, a formatted table, a picture, or a bit map, depending on the source application. Microsoft Excel data, for example, can appear in a number of forms. If you copy a range of Microsoft Excel cells and then use **E**dit Paste **S**pecial to paste them into a Word for Windows document, you see the following alternatives in the Data Type dialog box (refer to fig. 21.4):

- *Object*. The data is an embedded object with all data stored in the object. No link is maintained with the source document. This data type is available only through the **P**aste button, not with the Paste **L**ink button.

- *Formatted Text (RTF)*. Text transfers with formats. Worksheets appear formatted as tables. You can edit or reformat data. If you choose Paste **L**inks, a LINK field is inserted that links to the source document. If you choose **P**aste, the data appears as unlinked text.

- *Unformatted Text*. Text is unformatted. Worksheets appear as unformatted text with cells separated by tabs. You can edit or reformat data. If you choose Paste Links, a LINK field is inserted that links to the source document. If you choose Paste, the data appears as unlinked text.

- *Picture*. Pictures, text, database, or worksheet ranges appear as a picture. You can format them as pictures, but you cannot edit text in Word for Windows. Unlinking changes them to Microsoft Draw objects. If you choose Paste **L**inks, a LINK field is inserted that links to the source document. If you choose **P**aste, the picture becomes an object that you can edit with Microsoft Draw.

- *Bit map*. Pictures, text, or worksheet ranges appear as a bit-map picture. You can format them as pictures, but you cannot edit text in Word for Windows. Resolution is poor. If you choose Paste

Links, a LINK field is inserted that links to the source document. If you choose **P**aste, the picture becomes an object that you can edit with Microsoft Draw.

If you choose the **P**aste button, the text or graphic is inserted in the Word for Windows document. Text becomes part of the document, just as if you typed it. Graphics become like pasted graphics. If you double-click a pasted graphic, it becomes an embedded object that you can edit with Microsoft Draw and resides in an EMBED field code.

If you choose the Paste Link button, a link is created to the source document, using a LINK field code such as the following:

```
{LINK ExcelWorksheet C:\\FINANCIAL\\FORECAST.XLS Result
    \* mergeformat \r \a}
```

In this example, the Result range within the Microsoft Excel worksheet was copied and pasted into the Word for Windows document as Formatted Text (RTF), as indicated by the argument, \r. The following arguments specify the form for linked data:

\r	Formatted Text (RTF)
\t	Unformatted Text
\p	Picture
\b	Bit map

T   I   P   Windows applications prior to Word for Windows 2 may produce a DDE or DDEAUTO field code instead of the LINK field code.

Passing Linked Documents to Other Computer Users

If an operator wants to change linked data, the source application and source document must be available. When you give a document containing links to another operator, make sure that they have access to the source documents and source application. If they do not, unlink the links or change the links to embedded objects.

If you unlink linked word processing or worksheet information, it becomes text, just as if you typed it directly in the destination document. If you unlink graphics, they become pictures or bit maps. When you unlink objects, the Word for Windows document remains relatively small. Unlinking documents is described near the end of this chapter.

Opening the Source Document

In your Word for Windows document, you can edit linked data such as text or numbers, but as soon as you update the link, your changes disappear. To change linked data so that it remains, you need to edit the source document. Because these links are DDE links, the source application and its document must be open or available when you edit the link. If the source application and document are not open when you attempt to edit the link, Windows opens them for you.

Follow these steps to open a source document that may be closed:

1. Select the entire linked data or graphic.

2. Choose the **Edit Links** command.

   The Links dialog box appears (see fig. 21.5). If you selected linked data in step 1, the appropriate link in the Links list will be selected. If you did not do step 1, or you want to open a different link, select the link from the Links list.

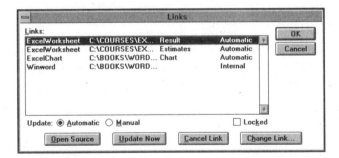

FIG. 21.5.

The Links dialog box.

3. Choose the **O**pen Source button. The source application opens.

4. Make your updates, edits, or formatting changes to the source document.

5. Save the source document and then close it if you have made all the changes you want.

If the link is automatic, the Word for Windows document updates immediately. If the link is manual, you must update the linked data to see the change. Update linked data by selecting it and pressing F9.

T I P   To preserve manually applied formatting during an update to linked data, use the * mergeformat and * charformat field switches described in Chapter 18. To preserve wide titles in a table, do not merge cells to give a title extra width in a cell. Instead, change individual cell widths to allow space for a wide title.

Converting Linked Data

To convert linked information to text a graphic, select the linked information and then press Shift+Ctrl+F9 to unlink. The information changes into text, a picture, or a bit map as if you had pasted it and not past linked it. You can use the Edit Link command with the Cancel Link button to achieve the same effect.

Embedding Data

The Insert File and Insert Picture methods of integrating data into Word for Windows use information inserted from files or imported from graphic files. The Paste Special method with a Paste Link uses DDE to link with other Windows applications that are running. When you use linked documents, however, you must keep track of the location of the source files, make sure that the source files' names do not change, and make sure that anyone receiving your Word for Windows document receives all the source files. You can avoid these file management problems by embedding the linked data directly within the Word for Windows document.

If you have worked with the WordArt, Microsoft Draw, or Microsoft Graph applets, you are familiar with embedded objects and how they work. Although these programs are applets (small applications), other major applications with Object Linking and Embedding (OLE) capabilities can embed their data into Word for Windows.

The advantages of embedding objects from Windows applications are as follows:

- File management and tracking of source documents is not a problem.

- Linked data is not destroyed when a source document cannot be found during an update.

■ Updated objects immediately reflect the changes.

Embedding objects has the following disadvantages:

■ The computer must have enough memory to run both applications simultaneously.

■ The Word for Windows document becomes large, containing the Word for Windows document and all the embedded data for the worksheet, chart, or graphic.

Creating an Embedded Object

You can create embedded objects in two ways. Both methods produce the same results.

To insert an embedded object, follow these steps:

1. Position the insertion point in the destination document where you want to insert the object.

2. Choose the **Insert Object** command. The Object dialog box appears and lists the types of objects you can embed (see fig. 21.6).

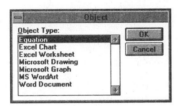

FIG. 21.6.

The Object dialog box lists the types of objects you can embed.

3. From the **Object** Type list, select the type of object you want to insert, and then choose OK or press Enter.

4. Create the data you want in the object. If a blank worksheet opens, for example, create the worksheet. If a blank drawing window appears, draw what you want as the new object.

5. Use one of the following techniques to embed the object, as appropriate to the application creating the object.

Choose the **File Exit** and Return command to close the application and update the embedded object.

or

Close the document window containing the object to close the object but keep the application open.

or

Choose the **File Update** command to update the embedded object but keep the application and object open.

If necessary, press Alt+Tab to return to your Word for Windows document.

An object will appear in the **O**bject List only if the application you use to create the object is registered with Windows and is capable of producing OLE objects. Figure 21.6 shows chart and worksheet objects from Microsoft Excel.

You also can create an embedded object by copying the object from an application that supports OLE and then choosing the **E**dit Paste **S**pecial command. From the Paste Special dialog box, select Object as the **D**ata Type and then choose OK.

Editing Embedded Objects

Embedded objects are easy to edit. With the mouse, just double-click the embedded object. With the keyboard, select the object and then choose the **E**dit *application* Object command at the bottom of the Edit menu. If not open, the application will open; if open, the application will activate. The object will load so that you can make changes.

To exit the object after you edit or format it, use the same procedures used to exit when you created it:

Choose the **F**ile E**x**it and Return command to close the application and update the embedded object.

or

Close the document window containing the object to close the object but keep the application open.

or

Choose the **File Update** command to update the embedded object but keep the application and object open.

If necessary, return to your Word for Windows document by pressing Alt+Tab.

Converting Embedded Objects

Embedded objects create large files and consume memory. If you no longer need to edit or update an embedded object, convert it to the equivalent of pasted data. To convert an embedded object into text, a picture, or a bit map, select the object and then press Shift+Ctrl+F9.

Managing Links

Keeping track of the many links into a large or complex document can be a difficult task. You can use the Edit Links command to make the job easier. When you choose Edit Links, the Links dialog box, shown in figure 21.7, opens and displays a list of all the links, their type, and how they update. From the buttons and check box, you can update linked data, lock it to prevent changes, cancel the link, and change the file names or directories where the linked data is stored.

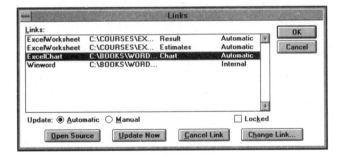

FIG. 21.7.

The Links dialog box.

Updating Links

To update individual links in a document so that the destination file receives new information, select the linked text or graphic and then press F9. To update links selectively without scrolling through the document, choose the Edit Links command. When the Links dialog box appears, select the links you want to update (use Ctrl+click to select multiple links), then choose the Update Now button.

When you want to update all the links in an entire document, select the entire document by pressing Ctrl and clicking in the left boundary, or press Ctrl+5 (numeric pad). Then press the F9 key or choose the Edit Links command and choose the Update Now button.

Changing between Automatic and Manual Links

Using the **Edit Paste Special** command creates an automatic link; pasted data normally updates immediately when the source information changes. This automatic updating process can slow down your computer's operation if changes are frequent.

If you do not need to see every change, however, you can change an automatic link to a manual link by following these steps:

1. Select the linked data or graphic.

2. Choose the **Edit Links** command.

3. Select the Update option that specifies when the link updates.

   Select **M**anual if you want to specify when the link is updated.

   Select **A**utomatic if you want the link to update when the source data changes.

4. Choose OK or press Enter.

To update a manual link, select the linked information and press F9. To prevent a link from updating, lock the link, as described later in the section "Locking a Link."

Unlinking Inserted Files or Pictures

Suppose that you no longer want a linked object to change when the source changes. You can unlink the source document and change the object into normal text or a graphic. Select the field code that creates the link and press Ctrl+Shift+F9 or choose the **Edit Links** command, select the link you want to unlink, and choose the **Cancel** button.

Editing Links When Names Change

If a source's location, file name, or range name changes, you need to update the field code that creates the link to reflect the new directory and file name. To update a linking field, choose the **Edit Link** command, select the link you need to edit, and then choose the **Change Link** button to display the Change Link dialog box (see fig. 21.8). From this dialog box, you can edit the **A**pplication, **F**ile Name, or **I**tem (range name or bookmark) text boxes to match the application, path, file name, and range name for the new source. The **A**pplication edit box cannot be edited for links created with **I**nsert **Fi**le or Insert **P**icture.

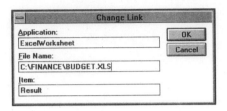

FIG. 21.8.

The Change Link
dialog box.

If you are familiar with the operation of field codes, you can display the field code and edit it directly. Remember that two backslashes are needed to separate subdirectories in a path name within a field code.

Locking a Link

You may want to prevent accidental updating of a link but still be able to update at your discretion. You can do this by locking or unlocking the related field code. To lock or unlock a field, select the field and press Ctrl+F11 (Lock Field) or Ctrl+Shift+F11 (Unlock Field). You also can lock or unlock a field by choosing the **E**dit Link command, selecting the link you want to lock or unlock, and then selecting or clearing the Loc**k**ed check box. (If your keyboard does not have an F11 key, press Alt+Ctrl+F1 to lock the field, and Alt+Ctrl+Shift+F1 to unlock the field.)

From Here . . .

This chapter gives you the techniques you need to create complex documents created from data from many sources. Word for Windows and the Windows programs with which it can exchange data create the most powerful document building system available.

For additional information on the INCLUDE, IMPORT, LINK, and EMBED commands, refer to the field codes in Chapter 18. If your compound documents are large or you need to include page numbers, headers, and footers, Chapter 20 describes how to assemble large documents from pieces contained in many files.

Troubleshooting

W ord for Windows includes many powerful, easy-to-use features. You may have problems or questions, however, when using some features. If you are unsure how to resolve a problem, Word for Windows' on-line help feature can be useful. To go into Help for specific information from a dialog or alert box, press F1. When a dialog box is not displayed, press F1 or choose the **H**elp **I**ndex command for general Help. To find information quickly in Help, use the **S**earch button.

This chapter provides you with answers to questions commonly raised when working with Word for Windows.

Operating Word for Windows

Problem: You choose a T**oo**l command such as **S**pelling, **H**yphen-ation, **G**rammar, **T**hesaurus, or a Form**a**t command involv-ing an object such as Draw, Graph, Equation Editor, or WordArt, and a dialog box displays a message telling you that Word for Windows cannot locate the command or feature.

Solution: Many Word for Windows features are optional during Word for Windows' installation process. If a feature or command you want to use has not been installed, you can run the Word for Windows installation procedure again and select only the options you want to install. Run Word for Win-dows' installation program by double-clicking on the Word

Setup icon in the Word for Windows group window of the Program Manager. Instructions appear on your screen at the beginning of the installation process and prompt you to select the options you want to install. Follow the instructions that appear to complete the installation process.

Problem: A dialog box displays an error message that you don't understand.

Solution: Press F1. A help window appears with an explanation of the error. Read the help window and follow the recommendations to resolve the problem.

Problem: You want to open a file from another application, but the file is not listed in the File **N**ame box.

Solution: The **F**ile **O**pen command assumes that you want to open a Word for Windows document or a file with the extension DOC. To see all files in the current directory, replace `*.DOC` in the File **N**ame box with `*.*` or select All Files from the List Files of **T**ype drop-down list.

Problem: You want to save your document in another file format. The file format you want is not listed in the Save File As **T**ype drop-down list.

Solution: When Word for Windows was installed, the file format conversion you now want to select was not installed. Reinstall Word for Windows, but select only the conversion filters you want for installation. You don't have to reinstall all of Word for Windows.

Problem: Different documents display different commands on the menus, or not all commands are visible on the menus.

Solution: You may have opened a document based on a template that contains customized menus. Templates are guides for specific types of documents and can have styles, macros, tools, and custom menus attached (see Chapter 30). The chapters in Part IV, "Customizing Word for Windows," explain the features that can change the appearance or capabilities of Word for Windows.

Editing and Formatting

Problem: Text changes its formatting when you press the Del or Backspace keys.

Solution: Word for Windows stores paragraph formatting in the paragraph mark at the end of each paragraph. If you delete the paragraph mark of a particular paragraph, it takes on the format of the following paragraph. Choose the Edit Undo command immediately to reverse the deletion and restore the paragraph formatting.

To repair the paragraph, reformat it or copy a paragraph mark from a similar paragraph and paste it at the end of the problem paragraph.

To avoid deleting a paragraph mark inadvertently, turn paragraph marks on by choosing the paragraph mark button at the right end of the ribbon. Or turn on nonprinting characters by choosing the Tools Options command and selecting the All check box in the View Category.

Problem: A message appears, informs you that you don't have enough memory for a large clipboard, and asks whether you want to discard the clipboard.

Solution: After you cut or copy information, it is stored on the clipboard. Discarding the clipboard clears its contents. In most cases, the clipboard contains the information you last cut or copied. If you no longer need this material, discard the clipboard. If you need the information, reduce memory use and recut or recopy the information (see the section "Improving Word for Windows Performance" later in this chapter).

Arranging Text and Graphics

Problem: When moved, a framed group of paragraphs or a table loses its link.

Solution: Framing and moving part of a linked group of paragraphs or a table breaks the link. Choose the Format Frame command and select the Remove Frame button to restore the moved item to the linked group.

Problem: A framed paragraph appears as vertical characters in the frame or in a cell table.

Solution: If the framed paragraph or the table cell contains indents, the indentation may be too wide for the frame or cell, leaving no room in the frame or cell. Choose the Format Paragraph command or use the ruler to remove or reduce the indents until the text fits correctly.

Problem: Text doesn't flow around a positioned frame.

Solution: The amount of space between the frame boundary and the text boundary must be at least 1 inch. Choose the Format Frame command and confirm that the Around option in the dialog box is selected. The Frame dialog box also enables you to change the frame width. You can reduce the frame width to allow enough space for text to wrap around the frame.

Problem: Text inside the frame appears cut off.

Solution: If the screen font doesn't match the fonts available in your printer, the text may not fit correctly in the frame and appear cut off. Choose the Format Character command to change the font of the text inside the frame to a font your printer can print. If you have the TrueType fonts, see Appendix C.

Problem: Unwanted automatic page breaks leave a partially filled page.

Solution: A paragraph or section break format can create unwanted page breaks. Position the insertion point before the unwanted page break. Choose the Format Paragraph command. Clear formatting options such as Page Break Before, Keep with Next, or Keep Lines Together.

Also check the Insert Break command to see that section breaks have not been set to Next Page. You may want the Continuous option.

Problem: Inserted graphics print well, but they appear as blanks on-screen.

Solution: To see graphics on-screen as you work, choose Tools Options View Category and select the Line Breaks and Fonts as Printed check box. Word for Windows operates faster when you don't display the graphics.

Adding Footnotes, Annotations, and Bookmarks

Problem: A footnote reference in the footnote pane cannot be deleted.

Solution: To delete a footnote, you must delete the footnote reference mark in the document. Word for Windows deletes the text in the footnote pane associated with the deleted footnote. Footnotes are renumbered when a footnote is deleted.

Problem: Deleting text in the annotation pane does not delete the annotation.

Solution: To delete an annotation, you must delete the annotation mark in the document.

Problem: Word for Windows cannot go to a bookmark because after you edited the bookmark, its contents disappeared.

Solution: When you delete, move, or replace a character that marks either end of a bookmark, you delete the bookmark. To prevent this problem, create bookmarks by including the space on either side of the text, the number, or the date being marked. When you change data within the bookmark, do not change, move, or delete the spaces that mark the bookmark boundaries. When you copy or move a bookmark, be sure that you include the characters that mark the boundary.

Printing

Problem: The fonts that appear on-screen are different from the fonts that appear when printed.

Solution: Two kinds of fonts exist: screen fonts and printer fonts. Fonts that the selected printer cannot print may appear on-screen. If you use TrueType, the problem of screen fonts not matching printer fonts is resolved automatically. (See Appendix C for details on TrueType.) When screen and printer fonts don't match, the printed document looks different from the document on-screen. To prevent this problem, you can make fonts appear on-screen as they appear when printed. Choose the **Tools Options** command and select the **View** Category, the Linebreaks And Fonts As Printed option.

Problem: Text extends beyond the right margin on-screen.

Solution: You may have selected a printer font that does not have a corresponding screen font. Choose the **Tools Options** command and clear the Linebreaks and Fonts As Printed check box. If you continue to have problems, you may have installed the wrong fonts for your monitor type. To check the type of installed fonts, choose the font icon in the Windows Control Panel. For more information on fonts, see the Appendix C.

Problem: The Print Preview command is not available and installed fonts are not listed in the font list.

Solution: Be sure that you have installed and selected a printer from within Word for Windows. If you add a new printer or change the configuration on your current printer using the Control Panel, you must reselect your printer from within Word for Windows. To select a default printer, choose the printer icon in the Control Panel.

Problem: Your printer does not print with its available font and graphics capabilities.

Solution: Installing and configuring a printer installs the generic printer of a certain class or brand. You may not have installed the specific printer model. After installing an HP LaserJet Series III through the Control Panel, for example, you still need to open File Printer Setup and define the type of printer, its available memory, the installed font cartridges, and the desired print resolution.

Problem: You are unsure which fonts, sizes, and graphics capabilities are available on your currently selected printer.

Solution: Choose the Tools Options View Category command and select the Line Breaks and Fonts as Printed check box to ensure that your printer can print the fonts, sizes, and graphics you use. If your printer cannot print graphics, the graphic shows on-screen as a blank. This option also produces a preview that shows how the document will print.

When you choose Format Character, the fonts and sizes available on the selected printer appear. This feature prevents you from selecting fonts the printer doesn't have.

If you open a document that was formatted on a different printer with different fonts, and you have the Line Breaks and Fonts as Printed option turned on, Word for Windows displays the document using the fonts that will be used in the printer. The ribbon shows the name and size of the original font even though it cannot be printed.

To create a document and print it on a printer that has different capabilities, turn off the Line Breaks and Fonts as Printed option. You now can use all of Word for Windows' features even if your printer cannot print them. Or you can install and select a printer's driver so that you can see how the document will print.

Problem: Some documents print correctly in the portrait (vertical) page orientation but print with incorrect fonts in the landscape (horizontal) orientation.

Solution: Laser printers use font cartridges to store additional fonts. Your laser printer or its font cartridges may contain fonts for portrait orientation but not for landscape orientation. If you have TrueType fonts available, you may want to use them. See Appendix C for more information on TrueType.

Using Styles

Problem: When you change your Normal style, all the heading styles change.

Solution: Heading styles are based on the Normal style. Changing Normal style changes the base style for the Heading styles. You need to redefine each Heading style.

Problem: You apply a style to a sentence and the style formats the entire paragraph.

Solution: Styles always apply to paragraphs. To format a sentence, you must format it manually or change it into its own paragraph before applying the style.

Improving Word for Windows' Performance

Problem: A message says you do not have enough memory to complete an action. This message has appeared at different times, such as when you're placing pictures, using the Equation Editor or Draw, displaying the ruler, and saving or running a macro. Pictures may display with their outline only. Macros may not run.

Solution: You need to increase the amount of memory available. When Word for Windows begins to run low on memory, you see messages warning you that commands or actions cannot be completed. To gain more memory, use one or more of the following techniques:

■ If you must work with multiple files open, save all the open files with the File Save All command.

■ Close unneeded applications.

■ Close unneeded documents. To gain the most memory, close all documents except the one you are working in.

■ Turn off background repagination with the Tools Options General Category command and unselect the Background Repagination check box.

■ Turn off unnecessary screen display items. Use the Tools Options View Category command to turn off the scroll bar, status bar, and set the style names area to zero. Turn on the Picture Placeholders check box to replace graphics with a blank placeholder on screen. Use the View Ribbon, View Ruler, and View Toolbar commands to turn off the ribbon, ruler, and toolbar.

■ Change to draft view with the View Draft command.

■ Put tables in other documents, and then use Insert File to include them.

■ Keep documents smaller than twenty pages, then link them together as described in Chapter 20.

■ Exit Word for Windows, remove any terminate-and-stay-resident (TSR) programs that may be operating, and restart Word for Windows with the document you need.

■ Follow the Windows speed-up techniques described in the Windows manuals and in the README.TXT files in the \WINDOWS directory. You can open these files with Word for Windows.

Using Fields

Problem: When you type field codes, they don't always work even though they look correct.

Solution: One of the most common reasons for this problem is that you have typed the braces—{ }. To enter these braces you must press Ctrl+F9.

Use the **Insert Field** command to insert field codes if typing them doesn't work. This procedure helps you get information in the correct order and also puts the correct number of space characters between different parts of the field code. Incorrect spacing and incorrect spelling are two common errors for typed fields.

Problem: General switches in field codes do not format results as they should.

Solution: Check for one of these problems:

- Ensure that you used a backslash (\ ) for the switch and not a forward slash (/).

- Update the field by selecting it and pressing F9 to ensure that the switch has a chance to change previous results.

- Ensure that the field produces a visible result that can be formatted with a switch.

Problem: After you type a field code, the result does not appear.

Solution: This problem can be caused by one of three things:

- The field code you entered is one that does not produce a visible result. Check the field codes description to see whether a result should appear.

- The field needs to be updated. To update most fields, you select the field and press F9, or choose the **File Print** or **File Print Merge** command. Not all field codes produce a result as soon as they are entered.

- You tried to enter the field characters by typing braces { }, which are not field characters. To enter field characters, you must press Ctrl+F9 (Insert Field). If you already typed the field type and its information, remove the incorrect braces, select the field type and its information, and press Ctrl+F9. Word for Windows encloses your selection in field characters, { }. Press F9 to update the field.

Problem: When you use the {ask} or {fillin} field to display a dialog box that prompts for text, the first word of the prompt appears in the dialog box.

Solution: If the prompt is longer than one word, you must enclose the entire prompt in quotation marks.

Problem: When you use the {macrobutton} and {gotobutton} fields, the text in the buttons doesn't appear correctly in the document.

Solution: Unlike most other field codes, the {macrobutton} and {gotobutton} fields don't require that you enclose the button text in double quotation marks.

Problem: When you press F11 or Alt+F1 to select the next field code, the insertion point disappears.

Solution: When the next field code has results, the insertion point moves to those results and selects them. If no results are available and if you are not viewing the field codes, you cannot see the insertion point when it moves. Press Shift+F9 to see the selected field code.

From Here . . .

For information about troubleshooting topics other than those topics listed here, or for troubleshooting advanced topics such as macros, refer to the chapters covering those topics. Watch for tips in those chapters.

Using Graphics and Charts

PART

III

OUTLINE

Inserting Pictures in Your Document

With Word for Windows, you can illustrate your ideas with pictures created in a graphics program. If a picture is worth a thousand words, think how much typing you may save! Even if your picture is worth somewhat less than a thousand words, illustrating your document with graphics can make your pages more appealing—and that appeal can mean readers pay more attention to your words. Figure 23.1 shows a brochure enhanced with graphic elements.

Pictures you insert into your Word for Windows documents come from many sources. Some come from a stand-alone graphics program, which you can use to create illustrations ranging from the simple to the sophisticated. Some pictures come from clip art packages that provide you with ready-to-use artwork. Some—including photographs—come from scanners that digitize artwork for use in a computer.

All of the pictures you insert come from a source outside of Word for Windows. That makes them different from the graphic objects you create using one of Word for Windows' three built-in graphics programs—Microsoft Draw, Microsoft WordArt, and Microsoft Chart.

(You can learn about each of these built-in programs in Chapters 25, 26, and 27, respectively.) Using one of the built-in graphics programs, you create a graphic that exists only as a part of your Word for Windows document.

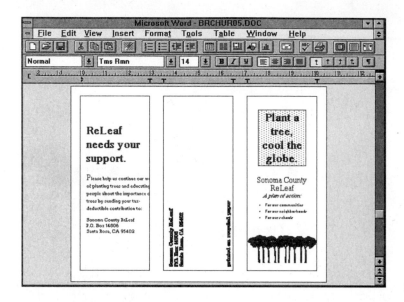

FIG. 23.1.

A picture can make your document more appealing to readers.

You can include pictures created with any graphics program available for the PC (such as CorelDRAW, Windows Paintbrush, PC Paintbrush, or Micrografx Designer) as part of documents created in different programs. For example, pictures created with a stand-alone graphics program often are included in newsletters, flyers, and brochures created with the desktop publishing program Aldus PageMaker. Stand-alone graphics programs often are more powerful than the simple built-in programs that come with Word for Windows.

Reviewing Compatible Formats

Word for Windows is compatible with many of the most frequently used graphics programs. You can import pictures created by any of these programs, or that are in any of these formats:

Program format	File extension
PC Paintbrush	PCX
Tagged Image File Format	TIF (scanned images)
Windows Metafile	WMF
Encapsulated PostScript	EPS
Windows Paintbrush	BMP
Windows Bitmaps	BMP
Computer Graphics Metafile	CGM
HP Graphic Language	HGL
DrawPerfect, WordPerfect	WPG
Micrografx Designer	DRW
Micrografx Draw	DRW
AutoCAD 2D	DXF
AutoCAD Plotter	PLT
Lotus 1-2-3 Graphic	PIC

Don't despair if your favorite graphic program isn't listed. Many programs easily export a graphic (or even part of a graphic) from its native format to a commonly used format. CorelDRAW saves files in its own format with the extension CDR, for example, but can export files as PCX, TIF, WMF, EPS, PIC, and other formats.

Installing the Import Filters

To import pictures into a document, Word for Windows uses special "import filters." One filter is required for each type of file you want to import. If you selected the Complete Setup option when you installed Word for Windows, all the graphic import filters were installed in your system. If you selected a custom installation, you may not have installed all the filters. To see which filters are installed (and consequently which types of graphics you are able to import), choose the Tools Options command. Under Category, select WIN.INI, and in the Application box, select MS Graphic Import Filters. If you cannot read the full line in the Startup Option list, select the item and then use the arrow keys to scroll through the item in the Setting text box. If you need to install an additional graphic filter, refer to Appendix C for detailed information.

Inserting Pictures

You can insert a picture into the text of your document, into a frame, or into a table. Inserting a picture directly into your text is the simplest way to get an illustration into your document. Other techniques, however, offer advantages. Inserting a picture into a frame is useful when you must leave an empty frame in your document as a placeholder until you finish your picture (or get it from someone else). Inserting a picture in one cell of a table enables you to position it adjacent to a caption in the next cell.

There are two ways to insert a picture into your document. You can use a command that asks you to locate the file name and then inserts the picture from disk. (Using this method, you don't even need to own the program used to create the picture.) Or you can open the program used to create the picture, copy the picture into the Windows clipboard, and then paste the picture into your Word for Windows document.

Inserting Pictures Using a Command

You can insert a picture into your document without ever opening the program you used to create the picture. As when opening or saving a Word for Windows file, you must locate the file to insert a picture.

To insert a picture using a command, follow these steps:

1. Position the insertion point where you want to insert the picture.

2. Choose the **Insert Picture** command. The Picture dialog box appears (see fig. 23.2).

3. Locate your file.

   If the drive containing your picture file is different from the current drive, select the drive containing your file from the Drives list.

   From the **Directories** list, select the directory containing your picture file.

4. From the File **Name** list, select the picture file you want to insert.

   If you want to restrict the File **Name** list to a particular file type, select the file type you want to list in the List Files of **Type** box.

5. If you want to see the picture before you insert it, choose the Pre-view button. A miniature version of your picture appears in the Preview Picture box. If you want help finding your file, choose the Find File button and use the Find File features to find your file.

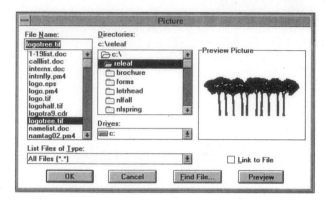

FIG. 23.2.

The Picture
dialog box.

6. If you want to link your picture to its original file, select the **Link** to File option. **Link** to File is discussed in the section "Working with Linked Pictures" later in this chapter and in Chapter 21.

7. Choose OK or press Enter.

When you insert a picture into your Word for Windows document, it falls into place at the location of the insertion point. If you add or delete text preceding the picture, the picture moves with the edited text. Unless you frame and position the picture, it stays with the text. For details about positioning a picture independently of the text, refer to Chapter 24.

 NOTE   If you format a paragraph to have line spacing of an exact amount—one inch, for example—and you insert into that paragraph a two-inch-tall picture, you won't see all of the picture. You can reformat the paragraph containing the picture for Auto line spacing, or set the line spacing to At Least any amount. (For details, refer to Chapter 6.)

Inserting Pictures from the Clipboard

Sometimes the easiest way to get a picture you created using a graphics program into Word for Windows is to copy it in via the clipboard. You can even link the picture to the original when you paste it in so that you can update the imported picture if you later make changes to the original. (See the later section "Working with Linked Pictures" and Chapter 21.) To link a picture, the graphics program must support DDE (dynamic data exchange).

To copy a picture into your document, follow these steps:

1. Start your graphics program, and open the file containing the picture you want to copy into your Word for Windows document.

2. Select the picture.

3. Choose the **E**dit **C**opy command.

4. Switch to your Word for Windows document.

5. Position the insertion point where you want to insert the picture.

6. Choose the **E**dit **P**aste command.

    or

    Choose the **E**dit Paste **S**pecial command to link the picture to the original file. From the Paste Special dialog box select **D**ata Type Picture, and then select Paste Link. For detailed information about how to use Paste Link, refer to Chapter 21.

Working with Pictures

Because Word for Windows is a word processing program, a picture behaves much like a text character when you first insert it. The picture is embedded in the text and stays with the text.

After you insert a picture into your document, however, you can manipulate it in many ways. You can scale the picture to a smaller or larger size, either proportionally or not. You can size it to the exact dimensions you want. You can crop the picture, cutting away portions you don't want to use. You can add a border. You can disassociate a picture from the text where you inserted it, freeing it for positioning anywhere on the page. You can wrap text around the picture, or group it with a caption or another object. To learn how to position or frame a picture, refer to Chapter 24.

You can work with pictures in any view. The page layout view shows you exactly where the picture is positioned and how text wraps around it. Working with pictures in the page layout view can be slow, however, as even the fastest computers slow down when scrolling past a graphic. The normal view displays the picture at the left margin and scrolls a little more quickly than the page layout view. The draft and outline views display only an empty box the size of your picture and scroll even faster.

Selecting Pictures

Before you change a picture, you must select it. When a picture is selected, it has selection handles on all four corners and sides—eight in all (see fig. 23.3). With a mouse, you can use the selection handles to size, crop, or scale the picture.

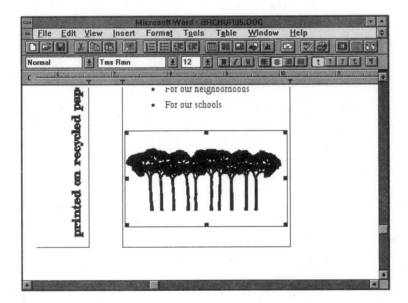

FIG. 23.3.

A selected picture has eight selection handles.

To select a picture with the mouse, follow these steps:

1. Display the picture on your screen.

2. Click on the picture with the mouse pointer.

To select a picture using the keyboard, follow these steps:

1. Position the insertion point to one side of the picture.

2. Press Shift+left-arrow key (to select a picture to the left of the insertion point) or Shift+right-arrow key (to select a picture to the right).

Clicking on an inserted picture selects it. Double-clicking on a picture often has a very different effect: it brings up a graphics program, such as Microsoft Draw, in which you can edit the picture. (This happens because of Word for Windows' OLE technology.) If Microsoft Draw pops up, then you close the program—whether or not you have edited the picture—and the picture's format changes. It becomes an embedded Microsoft Draw object rather than a simple inserted picture. If you display field codes, you will see that your picture is referenced by a field code that specifies the type of object the picture has become.

Scaling, Sizing, and Cropping Pictures

After you insert a picture into your document, you can scale the picture to a smaller or larger size, size it to the exact dimensions you want, or crop away parts of the picture you don't want to use.

You can change the dimensions of a picture in three ways:

- Scaling the picture larger or smaller by a percentage (proportionally or nonproportionally)
- Sizing the picture to fit specified dimensions
- Cropping part of the picture

You can make any of these changes with the mouse or a keyboard command.

Scaling, Sizing, and Cropping Using the Mouse

Using the mouse to scale, size, or crop a picture is visual: it enables you to see how your changes look while you're making them. At the same time, you can monitor your picture's dimensions because a readout in the status bar tells you its exact size. If you use the mouse to change a picture and later want to see what its dimensions are, select the picture and choose Format Picture. The entries in the Crop, Scaling, and Size groups tell you the picture's current dimensions.

To change a picture, you select it and drag the small black selection handles that appear on the sides and corners of the picture. After you select the picture and move the mouse pointer over the selection handles, the pointer turns into a two-headed arrow (see fig. 23.4).

Each of the eight selection handles surrounding a selected picture has a specific purpose. The corner handles enable you to scale or crop from two sides. The side handles enable scaling and cropping from just one side. Any time you drag a handle, the opposite handle stays anchored to its current position.

When you drag a handle toward the center of the picture, you make the picture smaller. When you drag the handle away, you make the picture bigger. (If you're cropping, you add a blank border after you pass the picture's original edges.)

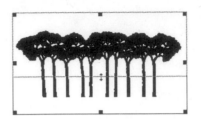

FIG. 23.4.

The two-headed arrow enables you to drag a selected picture's handles to size, scale, or crop the picture.

As you drag the handles to scale or crop the picture, you see a dotted-line box that represents the picture's new size and shape. When you release the mouse button, the picture snaps to fit inside the box.

To scale a picture using the mouse, follow these steps:

1. Select the picture.

2. Move the mouse pointer over a square, black selection handle until it turns into a two-headed arrow.

3. Drag a corner handle to scale the picture proportionally or drag a side handle to scale a picture nonproportionally (see fig. 23.5). The status bar reads Scaling and gives the picture's proportions. (Proportional changes keep the height and width proportions the same.) Release the mouse button.

To crop a picture, follow these steps:

1. Select the picture.

2. Hold down the Shift key.

3. Drag any square, black selection handle. Notice that the status bar reads Cropping and gives the picture's dimension.

4. Release the mouse button.

    Figure 23.6 shows the cropped figure.

Scaling, Sizing, and Cropping Using the Picture Dialog Box

You can use the Picture dialog box to scale, size, or crop a picture. The Picture dialog box includes boxes in which you must enter measurements. Each box has up and down arrows to its right; you can click on the up arrow to increase the measurement, or click on the down arrow to decrease the measurement.

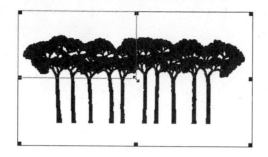 

FIG. 23.5.

Dragging a picture's selection handle scales it smaller or larger.

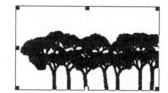

FIG. 23.6.

Cropping a picture means cutting part of it away.

To scale, size, or crop a picture using the Picture dialog box, follow these steps:

1. Select the picture.

2. Choose the Format Picture command. The Picture dialog box appears (see fig. 23.7).

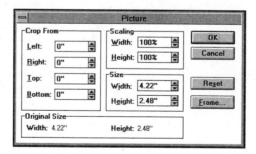

FIG. 23.7.

The Picture dialog box.

3. If you want to crop your picture, in the Crop From group enter the crop amount in the Left, Right, Top, or Bottom box (or click the up or down arrows to increase or decrease the crop amount).

To crop one-half inch off the bottom of the picture, for example, type *.5* in the **B**ottom box. To crop one-quarter inch off the right side as shown in figure 23.8, type *.25* in the **R**ight box.

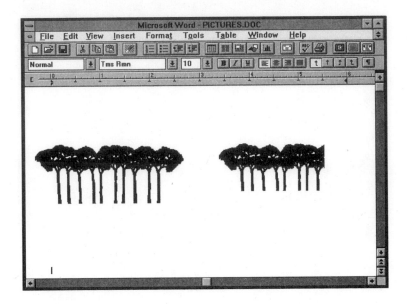

FIG. 23.8.

The picture on the right has been cropped.

4. If you want to scale your picture, in the Scaling group of the Picture dialog box enter a percentage by which you want to scale the picture in the **W**idth and/or **H**eight boxes.

    To scale the picture to half its original size, for example, type *50* (for 50%) in the **W**idth box and *50* in the **H**eight box. To double its size, type *200* (for 200%) in both boxes (see fig. 23.9).

    Typing the identical scaling amount keeps the scaled picture proportional. If you type a different scale in the **W**idth and **H**eight boxes, the picture is distorted.

5. If you want to resize your picture, in the Size group enter an exact size for your picture in the **W**idth and **H**eight boxes.

    If you want your picture to be exactly three inches wide, for example, type *3* in the **W**idth box; if you want it two inches tall, enter *2* in the **H**eight box.

    To help you avoid distorting the picture, its original dimensions are listed in the Original Size box at the bottom of the Picture dialog box.

6. Choose OK or press Enter.

The percent you enter in the Scaling boxes is always a percent of the original size, not a percent of the previous percent; therefore, it is easy to return to the original size.

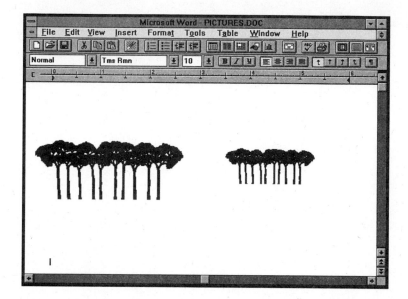

FIG. 23.9.

The same picture can be scaled to different sizes.

T I P   You can select a negative crop distance to crop *out* from the edge of the picture, creating a blank border around the picture. To add a one-quarter inch border on all sides of the picture, for example, type –.25 in the **L**eft, **R**ight, **T**op, and **B**ottom boxes.

Resetting the Picture

You can easily reset your picture to its original dimensions (even if you changed it with the mouse instead of with the Picture dialog box) by following these steps:

1. Select the picture.

2. Choose the Format Picture command.

3. Choose the Reset button.

Adding Lines or a Border

Unless a border is part of your original composition, pictures arrive in your document with no lines around their edges. You can easily add a border. A border can be a box, a shadowed box, or lines on any combination of sides. Many line styles and colors (if you have a color system) are available.

To add lines or a border to a picture, follow these steps:

1. Select the picture.

2. Choose the Format **B**order command. The Border Picture dialog box appears (see fig. 23.10).

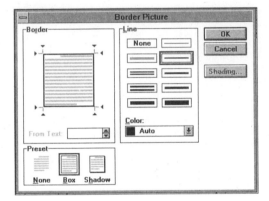

FIG. 23.10.

The Border
Picture dialog
box.

3. If you want lines on any side or sides of the picture, use the Border group. Click on the side of the sample picture where you want a line to appear. (Selected sides have black, triangular selection handles at each end.) Hold Shift to select multiple sides or to unselect a selected side. To use the keyboard, select Border and press any arrow key to cycle through varying combinations of lines.

    or

    If you want a box or shadowed box, select **B**ox or S**h**adow (with a mouse, just click on the appropriate icon) from the Preset group.

4. From the **L**ine group, select the line style you want for the selected line (or lines) or border.

5. From the **C**olor list, select the color you want the selected line (or lines) or border to be (you can type the first letter of the color you want to select).

6. Choose OK or press Enter.

To remove a line or border from a picture, follow these steps:

1. Select the picture.

2. Choose the Format Border command.

3. To remove a line, select the line you want to remove from the Border group, and then select None from the Line group. (Refer to step 3 in the preceding instructions for adding a line or border.)

   or

   To remove a box, or to remove all lines, select None from the Preset group.

4. Choose OK or press Enter.

Moving or Copying a Picture

Moving and copying a picture is much the same as moving or copying text in your document. To copy a picture, select it, choose the **Edit Copy** command (Ctrl+C or Ctrl+Ins), move the insertion point where you want to copy the picture in your document, and choose **Edit Paste** (Ctrl+V or Shift+Ins).

To move a picture, select it, choose **Edit Cut** (Ctrl+X or Shift+Del), move the insertion point where you want to move the picture, and choose **Edit Paste** (Ctrl+V or Shift+Ins).

You also can move a picture with the mouse. Position the mouse pointer over the selected picture, click and hold the left mouse button, drag the picture to its new location, and release the mouse button. As you drag the picture, the mouse pointer appears as a pointer with a small box, and a dotted vertical line indicates the picture's new position. (This technique works for any text or object you select.)

To copy a picture from its original location, select the picture, press and hold the Ctrl key, and drag the picture to its new location.

When you move or copy an unframed picture by using the techniques described in this section, the picture remains linked to the text in your document. It's like a character: if new text is added above the picture, the picture moves down; if the paragraph containing the picture is centered, the picture is centered with the paragraph. If you frame a picture, however, you can unlink it from the text and freely move it around in your document as an independent object. You can even specify that text should wrap around a framed picture, or frame a picture together with text, such as a caption, so that the two move together. To learn more about frames, refer to Chapter 24.

T I P

Editing Pictures with Microsoft Draw

Microsoft Draw is an OLE (object linking and embedding)-based drawing program included with Word for Windows. You can use Microsoft Draw to edit many types of pictures. Basic instructions for getting in and out of Draw are included in this section. Refer to Chapter 25 for in-depth details about using the program.

You can easily find out whether your picture is compatible with Microsoft Draw: simply double-click on the picture and if Draw starts, your picture is compatible. Microsoft Draw uses OLE technology to directly start a program when you double-click on one of its objects.

To edit pictures with Microsoft Draw, follow these steps:

1. Double-click the picture to edit. Microsoft Draw pops up on your screen if your picture is compatible with it (see fig. 23.11).

   or

   Select the picture and choose the Edit Microsoft Drawing **O**bject command.

2. Make your changes to the picture.

3. Choose the **F**ile **U**pdate command to update the picture in Word for Windows without closing Microsoft Draw.

or

Choose the **F**ile E**x**it and Return command to update the picture and exit Microsoft Draw.

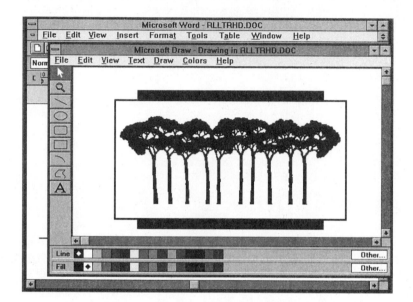

You can use the OLE-based Microsoft Draw to edit pictures.

Microsoft Draw is directly compatible with files formatted as WMF (Word Metafile) and BMP (Bitmap) graphic files. You can use Draw to open many other types of files as well (including TIF, PCX, EPS, and others) but two things happen: first, the file is converted to a Draw-format file; second, in the conversion, much of the original file's detail and resolution might be lost. If you need to retain quality, use the original graphic program to edit your picture.

From Here . . .

In this chapter you learned that you can insert pictures created in stand-alone graphics programs into your Word for Windows document. You learned that when inserted, you can scale a picture to the size you need, crop away unnecessary portions, add a border, edit the picture, and even link a picture to its original.

Many programs you can use to create sophisticated pictures are available, as are collections of computer "clip art," or pre-existing art you can use to illustrate your document. To find out about some of these programs, refer to "The Windows Shopping Guide" in Que's *Using Windows 3*.

One of the most important steps you can take with a picture is to frame it so that you can position it freely on your page and so that text can wrap around it. To learn about framing and positioning, refer to Chapter 24.

You can edit many types of pictures using the built-in program Microsoft Draw. To learn how to use Draw, refer to Chapter 25.

Finally, pictures are a very important component of desktop publishing. To see how you can use pictures creatively in your documents, refer to Chapter 28.

Framing and Positioning Text and Graphics

W ord for Windows has many features that help make your pages look better—borders add graphical appeal to text; columns make text more readable; pictures add interest to stories. Frames, however, take your document a step further: with frames, you can leave behind traditional word processing and enter the world of page layout.

In Word for Windows, you can frame many types of objects, including text, tables, pictures, captions, charts, equations, and even blank space (in case you want to add non-computer art to your document after you print it). You can frame objects singly or together (you can frame a picture with a caption, for example). You can add lines and borders to your framed objects.

After you frame an object, you can position it anywhere you want on the page—like hanging a picture on a wall. You can drag it into position with a mouse or specify its precise position on the page with a command. By positioning a framed object on the page, you free the object from its surrounding text. Frames are a critical tool in helping you use Word for Windows to design a pleasing, professional, and creative page layout.

Creating, Selecting, and Removing Frames

Framing text or an object sets it apart from the rest of your document. You can frame a paragraph, add a border around it, and move it into the left margin of a report. The paragraph becomes a graphic element on the page and attracts the reader's attention. You can frame a picture and a caption together and move them into the middle of a page so that text wraps around them. The picture and caption exist as a unit, so they aren't separated when you later edit your document (see fig. 24.1 for examples of frames).

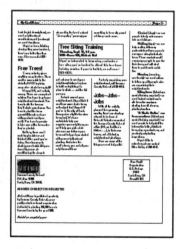

FIG. 24.1.

Framed text and graphics.

To create a frame, you simply select the object—or objects—you want to frame and choose the Insert Frame command or the Frame button on the toolbar. You can create a frame in any view. Page layout is the only view, however, that accurately shows where a frame is positioned in your document and how text wraps around the frame. If you create a frame in the normal view, Word for Windows displays a dialog box to suggest that you switch to page layout view . The following sections describe how text and objects behave inside (and outside) a frame, how to select frames so that you can edit or position them, how frames look in different views, and how you can remove a frame (and what happens when you do).

Framing Text

You can frame any amount of text—from one character to an entire page. When you first frame selected text, the frame is the same size as the text. If you change the size of the frame, the text wraps to accommodate the frame's new dimensions. After you frame text, it becomes an object you can move, border, and shade.

In page layout view, you can see your frame interact with the rest of the text on the page. You can see how frames appear in the normal, draft, and outline views in the section "Working in Different Views" later in this chapter.

To frame text, follow these steps:

1. If you're not in page layout view, choose the View Page Layout command.

2. Select the text you want to frame.

3. Choose the Insert Frame command or choose the Frame button on the toolbar. Selection handles appear around the edges of your framed text (see fig. 24.2). When you frame text, Word for Windows automatically adds a border.

   If you are in the normal view when you insert a frame, Word for Windows displays a dialog box suggesting that you switch to the page layout view (see fig. 24.3). Choose Yes.

Framed objects that are selected have eight selection handles on the corners and sides. Selection handles appear as small, black squares, which you can use to resize your frame. (See the section "Sizing and Cropping Frames" later in this chapter.)

If you frame only part of a paragraph, then the framed text becomes a separate paragraph and moves outside of the paragraph it's within. You then can move the framed text anywhere on the page (see the later section "Moving and Positioning Frames").

When you first insert a frame around selected text, the frame is the same width as the margins or column and the same height as the text. You cannot change the width of the frame by changing the width of the text—if you indent the paragraphs inside the frame, they are indented from the frame. You can change the height of a frame, however, by changing the text—if you increase the size of the text inside a frame, or add a line or two, the frame grows taller to accommodate your changes.

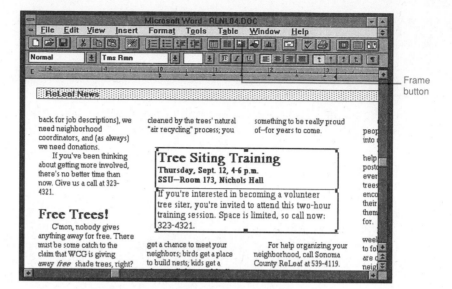

Frame
button

FIG. 24.2.

Framed objects
have selection
handles on the
corners and
sides.

FIG. 24.3.

If you insert a
frame in normal
view, Word for
Windows
suggests that
you switch to
page layout
view.

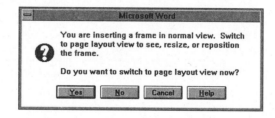

If you change the size of a frame, the text wraps to accommodate the new size because text wraps to fit its boundaries (whether they are margins, indents, columns, or a cell in a table). If you frame a paragraph to use as a pulled-quote in a newsletter, and then resize the frame to make it narrower, for example, the text within the frame wraps to accommodate the frame's new width. The frame grows taller because the wrapped text occupies more vertical space. For more details on sizing frames, refer to the later section "Sizing and Cropping Frames."

T I P

You can indent a paragraph inside a frame, but consider the implications: if you have a two-inch-wide frame and the text inside the frame has one-inch left and right margin indents that you set before inserting the frame, you get a frame containing a vertical string of characters trying to fit within your impossible specifications (see fig. 24.4). To fix it, reduce the indentations or widen the frame.

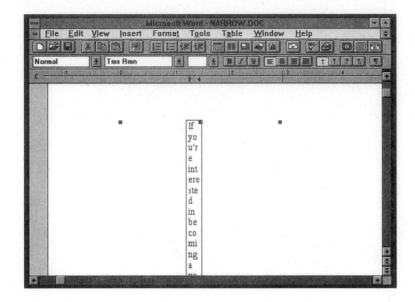

FIG. 24.4.

A frame containing text with indents that are too wide.

You also have control of the text around the outside of a frame. You can specify whether text wraps around the frame or not, and how far from surrounding text the frame appears. See the upcoming sections "Wrapping Text around a Frame" and "Moving and Positioning Frames."

Framing Tables

Framing a table is like framing text: you select a row or the entire table and insert the frame. You cannot frame just a cell—if you select a cell and choose the **Insert Frame** command, you frame the entire row containing the selected cell. You also cannot frame a single column in a table—if you select a column and insert a frame, you frame the entire table.

To frame a row or a table, follow these steps:

1. Select the row you want to frame, or select the entire table.

To frame	Select
A row	One cell or an entire row
A table	One column or the entire table

2. Choose the **Insert Frame** command or choose the Frame button on the toolbar.

Because you just inserted the frame, it is selected, and the eight selection handles appear on the corners and sides of the frame (see fig. 24.5). You can use these handles to resize the frame.

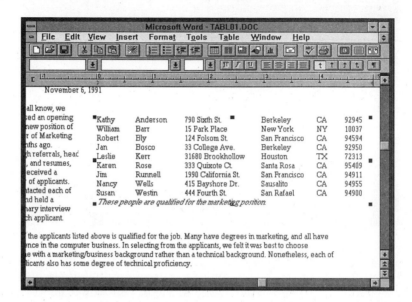

FIG. 24.5.

A newly framed table.

Framing a table makes it a movable object on your page. In a report, for example, you may want to center a table containing pertinent data to give it prominence on the page. Or you may want the flexibility to move the table around to different locations on the page, to see what looks best. You can move a framed row to a different location on the page and make it a separate table.

Framing Pictures and Other Graphic Objects

If you select an inserted, embedded, or copied picture or other graphic into your document (such as a Microsoft Draw object or a piece of clip art), the graphic's selection handles look much like a frame's selection handles. You can use the selection handles to resize or crop the graphic, to move it to another place in the text, or to add a border. Despite the graphic selection handles, however, the graphic has no frame. To position your graphic freely on the page or wrap text around it, you must add a frame.

To frame a picture or graphic, follow these steps:

1. Select the graphic.

   Mouse: Simply click on the graphic.

   Keyboard: Position the insertion point next to the graphic, and press Shift+up- or down-arrow key to move the insertion point across the graphic.

   A selected graphic appears with selection handles (if you've selected it by clicking with the mouse) or reversed (if you've selected it with Shift+arrow key and included the paragraph end mark in your selection).

2. Choose the **Insert F**rame command or choose the Frame button on the toolbar.

You can remove a frame from a graphic (see the upcoming section "Removing a Frame"). If you remove a frame, however, the graphic loses its position. To later reposition the graphic with the Forma**t F**rame command, first frame the graphic.

Selecting a Framed Object

In most Windows programs, as in many other programs, you must select an object before you can do something to it so that the program knows where to apply your actions. In Word for Windows, before you can move, border, size, position, or wrap text around a framed object, you first must select it.

You can select a framed object using the mouse or the keyboard. Usually, the easiest way is to use the mouse. Text is an exception because you can position the insertion point inside the framed text and choose the Forma**t F**rame command to select the frame.

A selected frame appears with black selection handles on its corners and sides. If you move the mouse pointer across the selected frame, the arrow or insertion point changes. On top of the selection handles, the insertion point turns into a two-headed arrow (used to size the frame); on top of the border surrounding the frame, it turns into a four-headed arrow (used to move the frame). See the section "Moving and Positioning Frames" later in this chapter for details.

To select a frame with a mouse, follow these steps:

1. Choose the **View P**age Layout command if it isn't already selected.

2. Click anywhere inside the frame, or on the frame's border.

You can select a framed object by clicking on the object, but to select a text frame, you must click on the frame's border.

To select a frame containing text with the keyboard, follow these steps:

1. Position the insertion point inside the frame.

2. Choose the Format Frame command.

3. Make your frame formatting choices, then choose OK or press Enter.

T I P   Sometimes selecting framed text is easiest in normal view. Because a text frame remains linked to its surrounding text by default, moving the insertion point left and right using arrow keys may bypass the framed text for awhile—until you arrive at the frame's location. To use arrow keys to move the insertion point into a frame containing text, position the insertion point above or below the text (rather than to the right or left) and press the up- or down-arrow key.

To select a frame containing a graphic with the keyboard, follow these steps:

1. Display page layout view by choosing the View Page Layout command.

2. Position the insertion point exactly next to the graphic and press Shift+left- or right-arrow key so that the insertion point moves across the graphic.

or

Position the insertion point inside the text above or below the graphic and press the up- or down-arrow key.

Working in Different Views

In page layout view, you can see where framed objects are positioned and how the text wraps around them (see fig. 24.6). In any view besides page layout, a framed object or text appears at the left margin with one or more small black squares at the left margin (see fig. 24.7). You usually work with frames in page layout view.

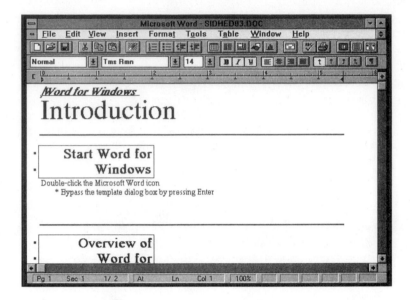

FIG. 24.6.

In page layout view, a framed object appears in place in your document.

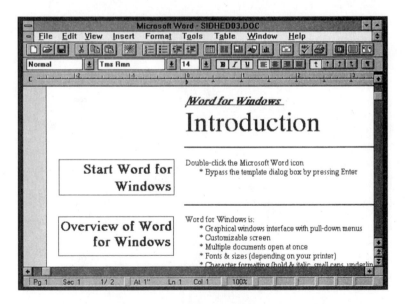

FIG. 24.7.

In normal view, a framed object appears with black squares in the left margin.

You can select a framed object in any view, and you can format it in any view with the Format Frame command (options include sizing the framed object, positioning it, and wrapping text around it). You can even insert a frame in normal view, although Word for Windows advises you to switch to page layout view. In normal, draft, and outline views, however, you see the framed object aligned to the margin, not positioned. You cannot move the object by dragging it with the mouse, as you can in page layout view.

Working in normal or draft view is faster—and indeed, that's the purpose of having these views. Anything graphical takes longer to redraw on your computer screen—in Word for Windows or any other program. If you're working very fast and you're on a deadline, do your layout in page layout view, and switch to normal or draft view for typing.

Inserting a Blank Frame

Sometimes you want to insert a blank frame to leave a space for a photograph or artwork to be inserted during copying or offset printing. When you create a blank frame, you must specify its size.

To insert a blank frame, follow these steps:

1. Make sure that no text, table, or other object is selected.

2. Choose the **Insert Frame** command or choose the Frame button on the toolbar. A crosshair appears on your screen, and a message in the status bar at the bottom of the screen reads Click and drag to insert frame (see fig. 24.8).

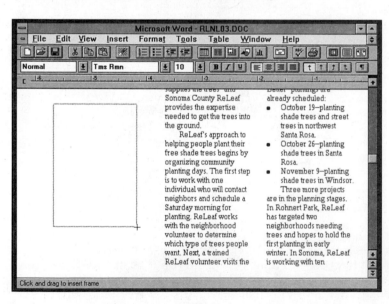

FIG. 24.8.

When you insert a blank frame, you must define its size.

3. Insert the frame with the mouse or keyboard.

   Mouse: Click and hold the left mouse button where you want to start the frame, drag to where you want the frame to end, and release the button.

   Keyboard: Use the arrow keys to position the crosshair where you want to start the frame, press Enter, use the arrow keys to move the crosshair where you want the frame to end, and press Enter again.

   To create a frame in larger increments, press Shift+up arrow or Shift+down arrow, or press Tab (to move the crosshair in increments the size of your default tab stops), or press Shift+Tab (to move backwards in tab stop increments).

When you insert an empty frame, it arrives with the insertion point flashing in the upper left corner (depending on the current paragraph formatting, of course). If you type text in the frame now, the text wraps to fit the size of the frame (and the frame expands as you continue typing). You also can use the **I**nsert commands to insert a picture, file, or other object (or objects) in the frame at this time.

Like text, a blank frame is automatically formatted with a border. Use the Forma**t B**order command to change the frame's border.

Removing a Frame

Removing a frame does not remove its contents. You can remove a frame from a paragraph or a table, for example, and even though the frame is gone, the paragraph or the table is still there.

Removing a frame does remove frame formatting. If text is wrapped around the framed paragraph, it doesn't wrap after you remove the frame. If the framed table was positioned in the center of the page, it moves back to where it was before you inserted the frame.

To remove a frame, follow these steps:

1. Select the framed object, or select the blank frame.

   For text, position the insertion point inside the framed text.

2. Choose the Forma**t F**rame command.

3. Choose the **R**emove Frame button.

A frame is a paragraph-level formatting command, and like a paragraph, the paragraph mark at the end of a frame stores the information defining the frame. If you delete the paragraph mark, you delete the frame (but not the paragraph). If you position the framed text, the text loses its position and moves back to where you inserted it. If two paragraphs are in a frame, and you delete the paragraph mark for the second paragraph, then the second paragraph moves outside of the frame, and the first stays in.

Wrapping Text around a Frame

If a frame is smaller than the page or column it's in, you may want to wrap text around it. By default, when you first insert a frame, the surrounding text wraps around the frame.

Text wraps around a frame no matter how many columns of text are on a page (see fig. 24.9). In order for text to wrap, however, at least one inch of text must be on the left or right of the frame.

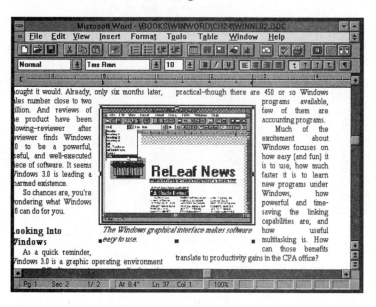

FIG. 24.9.

By default, text wraps around a frame.

To wrap text around a framed object and specify the distance between the frame and text, follow these steps:

1. Select the frame.

2. Choose the Format Frame command. The Frame dialog box appears (see fig. 24.10).

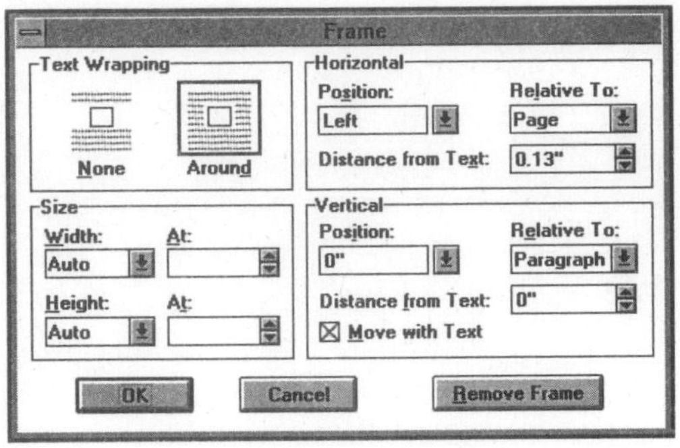

FIG. 24.10.

The Frame
dialog box.

3. In the Text Wrapping group (top left), select the Around option.

4. From the Horizontal group (top right), select the Distance from
    Text option. Type, in decimal numbers, the distance you want
    between the frame and the text to its left and right; or click the up
    or down arrows to increase or decrease the distance.

5. From the Vertical group (bottom right) select the Distance from
    Text option. Type, in decimal numbers, the distance you want
    between the frame and the text above and below; or click the up
    or down arrows to increase or decrease the distance.

6. Choose OK or press Enter.

The Distance from Text options usually are measured in decimal
inches. If you want to use some other measurement system, however,
type the distance measurements in the appropriate increments followed by the appropriate abbreviation (*pt* for points, *pi* for picas, or *cm*
for centimeters). You can change your measurement system by choosing the Tools Options command and selecting the General Category.
Then from the Measurement Units list, select inches, centimeters,
points, or picas.

If later you don't want text to wrap around the frame, select the frame
and choose Format Frame. Select the None option from the Text Wrapping group. Deleting the frame also causes text to no longer wrap
around the object.

If you specify a wide Distance for Text, you may create a space
around the frame that is too narrow for text. Remember that you
need at least an inch of space to the left or right of a frame in order
for text to wrap there. If text doesn't wrap around your frame, make
the distance from text smaller, or make the frame narrower.

T I P

Sizing Frames

When you first insert a frame around text or an object, the frame is selected. Square black selection handles appear on each corner and side of a selected frame—eight in all. The frame is the same size as the text or object. (Text frames are as wide as your margins or column. If the text is indented, a frame is wider than the indented text.)

You can size a frame proportionally so that it becomes larger or smaller but keeps its shape, or nonproportionally so that it stretches into a new shape. Using a mouse, drag the handles to size the frame. With the keyboard, use the Format Frame command to reshape a frame.

Although frames, by default, are the size of the object they contain (or the width of the text margins), you can resize them to the same size as their contents or to a different size. If you set the frame size to Auto, the frame adjusts to accommodate the text or object it contains. You can scale a picture larger, for example, and the frame adjusts to fit. If you specify a measured size for the frame, however, the frame may be larger or smaller than the object it contains. If it is smaller, it may hide part of the frame's contents. If the frame contains a graphic, the graphic is cropped; if the frame contains text, some words may be hidden.

The only way to make a frame larger or smaller than its contents is to use the Format Frame command and set an exact size for the frame. Scaling a graphic with the mouse scales the graphic, not the frame, and the frame adjusts to fit. When you use the mouse to scale a text frame, you can change the frame's shape, but not its volume—the frame always adjusts to fit the size of the text.

Sizing Frames with a Mouse

You can use a mouse to size a frame that encloses text or a graphic object such as an inserted picture or an embedded equation. You can easily select and size a text frame by using the mouse. The text adjusts to fit. (If you make the frame too large for the text, the frame will include a blank space at the end of the text; if you try to make the frame too small, it adjusts to fit the text.)

When you use a mouse to size a graphic frame, however, you probably are resizing the object, not the frame. On a newly framed graphic, the frame is by default the same size as the object. When you select the frame, you really are selecting the object; thus you are sizing the object. The frame adjusts to fit the resized object (unless you earlier specified an exact measurement for the frame).

You can select a frame around a graphic object rather than the graphic itself only when the frame is larger than the graphic. The frame might be larger than the graphic if your graphic is framed together with text (such as a caption) or if you have used the Format Frame command to specify for the frame an exact measurement which is larger than the graphic. You learn how to do that in the next section.

To size a frame, follow these steps:

1. Select the frame so that the black selection handles appear on all four sides and corners.

2. Move the mouse pointer over one of the selection handles so that it turns into a two-headed arrow (see fig. 24.11). This arrow is the sizing arrow.

FIG. 24.11.

The two-headed sizing arrow for the frame.

3. Click and hold the left mouse button, then drag the sizing arrow to reshape the frame. A dotted-line box shows you the frame's new shape as you drag the arrow.

4. Release the mouse button when the frame is the size you want.

Be careful: if you specify an exact size for a text frame and later resize the frame by using the mouse, you *can* size the frame smaller than text. The reason is that the frame is still set to an exact size in the Frame dialog box, and you now are changing the exact size.

T I P

Sizing Frames with the Keyboard

Using the Format Frame command to size or crop a frame has two advantages: you can specify the frame's precise dimensions; and you can size the frame around a graphic, rather than size the graphic itself.

If you choose the Format Frame command to display the Frame dialog box, you see that the Width and Height options in the Size group (bottom left of the dialog box) are set to Auto. The frame is set to the same size as its contents, so if you change the size of the object, the frame adjusts to be the same size. You can make the frame a fixed size, however. You can make the frame's width and height the exact size you want with the Exactly option, specifying the frame's exact dimensions (see fig. 24.12). You also can use the At Least option to specify that the frame be at least a certain height (see fig. 24.13). (This feature is most useful for text, when you want the frame to be an exact width, and you want it to be at least a certain height, but always tall enough to include all the text.)

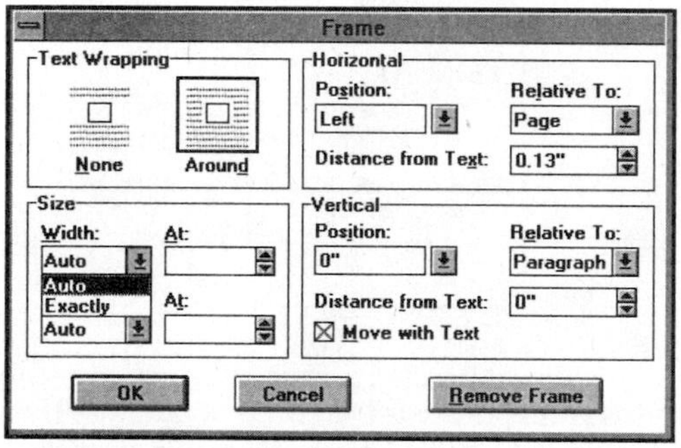

FIG. 24.12.

The Frame dialog box with a new frame's width set to Auto.

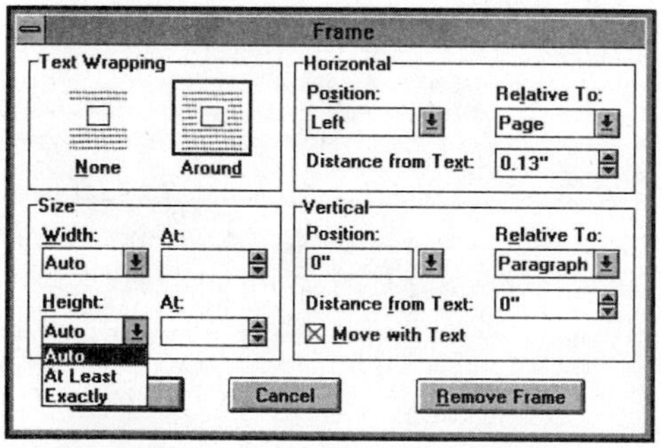

FIG. 24.13.

The Frame dialog box with a new frame's height set to Auto.

If you make a frame an exact size rather than the auto size, the frame is likely to be a different size than its contents. If the frame is larger than its contents, you insert a blank space below the contents. If the frame is smaller than the contents, you hide, or crop, part of the contents. The text or graphic itself does not change size. (If you want to change the size of a graphic, use the mouse technique described in the preceding section to drag the selection handles, or use the Format Picture command.)

To size a frame with the keyboard command, follow these steps:

1. Select the framed text or object. The square black selection handles appear.

2. Choose the Format Frame command. The Frame dialog box appears.

3. Select **Width** and **Height** options in the Size group.

Option	Function
Auto	Sizes the frame so that it is the same size as the framed object.
At Least (**Height** only)	Makes the frame at least as tall as you specify, but always tall enough to include the entire text or graphic.
Exactly	Makes the frame exactly the size you specify.

4. If you select Exactly for your **Width**, specify the exact width of your frame in the **At** box. Type in the width, or click the up or down arrow to increase or decrease the width.

5. If you select At Least or Exactly for your **Height**, specify the minimum or exact height of your frame in the **At** box. Type in the height, or click the up or down arrow to increase or decrease the width.

You may want to size a frame larger than the object it contains to add another object or more text inside the frame. Using this technique, you can create space for a caption underneath a graphic, for example.

T I P

Positioning Frames

A frame separates an object from the text on a page so that you can move the object independently. Word for Windows by default positions a framed object relative to the text surrounding it, not relative to the page. (You can easily override this default.) Every framed object also retains its connection to its roots—if you remove the frame, the object moves back to the beginning of the current paragraph.

You can position a framed object in two ways: you can select and drag it with the mouse, or you can select the object, choose the Format Frame command, and specify its precise position on the page.

A frame can contain more than one object. A frame often contains both a picture and a caption, for example. You can link two objects with a frame, and move them as a unit.

T I P   Use the View buttons on the toolbar to help you position objects. The Zoom Page Width button (last button on the right) shows the full width of a page and is helpful when you want to see where you're moving a framed object. Similarly, you can use the View Zoom command to zoom to a larger percentage when you want a closer look at how text wraps around a frame.

If a framed object is linked to another program, and you move part of it (for example, the caption) away from its original position, you break the link for the part of the text you moved. Similarly, if you designate a framed object as a bookmark, and you move part of the bookmark, then you remove the part you moved from the bookmark. If you frame and move the entire bookmark, however, Word for Windows remembers the bookmark and still finds it, even in its new position.

Moving a Frame with a Mouse

Using a mouse is probably the easiest way to move a framed object. It isn't as precise, however, as positioning the frame using the Frame dialog box (discussed in the next sections on positioning a frame).

By default, framed objects move with their surrounding text. If you add or delete text near the framed object, causing the text to move up or down on the page (or even to the next page), the object stays with its related text. If you want a framed object linked to its position on the page, regardless of where the surrounding text moves, choose the Format Frame command, and unselect the Move with Text option. (The option is unselected if no X appears in its box.)

To move a framed object with the mouse, follow these steps:

1. Select the framed object you want to move.

2. Move the mouse pointer over the frame until it turns into a four-headed arrow (see fig. 24.14).

FIG. 24.14.

The four-headed move arrow.

3. Click the left mouse button, drag the framed object to its new location, and release the mouse button. Even on a fast PC, graphics can be slow to redraw on-screen.

As you move a frame, the first word of the surrounding paragraph is underlined to help you know with which text the frame is associated.

T I P You can use Word for Windows' automatic scrolling feature to move a framed object from one page to another. In any view, select the object you want to move, drag it to the top of the screen (if you want to move it to the preceding page) or to the bottom of the screen (if you want to move it to the next page). By "pushing" the object into the top or bottom of your screen, you cause the text to scroll. If you continue holding the mouse button, the pages continue to scroll, and the frame continues to move. Release the mouse button when you get to the page where you want to move your framed object. If the status bar is displayed, you can see what page you're on when you release the mouse button.

Positioning a Frame Horizontally

Positioning a frame with a command is different from dragging it with a mouse. Dragging is visual, but it's not precise. When you position a frame by using a command, you specify exactly where it appears on the page and what you want it positioned relative to. You can center the frame horizontally relative to the page or a column, for example, or you can position it relative to the outside margins in a facing-page layout.

To position a frame horizontally, follow these steps:

1. Select the framed object.

2. Choose the Format Frame command. The Frame dialog box appears (refer to fig. 24.10).

3. In the Horizontal Position box, select the horizontal position for your frame.

Select	To position the frame
Left	At the left side of the margin, page or column
Right	At the right side of the margin, page or column
Center	Centered between the left and right margins, page edges, or column edges
Inside	At the inside edge of the margin, page, or column
Outside	At the outside edge of the margin, page, or column

4. In the Relative To box, select the boundary you want your frame positioned relative to.

Select	To position the frame relative to
Margin	The left or right margin
Page	The left or right edge of the page
Column	The left or right edge of the current column

5. In the Distance from Text box, type the amount of space you want between the frame and the text on the left and right sides of the frame, or click the up or down arrows to increase or decrease the distance.

6. Choose OK or press Enter.

Positioning a Frame Vertically

Positioning a frame vertically anchors it somewhere between the top and bottom of the page. Unless you unselect the **M**ove with Text option, however, the frame moves with its surrounding text. If the text moves to the next page, so does the frame—but it remains positioned in the same relative place.

If you center a frame vertically between the top and bottom margins, for example, then add so much text before the frame that its surrounding text moves to the top of the next page, the frame also moves to the next page, but it is still centered on the page.

To position a frame vertically on the page, follow these steps:

1. Select the frame.

2. Choose the Forma**t F**rame command. The Frame dialog box appears.

3. In the Vertical Position box, select or type the vertical position for your frame.

Type or Select	Positions the frame
A distance in inches	At a measured distance from the margin, page, or paragraph
Top	At the top margin, top of the page, or top edge of the paragraph

Type or Select	Positions the frame
Bottom	At the bottom margin, bottom of the page, or bottom edge of the paragraph
Center	Centered between the top and bottom margins or page edges, or centered between the top and bottom of the paragraph

4. In the Relative To box, select the boundary you want the frame positioned relative to.

Select	Positions the frame relative to
Margin	The top or bottom margin
Page	The top or bottom edge of the page
Paragraph	The top or bottom of the current paragraph

5. In the Distance from Text box, type the amount of space you want between the frame and the text above or below the frame. Or click the up or down arrows to increase or decrease the distance.

6. If you don't want the frame to move with its surrounding text, unselect the **M**ove with Text option so that no X appears in the option box.

   With this option unselected, the frame stays anchored to its spot on the page, no matter how the text moves. If you select this option, a frame moves with its surrounding text.

7. Choose OK or press Enter.

Positioning a Frame in a Margin

Because you can move or position a frame independently of the text on the page, you can move it into the margin (or partially into the margin) with text wrapping around it. You can create an empty frame, for example, fill it with a color, and move it to the top left of the first page of a newsletter to give the masthead a graphic effect. Or you can use a style to format tips in a training document as italicized and positioned in the inside margins. Perhaps your document's style is to include headings in the left margin of each page (see examples in fig. 24.15). Positioning text in a margin can give it emphasis in your document; positioning a graphic in a margin can make your page more interesting. Be creative!

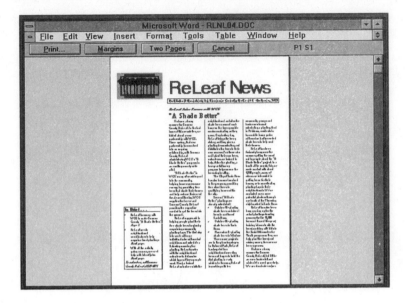

FIG. 25.15.

You can
position frames
in the margins.

When you position a frame in a margin, remember your printer's limitations. Most laser printers cannot print within one-quarter of an inch from the paper's edges.

If you're working with facing pages, you can position a frame relative to the inside or outside page edges. (For information about creating facing pages, refer to Chapter 8.)

Unless you unselect the **M**ove with Text option in the Frame dialog box, your frame moves with its surrounding text. If your document contains subheadings you intend to frame and position in the left margins, for example, then the subheads move up or down with the text to their right. If you create "sideheads," you want the headers to move with the text. Create a style for your sideheads to save time and ensure consistency in your document.

From Here . . .

Frames separate text or an object from the text in your document and enable the framed object—or objects—to move independently. You can position a frame anywhere on a page, even in the margins. Using a frame, you can wrap text around an object or group of objects.

One of the most common objects to frame is an inserted graphic. To learn about working with graphics, refer to Chapter 23. You also can frame a chart from the Microsoft Chart program; refer to Chapter 27.

Or you may frame a picture drawn with Microsoft Draw or Microsoft WordArt; refer to Chapters 25 and 26.

One of the most important uses of frames and positioning is in desktop publishing. Frames turn Word for Windows into a program that rivals desktop publishing programs like PageMaker for simple projects. To learn how you can use frames in desktop publishing, refer to Chapter 28.

Working with Microsoft Draw

An illustrated page can be much more interesting—and much more informative—than a page with only words. With Microsoft Draw, a program that comes free with Word for Windows, you can illustrate your document without ever leaving Word for Windows. Although Microsoft Draw is a simple program meant to accessorize Word for Windows, it is nonetheless powerful enough that it may be the only drawing program you need.

OLE, which is a new concept in Windows software, stands for *object linking and embedding*. OLE means that you can easily access one program from within another. To access Microsoft Draw from within Word for Windows, for example, you choose a command to insert a Microsoft Draw object, and Microsoft Draw pops up. You create your drawing, exit Microsoft Draw, and Draw embeds your drawing into your Word for Windows document. The drawing remains linked to Microsoft Draw, however; if you want to edit the drawing later, you double-click the drawing to pop up Microsoft Draw again.

The OLE concept works with other programs besides Microsoft Draw. You can, for example, embed an Excel chart in a Word for Windows document with an OLE link (Excel is Microsoft's spreadsheet program).

For details on integrating with other programs, see Chapter 21. The programs WordArt (for manipulating text), Equation (for writing scientific and mathematical equations), and Microsoft Graph (for creating graphs) also are, like Microsoft Draw, OLE-based programs that come free with Word for Windows. Any other major application that supports OLE can access other OLE-based programs in the same way that Word for Windows accesses Microsoft Draw.

Understanding Graphics Programs

Two general varieties of graphics programs are available: object-oriented drawing programs and bit-mapped painting programs. Microsoft Draw is an object-oriented drawing program. It creates objects on the screen, including squares, circles, lines, and freeform shapes, which can be edited, moved around, and layered on the screen. (See fig. 25.1 for an example of an illustration created with Microsoft Draw.) In contrast, a bit-mapped painting program, such as Microsoft Paintbrush, which comes free with Windows, works in a single, flat layer on your screen; shapes you create using Paintbrush can be erased and redrawn, but not edited. Each type of program has its benefits.

FIG. 25.1.

An illustration created with Microsoft Draw.

Starting and Exiting Microsoft Draw

As an OLE-based accessory program for Word for Windows, Microsoft Draw works only from within Word for Windows (or from within other applications supporting OLE technology). To start Microsoft Draw, you first must open a Word for Windows document, or start a new document.

To start Microsoft Draw, follow these steps:

1. Open a Word for Windows document or create a new document.

2. Position the insertion point where you want to insert your drawing.

3. Choose the **Insert O**bject command. The Object dialog box pops up (see fig. 25.2).

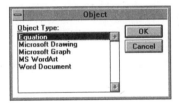

The Object dialog box.

4. Select Microsoft Drawing.

5. Choose OK or press Enter. Microsoft Draw pops up in a new window on your screen.

As an alternative, you can start Microsoft Draw by positioning the insertion point where you want to include a drawing and choosing the Insert Drawing button on the toolbar (see fig. 25.3).

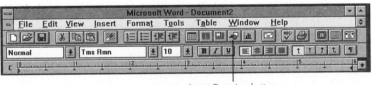

Insert Drawing button

The Insert Drawing button on the toolbar.

To add your Microsoft Draw drawing to your Word for Windows document, do one of the following:

- In Microsoft Draw, choose the File Update command to add your picture to your Word for Windows document (or update the existing picture) without exiting Microsoft Draw.

- Choose the File Exit and Return to Document command to add your picture to your Word for Windows document (or update the existing picture) and exit Microsoft Draw. A dialog box pops up asking whether you want to update your Word for Windows document. Choose **Yes**.

If you want to exit Microsoft Draw without adding the picture to your Word for Windows document, choose the File Exit and Return to Document command, and when the dialog box pops up asking whether you want to update your document, choose **No**.

Updating your drawing does not save it, however. To save your drawing, you must save the Word for Windows document that contains your drawing. Your drawing exists only as part of your Word for Windows document.

You also can use Microsoft Draw to edit an existing drawing in your document. Draw is compatible with several file types—even files that were not created with Draw (for details on inserted pictures, see Chapter 23).

To use Microsoft Draw to edit an existing drawing, do the following:

Double-click the picture.

or

Select the picture and choose the Edit Microsoft Drawing **Object** command.

or

Select the picture and choose the Insert Drawing button on the toolbar.

T I P   When you exit Draw and return to your document, you normally see your drawing in your document. If the View Field Codes command is selected, however, you see a field code in place of your drawing. Choose the View Field Codes command again.

Understanding the Microsoft Draw Screen

If you have ever used a graphics program before, you probably will find that the Microsoft Draw screen looks familiar (see fig. 25.4). Even if you haven't used a graphics program, the screen is intuitive.

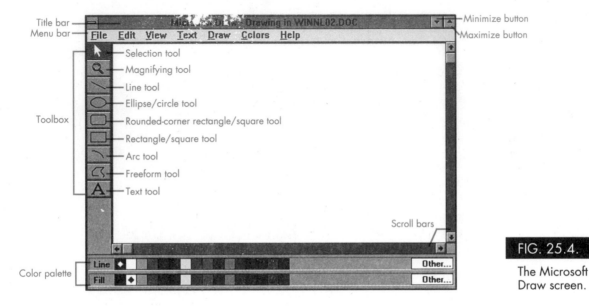

FIG. 25.4.

The Microsoft Draw screen.

Along the top of the Microsoft Draw window are the title and menu bars, as in every Windows program. On the left side is the toolbox: these are the tools you use to create your drawing. On the bottom is a color palette: you use the top half of the palette to choose line color, and you use the bottom half of the palette to choose fill color. On the right and bottom sides of the screen are the familiar scroll bars that enable you to move around on your drawing (which is a total of 22 by 22 inches wide).

The general process for creating a drawing is to select menu options to set defaults, select the tool you want to use, select colors from the palette, and draw your picture in the drawing area. You can edit any object after you create it. For details about using the tools, palette, and menu options, refer to the following sections in this chapter.

Although you can operate most Windows programs with a mouse or the keyboard, you must use a mouse to use Microsoft Draw. Some keyboard techniques and shortcuts are available in the program, but most operations depend on a mouse.

If you want the Microsoft Draw window to appear full-size on your screen, you can click the Maximize button at the top right of the Microsoft Draw window. Use Windows techniques to move between the Draw window and the Word for Windows window. To learn more about basic Windows techniques, refer to Chapter 1.

Scrolling the Drawing Page

Although you can see only a portion of it, the Microsoft Draw page measures 22 by 22 inches. Use the horizontal scroll bar at the bottom of the screen to scroll left and right on the page, and use the vertical scroll bar at the right to scroll up and down on the page.

Although scrolling enables you to view a part of the Microsoft Draw page that currently is hidden, it doesn't enable you to draw an object that is larger than the drawing area, or to select a group of objects that extends beyond the drawing area. To do either of those things, you can zoom out to see more of the page by using the Magnify tool, described in the section "Zooming In and Out with the Magnify Tool" later in this chapter.

Working with the Grid and Guides

Before you begin your drawing, you should know about two helpful drawing aids: the grid and the guides.

The *grid* is a sort of magnetic measurement system underlying your drawing. It's like an invisible piece of graph paper with magnetic lines— 12 lines per inch both vertical and horizontal—that snap your drawing tool to twelfth-inch increments, forcing you to draw objects that conform to the grid. Using the grid is important when you want to ensure accurate sizing and when you want to align objects accurately to one another.

Guides also are helpful for precise drawing. When you turn on the guides, two guides appear as intersecting dotted lines in the middle of the drawing area. You can move each guide independently by dragging it with the Selection tool. As you drag a guide, its distance from the top of the page (horizontal guide) or left of the page (vertical guide) appears at the arrow's location. By holding down the Ctrl key, the measurement starts from zero at the guide's starting location, making it easy to measure the size of an object. If the grid is turned on, the guides move in increments of 1/12 of an inch—the increments in which the grid is measured.

To turn on the grid, choose the **D**raw Snap to Grid command. To turn on the guides, choose the **D**raw Sho**w** Guides command.

Both the grid and the guides are commands you toggle on and off using the **D**raw menu. A checkmark appears to the left of each command when it's turned on. To turn off the grid or guides, select the command a second time (so that no checkmark appears to its left).

To move a guide, drag it with the Selection tool. To measure an object using the guides, follow these steps:

1. Drag the guide to one end or side of the object you want to measure.

2. Hold Ctrl while you drag the guide with the Selection tool; watch the measurement that appears on your screen.

Choosing a Frame, Fill, Pattern, or Line Style

Each object you draw with Microsoft Draw is a line or a shape. Lines have only one component: line style. Shapes have two components: a frame (the line around the shape's edges) and a fill. You can draw a line in any of several line styles. You can draw a shape that is framed or unframed and filled or not filled. You can choose any line style for a framed shape, and you can choose from several patterns for a filled shape.

You make all these choices from a menu, and you can choose them at one of two times: *before* you draw an object, so that your choices become defaults and apply to any subsequent shapes you draw; or *after* you draw and select an object or objects, so that your choices apply only to the selection.

Just remember this rule: if no object is selected, choices you make about frame, fill, pattern, and line style become defaults and apply to future objects you draw. If any object is selected, however, your frame, fill, pattern, and line style choices apply only to the selection.

Frame, fill, pattern, and line style choices are made through the **D**raw menu. The Frame**d** and **F**illed commands toggle on and off: they're on if a black diamond or checkmark appears to the left; they're off if nothing appears to the left. A black diamond indicates that Frame**d** or **F**illed is selected as a default; a checkmark indicates that it is selected for the currently selected object or objects. If two objects with conflicting frames or fills are selected, no mark appears to the left of the Frame**d** or **F**illed command.

The **P**attern and **L**ine Style commands have submenus (see fig. 25.5) from which you can choose a pattern (which fills any filled shape) or a line style (which frames any framed shape). These commands also toggle on and off, with a black diamond indicating a default choice, and a checkmark indicating the status of the currently selected object or objects.

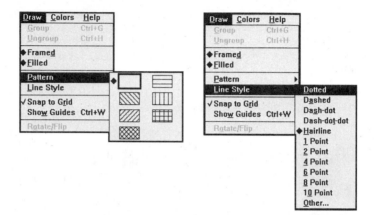

FIG. 25.5.

The Pattern and Line Style commands have submenus.

To specify **F**rame**d**, **F**illed, **P**attern, or **L**ine Style, follow these steps:

1. Make sure that no object is selected if you want all future objects to be framed or filled, or if you want to include a pattern or line style in all future objects (in other words, if you want to set a default).

    or

    Select the object or objects for which you want a frame, fill, pattern, or line style.

2. Choose the **D**raw **F**rame**d** command to frame an object or objects.

    or

    Choose the **D**raw **F**illed command to fill an object or objects.

    or

    Choose the **D**raw **P**attern command and select a pattern from the Pattern submenu to fill an object or objects with the pattern.

    or

    Choose the **D**raw **L**ine Style command and select a line style from the Line Style submenu to frame an object or objects with the line style.

Color is another important component in the drawings you create with Microsoft Draw. Lines and the borders around framed shapes are drawn in the color you select from the Line palette at the bottom of the screen. Fills and patterns appear in the color you select from the Fill palette at the bottom of the screen. To select a Line or Fill color, just click the color you want. Like other choices you make in Draw, you can choose colors *before* you begin your drawing (so the colors become the defaults for any subsequent lines or shapes you draw) or *after* you draw and select a line or shape (so the colors apply only to the selection). In the color palette, default colors appear with a diamond; colors for the currently selected object appear with a checkmark. To learn more about using colors, see the later section in this chapter on "Working with Color."

Using Microsoft Draw Drawing Tools

Each of the tools in the Microsoft Draw toolbox has a specific use. Some tools have more than one function: for example, with the Ellipse tool you can draw an oval or a perfect circle; with the Rectangle tool you can draw a rectangle or a perfect square; with the Freeform tool you can draw a line or a closed polygon. To use a tool, you first must select it.

To select a tool from the toolbox, click the tool icon in the toolbox. After you select a tool, move the pointer into the drawing area. The pointer changes from an arrow into some other tool. For drawing most objects, the pointer turns into a crosshair. You can use your drawing tool (or text tool, if you have selected the Text tool from the toolbox) to create your drawing, as explained in upcoming sections in this chapter. Refer to figure 25.4, which shows the nine drawing tools.

You can choose the Edit Undo command to undo your most recent screen action.

Figure 25.6 shows examples of framed and filled shapes created by using a variety of tools, line styles, patterns, and colors.

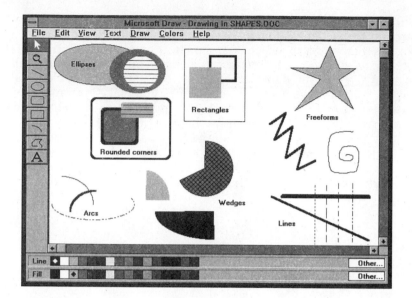

FIG. 25.6.

A sampling of framed and filled shapes using a variety of line styles and patterns.

Selecting with the Pointer Tool

The Selection tool selects text and objects in your drawing, usually so that you can edit them in some way. Because the primary purpose for using the Selection tool is for editing, the tool is described briefly here and in detail in the upcoming section, "Manipulating Text and Objects."

You can use the Selection tool in one of two ways. You can simply point to the single object you want to select and click the left mouse button, or, to select multiple objects, you can use the Selection tool to draw a box, or *marquee*, around the group of objects you want to select.

The Selection tool is particularly important because of one guiding principle that applies in nearly every Windows program: *select, and then do.* You first must *select* an object before you can *do* something to it. By selecting an object (or objects, or text), Microsoft Draw knows where to apply what you do.

To select an object or objects, follow these steps:

1. Click the Selection tool in the toolbox.

2. Point to the object to select and click the mouse button (hold Shift to select several objects).

    or

Drag the Selection tool in a box around a group of objects you want to select. The box appears as a dotted line while you hold down the mouse button and disappears when you release the mouse button. Be sure to enclose completely each object you want to select.

Selected objects have selection handles on each corner or end.

Many tools in the toolbox revert to the Selection tool after you use them. After you draw a box and click somewhere else in the drawing area, for example, the box crosshair turns into the Selection arrow.

Zooming In and Out with the Magnify Tool or View Command

When you first start Microsoft Draw, you see your page in full size—and your drawing is in the actual size it will be when printed. You may want to zoom out and see more of your page, however, especially if your drawing is larger than the drawing area. Or you may want to zoom in and get a close-up look at part of your drawing, particularly if you need to do some detailed editing.

Microsoft Draw offers seven different magnification levels for your picture: 25%, 50%, 75%, Full size, 200%, 400%, and 800%. You can draw and edit at any magnification. The available magnifications are listed in the View menu. The same choices also are available through the Magnify tool, which offers two advantages. First, the Magnify tool is easy to use—you just point and click. Second, it offers more control—when you point at an object and click the Magnify tool, you zoom in to that specific location on your screen. Using the View menu, you zoom in to the object you most recently created, regardless of where you want to be.

To magnify your drawing using the Magnify tool, follow these steps:

1. Select the Magnify tool from the toolbox.

2. Position the Magnify tool over the place in your drawing where you want to zoom in or zoom out.

3. Click the left mouse button to zoom in to the next higher magnification.

   or

   Hold Shift and click the left mouse button to zoom out to the next lower magnification.

4. Click repeatedly to continue zooming in or out.

To magnify or reduce your drawing through a menu, choose the **View** menu and select 25% **Size**, **50%**, **75%**, **Full Size**, **200%**, **400%**, or **800%**.

Drawing Lines

The Line tool enables you to draw straight lines. Your line appears in the default Line palette color (the color in the top of the color palette with a black diamond inside it), and in the selected Line Style (the Line Style in the **Draw** menu with a black diamond to its left).

To draw a line, follow these steps:

1. Select the Line tool from the toolbox.

2. Move the pointer into the drawing area.

3. Position the crosshair where you want to start your line.

4. Click and hold the mouse button.

5. Drag the crosshair to where you want to end your line.

6. Release the mouse button.

A newly drawn line has selection handles at each end, which you can use to edit the line (see the section later in this chapter on "Viewing, Selecting, and Manipulating Text and Objects"). When you finish drawing a line, you can click the mouse button anywhere in the drawing area to deselect the line you just drew and choose the Selection tool from the toolbox.

Two constraint keys, Shift and Ctrl, can help you keep a line straight, or enable you to draw a line from the center outward. To constrain your line to a 45 or 90-degree angle (especially when you want a perfectly horizontal or vertical line), hold the Shift key as you draw the line. To draw your line from the crosshair outward in both directions, hold the Ctrl key as you draw.

Drawing Ellipses, Circles, Rectangles, and Squares

Three tools enable you to draw round and square shapes. The Ellipse tool draws ellipses (ovals), or, when you hold the Shift key, circles. The Rounded-corner rectangle tool draws rectangles with rounded corners, or squares if you hold the Shift key. The Rectangle tool draws rectangles, or, when you hold the Shift key, squares. For each tool, holding the Ctrl key as you draw enables you to draw from the center outward, rather than from one corner to another.

Before you begin drawing an ellipse or rectangle, check your defaults in the **Draw** menu for Framed and Filled shapes and for Patterns and Line Styles (for details about these choices, refer to the earlier section on "Choosing a Frame, Fill, Pattern, or Line Style"). Also check your default colors in the Line and Fill palette. Set your defaults to what you want before you start drawing, or plan to edit the objects you draw later.

The process for drawing ellipses, circles, rectangles, and squares is the same. To draw an ellipse, circle, rounded-corner rectangle, rounded-corner square, rectangle, or square, follow these steps:

1. From the **Draw** menu, choose the Frame**d** command if you want your shape to have a border or choose the **F**illed command if you want your shape to be filled. Select the **P**attern or Line Style you want. Select the Line color and Fill color you want from the color palette.

2. Select the Ellipse tool to draw an ellipse or circle.

   or

   Select the Rounded-corner rectangle tool to draw a rounded-corner rectangle or square.

   or

   Select the Rectangle tool to draw a rectangle or square.

3. Move the tool into the drawing area, where it becomes a crosshair.

4. Position the crosshair where you want your shape to start.

   Hold Shift if you want to draw a perfect circle or a perfect square shape. Hold Ctrl to draw from the center outward.

5. Click and hold the mouse button, and drag to draw your shape.

6. Release the mouse button when your shape is correct.

A shape you have just drawn has selection handles at each corner, which you can use to edit the shape (see the section "Viewing, Selecting, and Manipulating Text and Objects" later in this chapter).

When you finish drawing an ellipse or rectangle, you can click the crosshair anywhere off the object to deselect the shape tool and select the Selection arrow.

Drawing Arcs and Wedges

An arc, as drawn in Microsoft Draw, is one quarter of an ellipse or circle. If the **Draw Filled** command is not selected, an arc is simply a line drawn in the selected Line Style and Line color. With the **Draw Filled** command selected, an arc is a wedge filled with the selected Fill color and with any **Pattern** selected in the **Draw** menu.

You can change the frame, fill, pattern, and line style for any object later; see the section "Viewing, Selecting, and Manipulating Text and Objects."

As with all the tools, two constraint keys can help you draw. By holding the Shift key, your arc or wedge will be a quarter of a perfect circle (rather than an ellipse). By holding the Ctrl key, you will draw your arc from the center (rather than from one corner to another).

The process of drawing an arc is similar to that of drawing any shape in Microsoft Draw. To draw an arc, follow these steps:

1. From the **Draw** menu, choose the Frame**d** command if you want your arc to have a border or choose the **F**illed command if you want your arc to be filled. Select the **P**attern or **L**ine Style you want. Select the Line color and Fill color you want from the color palette.

2. Select the Arc tool from the toolbox.

3. Move the tool into the drawing area, where it becomes a crosshair.

4. Position the crosshair where you want to start your arc.

   Hold down the Shift key if you want to draw a perfect quarter-circle arc. Hold the Ctrl key to draw from the center outwards.

5. Click where you want to start the arc, and drag to where you want to end the arc.

6. Release the mouse button.

As with all tools, you can drag the crosshair in any direction as you draw; to draw an arc that shows the bottom half of a circle or ellipse, drag the crosshair upward.

Drawing Freeform Lines and Polygons

The Freeform tool is one of the most versatile tools in the toolbox. With the Freeform tool, you can draw a squiggle, a jagged line, or a closed polygon.

Only one constraint key works with the Freeform tool. Holding Shift while you draw forces line segments to be on the horizontal, vertical, or 45-degree axis. Even while you're drawing a curved line, holding Shift forces all segments of the line to be on one of these axes.

As with all tools, check your defaults before you begin drawing. Check the **Draw** menu to see that **F**illed and Frame**d** are set as you want them, and that the correct **P**attern and **L**ine Style are selected; check the palette to be sure that the correct Line and Fill colors are selected.

You can change the frame, fill, pattern, and line style for any freeform object later; see the "Viewing, Selecting, and Manipulating Text and Objects" section. You can use a special technique to change each individual segment of a polygon.

To draw a jagged line or closed polygon with the Freeform tool, follow these steps:

1. Select **D**raw Frame**d** for a framed polygon, or **D**raw **F**illed for a filled polygon. Select your **P**attern, **L**ine Style, and color defaults.

2. Select the Freeform tool from the toolbox.

3. Move the tool into the drawing area and position the crosshair where you want your jagged line or polygon to begin.

4. Click the mouse button to anchor the first end of the line or polygon.

5. Move the crosshair to the second point on your line or polygon and click again.

6. Continue moving the crosshair and clicking the mouse button to define each point on your line or polygon.

7. Double-click the last point of your line to complete the line.

    or

    Double-click the first point of your polygon to join the last point with the first and create a closed polygon.

To draw a curving line or closed curving freeform shape, follow these steps:

1. Select **D**raw Frame**d** for a framed freeform shape, or **D**raw **F**illed for a filled freeform shape. Select your pattern, line style, and color defaults.

2. Select the Freeform tool from the toolbox.

3. Move the tool into the drawing area and position the crosshair where you want your curving line or freeform shape to begin.

4. Click and hold the mouse button where you want to start your line or shape. Wait until the crosshair turns into a pencil.

5. Still holding down the mouse button, drag the pencil around in the drawing area to draw your line or shape.

6. When you reach the end of your line, double-click the mouse button.

or

To close the shape, double-click the line's beginning point.

Adding and Editing Text

A picture may be worth a thousand words, but sometimes words can help clarify your point. You can easily add text to your Microsoft Draw drawing, selecting its font, style, and size. Later, you can select and edit your text as needed.

You can type only a single line of text in Microsoft Draw. If you reach the end of the screen, text does not wrap, and you cannot press Enter to start a new line. To stack lines of text, you must type each line separately and drag each line into place using the Selection arrow. Using Microsoft Draw's Snap to Grid feature (in the **D**raw menu), however, enables you to easily stack lines of text evenly.

Like any object, Windows' "select, and then do" principle applies to text: if you want to do something to an object, you first must select the object. If you don't select an object first, then what you do becomes the new default and applies to anything you do subsequently.

Because moving text is no different from moving other objects, techniques for moving text are discussed later in this chapter, in the section "Copying, Moving, and Deleting Text and Objects."

Typing Text

To enter text in your drawing, follow these steps:

1. Choose your text defaults (if a shape is selected in your drawing, you cannot choose text defaults—unselect the shape). From the **T**ext menu, select any of these commands:

Command	Result
Plain (or press Ctrl+T)	Plain, with no formatting
Bold (or press Ctrl+B)	Boldface
Italic (or press Ctrl+I)	Italicized
Underline (or press Ctrl+U)	Underlined
Left	Left aligned
Center	Centered
Right	Right Aligned
Font (then select the font	A different font you want from the submenu of available fonts)
Size (then select the	A different size size you want from the submenu of available sizes)

Three of the choices in the **Text** menu—**B**old, **I**talic, and **U**nderline—are style choices, which can be combined. You can type text that is both bold and italicized, for example, or that is underlined and bold. Each style choice selected for the current text has a checkmark to its left. To remove all style choices at once, select the **P**lain style.

2. From the Line color palette at the bottom of the screen, select a color for your text.

    If the color palette is not visible, choose the **C**olors Show **P**alette command to display it.

3. Select the Text tool from the toolbox.

4. Move the tool into the drawing area, where it turns into an I-beam. Position the I-beam where you want the left margin of your block of text.

5. Click the mouse button to insert the cursor where you want your text to start.

6. Type the text.

    If you want, you can press Shift+Ins to insert text from the clipboard (even if the text was typed in a different program). Just remember that in Microsoft Draw you can have only one line of text at a time.

7. Press Enter, or click the mouse button somewhere off the text to end the text block. The text block is selected and the Selection tool is selected.

T I P   Colored text sometimes looks best superimposed over a background of a different color. You can accomplish this effect by choosing one color for your text, then drawing a shape around the text that is filled with a different color, and using the **E**dit menu to send the shape to the back of the text. For best readability, be sure that you provide plenty of contrast between the two colors you choose.

Editing Text

To edit text, you first must select the text. Text is selected automatically after you type it and press Enter or click outside the text. If the text you want to edit is not currently selected, point to it with the Selection tool and click the mouse button.

Like any selected object, selected text has selection handles at each of its four corners. The selection handles indicate that you can move or edit the text.

You can change text style, alignment, font, or size by choosing commands from the Text menu, and choose a different color from the Line palette at the bottom of your screen. Or you can change the words by deleting, inserting, or retyping characters.

To change the words in a text block, you first must get the insertion point inside the selected text. You cannot just click the text to get the insertion point inside it. To get the insertion point inside the text, follow these steps:

1. Select the text block by clicking it with the Selection arrow.

2. Choose the **E**dit E**d**it Text command.

   or

   Double-click the text block.

   An insertion point appears inside the text block. Using the double-click method, the insertion point appears exactly where you double-click.

3. Edit the text using standard editing techniques.

   Press the Backspace key to erase characters to the left, Del to erase characters to the right; you can select text and retype it; or you can cut, copy, and paste text using commands from the **E**dit menu.

4. Press Enter or click outside the text block to complete the editing process.

Working with Colors

If you have a color monitor, you will really enjoy Microsoft Draw's colors. The Line and Fill palettes contain up to 16 solid colors (Windows' limit) and seemingly limitless "dithered" colors blended from the available solid colors. You can apply these colors to any object you create— text or shapes. (If you see less than 16 colors, it's because your PC supports fewer colors.)

The color palette at the bottom of the Microsoft Draw window contains colors for Line (top of the palette) and Fill (bottom of the palette). The colors with a black diamond inside them are the defaults—they will be applied to all objects you create. When you later select objects you created earlier, you may see a checkmark inside a color—this means the color is applied to the selected object.

You can change your color palette in two ways. One way is to click the Other button at the right end of the Line or Fill palette. The other way is to use the **C**olors menu. You can add new colors to your palette or change existing colors. You can save palettes you like to use in future drawings. Techniques are described in the next few sections.

To enlarge your screen space, you can hide the color palette. If the palette is displayed and you want to hide it, choose the **C**olors Show **P**alette command. To display the palette, choose the command a second time—the Show **P**alette command toggles on and off; you see a checkmark to its left when it's on.

Coloring Text and Objects

The default color in the Line palette is applied automatically to text, lines, the frame around framed objects, and the foreground in any patterned fill. The default color in the Fill palette is applied automatically to the fill in any filled shape, and to the background in any pattern fill.

Whereas default color choices apply to any object you create, you can just as easily change the Line or Fill color of an object or text you created earlier. Simply select the object (or objects) and choose the Line or Fill color you want. Colors change only for the selected object or objects.

To select a Line or Fill color as a default, or to change the Line or Fill color for a selected object, follow these steps:

1. If you want to change the default Line or Fill color, make sure that no object is selected (an easy way to do that is to select the Selection tool, which cancels all selections).

   and/or

   If you want to change the Line or Fill color for one or more specific objects, select the objects.

2. Click the Line color you want in the top half of the color palette.

   and/or

   Click the Fill color you want in the bottom half of the color palette.

Using Blended Colors

Although your initial color palette contains only up to 16 solid colors, you can paint your objects with a rainbow of blended colors. Working with blended colors requires that you use the most colorful dialog box in Microsoft Draw—the Other Color dialog box (see fig. 25.7). The Other Color dialog box offers a rainbow of colors you can add to your palette or apply to the selected objects. (If you access this dialog box through the Colors menu, its title instead is Add Color.)

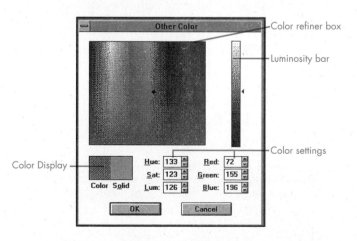

FIG. 25.7.

The Other Color dialog box.

When you're blending colors, you may want to understand how computers work with color. Computers understand color in terms of light—
not pigment. So forget what you have learned about color wheels: for
example, in a computer's mind, pure red and pure green combine to
make yellow; pure red, pure green, and pure blue combine to make
white. Computers use an additive system for blending colors, whereas
pigments use a subtractive system.

You can blend a color using the Other Color dialog box in three ways:

- You can select a color from the Color refiner box (the rainbow-
  colored box) and select a luminosity from the Luminosity bar.

- You can blend your own color by setting its hue, saturation, and
  luminosity.

- You can blend your own color by setting its levels of red, green,
  and blue.

In the next section, you learn how you can add blended colors to your
palette.

You can use the Other Color dialog box to add a color to your objects
by following these steps:

1. Select the objects whose line or fill colors you want to change.
    Choose Other from the Line or the Fill palette. The Other Color
    dialog box appears.

2. To select the color, use the Color refiner box (the large, rainbow-
    colored box).

    Click the color you like, or, holding the mouse button, drag the
    black diamond selection icon onto the color you like (the color
    display shows the selected color).

3. To set your selected color's luminosity, or value (how dark or
    light it is), use the Luminosity bar (vertical bar to the right of the
    rainbow-colored refiner box).

    Drag the black triangle icon up to select a lighter color, drag down
    to select a darker color, or click the area of the bar you want to
    select.

    Click the Solid box (right side) to select the solid color, rather
    than the dithered color.

4. To select a color by hue (color), saturation (amount of color), and
    luminosity (brightness), select values from 0 to 240 in the Hue,
    Sat, and Lum boxes (type the value or select the up and down
    arrows to increase or decrease the value). Values range from 0

(red hue; no saturation, or black; and no luminosity, or black) to 240 (red hue, full saturation, or pure color; and full luminosity, or pure white).

5. To select a color by blending hues, select values from 0 to 240 in the **R**ed, **G**reen, and **B**lue boxes (type the value or select the up and down arrows to increase or decrease the value). Values range from 0 (no hues, or black) to 240 (pure hue, or white).

6. To see the color you have selected—if it's not one of Windows' 16 solid colors, you see a dithered color blended of Windows' 16 colors—look at the Color/Solid box (below the Color refiner box).

Editing the Palette

You can add blended colors to your initial palette, and you can change the existing colors and delete colors in your palette. To edit the palette, you use the Colors menu, which accesses the Other Color dialog box described in the previous section (the dialog box is named Add Color, however, when you're editing the palette). Refer to the previous section for a description of the Add Color dialog box.

When you edit your palette using the **C**olors menu, you change the Line and Fill palettes simultaneously.

To change, add to, or delete colors from the palette, follow these steps:

1. Choose the **C**olors **E**dit Palette command.

   The Edit Palette dialog box appears (see fig. 25.8), displaying the colors in the current palette as well as many blank spaces where you can add new colors (notice that 100 spots are available for colors).

2. Select the existing color you want to change or delete.

3. Choose **C**hange to change the color you have selected, choose **A**dd to add a color to the next available blank space, or choose **D**elete to delete the selected color.

   If you add or change a color, you advance to the Add Color dialog box, described in the previous section.

4. Make your choices in that dialog box, and choose OK or press Enter. You return to the Edit Palette dialog box.

5. Choose OK or press **E**nter.

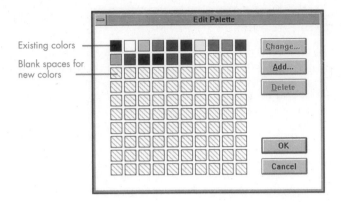

Existing colors

Blank spaces for
new colors

FIG 25.8.

The Edit Palette
dialog box.

The Edit Palette dialog box offers a couple of shortcuts: you can simply double-click the color you want to edit; and you can drag an existing color to a new square in the color grid to rearrange your palette.

You can have up to 100 colors on your palette, as you have seen in the Edit Palette dialog box. If you have more colors than can fit on your screen, you see scrolling arrows at the left and right ends of your on-screen palette. Click those arrows to see more of your palette.

If you have used the on-screen palette to change the color of one specific object in your drawing, you later can add that color to your palette.

To add an existing object's color to your palette, select the object whose color you want to add to the palette. Choose the **Colors Add Colors From Selection** command.

If your object contains both a new Line and a new Fill color, both are added to your palette.

Saving and Opening Palettes

When you first start Microsoft Draw, the Line and Fill color palette is displayed at the bottom of the drawing area. It contains 16 solid colors (or fewer, if your PC supports fewer). But you can get a different palette (Microsoft Draw includes several) and you can save a palette you have created yourself, making it available the next time you use Microsoft Draw. This is the way you can share colors among drawings.

To save your custom palette, follow these steps:

1. Choose the **Colors Save Palette** command.

2. Enter an eight-character file name. Microsoft Draw supplies the extension PAL.

   Microsoft Draw saves the currently displayed color palette in the MSDRAW directory by default; you can save it in a different directory if you want, but, if you do, your palette will not show up automatically when you choose the **G**et Palette command later.

3. Choose OK or press Enter.

T I P   You can create a palette in Microsoft Draw to use in Windows Paintbrush, if the palette contains no more than 28 colors. Paintbrush uses palettes in the same file format as Microsoft Draw (with the same extension), but Paintbrush looks for palette files in the Windows directory. To distinguish your Microsoft Draw palettes from Paintbrush, first change to the MSAPPS subdirectory, and then to the MSDRAW subdirectory.

To get an existing palette, do the following:

1. Choose the **C**olors **G**et Palette command. The Get Palette dialog box appears.

2. In the **F**iles list box, select the palette you want to open.

   Change the directory if your PAL file is stored somewhere besides the MSDRAW directory.

3. Choose OK or press Enter. The new palette is displayed on your screen.

Manipulating Text and Objects

After you draw objects and type text in Microsoft Draw, you can manipulate your drawing in many ways. Everything you create—even text—is an object you can move, layer, or group with other objects. You can resize, reshape, rotate, and flip shapes or grouped shapes (but not text). Microsoft Draw's object-editing capabilities enable you to produce complex and interesting works of art, like the one shown in fig. 25.9.

You can choose the **E**dit **U**ndo command to undo your most recent screen action.

FIG. 25.9.

By creating and editing objects, you can create complex and interesting works of art.

Selecting Text and Objects

Before you can edit any object, you first must select it. When selected, an object has selection handles on its four corners (even non-rectangular shapes have four selection handles arranged in a rectangle around the outside of the object). You can drag these handles to resize or reshape a selected object.

To review briefly, you can select an object by selecting the pointer tool (the arrow) and clicking the object or by drawing a selection marquee around a group of objects you want to select (for details, refer to the earlier section "Selecting with the Pointer Tool"). You can select all the objects in your drawing by choosing the Edit Select All command.

Resizing and Reshaping Objects

You can change the shape and size of any selected object, with the exception of text, by dragging the selection handles. Two constraint keys—Shift to retain proportions; Ctrl to resize and reshape from the center outwards—apply. As you're resizing or reshaping the object, a dotted-line bounding box shows you the object's new size or shape.

To change an object's size or shape, do the following:

1. Select the object.

    You cannot resize or reshape multiple objects simultaneously unless you first group them (see the upcoming section on "Grouping and Ungrouping Text and Objects").

2. To reshape an object, drag any corner handle to a new shape; release the mouse button when the bounding box shows the shape you want.

    or

    To resize the object, keeping it proportional, hold the Shift key while you drag a corner handle.

Copying, Moving, and Deleting Text and Objects

You can easily move an object or a text block. Just click it and drag it to its new location. Because you can drag only as far as the edge of the drawing area, you may want to zoom out so that you can move on a larger area of the page. You can move a selected group of objects together by dragging one of the objects.

As you're dragging an object to move it, you see one of two things on your screen. If you drag fast, you see a dotted-line bounding box that represents the position of your speeding object (the object reappears when you release the mouse button). If you drag slowly, you see a ghost of the moving object.

If you prefer, you can use the standard Windows **E**dit **C**ut, **E**dit **C**opy, and **E**dit **P**aste commands to copy and move selected objects using the clipboard. This technique is useful when you want to copy or move objects between drawings or between distant spots on the same large drawing. Because you can switch between programs in Windows by sharing the clipboard, you also can use this technique to copy or move a drawing from Microsoft Draw into another program besides Word for Windows.

To copy or move objects, follow these steps:

1. Select the object or objects you want to copy, move, or delete.

2. To move an object, choose the **E**dit **C**ut command.

    To copy an object, choose the **E**dit **C**opy command.

3. Move to where you want the object moved or copied.

4. Choose the **E**dit **P**aste command.

To remove an object, select it and choose the **E**dit C**l**ear command, or just press the Del or Backspace key.

Working with Layers

Like most drawing programs, Microsoft Draw enables you to work in layers. That is, you can create two or more objects and stack them on top of one another. Menu commands (and keyboard shortcuts) enable you to bring a selected object to the front or send it to the back of other objects.

Classic examples of layering are a shadow box, which is usually a white box overlapping a darker box of the same size, and text on a different color background.

To move an object to a different layer in your drawing, do the following:

1. Select the object or objects you want to send to the back or bring to the front of another object.

2. To bring the object to the top layer, choose the **E**dit Bring to **F**ront command (or press Ctrl+=).

   To send the object to the bottom layer, choose the Edit Send to **B**ack command (or press Ctrl+–).

If you know an object is hidden somewhere behind some other object, and you want to find it, choose the **E**dit Select **A**ll command to select all objects, and look for the hidden object's selection handles. To reveal the hidden object, you must move the top object (or objects) to the back of the stack, or just drag the top object off the object you're trying to find.

T I P

Editing a Freeform Shape

You can edit a freeform shape in one of two ways. You can resize or reshape it as described in the earlier section on "Resizing and Reshaping Objects." This technique leaves the freeform object in the same general shape (although by dragging its corner handles, you may condense or expand the shape if you don't hold down the Shift key to keep it proportional).

You can use a unique way to edit a freeform shape (in other words, actually edit the segments that make up the shape). You use the Selection tool and then a menu command to display control handles you can use to reshape the freeform shape. (While you're editing a freeform object, it appears on-screen as an empty shape with a thin black frame.)

To edit a freeform shape, follow these steps:

1. Select the shape by clicking it with the Selection tool. Four selection handles appear on each corner.

2. Choose the Edit Edit Freeform command. Control handles appear at the end of each segment of the freeform shape.

3. Drag any control handle to change the freeform's shape.

   To add a control handle, hold Ctrl (the arrow turns into a plus sign inside a circle) and click anywhere on the freeform's edge.

   To remove a control handle, hold Ctrl and Shift (the arrow turns into a minus sign inside a square) and click any existing control handle.

4. Press Enter or click anywhere outside the freeform to hide the control handles.

As an alternative to selecting the freeform shape and then choosing the Edit Freeform command, you can simply double-click the freeform to display the control handles.

Editing an Arc or Wedge

Like a freeform shape, you can edit an arc or wedge in two ways. You can select it with the Selection tool and resize or reshape the arc by dragging the corner handles (hold the Shift key as you drag to keep the arc proportional). Or, you can change the arc's degree by first selecting it with the Selection tool, and then choosing a menu command to display special control handles.

To change a wedge's or an arc's degree, follow these steps:

1. Select the arc or wedge by clicking it with the Selection tool. Four corner handles appear.

2. Choose the Edit Edit Arc command. Two control handles appear—one at each end of the arc or wedge.

3. Drag either control handle in a clockwise or counterclockwise manner to change the degree.

4. Click outside the arc to deselect it.

As an alternative to selecting the arc and then choosing the Edit Arc command, you can simply double-click the arc to display the control handles.

Grouping and Ungrouping Text and Objects

If you want to turn several objects into one (to easily copy, reshape, or move them together, for example), you can select and group them. You then can edit the objects as a single object (although you cannot resize, reshape, rotate, or flip text included in the group). Later, you can ungroup grouped objects (if you have resized a group, the ungrouped objects will be the new size).

To group objects, follow these steps:

1. Select all the objects you want to group (hold Shift while you click each object you want to select, or draw a selection marquee around a group of objects).

2. Choose the Draw Group command.

To ungroup a grouped object, do the following:

1. Select the grouped object.

2. Choose the Draw Ungroup command.

Rotating and Flipping Objects

You can rotate a selected object (or selected group) in 90-degree increments to the left (counterclockwise) or right (clockwise). You can flip an object vertically or horizontally. You cannot rotate or flip text.

To rotate or flip an object, follow these steps:

1. Select the object.

2. Choose the Draw Rotate/Flip command and select Rotate Left, Rotate Right, Flip Horizontal, or Flip Vertical.

Importing and Editing Clip Art and Other Pictures

You can import many types of graphics into Microsoft Draw. Among the most interesting are a series of clip-art images that come with Microsoft Draw, which you can import and disassemble to use in whole or in part. Browse through the various clip-art files to see what you find.

To import a picture, follow these steps:

1. Choose the **File I**mport Picture command. The Import Picture dialog box appears.

2. Select the file you want to import from the Files box (change the directory if necessary).

Clip-art files are located in the subdirectory CLIPART, located inside your Word for Windows directory. These files have the extension WMF, indicating that their format is Windows metafile.

You also can import BMP, PCX, and TIF files. If you import object-oriented images, you edit them the same way you edit any Microsoft Draw object. You also can import bit-map files (such as those created in Microsoft Paintbrush). Microsoft Draw converts the bit maps into objects, which you can resize, reshape, or recolor. To restore a bit-map image to its original size or shape, you can select it and double-click any corner handle.

Updating Your Word for Windows Document

You can get your drawing back into Word for Windows without closing Microsoft Draw or by closing Microsoft Draw at the same time you update your Word for Windows file. To save your drawing, you must be sure to save your Word for Windows file after you update the drawing.

To update your Word for Windows document, choose the **File U**pdate command to update your Word for Windows document without closing Microsoft Draw or choose the **File E**xit and Return to Document command to update the Word for Windows file and exit Microsoft Draw.

From Here . . .

Microsoft Draw is a simple but very powerful program you can use to create original works of art to illustrate your Word for Windows document or to edit existing art. You can even use the clip art that comes with Microsoft Draw as the basis for your own drawings.

One of the most obvious uses for drawings is to illustrate newsletters, brochures, flyers, forms, and much more using desktop publishing techniques. To learn more, refer to Chapter 28.

If you want to add a frame around your entire drawing after it's in Word for Windows, you can select the drawing and choose a border. Refer to Chapter 23 to learn how to select and border a graphic.

When you first insert a drawing into your document, it appears at the current location of the insertion point. To move the drawing independently of the text, you must frame it. See Chapter 24 about positioning text and graphics.

If you want, you can include a drawing in a table. See Chapter 12 to learn about creating tables.

Turning Words into Pictures with WordArt

Words don't always function strictly as abstract symbols that we read for meaning. Words sometimes work as graphics, not only conveying meaning, but also attracting attention and creating memorable images. You see examples of words used as graphics every day: pulled-quotes in magazines lighten a page of text and attract attention to important points; logos incorporate words in symbols that you recognize without even reading; decorated words embellish the mastheads in newsletters; special text effects add interest to the covers of record albums.

With WordArt, you can turn words into pictures, add shadows and colored backgrounds, stretch and condense letters, angle text, turn words on end, and arrange words in a circle. Figure 26.1 shows just one example of how using WordArt enhances a document.

WordArt, like Microsoft Draw and Microsoft Graph, is an OLE-based, add-in program that comes free with Word for Windows. OLE (object linking and embedding) means that the WordArt objects inserted in your document contain all the data necessary to edit the object. When you edit the WordArt objects, the image in your Word for Windows document updates to reflect the changes. WordArt is not a stand-alone program that you can run by itself; you must run WordArt within Word for Windows or other Windows programs that support OLE. You cannot create a separate WordArt file. WordArt images are part of your Word for Windows file.

Starting and Exiting WordArt

WordArt is a program you run from within Word for Windows. WordArt embeds a WordArt object at the insertion point. See the later section in this chapter, "Editing a WordArt Image," to learn how you can change your image after it is in your document.

To start and edit WordArt, follow these steps:

1. Position the insertion point where you want to embed the WordArt image.

2. Choose the **I**nsert **O**bject command.

   The Object dialog box appears (see fig. 26.2).

3. Select MS WordArt and choose OK.

   or

   Double-click MS WordArt.

The Microsoft WordArt dialog box appears. (See the next section, "Understanding the WordArt Dialog Box.")

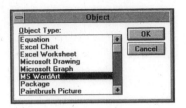

FIG. 26.2.

The Object
dialog box.

4. Create your WordArt image. (Refer to "Creating a WordArt Image" in this chapter.)

5. Choose **A**pply to insert your image or update an existing image in your Word for Windows document without exiting WordArt.

   or

   Choose OK to insert your image or update an existing image in your document and exit WordArt.

Remember that a WordArt image cannot be saved by itself. To save your WordArt image, save your Word for Windows document.

Usually, when you add a WordArt image to your document, you see the image on your screen. If you see a field code, however, the **View** Field **C**odes command is selected. To see the WordArt image, choose the **View** Field **C**odes command again.

T I P

Understanding the WordArt Dialog Box

WordArt contains one screen. Although a separate program, WordArt doesn't appear in a Window. Instead, it has a single dialog box similar to the one shown in figure 26.3.

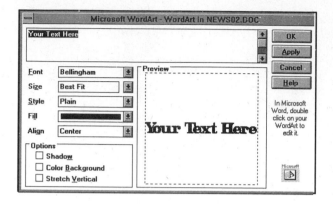

FIG. 26.3.

The WordArt program has only one dialog box.

At the top of the dialog box is a text entry area with sample text selected. Below and to the right of the text area is the Preview screen, which displays a preview of the choices you make. To the left of the Preview screen are options you use to manipulate your text. The Font, Size, and Fill lists enable you to set the appearance of your text; the Style list enables you to stretch, tilt, flip, arch, and stand text on end; and the Align list sets the alignment of text within the text frame. The Options box is below these lists. By selecting choices from the Options box, you can enhance text.

T   I   P
If you're editing existing text, you must choose the Apply button to see your changes in the Preview box. Choosing Apply also inserts the image into your document or updates the existing image.

Creating a WordArt Image

WordArt enables you to enhance any document with words transformed into graphic images. With a few simple techniques and a little imagination, you can create a brochure, letter, or report that is both eye-catching and eye-pleasing. Using WordArt is as simple as entering text, applying special effects, and editing to your satisfaction.

Entering Text

When you are creating a new WordArt image, you first must enter the text. When you start the program to create a new image, the text entry area contains the sample words Your Text Here. Type your own text to replace the selected sample text. You can press Shift+Ins to insert text from the clipboard into the text entry area.

The text you enter appears in the font selected in the Font list box. The Font list contains 19 different fonts, from Anacortes to Wenatchee. These fonts are graphic fonts specific to WordArt and are not the same as the fonts built into your printer. Each font is styled after a popular typeface.

After you insert your text into the text entry area, you can use any standard Windows text editing convention. You can select several words or lines by dragging the mouse across the text, for example, or you can select a single word by double-clicking. You can click the mouse button to position the insertion point, press Backspace to delete text to the left of the insertion point, or press Del to delete text to the right of the insertion point. Pressing Enter ends a line.

As you enter text, it appears in the text box at the top of the screen. You must choose the Apply button to see your changes in the Preview box.

Because the Preview box shows the appearance of each font, you can test how your WordArt image appears with different fonts by clicking on the down arrow next to the Font box and scrolling through the list. Click on the font you want. To use the keyboard, press Alt+F and use the up- and down-arrow keys to select a font. Watch the Preview box to see the appearance of your text with each font.

The text you enter appears in the font size selected in the Size box. WordArt offers a range of sizes from 6 points to 128 points. You also can type your own font size. To enable WordArt to select the size that best fits the WordArt frame, select Best Fit from the Size list.

Applying Special Effects

WordArt offers many ways to graphically enhance words. You can change the style by arching or flipping the words; you can change the fill or color; and you can align the words to fit the frame in many different ways. You also can add a drop shadow to words, add a colored background, or stretch the words vertically.

To apply effects to text, follow these steps:

1. From the **Style** list, select a style.

   The choices in the **Style** list release you from the typical text baseline. These choices include the following:

Selection	Result
Top to Bottom	Stands text vertical, with the first letter on top
Bottom to Top	Stands text vertical, with the first letter on the bottom
Plain	Removes all styles
Upside Down	Inverts text
Arch Up	Fits text to the top of a circle
Arch Down	Fits text to the bottom of a circle
Button	Arches up the first line of text, arches down the third line, and leaves the second line of text horizontal
Slant Up (Less)	Slants text slightly upward
Slant Up (More)	Slants text upward by about 45 degrees
Slant Down (Less)	Slants text slightly downward
Slant Down (More)	Slants text downward by about 45 degrees

2. From the **Fill** list, select a color for your text.

   If your PC supports the full Windows palette, 16 colors, including black, white, and two shades of gray, are listed. If your PC supports fewer colors, however, fewer colors are displayed.

3. From the **Align** list, select a text alignment.

Selection	Result
Left	Aligns text in your WordArt image to the left
Center	Aligns text in your WordArt image to the center
Right	Aligns text in your WordArt image to the right side of the frame

Selection	Result
Letter Justify	Spaces the letters out to fill the frame
Word Justify	Spaces words equally from the left to right edges of the frame
Fit Horizontally	Stretches the text out to fill the frame

Letter and Word Justify change the spacing, not the appearance, of the text. Fit Horizontally, in contrast, stretches the actual characters, distorting those letters smaller than the frame. To see the difference of Fit Horizontally, select a small point size for short lines of text.

4. From the Options group, select Shadow, Color Background, or Stretch Vertical to design further your WordArt image.

Selection	Result
Shadow	Adds a black drop-shadow to text
Color Background	Includes a colored background. If the text is any color besides white, the background color is light gray; if the text is white, the background color is black.
Stretch Vertical	Stretches the text vertically to fit the frame. (This option is similar to the Fit Horizontally alignment option, except that Stretch Vertical does up and down what Fit Horizontally does side to side.)

Options are selected if an X appears inside the box to their left.

5. Choose Apply to see your changes in the Preview box.

Figure 26.4 shows several examples of how you can stretch, squeeze, and enhance text in WordArt.

Editing a WordArt Image

You can edit your WordArt image in two ways: You can start WordArt and make changes to the image itself, using any of the techniques described earlier in this chapter; or you can manipulate the WordArt image in Word for Windows. For example, you can select the WordArt image and drag its corner handles or choose the Format Picture command to change its size. (To learn more about editing pictures, see Chapter 23).

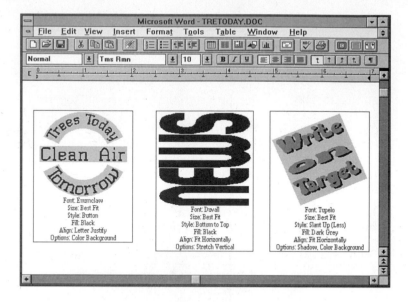

FIG. 26.4.

You can stretch, squeeze, and enhance text in different ways.

To edit a WordArt image in your document using WordArt, follow these steps:

1. Double-click the image to bring up WordArt.

   or

   Select the WordArt image and choose the **E**dit MS WordArt Object command.

2. Make changes in the Microsoft WordArt dialog box.

3. Choose **A**pply to apply your changes to the Preview box and the Word for Windows document.

   or

   Choose OK to apply your changes and exit WordArt.

A WordArt image is the same as a picture in your Word for Windows document; therefore, you also can edit the image by using Word for Windows editing techniques. You can add a frame to the image to position the WordArt image anywhere on the page and wrap text around it. You can add a border around your WordArt image. You also can resize, reshape, or crop the image as you would a picture and later reset the image to its original size.

From Here . . .

In this chapter you learned to use MS WordArt to change words into pictures by creating and editing a WordArt image. You also learned that WordArt doesn't restrict your editing to only WordArt techniques. WordArt also enables you to manipulate the image with Word for Windows editing techniques.

Chapter 23 contains information on reshaping, resizing, and scaling pictures. In Chapter 23, you also can find information on adding a border to your WordArt image. To frame a WordArt image, enabling you to position the image freely on the page and wrap text around it, read Chapter 24.

Because WordArt images are used in newsletters, ads, brochures, and many more publication-quality documents, be sure to take a look at Chapter 28 to see how to illustrate publications with your WordArt creations.

Working with Microsoft Graph

With Microsoft Graph you can create informative and impressive charts for your Word for Windows documents. An overwhelming table of numbers can become a chart that shows important trends and changes. You can relegate the detailed numeric table to a location where it doesn't slow down communication. Figure 27.1 shows a Word for Windows document enhanced by a chart. Microsoft Graph is not just a small charting application; it has the capability of Microsoft Excel, the most capable Windows spreadsheet, graphics, and database program.

Microsoft Graph is an *applet*. Applets are small applications designed to work with Windows programs that have Windows Object Linking and Embedding (OLE) capability. Applets add additional features to OLE-capable applications. Microsoft Graph is a separate program that embeds charts and their data into Windows applications such as Microsoft Word for Windows.

Charts embedded into a Word for Windows document contain the chart and the data that creates the chart. When you activate Microsoft Graph, it loads the selected chart and its data so that you can make changes. You cannot save the chart or data separately; they are embedded into your Word for Windows document.

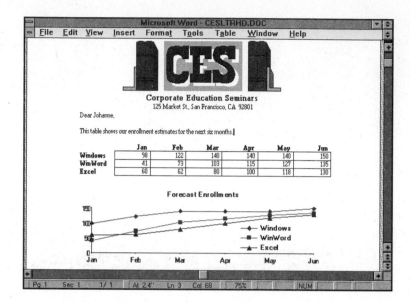

FIG. 27.1.

A Word for Windows document enhanced by a chart.

T I P Many of the tips found in the charting chapters of Que's book *Using Excel for Windows, Special Edition*, also work in Microsoft Graph.

Creating a Chart

Charts are created from data entered into a data sheet. With Microsoft Graph, you can create a new chart in Word for Windows in a number of ways. The text and numbers in the data sheet can be selected from a table in the Word for Windows document; typed into Microsoft Graph; copied in from any Windows document; imported from a Microsoft Excel, Lotus 1-2-3, or text file; or read in from an existing Microsoft Excel chart.

To start Microsoft Graph using the mouse, click the I-beam where you want the chart to appear in your document, and then click on the Chart button in the toolbar.

To start Microsoft Graph using the keyboard, move the insertion point to where you want the chart to appear in your document and choose the **Insert O**bject command. Select the Microsoft Graph object from the list in the Object dialog box, and then choose OK.

Microsoft Graph opens in an application window on top of your Word for Windows application. Microsoft Graph opens with default data in the data sheet and chart (see fig. 27.2). The chart reflects the data in the sample data sheet. (If you select data in a Word for Windows table before starting Microsoft Graph, the table's data is used.) If you change the data in the data sheet, you change the chart. When you close the Microsoft Graph application, you can embed the chart and its related data into your document.

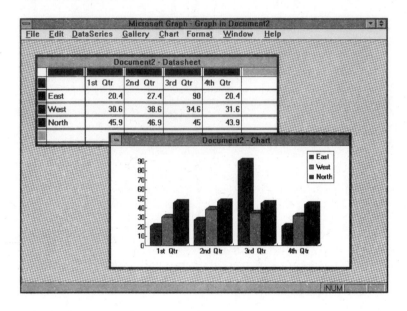

FIG. 27.2.

A sample data sheet and chart.

In Microsoft Graph, you can change the data in the sheet in many ways. You also can choose different types of charts from the **G**allery menu. From the **C**hart menu, you can add or remove from a chart items such as legends, arrows, and titles. You can change the appearance or position of selected chart items or data in the sheet by using the commands in the Forma**t** menu.

Understanding the Data Sheet Layout

The data points from the data sheet are plotted as *markers* in the chart. Markers appear as lines, bars, columns, data points in X-Y charts, or slices in a pie chart. Microsoft Graph usually uses its default settings. A row of *data points*, therefore, appears in a chart as a *series* of markers. A series of values appears in the chart connected by a line or as bars or columns that have the same color. In figure 27.3, for example, the row labeled East corresponds to one line in the 3-D line chart.

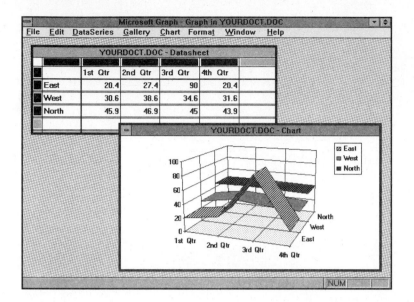

FIG. 27.3.

By default each row of data translates to a series of data points in the chart.

In this default orientation, known as Series in Rows, the text in the first row of the data sheet becomes the *category names* that appear below the *category (X) axis* (the horizontal axis). The text in the left column becomes the *series names*, which Microsoft Graph uses as labels for the legend. (The *legend* is the box that labels the different colors or patterns used by each series of markers.) If you change orientation and want to return to the default orientation, choose the **DataSeries** Series in **R**ows command

If your data on the data sheet uses the reverse orientation so that each data series goes down a column, you must choose the **DataSeries** Series in **C**olumns command. The category names (x-axis labels) are taken from the left column of the data sheet (see fig. 27.4). The series names (legend labels) are taken from the top row.

When you create a Microsoft Graph chart, be sure that you have text for each series name (legend labels), text for each category label (x-axis), and a number for each data point.

Typing Data for a New Chart

To manually create a chart, type over the numbers and text that appear in the default data sheet. When you change the default data sheet, you update the chart.

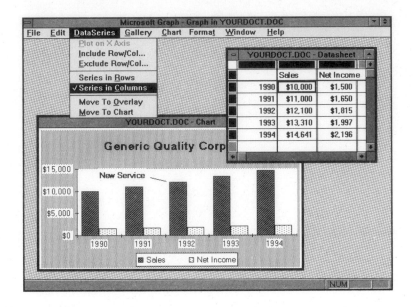

FIG. 27.4.

A data series
with a column
orientation.

If you change numbers or text in the data sheet after you open it, you
make corresponding changes in the chart. Rows or columns of data you
add to the data sheet are included in the chart. Later sections in this
chapter describe methods for editing data and for including or excluding rows or columns from the chart.

Creating Charts from a Table

In a Word for Windows' document, you can quickly convert data in a
table into a chart. Figure 27.5 shows a table and its subsequent chart in
a document.

To create a chart from a table in a Word for Windows' document, follow
these steps:

1. Enter in the table the data and text in the layout you want in a
   Microsoft Graph data sheet.

   Use the Table menu to insert and format a table.

2. Select the table.

3. Click on the Chart button in the toolbar or choose the Insert
   Object command. Select Microsoft Graph from the Object Type
   list, and then choose OK.

   Microsoft Graph starts. After a moment, Microsoft Graph will load
   the table's data into the data sheet. The chart updates.

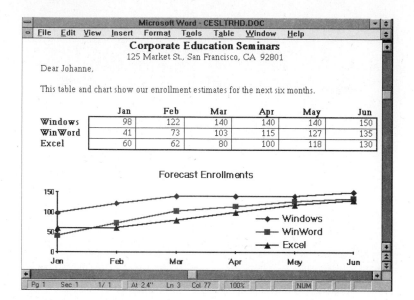

FIG. 27.5.

A table and its subsequent chart in a document.

4. Format, modify, and size the chart and data sheet. If your data series are in columns, you need to choose the **DataSeries** Series in **Columns** command.

5. Choose the File **Exit** and Return to Document command.

6. To update the chart in the document, choose **Yes** at the prompt.

Microsoft Graph closes. A blank line is inserted after the table, and then your chart is inserted.

Copying Data from Word for Windows or Other Applications

You can copy data from applications and paste it into the data sheet to create a chart. You can create a chart, for example, from a series of text and numbers aligned on tabs in Word for Windows, or you can copy a range of cells from a Microsoft Excel worksheet. (The later section, "Importing Excel Charts," describes how to import a range from Microsoft Excel or use a Microsoft Excel chart as a basis for a Microsoft Graph chart.)

You must separate data and text in a word processing document by tabs for the information to copy into separate data sheet cells. Figure 27.6 shows the same Word for Windows document as in figure 27.5, but the data and labels are separated by right-align tabs. You must arrange data and text as you want it to appear in the Microsoft Graph data sheet.

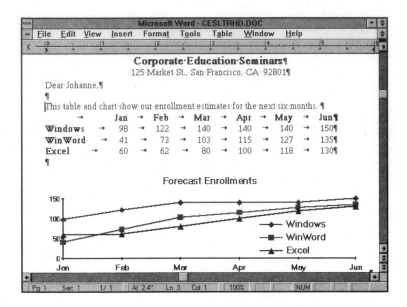

FIG. 27.6.

Data and labels separated by tabs.

To copy data from a document or Microsoft Excel worksheet and create a chart, follow these steps:

1. Select the tabbed data or range of Microsoft Excel cells. Choose the **E**dit **C**opy command.

2. Move the insertion point to where you want the chart, and then click on the Chart button or choose the **I**nsert **O**bject command. Select Microsoft Graph from the list, and then choose OK.

3. Activate the data sheet and erase all existing data by choosing the **E**dit Select **A**ll command or pressing Ctrl+A. Then choose the **E**dit **C**lear command or press the Del key. When the Clear dialog box displays, choose OK or press Enter.

4. Ensure that the top left cell in the data sheet is selected, and then choose the **E**dit **P**aste command.

   The data is pasted into the data sheet, and the chart updates.

5. Format, modify, or size the chart and data sheet as necessary.

6. Choose the **F**ile E**x**it and Return to Document command.

7. Choose **Y**es when asked whether you want to update the chart in the document.

   The chart is inserted at the insertion point.

Importing Worksheet or Text Data

You may want to use data you have in an ASCII text file, or Microsoft Excel or Lotus 1-2-3 worksheet for a chart. You can save time by importing this data directly into the Microsoft Graph data sheet.

To import data into the data sheet, follow these steps:

1. Erase all unwanted data from the data sheet, and then select the cell where you want the top left corner of the imported data. If you are importing an entire chart's worth of data, select the top left cell of the data sheet.

2. Choose the **F**ile **I**mport Data command. The Import Data dialog box appears (see fig. 27.7). Find and select the file from which you want to import data.

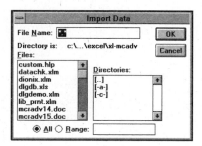

FIG. 27.7.

The Import Data dialog box.

3. Specify the amount of data you want imported. To import all data, choose the **A**ll button. To import a range of data, enter the range or range name in the Range box. Use a range format such as A12:D36.

4. Choose OK or press Enter.

To import data from a worksheet, you must have the worksheet converter files loaded. If they are not loaded, run the Word for Windows Setup program. (The icon is in the Word for Windows program window.) Select the options to install the converters you choose without reinstalling all of Word for Windows. You need your original Word for Windows installation disks to do this.

Importing a Microsoft Excel Chart

With Microsoft Excel, you can create mathematical models that generate charts which can be linked to Word for Windows documents. If you change the worksheet, you change the chart. These changes are reflected in the Word for Windows' document. (This concept is described in Chapter 21.) Importing a Microsoft Excel chart into Microsoft Graph so that the chart can be embedded into the Word for Windows document has other advantages. Embedded charts keep the data with the chart so that another person can update the chart without having Microsoft Excel or the original Microsoft Excel worksheet. Links are not broken if the source worksheet or chart in Microsoft Excel is renamed or moved to a different directory.

To import a Microsoft Excel chart and the chart's related data, follow these steps:

1. Move the insertion point to where you want the chart, and then start Microsoft Graph by clicking on the Graph button in the toolbar, or by choosing the **I**nsert **O**bject command.

2. Choose the **F**ile **O**pen Microsoft Excel Chart command. To overwrite existing data in the data sheet, choose OK when prompted.

    The Open Microsoft Excel Chart dialog box appears (see fig. 27.8).

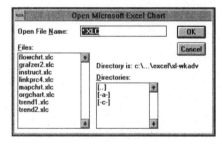

FIG. 27.8.

The Open Microsoft Excel Chart dialog box.

3. Select the drive, directory, and file name of the Microsoft Excel chart, and then choose OK. Microsoft Excel charts use the file extension XLC.

    The chart opens in Microsoft Graph and the associated data appears in the data sheet. Data series that were in rows in Microsoft Excel are in columns in the Microsoft Graph data sheet, but the chart will be correct.

Editing Existing Charts

Updating existing Microsoft Graph charts in a Word for Windows document is easy. With a mouse, double-click on the chart. With the keyboard, select the chart by moving the insertion point next to the chart, and then pressing Shift+arrow across the chart. After the chart is selected, choose the Edit Microsoft Graph Object command.

Microsoft Graph opens and loads the data and chart. You then can use any of the procedures described in this chapter to modify your chart or data.

Entering Data for Overlay Charts

Overlay charts overlay one two-dimensional chart type on another. They make it easier to see relationships between different types of data or data with widely different scales.

Overlay charts consist of a *main* chart (the underlying chart foundation that uses the Y-axis on the left) and an overlay chart (the overlay that covers the main chart and uses a second Y-axis on the right). You can create an overlay chart by choosing the Gallery Combination command. You also can create an overlay chart from existing charts by selecting a data series (line, bar, or column) and choosing the DataSeries Move to Overlay command. The selected series is moved out of the main chart and into the overlay chart.

The Gallery Combination command divides the number of data series in half. The first half creates the main chart, and the second half creates the overlay chart. When the total number of series is odd, the main chart receives the large number of series.

Editing the Data Sheet

Working in the data sheet is similar to working in a Word for Windows table or a Microsoft Excel worksheet. Because the data sheet cannot be printed, it does not have a wide range of font formatting options. Another difference is that cellular data may be edited directly in a cell or within an editing box.

Selecting Data

Moving and selecting cells in the data sheet uses many of the same techniques used in Microsoft Excel. If you are using a mouse, you can use the scroll bars to scroll to any location on the data sheet. To select a cell, click on it. To select multiple cells, drag the mouse across them. To select a row or column, click on its header. To select multiple rows or columns, drag across the headers. To select all of the cells in the data sheet, click in the blank rectangle at the top left corner where row and column headings intersect. (Selecting the entire worksheet and pressing Del erases the entire worksheet.)

If you are using the keyboard, use the keys shown in the following tables to move the insertion point or select cells and the cells' contents.

To move	Press
A cell	Arrow
To first cell in row	Home
To last cell in row	End
To top left data cell	Ctrl+Home
To lower right data cell	Ctrl+End
A screen up/down	Page Up/Down
A screen right/left	Ctrl+Page Up/Down
To select	Press
A cell	Arrow
A range (rectangle)	Shift+arrow or F8 (enters Extend of cells mode). Arrow, and then F8 (exit Extend mode)
A row	Shift+space bar
A column	Ctrl+space bar
The datasheet	Shift+Ctrl+space bar or Ctrl+A or **Edit Select All**
Undo selection	Shift+backspace or move

Replacing or Editing Existing Data

The easiest way to replace the contents of a cell is to select the cell by moving to it or clicking on it, and then typing directly over the cell's contents. When you press Enter or select a different cell, the change takes effect.

To edit the contents of a cell, select the cell by moving to it or clicking on it. Press F2, the Edit key, or double-click on the cell. A simple edit box appears and shows the contents of the cell. You can edit the cell's contents as you would the contents of any edit box. After you finish editing, choose OK or press Enter.

Inserting or Deleting Rows and Columns

Microsoft Graph expands the chart to include data or text you add in rows or columns outside the originally charted data. If you add rows or columns of data and leave blank rows or columns, Microsoft Graph does not include the blank rows or columns as part of the chart.

To insert or delete rows or columns in the data sheet, select the rows or columns where you want to insert or delete, and then choose the **Edit Insert** Row/Col or the **Edit Delete** Row/Col command. The shortcut keys for inserting and deleting are Ctrl++ (plus) and Ctrl+ – (minus), respectively. A dialog box appears if you do not select an entire row or column and asks you to select whether you want to affect the rows or columns that pass through the selected cells.

The Microsoft Graph data sheet cannot have more than 256 columns or 4000 rows. If you need a larger data sheet, create the chart in Microsoft Excel or an advanced charting application and link or paste it into Word for Windows.

Copying or Moving Data

Copy or move data in the data sheet using normal Windows techniques. Select the cells you want to copy or move, and then choose the **Edit Copy** or **Edit Cut** command. (The shortcut keys are Ctrl+C and Ctrl+X, respectively.) Select the cell at the top left corner of the area where you want the data to be pasted and choose the **Edit Paste** command or press Ctrl+V. The pasted data replaces the data it covers. To undo the paste operation, choose the **Edit Undo** command.

Including and Excluding Data from a Chart

When you add data or text to the data sheet, Microsoft Graph immediately redraws the chart, even if the data is not touching the preceding data. This is inconvenient if you want to exclude some rows or columns from the chart.

You can see which rows and columns of data are included because their row or column heading is darkened. Excluded rows or columns are grayed.

To include or exclude a row or column with the mouse, double-click on the row or column heading. The double-click toggles the row or column between included and excluded.

To include or exclude a row or column with the keyboard, select the entire row or column and then choose the **D**ataSeries **I**nclude Row/Col or the **D**ataSeries **E**xclude Row/Col command.

Changing Data by Moving a Graph Marker

Microsoft Graph enables you to move column, bar, lines, or X-Y markers on 2-D charts. As you move the data point, the corresponding data changes in the data sheet—convenient for smoothing a curve so that it matches real-life experience or for "fudging" numbers so that they fit the results you want.

To change values on the datasheet by moving markers on the chart, follow these steps:

1. Open the worksheet and chart. Activate the chart. The chart must be a two-dimensional column, bar, or line chart.

2. Hold down the Ctrl key and click on the column, bar, or line marker you want to change. A black handle appears on the marker.

3. Drag the black handle to the new height. When you drag the black handle, a tick mark on the vertical axis moves, showing you the value of the new location.

4. Release the mouse when the marker is at the location you want.

The corresponding data in the data sheet changes.

Changing the Chart Type

When Microsoft Graph first opens, the chart appears as a three-dimensional column type of chart. Many different chart types are available, but you have to select the appropriate one.

Try to choose the appropriate chart type before you begin customizing. To change the chart type after you customize, follow the procedure described in the later section, "Customizing an Existing Chart Type."

Selecting the Original Chart Type

When you build charts, you can use any of the 81 predefined chart formats. The easiest way to create charts is to select the predefined chart closest to the type you want. You then can customize the predefined chart until it fits your needs. To use a predefined chart, follow these steps:

1. Select the **G**allery command.

2. From the menu, choose one of these charts:

Area	Com**b**ination
Bar	3-D Area
Column	3-D Bar
Line	3-D **C**olumn
Pie	3-D Line
X-Y (**S**catter)	3-D Pie

After you make your choice, the Chart Gallery dialog box appears. This dialog box shows the different predefined types of charts. Figure 27.9 shows the gallery available for 3-D column charts.

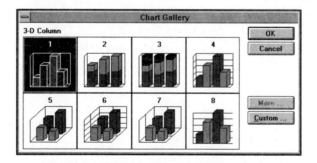

The gallery of predefined formats for 3-D Column charts.

3. To select a chart type, click on its square or type its number.

4. If you do not see the type you want and the **More** button is not grayed, choose the **More** button to see additional formats of this type.

5. If you want a variation from the chart types shown, choose the **Custom** button.

   The Format Chart dialog box appears (see fig. 27.10). Select options to modify the chart type. This dialog box is different for each chart type.

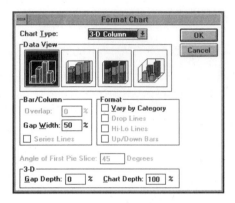

The Format Chart dialog box.

6. Choose OK or press Enter.

You can access the customizing options available through the **Custom** button in step 5 at any time by choosing the Forma**t** **C**hart or Forma**t** **O**verlay command.

> To select the chart type you want, double-click the box in the Gallery containing the chart. This technique selects the type and chooses OK.
>
> **T I P**

The following table describes the two-dimensional chart types available through the Gallery menu.

Chart	Description
2-D Line Chart	Compares trends over even time or measurement intervals plotted on the category (X) axis. (If your category data points are at uneven intervals, use an X-Y scatter chart.)

Chart	Description
2-D Area Chart	Compares the continuous change in volume of a data series.
2-D Bar Chart	Compares distinct (noncontinuous) items over time. Horizontal bars show positive or negative variation from a center point. Frequently used for time management.
2-D Column Chart	Compares separate (noncontinuous) items as they vary over time.
2-D Pie Chart	Compares the size of each of the pieces making up a whole unit. Use this type of chart when the parts total 100 percent for the first series of data. Only the first data series in a worksheet selection is plotted.
X-Y (Scattergram) Chart	Compares trends over *uneven* time or measurement intervals plotted on the category (X) axis.
Combination Chart	Lays one chart over another. These charts are useful for comparing data of different types or data requiring different axis scales.

The following table describes the three-dimensional chart types available through the Gallery menu.

Chart	Description
3-D Area Chart	Uses 3-D area charts for the same types of data as those used in 2-D area charts.
3-D Bar Chart	Uses 3-D bar charts for the same type of data as those used in 2-D bar charts.
3-D Column Chart	Uses 3-D column charts for the same types of data as those used in 2-D column charts. You can create 3-D column charts with the columns adjacent to each other or layered into the third dimension.
3-D Line Chart	Uses 3-D line charts for the same types of data as those used in 2-D line charts. 3-D line charts also are known as *ribbon charts*.
3-D Pie Chart	Shows labels or calculates percentages for wedges. Only the first data series from a selection is charted as a pie. Wedges can be dragged out from the pie.

Customizing an Existing Chart Type

You can save yourself work by deciding on the type of chart you want before you customize it. Use the **G**allery command to try different types of charts, and then customize the one you decide to use. If you use the **G**allery command to change the chart type after you customize a chart, you may lose some of your custom selections.

To change or customize a chart type without losing custom formatting, choose the Forma**t** **C**hart or Forma**t** **O**verlay command, and then select from the available options. The Forma**t** **O**verlay command is only available when the chart is a combination chart.

Forma**t** **C**hart changes the basic type or customizes the main or background chart. Forma**t** **O**verlay changes or customizes the overlay chart. Figures 27.11 and 27.12 show the Format Chart and Format Overlay dialog boxes that enable you to customize the main or overlay charts. Both use the same options.

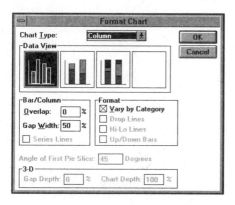

FIG. 27.11.

The Format Chart dialog box.

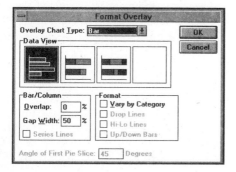

FIG. 27.12.

The Format Overlay dialog box.

Options in the Format Chart and Format Overlay dialog boxes are available only when appropriate for the type of chart that is active. The options include the following:

Option	Description
Chart **T**ype	Changes the basic chart type to one of the types shown in the Gallery menu and retains custom formats.
Data **V**iew	Changes the type of marker or axis presentation within a specific chart type.
Bar/Column **O**verlap	Enter a positive number as the percentage you want bars or columns to overlap. 50 is full overlap. A negative number separates individual bars or columns.
Bar/Column Gap **W**idth	Specifies the space between groups of bars or columns. Measured as a percentage of one bar or column width.
Format **V**ary by Category	Specifies a different color or pattern by category for each marker in all pie charts or any chart with one data series.
Format Drop Lines	Drops a vertical line from a marker to the category (X) axis. Used on line or area charts.
Format Hi-Lo Lines	Draws a line between the highest and lowest lines at a specific category. Used on 2-D line charts.
Format Up/Down Lines	Draws a rectangle from the opening price to closing price on open-high-low-close types of line charts used to track stock prices.
Angle of First Pie Slice	Specifies the starting angle in degrees for the first wedge in a pie chart. Vertical is zero degrees.
3-D Gap Depth	Specifies the spacing in depth between markers as a percentage of a marker. 50 changes the space of the depth between markers to 50% of a marker width.
3-D Chart Depth	Specifies how deep a 3-D chart is relative to its width. Enter a number as a percentage of the chart width. 50 makes the depth 50% of the width. Number must be between 20 and 2000.

If you did not choose a combination chart as your first chart type, you still can change your chart to include an overlay. To add data series to an overlay or to create an overlay, select the data series in the data sheet or select the markers in the chart. Choose the DataSeries Move to Overlay command.

If the chart did not have an overlay before, it will not have a line overlay. When a data series is added to the overlay, its heading in the data sheet shows a large white dot. To change the format of an overlay, use the Format Overlay command as described earlier in this section.

To remove a data series from the overlay, select the data series or the markers, and then choose the DataSeries Move to Main command. To completely remove an overlay, move all of the data series in the overlay back to the main chart.

Formatting the Data Sheet

Formatting the data sheet is important for more reasons than making data entry easier and more accurate. The format of the numbers and dates in the chart are controlled by their format in the data sheet.

Adjusting Column Widths in the Data Sheet

When numbers are entered in unformatted cells, they appear in General format. If the column is not wide enough to display the full number, the number's format changes to scientific format. 6,000,000, for example, changes to 6E+6. When a number is too large to fit in a cell, the cell fills with # signs.

Microsoft Graph uses the same numeric and date formatting methods as Microsoft Excel and the same as many of the numeric and date formatting switches used with Word for Windows' field codes. It has all of Microsoft Excel's custom numeric and date formatting capability.

To adjust column width with the mouse, move the pointer over the line separating the column headings until the pointer changes to a two-headed arrow. Drag the column separator line to the column width you want and release the mouse button.

To adjust column width by keyboard, select cells in the columns you want to adjust, then choose the the Format Column Width command. The Column Width dialog box appears. In the Column Width edit box, type a number representing the width of the column, and then choose OK.

You can return column widths to their standard setting by choosing the Standard Width check box in the Column Width dialog box.

Formatting Numbers and Dates

Microsoft Graph has many predefined numeric and date formats. You can choose from these formats to format the data sheet and chart or to create your own custom formats.

The format of the first data cell in a series defines the numeric or date format for that series in the chart. You can even enter a date such as 12-24-92 as a label for a category axis. You can then format the cell with a different date format (such as *d-mmm*, and the date appears as 12-Dec).

To format data cells, follow these steps:

1. Select the data cell or range you want to format. You can select entire rows or columns at one time.

2. Choose the Format Number command.

   The Number dialog box displays a list of different numeric and date formats.

3. Select from the list the numeric or date format you want to apply to the selected data cells.

4. Choose OK or press Enter.

The items in the list may appear strange until you understand the symbols used to represent different numeric and date formats. The characters in the list are as follows:

Character	Example	Entry	Result
#	#,###	9999.00	9,999

is a position holder for commas. It *will not* represent blank values, such as the trailing zeros to the right of the decimal.

0	#,###.00	9999.5	9,999.50

0 is a position holder for leading or trailing zeros.

$	$#,###	9000.65	$9,001

$ displays a dollar sign. Values are rounded up because of no trailing zeros.

()	0.00 ;(0.00)	5.6	$5.60
		-9.834	($9.83)

() parentheses are used to enclose negative numbers.

m	mmm	12	Dec

Represents months (m = 6, mm = 06, mmm = Jun, mmmm = June).

Character	Example	Entry	Result
d	dd	6	06

Represents days (d = 6, dd = 06, ddd = Tue, ddd = Tuesday).

yy	yy	1991	91

Represents years (yy = 93, yyyy = 1993).

h or m	hh:mm AM/PM	6:12	06:12 AM

h represents hours, m following h represents minutes, AM/PM indicates 12-hour clock, no AM/PM indicates 24-hour clock.

Microsoft Graph also enables you to format numbers and dates with a different format for positive or negative numbers. A semicolon separates positive and negative formats. For example,

$#,##0.00 ;($#,##0.00)

produces different formats for positive and negative numbers. For example,

The number	Appears as
89875.4	$89,875.40
–567.23	($567.23)

When a negative format is enclosed in parentheses, the positive format usually has a space between the last digit and the semicolon. This space leaves a space at the end of the positive number to balance the trailing parenthesis on a negative number and helps positive and negative numbers align when a column has right alignment.

Custom Formatting of Numbers and Dates

If the format you need is not in the Number Format list, you can create your own custom formats by typing them into the Format text box. Use the same characters as those used in the predefined formats. After you create a custom format, it appears at the bottom of the Number Format list so that you can reuse it. Que's book *Using Excel for Windows, Special Edition*, covers creating custom formats extensively.

Adding Items to a Chart

You can add many items to your Microsoft Graph charts that make them more informative and easier to read.

Some of the items you add are movable and some are fixed. Items fixed in position appear with white handles at their corners when selected. You cannot move or resize them. You can move or resize items that display black handles when selected.

Adding Titles and Data Values

You can use the **C**hart menu to add or delete most items from a chart. To add a title or data point to a fixed location on a chart, for example, follow these steps:

1. Choose the **C**hart **T**itles command.

   The Chart Titles dialog box appears (see fig. 27.13).

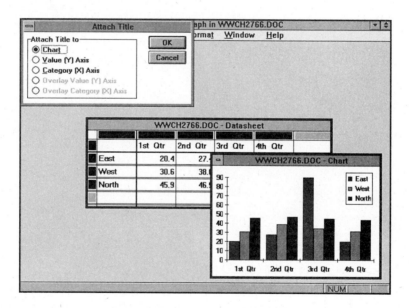

FIG. 27.13.

The Chart Titles
dialog box.

2. Select one of the option buttons.

3. Choose OK or press Enter.

   If you choose Chart or one of the axis options, a default title of Title, X, Y, or Z appears at the appropriate location in the chart.

4. While that default title is selected, type the text you want. Press Enter to move to a second line. Edit using normal editing keys.

5. To finish the text, Press Esc or click outside the text.

    To remove fixed text, select the text and then press the Del key or choose the **E**dit Cl**e**ar command.

To attach numbers or labels that move with the data point in a bar, column, or line chart, follow these steps:

1. Choose the **C**hart **D**ata Labels command.

2. Select the Show **V**alue or Show **L**abel option. If you are working with a pie chart, the Show **P**ercent option may be chosen.

3. Choose OK or press Enter.

To delete data point values or labels, select them and press Del, or choose the **C**hart Data Labels command and select the None option.

Adding Floating Text

Floating text can be used to add comment boxes or it can be used to create boxes for embellishing or covering parts of a chart.

To add floating text, make sure that no other text is selected and then type. Your text appears in a floating box surrounded by black handles. To complete the box, click outside it or press Esc.

The black handles on selected text indicate that you can resize and move the enclosing box by dragging it to a new location or dragging a handle to resize the box. You can format floating text boxes to include colors and patterns.

To select text with the keyboard so that it can be formatted, press the arrow keys until the text you want formatted is enclosed by black or white handles. Floating text cannot be moved by keyboard.

To edit the text in a floating text box, click on the text to select it, and then click where you want the insertion point. To delete a floating text box, select the text and then press the Del key, or use **E**dit Cl**e**ar. If you are using a keyboard, you must retype the text.

Adding Legends, Arrows, and Gridlines

To add a legend, choose the **C**hart Add **L**egend command. The legend appears. Notice that the legend is enclosed with black handles. To move a legend, select it and then choose the Forma**t** **L**egend command, or drag the legend to a new location and release it.

To change the labels used in the legend, change the series labels in the data sheet. You cannot resize a legend.

To add arrows to your charts, make sure an arrow is not selected, and then choose the **Chart Add Arrow** command. If an arrow is selected, the **Chart Delete Arrow** command replaces the **Chart Add Arrow** command. Notice that arrows have black handles at either end so that you can resize them. To move an arrow, drag with the pointer on the arrow's shaft. You can format arrows with different heads, thicknesses, or as a line.

To add gridlines to a chart, choose the **Chart Gridlines** command. The Gridlines dialog box that appears has many check boxes for vertical and horizontal gridlines. To delete gridlines, choose the **Chart Gridlines** command again and clear the check boxes for the gridlines you don't want.

Formatting the Chart and Chart Items

After you select a predefined chart format and add chart items, you can customize your chart. You can change the colors, patterns, and borders of chart items; the type and color of the fonts; the position and size of some chart items; and you can add lines, arrows, titles, legends, and floating text. By selecting an axis and then a format command, you can change the scale and the appearance of tick marks and labels. You also can rotate 3-D charts and create picture charts, in which pictures take the place of columns, bars, or lines.

Customize charts by selecting an item in the chart, and then choosing a format command, as in the following steps:

1. Select the chart item you want to customize by clicking on it or by pressing an arrow key until the chart item is selected.

2. Choose the Format menu and command to format the item.

3. Select the changes you want to make from the dialog box that appears.

4. Choose OK or press Enter.

Sizing Your Chart

Your charts look best in Word for Windows if you resize the chart in Microsoft Graph. Resizing the chart in Word for Windows changes the size, but does not correct text placement, readjust the scale, and so on. By sizing the chart in Microsoft Graph before you update it in Word for Windows, you use Microsoft Graph's capability to reposition and resize elements in the chart

Change the size of the chart as you would the size of any window. Drag its borders or corners with the mouse. Choose the **S**ize command from the Document Control Menu, press Alt+- (hyphen), and then press the arrow keys to resize the window. Make the chart's window the size you want the chart when pasted into the Word for Windows document.

Although you can change the magnification of the graph, it does not change the size of the chart when pasted into the document. Magnifying is useful when you format or position text or arrows. To magnify or shrink your view of the chart, select the **W**indow menu and choose a percentage to magnify or shrink.

Changing Patterns and Colors

To add patterns or colors to an item, choose the Forma**t P**attern command, and then select the colors, patterns, shading, and line widths you want for the item. With a mouse, double-click on an item to display the item's Pattern dialog box.

To return to the default colors, patterns, and borders, select the chart items you want to change, choose the Forma**t** Patterns command, and then select the Automatic option.

T I P   You are limited to sixteen colors but can blend them to create your own colors. To create your own color palette, choose the Format Color Palette command. When the Palette dialog box appears, select the color you want to replace, and then choose the Edit button. When the custom palette appears, type in new color numbers or click in the palette, and then choose OK. The custom color replaces the color you previously selected. To return to the original color settings, choose the Default button.

Formatting Fonts and Text

One font, size, and style are used by the entire data sheet. Each text item in the chart, however, can have a different font, size, or style.

To change an item's font, size, or style, select the item, and then choose the Format Font command. Select the font, size, or style you want. With a mouse, double-click on the item, and then choose the Font button to tunnel through to the Font dialog box. The Font dialog box looks like other Font dialog boxes in Word for Windows but enables you to select different types of character backgrounds.

To rotate or align text, such as the text on an axis, select the text or axis, and then choose the Format Text command. Select the text orientation from the options and choose OK.

Formatting Axes

Microsoft Graph automatically scales and labels the axes, but you can select any axis and change its scale, how frequently labels or tick marks appear, or the orientation and font of text.

Microsoft Graph scales charts to even amounts. To rescale your charts, select the axis (vertical or horizontal) and then choose the Format Scale command. (A shortcut is to double-click on an axis. When the Pattern dialog box appears, choose the Scale button.) A different dialog box appears, depending on which axis you select. If you select the Category (X) Axis, you can change tick marks types and spacing or labels spacing along the horizontal axis. If you select the Value (Y) Axis, you can change the vertical axis' beginning and ending values, the amount of increments and type of tick marks. Figure 27.14 shows the Format Axis Scale dialog box for the Value (Y) Axis where the end points and increments can be adjusted.

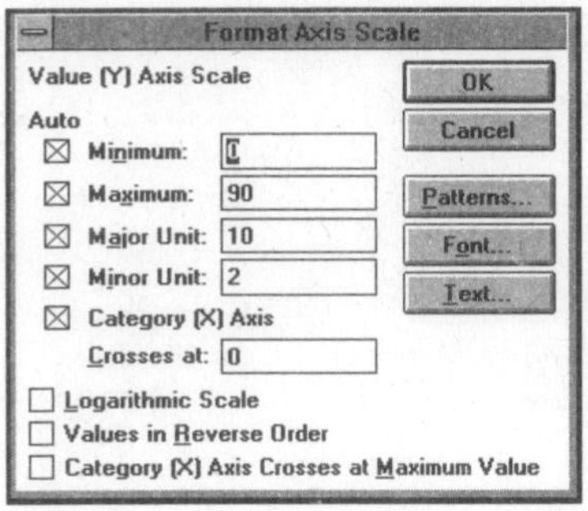

FIG. 27.14.

Format Axis Scale dialog box for the Value (Y) Axis.

To thin out the number of tick marks or overlapping labels along the category (X) axis, select the axis, and then choose the Format **S**cale command. Select the text boxes for either or both Number Of Categories (or Series) Between Tick **L**abels and Number of Categories (or Series) Between Tick Mar**k**s. If you enter five in a box, for example, every fifth tick mark and label is displayed. Choose OK or press Enter. Figure 27.15 shows the Format Axis Scale dialog box for the Category (X) Axis where you can adjust the frequency of data labels and tick marks.

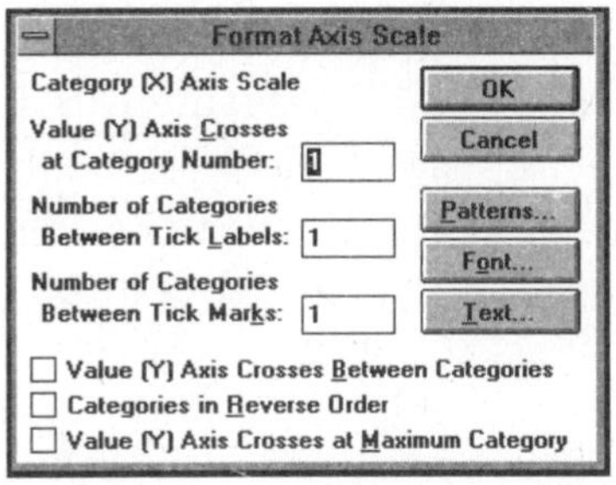

FIG. 27.15.

The Format Axis Scale dialog box for the Category (X) axis.

To change how tick marks appear on an axis scale, double-click on the axis or select the axis, and then choose the Forma**t P**attern command.

Rotating 3-D Charts

If your 3-D chart appears so that you do not have a good point of view to see all of it, you can rotate the chart to show the angle you want (see fig. 27.16). To rotate a 3-D chart, follow these steps:

1. Choose the Forma**t 3**-D View command. The Format 3-D View dialog box appears (see fig. 27.16).

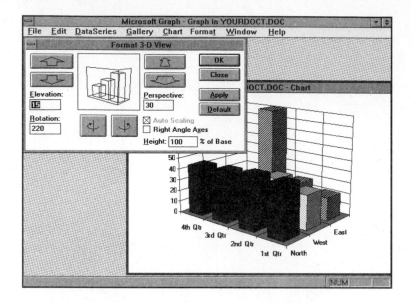

FIG. 27.16.

The Format 3-D
View dialog box.

2. Select the Elevation, Perspective, or Rotation buttons by clicking
   on them or typing values into them. Changing their values affects
   the wire frame sample chart.

3. When the wire frame sample is oriented so that you can see the
   chart as you want, choose OK or press Enter.

The Apply button enables you to apply the new orientation to the chart
and keep the dialog box open, which is helpful for experimenting.
Choose the Default button to return to the original orientation.

Exiting or Updating Graphs

You can keep Microsoft Graph open and update the chart in Word for
Windows, or close Microsoft Graph and update the chart. Updating the
chart embeds the chart and its data in the Word for Windows document. The chart and data cannot be saved separately. They must be
saved as embedded objects within the Word for Windows document.

To see how your chart or its changes will appear in the Word for Windows document, you do not need to close Microsoft Graph. To keep
Microsoft Graph open and update the new or existing chart in the document, choose the File Update command.

When you exit Microsoft Graph, you are given a chance to update the
new or existing chart in Word for Windows. To exit Microsoft Graph,

choose the File Exit and Return to document command. If you made changes since the last update, you are prompted to update the chart in the document. Choose Yes to update the chart.

From Here . . .

If you are familiar with charting in Microsoft Excel, use what you learned in Microsoft Excel to learn about Microsoft Graph. For more detailed information on Microsoft Graph, refer to the book *Using Excel for Windows, Special Edition*, published by Que Corporation. Many of the descriptions, tips, and tricks used in this best-selling book apply to Microsoft Graph.

To learn more about handling the chart as an embedded object, read Chapters 23 and 24. They describe how to position and format pictures and objects.

Desktop Publishing with Word for Windows

A s word processing programs, such as Word for Windows, become increasingly able to handle graphics, they become increasingly similar to desktop publishing programs.

Desktop publishing is simply the integration of text and graphics on a page to create a pleasing page layout. Typically, graphics are of two kinds—those created by the word processing or desktop publishing program, such as lines and boxes, and those imported from other programs, such as scanned photographs and pictures created in Microsoft Draw. Text typically includes a variety of type styles and sizes and may be arranged in columns.

With Word for Windows, you have all you need to create attractive desktop published documents. Word for Windows manages many types of graphics. You can draw lines and boxes, and shade or color boxes and paragraphs. Microsoft Draw, the powerful drawing (and coloring) program, WordArt (ideal for creating logos), and the Equation Editor (perfect for scientific publications) are easily accessible from within Word for Windows.

You can import many types of graphics into your Word for Windows document, including those you scan with a scanner, those you create in another illustration program, or those you select from a clip-art collection. After you add a graphic to your Word for Windows document, you can reshape, resize, and crop it, and you can position the graphic exactly where you want on the page and wrap text around it.

Word for Windows also has powerful text-handling capabilities. Depending on the capabilities of your printer, you have access to many different fonts, sizes, and styles. You can arrange your text in columns and split your document into sections with different numbers of columns. You can turn text into a graphic by framing it and positioning it precisely where you want on the page. You can wrap text around any object, whether the object is text, a table, or a picture.

If you have a laser printer, you can print documents at 300 dpi resolution—exactly what you need for many publications. If you need even better resolution, you can print at 1200 or 2400 dpi on a Linotronic typesetting system, available at service bureaus in most cities.

All of these capabilities add up to desktop publishing. Although Word for Windows isn't ideal for every desktop publishing job, it is suitable for many of the simple projects you do in your day-to-day work. As you learn in this chapter, you can use Word for Windows to create newsletters, advertisements, brochures, letterheads, and much more. This chapter shows you how to use the skills you have learned up to now to produce these types of projects, and refers you back to the chapter that explains the skills required, in case you need to brush up.

As you look through these examples, remember that you can accomplish any layout goal in many ways. You can create the effect of columns on your page, for example, by inserting true columns or by creating a table. In some situations, true columns are the better choice; in others, a table is easier to work with.

The most important rule to remember about desktop publishing with Word for Windows is to keep it simple. When all's said and done, Word for Windows isn't a desktop publishing program. It's a word processing program that enables you to insert and move graphics, format text, and lay out pages in columns. Because Word for Windows is a word processing program, it's oriented to words and treats graphics as though they were a special type of character or paragraph. A true desktop publishing program, on the other hand, is more like a graphics program, which treats words as a special type of object on the page. Therefore, as you're planning your desktop publishing project, be flexible. Work with Word for Windows' strengths as a word processor, appreciate its talents as a desktop publisher, and keep your designs simple and elegant.

Creating a Simple Newsletter

The newsletter shown in figure 28.1 is a simple project you can easily produce with Word for Windows. The newsletter is created in two sections. The drop cap is produced by enlarging and framing the letter *I* at the beginning of the story. An empty box in the middle of the page serves as a placeholder for a traditional photograph, which will be added after the newsletter is printed. The box is framed along with its caption. At the bottom of the page is a running footer.

The PC Reporter

Winter Issue

Shedding a Little Light on Windows

by Karen Rose

If you haven't heard enough about Windows that you're at least *thinking* about it, you may soon find yourself out in the dark.

Since its announcement, Windows has sold many more copies than even its ever-optimistic manufacturer Microsoft thought it would. Already, sales number close to five million. And reviews of the product have been glowing–reviewer after reviewer finds Windows to be a powerful, useful, and well-executed piece of software. It seems Windows is leading a charmed existence.

So chances are, you're wondering what Windows can do for you.

Looking Into Windows

As a quick reminder, Windows is a graphic operating environment for your PC. It presents your applications in "windows" on your screen, and supplies a graphical interface shared by all Windows applications. Programs work with the aid of pull-down menus, dialog boxes, and visual icons, and much of what you do in Windows programs can be managed by a hand-held mouse. Important features of Windows include multitasking–the ability to run multiple programs simultaneously, and DDE (dynamic data exchange)–the ability to link data between applications. (To learn more about Windows, refer to our June review.)

There are three ways you can implement Windows in your office. If you currently have a DOS-only office, and don't plan to buy Windows programs like Excel or Word for Windows, you can run Windows if you have 286-based PCs (Microsoft tells you it's possible to run Windows on an 8088, but hey, your grandfather could enter the Boston Marathon too . . .). A better solution is a mixed environment of DOS applications and Windows applications both running under Win-

dows. The best solution is an all-Windows environment, in which all the programs you use are designed to work with Windows. But for most CPA offices, the all-Windows solution isn't practical–though there are 750 or so Windows programs available, few of them are accounting programs.

Much of the excitement about Windows focuses on how easy (and fun) it is to use, how much faster it is to learn new programs under Windows, how powerful and time-saving the linking capabilities are, and how useful multitasking is. How can those benefits translate to productivity gains in the CPA office?

The Windows graphical interface makes software easy to use.

Financial Publishing

One of the great advantages to a graphic working environment is that it allows for programs that are more graphical–programs that include drawing tools, varied fonts, and instant charting, and that not only have the ability to mix text and graphics on the page, but that have the ability to display that page on screen in much the same way it will look when printed (known as WYSIWYG, or "what you see is what you get"). You have those capabilities in spreadsheet programs like Lotus 1-2-3 (with Allways in releases 2.2 and 3.0, and with Impress in release 3.1) and Excel (a true Windows program). But your office support staff may not be as fluent in a spreadsheet program as they are in the word processing program they use every day. And Windows makes it very easy to pull together financial information from multiple sources for publishing in a word processing program.

There are several advantages to automating the financial publishing process with Windows.

Published Quarterly for Clients of Ron Person & Co.—Page 1
"Specializing in Windows Software"

The procedures to create *The PC Reporter* newsletter shown in figure 28.1 are outlined in the following paragraphs.

To create the masthead, follow these steps:

1. Type the newsletter name.

2. Make the newsletter name bold, and then enlarge and center the name (Format Character and Format Paragraph, or ribbon).

3. Type, italicize, and center the subtitle.

4. Select the newsletter name and subtitle, and border them together, using a drop shadow box (Format Border).

To create the title of the article, follow these steps:

1. Type the article title.

2. Make the title bold. Then enlarge the title, leaving it left-aligned.

3. Type and italicize the byline.

4. Enter a blank line after the byline.

5. Enter a continuous section break below the byline.

To create the text of the article, follow these steps:

1. Type the article.

2. Redefine the Normal style to include formatting choices you want for the text (such as a quarter-inch first line indent, alignment, font style and size) (Format Style).

3. Create a style called Subhead to format all the subheadings consistently.

To create the two-column layout, follow these steps:

1. Place the insertion point inside the second section (inside the text of the article).

2. Choose two columns with a line between.

To create the drop cap, follow these steps:

1. Select the letter *I* at the beginning of the article.

2. Frame the letter *I* (Insert Frame, or Frame button on toolbar).

3. Position the frame horizontally to the left relative to the column, and vertically at 0 (zero) inches relative to the paragraph. Let it move with the text. (Make all of these choices using the Format Frame command.)

To create the running footer, follow these steps:

1. Display the footer and type the text as shown in figure 28.1, including automatic page numbering.

2. Select the first line of the footer and format it to include a border across the top.

To create the empty box with a caption, follow these steps:

1. Position the insertion point somewhere on the first page.

2. Insert a frame (Insert Frame, or Frame button), and draw it to the size you want at the left margin (to make it easier to add a caption). The insertion point is inside the frame.

3. Press Enter enough times to move the insertion point to the bottom of the frame.

4. Type the caption.

5. Select the caption and format it with no border (Format **B**order None).

6. Select the frame (which includes the caption) and position it where you want it (Forma**t F**rame).

You can use the following steps as an alternative method for creating the empty box with a caption:

1. Position the insertion point somewhere at the left margin.

2. Press Enter enough times to create a blank space as tall as you want your box.

3. Type the caption.

4. Select the empty spaces and border them with a box (Format **B**order).

5. Select and frame the caption and the box (**I**nsert **F**rame).

Position the frame—with its caption—where you want it on the page. In this case center it horizontally and manually position it vertically).

The template for this newsletter includes a masthead, dummy title text, a continuous section break below title, columns with line between, a few lines of dummy text for the article, a drop cap, redefined Normal style, subhead style, and a footer.

The following paragraphs provide tips you can use when creating a simple newsletter.

Views: Work in the page layout view (View Page Layout) so that you can see columns side by side; so you can see graphics where they are positioned; and so you can drag framed objects on the page using a mouse. (In the normal view, by contrast, everything appears at the left margin.) By seeing your page as it will look when printed, you are a better judge of your layout's visual impact. (See Chapter 4.)

Font Styles: You can combine many font styles, and depending on what's available in your printer, you may have many different fonts from which to choose. Don't get carried away; use font styles like bold and italic sparingly and meaningfully (subheadings are bold, titles italic, for example). Remember that ALL CAPS and <u>underlining</u> are conventions left over from the days of the typewriter, when bold and italic were unavailable. (See Chapter 5.)

Number of Columns: No steadfast rule exists about how many columns you should have in your publication, but a general guideline is that a column should be at least an alphabet and a half wide (about 40 characters). If your text is small, you can have more columns; if text is large, use fewer columns. The narrower the column, the more important hyphenation becomes. (See Chapter 9.)

Hyphenation: Hyphenate words individually (Ctrl+hyphen inserts a discretionary hyphen), or hyphenate your entire document at once (Tools Hyphenation). Hyphenation makes left-aligned text less ragged and helps prevent wide spaces between words in justified text. (See Chapter 9.)

Alignment: Left-aligned text is less formal in appearance than justified.

Framing and Positioning: You can frame anything—from a single character to a group of paragraphs to a graphic (Insert Frame or Frame button). After an object is framed, it is freed from the text: you can position it anywhere on the page, with text wrapping around the frame (Format Frame or drag with mouse).

Borders and Shading: Included in the Format Border command are several styles of graphics useful in desktop publishing. A border can be a line, such as a heavy line below a company name in letterhead. It can be an empty box, where you add hand-drawn art or a photo after you print. A border also can be a box around a floating pulled-quote in a newsletter, or a border can be shading behind text in an ad. Use borders in your desktop publication to easily add a touch of graphics to a text-heavy document.

Movable Boxes: Create a movable box by framing and sizing it, and then turning off Move with Text in the Frame dialog box. Drag the box wherever you want it on the page (or on the next page). You can leave the box empty (to add a photo or line drawing after you print, for example) or you can insert text or a picture, which will conform to the frame's size.

Creating a Three-Fold Brochure

The three-fold brochure shown in figure 28.2 is created using a landscape-oriented layout with three-row tables on two pages. Using tables enables each panel of the brochure to exist as an independent unit. With tables, you also can more easily border each panel separately and identically.

ReLeaf needs your support.

Please help us continue our work of planting trees and educating people about the importance of trees by sending your tax-deductible contribution to:

Sonoma County ReLeaf
P.O. Box 14806
Santa Rosa, CA 95402

Sonoma County ReLeaf
P.O. Box 14806
Santa Rosa, CA 95402

printed on recycled paper

Plant a tree, cool the globe.

Sonoma County ReLeaf
A plan of action:

- For our communities
- For our neighborhoods
- For our schools

THE GREENHOUSE EFFECT:
HOW YOU CAN DO YOUR PART

The greenhouse effect is slowly but dangerously heating up our planet. It's going to take some lifestyle changes, including energy conservation, to help reverse the buildup of carbon dioxide in our atmosphere.

SONOMA COUNTY RELEAF INVITES YOU TO DO YOUR PART:

- PLANT drought-tolerant trees on the southeast, southwest, or south sides of your home.
- ORGANIZE your neighbors to plant trees on your street.
- DRIVE a fuel-efficient car.
- CARPOOL or use public transit whenever possible.
- WALK or ride a bicycle for short trips.
- SWITCH off lights and air conditioning whenever possible.
- LOWER your thermostat to 68 degrees.
- RECYCLE glass, aluminum, and paper to save energy and trees.
- COMPOST your yard waste and kitchen scraps to reduce trash.

FOR MORE INFORMATION CALL:
Sonoma County ReLeaf
(707) 539-4119

California ReLeaf is a grassroots effort to plant and care for 20 million trees in towns and cities throughout the state by the year 2000.

Sonoma County ReLeaf as part of this statewide campaign has the following objectives:

- To educate about the implications of the global warming trend.
- To participate in the California ReLeaf campaign by planting thousands of trees around our homes, offices, shopping centers, streets, and highways.
- To encourage people through the act of planting a tree to enact their commitment to caring for our environment and the future of our earth.

Enclosed is my contribution to Sonoma County ReLeaf. Contributions will support tree plantings, community outreach, and education.

❑ $25
❑ $50
❑ $100
❑ $ ___

All contributions are tax-deductible. Make checks payable to ReLeaf:
ReLeaf/Friends of the Urban Forest
P.O. Box 14806
Santa Rosa, CA 95402
Please send me information on the following:
❑ Tree list and how to plant and maintain trees.
❑ Global warming fact sheets.
❑ How to organize neighborhood tree plantings.
❑ Energy conservation information.
Name_____
Address_____
City_____
State _____ Zip _____
Phone_____

FIG. 28.2.

A three-fold brochure created with tables.

The brochure's front panel includes a bordered paragraph, a bulleted list, and an inserted picture. The back panel (the mailing panel) has sideways text created in WordArt. Inside panels include bulleted lists and raised initial caps. The rightmost inside panel (a form for readers to mail in) includes a name and address area with lines created by using right-aligned tabs with an underlined tab leader.

In creating the page layout for a brochure, consider that you want each panel of the brochure to have equal left and right margins. That means you need to be able to divide the landscape-oriented page into three columns, with gutters (spaces between the columns) equal to twice the width of the left and right margins (when you fold the brochure, each panel gets half of a gutter—you want that to equal the width of the margin). On a standard 11-inch page width, the math doesn't come out evenly, so this design is a compromise: the margins are a little wider than the folded gutters.

In designing your own brochure, be sure to plan your math carefully before you begin the page layout. Changing your measurement system can be helpful; for example, measured in picas, an 11-inch page is 66 picas: if you include 2-pica margins and 4-pica gutters, you get 3 columns that are each exactly 18 picas wide.

The procedures to create the three-fold brochure shown in figure 28.2 are outlined in the following paragraphs.

1. Open a new document.

2. Set up the page for landscape orientation and set all margins to .4 inches (Format Page Setup).

To create the tables that form the framework for pages 1 and 2 of the brochure, follow these steps:

1. Insert a table with five columns (Table Insert Table, or the Table button on the toolbar).

2. Set the width for each column manually (Table Column Width, or the ruler), as follows:

Columns 1, 3, and 5	3 inches (the brochure panels)
Columns 2 and 4	.6 inches (the gutters)

3. Set the row height manually (Table Row Height). Set all rows to 7.6 inches tall (.1 inch shorter than the bottom margins).

4. Select columns 1, 3, and 5 and add a box border to each (Format Border).

To create the front panel (the right side of page 1), follow these steps:

1. Type and center the boxed text. Indent the text from both sides.

2. Select the text and add a box with shading (Format **B**order). Because you indented the text, the box will be narrower than the cell.

3. Type the remaining text, formatting it as shown in figure 28.2, or as you want.

4. Insert a picture at the bottom of the cell (Insert **P**icture). The picture will conform to the cell width, but you may want to further size or crop it.

To create the rotated text on the center mailing panel, follow these steps:

1. Position the insertion point about halfway down the page by pressing Enter several times.

2. Insert a new WordArt object (Insert **O**bject, MS WordArt).

3. Type the text of the return address and select the style Bottom to Top. Choose OK. Include more or fewer blank spaces above the return address to position it near the bottom of the cell. Double-click the return address to edit it, if necessary.

To create the raised initial cap used on the inside panels, follow these steps:

1. Select and enlarge the first letter in any paragraph.

2. Select the entire paragraph containing the raised first cap and set the paragraph line spacing to Exactly 1.5 lines, to maintain consistent spacing throughout the paragraph (Format **P**aragraph). Otherwise, the one large letter in the first line will cause more space to appear below the first line than below the remaining lines.

   After printing, check that you have enough line spacing to accommodate the size of your initial cap—if the top of the letter is cut off, you need to increase the line spacing.

To create bulleted lists, type the lists with no formatting. Select the lists, and then choose the Bulleted List button in the toolbar.

To create the check boxes in the reader response form, insert a symbol that looks like a box at the beginning of each item (Insert **S**ymbol).

To create the lines for the name and address in the reader response form, follow these steps:

1. Select the text for which you want to create lines.

2. Set a right-aligned tab at the right margin (Format **T**abs). Include an underlined leader for the tab setting.

3. In the text, press Ctrl+Tab to insert a tab stop. (Pressing Tab alone in a table causes the insertion point to move to the next cell.)

The template for this brochure includes the page setup, the tables on pages 1 and 2, and the borders around each panel.

The following paragraphs provide tips you can use when creating a newsletter.

Zooming: The center of the three Zoom buttons on the toolbar is View Zoom 100, which switches you to a full-size normal view. For desktop publishing, however, you probably want to work in page layout view most of the time. Consider replacing View Zoom 100 with View Zoom instead (Tools Options, Category Toolbar). View Zoom is a pull-down button that enables you to zoom quickly to any magnification in the page layout view. (See Chapter 29.)

Line Spacing: In typesetting terms, line spacing is called *leading* (pronounced "ledding"), referring to strips of lead inserted between lines in the days of metal type. Use Word for Windows' Format Paragraph command, adjusting the Line Spacing At option, to precisely control the spacing between lines of text in a paragraph. Use automatic line spacing for lines of average length (about one and one-half alphabets); decrease the spacing for large size text; increase the spacing for longer lines of text. Use an exact line spacing when you want all lines spaced the same in a paragraph with text of varying sizes. (See Chapter 6.)

Bullets and Numbering: The toolbar includes a Numbered List button and a Bulleted List button. Use these buttons to quickly number or bullet a list, or choose the Tools Bullets and Numbering command for access to a greater number of numbering and bulleting options. (See Chapter 6.)

Pictures: You can include many types of pictures in your publication, including TIF (the format most scanners use), BMP, PCS, EPS (formats used by many drawing programs), and others (Insert Picture). You also can copy pictures from programs not compatible with Word for Windows and paste them into your document. When inserted, pictures conform to the boundary they fall into; for example, a picture inserted into a table automatically is no wider than the cell. (See Chapter 23.)

Creating Stationery

The stationery shown in figure 28.3 includes text and graphics in the headers and footers. The headers and footers use symbols from the Symbol font set. The logo is created in WordArt. The first page of the stationery document is an envelope with different size, margins, paper orientation, and paper source from the second page. Following a section/page break, the second page is a standard letter-sized page.

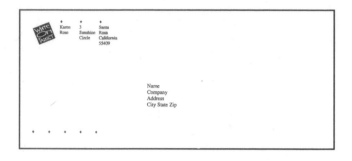

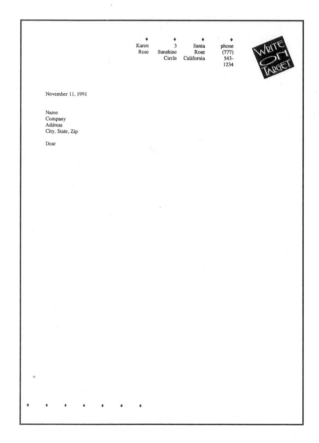

FIG. 28.3.

Stationery with text and graphics in the headers and footers.

To print the envelope and letterhead so that it can be taken to a commercial printer for volume printing, delete the dummy text, but leave the Section/Next Page break between pages 1 and 2.

The process for creating stationery is outlined in the following paragraphs.

1. Create a new template (**F**ile **N**ew **T**emplate).

2. Create an envelope (**T**ools Create **E**nvelope, or Envelope button on the toolbar, then **A**dd to Document).

Because you will be working with frames, headers, and footers, you may find it helpful to use the **T**ools **O**ptions command to turn on **T**ext Boundaries while you're creating your stationery. For the easiest working view, choose **V**iew **P**age Layout, and choose **V**iew **Z**oom **P**age Width.

To create the envelope, follow these steps:

1. With the insertion point on the first page of your document—the envelope—create a header that is different on the first page (**V**iew **H**eader/Footer, Header). Set it .25 inches from the edge.

2. Create the WordArt logo (**I**nsert **O**bject, MS WordArt). The logo shown uses these settings:

Font	Langley
Size	Best Fit
Style	Slant Up (Less)
Fi**ll**	White
Ali**g**n	Fit Horizontally
Options	Shado**w** and Color **B**ackground

3. Select the logo and size it to 45% (Forma**t** Pictu**r**e) and frame it (**I**nsert **F**rame or Frame button on toolbar). The frame is positioned at the left margin by default.

4. Set left-aligned tabs for the return address (Forma**t** **T**abs or ruler). Type the return address, including a symbol from the Symbol font on the first line (**I**nsert **S**ymbol).

5. Create the footer for a different first page (**V**iew **H**eader/Footer, Footer). Set it .25 inches from the edge. Set left-aligned tabs every quarter inch, and insert a symbol at each tab stop. .

6. Type dummy text for the address, if you want.

To create the letterhead, follow these steps:

1. Move the insertion point to the second page of your document— the letterhead page. Change the top margin to 2 inches (Forma**t** Page Set**u**p).

2. Create the header (View **H**eader/Footer, Header).

3. Create the WordArt logo, using the same specifications as for the envelope. Reduce it to 80% size.

4. Frame the logo and position it at 5.5 inches relative to the margin (Format **F**rame, Horizontal Position Left, Relative to Margin). Or if you prefer, just drag the framed logo where you want it.

5. Set right-aligned tabs for the return address, and type it as you did for the envelope.

6. Move to the text area of the letterhead, and on the first line include a date field (Insert Fie**l**d, Date). Add dummy name and address text, if you want.

7. Create the footer (View **H**eader/Footer, Footer). Set left-aligned tabs for the symbols, and include a first line hanging indent so that the first symbol appears to the left of the left margin. Insert the same symbols you used for the envelope.

This project is designed to be a template.

The following paragraphs provide tips you can use when creating letterheads.

Zooming: Zoom in to work on a project's details and zoom out to view your publication as a whole. You can zoom in and out using the **V**iew **Z**oom command, or using any of the three Zoom buttons at the right end of the toolbar. The rightmost button, View Zoom Page Width, zooms you in to see the entire page width, in whichever view you're working in. (See Chapter 4.)

Embedded Objects: Using the **I**nsert **O**bject command, you can access several programs that enable you to embed an object directly into your document. You can later edit the object in its original program by simply double-clicking on it, or by choosing **E**dit O**b**ject. Besides MS WordArt, you can create embedded drawings with Microsoft Draw; equations with Equation, and graphs with Microsoft Graph. (See Chapters 25 and 26.)

Creating an Ad

The simple ad in figure 28.4, designed to appear in a newspaper, is built within a table. The table is a custom size (smaller than a page) and includes two rows and two columns. Like the brochure, the ad probably could have been created with columns, section breaks, and positioned pictures. Using a table conveniently divided the page into individual sections, however, and didn't interfere with the layout. In this layout, the cells of the table can be as tall as necessary, as long as the table doesn't extend over the bottom of the page.

FIG. 28.4.

An ad created in a table.

The graphic in the ad was created using the Microsoft Draw add-in program that comes with Word for Windows.

The procedure for creating the simple ad shown in figure 28.4 is outlined in the following paragraphs.

To create the layout, create a new file and set page orientation to landscape. Set top and bottom margins to 1.75, and left and right margins to 2 inches (Format Page Setup).

To create the table, insert a two-column, two-row table on the page (Table Insert Table). Select the entire table and add a border around the outside edge only (Format Border).

To create the picture area in the top left cell, insert a picture (Insert Picture). Although the picture will fit the cell, you can resize it if you want. Add a border around the picture (Format Border).

To create the headline in the top right cell, type the headline in Avant Garde or Helvetica. Make the text 64 points, and set the line spacing to exactly 58 points (type *58 pt* in the Paragraph dialog box). The slightly reduced line spacing, or *leading*, tightens up the lines just a bit, which often improves the appearance of large headlines.

To create the schedule, follow these steps:

1. At the top of the bottom left cell, type the headline and the second line.

2. Select the headline text, and format it with a border below the paragraph (Format Border).

3. Set right tabs near the right edge of the cell. Include a dotted leader (Format Tabs). Type the schedule (remember to press Ctrl+Tab to insert a tab in a table).

4. Type the line of text below the schedule. You create the em dash by turning Num Lock on, holding the Alt key, and typing the number *0151* on the numeric keypad, or by selecting an em dash from the Symbol dialog box (Insert Symbol).

To create the shaded text, follow these steps:

1. Type the text of the paragraph in the bottom right cell.

2. Select the first letter in the paragraph and make it larger.

3. With the insertion point inside the paragraph, set the line spacing for Exactly 1 li, or a little more as needed (if it's too little, the top of the enlarged initial cap will be cut off).

4. Select the text of the paragraph (be careful not to select the entire cell).

5. Shade the paragraph (Format Border Shading). If you don't select just the text of the paragraph, you will shade the entire cell.

Save this document as a template, removing just the picture (you can leave its framed border). The rest of the text in the ad can serve as dummy text, and save you the time to set tabs, line spacing, a raised initial cap, and so forth.

The following paragraphs provide tips you can use when creating ads.

Fonts: Fonts are either serif, with flourishes at the end of each stroke in a letter, or sans serif, made up of straight lines. A common serif font is Times Roman, as used in the ad's schedule and shaded paragraph. Serifs tend to "knit" letters together as words; you often see serif fonts used in newspapers and magazines. A common sans serif font is Helvetica, similar to the Avant Garde font used in the ad's headline. Sans serif fonts are clearer at a distance. Use serif fonts in blocks of text for reading; use sans serif fonts for headlines and signs. (See Chapter 5.)

Kerning and Tracking: Kerning is the spacing between individual letters; tracking is the spacing between all characters in a line. Although character spacing is part of a font's design, sometimes you need to tighten up the spacing between individual letters in large titles, where a too-wide space becomes obvious, and sometimes you need to tighten up a line to make it fit. To change kerning, select two letters; to change tracking, select a line or more of text; for both, choose the Format Character command and adjust the Spacing option.

Tables: Tables provide a grid-like framework into which you can incorporate text, graphics, lines, boxes, and shading (but not frames). A table is useful in structuring publications that require rigidly separated parts. Remember that cells in a table don't have to be all the same size and that each cell can have its own border characteristics.

Editing Pictures: You can alter any graphic you've included in your publication. You can change the size or shape, or crop a graphic using the Format **P**icture command or by dragging its edges with a mouse (cropping is useful when you want to cut away the edges of a scanned photograph). You can add a border using Format **B**order. In many cases you can edit the actual picture with Microsoft Draw—even if it wasn't created with Draw—by double-clicking on the picture or selecting it and choosing **E**dit **O**bject. (See Chapters 23 and 25.)

Picture Placeholders: When you're working with pictures that slow down scrolling, insert and size them. Then, under View in the Options dialog box, choose the Show Text with Picture Placeholders option.

Line Spacing: When you set line spacing for an exact number of lines, li refers to a specific line size of 12 points. It works for text that's 12 points. But a setting of Exactly 1 li in 64 point condenses the lines of text to nonreadability. To set large size text for an exact line spacing, don't use points. To get condensed line spacing, set the lines as solid. For 24-point text, for example, set the line spacing for Exactly 24 pt. In large type, the solid setting may still be too loose; set the spacing a little smaller than the text point size. For 64-point type, for example, you can set the line spacing for Exactly 58 pt.

Table Borders: To border or shade a paragraph inside a table, select the text of the paragraph before you choose the border or shading. When you do this, it leaves a bit of white space between the paragraph border and the edge of the table cell. If you don't select the text, you will border or shade the whole cell. To make the paragraph border smaller, you can indent the paragraph's margins.

Keep it Simple: The most important tip for any desktop publishing project is to keep it simple. Plan your project ahead and try to think of the easiest way to accomplish each of your formatting goals. If you cannot think of an easy way to do your project, consider simplifying your design. Save experimentation for when you have the time.

Creating a More Complex Newsletter

ReLeaf News, shown in figure 28.5, is a fairly complex newsletter—not a project for the faint of heart. This newsletter includes an inserted graphic on page 1; a WordArt graphic (the word *NEWS* in the masthead); two text sidebars (pages 1 and 2) that have been bordered, framed, and positioned; a section break; columns with lines between; headers that include graphics and may be different on odd and even pages (if you want more than two pages for your newsletter); and a table including graphics and bordered text (the mailing box on page 2 is a table).

You can use different approaches to achieving the same visual result with this newsletter. The masthead in this example is set up with a negative first line indent and tabs; instead, it could be set up as a separate section with a wide left margin, with the left graphic framed and positioned manually inside that wide margin, and the right graphic framed and positioned manually at the top right margin. Either method would accomplish the goal of having the word *ReLeaf* start at exactly the same horizontal position on the page as the newsletter text below it.

To create the *ReLeaf News* newsletter, you must start a new document. Set the left and right margins to .625; set the top margin to .5, and set the bottom margin to .75. Margins for this newsletter are set so that the columns are measured in increments of 1/8 inch (the same as the Word for Windows ruler is measured). (If you want to create a multipage newsletter, choose Facing Pages and set the inside margin to .75 and the outside margin to .5).

Set the view to page layout, and select the Zoom Page Width button at the far right end of the toolbar so that you can see the full page. Turn on paragraph markers.

To create the negative (hanging) indent and tab for the masthead, follow these steps:

1. Set a hanging first line indent of minus 1.875, or 1 7/8 (Forma**t P**aragraph, or the ruler).

    This measurement equals the width of a column plus the width of a gutter. It ensures that the name of the newsletter begins at exactly the same horizontal position as the first column of text in the newsletter.

2. Set a right tab at the right margin. This is to align the NEWS WordArt object to the right margin.

ReLeaf NEWS

Published Quarterly by Sonoma County ReLeaf ✱ Autumn, 1991

ReLeaf Joins Forces with WCG

"A Shade Better"

It's been a busy summer for Sonoma County ReLeaf. In the last issue of this newsletter, we hinted about a new partnership with WCG. Since spring, that new partnership has evolved into an ongoing relationship, with Sonoma County ReLeaf administering WCG's "A Shade Better" program in an exciting county-wide pilot.

"A Shade Better" is WCG's way of reaching out into the community, helping homeowners save energy by providing free trees that shade their homes and help reduce their need for air conditioning. WCG supplies the trees—and Sonoma County ReLeaf provides the expertise needed to get the trees into the ground.

ReLeaf's approach to helping people plant their free shade trees begins by organizing community planting days. The first step is to work with one individual who will contact neighbors and schedule a Saturday morning for planting. ReLeaf works with the neighborhood volunteer to determine which type of trees people want. Next, a trained ReLeaf volunteer visits the neighborhood and sites the shade trees around each home so the trees provide maximum shading as they grow. On planting day, ReLeaf brings the trees, stakes, and ties, gives a planting demonstration, and distributes the trees to their new owners. For those who can't plant their own trees, volunteers are trained to help. After the planting, a two-year follow-up program helps ensure the trees stay healthy.

The City of Santa Rosa has also become involved in the program, providing free street trees to qualifying homes within the city.

Several "A Shade Better" plantings are already scheduled:

- October 19—planting shade trees and street trees in northwest Santa Rosa.
- October 26—planting shade trees in Santa Rosa.
- November 9—planting shade trees in Windsor.

Three more projects are in the planning stages. In Rohnert Park, ReLeaf has targeted two neighborhoods needing trees and hopes to hold the first planting in early winter. In Sonoma,

ReLeaf is working with ten community groups and businesses toward scheduling a planting. And in Petaluma, residents in two mobile home parks will receive badly-needed shade trees to help cool their homes.

ReLeaf has been furiously busy over the summer getting the word out to people about the "A Shade Better" project. In a booth at the county fair, we made contact with about 1,000 people, many of whom are interested in getting trees for their homes, or in coordinating planting days in their neighborhoods. We've contacted even more potential planters through our booth at the Thursday night market in Santa Rosa.

ReLeaf has also been busy gearing up for the actual plantings—locating growers for the 15,000 trees we'll need this year; training interns to site the trees; working with kids in the Social Advocates for Youth program so they can help plant the trees; and raising money for our non-tree expenses.

It's been a busy summer for Sonoma County ReLeaf,

In Brief . . .

- ReLeaf teams up with WCG to make Sonoma County "A Shade Better." *Page 1.*
- ReLeaf needs neighborhood coordinators to help organize local plantings. *Back page.*
- With all the activity going on now, we need help with lots of jobs. *Back page.*

To volunteer, call Sonoma County ReLeaf at 323-4321

FIG. 28.5.

A complex newsletter.

To create the graphic area at the top left of the newsletter, you insert the graphic and size it so that it is no wider than the negative first line indent (**I**nsert **P**icture).

To create the newsletter name, follow these steps:

1. Press Tab to advance the insertion point to the left margin marker.

2. Type the newsletter name, *ReLeaf*.

but it'll be an even busier fall and winter. We need your help. We need volunteers (see back for job descriptions), we need neighborhood coordinators, and (as always) we need donations.

If you've been thinking about getting more involved, there's no better time than now. Give us a call at 323-4321.

Free Trees!

C'mon, nobody gives anything away for free. There must be some catch to the claim that WCG is giving away *free* shade trees, right?

Wrong! OK, not entirely wrong. There are a couple of catches. You have to get your neighborhood involved. You have to site the trees so they'll shade your house. You have to plant the trees yourself (though we have willing volunteers if you can't). You have to promise to take care of the trees after they're planted.

But hey, those aren't such tough catches—and think of all the good you're doing. Your house gets shade; your electric bill goes down if you use air conditioning; the air gets cleaned by the trees' natural "air recycling" process; you get a chance to meet your neighbors; birds get a place to build nests; kids get a place to climb . . . and the list goes on.

So look around your neighborhood. If you think it could use some shade trees, call us (and don't forget—if you're in the city of Santa Rosa you're eligible for street trees, too). We have materials to help you organize your neighbors, and we'll help you pick a date when we can deliver your trees and

help get you started with your neighborhood planting. And when the work's done, you and all your neighbors will have something to be really proud of--for years.

For help organizing your neighborhood, call Sonoma County ReLeaf at 323-4321.

Jobs—Jobs—

Tree Siting Training
Thursday, Sept. 12, 4-6 p.m.
SSU—Room 173, Nichols Hall

If you're interested in becoming a volunteer tree siter, you're invited to attend this two-hour training session. Space is limited, so call now: 323-4321.

Jobs

With all the activity planned for upcoming months, there's no shortage of work to be done at ReLeaf. Volunteers work at the Sonoma County ReLeaf office (OK, so it's Ellen's kitchen . . .), in their own homes, and at Saturday neighborhood plantings.

Here are some of the things we need help with:

Clerical (days)—we need people to help enter names into our database.

Mailing (days)—we need help mailing follow-up postcards four times a year to everyone who plants shade trees. These reminders will encourage people to care for their trees, and will alert them to problems to watch for.

Phoning (evening, weekends)—we need callers to follow up with people who are organizing their neighborhoods.

Siting trees (Saturdays; special training required)—we need trained volunteers to site trees for maximum shading benefit at every planting location.

"A Shade Better" event team members (Saturdays; special training required)—we need people to help staff the information table, distribute trees, sign up volunteers, and conduct post-planting inspections. If you'd like to volunteer, please contact Ellen Davidson at 538-4547.

Sonoma County ReLeaf
P.O. Box 14806
Santa Rosa, CA 95402

ADDRESS CORRECTION REQUESTED

ReLeaf News is published quarterly by Sonoma County ReLeaf, a non-profit, volunteer-based organization dedicated to planting 350,000 trees in Sonoma County by the year 2000.

printed on recycled paper

Non-Profit
Organization
U.S. Postage
PAID
Santa Rosa, CA
Permit # 000

3. Select the name and change the font to Helvetica, the style to Bold, and size to 80 points (Forma**t C**haracter, or ribbon).

To create the sideways *NEWS* in the masthead, follow these steps:

1. Press Tab to advance to the right tab marker on the right margin.

2. Insert a WordArt object (**I**nsert **O**bject, MS WordArt). Type the word *NEWS* and include the following settings:

Font	Duval
Size	Best fit
Style	Bottom to Top
Fill	Black
Options	Stretch Vertical

To create the subtitle, follow these steps:

1. Press Enter after inserting the WordArt object *NEWS*.

2. Change the first-line indent to 0, but leave the left indent set at 1.875 (Format **P**aragraph, or ruler).

   This way, when you box and shade the subtitle, the box will be only as wide as the newsletter masthead, rather than as wide as the page.

3. Type the text and format it as bold and centered. Insert a symbol to separate the date from the publisher's line **I**nsert **S**ymbol).

4. Press Enter three times.

   Leaving blank lines now, rather than after you border the subtitle, moves the insertion point outside the area to be bordered. If you press Enter after you add the border, you will carry the border with you to the next line.

5. Select the subtitle text and border it with a box and shading (Format **B**order).

To create the first article title, follow these steps:

1. Position the insertion point two lines below the subtitle (one blank line should remain below the title line).

2. Type and format the title.

   For typesetting quotes, turn on Num Lock and use ANSI characters as follows: to create an open quotation mark, hold Alt while you type the numbers *0147* on the numeric keypad; for a close quotation mark, hold Alt and type *0148*.

To create the columns, follow these steps:

1. Move the insertion point below the title (if you do this by pressing Enter at the end of the title, you will have to remove the title's character formatting).

2. Enter a continuous section break (**I**nsert **B**reak, Continuous). The continuous break enables you to insert columns.

3. Remove the paragraph indent (Format Paragraph, or ruler).

4. Change the top margin to 1 inch and apply the margin to the section (Format Page Setup, Apply To This Section). This setting will not affect page 1, whose top section has a 1/2 inch top margin, but will take effect on page 2.

5. Change the number of columns to 4 with a line between (Format Columns, Number of Columns 4, Line Between).

To create the boxed sidebar on page 1, follow these steps:

1. Type the text of the sidebar and format the characters to the right size and style.

2. Press Enter once at the end to leave a blank line.

   This blank line enables you to more easily select the text to go in a box. Move the insertion point outside the box to continue with the text of the article.

3. Select the paragraphs to be bulleted and select the Bulleted List button in the toolbar.

4. Select just the first line in the boxed text and format it with a line in the middle (Format Border).

5. Select all the text (not including the blank line at the end) and format it with a boxed border (Format Border).

6. Select all the text and insert a frame (Insert Frame or the Frame button on the toolbar). Position the frame vertically at the bottom of the column (Format Frame, Vertical Position Bottom Relative to Margin, Distance from Text zero).

To create the newsletter text, follow these steps:

1. Move the insertion point to the blank line following the sidebar and insert a column break (Insert Break, Column Break). This break moves the text to the top of the next column.

2. Type the newsletter text.

   To include em dashes (wide hyphens used in punctuation) turn on Num Lock and hold Alt while you type the numbers 0151 on the numeric keypad.

3. Insert a header, and make the first page different with no header (View Header/Footer, Header, Different First Page).

   To format the header, type *ReLeaf News* at the left margin, insert a right tab stop at the right margin, press Tab, and insert the automatic page number field (Insert Field, Page in page layout view; choose the Data button if you're in normal view). Select the header and format it for a box and shading (Format Border).

If you're creating a newsletter longer than two pages, use facing pages (Format Page Setup, Facing Pages) and include different odd and even headers; position the page number on the outside of each page.

To create the boxed text on page 2, follow these steps:

1. Insert a blank frame on page 2; drag it to be the width of two columns. (Make sure that not text is selected and choose Insert Frame.)

2. Type and format the text inside the frame.

3. Select and border the frame (Format Border), and then position it horizontally in the middle of the page and vertically at whatever distance you want it from the top of the page (Format Frame).

   (You can easily do this by dragging the frame into the correct approximate location, and then formatting the frame to be centered horizontally, leaving the vertical measurement as it is in the Frame dialog box). Turn off the Move with Text option.

   To create the line that doesn't touch the edges of the box, on a blank line add a tab stop at the right margin, and either include an underlined tab leader and press Tab to draw the line, or press Tab and then select the line and format it with an underline.

To create the mailer on page 2, follow these steps:

1. Insert a continuous section break (Insert Break, Continuous) at the end of the text to balance the columns. Reset the text to one column (Format Columns, Columns button on toolbar).

2. Insert a two-column table at the bottom of page 2 (Table Insert Table, or Table button on toolbar).

3. In the left column include the graphic and text as shown.

4. In the right column, type the text of the postal indicia. Select the text and border it with a box (Format Border). With the text still selected, change its left and right indents to make the box the size you want (Ruler).

5. Select the table (Table Select Table) and format it with a boxed border (Format Border).

6. With the table still selected, frame it (Insert Frame) and position it at the bottom of the page (Format Frame). Turn off the Move with Text option.

For this template, include the page layout, the newsletter masthead and subtitle, the page 1 sidebar, the column break at the beginning of the newsletter text, a few lines of formatted dummy text, and the header.

The following paragraphs provide tips you can use when creating more complex newsletters.

Font Sizes and Styles: The fonts and font sizes you have available depend on what's built into your printer (or added in via cartridge or downloadable fonts). Be sure the font, size, and style you choose convey meaning to readers. For example, all the headlines in your newsletter may be 24-point bold Helvetica; all the subheadings 12-point bold Times Roman; and all the text may be 10-point Times Roman. Using fonts consistently gives readers visual cues that make reading easier. (See Chapter 5.)

Special Characters: Use typesetting characters properly. Use an em dash—a wide dash—in punctuation. Use typesetting quotes rather than the straight quotes from the keyboard. You can insert these characters as ANSI numbers, or as symbols. (See Chapter 5.)

Styles: One of the best ways to ensure consistent formatting is to use styles—sets of remembered formatting commands you can apply at the touch of a few keys, and can change just as easily (which changes all text associated with the style). To make your styles available to each issue of a newsletter, create the styles in the newsletter template. (See Chapter 11.)

Headers and Footers: Headers and footers often function as a publication's running heads and running feet. Remember that you can have different headers and footers on the first page than on the remaining pages—often useful in a newsletter, where you don't want headers and footers on the first page. Headers and footers can contain graphics and frames. (See Chapter 15.)

Column and Section Breaks: A column break causes text following the insertion point to start at the top of the next column. A section break divides a document into regions that can have different numbers of columns, and different headers and footers. Use the **I**nsert **B**reak command to tightly control how and where text appears in your publication. (See Chapters 7, 8, and 13.)

Balancing Columns: Sections divide a document into different regions, each of which can have a different number of columns. The last column on a page may not reach the bottom of a page, however, if not enough text fills the page. Insert a continuous section break (**I**nsert **B**reak Continuous) at the end of the text to balance columns on a page.

Templates: A template can save you the time of reconstructing the basics of any publication—especially a periodical like a newsletter. A template can include text and graphics, styles, mastheads, headers and footers, staff boxes, and anything else that repeats from issue to issue. (See Chapter 30.)

Viewing: When you're working on a layout with facing pages, choose Print Preview occasionally and display both pages to see how facing pages work together.

Turn on paragraph markers so that you can see paragraph markers, tab markers, section breaks, column breaks, and so on.

Lines inside a Border: To create a line inside a text frame, select the text under which you want a line, open the Border Paragraph dialog box, select the middle line in the Border graphic, and select a line width for the line. This line extends from one side of the border to the other.

To create a line inside a frame that is not as wide as the frame, enter a blank line and set a right-aligned tab stop at the right margin with an underlined tab leader, and press Tab on that line. Or you can set the tab without a leader, and then select the blank line and format it to include an underline.

Movable Lines: Create a movable line by inserting a right tab stop at the right margin of the line, pressing Tab, selecting the line, and choosing a bottom border. Reduce the height of the line's frame by selecting the entire line (not the frame) and, in the Paragraph dialog box, making the line spacing Exactly .25 li or .5 li—whatever height you need. Or, select the frame and set the height manually.

Preserving Formatting: Section breaks and paragraph markers contain the formatting for the section or paragraph preceding them. Don't delete breaks or markers. If you do delete a section break or paragraph marker, the text before and after the break or marker merges, taking on the formatting selections of the following text. Choose Edit Undo to reverse such a mistake. The best way to avoid deleting a section break or paragraph marker accidentally is to display them while you're working. To view your document without the break or marker symbols (as you should occasionally, to see how it really looks), choose Print Preview or turn the markers off for a moment.

Moving Pictures: If you insert a picture and later move the original, Word for Windows won't be able to find it. Word for Windows uses fields to insert pictures. If you move the original picture, you should view the fields in your document and edit the path that locates the original picture to reflect its new location.

Typesetting: For typeset-quality printing, take your Word for Windows disk to a service bureau that has a Linotronic typesetter and supports Word for Windows. The price for printing is generally around $10 per page (be sure to proofread your laser-printed pages carefully before you do this). If your file includes graphics, be sure to include the original graphics on the disk along with your Word for Windows file. Ask your service bureau what tips they can suggest before you prepare your disk.

From Here . . .

Throughout this book are chapters describing how to use the techniques you need for desktop publishing with Word for Windows. You should master editing, as well as character, paragraph, section, and page formatting (Chapters 4 through 9). You should become familiar with previewing and printing your documents (Chapter 10). You should understand how styles can save formatting time (Chapter 11).

You should learn how to work with tables and columns (Chapters 12 and 13), and you should learn all you can about frames, borders, and graphics (Chapters 23 through 26). You should understand the importance of templates in desktop publishing (Chapter 30).

But most of all, in order to master desktop publishing with Word for Windows, you should be creative, and be willing to experiment. Think about how you can use what you have learned; dare to try new techniques. Set aside some time just to play with the program, to see what it can do. For practice, try the projects presented in this chapter, but then branch out on your own to develop your own publication-quality documents.

Customizing Word for Windows

PART

IV

OUTLINE

Customizing Program Features

Using Templates

Creating and Editing Macros

Customizing Program Features

W ith the Tools Options command, you can customize a wide range of Word for Windows' options and appearance. You can customize the screen display. You can customize the way Word for Windows saves your documents and checks your spelling. You can add commands to the menu and add tools to the toolbar. You can even make your own shortcut keys. Invest some time in learning this part of Word for Windows; you will be rewarded with greater efficiency.

Using the Tools Options Command

The Tools Options command enables you to customize Word for Windows. Choosing Tools Options brings up the Options dialog box, which contains all of the Word for Windows setup options and preferences. The Options dialog box displays many customizable features, which are grouped together in categories. The Options dialog box displays different contents depending on the category you choose. Figure 29.1 shows the Options dialog box with the View Category selected.

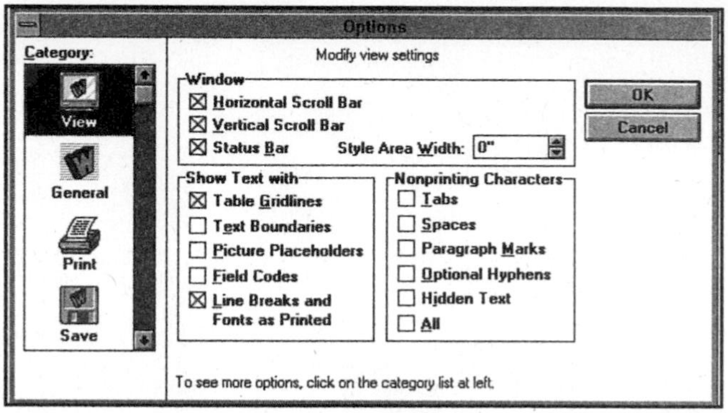

FIG. 29.1.

The Options dialog box with the View Category selected.

> **T I P**
>
> Think of the Tools Options dialog box as a gathering place for all of Word for Windows' customizable features.

You probably have seen the Options dialog box before. You can bring up this dialog box from several other points in the program. You learned in Chapter 10, for example, that choosing the **O**ptions button in the Print dialog box brings up the Options dialog box but displays only the Print Category.

Notice that the Options dialog box includes a scrollable list of categories. Each category is represented by an icon. When you tunnel into the dialog box by another route—from the Spelling dialog box, for example—the **C**ategory box presents a single appropriate icon instead of the entire list.

The first time you choose **T**ools **O**ptions after installing Word for Windows, the View Category is selected in the **C**ategory list box. To select a different category, click on the category's icon with a mouse or press Alt+C, then press the up- or down-arrow keys. As you move through the icons in the **C**ategory list box, the options panel, which occupies most of the Options dialog box, changes to reflect the currently selected category.

Customizing the View and Windows Display

Select the View icon to control the type of information displayed in the document window—scroll bars, boundary markers, and nonprinting characters, for example. Chapter 4 covers this procedure.

The only View option not introduced so far is Style Area Width. By entering a number in this edit box, you tell Word for Windows to create an area that displays the style name of each paragraph along the left boundary of the text. The width of the style area depends on the value entered in the Style Area Width text box. The style area displays only in normal view. Figure 29.1 shows the View Category within the Options dialog box.

Table 29.1 describes the options that customize the screen display.

Table 29.1. View Options

Options	Description
Window options	
Horizontal Scroll Bar	Toggles the horizontal scroll bar on or off.
Vertical Scroll Bar	Toggles the vertical scroll bar on or off.
Status **B**ar	Toggles the status bar on or off.
Style Area **W**idth	Sets the width of an area in the left boundary to show style names for each paragraph. Set to zero to close it.
Show Text With options	
Table **G**ridlines	Toggles dashed lines around cells and tables on or off.
Text Boundaries	Toggles a dashed line around margins, objects, and frames in page layout view on or off.
Picture Placeholders	Replaces a full picture with a dashed box. Improves performance when only boxes are shown.
Field Codes	Toggles the display between showing field codes or results on or off.
Line Breaks and Fonts as Printed	Shows the document as it will print on the current printer. The display reflects the fonts, font sizes, and features available in the printer.
Nonprinting Characters	
Tabs	Toggles the display of tabs as left arrows on or off.
Spaces	Toggles the display of spaces as dots on or off.
Paragraph **M**arks	Toggles the display of paragraph marks on or off.
Optional Hyphens	Toggles the display of optional hyphens as a dash with a crooked end on or off.
Hidden Text	Toggles the display of hidden text on or off.
All	Toggles the display of all the characters and marks described above on or off.

Customizing Editing and Help

The General options panel shown in figure 29.2 controls certain editing options and various personal preferences. Table 29.2 explains the options more fully.

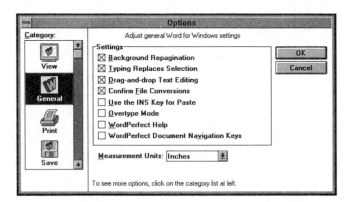

FIG. 29.2.

The Options dialog box with the General Category selected.

Table 29.2. General Options

Settings options	Description
Background Repagination	Updates the page breaks continually as you edit the document. Word for Windows operates faster when this option is off. To repaginate when the option is off, choose the T**o**ols Re**p**aginate Now command.
Typing Replaces Selection	Replaces the selected text as you type or when you paste.
Drag-and-drop Text Editing	Enables you to drag selected text to a new location without using the cut, paste, or copy commands.
Confirm **F**ile Conversions	Displays a message when you open a file in another format indicating whether the file successfully converted to Word for Windows formatting.
Use The INS Key For Paste	Uses the Ins key to insert the contents of the clipboard at the insertion point.
Overtype Mode	Enables you to type over text without selecting it.
WordPerfect Help	Provides help screens and keystroke demonstrations for WordPerfect commands.

Settings options	Description
WordPerfect Document Navigation Keys	Enables you to move around documents using WordPerfect cursor-movement keys.
Measurement Units list box	Determines the unit of measure (inches, centimeters, points, or picas) you use when changing margins, tabs, and position settings.

Customizing Print Options

You can use the Print Category options shown in figure 29.3 to control the printing options. Chapter 10 shows you how to use the Include With Document options group to specify which information in the document to print. Table 29.3 explains the Print panel options.

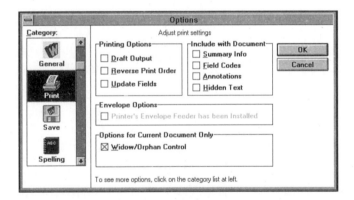

FIG. 29.3.

The Options dialog box with the Print Category selected.

Table 29.3. Print Options

Options	Description
Printing Options	
Draft Output	Prints in lower resolution draft mode. Speed is faster.
Reverse Print Order	Prints pages in reverse order to make collating easier when pages come out print side up.
Update Fields	Updates fields as the document prints.

continues

Table 29.3. (continued)

Options	Description
Include with Document	
Summary Info	Prints summary information on separate pages.
Field Codes	Prints field codes as text with the document.
Annotations	Prints annotations on separate pages.
Hidden Text	Prints hidden text with the document.
Envelope Options	
Printer's **E**nvelope Feeder has been Installed	Indicates that an envelope feeder can be used.
Options for Current Document Only	
Widow/Orphan Control	Avoids printing a solitary line at the top or bottom of a page.
Use **T**rueType	Prints with TrueType fonts when they are available in Windows. See Appendix C for more information on TrueType and fonts. (Option does not display if TrueType unavailable, as in Windows 3.0.)

Customizing How Files Save

The Save options shown in figure 29.4 control Word for Windows' default options for saving documents. Table 29.4 explains the Save options. See Chapter 3 for more details on saving and its options.

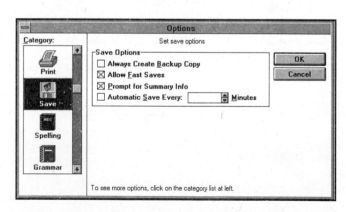

Table 29.4. Save Options

Save Options	Description
Always Create **B**ackup copy	Saves the prior saved version of the file under the same file name with a BAK extension. This option cannot be chosen with the Allow **F**ast Saves option.
Allow **F**ast Saves	Uses Word for Windows' *fast saving* method (saves only the changes made since the most recent time you saved the document). Documents saved with Fast Save may not convert correctly to other formats. (This option cannot be used when Always Create **B**ackup Copy is selected.)
Prompt for Summary Info	Displays the Summary Info dialog box the first time you save the document and when you choose the Save **A**s command.
Automatic **S**ave Every	Causes Word for Windows to save the document at intervals you specify in the **M**inutes box.

Customizing Spelling Options

Select the Spelling icon to control Word for Windows' spell-checking procedures (see fig. 29.5). You also can select this category by choosing the Options button in the Spelling dialog box. Table 29.5 explains the spell-checking rules. Chapter 9 describes spelling features in more detail.

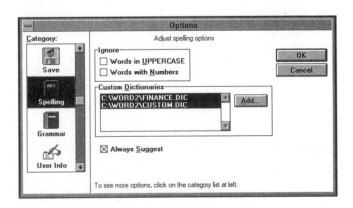

FIG. 29.5.

The Options dialog box with the Spelling Category selected.

Table 29.5. Spelling Options	
Options	Description
Words in UPPERCASE	Ignores words consisting of uppercase letters—useful when spell-checking a document with many acronyms.
Words with Numbers	Ignores words that include numeric characters.
Custom Dictionaries	Refers to the appropriate custom dictionary or dictionaries (maximum of four selected at the same time) when spell-checking a document.
Always Suggest	When spell-checking, the dialog box displays a list of suggested substitutes when it finds a word not in the dictionaries.
Add	Brings up a dialog box where you can enter the path and name of an alternative dictionary file.

Customizing Grammar Options

Select the Grammar Category to indicate the types of grammatical errors you want Word for Windows to find when you choose the Tools Grammar command. Figure 29.6 shows the dialog box with the Grammar Category selected. You also can select this category by choosing the Options button in the Grammar dialog box. Table 29.6 explains the grammar options. For more details about using the grammar options, refer to Chapter 9.

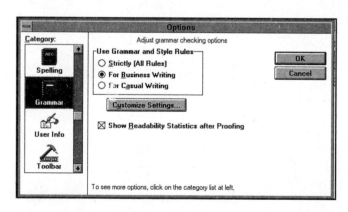

FIG. 29.6.

The Options dialog box with the Grammar Category selected.

Table 29.6. Grammar Options

Options	Description
Strictly (All Rules)	Applies all grammatical rules.
For **B**usiness Writing	Uses rules appropriate for business correspondence.
For C**a**sual Writing	Uses rules appropriate for casual letters.
C**u**stomize Settings	Displays a dialog box in which you select the grammar and style rules to be included in each of the preceding three options. This option is described later in this section.
Show **R**eadability Statistics after Proofing	Displays numeric measures of the document's readability.

When you choose the C**u**stomize Settings button, the Customize Grammar Settings dialog box appears. From this dialog box you can specify exactly which grammatical rules are used during the grammar check. If you are unsure of a rule, select the rule and choose the **E**xplain button. As you select a grammar option, the Grammar Explanation window explains what that option does (see fig. 29.7). To close the Grammar Explanation window, press Alt+F4.

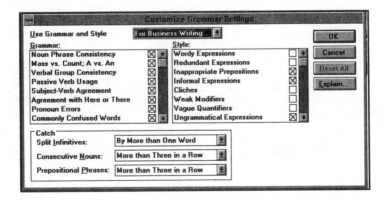

FIG. 29.7.

The Customize Grammar Settings dialog box.

Customizing the User Info Options

Select the User Info icon to enter the default author name (see fig. 29.8). Word for Windows enters this name in the document summary information when you save files. You also can enter a return mailing address for envelopes in this dialog box. Table 29.7 describes the User Info options.

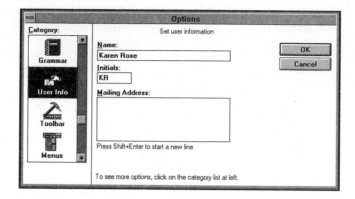

FIG. 29.8.

The Options
dialog box with
the User Info
Category
selected.

Table 29.7. User Info Options

Options	Description
Name	Enter the name you want as the author for the {author} field code.
Initials	Enter your initials.
Mailing Address	Enter the mailing address you want to display in Word for Windows' envelope feature.

Customizing the Toolbar

The toolbar makes Word for Windows even easier to use. You can add
your own tools representing menu commands or macros you write or
record. Figure 29.9 shows the Options dialog box for the Toolbar Category. Chapter 31 describes how to rearrange, add, or remove tools
from the toolbar.

You can customize the toolbar to contain your most frequently used
commands or macros (see table 29.8).

Table 29.8. Toolbar Options

Options	Description
Tool to Change	Select the tool or space you want to change.
Button	Displays all the buttons you can add to the toolbar.

Options	Description
Commands/Macros	Displays a list of all commands or macros that can be assigned to the tool you choose. This list and its title change depending on the Show Commands and Show Macros option selected.
Show Commands	Specifies that the Macros list shows built-in commands.
Show Macros	Specifies that the Commands list shows macros within the active document or template.
Context Global	Changes the toolbar for documents associated with the default template, NORMAL.DOT.
Context Template	Changes the toolbar for documents originating from a specific template.
Description	Describes the macro or command you have selected.
Change	Replaces the tool you selected in the Tool to Change list with the tool you selected from the Button list.
Reset Tool	Returns tool to its original setting.
Reset All	Returns all tools to their original settings.

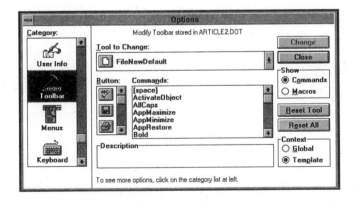

FIG. 29.9.

The Options dialog box with the Toolbar Category selected.

Customizing Menus and Commands

Word for Windows is the first fully programmable and customizable word processor. You can customize Word for Windows for specific tasks using custom menus, commands, toolbars, and features.

For example, you can customize Word for Windows as a legal word processor tightly integrated with a document tracking system, as the front-end for an electronic mail system, and as a financial publishing system that downloads financial data, analyzes it with Microsoft Excel and publishes the result in a book format. The keystone for these new systems is Word for Windows' customizable menus and commands. Tailor Word's menus to specific tasks by adding commands or macros to menus through the use of the options in the Menu Category (see fig. 29.10). These options are described in table 29.9. For more information on customizing menus, refer to Chapter 31.

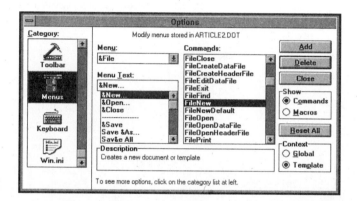

FIG. 29.10.

The Options dialog box with the Menus Category selected.

Table 29.9. Menu Options

Options	Description
Menu	Menu on which command is added or removed.
Menu Text	Command name as seen on menu. Select the command to which you want to assign a macro or type a new command name to be added to the bottom of the menu. Precede the active letter with an & symbol.
Commands/Macros	Built-in commands or macros appear in this list so that you can link them to the menu and command specified in the Menu and Menu Text lists. Controlled by Show options. Select the command you want to add to or delete from the menu.
Description	Describes the command or macro selected.
Add	Adds Menu Text to the menu as a new command and assigns the selected command or macro to that menu command.
Delete	Deletes the selected command or macro from the menu.

Options	Description
Reset All	Returns all menus to the default menus.
Show **C**ommands	Displays the built-in commands in the Commands list.
Show **M**acros	Displays your macros in the Commands list.
Context **G**lobal	Makes the menu changes globally, NORMAL.DOT template, so all default documents have the change.
Context Tem**p**late	Makes the menu changes to the template for the active document so that menu changes occur for documents originating from that template only.

Changing the WIN.INI File

Select the WIN.INI option to change parameters in the WIN.INI file. With the WIN.INI dialog box, you can more easily change the WIN.INI file and have the parameters immediately affect Word for Windows. Table 29.10 describes the WIN.INI options. Figure 29.11 shows the start-up path for Word for Windows being changed.

> If you are unfamiliar with the settings in the WIN.INI file, do not change them. Always keep a copy of your WIN.INI settings. Never make changes to the WIN.INI without having a copy of the current WIN.INI file. The WIN.INI file is located in the WINDOWS directory. You can learn more about the WIN.INI file by reading the text file named WININI.TXT.

T I P

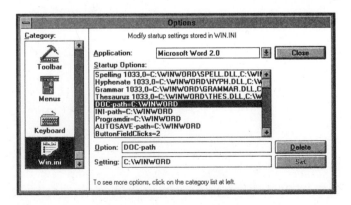

FIG. 29.11.

The Options dialog box with the WIN.INI Category selected.

Table 29.10. WIN.INI Options

Options	Description
Application	Specifies the particular program whose WIN.INI entries are to be changed.
Startup Options	Specifies the location of important program files on your hard disk. For example, you can set the location of Word for Windows' startup directory, the directory in which Word looks for templates or the directory used during automatic saves.
Option	Displays current option for editing.
Setting	Displays current option setting for editing.
Close	Closes the dialog box.
Delete	Deletes the selected item from the Startup Options list box.
Set	Saves the change(s) you made to the WIN.INI file.

Some of the different options you can add or change within the WIN.INI Category include the following:

Option	Description
DOC-PATH=*path*	Specifies the startup path name. Word for Windows starts up in this directory.
DOT-PATH=*path*	Specifies the directory for templates. Templates in this directory appear in the template list when you choose the File New command. Add this command to each network user's WIN.INI so that they can customize their own templates without affecting other users on the network.
INI-PATH=*path*	Specifies the location of the WINWORD.INI file that stores Word's global settings. On a network, each user should have their own copy of the WINWORD.INI so that they can keep their own settings. List this directory in the PATH statement in a user's AUTOEXEC.BAT file prior to network directory containing Word. Delete WINWORD.INI from the network directory. On startup, Word re-creates a WINWORD.INI in the user's directory if one does not exist.

For additional information on modifying the WIN.INI and installing Word on a network, open and read the README.DOC file located in the directory in which you installed WINWORD.EXE.

Customizing Keyboard Shortcut Keys

Shortcut keys give you the power to get work done more quickly. Word for Windows has many built-in shortcut keys. If you need a shortcut key for a command that doesn't have one, or to run a macro you write or record, you can assign your own shortcut keys. Figure 29.12 shows the Options dialog box to add or remove shortcut keys. Table 29.11 explains the Keyboard Category options.

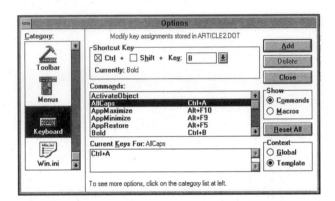

FIG. 29.12.

The Options dialog box with the Keyboard Category selected.

Table 29.11. Keyboard Options

Options	Description
Ctrl	Specifies Ctrl as one of the combination keys.
Shift	Specifies Shift as one of the combination keys.
Key	Specifies the keyboard key. Use the pull-down list if you aren't sure of valid keys.
Currently	Displays the command or macro currently assigned to the keystroke combination you enter.
Commands/Macros	Shows the list of built-in commands or macros and their shortcut keys.
Current Keys For	Shows the existing key assignment for the command or macro selected in the Commands list.
Show Commands	Shows built-in commands in the Commands list.
Show Macros	Shows macros in the Commands list.

continues

Table 29.11. *(continued)*

Options	Description
Context **G**lobal	Specifies that the keystroke assignment apply globally.
Context Temp**l**ate	Specifies that the keystroke assignment apply to the document from a specific template.
Add	Assigns the keystroke to macro or command you selected.
Delete	Removes a keystroke from the macro or command you selected.
Reset All	Resets all shortcut keys involving commands and macros for the active document.

From Here . . .

Word for Windows is a flexible program. You can install it to be a simple word processor or the most powerful word processor available. You also can customize Word for Windows to fit your preferences.

Word for Windows is one of the most customizable and programmable word processors available. In addition to the customizable features in the **T**ools **O**ptions command, you can create a template that contains formatting, text, menus, glossaries, styles, macros, and toolbars for a specific type of work or document. When you open a template, all the text, tools, and features you need for the document are ready. Templates are described in Chapter 30.

If you are familiar with the BASIC programming language or need to expand the work that macros do, be sure to read Chapter 31. In Chapter 31 you learn to use the macro recorder to create your own custom commands and add them to a shortcut key, menu command, or tool on the toolbar.

Using Templates

Templates can save you work and increase the consistency of any documents you create on a frequent basis. Templates act as a guide or pattern for documents of a specific type, such as form letters, letters of engagement, invoices, contracts, or proposals.

All documents in Word for Windows are based on a template. Even the default new document is based on a template, NORMAL.DOT. The NORMAL.DOT file contains the formatting and default settings for the new document you open when you choose File New.

A *template* is a file that contains the parts of a document and features used for a specific type of document. Word for Windows templates can contain text, pictures, graphs, formatting, styles, glossaries, field codes, custom menu commands, tools on the toolbar, shortcut keys, and macros. You can put text, formatting, and settings you use repeatedly for a specific task into a template.

When you open a new document, all the contents and features of the template are transferred to the new untitled document. The original template remains unaltered on disk.

Your company might want to use Word for Windows templates for proposals and reports. The templates ensure that all their reports have the same format and layout. When certain phrases and names are placed in glossaries, the company ensures that they always will be typed the same way. All table and figure formatting, tables of contents, and indexes look the same from report to report because they are created and formatted with macros and styles attached to the template.

Many companies use templates to prepare interoffice memos and FAX cover letters. The headings and document formatting are predefined and, therefore, are standardized. FILLIN fields prompt the operator for entries. The DATE and AUTHOR fields can be used to enter the current date and name of the operator automatically.

Word for Windows comes with several predesigned templates that can be used as a basis for your own business documents, including press releases, FAX cover sheets, and reports. You can modify the Word for Windows templates to meet your needs, or you can create your own templates from scratch.

Setting Default Formats in the Normal Template

Word for Windows bases its default settings for a new document on a template stored in the file NORMAL.DOT. All documents you create by choosing File New and pressing Enter are based on the Normal template. Settings, such as the style, font type and size, margins, and other formats, are set in this file. If you want to change a default setting for new documents, you change the setting in the NORMAL.DOT template. Later sections in this chapter describe how to change these settings.

When you choose the File New command, a dialog box appears showing a list of templates (see fig. 30.1). Notice that the Normal template in the Use Template list is selected automatically.

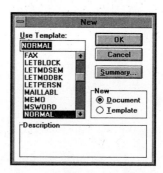

FIG. 30.1.

The File New dialog box.

When you open a new document based on the Normal template, Word for Windows creates a new document that is the same as the Normal template. The template remains on disk and does not change.

> Selecting the New File button on the toolbar is a quick way to create a new document based on the Normal template. Selecting this button skips the dialog box that appears when you choose the File New command.
>
> **T I P**

Using Word for Windows' Predesigned Templates

If you want to base your new document on a template other than the Normal template, select the template from the Use Template list in the File New dialog box. The templates are listed in alphabetical order. The Description area below the list provides a brief description of the selected template.

Word for Windows comes with a variety of predesigned templates you can use to create many typical business documents. Many of the templates use custom menus, display custom dialog boxes, and contain glossaries and macros that execute frequently used procedures. The predesigned templates are described in table 30.1.

Table 30.1. Predesigned Word Templates

Template	Function
ARTICLE2.DOT	Prepares a manuscript for a magazine article in accordance with the guidelines of the *1991 Writer's Market*.
DATAFILE.DOT	Contains macros and toolbar buttons to help you manage print-merge data files.
DISSERT2.DOT	Prepares a document for writing a dissertation.
FAX.DOT	Contains the format and text for a FAX cover sheet.
LETBLOCK.DOT	Contains prompts and format for standard block style business letter.

continues

Table 30.1. *(continued)*

Template	Function
LETMDSEM.DOT	Contains prompts and format for modified semiblock business letter.
LETMODBK.DOT	Contains prompts and format for a modified block letter.
LETPERSN.DOT	Contains format for personalized modified block letter.
MAILLABL.DOT	Creates a mailing-label form for many types of Avery labels. Use for manually typed or merged labels.
MEMO2.DOT	Contains layout for creating a business memo.
MSWORD.DOT	Contains Word for DOS keyboard remapping.
OVERHEAD.DOT	Contains prompts and layout for creating overhead slides.
PRESS.DOT	Contains prompts and layout for creating a press release as prescribed by the *AP Stylebook*.
PROPOSAL.DOT	Contains prompts and commands for creating a formal business proposal.
REPLAND.DOT	Contains prompts and layout for creating a standard report in landscape orientation.
REPSIDE.DOT	Contains prompts and layout for creating a report with sideheads (headings to the left of the body copy).
REPSTAND.DOT	Contains prompts and layout for creating a standard report in portrait orientation.
TERM2.DOT	Contains layout for writing a term paper.

If your File New dialog box does not display the templates listed in this table, the templates may not have been installed when you installed Word for Windows. You can rerun the installation procedure and choose to install the templates. Templates use a DOT extension and are stored in the same directory as the Word for Windows program, WINWORD.EXE. This directory is usually the C:\WINWORD directory.

Figure 30.2 shows a FAX cover sheet being created from the FAX.DOT template. After completing the FAX Cover Sheet dialog box, the rest of the template is filled in.

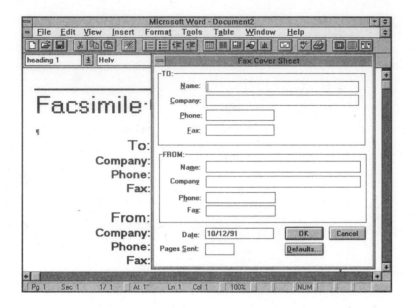

FIG. 30.2.

A document being created from the FAX template.

You can use the MAILLABL template to create labels for many Avery mailing-label sheets (see fig. 30.3).

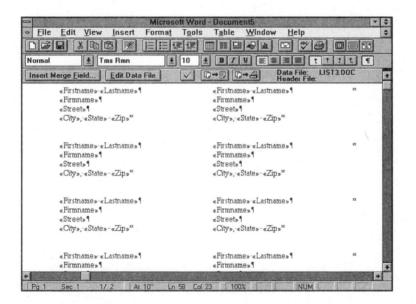

FIG. 30.3.

The MAILLABL template.

Changing an Existing Template

Templates can be modified to incorporate the specific text, graphics, styles, formatting, glossaries, and macros you need for your documents. This feature is handy for modifying the predefined templates to fit your needs or for modifying templates you have created.

The templates that come with Word for Windows are designed to handle many of the daily business transactions you may face. You can modify the templates to fit your business formats more closely, however, or to add glossaries and styles specific to your needs. You may want to use the MEMO2.DOT template for creating interoffice memos, but the template may not include glossary entries of words or text used in your department. You can modify MEMO2.DOT to include your own glossary entries, change the format to fit your needs, and edit the boilerplate text.

All new documents include the modifications or edits made to their template. Existing documents created before the template was modified, however, change only partially. Some of an existing document's features update to reflect the changes in its template and some of its features do not.

Changes in a template that transfer to existing documents based on the earlier template are as follows:

- Glossary entries
- Macros
- Menus
- Shortcut keys
- Toolbar tools

Although styles do not transfer from a changed template to its existing documents, you can merge styles between documents or between documents and templates. (Merging styles is discussed later in this chapter.)

Changes in a template that do not transfer automatically to existing documents based on that template are as follows:

- Template text
- Section formatting
- Page setup formatting
- Styles

To edit an existing template, follow these steps:

1. Choose the **File Open** command.

2. Enter the template name, with the extension DOT, in the File **Name** box.

   If you aren't sure of the file name, select Document Templates (*.DOT) from the List Files of **Type** pull-down list. All document template files in the current directory (those using the *.DOT extension) appear in the File **Name** list (see fig. 30.4). Select the template file from the list.

   Template files are stored in the same directory as the Word for Windows program files. This is usually the C:\WINWORD directory; however, it may be different for your company or if you are on a network.

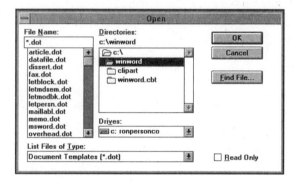

FIG. 30.4.

Opening a document template file in the WINWORD directory.

3. Choose OK or press Enter.

4. Edit the template to include the text, formatting, styles, glossaries, macros, shortcut keys, or tools you want to include in all the documents based on the template.

5. Choose the **File Save** command to save the template with the changes you made.

If a template required much work to create and is important to your business, you should make copies of it on disk and store it away from your computer. This prevents the template's loss in case of accidental erasure, theft, or fire.

T I P

Changing Template Formats from within a Document

Default settings are format settings specified when a document opens—settings such as which font and font size are used when you first begin to type. Default settings can be changed in two ways. You can modify the template on which a document is based, or you can change some formats within a document and transfer the changes back to the template so that the changes become new defaults.

The types of changes that can be transferred from a document back to its template are found in the Format Character, Format Language, or Format Page Setup commands.

To make format changes in a document and transfer those changes back to the originating template, use the following steps:

1. Open a new or existing document based on the template you want to change.

2. Choose the Format Character, Format Language, or Format Page Setup command.

   Figure 30.5, for example, shows the Format Character dialog box.

The Character dialog box.

3. Select the formatting options you want to define as default settings on the template.

4. Choose the Use as Default button. A dialog box appears asking you to confirm the update to the template.

5. Choose Yes or press Enter to update the document's template file with the selected default settings.

Transferring Styles between Templates and Documents

A *style* is a named combination of formatting commands. If you create a style in a document, the style is available in only that document. You may want styles in a document, however, to be available for any new document originating from a template. Or you may want some styles accessible by all documents no matter which template they came from. To do this, you have to transfer styles.

You can transfer styles between documents and templates in two ways: As you change or define a style in a document, you can select a check box and the style will be added to the document and the original template; or you can merge styles between the active document and a template.

Transferring Styles to a Template As You Create Them

If you want the styles you create in a document to transfer back to the template on which the document is based, select Format Style and choose the **D**efine button (see fig. 30.6). In the expanded Style dialog box, change or create a style, and then select the Add to Template check box. Finally, choose the **A**pply button. (Make sure that you change or define a style *before* selecting, or reselecting, the Add to Template check box.)

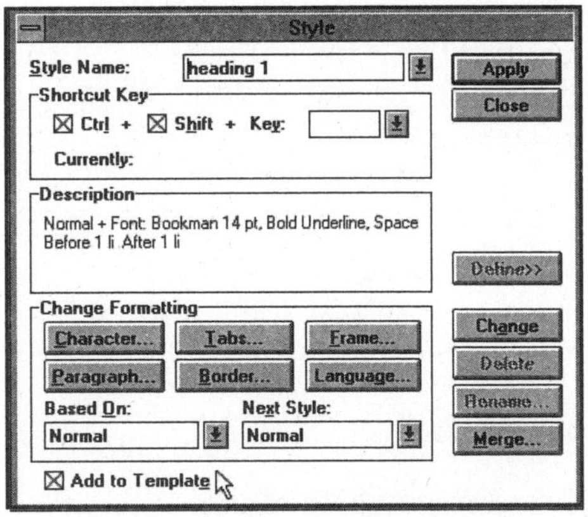

FIG. 30.6.

The Style dialog box.

Merging Styles between the Active Document and a Template

To avoid having to redefine styles on documents that have already been created, you can merge *all* of the styles between documents and templates. Styles you add to a template do not appear automatically in documents already created from that template. If a style is created on the MEMO.DOT template file, for example, the style will be available in all new documents based on the Memo template. The style will not be available, however, for memos created before the template was changed. If you are unfamiliar with creating and using styles, refer to Chapter 11.

To solve the problem of passing newly added styles from a template to existing documents, you should learn how to merge styles between the active document and a template.

 You must be careful! Merged styles replace existing styles of the same name. When you merge styles, you merge all styles; you cannot merge selected styles.

For detailed information about how to merge styles between documents and templates, refer to Chapter 11's section titled "Sharing Styles among Documents."

Creating a Template

Although Word for Windows comes with many predesigned templates, you may have a document or form that does not fit any of the templates. You can create a new template, or you can create a template based on an existing document.

Creating a New Template

You can create a template in much the same way as you create any document. To create a new template, follow these steps:

1. Choose the **File New** command.

2. Select the New **T**emplate option.

3. Choose OK or press Enter.

    The title bar displays Template rather than Document.

4. Lay out and format the template as you would a document. Include text that will not change between documents. The template can contain text and graphics you want to appear on all documents, formatting and styles, glossary entries, macros, new commands, shortcut keys, and new toolbar tools.

5. Choose the **File Save** command.

6. Enter a name for the template in the File **Name** box. The extension DOT is assigned to templates. All document template files are stored in the Word for Windows program directory unless you specify otherwise.

7. Choose OK or press Enter.

Template files normally are stored in the Word for Windows program directory (usually C:\WINWORD) if you want to select the template from the list in the **File New** dialog box.

You can specify the path where Word looks for templates. The templates it finds appear in the **Use** Template list of the File New dialog box.

This capability is especially useful when Word for Windows runs on a network. It enables each user to keep his or her own templates in private directory or on a local hard drive. This prevents modifications of a user's templates from affecting everyone's templates.

To set up a directory for templates, first create the directory in which templates will be stored. Start Word for Windows, and choose the **T**ools **O**ptions command. Choose the WIN.INI **C**ategory. Select Microsoft Word 2.0 from the drop-down **A**pplication list. Use the methods described in Chapter 29 to add or edit a DOT-path line in the **S**elect Options list. Your DOT-path should appear similar to the following:

> DOT-path = D:\TEMPLATE

You can create a new template based on an existing template by choosing the **File New** command and selecting the New **T**emplate option. Select from the **Use** Template list a template you want to use as the starting point. Save the template with a new name. Word for Windows automatically saves the file as a template with the DOT extension.

T I P

Creating a Template Based on an Existing Document

You already may have a document that contains most of the text, formatting, and settings you want to use in a template. Rather than re-create the document on a template, Word for Windows enables you to create a template based on the existing document.

To create a template based on an existing document, follow these steps:

1. Choose the **File New** command.

2. Select the New **T**emplate option.

3. Type the path and file name of the document you want to use as the template in the **U**se Template box. For example, type *c:\reprts\qtr1.doc* (see fig. 30.7).

Enter the name of an existing document you want a template based on.

4. Choose OK or press Enter.

   In the title bar, notice that the file opens as a template but contains all the document's text, formatting, glossaries, styles, macros, commands, shortcut keys, and tools.

5. Make the necessary changes to the template.

6. Choose the **File S**ave command and enter a file name with a DOT extension for the template.

7. Choose OK or press Enter.

Attaching a Template to a Document

If you are working on a document and decide you want to have access to all the features in another template, you can attach the document to that template. Attaching a new template does not change the existing document text, but it does change specified settings, such as glossaries, macros, menu commands, margins, shortcut key assignments and tools. (Styles do not transfer.)

To attach a template to an existing document, follow these steps:

1. Choose the **File Template** command.

   The File Template dialog box displays the current template to which the document is attached (see fig. 30.8). The default template is Normal.

The Template dialog box.

2. Select from the Attach **D**ocument To drop-down list the template to which you want to attach the document.

   Select from among the following options for storing new glossaries and macros:

Option	Description
Global	Stores all new glossaries and macros with the NORMAL.DOT template. Beware! Choosing this option can add unwanted items to NORMAL.DOT, the template that contains all default settings.
With Document **T**emplate	Stores all new glossaries and macros with the selected template.
Prompt for Each New	Displays a dialog box each time you create a new glossary entry or macro, giving you a storage option.

3. Choose OK or press Enter. The active document will contain the settings of the selected template.

From Here . . .

Templates are just one of the ways professional writers can ensure that their documents are consistent. Some other features you can use alone or incorporate with templates include styles, fields, forms, glossary entries, and all the customizing features, such as macros, shortcut keys, custom commands, and tools on the toolbar.

Styles enable you to change formats easily throughout a document. Styles are described in detail in Chapter 11. Glossaries store commonly used terms. Glossaries are described in Chapter 9. Your templates can include field codes that automatically enter dates or prompt you for data. If you want to learn how to insert or manipulate field codes and their results, read Chapter 18. Macros are automated procedures that you create. You can attach a macro to a menu command, to a shortcut key, or to a tool on the toolbar. To learn more about macros, read Chapter 31.

31

Creating and Editing Macros

Word for Windows macros enable you to automate frequent procedures and command choices with a minimum of effort. The easiest way to create a macro is to record your keystrokes and commands with the macro recorder. You also can build macros from scratch using WordBASIC, the programming language that comes with Word for Windows. You can test and modify your macros using Word for Windows' macro editor.

Macros are the basis for customizing Word for Windows. Using the Tools Options command, you can attach macros or Word for Windows' built-in commands to toolbar buttons, menu commands, or shortcut keys. You can turn Word for Windows into a word processor specially designed to handle the work you face.

In some word processors, all automation must be done with macros. Word for Windows is more powerful and flexible. Word for Windows also gives you styles, field codes, and a glossary to make your work easier. Many of the tasks performed by macros in other word processors can be done more efficiently with these features:

Feature	Function
Styles	Applies complex formatting multiple times
Field codes	Automates entries such as the current date or filling a form
Glossaries	Repeats frequently used text or pictures

If you need to accomplish a mix of these features, or automate an entire task involving multiple features, then use macros.

Working with Recorded Macros

Macros can be recordings of keystrokes and commands or sophisticated programs you build. Even simple recorded macros can improve your work efficiency significantly. Some of the simple tasks and procedures you can automate with a macro and its shortcut key are as follows:

- Opening, selecting, and updating a document filled with field codes

- Modifying the Tools Create Envelope command so that it uses the default options and immediately prints

- Adding custom zoom or edit buttons to the toolbar

- Creating a shortcut key to toggle table gridlines on or off by using the built-in Table Gridlines command

Deciding How Your Macro Will Work

Before you create a usable macro, you need to decide whether it affects a specific portion of the document or the currently selected portion. If the macro always affects a specific part of a document, insert bookmarks in the document that name the specific text or graphic so that the macro can find these parts easily.

You also must decide whether you want to make a *global macro* (a macro that can be used with any document) or a *template macro* (a macro that can be used only with documents based on that template).

Specifying Where Macros Are Stored

Macros are stored in three different ways—as commands, global macros, or template macros. *Commands* are built-in macros stored within the Word for Windows program, WINWORD.EXE. Many of these built-in macros are the same menu commands, such as FileNew or Bold. Many of these commands that do not exist on the menu, however, are useful when added to a shortcut key or toolbar button or used within one of your macros. Macros that you record or program are stored as a *global* or *template* macro. Global macros are stored with the NORMAL.DOT template and are available to all documents and templates. Template macros are stored with a specific template and are available to only those documents that are based on that template.

Storing a macro as a global macro ensures that it is available in all documents. If you store too many macros as global macros, however, you clutter your NORMAL.DOT file with macros used for a specific purpose or for a specific document. You should save macros designed for a specific purpose with the appropriate template. Save macros as a global macro only when they need to be shared by many documents.

T I P

Before you begin recording or programming macros in Word for Windows, you will want to define the *context*, or where macros will be recorded. When Word for Windows is first installed, by default you are always asked where you want the macro saved—globally (NORMAL.DOT), or to the template for the active document.

To specify where you want your macros stored as you record or program them, follow these steps:

1. Choose the **File Template** command.

    The Template dialog box appears (see fig. 31.1).

FIG. 31.1.

The Template dialog box.

2. Select one of the following storage options from the Store New Macros and Glossaries As option group.

Global (Available to All Documents). Macros are stored in the NORMAL.DOT template and will be available to documents based on any template.

With Document Template. Macros are stored with the template on which the active document is based. If the active document is based on the Normal template, then the macro will be stored as a global macro.

Prompt for Each New. When you begin the recording, a dialog box will prompt you for whether the macro should be a global macro (stored in NORMAL.DOT) or a template macro (stored in the template of the active document). If the active document is based on NORMAL.DOT, you will not be prompted.

3. Choose OK or press Enter.

If the active document is a document based on NORMAL.DOT, the macro is assumed to be a global macro and will be saved in NORMAL.DOT. You will not be prompted for where the macro should be saved.

When Word for Windows is first installed, the default is the **P**rompt for Each New option. If you are working with a mix of both templates and normal documents, this is the most convenient setting to use.

Recording a Macro

When you record a macro, you are asked for a name and shortcut key for the macro. Word for Windows then records each key you press, selection you make, and command you choose. You cannot select text or move with the mouse during recording.

To start the macro recorder, follow these steps:

1. If you plan to use the macro with a template, open a document based on that template. If you plan to make the macro global, open any document.

2. Choose the **T**ools **R**ecord Macro command.

   The Record Macro dialog box appears (see fig. 31.2).

3. Type the macro's name in the **R**ecord Macro text box.

   Enter a descriptive name, even if you plan to use the macro only in your current session. Macro names must begin with a letter and can be up to 32 characters long. Do not use spaces. A combination of upper- and lowercase letters is best (PrintEnvelope, for example).

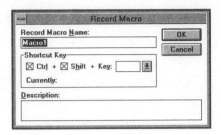

FIG. 31.2.

The Record
Macro dialog
box.

4. If you want to use a shortcut key to run the macro, select a combination of the Ctrl, Shift, and Key boxes.

   You can use any combination of Ctrl+Shift+Key or Ctrl+Key for your shortcut. The best solution is to use Ctrl+Shift+key shortcuts for your macros and reserve the Ctrl+key shortcuts for those macros built in to Word for Windows. In the Key drop-down list, you can see that you can assign a macro to keys other than letters. If you choose a key that has an assignment, that assignment displays to the right of Currently:

5. Enter a brief descriptive line in the Description text box to help you remember what the macro does.

6. Choose OK or press Enter.

7. If you selected the Prompt for Each New option in the File Template dialog box, the Macro dialog box in figure 31.3 prompts you for where you want to store the macro. Choose Store Macro as Global or In Template. Choose OK or press Enter.

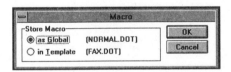

FIG. 31.3.

The Macro
dialog box.

8. Execute the commands and procedures you want recorded.

9. Choose the Tools Stop Recorder command to turn off the macro recorder. The REC indicator in the status bar disappears.

While the macro recorder is on, all of the keys you press and commands and options you choose are recorded. If the status bar is turned on, you see a REC indicator at the lower right corner of the screen.

Mouse actions are limited while the recorder is on. You can choose commands, but you cannot move or select within the document. You can use Microsoft Drawing or Microsoft Graph when you are recording a macro, but only the work you do in Word for Windows (such as inserting a graphic or resizing a chart) is recorded.

If you make minor mistakes while the recorder is on, you don't have to stop the recording session. You can leave the recorder on, correct the mistakes, and leave the macro with these corrections. You also can edit the macro later to remove the mistakes.

You cannot use the mouse to go to specific areas of the document when recording a macro. If you name specific locations in the document with bookmarks before recording, however, you can use the Edit Go To command or the F5 key to select that bookmark while recording.

Recording a Sample Macro

The following procedure illustrates how easily you can record a macro. Follow these steps to record a macro that turns off the View settings in the Tools Options dialog box so that you have the maximum screen area for typing:

1. Choose the Tools Record Macro command.

2. Type *ViewMaxSpace* in the Record Macro Name text box.

3. Enter *Turns off View settings for maximum typing space* in the Description text box.

4. Choose OK or press Enter.

5. If the active document is based on a template other than NORMAL.DOT and you selected Prompt for Each New in the File Template dialog box, you are prompted for the context of the recorded macro. Choose Store Macro Global so that this macro can be used with any document. Choose OK or press Enter.

The macro recorder is now on. Follow these steps to tell Word for Windows the commands and options to record:

1. Choose the Tools Options command.

2. Select the View category.

3. Clear all of the options in the Window group—scroll bars and status bar. If an option is already cleared, leave it. The clear setting is recorded.

4. Choose OK or press Enter.

5. Choose the Tools Stop Recorder command.

Keep the ViewMaxSpace macro you just recorded; you will use it when you learn how to edit a macro.

Running a Macro

After you record a macro, you should test it. Save your document so that if the macro doesn't do what you wanted, you can recover your saved work.

To run or play back a macro, choose the Tools Macro Run command. You also can use this option to run built-in commands, including commands not shown on Word for Windows' menu or toolbar.

To run a macro, follow these steps:

1. Activate a document on which the macro is designed to work. If the macro is designed to work with items preselected, select those items. (Macros do not run if the macro editor window is active.)

2. Choose the Tools Macro command.

3. In the Macro dialog box, select from the Show group the type of macro you want to run—Commands, Global Macros, or Template Macros.

4. Select or type the macro or command name in the Macro Name list box.

5. Choose Run.

If you assigned a shortcut key to your macro, you also can run a macro by doing step 1 in the preceding steps, then pressing the macro shortcut key.

If your macro does not run correctly, you can record it again or correct it with the following editing techniques.

Editing a Macro

The macro you record is kept as macro commands. You can see and edit these commands much like a normal document. By editing a macro, you can remove commands recorded by mistake, modify recorded commands, or make your macros more efficient.

You can view or edit your recorded macro, ViewMaxSpace, by following these steps:

1. Choose the Tools Macro command.

    The Macro dialog box appears (see fig. 31.4).

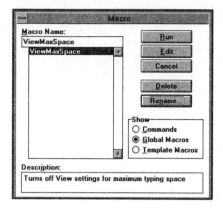

FIG. 31.4.

The Macro
dialog box.

2. Select from the Show group where the macro is stored. (The ViewMaxSpace macro just recorded was a **G**lobal Macro.)

3. Select or type the name in the **M**acros Name text box or list.

4. Choose **E**dit.

Figure 31.5 shows the newly recorded macro, ViewMaxSpace, in the macro editing window.

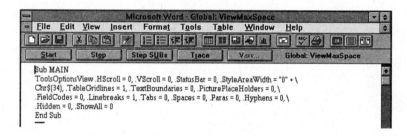

FIG. 31.5.

The recorded
macro,
ViewMaxSpace,
in the edit
window.

When you open a macro for viewing or editing, Word for Windows displays a macro editing bar at the top of the screen. The buttons on the bar are helpful when you troubleshoot macros.

At the right side of the edit bar you see the name and context of the macro being displayed—Global: ViewMaxSpace. The macro begins with the words Sub MAIN and ends with End Sub. All macros within WordBASIC are considered *subroutines* (subprograms) that run under Word for Windows. In your recording you choose the **T**ools **O**ptions command and the View category. Notice that the first statement is ToolsOptionsView. Each item that follows ToolsOptionsView corresponds to an edit box, option button, or check box in the View dialog box. Notice that .HScroll=0 corresponds to the Horizontal Scroll check box being turned off. If the item was .HScroll=1, it would correspond to the Horizontal Scroll check box being turned on. The pieces of code and how to get explanations of them from Help are described later in this chapter.

When you are in the macro editor, use standard Word for Windows editing procedures and menu commands to edit, type, or delete macro statements and functions. Tabs are in fixed locations and you cannot format the macro code.

The capability to edit macros is useful even if you only record macros and never program in WordBASIC. With simple edits you can correct typographical errors, delete commands, copy macros or parts of macros from one document or template to another, and reorganize a macro by cutting and pasting.

While a macro is open, the macro edit bar remains on-screen. You can switch between macro windows and other document windows like you would change between any Word for Windows documents; choose the document from the **W**indow menu or click on an exposed portion, or press Ctrl+F6.

To close your macro editing window, activate the macro's window. Then choose the document control menu icon by pressing Alt, - (hyphen). Choose the **C**lose command. This closes the window and keeps the macro in memory. (It does not save the macro to disk.) If you choose the **F**ile **C**lose command instead, you close the macro window and the document containing the macro.

Saving Macros

Your new macro is stored in memory but is not automatically saved to disk. You can lose your macro if you forget to save it. Template macros must be saved before you close the template to which they are attached; global macros must be saved before you exit Word for Windows. Just as you save preliminary versions of documents every fifteen minutes or so, occasionally save versions of your macros to protect against accidental deletion.

To save a macro to disk, choose the **F**ile Sav**e** All command. The Sav**e** All command goes through your open templates and documents, including any macros you opened to view or edit, and determines whether they have been newly created or changed. Word for Windows prompts you to specify whether to save the changes and newly created macros. You are given a chance to save documents that have changed and templates that have macros added to them.

Word for Windows displays a prompt similar to the one in figure 31.6 when you are prompted to save a global macro.

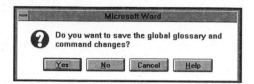

FIG. 31.6.

Save macro
changes to disk.

Word for Windows specifies the name and the template of your macro in the dialog box when prompting you to save a macro with a template, as shown in figure 31.7.

FIG. 31.7.

The prompt for a
template macro
shows the name
of the DOT file.

Choose **Yes** to save a macro. If you choose **No**, your macro will remain in memory and can be used, but has not been saved to disk.

When you close a document that has an unsaved template or global macro, you are prompted one last time if you want the macro saved. If you choose **No**, the macro will be lost.

Understanding Dialog Box Options in Macro Recordings

One of the most familiar features of the Word for Windows program is its reliance on the dialog box to store information from the user. A dialog box is composed of one or more dialog elements: check boxes, text boxes, option buttons, and so on. When you make a selection in a dialog box, Word for Windows stores this information as a value in a *dialog record*. You can use dialog records to toggle commands on or off, or to change the entries in text boxes.

Understanding Dialog Records

Each time Word for Windows displays a dialog box, it creates a dialog record in memory. The dialog record contains a data field for each element in the dialog box, such as a text edit box or a check box.

The following is a simple convention for identifying the fields and related values within a dialog record that you may have observed when recording macros:

```
CommandName .Field1 = Value, .Field2 = Value,...
```

In this convention, CommandName is the menu and command that, when chosen, displays the dialog box. Each field, such as .Field1, corresponds to an element within the dialog box—for example, the name of a check box. The value for each field describes the condition of that field—1 or 0 if a check box is selected or cleared, for example, or quoted text for the contents of an edit box.

As an example, examine the familiar Format Character dialog box shown in figure 31.8 after a user's entries and selections.

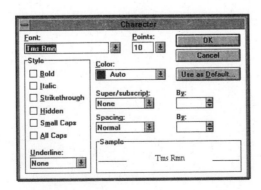

FIG. 31.8.

The Format Character Dialog Box.

Figure 31.9 shows the recorded version of the same entries and selection in the Format Character dialog box.

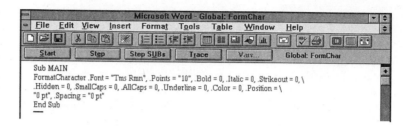

FIG. 31.9.

The recorded
version of the
Format Character
command.

Note that the recorded macro is a straightforward guide to the user's selections within the dialog box. Each option in the dialog box is represented by a field in the recorded macro.

Field names are preceded with a period, string values are enclosed in quotation marks, and select or cleared values for Bold, AllCaps, and so on, are identified by a 0 for clear and a 1 for selected. When a field (Color, for example) requires the user to choose from among several values in a list, the number of the selected value is stored in the field. (As in many instances when dealing with computer languages, you should start counting at 0, not 1). Auto is the first choice in the Color list box, so the Color field's value is 0.

Selecting or Clearing Dialog Box Options

Earlier in this chapter you recorded the macro ViewMaxSpace. In this macro you chose the Tools Options command, selected the View Category, and cleared the status bar and horizontal and vertical scroll bars. Figure 31.10 shows the recorded version of this process with most View settings cleared.

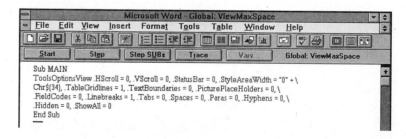

FIG. 31.10.

Recorded version
of the Tools
Options View
command.

To create a macro that turns on the vertical scroll bar, you can record the macro again, this time selecting the **Vertical Scroll Bar** check box. But an easier solution is available.

To create a macro that turns on the vertical scroll bar, simply change the corresponding dialog field value, .VScroll, from 0 to 1 (from clear to selected). The new macro looks like the macro shown in figure 31.11.

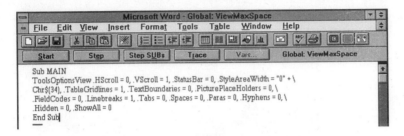

FIG. 31.11.

Changing the .VScroll value in a recorded command.

This macro not only turns on the vertical scroll bar option, it also affects the other View settings. Because you care about only the .VScroll field, the rest of the field settings can be removed from the macro. Use normal editing methods to delete unwanted fields and values. The resulting macro, called VScrollOn, is simple and to the point:

```
Sub MAIN
ToolsOptionsView .VScroll = 1
End Sub
```

You probably can guess what the reverse of this macro would be—a macro to turn off the vertical scroll bar. The VScrollOff macro looks like this:

```
Sub MAIN
ToolsOptionsView .VScroll = 0
End Sub
```

Now you have two macros—one that turns the vertical scroll bar on, and another that turns it off. The other values in the View dialog box are not affected. In the next section, you learn about a programming construct that enables you to combine these two macros into one.

Getting Help on Macros

Word for Windows contains extensive help for macros. You can choose the **Help Help Index** command to see the index of major help topics. To get an overview and detail on specific procedures, select the underlined topic *WordBasic Programming Language* by clicking on it or by pressing the Tab key until it is selected, and then press Enter.

You also can get information about a specific macro statement or function. For example, you may have recorded a macro and need to know which field values are appropriate to turn a dialog option on or off. To find out about a specific field, macro statement or function, open the macro in a macro edit window, move the insertion point into the macro statement or field you need information about, and press F1 (Help). Figure 31.12 shows the help screen for the Bold macro statement and function. The numeric values that can be used or returned by Bold are shown.

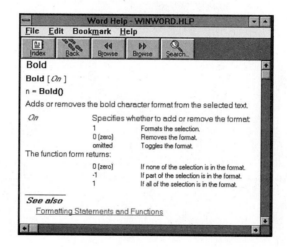

FIG. 31.12.

Get help about a macro function or statement by selecting it and pressing F1.

Troubleshooting Macros

Even the best programmers usually have a few errors (or bugs) in their programs at first. Long, complex macro recordings or manually entered WordBASIC programs are more prone to errors than short recordings, but any macro can contain an error that prevents it from working properly. Fortunately, Word for Windows contains special troubleshooting tools to help you find problems and correct them.

Using the Word for Windows Debugger

When you choose the Tools Macro Edit command and select a macro to edit, Word for Windows automatically switches to a troubleshooting or "debugging" mode. The macro edit bar appears at the top of the screen to aid you in testing and troubleshooting your macros. The buttons on this bar enable you to control the operation of your macro, constraining its operation to one statement or subroutine at a time. As the macro runs, you can watch its effect on a target document and isolate problems as they occur. This process is much easier than running a macro and seeing it zip through its operations, only to stop abruptly and display a macro error message.

To debug your macro, you need to run it from within a target document. The easiest way is to put a target document in one window and the macro in another, and then use one of the step buttons to watch how each macro statement affects the document.

To make troubleshooting easier, set up the macro and document in two windows. Make sure that you open your macro using the **T**ools **M**acro Edit command, and then follow these steps:

1. Choose the **W**indow **A**rrange All command to see multiple documents.

2. Reposition and size the windows so that each takes half the screen, one above the other.

3. Activate the document window you want to work in by clicking it or by pressing Ctrl+F6 (Next Window) or Shift+Ctrl+F6 (Previous Window).

Each button in the edit icon bar can help you see the macro's effect on the document. To operate these buttons by keyboard, press Alt+Shift+the underlined letter. Table 31.1 describes the buttons in the edit bar.

Table 31.1. Using the Edit Bar

Button	Function
Start/**C**ontinue	Runs the active macro or continues the macro after a pause. If the macro has paused for a step or trace, the **S**tart button appears as **C**ontinue.
Step	Runs the macro on the target document one statement at a time, highlighting the statement being executed, and then pausing until the St**e**p button is pressed again.
Step SUB	Runs the macro on the target document one subroutine at a time, pausing on the first line of the subsequent subroutine until the Step SUB button is pressed again.
Trace	Runs the macro from start to finish, highlighting each statement as it executes.
Vars	Shows the current values of the variables used in the macro and provides a way to reset the variable assignments during macro execution.

If an error or alert box displays, press F1 for help with that macro statement or function.

Managing Macros

After awhile, you may have accumulated macros you really don't need. Others may be poorly named (can you remember what *Macro7* does?) or better suited to another template. You should keep your macros up-to-date and well organized. This section discusses how to manage your macros.

Deleting Macros

To delete a macro, follow these steps:

1. If the macro is a template macro, open the template or a document attached to it. If the macro is a global macro, open any document.

2. Choose the Tools Macro command.

3. Select the macro or command type—Commands, Global Macros, or Template Macros—from the Show group, then select the macro or command from the Macro Name list.

4. Choose the Delete button.

5. Choose Close.

You cannot delete a macro that is in an open edit window. If you delete a macro currently assigned to the menu or toolbar, Word for Windows unassigns the macro when it is deleted. All of your changes are stored in memory until you save them to disk (see "Saving Macros" earlier in this chapter).

Renaming Macros

To rename a macro, follow these steps:

1. If the macro is a template macro, open the template or a document attached to it. If the macro is a global macro, open any document.

2. Choose the Tools Macro command.

3. Select the macro or command type—**C**ommands, **G**lobal Macros, or **T**emplate Macros—from the Show group, then select the macro or command from the **M**acro Name list.

4. Choose the Re**n**ame button.

   The Rename dialog box appears.

5. Type the new name in the New Macro **N**ame text box.

6. Choose OK or press Enter.

7. Choose Close or press Enter.

Creating Automatic Macros

After you complete your macro, you can give it a special name that signals Word for Windows to run the macro automatically at certain times. Table 31.2 describes Word for Windows' five automatic macros.

Table 31.2. Running Macros Automatically

Macro name	Function
AutoExec	Global macro that runs when you start Word for Windows. For example, the macro could change to a selected directory, prompt the user for preferences, or prompt for a document or template to start up in.
AutoExit	Global macro that runs when you exit Word for Windows. For example, closes applications that Word for Windows macros opened, or automatically opens another application.
AutoNew	Global or template macro that runs when you create a new document based on the template containing AutoNew. For example, displays an instruction message to help new users or update fields in a new document.
AutoOpen	Global or template macro that runs when you open an existing document. For example, updates fields in an existing document, or automatically inserts text from a specified file.
AutoClose	Global or template macro that runs when you close a document. For example, saves a changed document to a predetermined file name.

To prevent an automatic macro from running, hold down the Shift key when you perform the action that starts the macro. To prevent AutoOpen from running when you open a document, for example, hold down the Shift key while you choose the OK button from the **File O**pen command.

As table 31.2 indicates, automatic macros are especially useful for performing operations that set up a document when it opens. A handy use of the AutoNew macro, for example, is to update all fields in a document when the document opens from a template. This is especially useful for templates containing date and time fields and {fillin} field codes. The macro may appear as follows:

```
Sub MAIN
   EditSelectAll
   UpdateFields
   StartOfDocument
End Sub
```

This macro is useful when saved as an AutoNew macro with a template used for forms and containing field codes such as {fillin}. When a new document opens from a template having this macro, each field code is updated. For example, all the {fillin} input boxes are displayed in turn.

Customizing the Toolbar, Menus, and Shortcut Keys

Part of Word for Windows' power comes from the capability it gives you to remake Word for Window's menus, toolbar, and shortcut keys to take advantage of the macros you create. You can add your own macros to the keyboard, menus, and toolbar. You can remove unneeded built-in commands, move commands to other places, or add some of the many macros and commands included with Word for Windows that are not included in the standard Word for Windows screen.

Custom key assignments, menus, and toolbars combined with Word for Windows' easy-to-create macros enable you to build a word processor tailored to the work you do. This capability also holds a danger: you have the potential to modify the global menus and keyboard assignments so much that Word for Windows becomes difficult for other operators to use. For this reason, you probably should assign your menus, toolbar buttons, and key assignments to templates rather than to assign them globally.

Differentiating between Global and Template Customizing

Assigning your macros or the built-in commands to menu commands, toolbar buttons, or shortcut keys may cause conflicts.

An assignment you make at the global level may conflict with one you make in a template. Suppose that you assign Ctrl+C to the **E**dit Cu**t** command in your template, but Ctrl+C is already assigned to **E**dit **C**opy at the Global level. To avoid confusion, Word for Windows follows a strict hierarchy: template assignments always take precedence over assignments at the Global level.

A global macro and a template macro can have the same name. In assignments to a menu or the toolbar, Word for Windows recognizes duplicate macro names and eliminates them from the list box from which you select macros. When you make an assignment for a template, global macros are hidden from view, giving the template macro precedence. Word for Windows lists both names in keyboard assignments, but doesn't distinguish the template macro from the global macro.

Assigning Commands and Macros to Shortcut Keys

Shortcut keys enable you to perform routine operations quickly without moving from the keyboard to the mouse. You should consider assigning shortcut keys to frequently used menu options.

Assigning Global Shortcut Keys

Many of Word for Windows' commands and options are assigned to shortcut keys in the default template, NORMAL.DOT. Pressing Ctrl+B applies boldface to selected text, for example, and pressing Ctrl+F2 increases the font size of a selection. These key combinations are global.

If you did not assign a key combination to a macro when it was created, you can assign it with the following procedure. To assign key combinations to existing commands or macros in the global context, follow these steps:

1. Choose the **T**ools **O**ptions command and select the Keyboard Category. The Options Keyboard dialog box appears (see fig. 31.13).

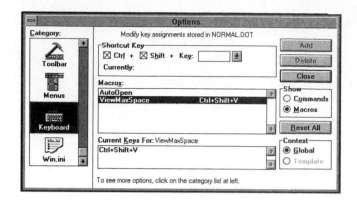

FIG. 31.13.

The Options
dialog box with
the Keyboard
Category
selected.

2. Select **Co**mmands or **M**acros from the Show options to see a list of built-in commands or available macros.

3. Select **G**lobal from the Context options.

   You can make global assignments from within any document or template in Word for Windows. If you are working in a document based on NORMAL.DOT, Global is the only context option available. If you are working in a document attached to a custom template, selecting Global from the Context options constrains the list of macros to global macros.

4. Select a command or macro from the Comma**n**ds/Macro**s** list box.

   Notice that current global key assignments appear to the right of the command or macro names. When you select a command or macro from the list box, all global key assignments appear in the Current **K**eys For box.

5. In the Shortcut Key check boxes, select a key combination.

   Press a combination of function keys: the Ctrl key, or Shift+Ctrl. If you select a combination already in use, Word for Windows displays the macro or command assigned to the combination to the right of `Currently:`.

6. Choose **A**dd.

7. Continue to make more shortcut key assignments, or choose Close.

To return to the default keyboard assignments, choose the **R**eset All button. Word for Windows removes any global assignments you made and restores the original set of shortcuts.

> Replacing the global key assignments that come with Word for
> Windows may confuse other users of your system. If you want to
> save your personal shortcut keys globally, use Shift+Ctrl+letter for
> your new assignments so that you leave Word for Windows'
> Ctrl+letter shortcuts intact.
>
> **T I P**

Assigning Template Shortcut Keys

Key combinations assigned to a template enable documents based on
the template to have shortcut keys specific to the template. Template
shortcut keys take precedence over global shortcut keys with the same
key combination.

To assign commands or macros to the keyboard in the template context, follow these steps:

1. Open your template or a document based on that template.

2. Choose the Tools Options command and select the Keyboard
   Category.

3. Select Commands or Macros from the Show options.

4. Select Template from the Context options.

   Remember, the macros list contains all macros available (global
   and template). If a global and template macro have the same
   name, both appear in the macro list.

5. Select a command or macro from the Commands/Macros list box.

   Notice that current key assignments, global and template, appear
   to the right of the command or macro names. When you select a
   command or macro from the list box, key assignments appear in
   the Current Keys For box.

6. In the Shortcut Key check boxes, select a key combination.

   Press a combination using function keys, the Ctrl key, or
   Shift+Ctrl. If you select a combination already in use, Word for
   Windows displays the currently assigned macro or command to
   the right of Currently:.

7. Choose Add.

8. Choose Close.

T I P   When you make key assignments in the template context, a global and template macro may have the same name. Duplicate names appear twice in the Macros list. You cannot readily identify which macro is global or template—something to keep in mind when naming new macros.

If you think that you may be assigning a template macro to the keyboard, consider giving the template macro a unique name to differentiate it from a global macro. If you created a global macro named *MakeIndex*, for example, and you want to create a variation of this macro at the template level, name it *TMakeIndex*, or something similar.

Removing Shortcut Keys

To remove the shortcut key assignment from a command or macro, repeat the steps for assigning keys, but instead of entering a key combination, select the key combination in the Current **K**eys For list box and choose the **D**elete button.

Assigning Commands and Macros to the Toolbar

You can access commands and macros added to the toolbar by clicking the mouse. Even if you don't create your own macros, you can add significantly to the toolbar's functions by adding commands you use often. If you frequently need to switch between viewing field codes and viewing their results, for example, add ViewFieldCodes to the toolbar. Or add ViewZoom to the toolbar to create a single tool that enables you to zoom to any percentage.

Before you add a command or macro to a button on the toolbar, you first must decide whether you want it to apply to all toolbars (global) or only toolbars specific to a template. To create a global assignment, open any document. To create an assignment local to a specific template, open the template or use the **F**ile **T**emplate command to attach your current document to the template.

To add or remove a command or macro assigned to a toolbar button, follow these steps:

1. Choose the Tools Options command, then select the Toolbar Category.

   The Toolbar Category of the Options dialog box appears (see fig. 31.14).

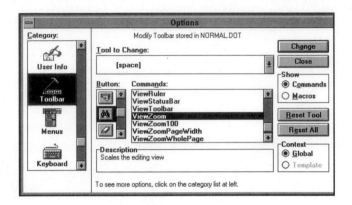

FIG. 31.14.

The Options dialog box with the Toolbar Category displayed.

2. Select Commands or Macros from the Show options.

3. Select Global or Template from the Context options.

   As noted, the macros list contains all macros available to the active template. If you are working in a template and choose the Template context, global and template macros show in the Commands/Macros list box.

4. Select a command or macro from the Commands/Macros list box. If you want to remove a current button from the toolbar and replace it with a space, select [space] from the list.

5. Scroll through the Tools to Change list until you find the button you want to change, and then select the button. The toolbar buttons appear in the list in the order they appear on the toolbar, starting with the far left and ending with the far right.

6. Scroll through the Buttons list and select a button appropriate for the macro you want to assign.

7. Choose Change. The toolbar immediately reflects your change.

8. Choose Close.

If you add the ViewZoom command to the toolbar, you can zoom from 25% to 200% with one button. This macro eliminates the need for the other three zoom tools.

T I P

If you want to restore the original assignment to a toolbar button, select the button in the **T**ool To Change list, and then choose the **R**eset Tool button. Choose **R**eset All to restore all button assignments.

Save toolbar changes the same way you save macros to disk. Choose **F**ile Sav**e** All and save changes to the global macros and glossaries or to the appropriate template (DOT) file.

Customizing the Menu

Many commands and macros built into Word for Windows are too useful to bury in the Tools Macro Run list but are not used frequently enough to merit assignment to the toolbar or shortcut keys. This category of commands or macros are probably best suited to the menus. You can add macros or commands to the global menu so that they are shared by all documents, or you can add them to a specific template so that only documents created from the template display the customized menu.

Assigning Macros and Commands to Menus

When you add a command to a menu, the command is always added at the bottom of the pull-down menu. Figure 31.15 shows the **F**ile menu with commands added for a custom macro named **C**hange Case.

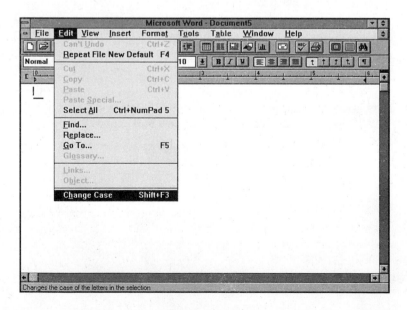

Just as you add space to the toolbar, you can add separator lines to a menu. A separator line is the line that crosses pull-down menus to separate groups of similar commands.

Before you customize a menu, open any document to change the global menu or open the specific template to change the menu associated with that template.

To add a macro or command to the menu, follow these steps:

1. Choose the T**o**ols **O**ptions command, then select the Menus **Cat**egory. The Options dialog box for menus appears (see fig. 31.16).

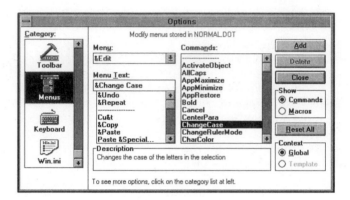

FIG. 31.16.

The Options dialog box with the Menus Category displayed.

2. Select **C**ommands or **M**acros from the Show options.

3. Select **G**lobal or **T**emplate from the Context options.

   As noted, the macros list contains all macros available to the active template. If you are working in a custom template and choose the **T**emplate context, global and template macros show in the Comma**n**ds/Macros list box.

4. Select a command or macro from the Comma**n**ds/Macros list box. To add a separator line to a menu, select the dashed line from the list.

5. Select from the Men**u** list the menu to which you want to add the macro or command. Menus appear in the list in the order that they appear on-screen (left to right).

6. In the Menu T**e**xt list box, type the name of the command or macro as you want it to appear on the menu. If the macro is already on the menu, a name is already selected in the Menu T**e**xt list.

Type an ampersand (&) before the letter you want underlined as the activating letter. Pick a letter that hasn't been used before in that menu.

7. Choose **A**dd.

8. Add another command or choose Close.

The macro description, displayed in the Description box at the bottom of the dialog box, appears in the status bar at the bottom of the screen when the new added command is selected from the menu. Any key combinations you assigned to the macro also appear to the right of the menu command name.

Removing Commands and Macros from Menus

To remove a command or macro from a menu, repeat the steps for assigning a command or macro to a menu, select from the Menu **T**ext list the menu item you want to remove, and choose **D**elete. The command is removed from the menu. Notice that when you remove a command, the other commands on the menu move up. To restore your menus to the original configuration provided by Word for Windows, select **R**eset All.

Using Word for Windows Sample Macros

Word for Windows has sample macros associated with the templates saved in the WINWORD directory during installation. You can copy these macros from the sample templates to your own documents or templates.

The C:\WINWORD\LIBRARY directory contains the document NEWMACRO.DOC. This document calls up powerful macros you can learn from and add to your global menus. You can see a demonstration of a macro by selecting from the list that appears and then choosing the **D**emo button. To add a macro to the global menu, click the **I**nstall button. Some of the extra menu commands available through the NEWMACRO.DOC macros include commands to accomplish the following tasks:

- Delete unused styles

- Convert other word processing files in batch mode

- Insert a table of authorities
- Create a concordance index
- Rotate columns in a table
- Insert smart quotes
- Start and activate Microsoft Excel

From Here . . .

Combined with the Tools Options Keyboard, Menu, and Toolbar commands, Word for Windows' recorded macros enable you to customize your word processing environment to fit the work you do.

Word for Windows also has styles, field codes, and glossaries to automate your work. These features are described in Chapters 11 through 20 and significantly increase productivity.

Installing Word for Windows

I n this appendix, you learn what hardware components are required
to run Word for Windows and how to install the program with different features.

Reviewing the Hardware Requirements

To provide acceptable performance in the Windows environment, your
computer system must satisfy the following minimum hardware
requirements:

- IBM Personal System/2 with 80286, 80386, or 80486 processors,
  AT, COMPAQ 286, 386, or 486 computers, or compatibles.

- Computers using 80286 processors should have a speed of at least
  12 Mhz. Computers with 8088 or 8086 processors do not have
  sufficient computing power for Word for Windows to operate
  efficiently.

- 2M or more of memory. Performance increases dramatically with at least 4M of memory where at least 1M is set aside for SMARTdrive.

- IBM EGA, VGA graphics card, Hercules graphics card, or other graphics cards and monitors compatible with Windows 3.0 or higher. The quality of display and performance of Word for Windows may vary significantly with the graphics card.

- Hard disk or file server.

- At least one floppy disk drive.

- DOS 3.0 or higher (as required by your system and network) for operation with Windows. More memory will be available with the use of DOS 5.0 or higher.

In addition, Word for Windows supports the following:

- The wide range of printers and plotters supported by Windows, including the Hewlett-Packard LaserJet-compatible and PostScript-compatible laser printers.

- A mouse.

- Memory management and disk cache systems supported by Windows. Windows comes with its own memory-management and disk-cache system, but memory managers from other software developers may better suit your network and memory-management needs.

- Major personal computer networks supporting Windows 3.0 or higher.

Installing Word for Windows

Before you install Word for Windows, you should install Windows 3.0 or higher. Windows is a separate software package that enables you to run Word for Windows, Microsoft Excel, and other Windows applications.

Before you begin the Word for Windows installation, check your hard disk and decide where you want to install Word. The default directory used during installation is C:\WINWORD. During installation, you are given a chance to change this directory. If you have an existing version of Word for Windows on the disk, the installation program gives you the option of overwriting it.

To install Word for Windows, follow these steps:

1. Protect your original disks from accidental change. On 5 1/4-inch disks, put a write-protect tab over the square cut notch on the edge. On 3 1/2-inch disks, slide the write-protect notch to the open position.

2. Start Windows.

3. Choose the File Run command from the Program Manager or File Manager.

4. When the Run dialog box appears, insert the Setup Disk 1 in drive A, type *a:setup*, and press Enter.

   Word for Windows setup runs as a normal Windows application. You can use the normal Windows mouse or keyboard operating techniques to make selections during installation. If you are not familiar with operating a mouse or with using the keyboard, you may want to review Chapter 1.

5. If this is the first time you have installed Word for Windows, a dialog box appears and prompts you for your name and company. Use the Tab key to move between edit boxes and press the Back-space key to remove errors. Click the Continue button or press Enter to continue.

   Figure A.1 shows the Setup dialog box, which asks for the path where you want Word for Windows.

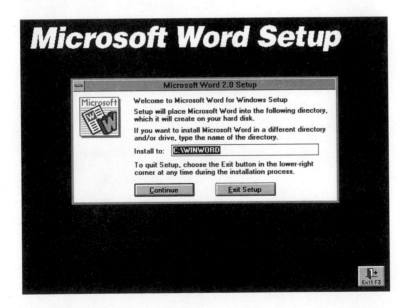

FIG. A.1.

The Setup dialog box.

6. In the Setup dialog box, type the path name of where you want to install Word for Windows, and then choose Continue or press Enter. To cancel, click the Exit Setup button or press the Esc key. The default path for installing Word for Windows is C:\WINWORD. If the path you type does not exist, you are asked if you want to create it.

   If Setup finds a different version of Word for Windows in the directory you specify, click the Continue button to overwrite it. To keep the existing version of Word for Windows and put the new version in a different directory, click the Change Directory button. Type a new path.

   The next dialog box that appears gives you an opportunity to choose how much of Word for Windows you want installed.

7. Click the box describing the type of installation you want. Using the keyboard, press the arrow keys to select a box, and then press Enter. You can choose one of three levels of installation (see fig. A.2).

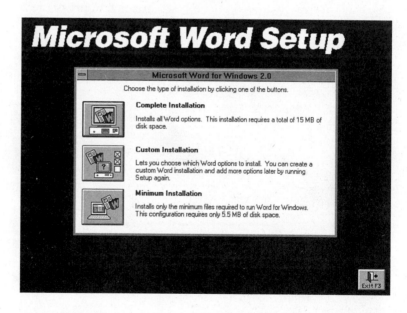

FIG. A.2.

Choose from three different levels of installation.

The choices shown in figure A.2 are as follows:

Selection	Description
Complete Installation	Installs all Word for Windows files. Approximately 15M of disk space is required. Gives you an opportunity to accept or reject automatically adding the Word for Windows path to the AUTOEXEC.BAT file.
Custom Installation	Installs only those portions of Word for Windows features that you select. Use this option to add features you have not installed previously. This option also enables you to see how much disk space is required for different features.
Minimum Installation	Installs only the basic Word for Windows files. Approximately 5.5M of disk space is required. You will have basic word processing features, but you will not have the additional features listed later such as Spell Checking, Microsoft Draw, Equation Editor, and so on.

T I P

If you later decide to add Word for Windows features that you did not install initially, you can rerun the Word for Windows setup and install the features you want.

If you are unsure which type of installation to choose, choose Custom Installation and read the rest of this appendix before completing the installation.

If you choose Custom Installation, the Word Setup Options dialog box appears (see fig. A.3).

In the Options dialog box, you can select all or part of different features. Each feature requires additional storage on your hard disk. The lower left corner of the dialog box shows you how much storage you have available and how much storage is required for the options you have selected. The different features you can install are as follows:

Feature	Description
Microsoft Word	Fundamental word processing
Tools	Miniature applications—applets—that run with Word for Windows. You can select which tools you want to add by clicking the Tools button.

Feature	Description
Proofing Tools	Word processing enhancements, such as spell checker, thesaurus, and grammar checker.
Conversions	Filters that enable Word for Windows to convert other word processing documents and graphics files automatically.
Online Lessons	On-line learning aids to help you learn features in Word for Windows.
Help	On-line help information for procedures, features, dialog boxes, and alert boxes.
Sample Files and Clip Art	Sample documents and templates for mailing lists, envelopes, labels, form letters, and graphic art you can insert into documents.

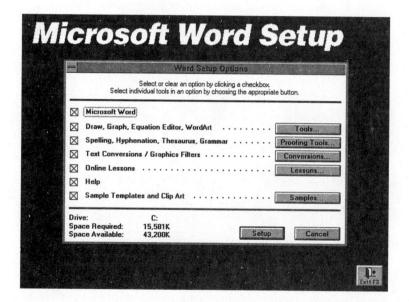

FIG. A.3.

Use the Word for Windows Setup Options dialog box to install or reinstall portions of Word for Windows.

With the mouse, click on check boxes of features you do not want so that the check box is clear. Click on a button, such as the Tools button, to display a set of partial features from which you can choose.

With the keyboard, press the Tab key to select features, then the space bar to turn a check box on or off. Choose a button, such as the Tool button, by pressing the Tab key until the button is selected, and then press the space bar.

8. Choose the Setup button when you finish selecting the features to be installed.

Following are some of the features available for each button in the Word Setup Options dialog box:

Button	Feature	Description
Tools	Microsoft Draw	Drawing program
	Microsoft Graph	Chart and graph program
	Equation Editor	Inserts equations
	WordArt	Title and word enhancement program
Proofing Tools	Spelling	Spelling dictionary
	Hyphenation	Hyphenation dictionary
	Thesaurus	Synonym list
	Grammar	Grammar checker
Conversions	Text with Layout (PC-8) Text with Layout (ANSI) RFT-DCA (IBM document interchange format) WordPerfect 5.0, 5.1	(Word processing and graphic)
	Word for DOS	
	Word for Macintosh	
	Word for Windows 1	
	WordStar 5.5, 5.0, 4.0, 3.45, 3.3	
	Lotus 1-2-3	
	Microsoft Works 2.0	
	Microsoft Excel	
	DrawPerfect Import Filter	
	DrawPerfect Export Filter	
	Micrografx Designer/Draw Filter	
	HP Graphics Language (HPGL) Filter	
	Computer Graphics Metafile (CGM) Filter	
	dBASE	
	Encapsulated Postscript (EPS) Format Filter	
	Tagged Image Format (TIF) Filter	

Button	Feature	Description
	PC Paintbrush (PCX) Filter	
	Lotus 1-2-3 Graphics (PIC) Filter	
	AutoCAD Format Filter	
	AutoCAD Plot File Filter	
	Write for Windows	
	Windows Metafile Filter	
Lessons	Getting Started	A short tutorial on using the mouse.
	Learning Word	Tutorials on major features in Word for Windows. Accessed through the Help menu.
Samples	Templates	Act as guides for creating mailing lists, labels, and so on.
	Clip Art	Numerous pictures that can be inserted in Word for Windows documents or edited with Microsoft Draw.

If you have Microsoft Excel or a previous version of Word for Windows already installed, you should make sure that you include the conversion filters for Microsoft Excel and Word for Windows 1.x. If you previously used WordPerfect or work with people who still use WordPerfect, you should install the conversion filters for WordPerfect 5.0, 5.1, DrawPerfect Import, and DrawPerfect Export.

Word for Windows will prompt you as to whether you want to manually change your AUTOEXEC.BAT file or if it should automatically update the file. If you choose to manually update the AUTOEXEC.BAT file, you should modify the path to include the directory containing WINWORD.EXE. A path that includes Word for Windows might look like the following:

```
PATH C:\EXCEL;C:\WINDOWS;C:\WINWORD;C:\VB;C:\DOS;C:\
```

You also will need to add a line that runs the Share utility. This utility is normally in the DOS directory, so the line you will add might appear as follows:

```
C:\DOS\SHARE.EXE
```

You can use the Windows Notepad accessory to open and modify the AUTOEXEC.BAT file. Save the file back to the root directory. Notepad automatically saves the file in text format. You will need to reboot your computer before the new AUTOEXEC.BAT takes effect.

As the Setup program installs Word for Windows, watch the top left corner of the installation dialog boxes. They will display descriptions of some of Word's most important features.

When Word for Windows is installed, make sure that you store your original and backup floppy disks in safe, but separate locations.

Converting Word Processor and Other Files

I n this appendix, you learn how to make the transition to Word for Windows smoothly and how to use Word for Windows with other word processing spreadsheet and database programs that still may be a part of your operations.

If you are experienced with a word processor, you may meet frustration in the first days of transition from your old word processing program to Word for Windows. Whenever people move from a known system to a similar but different system, they encounter learning interference. The old similar ideas and muscle memory get in the way of the new ideas and new muscle coordination. Within a few weeks of using Word for Windows, however, you will be handling more work with better quality and greater ease.

Converting Files from Word Processors, Spreadsheets, or Databases

Word for Windows is made for offices using a mix of word processors and spreadsheets from different software manufacturers. Because Word for Windows reads and writes the files of many major word processors, working in an office that has more than one word processor is not a problem for standard business writing. You also can insert all or portions of major worksheet and database files.

Word for Windows can read and convert files in the following word processor, spreadsheet, and database formats:

Program	Description
Microsoft Excel	XLS; Version 2 and 3
dBASE	DBF; II, III, III+, IV
Display Write and DisplayWriter	DCA/RFT
Microsoft Windows Write	WRI
Microsoft Word for DOS	DOC and styles
Microsoft MultiMate	Versions 3.3, 3.6, and Advantage II
Multiplan	SLK
Rich Text Format (stores formatting and graphics as ANSI characters)	RTF
Text Only (ASCII)	With or without line breaks
Text Only (PC-8)	With or without line breaks
Text with Layout	Column and tabs are preserved
Microsoft Word for Windows	DOC; Versions 1.0, 1.1, and 1.1a
Microsoft Word for the Macintosh	Version 4.0
Microsoft Works	WKS and WK1 files
Lotus 1-2-3	WKS Versions 1A and WK1 2.x
WordPerfect	Versions 4.1, 4.2, 5.0, and 5.1
WordStar	Versions 3.3, 3.4, 3.45, 4.0, 5.0, 5.5, and 6.0

During the Word for Windows installation process (described in Appendix A) you have the opportunity to select the types of converters you want to install on your hard disk. From your selections, Word for Windows copies the appropriate converters into the directory you specify for Word for Windows. The installation process also makes changes to the WIN.INI file, which contains start-up characteristics for Windows applications.

You can add converters after Word for Windows has been installed by running the Word Setup program.

You will need the original installation floppy disks. You will be given the opportunity to install selected filters rather than reinstalling all of Word for Windows.

When the conversion filters are installed, you can read or write to different word processing formats using the Word for Windows **F**ile **O**pen and **F**ile Save **A**s commands. Word for Windows converts the files as you open or save them.

When worksheet or database filters are installed, you can insert all or a portion of a worksheet or database by using the **I**nsert **F**ile command. The **F**ile Print **M**erge command uses worksheet or database files as the mail-merge data file. Data converts as it merges.

To open a file from another word processor, follow these steps:

1. Choose the Open button from the toolbar, or choose the **F**ile **O**pen command.

2. Type or select a file name in the File Name box. Use the Drives, Directories, or List Files Of Type boxes to find the document when necessary.

3. Choose OK or press Enter.

4. If a conversion dialog box appears asking which format the file is in, select the file format, and then choose OK.

The next time you save this document, it will be saved in the Word for Windows Normal format. If you have much editing to do, continue to save the document in Word for Windows format. When you are ready to send the document to a user who does not have Word for Windows, use the procedure listed at the end of this chapter to save the document to another word processing or spreadsheet format.

Inserting all or a portion of a worksheet or database file is described in Chapter 21.

If you want Word for Windows to always prompt you with the conversion format dialog box, choose the **T**ools **O**ptions command, and then choose the General icon from the **C**ategories group. When the Settings group appears, select the Confirm **F**ile Conversions check box.

Learning Specific File Conversion Details

When you install Word for Windows, technical documentation files are copied into the directory in which Word for Windows is installed. One of these files is CONVINFO.DOC, which contains information about installing file converters. The file also contains tables describing how features in non-Word for Windows file formats convert into Word for Windows documents and how features in Word for Windows documents convert to non-Word for Windows file formats.

To open, read, or print CONVINFO.DOC, follow these steps:

1. Choose the **File O**pen command.

2. Change to the directory containing WINWORD.EXE. This is normally the WINWORD directory.

3. Select the CONVINFO.DOC file and choose OK or press Enter.

Figure B.1 shows the top of the first page of the CONVINFO.DOC document. Clicking on the macro buttons shown in the document takes you to the topic printed on that button. To return to the top of the document from a topic, press Ctrl+Home. You can print this document as you would a normal Word for Windows document.

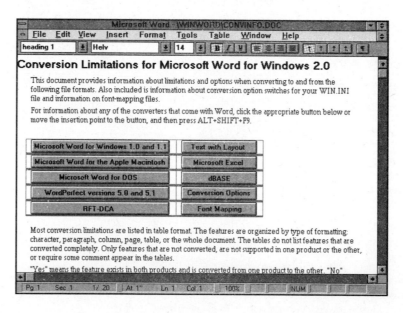

FIG. B.1.

CONVINFO.DOC contains information on how Word converts files.

CONVINFO.DOC contains feature tables like the one shown in figure B.2 that describe how features from different non-Word for Windows files convert into Word for Windows and how to convert out of Word for Windows back to another format.

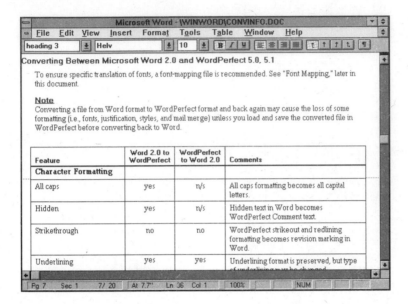

FIG. B.2.

Tables in CONVINFO.DOC describe how features convert into and out of Word documents.

Seeing Which Converters You Have Installed

When you install converters, the conversion files with the file extension CNV are copied into the same directory in which Word for Windows is installed. The installation program also modifies the WIN.INI file. The WIN.INI file is a text file that stores configuration information for Windows and some Windows applications.

You can see which converters are installed for Word for Windows by opening the WIN.INI file and examining a segment of that file that starts with the title [MSWord Text Converters]. WIN.INI can be found in the Windows directory. When you open the Windows directory, Word will ask if you want to convert the file from text. Choose OK to convert it.

Microsoft does not recommend modifying the [MSWord Text Converters] segment of WIN.INI. Instead, use the Word for Windows setup program to modify WIN.INI automatically. If you must make changes to the

WIN.INI, make a backup copy you can use in case your modifications do not work. When you save WIN.INI with your modifications, choose the **F**ile Save **A**s command and select Text Only (*.TXT) from the Save File as **T**ype pull-down list. WIN.INI must be saved as a text file.

Information in the [MSWord Text Converters] segment uses the following syntax:

```
Converter_class_name=application_name, filename,
    filename_extension
```

By looking in the WIN.INI, you can see the types of converters you have installed and where they are located. The following list shows a sample [MSWord Text Converters] segment:

```
[MSWord Text Converters]
Text with Layout=Text with Layout, C:\WINWORD\TXTWLYT.CNV,
    ans
RFTDCA=RFT-DCA, C:\WINWORD\RFTDCA.CNV, rft
WrdPrfctDOS50=WordPerfect 5.0, C:\WINWORD\WPFT5.CNV, doc
WrdPrfctDOS=WordPerfect 5.1, C:\WINWORD\WPFT5.CNV, doc
MSWordDos=Word for DOS, C:\WINWORD\WORDDOS.CNV, doc
WordStar 5.5=WordStar 5.5, C:\WINWORD\WORDSTAR.CNV, doc
WordStar 5.0=WordStar 5.0, C:\WINWORD\WORDSTAR.CNV, doc
WordStar 4.0=WordStar 4.0, C:\WINWORD\WORDSTAR.CNV, doc
WordStar 3.45=WordStar 3.45, C:\WINWORD\WORDSTAR.CNV, doc
WordStar 3.3=WordStar 3.3, C:\WINWORD\WORDSTAR.CNV, doc
MSBiff=Excel Worksheet, C:\WINWORD\XLBIFF.CNV, xls
MSWordWin=Word for Windows 1, C:\WINWORD\WORDWIN1.CNV, doc
DOS Text with Layout=DOS Text with Layout,
    C:\WINWORD\TXTWLYT.CNV, asc
MSWordMac4=Word for Macintosh 4.0, C:\WINWORD\WORDMAC.CNV,
    mcw
MSWordMac=Word for Macintosh 5.0, C:\WINWORD\WORDMAC.CNV,
    mcw
ATdBase=Ashton-Tate dBASE, C:\WINWORD\DBASE.CNV, dbf
Lotus123=Lotus 1-2-3, C:\WINWORD\LOTUS123.CNV, wk1 wk3
Multiplan=Multiplan, C:\WINWORD\MLTIPLAN.CNV, mp
WordPerfect 4.2=WordPerfect 4.2, C:\WINWORD\WPFT4.CNV, doc
WordPerfect 4.1=WordPerfect 4.1, C:\WINWORD\WPFT4.CNV, doc
Windows Write=Windows Write, C:\WINWORD\WRITWIN.CNV, wri
```

Modifying Conversion Options

You can control how some of Word's converters operate—how features convert or whether a feature converts. One section of the CONVINFO.DOC file describes the converters that can be modified. The modifiable converters are as follows:

Microsoft Word for the Macintosh
Microsoft Word for DOS
Microsoft Works
RFT-DCA
Text with Layout

Some of the ways in which these converters can be modified are whether mail-merge fields are converted, whether INCLUDE fields are converted, and whether you want a document to convert as close to the same print layout or with the greatest use of compatible features in Word for Windows.

CONVINFO.DOC describes the different options available for each of the modifiable converters. To see the modifiable section of these converters and where they are edited, do the following:

1. Choose the Tools Options command.

2. Select the WIN.INI Category.

3. Select the converter group name from the Application pull-down list (for example, TextLytConv).

4. Select the option you want to change in the Startup Options list.

5. Edit the parameters in the Setting edit box to be one of the settings described in CONVINFO.DOC.

6. Choose the Set button, and then choose Close.

Controlling Font Conversion in Documents

While Word for Windows converts font changes during conversion, it may not get the fonts correct. You can handle this issue in two ways. You can use the Edit Replace command to search for a specific font and replace it with a different font. Or you can use a font-mapping file that tells Word for Windows which font, size, and style to use for each change in fonts in the converted file.

Sample font conversion files are stored in the Word for Windows directory with the TXT file extension. These files contain a description of how to use the file and a sample mapping. For these files to be used during conversion, they must be in the Word for Windows directory and renamed or copied with the file extension DAT. Make sure that you save the modified and renamed file in text format.

Some of these mapping files map fonts according to each font change in the original font. For example, the first font may be Helv 12 pt, the second font may be Times Roman 14 pt, and so on. For font mappings that work this way, you may need a different DAT file for different word processing documents.

The font-mapping file names are a three-letter abbreviation for the format being converted, an underscore, and then a three-letter abbreviation of the format being converted to. The intermediary format for these conversions is Rich Text Format (RTF). Some of the TXT file containing font mapping information are as follows:

> To Word
> From Word
> RFT-DCA
> DCA_RTF.TXT
> RTF_DCA.TXT
> Microsoft Word 5, Macintosh
> MW5_RTF.TXT
> RTF_MW5.TXT
> Word for DOS
> PCW_RTF.TXT
> RTF-PCW.TXT
> WordPerfect 5.0/5.1
> RTF_WP5.TXT
> WP5_RTF.TXT

The following is an example of the WP5_RTF.TXT file that can be modified into a WP5_RTF.DAT file.

```
# This is a sample font mapping file for use with the
     WordPerfect 5.x
# converter for Microsoft Word for Windows. In order for this
     file to
# be used by the converter, it should be renamed WP5_RTF.DAT.
# Following the example below, place the WordPerfect font
     number at the
# beginning of a line, followed by a ';', followed by the font
     name Word
# should use. The first font used in a WordPerfect document is
     font
```

```
# zero, the next font is font one, and so on.
# Please see the documentation for further information on
    how to set
# up a font mapping file.
#
# Maps WP font #0 to Courier
0;Courier
# Maps WP font #1 to Tms Rmn
1;Tms Rmn
# Maps WP font #2 to Helvetica
2;Helv
The actual working part of the this file is,
0;Courier
1;Tms Rmn
2;Helv
```

Saving Word for Windows Documents to Another Format

Word for Windows can save files to the same word processing formats it converts. This feature is useful if you work in a company that uses different types of word processors. Word for Windows files cannot be saved back to worksheet or database formats.

Word for Windows needs the same conversion files described earlier to convert Word for Windows documents into other word processing formats. If you do not see the format you need in the Save File As Type box, rerun the Word for Windows installation program and install the filter you need.

To save a Word for Windows document to a non-Word for Windows format, follow these steps:

1. Choose the File Save As command.

2. Type the document name in the File Name text box. Use a different file name than the original file so that you do not write over the original file.

3. Select a file format from the Save File As Type pull-down box.

4. Choose OK or press Enter.

C

APPENDIX

Managing Fonts

With Windows and Word for Windows you can create documents that use the best capabilities of your printer. If you understand how Windows works with fonts, you can make the screen display match the printed result more closely.

A *font* is a set of characters with a consistent size and style. Times Roman 12 point and Helvetica 10 point, for example, are fonts. Windows is equipped with several fonts, and your printer may add more fonts. You also can purchase additional fonts for Windows and your printer.

Understanding Fonts

Windows 3.0 works with two different types of fonts: fonts designed to display on-screen (screen fonts) and fonts designed to print (printer fonts). This section describes both.

Windows 3.1 uses a different type of font technology that resolves many of the font problems inherent in Windows 3.0. This new font technology is called *TrueType* and is described later in this appendix.

Understanding Printer Fonts

Depending on how the fonts are stored, Windows deals with fonts used by the printer in three ways.

Resident fonts are built into the printer. Many PostScript printers, for example, have a standard set of thirteen typefaces. (PostScript is a page description language.) Each typeface contains many fonts, such as Times Roman, Times Roman Italic, Times Roman Bold, and so on. Hewlett-Packard LaserJet printers also have built-in fonts. The number of built-in fonts depends on the model of the printer. Some printers contain scalable fonts, also known as outline fonts, that generate many sizes from one font outline. Many users prefer resident fonts because they print the fastest and do not take up processing power or computer memory.

> **T   I   P**
>
> The available fonts may vary with the printer orientation (portrait or landscape). When you select a specific printer and configure it with the File Print Setup command, you tell Windows to look up from an internal list the resident fonts for that printer.

Cartridge fonts come in hardware modules that plug into a printer. They act as resident fonts. Each cartridge contains one or more sets of fonts. Cartridges usually are used with HP LaserJet-compatible printers. During printer installation or setup, you must select from a list the cartridges available to the printer to let Windows know which additional fonts are available. You can access this list of cartridge fonts through Word for Windows File Printer Setup command.

> **T   I   P**
>
> On HP LaserJet printers, you can select two cartridges in the printer setup dialog box. To select the second cartridge, hold Ctrl and click on the second cartridge with the mouse.

Soft fonts are generated by a software program and stored on your computer's hard disk or on the network. When soft fonts are needed, Windows sends the font information to the printer. The printer stores the font information in memory and composes a page. After the font is downloaded to memory, it stays in the printer. Soft fonts take up hard disk storage and slow down printing times. Most soft font generation packages have a font installer program that creates the fonts you request and stores the fonts in a directory on the hard disk. You must use the Windows Control Panel to install the soft fonts in Windows.

If soft fonts and cartridges cannot coexist in your printer, select
None as the cartridge when you use soft fonts.

T I P

Understanding Screen Fonts

Windows 3.0 uses three types of fonts on-screen. *System fonts* come
with Windows and are designed to match generic serif and sans serif
fonts. (Serifs are the small marks at the end of some characters' lines.)
System fonts also provide special characters. System fonts are used in
Windows' dialog boxes, titles, and so on, and to represent printer resident or cartridge fonts. Because a generic screen font that comes with
Windows may be slightly different from a specific printer font, the
screen appearance and the printed result of a font may be different.

A special form of *screen soft font* matches a printer font as closely as
possible. These fonts are stored in software files and are available with
soft fonts designed for the printer. Because these screen fonts are designed to match a specific printer's soft font, the on-screen display
closely matches the printed result. Soft font generation programs usually generate a printer font and screen font of a specific typeface, size,
and style at the same time, or the fonts are pregenerated on disk.
Screen fonts end with a FON extension.

Type management programs are designed to generate screen and
printer fonts simultaneously. These fonts are generated on the fly
rather than prebuilt like soft fonts, reducing the disk storage devoted
to prebuilt soft fonts and ensuring that screen displays are nearly an
exact match to printed results. Type management programs are slower
to print a page than some other forms of fonts. TrueType and the
Adobe Type Manager are type management programs. TrueType is
built into Windows 3.1. Adobe Type Manager is a program purchased
separately.

Understanding Your Printer's
Capabilities

Different printers have different capabilities. Some printers are not
capable of advanced features such as printing small capital letters, bi-
directional printing, landscape printing, or graphics. Some printers
require that you change the font to change from normal to bold or
italic, rather than formatting the existing font with a bold or italic style.

Windows is designed to use as much of your printer's capabilities as possible.

You must tell Windows which printer is connected and which extra features are available on that printer. If you install an HP LaserJet III printer, for example, during installation you still need to use the File Printer Setup command to tell Windows the amount of memory in the printer, which font cartridges are installed, and how the printer and envelope bins are handled.

If you are using a laser printer with expandable memory, be sure that you have correctly specified how much memory it has. If the printer doesn't have enough memory, or if you do not tell Windows additional memory has been installed, Windows may not be able to print a full graphic or page of text. If a full page will not print, lower the graphic print resolution in the setup dialog box and try it again.

Understanding How Windows Works with Fonts

When you run Word for Windows in Windows 3.0, two sets of fonts are used: screen fonts and printer fonts. If you print to a printer with resident fonts or cartridge fonts, Windows uses its screen fonts to display as closely as possible how text will appear on the page. The generic screen fonts that come with Windows 3.0 do not always represent accurately the size, shape, and spacing of the printer fonts. If you create and install custom screen fonts in Windows and print with soft fonts, Windows uses the custom screen fonts. These custom screen fonts enable Windows to more accurately represent the printed page. If the screen fonts and printer fonts do not match, the screen and the printed results may differ. (Custom screen fonts are created by soft font generation programs or are available on disk with cartridges.)

This difference between screen and printer fonts can cause numerous problems:

- Words wrap differently on-screen than they do in print.

- Titles or sidebars extend further than expected.

- On-screen text extends past the margin set in the ruler.

- On-screen text in tables overfills cells in tables.

- Bold or italic formatting causes lines to appear longer than they print.

Screen fonts and printer fonts also are mismatched when fonts unavailable in the printer are used on-screen. (In Word for Windows, you can select a font even if the font is not available on the current printer.) You can use this feature to create a document for printing on another printer. If you do use a font not available in the printer, Word for Windows attempts to substitute a similar typeface and size when it prints. If it cannot find the requested size, it substitutes the next smallest size font in the printer.

You can avoid these problems in several ways. First, use fonts available in the printer. If a font is in the current printer, a small printer icon appears to the left of the font name in the Font list from the ribbon or the Character dialog box. Second, make sure that you can see on-screen the affects of font substitutions. To see the affect of substituted fonts, choose the Tools Options command and select the View Category. From the View Category dialog box, select the Line Breaks and Fonts as Printed check box. Third, if you are using soft fonts or a font manager, make sure that you generate and install the screen fonts that go with the printer's soft fonts.

Installing and Deleting Soft Fonts

Soft fonts often generate the printer font and the screen font. The soft font software usually does three things: generates screen and printer fonts of the size and type you want, saves files for those fonts to the hard disk, and modifies Windows' WIN.INI file so that Windows knows which fonts are available and where they are located. When done correctly, you can see the new fonts listed in your font lists and print them. If font installation was incorrect or the font program did not install the fonts in Windows, you may be able to install them yourself.

You can check whether screen fonts are installed by looking for the appropriately named FON files in the PCLFONTS directory (for HP LaserJet-compatible printers) or the directory where fonts were installed. The PCLFONTS directory normally is located off of the root directory of your hard disk. Some printers, like the newer HP Series III LaserJet printers, have appropriate screen fonts built into the printer driver. You may have screen fonts available in the driver but see no FON files on disk.

Adding or Removing Bit-Mapped Printer and Screen Fonts

Some font manufacturers produce font generation and management programs that create files of predefined fonts for the screen and printer. These fonts are created with patterns of dots (bit maps) and are displayed or printed. Such fonts for printers subscribing to the Hewlett-Packard PCL format store their fonts in the PCLFONTS directory.

If the font generation software does not automatically modify Windows WIN.INI file, you cannot see the fonts in Windows that you have installed. You can install the screen fonts and printer fonts at the same time with the Printer Font Installer that is part of many printer drivers. The following procedures describe font installation for an HP Series III LaserJet printer:

1. Choose the File Printer Setup command.

2. Select the printer for which the fonts are designed from the Printer Setup dialog box, and then choose the Setup button.

3. Choose the Fonts button. The HP Font Installer dialog box appears.

   If the Fonts button is not displayed in the dialog box, the driver cannot install soft fonts. Check with Microsoft or the font manufacturer for instructions on installing the soft fonts.

   Currently installed fonts in the PCLFONTS directory appear in the left window of the dialog box.

4. Click on the Add Fonts button.

5. In the Add Fonts dialog box, type the drive and path name where the soft fonts are located and then choose OK. This usually is a floppy disk containing prebuilt fonts or a directory on the hard disk where fonts were stored by the font generation program.

6. Select from the right window the bit-mapped fonts you want to install into the PCLFONTS directory. You can select multiple fonts by clicking on them, or by pressing the up- or down-arrow keys and then pressing the space bar to mark them. Select a font again to unselect it.

7. Choose the Add button.

   Installed fonts appear in the left side of the window.

8. Choose OK twice to return to Word for Windows.

Do not delete font files without first uninstalling them. Deleting the files from disk does not tell the WIN.INI file that the fonts are no longer available. You must uninstall the font files, and then delete them.

Installing Screen Fonts

You can install or remove screen soft fonts by using the Font program in the Control Panel. Use the Font program to add or remove screen fonts that are separate from the printer soft fonts (if you are using font cartridges or if the font manufacturers release updated screen fonts after the printer fonts).

In Word for Windows you can install soft fonts from disk for Windows 3.0 with these steps:

1.ˑ Choose the Application Control Menu by pressing Alt+space bar or clicking on the Application Control icon. Choose the **Ru**n command.

2. Select the Control **P**anel option, and then choose OK.

3. From the Control Panel window, choose the Fonts item icon by double-clicking on it or by pressing the arrow keys to select it, and then pressing Enter.

4. Choose the **A**dd button.

5. From the Add Font Files dialog box that appears, change to the directory containing the fonts you want to add, select the files, and then choose OK.

6. From the Fonts dialog box, choose OK.

To remove fonts, uninstall them and then delete the files. To remove a font from Windows, follow steps 1 through 3, and then select from the Installed **F**onts list the font you want to remove, and choose the **Re**move button. When you are prompted to verify removing the font, choose **Y**es. After you have uninstalled the font, you can delete the file from the hard disk.

Do not delete font files before you uninstall them with the Font program in the Control Panel. Windows keeps a list of installed fonts within the WIN.INI file. When you use the Font program to add or remove soft fonts, you also are modifying the WIN.INI file. After you have uninstalled the font, you can delete the file.

T I P

Using TrueType

Most Windows 3.0 fonts are bit-mapped fonts—small dots used to create a character on-screen or in the printer. Bit-mapped fonts are created before you use them. These fonts require a large amount of disk space for storage and separate files to store the fonts used on-screen and the one used in the printer. Each font size requires a different bit map. Because of differences between the screen and printer fonts, the display may differ from the printed result.

Windows 3.1 includes a new built-in font technology called TrueType, a font management program that generates screen and printer fonts as they are needed. TrueType fonts are outline fonts. The outline of each character is stored as a mathematical formula that defines the lines and curves needed to create a character. Each character, whether on-screen or in the printer, is calculated when needed and for the typeface, size, and style needed. TrueType even uses the same fonts for different printers and plotters. You save significant disk space because fonts are not precalculated and stored on disk. When characters are sent to the printer, only those characters being used are sent, not the entire character set. Most importantly, the display on-screen shows how the printed result will appear.

When you install Windows 3.1, you install TrueType. You can continue to use your existing PostScript fonts, cartridges, or soft fonts. In the Windows 3.1 Font program (accessed from the Control Panel) and in each printer's setup dialog box are options and check boxes that enable you to control whether TrueType takes priority over other fonts. You also can map a TrueType font used on-screen to a resident, cartridge, or PostScript font in the printer. Sometimes doing so quickens printing.

Windows 3.1 includes 13 TrueType fonts (registered to The Monotype Corporation, PCC): Times New Roman, Times New Roman Bold, Times New Roman Italic, Times New Roman Bold Italic, Arial, Arial Bold, Arial Italic, Arial Bold Italic, Courier New, Courier New Bold, Courier New Italic, Courier New Bold Italic, and Symbol.

G

N

Free Catalog!

Mail us this registration form today, and we'll send you a free catalog featuring Que's complete line of best-selling books.

Name of Book _____

Name _____

Title _____

Phone ( ) _____

Company _____

Address _____

City _____

State _____ ZIP _____

Please check the appropriate answers:

1. Where did you buy your Que book?
   ☐ Bookstore (name: _____)
   ☐ Computer store (name: _____)
   ☐ Catalog (name: _____)
   ☐ Direct from Que
   ☐ Other: _____

2. How many computer books do you buy a year?
   ☐ 1 or less
   ☐ 2-5
   ☐ 6-10
   ☐ More than 10

3. How many Que books do you own?
   ☐ 1
   ☐ 2-5
   ☐ 6-10
   ☐ More than 10

4. How long have you been using this software?
   ☐ Less than 6 months
   ☐ 6 months to 1 year
   ☐ 1-3 years
   ☐ More than 3 years

5. What influenced your purchase of this Que book?
   ☐ Personal recommendation
   ☐ Advertisement
   ☐ In-store display
   ☐ Price
   ☐ Que catalog
   ☐ Que mailing
   ☐ Que's reputation
   ☐ Other: _____

6. How would you rate the overall content of the book?
   ☐ Very good
   ☐ Good
   ☐ Satisfactory
   ☐ Poor

7. What do you like *best* about this Que book?
   _____
   _____

8. What do you like *least* about this Que book?
   _____
   _____

9. Did you buy this book with your personal funds?
   ☐ Yes   ☐ No

10. Please feel free to list any other comments you may have about this Que book.
    _____
    _____
    _____

— que —

Order Your Que Books Today!

Name _____

Title _____

Company _____

City _____

State _____ ZIP _____

Phone No. ( ) _____

Method of Payment:

Check ☐   (Please enclose in envelope.)

Charge My: VISA ☐   MasterCard ☐

American Express ☐

Charge # _____

Expiration Date _____

Order No.	Title	Qty.	Price	Total

You can **FAX** your order to **1-317-573-2583**. Or call **1-800-428-5331**, ext. **ORDR** to order direct.
Please add $2.50 per title for shipping and handling.

Subtotal _____

Shipping & Handling _____

Total _____

— que —

BUSINESS REPLY MAIL
First Class Permit No. 9918   Indianapolis, IN

Postage will be paid by addressee

11711 N. College
Carmel, IN 46032

BUSINESS REPLY MAIL
First Class Permit No. 9918   Indianapolis, IN

Postage will be paid by addressee

11711 N. College
Carmel, IN 46032

Ruler Formatting Keys

Ctrl+Shift+F10 to activate the ruler; then:

Right arrow	Move cursor right	R	Set right indent
Ctrl+right arrow	Move cursor right in large increments	1	Select left-aligned tabs
Left arrow	Move cursor left	2	Select center-aligned tabs
Shift+left arrow	Move left of left margin	3	Select right-aligned tabs
Ctrl+left arrow	Move cursor left in large increments	4	Select decimal tabs
Home	Move to left margin (zero point)	Ins	Set a tab stop at cursor location
End	Move to right margin	Del	Delete tab stop at cursor location
F	Set first-line indent	Enter	Apply settings and deactivate ruler
L	Set left indent		

Outlining Keys

Alt+Shift+left arrow	Promote heading	Alt+Shift+hyphen or Alt+Shift+ – (with numeric keypad off)	Collapse text under a heading
Alt+Shift+right arrow	Demote heading		
Alt+Shift+up arrow	Move paragraph/ heading up	Alt+Shift+= or Alt+Shift++ (with numeric keypad off)	Show text under a heading
Alt+Shift+down arrow	Move paragraph/ heading down		
Alt+Shift+5 (on numeric keypad)	Convert to body text	Alt+Shift+1 through 9 (cannot use keypad)	Show through indicated numeric level
Alt+Shift++ (on numeric keypad)	Expand outline	Alt+Shift+A or * (on numeric keypad)	Toggle between showing all levels and showing all levels and all text
Alt+Shift+ – (on numeric keypad)	Collapse outline	Alt+Shift+ * (on numeric keypads)	Show all levels

Additional Keys

Esc	Cancel	Ctrl+Shift+hyphen	Insert nonbreaking hyphen
Enter	Begin new paragraph	Ctrl+Shift+space bar	Insert nonbreaking space
Shift+Enter	Begin new line	Tab	Move to next cell (table)
Ctrl+Enter	Begin new page	Ctrl+Tab	Insert tab character (table)
Ctrl+Shift+Enter	Begin new column/split table	Ctrl+Shift+*	Show all marks and field codes
Ctrl+ – (hyphen)	Insert optional hyphen		

Cursor-Movement Keys

Holding down the Shift key selects while you're moving.

Up arrow	Previous line	Home	Beginning of line
Ctrl+Up arrow	Previous paragraph	Ctrl+Home	Beginning of document
Alt+Up arrow	Previous page view region	Alt+Home	Beginning of table row
Alt+Shift+Up arrow	Previous page view region	End	End of line
Down arrow	Next line	Ctrl+End	End of document
Ctrl+Down arrow	Next paragraph	Alt+End	End of table row
Alt+Down arrow	Next page view region	PgUp	Show previous windowful
Alt+Shift+Down arrow	Move paragraph down	Ctrl+PgUp	Top of window
Left arrow	Previous character	Alt+PgUp	Top of table column
Ctrl+Left arrow	Previous word	PgDn	Show next windowful
Alt+Left arrow	Previous word	Ctrl+PgDn	Bottom of window
Alt+Shift+Left arrow	Promote heading	Alt+PgDn	Bottom of table column
Right arrow	Next character	Ctrl+5 (pad on or off)	Select entire document
Ctrl+Right arrow	Next word	Alt+5 (pad off)	Select table
Alt+Right arrow	Next word	Alt+Shift+5 (pad off)	Apply normal style
Alt+Shift+Right arrow	Demote heading		

Function Keys Used with Fields

Key	Function	Key	Function
Ctrl+Shift+F7	Update linked information in source	F11	Go to next field
		Shift+F11	Go to previous field
F9	Update field	Ctrl+F11	Lock field
Shift+F9	Toggle between field codes and field results	Ctrl+Shift+F11	Unlock field
Ctrl+F9	Insert field characters {}	Alt+Shift+D	Insert DATE field
Ctrl+Shift+F9	Unlink field	Alt+Shift+P	Insert PAGE field
Alt+Shift+F9	Simulates double-click on MACROBUTTON or GOTOBUTTON	Alt+Shift+T	Insert TIME field
		Alt+Shift+F	Insert MERGE field in main document

Paragraph Formatting

Key	Function	Key	Function
Ctrl+E	Center	Ctrl+R	Right align
Ctrl+G	Remove hanging indent	Ctrl+S	Apply a style (type or select name)
Ctrl+J	Justify	Ctrl+T	Create hanging indent
Ctrl+L	Left align	Ctrl+0 (zero)	Close space before paragraph
Ctrl+M	Indent	Ctrl+1	Single space lines
Ctrl+N	Unindent	Ctrl+2	Double space lines
Ctrl+O	Open space before paragraph	Ctrl+5	One-and-one-half space lines
Ctrl+Q	Remove direct formatting		

Character Formatting Keys

Key	Function	Key	Function
Alt+Shift+5 (on numeric keypad)	Apply normal style	Ctrl+K	Small caps
		Ctrl+P	Point size
Ctrl+A	All Caps	Ctrl+U	Continuous underline
Ctrl+B	Bold	Ctrl+W	Word underline
Ctrl+D	Double-underline	Ctrl+=	Subscript
Ctrl+F	Font	Ctrl++	Superscript
Ctrl+H	Hidden	Ctrl+space bar	Removes non-style formatting
Ctrl+I	Italic		

...rt ...le	Format Columns	Insert Frame	Insert Drawing	Insert Chart	Create Envelope	Check Spelling	Print	Zoom Whole Page	Zoom 100 %	Zoom Page Width

Shortcut Keys

A + sign in these tables indicates that you should hold down the first key while pressing the second key, as in Alt+A. A comma (,) indicates that you should release the first key before pressing the second key, as in Alt,A.

If your keyboard has only 10 function keys, use Alt+F1 for the F11 key and Alt+F2 for the F12 key.

Function Keys

Key	Function	Key	Function
F1	Help	F8	Extend selection/extend mode
Shift+F1	Help pointer (Context-sensitive help)	Shift+F8	Shrink selection
		Ctrl+F8	Size document window
F2	Move selection to insertion point on Enter	Ctrl+Shift+F8	Select column
Shift+F2	Copy selection to insertion point on Enter		
Ctrl+F2	Grow font	F9	Update field
Ctrl+Shift+F2	Shrink font	Shift+F9	Toggle field display
		Ctrl+F9	Insert field characters {}
F3	Insert glossary entry	Ctrl+Shift+F9	Unlink field
Shift+F3	Alternate between three letter cases	Alt+F9	Minimize Word window
Ctrl+F3	Cut to spike	Alt+Shift+F9	Simulate double-click on GOTOBUTTON or MACROBUTTON
Ctrl+Shift+F3	Insert from spike		
F4	Repeat previous command	F10	Activate menu
Shift+F4	Repeat search/Go To	Shift+F10	Activate annotation, header/footer, outline or macro bar
Ctrl+F4	Close active document window		
Alt+F4	Close Word	Ctrl+F10	Maximize document window
		Ctrl+Shift+F10	Activate ruler
F5	Go To	Alt+F10	Maximize Word window
Shift+F5	Go back to previous positions		
Ctrl+F5	Restore document window	F11	Next field
Ctrl+Shift+F5	Insert bookmark	Shift+F11	Previous field
Alt+F5	Restore Word window	Ctrl+F11	Lock field
		Ctrl+Shift+F11	Unlock field
F6	Next pane		
Shift+F6	Previous pane	F12	Save as
Ctrl+F6	Next document window	Shift+F12	Save
Ctrl+Shift+F6	Previous document window	Ctrl+F12	Open
		Ctrl+Shift+F12	Print
F7	Spelling		
Shift+F7	Thesaurus		
Ctrl+F7	Move document window		
Ctrl+Shift+F7	Update linked information to the source		

Toolbar Tools

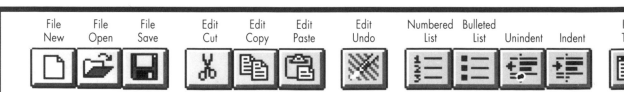

File New | File Open | File Save | Edit Cut | Edit Copy | Edit Paste | Edit Undo | Numbered List | Bulleted List | Unindent | Indent | In To

Moving in a Table

Enter	Start a new paragraph in a cell	Alt+PgUp	Move to top cell of current column
Tab	Move to next cell or start a new row if insertion point is in last cell of table	Alt+PgDn	Move to bottom cell of current column
		Up arrow	Move up one row
Shift+Tab	Move to previous cell	Down arrow	Move down one row
Ctrl+Tab	Insert a tab character in a cell	Arrow keys	Move within text in a cell, at cell edge to next cell, or at table edge into and out of table
Alt+Home	Move to first cell in current row		
Alt+End	Move to last cell in current row		

Mouse Actions

Many of the commonly used dialog boxes and features can be directly accessed by double-clicking specific areas in the Word window.

Hotspots on Screen

To	Double-click	To	Double-click
Open Character dialog box	On blank area in ribbon	Open the Options dialog box	On the toolbar background
Open Paragraph dialog box	Anywhere in upper half of ruler	Open the Macro dialog box	On the macro icon bar background
Open Tabs dialog box	On tab stop		
Open the Page Layout dialog box	On corners of page outside margin while in page layout view	Open footnote window	On footnote reference mark
		Split active window in half	On split bar
Open Section Layout dialog box	On any section mark or anywhere in lower half of ruler in margin view	Switch between maximized and restored	On title bar
Open Styles dialog box	On style name in the status area	Open application for an embedded object	On object
Open Go To dialog box	On page number in status bar		

Selecting

Function	Mouse Action
Position insertion point	Position pointer, click
Select text	Drag or click then Shift+click at end
Select word	Double-click
Select sentence	Ctrl+click
Select line	Click in selection bar (left edge)
Select paragraph	Double-click in selection bar (left edge)
Select object (e.g., picture)	Click object
Select block of text	Drag with right button
Select table row	Click in selection bar (left edge)
Select table column	Click right button

Outlining

Function	Mouse Action
Select heading	Click heading's icon on left
Select heading and text	Ctrl+click heading's icon
Promote heading	Drag icon to left
Demote heading	Drag icon to right
Move heading	Drag icon up or down
Demote heading to text	Click text icon in bar (two-headed arrow)
Expand heading	Double-click heading's icon
Collapse heading	Double-click heading's icon
Display to a level	Click numeric level icon
Display all text	Click All icon

Modifying Pictures

Function	Mouse Action
Scale (size) a picture	Select, drag black handle
Crop (trim) a picture	Select, Shift+drag black handle